Léonard Bourdon

A hostile sketch by Gabriel, probably early in 1794. According to J.-M.-B. Renouyier, *Histoire de l'art pendant la Révolution* (Paris, 1863), vol. 2, p. 371, as a young man Gabriel "avide des spectacles révolutionnaires . . . avait saisi à la Commune, à la Convention, ou dans la rue, à la pointe de son crayon et dans la coiffe de son chapeau, les physionomies qui l'avaient le plus frappé, et s'il les a chargées quelquefois, c'est uniquement par l'effet de la préoccupation du moment." Courtesy of Photothèque des Musées de la ville de Paris.

Léonard Bourdon

The Career of a Revolutionary, 1754-1807

Léonard Bourdon

The Career of a Revolutionary, 1754-1807

Michael J. Sydenham

Wilfrid Laurier University Press

This book has been published with the help of a grant from the Humanities and Social Sciences Federation of Canada, using funds provided by the Social Sciences and Humanities Research Council of Canada. We acknowledge the financial support of the Government of Canada through the Book Publishing Industry Development Program for our publishing activities.

Canadä

Canadian Cataloguing in Publication Data

Sydenham, M.J.
   Léonard Bourdon : the career of a revolutionary, 1754-1807

Includes bibliographical references and index.
ISBN 0-88920-319-9

1. Bourdon, Léonard, 1754-1807.   2. France—History—Revolution
1789-1799.   3. Revolutionaries—France—Biography.   I. Title.

DC146.B733S92 1999   944.04′092   C98-932829-5

© 1999 Wilfrid Laurier University Press
Waterloo, Ontario N2L 3C5

Cover design by Leslie Macredie using the Symbolic Insignia of
the First French Republic. From a private collection.

Printed in Canada

In Memoriam

Anne Margaret Lindsay Sydenham
3 May 1955 - 16 August 1999

Contents

List of Illustrations

Figures

Maps

Preface

The French Revolution was and remains deeply divisive. That is because it, more than any other modern revolution, was concerned with fundamentals. In and after 1789, many people were convinced that the almost accidental collapse of an antiquated state opened the way not only to improvements in the political and social orders but also to the creation of an entirely new world. Freed from the shackles of "tyranny" and "superstition," the goodness innate in all people was expected to flourish and sweep away every obstacle to human happiness. Furthermore, the more ardent revolutionaries soon became convinced that, if this did not happen immediately, then it could only be because the way was blocked by the opposition of those perverted by the past, whether they were foreign rulers, dispossessed aristocrats, or simply the apathetic, the selfish, and the corrupt. Such people therefore had to be enlightened by education and propaganda, silenced by coercion, or even eliminated along with all the other relics of the "old order." In short, rapid political change fostered the conviction that nature needed help in creating mankind in a new mould.

Representative of that attitude was Léonard Bourdon, a man whose lifelong objective was the general adoption of reforms that would make education both more humane and more realistic, a man who soon realized that educational, social, and political changes were inseparable. Moreover, although his extremism in practice may be questioned, he was also remarkably representative of the revolutionary period in many other ways. Initially, as le sieur Bourdon de la Crosnière, an innovator in education and the son of a notable advocate of economic reform, he was a typically liberal member of the administrative bourgeoisie into which he had been born. Later, between 1789 and 1792, as le citoyen

---

The note to the Preface is on p. 347.

Léonard Bourdon, an Elector of Paris, a "Patriot of 1789," and one of the "Conquerors of The Bastille," he personified the "spirit of 1789"; later again, both as a deputy and as a representative of the people sent on a mission to the provinces, he was one of those members of the National Convention who, as the Montagnards or "men of the Mountain," dominated the assembly and the whole of France during the critical year of 1793-94. And, like many of those who survived all the tempests of the time, he ultimately reconciled himself to becoming once again simply a servant of the state, directed though it was by an emperor, Napoleon.

That, however, is far from being a complete account of this ardent believer in liberty and equality. As the Revolution continued, the Montagnards became an increasingly isolated minority, and even among them Bourdon was exceptional because in 1795 he was one of the very few who did *not* repudiate their immediate past and reappear among the reactionaries in their time of triumph. Thus, he finally became representative only of those who were held responsible for all the bloodshed and abuses committed since 1789. Scorned as "Léopard" Bourdon, he was subjected for years to the abuse of journalists for whom scurrility had become second nature, and, although he subsequently had some success in rebuilding his career, his reputation was ruined.

That it has remained so is due less to the credulity of some popular writers than to the fact that few serious scholars have given their attention to those revolutionaries who were not of outstanding importance. Of late, moreover, and particularly since the conclusion of the Cold War, the temper of our own time has been toward universal tolerance, and many historians have become more inclined to concentrate on problems such as the incidence of disease than to concern themselves with those of political behaviour. Nevertheless, our understanding of the importance of the French Revolution may be thought incomplete because our appreciation of the conduct of many of the revolutionaries is often distorted by our almost casual acceptance of the propaganda of their enemies. In this context, this book is an attempt to ascertain the truth about one apparently typical individual, and, although I may have become increasingly sympathetic toward Bourdon, I have sought to maintain that approach throughout the work. If it has led to some rehabilitation of him, then that is the result rather than the intent of the inquiry.

The truth about Bourdon, however, is elusive. His parents were people of some small standing, and one of his brothers eventually obtained high rank, but we know virtually nothing of his private life beyond main features such as the fact that his wife, "*la femme* Bourdon," supported him resolutely in every adversity. The record that survives relates to his public life as an educational reformer, a political figure, and, finally, a public servant whose life ended abruptly and inexplicably.

Cumulatively, this public material is considerable, for Bourdon long continued to advocate his father's particular panacea for the economic ills of France; he constantly spoke and wrote about his own experimental school and his conception of enlightened education; and he was an active participant in many of the great events of the Revolution. Considered in detail, however, much of this material is repetitive. Although Bourdon often pleaded powerfully for the adoption of his economic and educational ideas, and even modified them in detail as times changed, they remained essentially unaltered. Moreover, just as he was a practitioner rather than an abstract theorist in education, so too he was politically a man whose career must be assessed as much by his activities as by what he said, for the primary written evidence is fragmentary. There is no single major source such as a diary or a body of sustained correspondence; some periods of his life are simply unrecorded; and at best his interventions in debate were occasional and usually brief. Indeed, the only really detailed written record of his day-to-day experiences relates to his visit to Hamburg in the first few months of 1798, when the Revolution was virtually over.

Furthermore, the secondary literature is so scanty that I have not attempted a serious historiographical survey of it. Here the decisive fact is that Bourdon lived throughout the Revolution. Although he developed with it, he remained true to his initial ideals; hence, in the course of time he, like a few others, became odious to every successive political group, from the royalists of 1789 to the turncoat reactionaries of 1795. Moreover, Bourdon was particularly unfortunate in that he incurred the bitter enmity of those who were well established in Orléans, the principal city in his constituency, and these people proved implacable in their determination to discredit him. Contemporary material about Bourdon is consequently uniformly hostile, and the tales circulated about him became embedded in tradition during the long predominance of the right that ensued. Indeed, these stories still come to the surface from time to time in popular histories and even in biographical dictionaries, the compilers of which are, with a few notable exceptions, apt to rely too much on the work of their predecessors. Also unfortunate for Bourdon, the resurgence of sympathy for the left among historians in the twentieth century has generally led to more concern with collective groupings and socio-economic developments than with individuals. In short, a biographer of Bourdon has no authorities either to emulate or to supersede.

One consequence of all this is that in this instance the search for truth has often been primarily a matter of deciding what really happened. If on some particularly controversial occasions my assessment of the evidence has perhaps erred in Bourdon's favour, then I can at least suggest that 200 years of misrepresentation and neglect excuse some such bias in the correction of it. Overall, however, this book is more factual than interpretative: although it ends with my conclusions, I have generally avoided abstractions and even, I hope, left readers reasonably free to determine the significance of Bourdon's role in the Revolution. Because I have also tried to show that his actions are comprehensible, some indication of the changing circumstances in which he acted is an integral part of his story; nonetheless, this book should not be seen as another history of the Revolution. Concerned with only one man, it can be no more than illustrative. Yet illustration is often instructive. Thus, the reader, who may on occasion be led, as I was, into some curious corners of revolutionary history, may also find that the experiences of an individual sometimes provide fresh perspectives on familiar material. Certainly, my own appreciation of the point of view of the Montagnards has been enhanced by this study.

At this point, I find it appropriate to reverse the usual practice by which authors acknowledge their indebtedness to others before recognizing their own responsibility for mistakes. I take full responsibility for all that is written in these pages, but the whole is perhaps even more predominantly personal than usual; just as there is no substantial work about Bourdon, so too there seem to be few historians to whom he is familiar and fewer still who know him as anything other than an advocate of educational reform.

I have nonetheless been encouraged by the interest of others, and scholars active in related fields have responded to my inquiries, volunteered helpful suggestions, or simply searched their files in vain on my behalf. Specifically, Michael Fitzsimmons prevented me from blundering too badly in my references to the legal profession; Rod Day supplied useful information about the foundation of the École des Arts et Métiers; Benjamin Kennedy helped me to find out more about Bourdon's secretary, William Duckett; and David M. Vess suggested the sources that I consulted for my tentative venture into medical history. I am also particularly appreciative of the assistance of John F. Bosher and James A. Leith, long-standing colleagues whose help in their different fields of expertise has been invaluable. Being far from a fluent speaker in French, I am equally grateful for the patience and courtesy of many archivists and librarians in France, busy people whose helpfulness was generally limited only by the relevant resources at their command. Still more patient were two hospitable scholars to whom I was introduced through the kindness and interest of Professor E. Ducoudray in Paris. I have indeed the happiest of recollections of Roland Gotlib, who taught me much about both the Section des Gravilliers and Bourdon, and of Agnès Thibal, whose work on la Société des Jeunes Français has proved an indispensable component of this book. Unfortunately, however, Raymonde Monnier's succinct and perceptive survey of that school was not available to me while I was writing.[1]

Although the lapse of time and the exigencies of my subject may excuse omissions in these acknowledgments, a failure to record the patience, encouragement and high professional abilities of my publishers would be unforgivable. Beyond praise, too, is the aid gladly given by my wife Jean, the lady who inadvertently married the French Revolution. She has been as enterprising in archival research as she has been persistent in reading and correcting endless drafts of my writing, and much of whatever merit this book may have is indeed due to her.

The Revolutionary Calendar

*A*fter the fall of the Bastille, 1789 was known as the First Year of Liberty. When royalty was abolished in France on September 21, 1792, the Fourth Year of Liberty became the First Year of the Republic, the two terms sometimes being used concurrently. When the Revolutionary Calendar was adopted in October 1793, its effect was retrospective to the first anniversary of the abolition of royalty, so that September 22, 1793, became the first day of Vendémiaire, the month of vintage, of the Second Year of the Republic. Thereafter, the months of the second year ran as follows:

Vendémiaire (vintage)	= September 22-October 21, 1793
Brumaire (fog)	= October 22-November 20
Frimaire (frost)	= November 21-December 20
Nivôse (snow)	= December 21-January 19, 1794
Pluviôse (rain)	= January 20-February 18
Ventôse (wind)	= February 19-March 20
Germinal (budding)	= March 21-April 19
Floréal (flowering)	= April 20-May 19
Prairial (meadows)	= May 20-June 18
Messidor (harvest)	= June 19-July 18
Thermidor (heat)	= July 19-August 17
Fructidor (fruit)	= August 18-September 16

The five additional days, September 17-21, were the *sans-culottides*. For dates between September 21, 1795, and March 20, 1796, add one day. For a full table of concordance, see, for example, J. Godechot, *Les institutions de la France sous la Révolution et l'Empire* (Paris: PUF, 1951), 666.

*R*eaders unfamiliar with the period 1789-99 may find it helpful to have here some approximate definitions of the names used in this book that are most likely to cause difficulty. They generally relate either to the Revolutionary Calendar or to political affiliations.

1. The Revolutionary Calendar

Because this calendar was in general use from 1793 onward, some references to it are inescapable, but specific dates in this text are generally matched with their Gregorian equivalents. Beyond that, the following occasions have acquired general significance and are commonly used by historians.

Thermidor, properly, refers to the overthrow of Robespierre on July 27-28, 1794 (Thermidor 9-10, Year II). More generally, it is often taken as the end of the Revolution as a progressive movement. By derivation, **Thermidorian** usually means reactionary, probably with some upper-class social connotation, and the name, **Thermidorians**, properly that of the men who combined to destroy Robespierre, is loosely applied to those who controlled France from mid-1794 to 1795 or even until 1799.

Germinal and **Prairial**, by contrast, imply the conclusion of the Revolution by the later suppression of popular democracy, these names being those of the two final risings of the people of Paris on April 1 (Germinal 12) and May 20-21 (Prairial 1-2) in 1795 (Year III).

2. Political Affiliations

These collective terms should be regarded with suspicion. In the revolutionary decade, it was believed that, if all men spoke freely as individuals, a general will for the well-being of the whole community would become apparent. Because any group allegiance was then seen as the expression of a partial or selfish interest, the names of parties, now necessary for historians, were usually terms of abuse applied to the real or supposed associates of prominent men by their opponents. They were also extremely elastic, often becoming equated with some ill-defined conspiracy. The principal terms used in this book are here given approximately in their chronological order.

Throughout the Revolution

Aristos was a common general term for those who opposed the Revolution, or any aspect of it, whatever their social standing. From the beginning of the Revolution, it was employed as the converse of **patriote**, one who supported the Revolution both politically and nationally.

In the Period of the National Constituent Assembly (1789-91)

The **Jacobins** rapidly became a major political force, and until 1795 the words *Jacobin* and *Revolutionary* became almost synonymous. Properly, these men were members of the Society of the Friends of the Constitution, which met in the Jacobin (Dominican) convent in Paris, but the name was also applied to those enrolled in any one of the host of affiliated societies throughout France. By repeated purges, by sustained correspondence with their affiliates, as well as by assiduous attention to public opinion, the Jacobins became immensely influential and, in effect, a shadow parliament. After the mother society was dispersed by force in November 1795, all Jacobins were persecuted as anarchists or terrorists.

The **Feuillants** were initially those Jacobins who seceded from the society in July 1791 because they believed that the body was becoming republican. They therefore tried to establish a new society of "true Jacobins" in the nearby convent of the Feuillants. Although that society was short-lived, the name was long used to designate constitutional royalists, particularly those of noble birth and liberal sympathies.

The **Cordeliers**, on the other hand, from 1790 to 1795, were members of the most notable independent club in Paris. Known from its first meeting place, the Franciscan or "Cordelier" monastery in the densely populated district of that name (later the Théâtre Français Section), this club was much more popular in composition, and it was correspondingly even more politically radical and democratic than the Jacobin Club.

In the Period of the National Legislative Assembly (1791-92)

The **Brissotins** were associated with J.-P. Brissot in his initially belli-cose attitude to the king and foreign powers and then in his reluctance to support radical republicanism. Opposed in all but the last of these policies to the Feuillants, they were also suspected of seeking to secure ministerial offices for their personal friends and of hoping to check the Revolution before bourgeois interests were jeopardized.

In the National Convention (1792-95)

The Brissotins are more usually referred to as the **Girondins** because Brissot was then less prominent than his friends from the previous assembly, men such as P.-V. Vergniaud and M.-E. Guadet, deputies of the Department of the Gironde. These men were soon identified with hostility to Paris and a "federalist" policy of enhancing the authority of the local departmental administrations. Partly on that account, and partly because they proved reluctant to condemn the king and accept the emergency measures necessary for success in war, they lost pre-dominance and were proscribed in June 1793.

The **Montagnards**, or "men of the Mountain," were deputies who occupied the highest tiers of seats and dominated the Convention after the expulsion of the Girondins. Commonly, but not invariably, Jacobins, their strength was initially based on close association with Paris, of which men such as Maximilien Robespierre (their principal speaker) and Georges Danton were deputies. Generally regicides, they are particularly identified with the Terror (q.v.), the exceptionally strong emergency government that won military victory for France in 1794, and they are sometimes seen as social democrats. After Robes-pierre was overthrown in July 1794, their influence waned rapidly, and they were generally persecuted after the early summer of 1795.

The **Dantonists** and the **Hébertists** were the two principal factions that challenged the Revolutionary Government when its monopoly of power was being consolidated and its vigorous policies were beginning to take effect. In the winter of 1793-94, the Dantonists pressed for some relaxation of the Terror, while a still more nebulous group linked to the Cordeliers supported the demands of J.-R. Hébert, a popular Parisian journalist, for still more savage repression. Robespierre, how-ever, saw both groups, whether "**Indulgents**" or "**Ultras**," as under-mining government, and he suspected, not without reason, that some of those concerned, the "**pourris**," were corrupt. In March and April 1794, these two groups were eliminated in succession.

During the Time of the Directory (1795-99)

As in the last year of the Convention (1794-95), government was controlled by those called, as appropriate, the **Thermidorians** or the **Directorials**. Their policy, which alternated between reactionary and liberal republicanism, was repeatedly challenged by those excluded from political life. Opponents on the right, which certainly included some constitutional monarchists, were then indiscriminately called "**royalists**," and those on the left, men who hoped to establish a freer and more egalitarian republic, were similarly labelled "Jacobins." In these pages, I have deliberately referred to the latter as **democrats** because the contemporary term was used as one of opprobrium.

3. Other Terms that May Cause Confusion

- The **appellants** were the deputies who voted in January 1793 for a referendum to decide the fate of the king, a course favoured by many Girondins.
- **Département/department** may be either an administrative area (e.g., the Côte-d'Or) or the administrative body itself.
- An **enragé** is any extremist, particularly one who demands sweeping measures to control prices, food supplies, and enemies of the people.
- **Fédération** and **fédérés** were initially highly patriotic terms that implied free association in national unity. Thus until late 1792 the federal forces that went to Paris were seen both as military reinforcements against counterrevolution and as identifying France with the patriots in Paris. By 1793, however, "federalism" had become a term of abuse signifying local independence and hostility to Paris.
- **Insurrection** may, but need not, mean an armed rising. A body that announced itself to be "in insurrection" was in effect saying that, because an emergency had arisen, all power reverted to the people, and it could therefore act independently of regular laws and authorities.
- The **parlements** were the highest courts of justice in France before the Revolution, the most important being the Parlement de Paris. Just as some provinces had their own assemblies, so some had their own high courts, and, while some people in 1789 hoped to standardize these institutions for every province, others (rightly) expected all to be abolished as inequitable.
- An **armée révolutionnaire** was an irregular popular force raised in some French towns in late 1793 to compel farmers and merchants to release stocks of grain for urban consumption. Such forces also sought public enemies and terrorized rural areas and "federalist" strongholds so much that they were abolished early in 1794.

- **Sans-culottes** may mean either the general mass of urban workers or, as it is used here, those of them who were particularly active in the political life of the sections.
- In 1793-94, a **terrorist** supported exceptionally strong government as the only possible means of saving France and the Revolution during a desperate crisis. That support implied acceptance of regulated repression by accredited government agencies, but manifestations of popular and spontaneous intimidation were deplored as anarchical. Least of all should terrorism be thought of as any attempt to intimidate or destroy government itself.

Abbreviations

AD	Archives départementales
AHRF	*Annales historiques de la Révolution Française*
AN	Archives nationales, Paris
AP	*Archives parlementaires de 1787 à 1799* (Paris, 1879-1913)
BHVP	Bibliothèque historique de la ville de Paris
BL	British Library, London
BN	Bibliothèque nationale, Paris
FHS	*French Historical Studies*
Moniteur	*Réimpression de l'ancien moniteur* (Paris, 1854)

1

A Reformer and His Son
(1754-89)

For good or ill, the ideas and attitudes characteristic of the French Revolution seem to have become accepted as an integral part of our own contemporary outlook. Partly, perhaps, for this reason, many historians are now primarily concerned to reassess the significance of the Revolution as a stage in a much longer process of social change. Thus, instead of the sudden triumph of a more-or-less capitalist bourgeoisie, we have the emergence in the early nineteenth century of a new elite of notables, men strangely similar to the *noblesse* of the ancien régime, and considerable efforts are being made to determine the extent to which the remarkably rapid rise of popular democracy in the Revolution was at least initially influenced, if not dominated, by middle-class people.

The predominance of such broad perspectives is perhaps in itself sufficient justification for consideration of the life of an individual revolutionary, Léonard Bourdon. Although his political importance was never as considerable as his notoriety, his almost continual activity throughout the revolutionary decade illustrates many particular aspects of those tumultuous years. His triumphs and tribulations, too, are a salutary reminder of the intensity of the conflicts that divided people during the Revolution—and that are still latent wherever "democracy" is too casually accepted. Moreover, his career provides an interesting case study in sociopolitical relationships; although Bourdon was indubitably an educated and enlightened man whose background was that of the administrative bourgeoisie, he was also for many months a spokesman for and champion of one of the most impoverished and turbulent parts of Paris, the densely populated Section des Gravilliers.

Notes to Chapter 1 are on pp. 347-50.

1

The history of his family, too, may be cited as exemplifying the evolution of the notabilities of nineteenth-century France. According to Chaix d'Est-Ange, the author of a recently republished compilation of genealogies,[1] the families of Bourdon de Vatry and de Saussay both sprang from a man of honourable rank in the eighteenth-century bourgeoisie, Louis-Joseph Bourdon des Planches, the father of Léonard; moreover, one of Léonard's brothers, Marc-Antoine Bourdon de Vatry, became a baron of the Empire in 1810 and was afforded a coat of arms by Louis XVIII in 1814. If we go further, we find that in the 1830s a *baronne* de Vatry, the widow of Marc-Antoine's elder son (Amédée Bourdon de Vatry, 1790-1831) became the *duchesse* d'Elchingen by remarrying into the family of Marshal Ney;[2] moreover, Marc-Antoine's younger son, Alphée de Vatry (1793-1871), a deputy of the Meurthe almost throughout the reign of Louis-Philippe, chose to retire to his chateau in the Oise rather than condone Louis-Napoleon's coup d'état.[3]

Although Léonard Bourdon himself eventually held an office of some importance in the service of Napoleon, our fashionable genealogist mentions him only briefly as that son of Bourdon des Planches who voted for the death of Louis XVI. To presume Léonard to be the black sheep of an honourable family is to follow a well-trodden path, for few of the general historians of the Revolution refer to him other than incidentally and in disparaging terms, and those writers whose sympathies are evidently with the right generally assert that he was at best thoroughly disreputable and at worst a particularly odious terrorist. On the other hand, even a cursory reading of this material soon suggests that neither neglect nor casual condemnation of Léonard Bourdon is satisfactory. Whereas many biographical dictionaries simply duplicate others in reiterating dubious evidence and the scabrous stories that (as may easily be discovered) were originally developed by reactionary journalists after 1795, a few, notably that by Kuscinski,[4] are both more informative and more interesting; so, too, are the biographical notes that appear in the works of scholars, such as Lacroix and Guillaume, who have studied particular aspects of the revolutionary period.[5] In these sources, we see a very different Bourdon, one who was not only a remarkably consistent revolutionary but also a prolific writer and the head of a school whose ideas about education were, and indeed still are, surprisingly advanced. Thus, in encountering Bourdon, we seem from the first to be meeting not one man but two, or at least a man of curiously complex character. Even though a full explanation of this apparent paradox probably lies beyond the sphere of a historian, the problem is one that demands investigation.

Inquiry, however, is by no means easy, and is often speculative, for the literature about Bourdon, if extensive, is fragmentary. Although a lurid account of one episode in his career was published in 1938 under the title *Le Léopard de la Révolution*,[6] no full-length biography exists, and most historians' references to him are brief and unsympathetic. Nor, with the exception of his rather repetitive writings about his educational plans, is there any single substantial body of primary material, for he left neither memoirs nor diary, and only a few of his private letters have survived. Even the record of his protracted public activity is defective: his interventions in debate were usually brief, and there are considerable gaps in the evidence as well as grave problems in interpreting the conduct and character of a controversial figure who lived through a deeply divisive decade. Identification, too, is often doubtful, the name Bourdon being common. Even in 1792-95, when Léonard was a comparatively well-known deputy in the National Convention, he was often confused with another deputy, his namesake François Bourdon; moreover, as is not unusual, if the name Bourdon is used alone, it can refer to either of these men or to someone else entirely.

Such uncertainty is so characteristic of the record of Léonard Bourdon's life that even the date and place of his birth long remained in doubt. Three biographical dictionaries published between 1815 and 1834[7] described Bourdon as a native of Orléans, presumably because he became identified for many people with that city during the Revolution. Then in 1835 Michaud, in the *Biographie universelle*, which is still a standard work, inexplicably but categorically stated that Bourdon was born in 1758 at Longné-au-Perche in the Orne. Successive reference works followed this authority, sometimes placing Longné in the Sarthe, until 1889, when Kuscinski recorded his discovery at Alençon of the registration of Léonard's baptism.[8] This irrefutable evidence reads:

> Le mercredi six novembre mil sept cent cinquante-quatre, par nous prêtre desservant soussigné, a été baptisé Louis-Jean-Joseph-Léonard, né de ce jour, à onze heures du matin, rue du Jeudi, en légitime mariage fils de Me Louis-Joseph Bourdon, s^r des Planches, conseiller du roi, greffier des commissions extraordinaires de son conseil et de dame Thérèse Joly, son épouse. Le parrain Me Joseph Bourdon, s^r des Planches, conseiller du Roi, commissaire aux saisies réelles. La marraine, dame Louise-Françoise Malassis, le père absent.
>
> Signé: BOURDON, Louise Malassis
> B.-F. de la BARTE, prêtre desservant

Thus, in 1754, when Léonard was born, Louis-Joseph Bourdon des Planches was apparently prospering as a royal administrative official. His territorial title, though no doubt initially a necessary means of identification, may well be illustrative of the practice by which many rising families acquired social status and perhaps ultimately some degree of nobility. His office of *conseiller du roi*, which demanded legal qualifications, was a venal one, more honorific than functional; however, as the *greffier* or registrar of one of the more-or-less-permanent commissions entrusted by a branch of the royal council with particular responsibilities, he would have had substantial legal and executive duties.[9] As recorded in the *Almanach royal*,[10] he held this position from 1749-50 to 1756-57, when he was some thirty-five years old, and it involved service in Paris, of which he seems—through several changes of address—to have been a lifelong resident.

Although little is known of Léonard's earliest years, a positive statement by his younger brother, Marc-Antoine Bourdon de Vatry, makes it possible to correct some common errors of identification. Confronted in 1794 with the accusation that his family had been active in support of the king in 1792, Marc-Antoine—then a popular figure in his own district of revolutionary Paris, the Section du Nord—denied the charge vigorously, identifying the family in the process.[11] There were, he explained, five brothers, of whom Léonard was the eldest and Charles, a merchant (*négotiant*) at Orléans, was the second; Marc-Antoine himself, as the third son, had two younger brothers, Thomas and Désiré. Any man may be credited with knowing his own family, so we see that Léonard was not, as is sometimes supposed,[12] a younger brother of François-Mathurin-Pierre Bourdon, who honourably fulfilled high administrative and judicial responsibilities in the Orne. Moreover, it was this man, F.-M.-P. Bourdon, not Léonard, with whom he has been confused, who was a deputy for some years in the national Conseil des Anciens.

Because Léonard Bourdon is also sometimes alleged to have been one of those who guarded Louis XVI when he was confined in the Temple in 1792, we may conveniently notice here that Marc-Antoine's repudiation of royalism indicates that it was in fact the fourth of the brothers, Thomas Bourdon, who was nominated as a guard by the Section du Nord.[13] Neither he nor Désiré, whom Marc-Antoine described as an official at Calais, need concern us further, and of Charles, the second brother, it suffices to say that there was indeed a manufacturer of porcelain called Bourdon du Saunai in Orléans in 1790, a man about whom a contemporary chronicler remarked: "il ne méritait pas d'avoir un monstre pour frère."[14]

Because these brothers had several sisters—shadowy figures whom we shall encounter only once, at a particularly dramatic moment in Léonard's career—the family was evidently a large one, and Bourdon des Planches's ability to give both Léonard and Marc-Antoine a good start in life seems indicative of his status and prosperity. According to Michaud (the *Biographie universelle*), Léonard was a fairly good student at a college in Orléans; but in 1795 he denied having ever lived in that city. Some legal studies may be presumed, even if it was probably by his father's influence that in 1779, at the age of twenty-five, he acquired an office of some distinction, that of an *avocat aux conseils du roi*.[15] By that time, he also had his own title, for in 1767 Bourdon des Planches had, with two associates, purchased a small islet called Crosnière at the mouth of the Loire, so that Léonard became known as Bourdon de la Crosnière.[16] As for Marc-Antoine, who was seven years younger but almost certainly the ablest of the family, he won considerable distinction at a renowned school, le Collège d'Harcourt, in Paris. Appointed, again probably by des Planches's influence, to a junior position in the public service, he became known to Admiral de Grasse, and at nineteen he became the admiral's secretary. After accompanying de Grasse to American waters and being present at the battle of The Saintes in 1782, he entered the Ministry of Marine, in which he rose steadily throughout the period of the Revolution.[17]

Interesting as they are, the details of the later life of Marc-Antoine, Bourdon de Vatry, cannot be considered here. Being more orthodox, and probably better balanced, than Léonard, he followed a more conventional path. Yet he remained one of Léonard's few loyal friends, and, because he jeopardized his own career on more than one occasion by his firm refusal to implement policies that he distrusted, we may reasonably expect his brother to have at least some measure of his consistency, courage, and obstinacy. On the other hand, fuller consideration of the life of Léonard's father is imperative, for Bourdon des Planches and Léonard Bourdon de la Crosnière remained so closely associated both before and during the Revolution that appreciation of the son is impossible without adequate understanding of the father.

In 1765, after a gap of seven years, the name of Bourdon des Planches reappears in the *Almanach* at a higher administrative level than before, that of *premier commis des finances*. Although he subsequently used this title as one of distinction, it does not mean that he was ever *the* principal secretary of the controller-general of French royal finances, a particularly important office. Rather, he was one of several permanent officials, each of whom was the head of staff in one of the various departmental offices into which the administration of finance was divided.[18] Thus for seven years his name appears in the *Almanach* as the *premier commis* of the bureau of M. Langlois, one of the Intendants of Finance, which was established in the Hôtel de Lautrec, quai Malaquais, and which was initially responsible, inter alia, for revenues derived from the monopoly afforded to the India Company. These years were probably those of the Bourdon family's greatest prosperity. Paid according to seniority, the *premiers commis* were exempt from basic taxation, the *taille*; they were given a tax-free annual bonus; and they were assured of a pension normally equivalent to salary.

Between 1771 and 1776, however, des Planches's career went seriously awry. The usual explanation is that des Planches was "dismissed by the *abbé* Terray, who had him imprisoned in the Bastille for the unauthorised printing of proposals of reform and for refusing to reveal the name of his printer."[19] The truth is both more complex and more interesting. In the first place, des Planches's name indeed disappears from the *Almanach* in 1772, but so does the whole bureau of Langlois.[20] This is not surprising, for the abolition of the monopoly of the India Company in 1769 meant that in 1770 the bureau was principally concerned with municipal matters, suggesting that it was becoming superfluous; moreover, Terray, the controller-general who from 1768 to 1774 enforced the financial measures that accompanied Maupeou's devastating attack on the *parlements*, was notoriously high-handed and even brutal in his methods. As for des Planches, probably he was either transferred to another bureau or simply retired as redundant. Although he may not have received a pension immediately, his right to 2,000 livres annually, with the reversion of half that sum to his wife, Thérèse Joly, was recognized by Calonne in 1784, and he is listed as being entitled to the same amount in an official return compiled in 1789.[21]

If not another story, the arrest of Bourdon des Planches in 1776, four or five years after his loss of office, is evidently no more than an indirectly related event. According to his own account,[22] as far back as 1760, when he had travelled with his family from Alsace to his home in Paris, he had been so impeded by constant delays that he had discussed his difficulties with various officials and had eventually drafted a scheme for the extensive reorganization of the service. Essentially his proposal was that two separate means of communication, commonly referred to jointly as *postes et messageries*, should be amalgamated. In itself, this was not unreasonable, for both now appear illustrative of the frustrating complexity of the old order. On the one hand, the mounted courier service, originally a royal means of expediting official documents, had gradually been extended to include the transport of small packages in light carriages, and it had been contracted and subcontracted out to private persons. On the other hand, the coaching service, originally developed privately for travellers, had come at least nominally under state control. Both of these branches, although to some extent supervised by a central bureau, were in fact largely run and financed privately, being regarded as lucrative investments by many interested persons, and Bourdon des Planches had no doubt that the result was duplication and delay. He was equally sure that compulsory fusion and improved state supervision would make it possible to place the posting stations closer together, so that the horses could easily go back and forth with either mail or passengers. Being the man that he was, he developed this plan in detail, considering it of immense potential value for the whole community.

Just as typically, from 1761 onward, he persisted in presenting his plan to a succession of ministers from the Duke of Choiseul to Turgot, who was controller-general from 1774 to 1776. Apparently all save Turgot did no more than refer it to some committee, and even Turgot, who preferred another plan, implemented it only in part. Exasperated by this constant frustration, des Planches had his manuscript printed and published,[23] thus defying both the general censorship and his particular obligations as a respected—if obviously importunate—royal servant.

At this time, moreover, des Planches almost certainly offended the authorities by expressing his opinion about the economy. This action was really more serious, for in effect he challenged the economic and financial policies of the government at a time when popular agitation and divisions in opinion made it unusually sensitive to criticism. At that time, one of the principal questions at issue was whether grain could be moved and sold freely throughout the kingdom or whether, as was the traditional practice, its distribution and sale should be subject to strict central control. Acting more by considerations of expediency than by any particular conviction, Terray had reimposed controls that had been relaxed by one of his predecessors, Bertin, in 1763-64; Turgot, however, whose appointment in 1774 by the new king, Louis XVI, seemed to symbolize the opening of an era of enlightened government, was a firm believer in the liberal economic ideas advocated by the Physiocratic school, and his first and most famous measure was the order of September 13, 1774, which restored freedom of trade in grain and flour. Followed as it was by a poor harvest, this order led to a sharp rise in prices and the widespread rioting known as *la guerre des farines* in the spring of 1775.[24] Turgot's further moves toward freer trade then antagonized many people whose interests were endangered; an outcry led to his dismissal in May 1776, and his immediate successor, Clugny, promptly reversed his whole policy. Thus, in September 1776, the date of the arrest of des Planches, the question of economic freedom or control, which involved enlightened ideas on the one hand and customary practice as well as the dictates of necessity on the other, was extremely divisive, as indeed it would be throughout the period of the Revolution.

That des Planches's own views were not fully formulated at this time matters little, for he would return repeatedly to the subject, publishing one pamphlet after another. Moreover, his first venture into the field, a letter published in 1775 in Amsterdam in irate reaction to an unknown author's observations on the grain trade, indicates his position.[25] Claiming that he had been considering the problem since 1769, he deplored both the official censorship and the private pressures that prevented freedom in discussion. On the other hand, he condemned complete freedom of trade still more strongly. Tracing the difficulties of the day back to Bertin's relaxation of controls in 1764, he asserted that such freedom (and, by implication, the current policy of Turgot) had led directly to speculation and hoarding, to severe shortages and prohibitive prices. The effect, he believed, was to foster artificial divisions of interest between the well-to-do and the poor, between the towns and the countryside—in which misery had led to widespread brigandage.

Although writings in a similar vein were plentiful, des Planches's letter bears the stamp of sincerity. "Get down from your carriage," des Planches calls, "for men in carriages travel too fast to hear the cry of the people and to see how much wretchedness there is." It is also imbued with his characteristic conviction that the measure he himself had in mind would prove a panacea, not only producing general prosperity and concord but also greatly increasing the revenues of the state. Although this remedy was not yet revealed, des Planches was evidently considering what he called "reasonable liberty," some beneficial blending of freedom and control. Whatever its merits, such a solution would have been, and was to be, offensive both to believers in regulation and to advocates of freedom.

Given these circumstances, it is hardly surprising that des Planches was sent to the Bastille, where his entry was registered on September 2, 1776.[26] There is, however, no apparent reason for ascribing his detention to Terray, who had been out of office for two years.[27] The order of arrest was in fact countersigned by Amelot (J.-A. Amelot de Chaillou);

as the secretary of state responsible for the royal household during the ministry of Turgot's immediate successor, M. d'Ogny (May to October 1776), he had some reputation for intermittent rigidity and for abusing his power to issue *lettres de cachet.*[28] The stated reason for des Planches's detention was his publication of proposals for the amalgamation of the posting services, but des Planches was also asked to explain his concern with the reorganization of the grain trade, and his justification of this concern may serve as a summary of his whole defence of his activities. He had, he said, "always sought to employ whatever free time he had for the benefit of his fellow-citizens."[29] He was, in short, respectful but not apologetic, and his detention, which lasted only two weeks, until September 19, would probably have been even shorter if he had not stubbornly refused to reveal the name of his printer. The period of imprisonment thus seems to have been not so much a punishment as a reprimand and a warning.[30] If so, then it was at least temporarily effective, for we have no further publications by Bourdon des Planches until 1785—by which time, surprisingly, he had been established for a year as the proprietor of a porcelain manufactory in the Faubourg Saint-Denis, this enterprise being under the protective patronage of the king's brother, the Count of Artois.[31]

The arrest and detention of des Planches in 1776 are sometimes supposed to have been bitterly resented by him and his sons. The affair certainly attracted some public interest, being seen as illustrative of the restrictive character of the government, but its effect on the family may be doubted. Des Planches had taken a conscious risk but did not suffer unduly: his professional career had already been interrupted, and thirteen more years would elapse before the beginning of the Revolution—when the imprisonment became almost a brevet of revolutionary respectability.[32] As we have seen, too, in 1779-80 des Planches still had sufficient influence and resources to secure promising appointments in the royal service for both Léonard and Marc-Antoine Bourdon.

Here it would be simple to repeat the traditional assertion that Léonard Bourdon was unsuccessful as a lawyer. That assertion would not do much to advance our understanding of him, for similar statements could be made about many men whose reputations in the Revolution stood much higher than his. The judgment, however, seems to have been drawn from an absence of evidence. What is known is that Bourdon retained office as an *avocat aux conseils du roi* until 1785, being listed for the last time in the *Almanach* of 1786;[33] that he then resigned his charge, by his own account, because he had become more interested in education; and that in 1781 he had been consulted in a dispute of some notoriety. These facts certainly do not suggest spectacular success. They may indicate a lack of interest in the practice of law. They do not, however, prove a lack of ability, and ability is apparent in his assessment of the one case in which we know him to have been involved, that of the Benedictine Congrégation de Saint-Maur.[34]

That dispute, like several others, really arose because many monks had become dissatisfied with the more austere practices of their rule, and their conflicts with their superiors led them to demand more say in the regional assemblies of representatives of their order. In particular, three monasteries in the province of Normandy protested to their provincial assembly that their priors had dominated or distorted the elections, thus ensuring that only their own nominees accompanied them to the assembly. The affair consequently went to the general chapter of the order, which first heard from a commission of inquiry most unsympathetic to the dissident monks and then became involved in problems of procedure. It was on these problems that Bourdon de la Crosnière was required to rule as a royal advocate, and his opinion, based both on the constitution of the order and on *les lumières naturelles*, seems to have been as acceptable as it was uncompromising. More surprisingly, perhaps, Bourdon ruled firmly in favour of the authority of the assemblies concerned. He considered that the reverend father who had headed the commission of inquiry had been fully justified in asserting his authority; that the three priors, though perhaps negligent in conducting the elections, were wholly wrong in refusing to retire while their conduct was under discussion; and that those who supported them in this regard were even more at fault. In Bourdon's view, such dangerous examples of disobedience could be explained only by some particular interest in promoting schism, and they should be firmly suppressed. Although at first glance this does not seem to be the attitude expected of a future revolutionary, it is perhaps an interesting anticipation of the conviction that the authority of a duly constituted assembly, as of its delegates, is sacrosanct.[35]

Exactly what Léonard Bourdon did between this consultation in 1781 and the final months of 1788 is uncertain. We know that he remained an *avocat aux conseils* until 1785. We know, too, that he was not, as was long supposed, the secretary and steward from 1780 to 1791 of Senac de Meilhan, a gentleman of some literary repute who soon became an *émigré*; that position was in fact held by a different Bourdon, an André-Joseph-Dominique.[36] On the other hand, it is likely that his attachment to the Congregation of Saint-Maur was of some duration. The Benedictine order in France having become much concerned with education, that congregation was responsible for six of the military schools established by Louis XV and Louis XVI for the training of potential officers, and it apparently required legal advice in its endeavour to reform these establishments. That Bourdon provided such guidance over a period is implicit in the opening words of his first publication, which appeared late in 1788.[37]

> In 1780, in difficult circumstances, the directors of the Congregation of Saint-Maur chose me as their counsel; I had the good fortune to justify their confidence. I was more than once in a position to appreciate the devotion with which this reputable body of scholars sought to fulfil the purposes of the government in the various military schools entrusted to their care.

From these and other remarks in the same publication, we may presume that from about 1780 on Bourdon was principally concerned with education and with the formulation of his own ideas about it.

Meanwhile, his father, Bourdon des Planches, whose thought on the economy of France had long been maturing, published four pamphlets: the *Projet nouveau* in 1785; *Bases pour taxer le pain* and the *Code fraternel* in 1787; and a letter to the king entitled *Au roi* in December 1788.[38] Because des Planches was concerned in all of them to advance, elaborate, and defend the single proposal on which his thought had focused, they may be considered together. In his view, the whole economy of the country depended on the price of grain; however, because farmers were subject to burdensome taxation, productivity was fairly low and prices were unduly high. This situation was aggravated by the freedom increasingly afforded lately to proprietors and merchants to sell grain as they wished either in France or abroad. That freedom, in his opinion, was founded on a foolish faith that "nature will do all," whereas he believed that it really fostered cupidity: speculators and monopolists profited, but scarcities increased prices still further, so that, despite the benevolence of the monarch, general misery and insecurity were straining confidence in the government. Des Planches was nevertheless sure that the situation could easily be transformed. First, producers should be freed from the burdens that restricted them, the multiplicity of imposts being replaced by a single tax on the sale of grain. Second, a single trading company, to be called the Company of France, should be created and given the responsibility of establishing and maintaining granaries in all principal towns. After a year, during which stocks would be built up, the company would be obliged to buy and sell grain at fixed prices determined in part through consultation with local authorities. Because the purpose of the company would be not only to maintain supplies in good and bad times alike but also to ensure that prices remained competitive, it would not have any monopoly of trade within France. It would, however, be sustained by the monopoly and complete control of the exporting and importing of grain between France and foreign countries.

This plan, developed in detail and accompanied by a draft in sixty articles of appropriate legislation, first appeared as the *Projet nouveau* in 1785. Published in Brussels, this booklet soon became available in Paris, for des Planches had been careful to obtain permission to explain his ideas to the public, and it apparently aroused considerable interest. A contemporary noted in 1786 that Bourdon des Planches was regarded as an oracle and praised in all the journals, and early in 1788 the *Mercure de France* particularly recommended the pamphlet to its readers.[39] The following three pamphlets were primarily replies to criticism. Thus, the *Bases pour taxer le pain* indicated how a basic price might be calculated, and the *Code fraternel* emphasized that the company would be compatible with internal freedom of trade. There is, however, an interesting change in its proposed composition. In 1785, des Planches suggested that forty directors be chosen by the king; by 1787, he had come to believe that the interest of the nation demanded unity, and the *Lettre au roi*, which included the request that all his works be put before the Estates-General due to assemble in May 1789, called for the reinforcement of the royal nominees by representatives chosen by each of the provinces of France, so that the company would be "directly in the hands of the nation."

Indicative as it is of the rapid evolution of opinion in the final months of 1788, this change of emphasis also exposes an aspect of des Planches's plan that was to become particularly contentious. As the *Mercure de France* remarked, his exposition was clear and interesting; as always, des Planches himself was convinced that his proposal would be universally beneficial, doubling the royal revenues even as it increased production, guaranteed reserves of grain, and substantially reduced the price of bread; however, how or by whom so considerable an undertaking could be effected in the desperate circumstances of the time was never made clear. Despite his carefully compiled statistics, the plan was unrealistic.

In contrast, Léonard Bourdon's consideration of education led in 1788 to the more modest proposal made in his *Plan d'un établissement d'éducation nationale*: the monarchy should sponsor the establishment of a new school where his ideas could be tested.[40] As Agnès Thibal has emphasized in a recent thesis,[41] Bourdon was always a practical man as well as a theorist. The ideas advanced in his *Plan*, the first of many brochures that he would write about education, nonetheless have far-reaching implications. This is not to say that Léonard was an original thinker: indeed, different strands in his conception of education may be traced back to writers such as Condillac, Helvétius, and particularly Rousseau, whose publication of *Émile* in 1762 had combined with the expulsion of the Jesuits from France in 1764 to stimulate protracted intellectual debate about teaching. Despite differences of purpose that subsequently emerged, he was probably also influenced by the example of *le chevalier* Pawlet, the founder of a school famous for its enlightened approach to the training of young gentlemen. Bourdon's exposition of his own views yet remains remarkably clear, forceful, and comprehensive.

Like his father, Léonard opened his argument with a description of the existing state of affairs, which he regarded as vicious in principle. He remembered his own childhood as a period of austerity, when he had often been angered by the arbitrary power of his teachers; moreover, although he was convinced that any school was infinitely better than private instruction, his observations of the work of the Congregation of Saint-Maur had convinced him that prevailing methods were totally wrong. He believed that pupils, condemned for long hours and long years to be passive recipients of abstract information, became so frustrated that discipline could be maintained only by severity, which in turn bred deceit. Thus, learning became despised, and the way of the teacher was so "sown with thorns" that "a state of perpetual war" existed between master and pupils. Yet, again like his father, Léonard shared the general conviction of the age that problems of this sort were essentially artificial and could easily be resolved if "nature and reason, two infallible guides," were trusted: "a simple natural means applicable to all times and places must exist."

Having this attitude, as well as "a natural sympathy for children," Léonard believed that a school should be a residential community in which young people are afforded ample opportunities to participate actively in a wide range of both cultural and technical studies and physical recreation. Within the specific times allocated to the various fields of activity, the pupils should be free to pursue the interests and skills that are most attractive to them, the teachers being guides and observers rather than simply instructors. To Léonard, however, all this was subordinate to the development of the child in a progressive social environment. In the school that he proposed to establish, all would be equal members of a self-governing community, electing their own officials, making their own laws through a general assembly, and distributing both awards and punishments (excluding corporal punishment) in a court of their own creation. The new regime, however, would not be without its own rigours: the day would begin at 5 a.m. and continue, with periods of recreation, until the lights were extinguished at 9 p.m.

These proposals obviously anticipated many of the ideas that are still seen as "advanced" in our own day—"free activity," "learning by experience," and so on—and schools closely akin to that planned by Bourdon, such as A.S. Neill's Summerhill, may still attract or repel observers. Fundamental to all these ventures is the belief that "education," taken as meaning the development of one or more aspects of individual character, is more important than "instruction," the imparting of knowledge and the development of the power of reasoning. Bourdon was emphatically in favour of "education," and he remained true to this conviction even when it became the most divisive of the issues involved in the revolutionaries' many debates about educational reform. Even in 1788, however, it seems that he was looking beyond the individual to the social order: he wrote about educating "social man"; he called his plan one for national education; and he constantly thought of the school, which he proposed to call la Société d'Émulation, as a society in miniature.[42]

Bourdon soon seemed to be succeeding in his initiative. Fully aware that a residential school with a wide curriculum would be expensive, he hoped to attract parents who were well placed and had high ambitions for their sons—a fact that has led some writers to point out that he was really offering egalitarian education only to the aristocracy.[43] To obtain both patronage and a nucleus of pupils, he realistically approached authority in the first instance, writing to J.-F. de la Tour du Pin Gouvernet, a well-known and liberally minded soldier, who was apparently sufficiently impressed to forward the plan to the Minister of War. According to Bourdon,[44] the minister put the proposal before the royal council on October 5, 1788, when the establishment of the school as a place of civil and military education, to be called la Société Royale d'Émulation, was authorized by letters patent.[45]

On the other hand, authorization and patronage were intangible assets, and no evidence has survived to substantiate Bourdon's later claim that the Minister of War gave him a written promise of a certain number of pupils. Nevertheless, Bourdon launched his venture with enthusiasm. The *Plan* and the royal Order in Council were published and distributed, together with a detailed prospectus of the new society, the latter indicating that it had premises ("l'hôtel de la société, rue des

Gobelins à Paris") and at least one member of staff (the director of military exercises). How many pupils had actually been enrolled by May 1789 is uncertain, but whatever the number Bourdon first appears in the records of the Revolution as an *instituteur*, a *maître de pension*.[46]

Assessment of Bourdon at this time of transition may begin with a brief consideration of two quasi-historical comments. First, Dr. Siegfried Bernfeld, a German educational psychologist, produced an article in 1930[47] in which he argued that Bourdon's revolutionary career was marked by hatred of authority and that it was the result of his failure to sublimate subconscious hatreds, particularly of his parents, developed during his childhood. This interpretation does not sit well with the historical facts. Léonard was not, as Bernfeld supposed, a young sprig of the nobility who renounced his rank and identified himself with the masses; his short reference in the *Plan* to his childhood does not seem to be specific enough to bear the weight imposed on it, and, as will be seen, he consistently associated himself with his father's continued efforts to effect economic reform. Second, Armand Le Corbeiller opened his account of Léonard's "assassination" in 1793 with a derogatory reference[48] to the supposedly slavish and hypocritical terms that Bourdon employed in addressing the king at the beginning of the Revolution. That both father and son approached the king in language that now seems unduly humble and adulatory is true, but such terminology was normal and universal at the time, when there was no thought of destroying the monarchy. Such language, of course, affords no guide to individual character.

More generally, the little that is known about his background and career before the Revolution does not suggest that Léonard Bourdon was a man likely to be an extremely violent and unscrupulous terrorist. His family seems to have been respectable, of some substance, and not without contacts with men of higher social rank. Like his father and his younger brother, Léonard was a professional man, and, although his abandonment of the law in favour of education may have caused him financial difficulty at the beginning of 1789, there is no reason to think of him, or to suppose that he thought of himself, as one who was failing in life. If due allowance be made for the exaggeration natural to one seeking to obtain government funds, his statement in 1791 that he had sacrificed "honourable and useful estate" to keep his school alive[49] is not unacceptable. Nor need too much be made of the fact that his father had lost his position at some time between 1772 and 1776 (when he was between fifty and fifty-four years of age) and been briefly confined in the Bastille in 1776, thirteen years before the Revolution.

Although that short period of restraint may have increased the family's awareness of the unpredictability of life at the time, no disloyalty or tendency toward violence appeared as its consequence. On the contrary, in the matter of the monasteries, Léonard seems to have been more inclined to maintain than to challenge authority.

Nonetheless, both he and his father were intelligent and well-educated men who could express themselves in powerful and convincing prose. Each, moreover, had formulated plans for a far-reaching reform and was convinced that the adoption of his particular principles would be beneficial beyond all measure. Although Léonard had only begun to make his presence felt, he was evidently as ready as his father to risk his career for the sake of these principles. Indeed, persistence taken to the point of obstinacy seems to have been a characteristic common to both men. That plans like theirs for the reorganization and reform of many aspects of French life soon proliferated, generally being advanced as panaceas, may be recognized, but this proliferation should not diminish appreciation of the fact that before the Revolution the Bourdons were active advocates of constructive, if naturally controversial, improvements in French life.

Yet they should not be seen simply as well-meaning reformers. On the contrary, many of their attitudes were revolutionary. Both Bourdons believed that most of the perceived ills in society sprang from a single cause, and both believed that a single and simple change would transform everything. True, Léonard's school was to be one in which his method would be demonstrated, and his father recognized that his own plan for the economy could not immediately be fully operative, but in neither approach was there any real suggestion of gradualness or of compromise. Moreover, the thinking of both men had a strong moral dimension: just as the environment, whether economic or educational, was the root cause of social evils, so too an easily effected alteration of it would be morally as well as physically beneficial. Unhappily such convictions may all too easily imply that all opposition may legitimately be condemned as morally reprehensible.

To the Bourdons, as to many other such men, 1789, the year of the first assembly of an Estates-General since 1614, thus seemed to be the opening of an age of unbounded opportunity for the people of France. In fact, however, they were soon confronted by a revolution far more extensive and much more violent than they or anybody else could possibly have anticipated. In responding to it, the Bourdons occasionally acted together, but Léonard, by thirty years the younger man, naturally became the more prominent of the two.

2

The Revolution of 1789:
The Political Activist

From 1789 onward, Léonard Bourdon's public life had two major themes. As a political figure, Bourdon was an ardent revolutionary. As an educationalist, he campaigned tirelessly for the development of his own school, which he believed ought to be a model for many others throughout France. This duality has inevitably fostered hostile criticism, for Bourdon can easily be condemned either as a teacher who exploited his pupils to promote his own political career, or as a politician whose only real purpose was to secure favours and financial support for his school. Although both views are plausible, their apparent incompatibility suggests that there may be some less superficial explanation of Bourdon's behaviour.

One obvious fact is that his educational and political activities, if sometimes interwoven, were more often pursued in succession. In 1789, when Bourdon was still an unknown man, the latter pattern predominated. Initially concerned simply with the foundation of his school, he was soon involved in the exciting events that occurred in Paris. At the end of the year, however, the gradual return of calmer conditions coincided with the resumption of his effort to advertise his ideas about education and to gain public support for his school, and this endeavour seems to have been his principal concern until the summer of 1792.

Although the winter of 1788-89 was a time of severe hardship and intense political debate about the composition and procedure of the forthcoming Estates-General, Bourdon presumably welcomed the new year with confidence. He had won royal patronage for his school; he probably believed, as he maintained afterward, that he had been promised financial backing by the royal government and that a nucleus

Notes to Chapter 2 are on pp. 350-52.

of pupils would be provided by the Ministry of War; and he certainly expected to attract the interest of many parents. Indeed, as early as January 4, Bourdon implored his printer to send him 100 copies of the *Plan*, which he had submitted to the king in 1788, together with 1,000 copies of the *Prospectus* that had accompanied it.[1] He hoped, moreover, that la Société Royale d'Émulation would be approved and expanded by the representatives of the nation who were to assemble at Versailles on May 5. In the address entitled *Aux États-Généraux: idées sur l'éducation nationale,*[2] Bourdon reiterated his earlier argument that existing methods of teaching were not only arbitrary and oppressive but also harmful both to the individual and to society. In his view, a premature appeal to reason and a constant emphasis on the acquisition of information had long prevented the development of any sense of social responsibility in schoolchildren.

On this occasion, however, Bourdon went further than before, emphasizing the importance of equality and optimistically suggesting that, because the Estates-General was to provide France with a constitution, it should also take steps to ensure that education appropriate to that constitution would eventually become freely available to the entire nation. Claiming that what he called "MY PLAN" showed how easily young people could be encouraged to live as equals under laws of their own making, Bourdon urged the deputies to study his proposals of 1788 and, if they approved of them, to see that the provincial assemblies[3] applied his principles and methods in all the colleges in their charge. This step, he asserted, could be financed simply enough by a redistribution of the excessive funds already allocated from lotteries or taxation to the military schools.[4] So aided, the colleges would be the foundation of a system of national education, and that would indeed be "une vaste et superbe monument" to the work of the Estates-General.

Nor was this all, for soon afterward Léonard Bourdon joined his father, Bourdon des Planches, in addressing another proposal to the assembly. *Aux États-Généraux: subsistence et impôt,*[5] published as the joint work of the Bourdons, is so closely akin to the earlier writings of the elder Bourdon that he may well be thought almost entirely responsible for it. Yet Léonard's participation on this occasion is not without significance, for the younger Bourdon was later to champion substantially the same recommendations and, in doing so, to acquire some repute as an economist in his own right.

As in the *Projet nouveau* of 1785, the first major recommendation in *Subsistence et impôt* was for the formation of a national body that would have the exclusive right to buy or sell grain beyond the frontiers and that would be responsible for establishing and maintaining throughout France public granaries for the purchase, storage, and sale of grain. Because the use of these granaries would be optional, freedom of trade would be preserved, but the evils of competition, such as private hoarding and speculation, would be ended because the granaries, replenished from abroad if necessary, would always have supplies and would constantly buy or sell at fixed prices. Abundance being thus assured, the second recommendation followed, again as in des Planches's earlier works. The multitude of dues and taxes hampering agriculture should be replaced by a single tax on grain (which would in practice be offset by allowance for it in the determination of prices at the granaries). This system would substantially reduce the cost of bread, which would so cut the costs of manufactured goods that the revival of agriculture and commerce would proceed simultaneously.

Thus far, the only notable difference between this proposal and des Planches's previous proposals for the "full and perfect regeneration" of the French economy is that the controlling national body now appears as distinct from the government, being entirely composed of representatives elected by the different regions of France. *Subsistence et impôt*, however, has an interesting preamble in which the Bourdons contend that the first duty of the Estates-General must be to ensure the provisioning of the markets and a reduction in the price of bread. Asserting that even the best of constitutions will not benefit those who die of starvation, they demand that the Estates-General immediately appoint an extraordinary commission with full powers to determine the price of grain and to purchase and distribute supplies for sale at that price. This imperative note may indicate the influence of Léonard, the younger and probably the more impatient man, but both Bourdons seem to be well aware of the sufferings of the poor and sincere in their belief that hardships could be mitigated by their proposed measures.

That neither of these projects for the regeneration of education and the economy in France could come to anything in 1789 now seems almost self-evident. In reality, the meeting of the Estates-General was occasioned by the bankruptcy of the treasury and accompanied by the total collapse of what remained of royal government. Moreover, even if the new assembly had not been inundated by a flood of equally ambitious long-term plans, it was—from the hour of its inauguration—wholly concerned with meeting the immediate political crisis precipitated by the government's determination to preserve the separation and independence of the three ancient orders, the clergy,

the nobility, and the commons. Only when the commons had succeeded in overcoming that determination by asserting the sovereignty
of the nation, and when the power of the people had been demonstrated by the Parisian revolt of mid-July, could even the essential features of a new and legitimate system of government be considered.
Nor, as far as la Société Royale d'Émulation was concerned, could the
time have been propitious for the foundation of a new residential
school in Paris, particularly as the costs to parents were to be considerable—a fact that Léonard Bourdon implicitly recognized by offering
one place in ten to the children of the poor without charge. Indeed,
despite its pretentious title and imposing address, in 1789 the school
probably had no more than a few pupils, if any at all.[6]

Nevertheless, it is worth repeating that Bourdon first appears in the
records of the Revolution as an *instituteur*, a *maître en pension*. These
records show that he was chosen, presumably on April 21, 1789, as
one of those members of the primary assembly of his district, Saint-
Marcel (Quartier de Sainte-Geneviève, in southeastern Paris), who
would attend the Assembly of Electors of Paris to elect deputies of the
city to the Estates-General. Because most of the documents about
these first primary elections in Paris were destroyed in 1871, we know
little of what happened in Saint-Marcel; however, when the electors
drew up a list of their membership in July, Bourdon de la Crosnière was
included, being identified as Directeur de la Société Royale d'Émulation pour l'Éducation Nationale. A slightly fuller record similarly
shows that Bourdon des Planches, described as an *entrepreneur de
manufacture de porcelaines*, was also chosen, being the sole representative of his district, Saint-Laurent (Quartier Saint-Denis, in northern
Paris).[7] Thus, both Bourdons became entitled to call themselves an
"Elector of 1789," a title that in due course became a hallmark of
devotion to the Revolution.

For a time, that title was indeed one of real significance, for both
the primary assemblies and the Electoral Assembly were in various
degrees bodies that acted in open defiance of the royal authority by
which they were convened. Although the size and social complexity of
Paris made particular electoral arrangements imperative, the relevant
decrees did not appear until March 28 (when the city was afforded
forty deputies, twenty of whom would be for the Third Estate) and
April 13 (when the franchise and electoral procedures were determined). These regulations were clearly reactionary, for by that time
ministers and officials were concerned to check the growing independence of the commons in general and of Paris in particular. The city was

divided into sixty districts, each of which was required to return one member to the Electoral Assembly for each 100 of those present and voting in its primary assembly; however, these districts, if often loosely associated with one or the other of the city's fifty-three parishes, were really artificial creations that stood apart from the established communal life of the guilds and *quartiers*. Moreover, the franchise was in effect restricted to the wealthiest third of the adult male population (about 50,000 of a population of some 600,000),[8] and the district assemblies were to meet once only, under official supervision and without formulating any statements of grievances (the *cahiers* that were drafted throughout the rest of France). In the tense and turbulent atmosphere of the time, such regulations made even attendance at the assemblies an act of some civic courage, and it is scarcely surprising that only 11,706 of those eligible to vote actually did so.[9]

The district assemblies generally showed astonishing independence, consenting to tutelage only when the officials sent to preside over them were willing to do what they wished. There was, as Jean-Sylvain Bailly, the astronomer and philanthropist who was soon to become the first mayor of Paris, noted, "a new atmosphere." Indeed, one district, the Barnabites, formally explained that "the regulations are not at all obligatory . . . since the right of explaining its demands [and] its complaints, and of giving a mandate to its Representatives, is inherent in every assembly of French citizens called together by the King to send a deputation to the Estates-General."[10] The proceedings of the districts that returned the two Bourdons seem to have been, so far as we know them, typical of such independence. In the District of Saint-Laurent, Bourdon des Planches was duly elected by seventy-six voters, who accepted a visiting officer as their president but proceeded to draw up a *cahier*, which des Planches personally deposited at the Hôtel de Ville on April 23. That Léonard Bourdon's Saint-Marcel was even less inclined to accept authority is also sufficiently apparent, for there the eighty-seven voters chose no fewer than six electors, and drafts of a *cahier*, which was presumably completed, remain on record.[11]

To what degree father and son were also socially representative of those men who were bold enough to become electors is perhaps more disputable. There were 407 electors (only 300 had been called for in the regulations), and the historian Ch. L. Chassin has classified Léonard Bourdon as one of eight who were concerned with education, a group that included two representatives of the University of Paris (an additional district). Des Planches similarly appears as one of six entrepreneurs.[12] Chassin's classification also indicates that, apart from a group of men who were previously officials, 15 percent of the membership of the Electoral Assembly was drawn from the liberal professions, whereas 34 percent came from commerce and manufacturing and 42 percent were men of the law.[13] The Bourdons were thus similar to other men in the assembly.

Their status there is another matter. In 1987, Michael Fitzsimmons showed that the influence of the Parisian Order of Barristers was pervasive in the elections and that no fewer than sixty-eight, or 16 percent, of the electors were members of that particularly prestigious order.[14] Thus, although the two Bourdons were evidently entitled to vote and hold office (at their own expense) both as taxpayers paying at least six livres in the poll tax and as men having professional qualifications, this broadly bourgeois standing would hardly have entitled them to be placed among "the élite of the bourgeoisie"—a contemporary description of the district assemblies.[15] Both men in fact resided in and represented districts inhabited by working people, Saint-Marcel in particular being part of the Faubourg Saint-Marcel, the home of some 30,000 *ouvriers* and a notoriously impoverished area. Moreover, although the primary assemblies generally seem to have shown concern for the plight of the poor while rigorously excluding those not enfranchised, discussion in Saint-Laurent was apparently concentrated on the matter closest to Bourdon des Planches's heart, the urgent necessity of reducing the price of bread and regulating its cost through a popularly elected body.[16] There is thus some probability that both father and son may have been more sympathetic than many other electors to the problems of the poor.

Unfortunately the Bourdons' political position within the Electoral Assembly must also be mainly a matter of presumption, for references to them in its recorded proceedings are rare. They were probably overshadowed initially by men of established reputation and perhaps by others who were, if not more radical, then at least quicker to make their presence felt in political life. The *procès-verbaux* of the assembly do not provide conclusive evidence of this relative obscurity, for these volumes were not finally compiled until 1790, and, as Bailly explains in his preface to them, the torrent of events soon became so overwhelming that it was often impossible for the secretaries to do more than keep notes of essentials.[17]

Nevertheless, the assembly as a whole clearly emerges as a remarkably united revolutionary body. In defiance of all authority, the members insisted on electing their own officers, on meeting apart from the nobility and the clergy of Paris, and on preparing an elaborate *cahier* of proposals for the future, all *before* the members elected their deputies to the Estates-General. Moreover, the results of this protracted process were momentous. The deputies of Paris, appearing belatedly at Versailles, played a decisive part in resolving the constitutional crisis by promoting the annexation of sovereign authority by the National Assembly, and in Paris the Electoral Assembly inevitably became involved both in national and in municipal affairs. Instead of dissolving when their formal work was finally accomplished on May 23, the electors resolved to reassemble at intervals to keep in touch with their deputies, and so they passed from preparing addresses in support of the National Assembly to protesting against what seemed to be a developing attempt to isolate and overawe Paris by military force. At the same time, as supplies of grain diminished and the price of bread soared, they increasingly accepted responsibility for the government and welfare of the capital. Indeed, by July 13, when Paris was in open revolt and complete anarchy was imminent, theirs was the only authority extant for the city as a whole.

Presumably the Bourdons participated in most if not all of this momentous process, the successive stages of which were marked by the electors' move from a room in the archbishop's palace to the Grand Salle of the Hôtel de Ville after June 28; by the establishment in terrifying circumstances of a Permanent Committee on July 13; by Louis XVI's recognition of Bailly as mayor and of Lafayette as commander of the newly formed National Guard on July 17; and by the decision on July 23 to convene a new assembly of 120 representatives, two from each of the sixty districts, to draft a new municipal constitution for Paris. More specifically, the names of both father and son are on one crucial list, that of the electors who were present at the Hôtel de Ville on July 14. Moreover, at the end of that month, both men were re-elected by their districts as members of the new representative assembly, which in effect became a provisional commune, and both were similarly chosen as members of the committee charged with drafting proposals for the new municipal constitution.[18] Beyond this information, we know of Bourdon des Planches only that he was one of those who on June 25 expressed the assembly's appreciation of a temporary meeting place (which implies that he may have been a member of the committee set up to find permanent accommodation) and that he was nominated by his district to a proposed delegation to welcome the king to Paris on July 17.[19]

References at this time to Léonard Bourdon are still scantier. They are, however, of interest. On May 8, the electors resolved to send

Map 1
Paris at the time of the Revolution

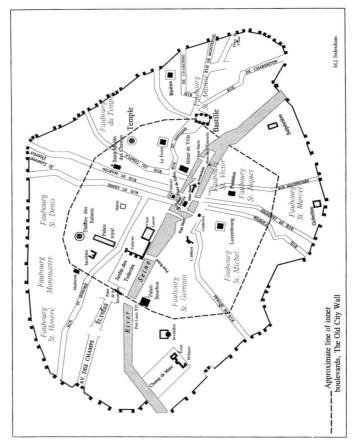

Source: Adapted from Michael Sydenham, *French Revolution* (London: Batsford, 1965).

delegations to the nobility and to the clergy of Paris, bodies that were then still meeting as separate chambers, to ask them to support a protest against the Royal Council's decision to ban Mirabeau's *Journal des États-Généraux*, the famous first number of which had just appeared. Although the electors' *Procès-verbal* does not mention Léonard in this context, the records of the *noblesse* show that he was one of the delegation to their assembly.[20] Delegations of this sort were frequent, but this one was of some importance. Originally appointed to present the *cahier* of the commons to the nobility, it was now also required to call for free reporting of parliamentary debates. His presence may thus indicate that Léonard was gradually acquiring a degree of prominence.

At approximately the same time, too, he published his first political pamphlet, apparently an expanded version of a proposal that he hoped to make, and perhaps actually made, to the Electoral Assembly on May 7.[21] This proposal amounted to a demand for the abolition of hereditary nobility. Although welcoming that order's acceptance of liability to taxation, Bourdon argued that its size had constantly been increased both by descent and by the purchase of title-bearing offices, so that the order had become burdensome to society; moreover, once merit and ability were recognized as the only valid qualifications for distinction between citizens, the inheritance of rank became an anachronism. After considering the possibility of establishing peerages for life only, Bourdon rejected it as likely to cause new social frictions without eliminating existing evils, so he recommended the replacement of hereditary titles by a completely new honour, a *brevet de citoyen utile* open to all but not transmissible from one generation to another. This honour, he believed, would be welcomed by the nobility, many of whom were already enhancing the traditional renown of their names by important public service, and he even suggested how recommendations for the award might be initiated by local assemblies and endorsed first by the provincial assemblies and then by the Estates-General.

Léonard Bourdon's first political publication is thus in part typical of its time. Written before June 17, when the Third Estate at Versailles, together with a few clergy and nobles, assumed all authority as the National Assembly,[22] it presumed that in the future the monarchy, the Estates-General, and the provincial assemblies would continue to exist harmoniously together. Although it echoes Sieyès's well-known indictment of the privileged orders as a tiny minority that monopolized honours, profit, and power, it is written in far more restrained terms, and it

may even be thought to be, within its compass, more realistic. It nevertheless suggests that its author felt strongly about the principle of
equality of opportunity, and its revolutionary nature is sufficiently evident in the fact that hereditary nobility and titles were not abolished
until June 19, 1790, more than a year later. Bourdon's attitude certainly would not have been popular in the Electoral Assembly of the
Third Estate of Paris, which retained remarkably respectful and even
cordial relations with the Assembly of the Nobility of Paris.

The implication of this relative radicalism is that Bourdon was
probably in more congenial company in the Provisional Commune that
succeeded the Electoral Assembly on July 25. This body was convened
both to ensure that the daily business of administration had more legitimacy and to prepare a plan for a properly constituted municipality.
Initially it consisted of 120 members, two being elected by each of the
sixty districts, and, as we have seen, both Bourdons were of this number—Léonard at this time being listed simply as an *ancien avocat au
conseils*, although his address, rue des Gobelins, remained that previously ascribed to his school.[23] On August 5, however, the new assembly was reinforced by a further sixty members, one additional person
being called for from each of the districts to compensate for the many
absences occasioned by committee work, and thereafter the Commune
was clearly a good deal more advanced in attitude than the Electoral
Assembly had been. True, many of the electors, like the two Bourdons,
were simply confirmed in office as representatives of the Commune,
but it is a reasonable assumption that these were men whose conduct
during the tumultuous days of mid-July was approved by their districts.
Moreover, among those newly elected were a number of notable
democrats, such as Brissot de Warville and the *abbé* Claude Fauchet,
and these men were soon engaged in the first round of a long conflict
with the mayor, Bailly, about the rights and powers of the assembly
relative to the authority of the mayor's own office on the one hand
and that of the districts on the other.[24]

As one of many attempts to settle that problem, which involved
not only the relationship between the executive and the legislative
powers but also a question fundamental to the whole Revolution, that
of reconciling representative and direct democracy, yet another municipal election soon had to be called. Thus, from September 18, 1789,
until October 8, 1790, the Provisional Commune consisted of 300
members, five from each of the districts, and once again both Bourdons were re-elected.[25] Although neither seems to have played any
notable part in the constitutional conflict, for a time both were active

members of the Commune, being particularly concerned in August and September 1789 with the vital and immediate matter of maintaining food supplies for Paris. Appropriately des Planches was soon a member of the Subsistence Committee, and, when that committee was reconstituted on September 8, Léonard also became a member, being appointed secretary the next day.[26] This was probably because he, with others, had already successfully fulfilled various commissions allocated to him by the Commune in its constant search for provisions.

At least one of these commissions merits fuller consideration as illustrative of the situation and of Bourdon's conduct at this time. It began on August 4, the date on which reports of extensive rural disorders moved the National Assembly at Versailles to adopt the momentous resolutions generally known as "the Abolition of Feudalism." That evening the Commune heard that two electors, Garin and Charton (respectively a master baker and a clothier), had been arrested in Provins, a fine old walled town fifty miles southeast of Paris, where they had been trying to buy grain for the capital. To such news the Commune, barely contriving to keep Paris fed from one day to the next, was highly sensitive. Four of its members—La Grey, de Sauvigny, Bourdon de la Crosnière, and La Chesnaye—were promptly appointed to go to Provins to conciliate its people, release the two electors, and secure the provisions. Told to take immediate steps to ensure that this deputation was well protected and successful, Lafayette, the commander of the armed forces of Paris, mustered 400 men and two cannons, and the Minister of War ordered the troops in garrison at Provins, a detachment of the Royal-Cravatte Regiment, to be prepared to support the expedition. Thus, although the four commissioners were instructed to express the Parisians' fraternal greetings to the people of Provins, "enfants de la même patrie," the Commune's force departed as if to suppress a rebellion.[27]

The record of events in Provins itself similarly suggests that serious conflict might well have occurred. Alarmed by rumours about the burning of crops by brigands, and as concerned as the Parisians about the adequacy of their own supplies, the people there had already taken up arms before the two electors, Garin and Charton, arrived at the head of a line of 150 empty coaches. Although the mayor at first refused to release anything until the amount of grain available had been properly calculated, the electors eventually drove off with sixty coachloads of cereals, disorder being prevented by the local police. Two days later, however, the electors are said to have returned with a force of fifty armed horsemen who called themselves "the Conquerors of the Bastille," and these men allegedly terrorized the town until they and the electors were themselves besieged in an inn by soldiers of the garrison. By the time peace was restored, the electors' cry for help had reached Paris; however, as this appeal failed to distinguish between the garrison and the townsmen, the Commune overreacted, and its display of force so alarmed Provins that the people there expected to have to defend themselves against an attack.[28]

That conflict was averted was due in part to the reluctance of the authorities in Provins to risk open hostilities with Lafayette's force, even though the major commanding the garrison urged resistance and an offer of support arrived from Troyes.[29] Nevertheless, according to the report that Bourdon gave to the Commune on August 16, the conduct of its commissioners was well designed to placate opposition. The Commune heard that as its force advanced the men were halted along the road by detachments, so that the last armed men were left some twenty miles from Provins. Advancing alone to Maison-Rouge, five miles from the town, the commissioners wrote to the local authorities to suggest a meeting. Once that suggestion was accepted, Bourdon was able to speak for his colleagues to a general assembly of about 800 people, assuring them that Paris sought only their superfluity, for which they would be paid in full, and disclaiming any intention of interfering in their own civic affairs. So effective was this address that Bourdon had subsequently to speak again to explain the rights and duties of citizens and the paramount importance of communal unity, and, still according to his own report, this appeal was so moving that all the local officials at once resigned, being immediately either re-elected or replaced by public voting.[30]

After this, harmony apparently prevailed. All agreed to assist the two electors in their work and to aid them if they were again molested, and on the eve of their departure the commissioners organized a civic festival for all comers. They then left for Paris amid acclamations and with the promise that the young men of Provins would soon follow them with all the grain that could be spared. Hence, the commissioners' only remaining anxiety was that the men of Provins would be received in Paris well enough to consolidate the new relationship between the two towns.[31] They need have had no fears, however; when the militia from Provins arrived with thirty wagonloads of wheat, they were met by Lafayette and a detachment of the National Guard, and they were afforded a reception by Bailly before being escorted by Léonard Bourdon to the opera, where the performance of the evening began again in their honour.[32]

Essentially this report by Bourdon seems to be reliable despite its explicit emphasis on his own activity, for it was a collective statement, written in the third person and signed by all four commissioners. True, the register of the Municipality of Provins gives a more mundane account, indicating that Bourdon's address interrupted an election that was already in progress and that the business raised by the commissioners from Paris was not considered until that election was finished.[33] Nor does the report to the Commune confirm a local story that the Parisian force had compelled adjacent villages to release grain that they had been withholding from Provins: it simply and not improbably claimed that once confidence had been restored many farmers had opened their granaries and begun to thresh and market the new harvest. However, if something on both sides be discounted as due either to the commissioners' tendency to exalt their own role or to the desire of Provins to record its independence, then the substance of Bourdon's account of how one potentially disruptive situation was resolved in 1789 is acceptable.

Although it is impossible to determine the exact extent of Bourdon's contribution to this small but spectacular success, his influence appears to have been considerable.[34] Bourdon also seems to have acted sensibly and with much more restraint than might be expected from one later to be of such ill repute. Still more notable is the appearance of this man, hitherto really remarkable only as an educational reformer, as an orator well able to rouse large numbers of ordinary people to enthusiasm for self-government and cooperation with Paris in a common cause. The provision of the civic supper in Provins and the visit to the opera in Paris are also characteristic, for Bourdon, if he was a bourgeois and an intellectual who was always inclined to be theatrical, also appears as one who took equality seriously and was blessed with the common touch.

By this time, too, Bourdon was gradually becoming more notable, the affair at Provins being but one of many commissions for the Commune with which he was concerned in August and September 1789. On August 22, he was again one of several members of that assembly who were sent into the countryside to increase the supply of provisions to Paris,[35] and on three occasions (September 2, 8, and 30) he was sent with others to Versailles to bring the concerns of the capital to the notice of ministers and the National Assembly.[36] Specific details of these assignments are elusive, but the advocacy of Parisian interests at Versailles was certainly a difficult matter. On the one hand, Paris was primarily concerned with the food situation, which—despite all endeavours—deteriorated so steadily that the Commune was constantly confronted by angry and intractable delegations from the districts, and there was always the possibility of a new general insurrection. The Hôtel de Ville therefore looked to Versailles for more explicit laws and more powers to enforce them, both to control trade and to maintain law and order. The deputies at Versailles, however, were much more inclined to favour economic liberalism than to encourage new regulation, and they were still far from ready to formulate definitive laws. Although in July they had won recognition as the National Assembly, they remained frustrated by the king's continued refusal to commit himself to any final and formal approval of "the Abolition of Feudalism" (August 4), the Declaration of the Rights of Man (August 27), and the Principles of Government (October 1), all of which were seen as the constitutional prerequisites of legislative progress. It is therefore worth remarking that on one of the three missions Bourdon and his colleague, Charpentier, should have won both the authority that they sought for the Commune and the praise of the principal minister, Necker, who particularly commended "the zeal and intelligence of the two delegates."[37]

Bourdon was also concerned with various other matters at this time, for until the size of the Provisional Commune was increased in mid-September, members' administrative duties were generally heavy. On August 13, for example, he was one of those called on to consider the problem of providing arms for the mixed force of volunteers and paid soldiers that was then being organized as the National Guard, and it seems that he subsequently wrote a paper of some length, now lost, about the larger problem of making the army more national in spirit.[38] On August 13, too, Bourdon made the first of the many public dramatic gestures by which his revolutionary career would be marked, offering two free places in his school, la Société Royale d'Émulation, to children whose fathers had died in the assault on the Bastille or in any other conflict for public freedom. Today this offer may seem suspect as advertisement, but it was seen at the time as an honourable and noble proposal, and the Commune publicized it accordingly.[39]

Whatever Bourdon's true motives on this occasion, his interest in the men who had been prominent in the attack on the Bastille, as well as in the welfare of their dependents, is certain. Indeed, from this time onward, Bourdon often described himself as a "Conqueror of the Bastille,"[40] and that title has naturally led historians to assume that he had participated in the fighting that led to the fall of the fortress.[41] My own inquiries, however, have not revealed any evidence either to substantiate or to refute that assumption. As we have seen, Bourdon was then one of the electors of Paris, and he was listed as present at the Hôtel de Ville on July 14, but such chaos reigned there that few individuals can be otherwise identified. Again, although in the course of the day the electors, or more precisely their Permanent Committee, sent three different delegations to the Bastille to assess the situation and to try to prevent violence, Bourdon was not a member of any of these delegations.[42] The only possible (and wholly speculative) conclusion is that, if he was among the combatants, then he joined them simply as a Parisian.[43] Curiously, however, his right to describe himself as he did is indisputable.

This apparent paradox becomes less perplexing once we realize that the siege of the Bastille was rapidly followed by the appearance of many claimants for the honours of victory. That some of them were impostors soon became obvious. On July 18, for example, there appeared before the electors a boy aged thirteen who asserted that he had been the fourth person to scale the walls of the fortress and the first to show a flag on its battlements, and it was not until he was confronted by some of the French Guards, who knew that there had been no such assault or displaying of a flag, that the electors could dismiss him as "a little liar."[44] After receiving a complaint about such impostors from three of those who had in fact been prominent in the fighting, the Commune on August 10 appointed four commissioners— Dusaulx, La Grey, Bourdon de la Crosnière, and Oudart—to determine the truth, and on August 13 these commissioners presented an initial report naming nine men whose claims to recognition were beyond dispute.[45] Almost simultaneously, however, Lafayette gave the assembly an account of a visit that he had made to the Faubourg Saint-Antoine, where he had seen badly wounded men and bereaved families reduced to destitution, and the Commune was so moved by this account that the commissioners' brief was extended to include consideration of all genuine cases of such suffering. After this, the occasion of Bourdon's offer of places in his school, the commissioners had to be reinforced by two more members, Thuriot de la Rosière and d'Osmond, for their task was evidently becoming formidable.[46]

Although to anticipate the outcome of this arduous and protracted work would be premature here, one aspect of it relates directly to the problem of Bourdon's later description of himself. The commissioners conducted their inquiry by co-opting those whom they had first identified, so that all who claimed to have been active participants in the attack were scrutinized by men who were undoubtedly "Conquerors of the Bastille."[47] The title thus became that of the commission itself, and, when a deputation of these *Vainqueurs de la Bastille* presented the final list of names to the National Assembly on June 19, 1790, they explicitly added "those of the commissioners chosen from the representatives of the Commune who have presided over their operations."[48] Moreover, Bourdon's name is included, with the endorsement "ancien avocat aux conseils, commissaire." Thus, the question of whether Bourdon was or was not present when the Bastille fell remains open, being even more disputable because some of the six commissioners, notably Thuriot, were certainly there, whereas others, notably Dusaulx—also noted as a *commissaire*—were not, but Bourdon's right to the title *Vainqueur de la Bastille* as an honorary one seems to be firmly founded. Indeed, Bourdon himself really claimed no more than this, for in 1792, in a brief recapitulation of his earlier career, he remarked: "The *procès-verbaux* of the Constituent Assembly included me in the number of the Conquerors of the Bastille."[49]

Still greater obscurity conceals Bourdon's activities during the second great rising to occur in 1789, that of the October Days, when the people of Paris, again exasperated by hunger and by suspicion of the court, marched to Versailles and compelled the royal family to return with them to the capital, captives in fact if not in name. That Bourdon played some part in this insurrection is probable. In the same recapitulation of his political activities, a pamphlet that he wrote when his revolutionary record was challenged by Marat in September 1792, he said: "On October 5, I compelled Lafayette to march to Versailles. On October 6, as a commissioner of the municipality, I conducted Louis the Last to Paris."[50] These claims might have been expected of him in 1792, when an impeccably patriotic record was politically imperative. They are nonetheless obvious exaggerations, commendable only in comparison with the still wilder statement by Bourdon's only biographer, Armand Le Corbeiller: "We meet him [Bourdon] again in the October Days, marching on Versailles at the head of a mob of women, and of men disguised as women, to bring the king back to Paris."[51]

On the other hand, the known facts do little more than limit the range of possibilities. On September 30, the Provisional Commune again resolved to send commissioners to Versailles to argue its case on various matters. One was the need for further legislation to penalize interference with the free movement of grain, and Bourdon, one of the eight commissioners,[52] may have been chosen because he was the secretary of the Subsistence Committee. Five unnamed members of this mission were still at Versailles on October 3, when one of the other three (who are also unidentified) reported to the Commune,[53] so a more general political consultation about bringing pressure to bear on the king was possibly then in progress. If so, and if, as his own state-ment implies, Bourdon was in Paris on October 5, then he was proba-bly one of the three who returned; nor would it have been uncharacteristic of him to look at a critical time to Paris rather than to the corridors at Versailles.

To go beyond this, however, would be to carry speculation too far. On October 5, Lafayette was indeed forced to lead the National Guard of Paris to Versailles, where its strength was decisive in forcing the king to capitulate, but he ordered the march only after almost eight hours of tumult, during which his life was repeatedly threatened by furious crowds and his own mutinous men.[54] Bourdon may well have sup-ported the more-or-less-nominal vote in the Commune that finally authorized the march; however, if he was one of those who had threat-ened Lafayette, then it is improbable that the Commune would have commissioned him the next day, as it did when it heard of the king's approach, to express its appreciative congratulations to the general.[55] For the rest, because he was not one of the four members of the assem-bly who had been appointed to accompany Lafayette to Versailles, one can only suppose either that he joined the returning procession after delivering his message of thanks or that he was simply one of those many members who followed their president and the mayor when they went out to welcome the king to Paris.

If Le Corbeiller's assertions are dismissed as fanciful, and those of Bourdon himself duly discounted as deliberate hyperbole, then the lat-ter's real role in this second insurrection in Paris seems to have been more prosaic than either glorious or discreditable. His political impor-tance at this time is perhaps more accurately indicated by more mun-dane evidence. On September 20, when the enlarged Commune was holding its first formal roll call, his re-election was challenged;[56] more-over, although those charged with verifying the voting (including his father, Bourdon des Planches) soon returned a decision "absolutely favourable" to him, he was only the twentieth and last of those elected in November to one of the Commune's principal committees, that charged with preparing a new municipal constitution.[57] And in 1789-90 he was apparently named only once more as a commissioner, one of the twelve who took the Commune's good wishes to ministers at the beginning of the new year.[58] Indeed, from this time onward, his only obvious participation in the work of this Commune was his sus-tained concern with identifying the heroes and victims of the fight for the Bastille. It is thus possible that his standing may have been diminished by violent behaviour during the October Days, but a simpler explanation of his withdrawal is that once comparative calm prevailed in Paris he probably gave increasing attention to his own affairs, particularly to his plans for education.

It was nevertheless in October 1789 that Bourdon first became notorious. Unwisely he identified himself and his school with a minor event that aroused great public interest, the appearance before the National Assembly of Jean (or Jacques) Jacob, the "Centenarian of the Jura." The existence of this aged peasant, whose baptism in a remote hamlet had been recorded in 1669, had somehow been discovered by Cérutti, a literary figure of some repute as a popular journalist, and in 1788 Cérutti's romanticized accounts of the man and his situation had stimulated much similar writing about the virtues of rural simplicity.[59] Then in 1789 it had occurred to someone that it would be appropriate, and presumably profitable, to produce Jean in Paris. Strangely enough, the old man survived the journey, nursed along the way by two members of his family and a doctor. On October 11, he was taken to the Tuileries to meet the king, an occasion that attracted little attention; and two weeks later, on October 23, his unexpected arrival was announced to the National Assembly, which had followed the king to Paris and was then meeting in the archbishop's palace.

The scene that ensued was both dramatic and embarrassing: although a visit in 1789 by a man who had been born in the early years of the reign of Louis XIV was indeed remarkable, the deputies were shocked by the spectacle of a man almost moribund, quite unlike the sturdy survivor portrayed by the press. Consequently a sudden silence prevailed until one deputy, aptly remarking that the visitor's great age had enabled him to witness the regeneration of France, proposed that a collection should be taken for the family. The president then announced a request from Bourdon de la Crosnière, "the author of a plan for national education that had previously been presented to the assembly." The author, he explained, wished to take the venerable old man to his patriotic school, where young people of all ranks could care for him with all the respect that they had been taught was due to the elderly.

It is to his credit that this was not the first occasion on which Bourdon had raised the possibility of having some old people in residence in his communal school: the *Plan* that he had submitted to the king in 1788 suggested including twenty such residents. His offer to accommodate Jean Jacob, presumably made before the centenarian's condition was apparent, may therefore be thought sincere. Moreover, there is no reason to suppose that he was one of those who had effected Jacob's removal from the Jura. Yet he evidently had advance knowledge of the presentation to the National Assembly, which suggests that he had some dubious acquaintances in what has well been called the literary underworld of Paris, and he was clearly concerned to exploit an opportunity to advertise himself and his establishment. The assembly's response to the president's announcement indicates that the deputies found Bourdon's proposal somewhat offensive, for the awkward interval that ensued was ended by Mirabeau's great voice: "Do as you will with the old man, but see that he remains free."

It is unlikely that the centenarian remained in Bourdon's charge for longer than was necessary for an artist named Flouet to complete a portrait of him at a window of the hôtel "de la Société d'Émulation de M. de Lacrosnière." Retrieved by his family, Jacob was established in a more central location near the Palais-Royal, and there he could be seen by the curious, presumably for some appropriate donation, until he died in January 1790. Bourdon's name was nevertheless tarnished by association with this discreditable affair, of which distorted versions were long afterward accepted as proof of his wickedness. In 1850, for example, Désiré Monnier, an annalist of the Jura, identified Léonard as a well-known charlatan, the man who purchased "our centenarian" from a granddaughter for 100 crowns and then let people see him at some small price per person until he died of exhaustion.[60]

However, if the Revolution had been satisfactorily concluded at the end of 1789, Bourdon's general record as a revolutionary would not have been particularly remarkable for either good or ill. Like his father, and like many other Parisians of the middle sort, Bourdon had represented his district at a critical time and had consequently become a member of the municipal assembly. In that capacity, he had served in committee, notably the vital Subsistence Committee, and satisfactorily fulfilled a number of missions of importance. Yet unlike Bourdon des Planches, who was a member of the council of the Commune and, by virtue of his age, sometimes presided over it, Léonard Bourdon did not become an *administrateur*.[61] His record, which shows that he was most obviously active during the particularly tense months of August and September, may indeed suggest that, although he would have readily worked to remedy particular cases of hardship, he did not find either administration or the routine of a representative's work congenial. Rather, it shows that he was able to respond energetically to the demands of a critical situation and to speak vigorously and convinc-

Fig. 1. The Centenarian of the Jura. An engraving showing Jean Jacob in 1789 at a window of Bourdon's first school, La Société Royale d'Émulation. Private collection. From G. Lenotre (L.-L. Gosselin), *Paris révolutionnaire: vieilles maisons, vieux papiers,* 6th series (Paris: Perrin, 1930).

ingly to large numbers of ordinary people, as he did at Provins. Thus, his re-emergence as a political activist in the still greater crisis of 1792 was presaged. At the end of 1789, however, his reputation, such as it was, seems to have been the outcome of his two offers of accommodation in his school, the one to two "orphans of the Bastille" and the other to old Jacob from the Jura. Probably well meant rather than well considered, both offers may easily be dismissed as mere advertising, but they also suggest that in Bourdon's mind political revolution and the development of a new form of national education were really different roads to the same goal. For Bourdon, education remained the true highway to the future, even though circumstances might make political action more immediately imperative.

Léonard Bourdon certainly seems to have been readier than his father to accept a postponement of his plans. Submitted initially to the Estates-General, his exposition of his ideas on education was merely acknowledged by the National Assembly in mid-September,[62] but he does not seem to have done anything more about this matter at the time. In the course of the summer, by contrast, Bourdon des Planches once again submitted his proposals for economic reform to the National Assembly, publishing them as the draft of a decree in which no fewer than fifty-seven clauses defined the operations of a new national administrative body or "Association Patriotique."[63] Thus, when the National Assembly's Committee of Agriculture and Commerce met on November 30 to consider the papers with which it had been presented, it found that four of fifteen proposals had come from Bourdon des Planches.[64] The Commune was similarly canvassed, for on September 15 the author requested a report on the proposals that he had distributed some weeks earlier.[65] The responses to the father, however, were no more encouraging than the acknowledgment given to his son, for the Commune simply suggested that des Planches submit his ideas to the Subsistence Committee—which was probably all too well aware of them already; moreover, on January 2, 1790, the National Assembly's Committee of Agriculture and Commerce recommended that the scheme be circulated to the municipalities of France for comment.[66] Thus, in 1789 both men encountered the fact that a free government may be just as evasive as a more arbitrary one, a truth that both would have many more opportunities to learn.

Neither, however, seems to have been unduly discouraged, for optimism and faith in the inevitability of human progress were characteristic of the age, and the Bourdons were nothing if not persistent. If the high hopes with which they had begun the year had not been fulfilled at its end by any real advance toward the achievement of their particular plans, then they had at least experienced the euphoria of freedom and witnessed the collapse of an order of things so complex that extensive changes were almost impossible. Moreover, although many people had been alarmed, and some had been irrevocably alienated, by lawlessness in the streets and by the apparently limitless pretensions of democracy at all levels, few could have foreseen the appalling difficulties that the National Assembly and its successors would have in implementing plans for the future. For the two Bourdons, as for most French people, hope in 1789 was deferred but not diminished.

3

$\mathcal{A}$ $\mathcal{F}$rustrated $\mathcal{R}$eformer (1789-92)

$\mathcal{I}$n 1789, Léonard Bourdon's principal interest was in political revolution, but for the next two and a half years the record of his
activities is dominated by his endeavour to establish his school on a
firm foundation and so to promote radical changes in education
throughout France. This distinction between education and politics
should not, however, be seen as absolute, for his pursuit of innovation
in education compelled him to seek substantial political support, and
that involved participation in political life. In all probability, too, Bourdon now became more convinced than ever that a real regeneration of
society demanded political as well as educational reconstruction.

Bourdon's evolution in 1790-92 indeed poses a historical problem
parallel to that raised by the collapse of the new constitutional regime.
In August 1792, that regime, the apparent fulfilment of such high
hopes and so much careful consideration by the National Assembly,
was destroyed by a second revolution, far more violent than the first,
and in that revolution Bourdon, a reasonably respectable member of
the bourgeois government of Paris at the end of 1789, was a prominent
popular leader and a man commonly identified with calculated bloodshed. Even if much allowance is made for the exaggeration and distor-
tion of his role by contemporary opponents and hostile historians, the
fact remains that in the course of the years between 1789 and
mid-1792 Bourdon, like many other French people, became a committed republican revolutionary.

Unfortunately no complete explanation of this transition is possible, for practically nothing is known of Bourdon's private life, and the
records of his public activity at this time are scanty. Consequently the
biographical studies that exist are either discreetly silent or simply

---

Notes to Chapter 3 are on pp. 353-58.

superficial in their treatment of the period. Thus, Armand Le Corbeiller, in introducing *Le Léopard de la Révolution*, presumes that there is no problem: Bourdon's whole record being one of personal failure and unrestrained violence, he naturally appears in August and September 1792 as almost personally responsible for the sacking of the Tuileries and the wholesale slaughter of helpless prisoners.[1] Moreover, among the many biographical dictionaries that I have consulted for this study, all but three move directly from October 1789, when Bourdon offered accommodation to Jean Jacob, the centenarian of the Jura, to the tumult of August 1792. Nor are the three exceptions really helpful in their references to the intervening period. The most recent, Roland Gotlib's entry in the bicentennial *Dictionnaire historique de la Révolution Française*, mentions the re-establishment of Bourdon's school in 1792;[2] in *La Grande encyclopédie* (1886-92), Aulard deals more fully with the same topic and includes Bourdon's statement of his activity in the crisis of July 1791; and in the *Biographie universelle* (1835), Michaud, probably echoing earlier works by Rabbe (1834) and Arnault (1821),[3] remarks that Bourdon's behaviour in the matter of the centenarian, being that of a mountebank, attracted the attention of agitators and led to his association with them.

Speculative though it is, this last assertion cannot be entirely ignored. As we have seen, Bourdon's anticipation of the appearance of old Jacob before the National Assembly does suggest that Bourdon knew some disreputable people, and, inclined to be theatrical, he may well have come to enjoy the society of extremists. Michaud's argument is nonetheless interesting only as a possible minor factor in Bourdon's development, for the suggestion that Bourdon was simply a weak man, easily led astray by evil associates, is incompatible with his subsequent record of political independence.

More tangible and more important is his sustained interest in the identification of the Conquerors of the Bastille and their dependents. Although Bourdon remained a member of the municipal assembly until September 1790, this was apparently the only official activity that he took seriously that year, and it would have brought him into contact both with active democrats and with the *menu peuple* of Paris. The matter, pending since August 1789, was revived in February 1790 by an appeal to the Commune of Paris for succour by twelve widows, and between March 26 and June 15 a Bastille Committee, composed of the commissioners of the Commune and men such as Bonnemère, Élie, and Maillard, well-recognized participants in the attack on the fortress, met frequently and in public to assess innumerable claims.

Although the minutes of these meetings do not reveal the extent to which particular individuals contributed to the discussions, they show that Bourdon was invariably present.[4]

The first result of the committee's work was the presentation to the National Assembly on June 19 of its final list of the 866 names of those whom it believed to be entitled to recognition for their sufferings or services on July 14, 1789. This total included seventy-three wounded or crippled and some twenty-five widows and orphans. The majority of those named, incidentally, have been identified as typically Parisian working people of the time—tradesmen, artisans, and wage earners. In enthusiastic response, the assembly decreed that distinctive arms and uniforms be immediately awarded to the survivors, who would be afforded a place of honour in the anniversary festival, la Fête de la Fédération. These men were also encouraged to form a separate company in the National Guard, to be known as the Conquerors of the Bastille, and the question of compensation to the severely wounded and the bereaved was referred to the assembly's Pensions Committee.[5]

To general surprise, though, the matter did not end at this point. There was, indeed, so great a clamour in Paris that the Commune feared that street fighting would begin and might even lead to civil war. Some people protested that the list was too long, comparatively few of those named having been really active in the assault on the Bastille. More particularly, soldiers of the French Guards, the garrison troops of Paris who had been incorporated into the National Guard after playing a decisive part in the Revolution of 1789, resented the honours to be afforded to the new company, and this resentment was also apparent in other established units. Thus, there was soon a general feeling that any list must be rejected because the fortress had been invested and conquered not by any particular group but by the people of Paris in general.[6] Focusing on the undesirability of awarding distinctive dress and insignia to anyone once the equality of all people had been recognized, this outcry shows how far popular opinion had moved in the previous year and how wide a gulf was opening between the more radical democrats and the relatively conservative members of the National Assembly.

Significantly Léonard Bourdon was prominent among those who succeeded in restoring concord on June 25. In the evening of that day, a large and tumultuous meeting of the Conquerors of the Bastille took place in the Church of the Quinze-Vingts in eastern Paris.[7] The mayor, Bailly, presided, and the question at issue was nothing less than whether the "Conquerors" should fight if necessary to uphold the

National Assembly's decree. Addressed first by Maillard and then by Bourdon, who spoke "d'abondance de coeur et mieux qu'on n'écrit ordinairement" and was long applauded, the assembly also heard appeals by Bailly and by democrats such as Dusaulx and Fauchet.[8] Yet it remained angry and inclined to call the eastern *fauxbourgs* to arms against the supposed plots of the aristocracy. A further speaker (de la Reynie) then transformed the situation by an extraordinarily effective speech calling for the voluntary renunciation of all distinctions and privileges. The substance of this speech was promptly (by prearrangement?) presented to the meeting by Bourdon as a long resolution addressed to the National Assembly. Acclaimed and accepted, this resolution was taken at once to the National Assembly by a deputation headed by Bailly, and there Bourdon himself read it to the deputies, who duly welcomed it as a noble sacrifice.

Bourdon's contribution both to identifying the most deserving and to averting a conflict about discrimination was thus considerable. Yet the final results of the whole inquiry were disappointing. At the end of 1790, the National Assembly approved its committee's recommendations regarding compensation, which can hardly be called munificent: four severely wounded citizens were paid 400 livres each, and twenty-five crippled citizens and one widow were afforded pensions for life of 200 livres.[9] A few days later, too, the Commune, taking advantage of a general decree against any unauthorized association of soldiers, forbade any continuation of meetings by the "Conquerors."[10] Nor does it seem that Bourdon's activity in the original inquiry did anything to improve his standing in the Commune: almost immediately after the danger of conflict was past, Bourdon and Dusaulx narrowly escaped a formal reprimand for signing an announcement, apparently emanating from the Bastille Committee, that had somehow appeared as an official public notice.[11]

In all probability, Bourdon's drift toward radicalism at this time was also related to a deterioration in his financial position and in that of his father. Neither the income nor the expenditure of either man can even be indicated here, but Léonard's claims for compensation from the government for the costs incurred in creating his school were to continue for years, and there were some signs that Bourdon des Planches was also encountering difficulties. The latter need not be exaggerated, for des Planches, who remained an active member of the Commune until it was reconstituted in October 1790, became in November a member of the new Electoral Assembly of Paris,[12] and eligibility for that position depended on a relatively substantial tax payment, the equivalent of ten days' labour. Moreover, in April 1790, the annual pension of 2,000 livres awarded to him in 1784 was confirmed by the National Assembly, as was the reversion of half that amount to his wife,[13] and in 1790-91 he published, presumably at his own expense, at least three pamphlets about the economy.[14] Nevertheless, after January 1790, when a considerable quantity of porcelain manufactured at his works was sold by auction,[15] we hear no more of that enterprise. No doubt the demand for porcelain, like that for other luxuries, had declined sharply after the October Days, when a great many wealthy people decided to emigrate. Again, in December 1790, he and Thérèse Joly (Madame des Planches) had to rearrange the repayment by instalments of debts amounting to 43,000 livres, which they owed to a business agent, and they were apparently much concerned to reserve their right to the possession of their residence in Paris.[16]

Despite the absence of detail, this state of affairs does a good deal to substantiate Léonard Bourdon's later statement that considerable help from his father had alone enabled him to finance his first school, la Société Royale d'Émulation. He also claimed that the cost of this school had been ruinous,[17] and his assertion is not to be dismissed, for, as we have seen, he had taken possession of expensive premises by the beginning of 1789, engaging at least a skeleton staff and advertising his establishment extensively. Nor, indeed, was it ever entirely dismissed. In January 1790, Bourdon made what seems to have been his first formal claim for compensation for the losses that he had incurred because, as he believed, the royal government had failed to honour its promises of support. This claim amounted to 39,053 livres, and twelve months later the National Assembly at least recommended the claim for consideration by its Pensions Committee.[18]

Fed though it was by this and later delays and difficulties, Bourdon's personal grievance against the government remained rooted in his conviction that it had betrayed him in 1788-89. Certainly Bourdon had been given neither money nor pupils, and he ascribed these deficiencies partly to the inherent duplicity of a royal and aristocratic regime and partly to growing ministerial suspicion of him as a man with dangerously advanced ideas.[19] If, however, there was deliberate procrastination, it could equally well have been his own fault, for he had not hesitated in seeking to replace the patronage of the Royal Council with that of the Estates-General and the National Assembly, and in that process he had re-emphasized the "national" character of his project.

Beyond such considerations, beyond even the fact that royal support for a new venture was bound to be minimal in 1789, there is the salient point that, whatever Bourdon believed, the government's commitment to him was never as great as he claimed. In fact, the Order in Council of October 5, 1788, had authorized him to form a civil and military school to be known as la Société Royale d'Émulation and assured him of the king's protection "s'il remplit l'espoir du public par l'exécution de son *Plan*." In other words, the school was to be established at Bourdon's own expense, and any assurances of further support were clearly conditional on its satisfactory development.[20] By securing l'Hôtel des Gobelins and the nucleus of a staff, Bourdon may have met the first of these requirements, but the second proved beyond his reach. Although he evidently intended to make the school spectacularly successful, his proposed provision of endless opportunities for voluntary studies and activities meant that the fees asked of parents were prohibitive.[21] Thus, whatever doubts ministers had about Bourdon's political activities were probably secondary to their reluctance to send pupils from extant military schools to an embryonic establishment.

From a wider perspective, there seems to be no reason to suppose that Bourdon's far more famous school, la Société des Jeunes Français, was simply a continuation of la Société Royale. By far the greater probability is that in 1790 Bourdon abandoned all hope of keeping the latter alive and thus resolved to make a new beginning.[22] Apparently—and fortunately well before the fuss about the poster for the Bastille Committee—his first approach was to the Public Establishments Department of the Municipality of Paris, which responded very favourably on March 29. Declaring that the promotion of his plan to familiarize young people with the principles of the Constitution was in the interest of the city and of all parents, the municipality invited all friends of the Constitution to work together to ensure that the experiment was successful.[23] So encouraged, Bourdon on April 6 presented the General Assembly of the Representatives of the Commune with his *Mémoire sur la nécessité de former une école d'expérience pour le partie morale de l'éducation publique*,[24] which was then referred to the Reports Committee; on May 31, too, he sought to win support at the highest level by speaking in person at the bar of the National Assembly.

On this occasion, Bourdon submitted to the deputies an array of documents, the principal one being the *Mémoire*, now entitled *Mémoire sur l'instruction et sur l'éducation nationale*[25] (one part of which he subsequently—and significantly—published simply as *Sur l'éducation nationale*).[26] Attached to the *Mémoire* was an essay on the education of heirs to the throne, advocating a way in which national supervision of such education could be exercised without detriment to parental rights. There was also a copy of the municipality's recent enthusiastic ruling of March 29 and, in forty-nine articles, the draft of a decree covering the organization of national education in publicly supported schools. Because the *Mémoire* incorporates much of Bourdon's *Plan* of 1788, the presentation on May 31 probably provides the most comprehensive statement of his views about existing education in France and what should be done to improve it.

In phraseology probably borrowed from Bourdon, but nonetheless typical of the time, the Municipality of Paris had spoken on March 29 of the importance of supporting his plans as a means of "preparing the regeneration of public education." Few people would have denied that the necessity for some such change was fast becoming imperative. France before the Revolution was in fact surprisingly well provided with schools, colleges, technical institutions, and universities.[27] Basic literacy, as measured by the ability of men and women to sign their names on marriage registers, had almost doubled during the eighteenth century, probably being over 75 percent for men and over 50 percent for women in the areas where it was most common, the towns of northern France. Just before the Revolution, too, some 50,000 pupils were receiving secondary education in 347 endowed colleges, and thousands more attended private schools, of which the number was increasing. Contemporaries and historians nevertheless agree that education at all levels was ill distributed and of variable quality.

Moreover, although many teachers were neither ordained priests nor men fully committed to a religious order, all education remained either controlled, or at least nominally supervised, by the Catholic Church. The monarchy had encouraged the development of military schools for the sons of officers, and on occasion it had issued general decrees about elementary education, but the latter really remained declarations of intent because the provision and financing of new schools was left to the initiative of the localities. At the least, therefore, there was a long-standing need for some substantial extension of facilities, for adequate administrative reform, and for more support from the state; moreover, after 1762, when the suppression of the Society of Jesuits in France deprived the church of its most important body of teachers, the necessity for changes of this sort became still more apparent.

The National Assembly, determined to reconstruct the whole administration of France, had no doubt that the organization of education was an integral part of its responsibility in providing the country with a constitution. Legislation, however, was necessarily dependent on the successful completion of other reforms, the most immediately important of which was the establishment of a completely new system of local government. By the end of February 1790, new departmental, district, municipal, and cantonal authorities had been created. By that date, however, the process by which the educational work of the church would be seriously, if not intentionally, disrupted was already well advanced. Having in August 1789 abolished seignorial dues and the church's tithe, two sources from which the income of many primary schools was directly or indirectly derived, the assembly confiscated all ecclesiastical property outright the following November, thus depriving the colleges of their endowments, and in February 1790 it simply suppressed all monastic congregations. These measures were indeed qualified by clauses affording temporary exemptions to those responsible for public education and promising that the social work of the church would be financed by other means, but the encroachment, if gradual, was still grave, and uncertainty was increased by the assembly's evident intention to reorganize the church itself. Thus, before the deputies had given any serious attention to education, the problem had become much more complex. What might have been a relatively simple matter, of supporting, supervising, and supplementing existing institutions, had become one of either replacing them or incorporating them into a completely new and comprehensive system, which would entail immense administrative difficulties and incalculable expenditure.

As always, however, the question of education involved problems more fundamental than those of its administration. Although secular subjects and attitudes seem to have become increasingly common in the schools during the final years of the old order, clerical teachers in general had long been predominantly concerned with instructing their pupils in religion and the classical languages. Ultimately their raison d'être was the preservation of the Catholic faith and the traditional values of a hierarchical society. The Revolution, however, was almost by definition a repudiation of those values. Opinions, of course, differed sharply. From the beginning, the counterrevolution was as real, if not as effective, as the Revolution, and there were innumerable variations of degree in the views of the revolutionaries themselves. Nevertheless, for many people, the old ideas were modified or superseded by the newer, and indeed heretical, belief that people were essentially malleable and consequently that it would be possible to improve and even to perfect society by the free and natural operation of human reason. By the middle of 1790, moreover, this attitude was fast becoming institutionalized: the Rights of Man had been proclaimed; nobility was abolished; the king in effect exercised conditional authority simply as a chief executive officer; and the National Assembly was striving to unify the nation both by rationalizing its entire administration and by establishing representative parliamentary government on the basis of extensive, if not yet complete, political democracy. Eventually, therefore, public education would have to be governed by the same convictions and directed toward the same social and political objectives.[28]

In this situation, debate about education, which had been stimulated in the 1760s by the near coincidence of the elimination of the Jesuits and the publication of Rousseau's *Émile*, was intensified. Publications were so abundant that, when the proposals received by the National Assembly were finally listed, Bourdon's material was in part overlooked and in part confused with that of another writer.[29] Yet the complexity of the subject and of national affairs in general effectively prevented progress. Belatedly the provision of education for all citizens was guaranteed in the completed Constitution. But it was not until September 1791 that a formal committee report was presented to the assembly by Talleyrand, and at that date the deputies had to refer the whole problem to their successors in the first Legislative Assembly. The *Mémoire* and the *Projet de décret* that Bourdon put forward in May 1790 thus seem in retrospect illustrative of the needs and attitudes of the time rather than of any immediately practical general reform.

Although Bourdon, an ardent revolutionary, probably believed that everything he proposed could be accomplished quickly, his approach to the National Assembly also seems in some respects to have been curiously unrealistic.[30] The *Mémoire* itself is general in nature, being essentially an expansion of the *Plan* of 1788, and the accompanying *Projet de décret*, which deals more specifically with the organization of a new national educational system, was—or at least soon became—almost commonplace in its allocation of the various levels of schools to corresponding levels in the new system of local government. Similarly the somewhat casual selection of subjects for study in each type of school is perhaps principally of interest as indicative of Bourdon's lack of concern for mere "instruction," as well as of his readiness to provide something for everyone, whether it was military training or religious education. Whatever Bourdon said to the deputies in his introductory discourse, here he makes no explicit plea for support for his own school, which he implied to be in existence, but his whole presentation seems to have been primarily another preliminary step toward the re-establishment of that school.[31] Indeed, the place apparently reserved for la Société Royale d'Émulation (or its successor) in Bourdon's new scheme of things is astonishing. At each educational level, from the lowest or cantonal level through the districts to the departments, public schools would be supervised by the one immediately above them, and crowning all and responsible for all would be a national school, where "a considerable number of free places" would be available for the best students (*sujets d'élite*) of the departmental schools. Of this national school, which would supersede and occupy the royal military school, Bourdon notes: "la Société Royale d'Émulation était destinée à en offrir le modèle."[32]

Whether or not his personal ambitions were as far reaching as that note implies, his attitude was certainly revolutionary. Always primarily concerned with "the moral part" of education (i.e., with fostering civic and patriotic responsibility), Bourdon averred that the new social and political order must ultimately depend on the emergence of people of a new kind, "worthy of the Revolution and able to sustain it." A fresh start in education was therefore imperative, and the assembly was exhorted to destroy the old system so that reconstruction could be complete ("tout renverser pour tout reconstruire").[33] Thus, the universities (which supervised some of the existing colleges) had to be suppressed, for only their elimination could ensure that the new order in education would not be tainted by their antiquated prejudices. Bourdon even held that for a transitional period one "indispensable measure" was the erection of an absolute barrier to all contact and communication between adolescents ("la jeunesse actuelle") and children below the age of ten ("la génération naissante"), who were still uncorrupted by the evils implicit in the old order.[34]

Nevertheless, Bourdon's extremism, which might be expected of one later to be reviled as a singularly savage terrorist, was tempered at this time by a certain respect for the rights of the individual. Although Bourdon defined his purpose—one might even say his mission—as "the regeneration of public education and the destruction, if possible, of private education,"[35] he recognized that, as France had become free, private tuition could not simply be banned; rather, the established prejudice in favour of it had to be eroded by the successful practice of the new schools. Similarly, although Bourdon evidently regarded orthodox Catholicism as irrational, in 1790 he proposed to leave the supervision of religious instruction in the schools entirely to the clergy; in religion, he maintained, freedom of opinion was sacrosanct. Still more surprisingly, he defined social virtue, certainly his principal objective in the education of each individual, as moderation in the use of all the human faculties.

In its essentials, Bourdon's approach to education was indeed remarkably enlightened. Few teachers would now quarrel with his demand for the creation of a Ministry of Education and a central body of general inspectors. Fewer still would object to his insistence that teachers should be carefully selected as members of an important profession and be correspondingly well paid and sure of a substantial pension. Beyond all such matters, however, lies Bourdon's conviction that there must be some fundamental fault in an educational system in which all the emphasis is on formal instruction and rigorous discipline. In his *Mémoire*, as in his earlier *Plan*, Bourdon condemns that approach as frustrating and futile: all too often, "the ten most precious years of life are wasted in learning a few words of a dead language."[36] Now, moreover, he could stigmatize the arbitrary imposition of abstract learning as being an integral part of the ancien régime: fostering subservience and deceit, it simply perpetuated the vices in which tyranny was rooted. Bourdon, however, would prohibit studies based on books until children were at least eight years old. Insisting that humans are born neither good nor evil, but simply ignorant, he asserts that the teacher must promote the natural development of all the senses by encouraging positive activities. For him, schools should be places in which freedom and physical exercise combine with work in an atmosphere of gaiety.

Furthermore, and again as in 1788, Bourdon constantly thought of the individual as a member of society. That all children should become familiar with the Rights of Man and with the new Constitution was for him a necessary part of the real education that they would gain by the experience of living in a school that was a self-governing society where all were free and equal. In such a society, the individual would grow in moral stature by realizing the importance of personal restraint, and all young people, by the daily practice of their rights and duties, would acquire the attitudes essential to citizenship in a constitutional state. Thus, in place of "schools of servitude," a real "apprenticeship for life" would fit a new generation for the responsibilities of a free society.[37]

Arguments advanced as passionately and persistently as these carry conviction. In 1790, too, Bourdon was able to address the

National Assembly as one who had been active in the Parisian Revolution of 1789 as an elected representative of the people, and he could legitimately claim that his advocacy of freedom, equality, and self-government in education had won official favour before the Rights of Man had even been formulated. Some later writers have indeed sought to show that the *Mémoire* of 1790—being appreciably more egalitarian—represents a marked advance from Bourdon's *Plan* of 1788. In 1790, Bourdon certainly presumed that his school and others like it would be open to all, whereas equality in la Société Royale d'Émulation would have applied principally to the sons of those able to afford substantial fees. The difference, however, is one of degree, not of principle, and to exaggerate it is to obscure the essential flexibility of his proposals. Again, Bourdon certainly went too far in attempting to frame a national system that would be permeated at all levels by social and political virtue but that apparently would be without adequate provision for formal learning. Yet his enthusiasm remains infectious. His proposals, in some respects simply representative of the spirit of the times, are more unusual in that they suggest a way in which education for the whole nation might become an enjoyable and even an informative experience in the patriotism appropriate to a free people. Moreover, Bourdon himself was peculiar in his readiness, whether expressed or implied, to put his ideas to the test of immediate practice in an experimental school. Certainly neither the sincerity of his beliefs nor the desirability of some measure of his methods need be questioned.

Although on May 31, 1790, Bourdon could make only a brief speech in introducing his texts, the assembly was probably impressed. Complimented by the president, he was invited to participate in the rest of the day's proceedings, and the *Mémoire* and the *Projet* were referred to the Constitutional Committee for further consideration.[38] There, however, they remained entombed until the following October, when Bourdon wrote directly to the committee requesting the return of what was probably his most valuable acquisition, the declaration of the Municipal Department of Public Establishments on March 29.[39] At the same time, he appealed again to the National Assembly, asking in the name of the Constitution to be afforded premises, financial support, and the authority to open a school in which the virtue of his ideas could be demonstrated.[40] On October 23, the assembly consequently renewed its call for a report from its committee, but even this call evoked no response until January 16, 1791, when the committee issued an interim statement explaining that it was bound by its order of business. Apart from recommending Bourdon's claim for reimbursement to the Pensions Committee, this report simply praised his zeal in anticipating the educational principles appropriate to the new Constitution.[41] Thus, all that Bourdon had achieved after almost a year of endeavour was a measure of publicity and the right to claim that his ideas were under consideration by the National Assembly.

Practically nothing else is known of Bourdon's activities in 1790[42] or of his attitude toward outstanding events such as the national Festival of Federation on July 14—whereas his brother, Marc-Antoine, evidently respected in the Saint-Laurent district, addressed the general assembly of its citizens on that occasion.[43] Even Léonard's sympathy for the National Assembly's most divisive measures, the Civil Constitution of the Clergy and the subsequent demand that all ecclesiastics should swear allegiance to the nation, can be gauged only by his general record. Indeed, at this time his father was the more active in public life. As a member of the municipal Conseil d'Administration, Bourdon des Planches was concerned with the complexities of taxation, and in April and May he became responsible for visiting two monasteries and three convents in order to list their contents. As one of the oldest members of the Conseil d'Administration, he continued on occasion to preside over its meetings, and in April and September he took part in delegations from the Commune to the National Assembly.[44]

Nor did the elder Bourdon relax his constant endeavours to propagate his concept of economic perfection, presenting his *Projet* to the National Assembly's Committee of Agriculture and Commerce in May and reiterating his arguments in a new pamphlet, *Dangers du serment fédératif relativement aux subsistences*.[45] This publication presumably arose from a fear that shortages might be caused by the festival on July 14, when delegates were to come to Paris from all parts of France to swear to uphold the law and to remain united in brotherhood. The brochure, however, was primarily a criticism of the assembly's decision in 1789 to allow free trade within France while maintaining controls over exports and imports. Because unrestricted freedom in buying and selling grain was for Bourdon des Planches synonymous with profiteering at the expense of the poor, that decision was most unpalatable to him. In the longer term, however, the repetition of his proposals for combining freedom with a carefully controlled system for the purchase, storage, and sale of surplus grain is less interesting than his assertion that the nation had allowed its faith in freedom ("notre religion") to imperil its immediate economic needs ("notre subsistence").

Map 2
The Sections of Paris

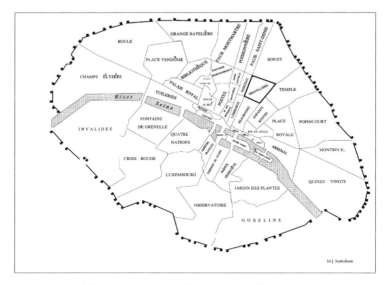

The names of the sections were often changed. Those most pertinent to the text are: Ponceau (Amis de la Patrie); Mauconseil (Bonconseil); Fbg. St-Denis (Fbg. du Nord); Beaubourg (Réunion); Enfants Rouges (Marais, Homme Armé); Roi de Sicile (Droits de L'Homme); Notre Dame (Cité); and Théâtre Français (Marat).

Source: Adapted from Michael Sydenham, *French Revolution* (London: Batsford, 1965).

Bourdon des Planches was also active in the summer of 1790 in implementing in his own district the new municipal constitution of Paris, by which the original sixty districts were replaced by forty-eight sections.[46] The relevant decrees were manifestly intended to curb popular democracy, for they sought to sever the connection between local assemblies and the sixty Parisian battalions of the National Guard and to restrict admission to the assemblies to "active" citizens (essentially those paying at least three livres a year in direct taxation) meeting for electoral purposes alone.[47] Although the boundaries of des Planches's district, Saint-Laurent, did not alter greatly when it became the Section Faubourg Saint-Denis, it is perhaps not surprising that des Planches was not elected to the new Commune that took office in October 1790.[48] Nor did Léonard Bourdon retain the seat that he had held for the Saint-Marcel district.[49] As we have seen, he seems to have neglected municipal administration in 1790, and before the end of that year he must have moved from Saint-Marcel (later, allegedly, clandestinely and as a debtor) to the vicinity of the Section des Gravilliers in central Paris.[50] On the other hand, both the Bourdons may be assumed to have shared the democrats' repugnance for the restriction of the franchise, and in December 1790 the names of both appear in the first recorded membership list of the most influential political association in the revolutionary period, the Society of the Friends of the Constitution, commonly called the Jacobin Club.[51]

The Club, which then had more than 1,000 members and over 200 affiliated "daughter" societies in provincial towns and cities,[52] held— and continued to hold—a central revolutionary position between more avowedly monarchical associations and those, like the Cordeliers Club, that were more localized, popular, and aggressively democratic. In the broadest terms, the Jacobins were educated and politically progressive townsmen of the middle sort, and that Léonard Bourdon was of their number from so early a date in the Revolution is interesting in itself. Moreover, although it is impossible to say how long before 1791 he had been in the Club, it was certainly there that he then sought support for his educational project. At some point, the *Mémoire* was submitted to the society, which appointed commissioners to consider it, and according to one of them, the young Duc de Chartres (later King Louis-Philippe), on February 17 Bourdon began to tell them about his plan at five o'clock and did not stop until eight.[53]

In their report, presented to the society by Alexandre de Beauharnais[54] on March 11, the ten commissioners (of whom six were deputies in the National Assembly) first praised Bourdon's general principles: all citizens had an equal right to education, and the education of young people should be both a happy experience and one largely concerned with preparing them to live in freedom. Wisely, however, the commissioners had concentrated their attention on a single part of Bourdon's material, that which they thought the most immediately important and practical. In their view, the distinctive feature of the proposals before them was that, long before the fundamentals of the new constitutional order had been formulated, Bourdon had anticipated their nature and had worked out a detailed scheme by which they could be applied in the daily life of a residential school. The concept of a community in which the teachers would simply guide elected representatives of the pupils in all matters of administration, while rules, rewards, penalties, and promotions were constantly reviewed by similarly constituted juries, was, as Beauharnais said, "drawn from nature itself and in harmony with the great social order." All that remained was to test it in practice, and for this great experiment a few months should suffice. Because this test could begin apart from any consideration of education in general, the commissioners proposed that one of the members of the society, the deputy Rabaut Saint-Étienne, should ask the National Assembly to set a specific date in the immediate future for hearing the report of its Constitutional Committee on Bourdon's proposals.

Although the society's approval of this resolution provides an interesting example of one way in which the Jacobins influenced national affairs, on this occasion the society did not materially advance Bourdon's position. Rabaut Saint-Étienne did prepare a detailed appreciation of his project, giving it high praise and preparing the draft of a decree by which Bourdon would have obtained premises, pupils, and the authorization that he sought as well as the promise of attention to his claims for compensation for his initial expenditure.[55] However, for some unknown reason, Rabaut failed to put his report before the National Assembly on March 31, the date that he had selected. So that something might be gained, Beauharnais contrived the next day, April 1, to speak briefly on Bourdon's behalf, presenting the assembly with the *Mémoire* and an accompanying letter to remind the deputies that the original approach to them had been referred to the Constitutional Committee; and, as Beauharnais proposed, the assembly formally accepted the *Mémoire* and referred it and the letter to the committee "pour en être rendu compte."[56] Thus, all again seemed irrevocably interred.

That Bourdon nevertheless strove to secure substantial public support is apparent in his publication at this time of the *Mémoire*, which was duly noted in the *Moniteur* on May 27. In June, too, the news that the king had escaped from Paris and that he had then been arrested at Varennes first caused Bourdon to effect a hasty revision of the piece annexed to his *Mémoire*, the *Essai sur . . . l'éducation des héritiers présomptifs de la couronne*. On June 25, the day that the king was brought back into Paris, this was re-rewritten as an *Essai sur l'éducation de Monsieur le Dauphin adaptée aux circonstances actuelles*,[57] a paper first submitted to the Constitutional Committee on June 26 and then published as *Idées sur l'éducation d'un prince royal*.[58] Taken together, these versions suggest that all was grist to Bourdon's mill, for their tenor is that the best education for a prince would be in a school where pupils representative of all the *départements* of France were habituated to equality and self-government. In the final version, written after the king had been suspended, this proposal is indeed represented as a completely new concept and one that would provide a new centre of national unity. Yet Bourdon's initial concern for safeguarding parental rights does not entirely disappear even in the *Idées*, which appeared after the deputies had decided on June 24 that the selection of a governor for the dauphin would be determined by the assembly and not by the king.

As was later remarked, however, Bourdon's efforts were further interrupted by the political crisis that followed the discovery of the king's escape.[59] That crisis also seems to have completed his disillusionment with the existing constitutional order. In this respect, of course, his feelings were widely shared; whatever Louis's real purpose in heading toward France's northeastern frontier, many people were convinced that the king meant to seek foreign aid in crushing the Revolution, and still more were sure that he had belied all his promises and could never again be trusted. Although the monarchy might still have been saved after the flight to Varennes, political activists throughout France were undoubtedly predisposed to a further and more drastic revolution. Bourdon, certainly, was of this mind. Addressing the Jacobins on July 14, 1791, he asserted that the king's arrest was welcomed only because it had prevented an immediate outbreak of war: "Tous les bons esprits, monarchistes d'hier ou républicains de demain, pensent qu'il faut que le roi soit jugé, pour pouvoir être déclaré déchu du trône."[60] His own view differed from this one only on procedure, for he held that, because public opinion had decided that Louis could not possibly remain king, he should first be deposed and then tried as a private citizen, without the benefit of constitutional inviolability.

At this time, too, Bourdon was again becoming more active, and certainly more prominent, in political life. On June 29, he rather surprisingly appears as a secretary of the Jacobin Club, a position to which members were elected every second week, and, although thereafter he seldom spoke at length, his interventions in debate became fairly frequent.[61] Moreover, meagre as it is, the evidence indicates that his role in the summer of 1791 was of no small importance to the survival of the Club. The position of the king being indeterminate, members were divided about the desirability of a restoration, a regency, or a republic, and these divisions became critical after July 15. Late in the evening of that day, a crowd headed by members of the popular Cordeliers Club invaded the Jacobin Club, demanding that it endorse a petition calling for the deposition of the king. Amid much tumult, those Jacobins who were still present agreed to prepare such a petition and to present it to the people on the Champ-de-Mars the next day, and Bourdon subsequently claimed that he was among those who collected signatures there on July 16.[62]

Whatever the truth of that assertion, the Jacobins' action proved highly compromising. On the one hand, their petition was imperative in tone but ambiguous in substance: demanding that the National Assembly recognize Louis's flight as being equivalent to his abdication, it called on the deputies to "provide for his replacement by all constitutional means," a phrase that left the way open for the retention of the monarchy by the creation of a regency—which would presumably be that of the popular but disreputable Duke of Orléans. To the republicans of Paris, however, this was virtually a betrayal. So few people were willing to sign the demand that the effort was abandoned; moreover, when the Jacobins learned that the National Assembly had just approved a decree by which the king would be reinstated as soon as he accepted the final form of the Constitution, the petition was suppressed as illegal. Even so, most members of the Club repudiated their colleagues' action as the attempt of a minority to commit the Society of the Friends of the Constitution to republicanism, and all these men seceded and sought to re-establish the society in a different location, the vacant convent of the Feuillants. Thus, the remaining Jacobins were discredited as being both too half-hearted for ardent republicans and too radical for moderate thinkers. Their situation temporarily deteriorated further on July 17, when the republicans sponsored a much more popular petition that openly rebuked the Assembly for ignoring the will of the sovereign people and demanded the convocation of a new assembly to bring the king to trial and to organize a new form of executive authority. This petition occasioned the notorious Massacre of the Champ-de-Mars, for the Commune proclaimed martial law and the crowd was dispersed by the National Guard at the cost of many lives. In the weeks that followed, advocates of law and order seemed to be triumphant, whereas the freedom of those who still upheld democracy, including even well-known deputies such as Robespierre, was in jeopardy.

In this situation, a handful of men, one of whom was Bourdon, gradually succeeded in re-establishing the Jacobin Club as the principal political association in France. Precisely how this renewal was achieved defies description.[63] Certainly the reputations and the abilities of a few principals such as Robespierre and Pétion, both of whom were notably democratic deputies, counted for much. Ultimately, too, the reaction itself was beneficial to the Jacobins, who were less compromised by their dalliance with republicanism than were the Feuillants by their association with the monarchy and with the bloodshed on July 17. Moreover, the Club boldly treated the secession as an opportunity to purge itself of political impurities, developing a process by which the surviving members nominated others for admission or re-admission subject to the scrutiny of a select but expanding committee. Thus, on July 27, Bourdon was one of six members who joined six others, deputies in the National Assembly, to form the Regenerative Committee, which eventually became a *grand comité* of seventy-two approved members.[64] At least equally important was the success of the crucial Correspondence Committee, of which Bourdon was a member from July 16 onward,[65] in convincing most of the affiliated societies throughout France that the Society of the Friends of the Constitution "séante aux Jacobins" were true patriots, whereas those "séante aux Feuillants" were at best deluded deviationists. Bourdon, who submitted some of this committee's letters to the Club for approval, also participated personally in negotiations with the Feuillants and helped to draw up new regulations for the "regenerated" Jacobin Club itself.[66] Thus, he contributed appreciably to its survival in July-August 1791 and hence to its subsequent attainment of even greater influence than before.

That Bourdon should have identified himself so completely with the Jacobins at this time is interesting, for his previous record does not suggest that he was greatly interested either in politics as such or even in vital questions such as the reorganization of the Catholic Church and the growing threat of war with Austria. Rather, he seems to have been single-minded and almost simplistic in outlook. Dominated by his great vision of an ideal form of education, and sure of the essential rightness of civil liberty and civic equality, he found in the Jacobin Club a society sworn to maintain such ideals but averse to endorsing particular policies before public opinion had become apparent. There his hostility to the monarchy, which he believed to have betrayed both him and France, and to what may perhaps be called the new bourgeois establishment, which seemed to be ruthless in its support of a property owners' constitution, probably inclined him to mix with men of extreme views.[67] Yet, although he was often interested in particular problems and instances of individual hardship, he usually remained content to leave debate to others.

This intimate association with the Jacobins soon proved to be of much importance to Bourdon, for in the autumn the influence of the Club increased considerably. Once Louis accepted the new Constitution on September 14, 1791, the National Assembly's work was done, and by October 1 its deputies were replaced by those of France's first regular parliament, the Legislative Assembly. Inevitably many of these new deputies—notably Brissot from Paris and Vergniaud, Gensonné, and Guadet from the Gironde—were Jacobins; conversely, because none of the men who had sat in the National Constituent Assembly was eligible for re-election, some of the latter—notably Robespierre and Pétion—were free to make the Club their principal forum. Ultimately the distinction between the Jacobins in the Legislative Assembly and those in the Club became deeply divisive;[68] more immediately, however, men such as Bourdon could expect that support for their ideas in the Club would be matched in the new parliament.

Yet in September 1791 it again seemed that all Bourdon's work to secure the school of his dreams would have to begin anew. As far as education was concerned, the new deputies inherited only a general report prepared by Talleyrand and the promise, recently written into the Constitution, that provisions would be made for the instruction of all citizens. Presented to the National Constituent Assembly on behalf of the newly created Committee of Public Instruction on September 10-11, 1791, the report urgently recommended a total reconstruction of education.[69] Schools, graded in levels to correspond with the new system of local authorities, and supervised by government inspectors, should make uniform instruction available to all, though free only at the primary level; there should also be more systematic provision of professional training in medicine, law, and military studies; and the whole should be constantly inspired by a new national institute of higher learning in Paris. Much of this, including the emphasis on the importance of inculcating patriotism and political morality, is at least reminiscent of the writings of Bourdon, who soon claimed that Talleyrand had written to him acknowledging the similarities of their views.[70] However much Talleyrand owed to Bourdon, though, his report—which of necessity was simply referred to the new National Legislative Assembly for further consideration—has rightly been praised for "the sophistication and amplitude with which it expresses much prevailing opinion."[71] It was evidently a better-balanced and more comprehensive survey of the country's needs than was the framework that Bourdon had provided for his own special pleading. Talleyrand, for example, gave careful consideration to the question of educating girls, then a highly controversial matter and one that Bourdon had dismissed as being entirely the responsibility of their mothers.[72]

Thus, in three years, Bourdon had won a certain reputation but had achieved nothing positive. His father, too, had found his most recent publications—*L'Anti-economiste* and *Réclamation d'un citoyen . . . pour une organisation dans le commerce des grains*[73]— disregarded by the authorities. Léonard nevertheless resumed his campaign with undiminished zeal, his first step being to renew his support among the Jacobins. On October 7, the Club approved a proposal made by the *abbé* Grégoire that all its affiliated societies should recommend Bourdon's establishment to their members.[74] According to the letter sent out by the Correspondence Committee over the signatures of men such as Collot d'Herbois, Pétion, Billaud-Varenne, and Robespierre, the new school would thus become for others what the Society of the Friends of the Constitution itself was for its daughter societies, a central point of correspondence and enlightened patriotism. Moreover, this letter was accompanied by a prospectus[75] announcing that protracted uncertainty about the future in education had caused la Société des Jeunes Français to decide to constitute itself (*se réunir*) without further delay. Thus, Bourdon, soon after to appear as the president of the same Correspondence Committee,[76] anticipated reality, being the more confident because he had apparently been assured that the Department of Paris would make the extensive premises of the Priory of Saint-Martin-des-Champs in the Section des Gravilliers available to him as "le plus propre à ce vaste établissement d'éducation." The prospectus, generally an effective but familiar reiteration of Bourdon's proposals, is also interesting because it shows that at this time the Jacobins expected the creation of the school to be accompanied by a considerable development in adult education. The proceedings of conferences for the instruction of artisans, day labourers, and countrymen were to be recorded, copied, and distributed throughout the primary schools of France for the benefit of local people, and twelve well-known Jacobins, including both Robespierre and Brissot, undertook to participate in these conferences.[77]

Having secured his base in this way, Bourdon renewed his appeals for official backing. Early in November, he wrote to the Legislative Assembly requesting early consideration of the report called for by the Constituent Assembly eighteen months previously, and at the same time copies of the *Mémoire* were distributed to the new Committee of Public Instruction.[78] Then on November 13 he again appeared personally before the representatives of the nation, supporting his plea by presenting them with the *Plan* that he had put before the Royal Council in 1788, and they again afforded him conventional honours and referred the matter to their committee.[79] Now, however, Bourdon was less patient than in the past. After no more than a few days, he asked the committee for an interview, and when he was heard on November 25 he specifically requested that the members give him official encouragement to open a school for pupils from all parts of France. The committee then appointed two of its members, Romme and Condorcet, to examine this demand.[80]

In all probability, it was in the hope of swaying the decision of these two commissioners that Bourdon again enlisted the support of the Jacobin Club. On December 4, a notice in the press indicated that the school would open between December 15 and January 1, 1792, and that a preparatory public meeting would be held at the Jacobins on December 8.[81] When that meeting took place, there was general approval of Bourdon's exposition, which was strongly supported by Collot d'Herbois, who presided, as well as by Billaud-Varenne and several other notable Jacobins.[82] This evidence, and the fact that at some point in November the Department of Paris had confirmed its undertaking to make the Priory of Saint-Martin available to Bourdon, have led some writers to suppose that he finally succeeded in establishing his new school at this date.[83] That belief, however, is almost certainly mistaken, for although he had the promise of premises he still had neither pupils nor official support. On December 16, moreover, the Committee of Public Instruction heard and accepted its commissioners' recommendation that Bourdon should be congratulated on his zeal and patriotism but that a report to the assembly about his proposal should be postponed indefinitely.[84] Examined dispassionately, the scheme probably seemed too ambitious, benefiting too few pupils; moreover, to so notable an advocate of rational thought as Condorcet, it no doubt seemed far too much concerned with the stimulation of sentiment. Indeed, the Legislative Assembly's contribution to educational reform is virtually identified with the report that Condorcet himself presented on April 20 and 21, 1792. At once liberal and systematic, his proposals long dominated the revolutionaries' debates about education, and they eventually formed the foundation of its reconstruction in France.[85] In 1792, however, Bourdon must have found their predominance particularly frustrating, for Condorcet's belief that civic virtue would naturally and necessarily follow the improvement of instruction, the development of the citizen's knowledge and skills, was the antithesis of his own convictions.

Bourdon should thus be seen at the beginning of 1792 as a man repeatedly complimented but constantly thwarted. At last, too, he seems to have become discouraged, for nothing more about his project is recorded until the end of the following May. Much the same might also be said of his father, who had hopefully submitted "divers mémorials" on the grain trade to the Legislative Assembly in November

1791.[86] As in 1789, father and son made a joint approach to the deputies in May 1792, but again their request to present the outline of a law beneficial to both farmers and consumers was set aside.[87] More remarkable is the fact that, although Bourdon is recorded as speaking at the Jacobin Club at intervals between January and June 1792, all his interventions were on relatively minor matters, such as his attempt to support the development of a quick-firing gun—which Robespierre condemned as inhuman.[88] In these months, the Club became bitterly divided between the supporters of Brissot and those of Robespierre. The schism in the Catholic Church, the intransigence of the émigrés, the outbreak of war, and the king's use of his right to veto legislation constantly increased tensions toward the breaking point of a second revolution, but Bourdon apparently remained silent unless something seemed to him to be an infringement on the rights of the common people. One can only suppose that the growing anger and impatience of all the revolutionaries of France matched and magnified his own.

In retrospect, it is particularly ironic that this man's long endeavour to found a school in which the true value of his ideas could be effectively demonstrated finally succeeded just as a new outbreak of political violence became imminent. On May 29, 1792, the Ministry of War informed Bourdon that his proposal had received royal approval and that he would initially be allowed to select fifty pupils from the number of those who had applied for admission to the military schools. For the maintenance of each of these pupils, he would be paid 1,000 livres annually, from which the equivalent of two months' payment could be drawn in advance on each enrolment. Furthermore, he was afforded one-quarter of the annual total, 12,500 livres, as an additional free gift, presumably meant to cover his initial expenses.[89] This seemingly sudden success may fairly be ascribed to Bourdon's initiative and persistence in promoting his cause and particularly to his skill in enlisting the support of so many different people and official bodies. Ultimately, however, the fact that the Minister of War at this date was Servan, a member of the so-called Patriot ministry and a friend of Brissot's friend Roland de la Platière, the Minister of the Interior, is surely an indication that it was the influence of the Jacobin connection that eventually prevailed.[90]

According to Bourdon's own statement, it was in May 1792 that la Société des Jeunes Français was established in the Priory of Saint-Martin-des-Champs.[91] Certainly Bourdon occupied some part of that building in June, for on June 1 he wrote to the Department of Paris complaining that about half the priory was being used by one of

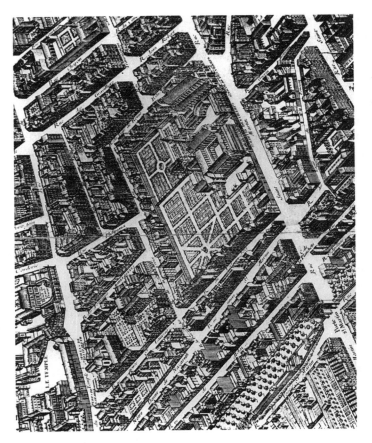

Fig. 2. The Priory of Saint-Martin-des-Champs. Bourdon's school and residence was situated in the upper right-hand corner of the rectangular precincts. Author's enlargement of a part of the Plan de Turgot. Courtesy of the Bibliothèque nationale de France, cartes et plans.

its agencies,[92] and the local police soon noted that he had fitted new locks to the clock tower and was about to improve the exterior plumbing.[93] On June 4, moreover, the Jacobins notified their affiliates of his success ("ce nouveau triomphe de l'égalité sur les privilèges") and urged them to inform Bourdon immediately if they knew of orphans whose parents had served the cause of liberty.[94] Presumably provision for the administration of the school and for the organization of its classes was also at least adequately advanced, for on June 25 Bourdon politely, if perhaps cheekily, invited the members of the assembly's Committee of Public Instruction to attend a public meeting about the physical education of the pupils.[95] Even so, it seems that they were enrolled only gradually, so that some months passed before the school achieved appreciable size.[96]

* * *

Bourdon's ideas and his attempt to implement them after mid-1792 are usually given at least some attention in general studies of education during the revolutionary decade. Occasionally, too, more detailed consideration of his views, publications, and school appears in academic journals. Here, however, this material will be considered as it occurs chronologically and in its appropriate relationship to Bourdon's less familiar participation in political affairs. La Société des Jeunes Français is also best seen in the context of events, for its character was certainly greatly affected by the fact that it both developed and declined during the most critical years of the Revolution. Indeed, because the summer of 1792 was dominated by the great crisis of a second insurrection, even the approbation that Bourdon had finally won may have come too late to allow his experiment a fair chance of enduring success.

More generally, the period between the Revolutions of 1789 and 1792 may be seen as one in which Bourdon's various contacts with the poor apparently enhanced his belief in equality and in the possibilities of progress that a truly egalitarian regime would offer. The period must also be seen as one of constant frustration for Bourdon. His educational proposals were frequently praised, but their implementation was repeatedly postponed, and the same was true for the economic plan with which both he and his father were associated. In all probability, he supposed these personal reverses to be due to the survival of a treacherous monarchy and the establishment of a quasi-aristocratic parliament, and thus came to equate his own dissatisfaction with the common belief that the king and an incompetent assembly were allowing France and the Revolution to drift toward disaster. Certainly his convictions combined with the circumstances of the day to cause him to immerse himself in the feverish political activity that culminated in the Revolution of August 1792, and thereafter his commitment to political problems (including that of education in general) was far more fully recorded than was his day-to-day administration of his own school.

4

Commitment to Revolution
(July to September 1792)

*I*n the summer of 1792, a new, republican, France repudiated the Constitution of 1791, destroying the monarchy and beating back the invading armies of Austria and Prussia. Although references to Léonard Bourdon's activities in this second eruption of revolution are more plentiful than those about 1789, the difficulty in assessing his character and determining his importance remains considerable. The profound divisions and unprecedented violence of the time inevitably exposed everyone of any note to accusations of misconduct, and all too often these accusations have become embedded in historical interpretations of the period. Moreover, even the most meticulous scholars are frequently thwarted by the fragmentary nature of the evidence. Much of real importance was not written down, and the destruction in 1871 of many records—particularly most of those of the sections of Paris—often makes it impossible to see the significance of specific events in their full context and proper perspective.

More particularly, a problem is posed by the apparently sudden appearance in July 1792 of Bourdon as the principal spokesman of the Section des Gravilliers, for he was a man of some status who had long been primarily concerned with the promotion of his ideas about education, and Gravilliers was by repute a notoriously turbulent part of revolutionary Paris. Yet, as we have seen, he claimed that his school was established in the Priory of Saint-Martin-des-Champs—which occupied a large part of the section—in May 1792, and the first membership list of the Jacobin Club indicates that he was living in the vicinity of Gravilliers in December 1790.[1] In September 1792, moreover, Bourdon asserted that he had been a resident of the section since the beginning of that year and that he had contributed to its renown as

---

Notes to Chapter 4 are on pp. 358-61.

"the revolutionary section" by printing the addresses in which it attacked Lafayette and the Directory of the Department of Paris.[2] Because attendance at the assemblies of sections was often surprisingly small, a gradual rise in Bourdon's influence is likely, even though his prominence became apparent only when agitation gained momentum in the summer of 1792.

Map 3
The Gravilliers Section

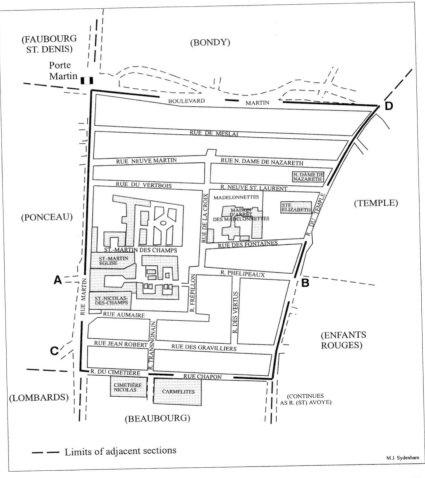

Today the area is traversed laterally from A to B by the Rue Réaumur and diagonally from C to D by the Rue de Turbigo. The abbey site is the Conservatoire national des arts et métiers.

It is also likely that the Section des Gravilliers was somewhat slower to become militant than is usually supposed. Situated in the northern centre of old Paris, the section was approximately square, bounded east and west by rue Saint-Martin and rue du Temple, and north and south by boulevard Saint-Martin and rue Chapon. Within this area, little more than 500 yards square, was a labyrinth of high-storied houses, many of which could be reached only through narrow roads and alleys. Enclosed passages and steep stairways led to the upper rooms, where the poorer folk lived as best they could. Home to some 25,000 people, Gravilliers has been represented as a singularly drab, congested, and impoverished district, and indeed it was one of the most densely populated parts of Paris. It seems, however, that the number of those actually destitute was relatively small, whereas the number of "active" citizens (3,252) was relatively high, and about half of the latter paid sufficient taxes to be eligible as electors and to hold administrative offices.[3]

Although it was not monolithic, the section certainly had a high degree of homogeneity. Recent research indicates that, although there were numerous literary and minor professional men, the typical unit in Gravilliers was either a family shop or a small workshop where a skilled artisan, probably aided by members of his family, employed a few apprentices and journeymen. Thus, there were many bakers and other tradesmen involved in the provision and distribution of food, and a high percentage of women worked as dressmakers and milliners or made ribbons. Even more characteristic of the section were the lock-smiths, watchmakers, jewellers, and craftsmen who made the small objets d'art peculiar to Paris. Gravilliers was thus predominantly, even perhaps par excellence, socially and economically *sans-culotte*, an area in which a multitude of working men and women, largely self-employed, lived closely together in differing degrees of poverty and relative affluence.

Such people were very vulnerable to any sudden shortage of food-stuffs and to increases in the cost of living: the price or availability of bread was in fact the index of their welfare. Being independent, they were also profoundly concerned to secure, and indeed to assert, the personal freedoms and the equality of status and opportunity proclaimed in the Declaration of Rights of 1789. Moreover, although they were quick to see problems in simple terms and to suppose that solutions should be sought in direct and even violent action, their condition stimulated strong aspirations for what would now be called the services of social welfare—particularly education.

Many of these considerations help to make Bourdon's popularity in Gravilliers more comprehensible. Although Bourdon was not a man of the people, he had joined his father in emphasizing the urgency of taking steps to ensure that cheap food was readily available to all, and he was in the process of establishing an egalitarian residential school in the best-known building in the section. Moreover, although prices were increasing, the time was not yet one of acute economic crisis.[4] In the summer of 1792, however, counterrevolution seemed to place all the achievements of 1789, to say nothing of the homes and lives of the people of Paris, in ever-increasing danger, and whatever his exaggerations Bourdon was a man of action and a man of 1789, entitled to call himself an Elector of Paris and a Conqueror of the Bastille. He was also an able writer and speaker who had shown himself capable of influencing people in the streets as well as members of the National Assembly, and he may be credited with being a sincere believer in liberty and equality, the ideals of the French Revolution. Although his influence in the section would soon be challenged by Jacques Roux, the much more militantly radical curate at the Church of Saint-Nicholas-des-Champs,[5] he was in many respects an appropriate representative of its people at a time of national crisis.

Bourdon, moreover, soon acquired political importance as a man able to maintain an effective liaison between the Section des Gravilliers and the Jacobin Club—that is, between a part of Paris having considerable physical force and the political society that had the most influence in the capital, as throughout France. Precisely how this connection was established is difficult to determine, but something may be surmised. Since mid-1791, there had been in Gravilliers a local political club or "popular society" that in and after 1792 was properly called la Société des Amis de la Loi et de l'Humanité. It was commonly known, however, from its place of meeting as la Société de la rue Vert-Bois. Lined on each side, despite its name, by a row of high, terraced houses, that road marked the northern boundary of the Priory of Saint-Martin-des-Champs. Although the date when Bourdon joined this now obscure society is unknown, it may well have been in the spring of 1792, when the club, having unsuccessfully applied for affiliation with the Jacobins, was afforded more appropriate recognition as a body having full rights of correspondence with them.[6] Certainly la Société de la rue Vert-Bois soon after became regarded both as an outpost of the Jacobins and as the personal stronghold of Léonard Bourdon.

His appearance as an active participant in popular agitation in the summer of 1792 is indeed illustrative of the growth of Jacobin and *sans-culotte* cooperation. That alliance developed rapidly during a period of dangers both real and supposed. Early in July, there was a great outcry in Paris because the mayor and the *procureur* of the city, Jerôme Pétion and P.-L. Manuel, were suspended from office by the Directory of the Department of Paris. Pétion, a prominent democrat since 1789, was then exceedingly popular; beyond that popularity, however, the suspension of both men symbolized the potential danger of reaction after June 20, when a huge crowd from eastern and south-eastern Paris, including many men carrying arms, had burst into the Tuileries, insulting and threatening Louis XVI for having exercised his right to veto legislation. Whether Pétion could have prevented or controlled this ugly and divisive demonstration is doubtful; that he was in sympathy with it is certain; and, not surprisingly, many people throughout France held him and the Municipality of Paris responsible for an outrage. Their protests, and particularly the brief appearance in Paris on June 29 of Lafayette, who had become commander of the Army of the Centre, nevertheless appeared to many others to be proof of the strength and menace of counterrevolution. Lafayette was expected to return at the head of his army, and the suspension of the mayor and the *procureur* seemed to be a sure sign that a coup d'état was imminent. In this situation, the Jacobins in the Legislative Assembly and in their own society naturally encouraged the widespread popular demand for the reinstatement of Pétion.

Bourdon's name, which still appears in the record of the Jacobin Club as M. Bourdon de la Crosnière, was first mentioned at this time on July 4, before Pétion had been suspended but while his conduct on June 20 was under investigation. On this occasion, the Club heard Bourdon read an address to Pétion from the Section des Gravilliers that amounted to a vote of confidence in him "by 25,000 good citizens."[7] This address, to the preparation of which Bourdon himself may well have contributed considerably, is of interest both because the Jacobins afforded it at least tacit approval and because it anticipated the arrival of further support by the *fédérés*, the contingents of National Guards then going to Paris to take part in the third Festival of Federation on July 14. Apparently the section (i.e., those who spoke for it) had read and approved Pétion's published account of his conduct, and, while his virtue and fidelity to freedom were extolled, the men attacking him were damned as tigers thirsting for blood and anticipating a massacre like that of July 17, 1791. The men of Gravilliers, however, were sure that neither they nor their "brothers from the departments" would tolerate the imposition of any veto on their oath to uphold freedom. Although there was much hyperbole in all this, the address to Pétion amounted to a promise to fight if need be: "We will live with you in freedom, or we will all die together."

Once the Department of Paris had decided to suspend Pétion, which it did during the night of July 6-7, Bourdon and the Section des Gravilliers were foremost among those who appealed on his behalf to the Legislative Assembly. The address of the Gravilliers on July 8 is known to have been prepared by Bourdon and an associate on July 7, and it was approved the next morning by some 300 "active" citizens of the section at an exceptionally well-attended general assembly held as usual in the chapter house of the Priory of Saint-Martin-des-Champs. The same day, the address, signed simply "Léonard Bourdon, président," was presented to the Legislative Assembly, together with a patriotic collection of about 3,000 livres in coin and *assignats*. Being in its immediate context an urgent demand by "more than 30,000 citizens" that Pétion and Manuel be exonerated, and the whole departmental directory dismissed, it won the imprimatur of the assembly. Significantly, perhaps, it was only then that it was taken to the Jacobin Club, where it was heard amid lively acclaim.[8]

Pressure of this sort from many parts of Paris soon had its reward, for Pétion was reinstated in time to appear as the hero of the hour at the national festival on July 14, and all but one of the members of the departmental directory were driven to resign. The Gravilliers address, much of which was probably written in Bourdon's words, must, however, also be seen in a wider perspective, for it attacked the departmental authority as being an integral part of a widespread counter-revolutionary conspiracy. Supposedly involved in it were the directories of many other departments, as well as Lafayette: all were seen as acting in the interest of a perfidious court, and the court itself was assumed to be directed by France's foreign enemies, particularly Austria. Thus, the address was fundamentally a fervent appeal to the National Legislative Assembly to act decisively to save the situation: "the destiny of a regenerated country, the fate of the most wonderful revolution ever effected, the liberty of the whole world is in your hands." If the deputies were bound by the Constitution, then recourse should be had to the ultimate sovereignty of the nation, the people first being told how their will could properly be made apparent.

In the circumstances, this address, noted in the assembly's record as being "most moving," was remarkably restrained. Apparently the king himself was seen as the conspirators' victim rather than as their master, and even the ultimate power of the people was presented as a means of maintaining legality, not as a threat of insurrection. In sharp contrast to this restraint was the inflammatory language used by others: for example, Brissot, nominally the principal deputy of the left, told the assembly the next day that "There is but one cause of national danger: one man has paralyzed the nation's forces. You have been taught to fear the kings of Prussia and of Hungary. Strike at the court of the Tuileries and you will overwhelm them!"[9] Something of the depth of the division within France is equally evident in an assertion made by DeJoly, perhaps the most liberal of the latest batch of ministers. When he and his colleagues reported their resignations to the assembly on July 10, he identified the Jacobin societies as the main source of national disunity and administrative paralysis.[10]

As Robespierre told the Jacobin Club in Paris on July 9, patriots had indeed two wars to sustain, one internal and the other external.[11] During July, as the armies of Austria and Prussia assembled at the frontiers of France in preparation for invasion, these "two wars" were increasingly seen as one. Whatever combination of causes may be found to explain the situation, the king, the one man who might have made French power more effective, had in fact resigned himself to temporizing until the sovereigns of Europe could restore him to some measure of independence. Similarly the National Assembly had become increasingly impotent. Torn between the dictates of legality and of necessity, the deputies were also deeply divided politically. The majority, those who strove to uphold constitutional monarchy, were constantly compromised by the inertia of their monarch, and those who were still at least nominally Jacobins and "patriots" were as constantly frustrated because, being in the minority, they could do no more than threaten the king with an insurrection. Thus, public anger became concentrated on both the king and the assembly, inertia and impotence being identified with treason. As the dangers of invasion— made explicit in the Brunswick Manifesto—became ever more menacing, so did a popular republican revolution become ever more certain.

Evidence of Bourdon's views and activities during the second half of July is nevertheless strangely slight. On one occasion, Bourdon spoke briefly in the Jacobins, deploring the assembly's disregard of information about the weakness of defences at the frontier,[12] and on July 28, without indicating any office, he signed a letter from Gravilliers to the mayor of Paris in which the section announced that its anxiety about the activities of "internal enemies" (i.e., those then strengthening the defence of the Tuileries) was so great that it had reinforced its guard on rue Saint-Martin.[13] Although the section, by constantly adjourning its meetings, had in effect been one of the first of those in Paris illegally to adopt the crucial practice of *permanence*, by which a popular assembly kept its hall open and met whenever necessary, the initiative in taking still more revolutionary measures came from other parts of Paris. Thus, the Section Théâtre Français, where Danton and his friends of the Cordeliers Club were dominant, resolved on July 30 to open its doors to the unenfranchised "passive" citizens, and on July 31 the Section Mauconseil, near neighbour to Gravilliers, explicitly renounced all allegiance to Louis XVI. As resolutions like these were promptly taken by delegates to other sections, the organization of joint addresses and communal actions developed apace. Nor could such activities easily be repudiated—once the National Assembly proclaimed the country to be in danger, as it did on July 22, its recognition of a state of emergency implied at least some measure of recourse to the sovereignty of the people.

The register of the Section des Gravilliers has long been lost, but Bourdon and "his" section certainly became more prominent and more militant during the final days of the monarchy. The section, one of those that were quick to adopt the resolutions of Mauconseil and Théâtre Français,[14] was probably swung toward extreme democracy by a great influx of "passive" citizens: its meetings were indeed said to have been attended by "almost 8,000" people on August 3 and by some 10,000 people on August 9.[15] Bourdon was one of the three commissioners of the section[16] who joined those of all the other sections in preparing the petition that Pétion presented to the National Assembly on August 3 as the whole city's essential demands: the immediate deposition of Louis XVI, the appointment of a provisional government, and the earliest possible convocation of a National Convention to determine the future of France. Probably because this was simply referred to the assembly's Commission of Twenty-One, the Section des Gravilliers drew up a further address, which Bourdon again signed as president and which he read to the National Assembly the next day, August 4. Claiming that the citizens of the section, preferring death to slavery, had thrice unanimously approved the motion that Louis be deposed, Bourdon argued that all constitutional difficulties would be resolved if the assembly acted simply as a jury of indictment: Louis could then easily be formally accused of misconduct and deposed pending a final judgment by the nation at large. Needless to say, this exposition of proper procedure was popular only with the public galleries and some extreme deputies, and considerable tumult followed Bourdon's conclusion. Reminding the assembly that the military situation made an immediate decision imperative ("If an instant is lost, France may be lost!"), Bourdon then ended with an open threat: "We leave you the honour of saving the country; but if you refuse to save it, we shall have to do so ourselves."[17]

That one so evidently an influential insurgent should appear on the night of August 9-10 as a delegate of his section in the body that became "the Commune of the Insurrection" is hardly surprising, but the extent and the importance of his participation in the creation of that body is far more difficult to determine. The Revolution of August 10 was certainly not the work of any one man. Just as certainly, Robespierre played a crucial role, first by formulating the two essential demands, for the deposition of the king and the election of a National Convention, and then by enabling the Jacobins, the *fédérés*, and the sections of Paris to work together toward a common purpose. Furthermore, historians are agreed that initiative gradually passed to the sections and that their establishment of a central committee of correspondence at the Hôtel de Ville, a step sanctioned by Pétion, had accustomed them to sending delegates there, just as they did on the night of August 9-10. Preparation apart, however, common action only becomes possible when particular people are willing to take the first step, and the identification of those who took the initiative on this occasion has long been a subject of dispute. There was so much uncertainty and confusion in the hours before the insurrection became recognizable that it may be impossible now to determine which section first acted decisively. Nonetheless, Bourdon's contribution to the formation of the new Commune may have been greater than is generally allowed.

One consideration here is that in mid-September a delegation of the Section des Gravilliers complained to the National Assembly about intrigues in the new Electoral Assembly of Paris against Bourdon, whom the delegates described as "the principal author of the Revolution of August 10."[18] That alone might be no more than recognition of the importance of Bourdon's influence within the section itself. It may, however, acquire more significance if it is associated with an unidentified "fragment" of evidence originally published by Maurice Tourneux as an appendix to his edition of the *procès-verbaux* of the Commune.[19] The main text of this paper was preceded by a note indicating that on July 25 various citizens, including the popular journalist Louvet and two close friends of Madame Roland, Lanthenas and Bancal,[20] had met in Bourdon's rooms, where Bourdon had made them aware of the necessity of a new revolution. For what it is worth, this note suggests that Bourdon may have done something to win over some of the more moderate patriots, for at this time all those named as his guests were more closely associated with Brissot than with Robespierre—and this meeting apparently took place the night before Brissot openly repudiated republicanism in the National Assembly.

Appreciation of the text of the fragment itself depends on recognition that August 9 was commonly known as the date at which an ultimatum would expire. Some days before, on August 3, the men of the Quinze-Vingts Section, within which lay much of the powerful and turbulent Faubourg Saint-Antoine, had resolved to march in arms on the National Assembly on August 5. At the request of the mayor, however, they had agreed on August 4 to await the response of the assembly to the Parisian petition that he had delivered to it the previous day. This postponement, however, had been explicitly conditional: "if justice and right are not done to the people by the legislative body before Thursday [August 9] at eleven o'clock in the evening, then at midnight the tocsin will ring and the drums will beat general quarters, and all will immediately rise up together."[21] The National Assembly obviously failed to meet the required condition, for on August 8 two-thirds of the deputies rejected one crucial proposal, for the impeachment of Lafayette, and on August 9 they resolved to suspend all discussion of petitions demanding the deposition of the king. Consequently the meeting held in the Quinze-Vingts Section that night was certainly critical, and it is to this meeting that the fragment refers.

Evidently the assembly was not simply one of the people of the section, for the fragment states that the commissioners of several sections were present, and a more formal record of its proceedings, which also refers to the presence of *fédérés*, names thirteen sections, including Gravilliers, whose commissioners were there. The "Proceedings" then note that

> it was decided, in order to save the country, and as a member of a section of Paris proposed, that three commissioners should be named by each section, to join the Commune and advise on prompt measures to save the public weal, and for this purpose it was decided that orders would be taken only from the assembled commissioners of the majority of sections.

The fragment amplifies this note by describing a large and dangerously disorderly meeting, "une multitude sans chef," that might easily have initiated an attack on the Tuileries Palace and then been cut to pieces. Moreover, the fragment names Léonard Bourdon as the man who proposed the plan for the formation of a central committee "composed of citizens sent by all the sections with full powers to save the public weal."

The distinction in these two accounts between a central committee that would be advisory and one that would have governing authority may be disregarded, for in practice the delegates of the sections who assembled at the Hôtel de Ville in the early hours of August 10 soon superseded the regular municipal council—a process in which Danton, a member of both bodies, played a major part. More interesting here is the positive, albeit unconfirmed, statement that it was Bourdon who proposed the method of political action first adopted by the assembly and then put into effect for the whole of Paris. The plan need not have been either particularly original or peculiar to him.[22] In fact, the ringing of the tocsin in Quinze-Vingts was temporarily stopped, and in the subsequent confusion other bells were rung and other, more central, sections acted in the way adopted by Quinze-Vingts. It is nonetheless not improbable that Bourdon had considerable influence at a decisive moment on the course of events in a substantial part of Paris. Nor is it irrelevant that he and Huguenin, the principal figure in the Quinze-Vingts Section, were among the most prominent members of the new Commune during its first days of revolutionary activity.

Still according to the fragment, Bourdon concluded his speech to the Quinze-Vingts assembly by proposing three measures, all of which were approved: with the exception of Pétion, Manuel, and Danton (the deputy *procureur*), all members of the regular municipality should be discharged; Mandat, the commander of the National Guard (and principally responsible for the defence of the Tuileries) should be arrested; and a new commander should be appointed. Because these steps now seem to be obvious, Bourdon's alleged proposal of them is probably important only for his insistence on their priority. Certainly, however, all three were effected during the early hours of August 10. The General Council of the old municipality was then suspended; Mandat was interrogated and consigned to prison—only to be shot down on the steps of the Hôtel de Ville;[23] and he was immediately replaced by the brewer Santerre, "the general of the Faubourg Saint-Antoine."

The extent to which Bourdon himself can be associated with any of the measures taken by the new Commune is nevertheless indeterminate. Although he was nominally a member of it until mid-September, he was active in its proceedings only for two weeks; moreover, although F. Braesch, the author of the most authoritative study of the new Commune, included Bourdon in his list of the twenty-one men whom he considered were most influential for the first few days,[24] the formal record predominantly shows that decisions were made by the assembly as a whole. Moreover, the days and nights were so turbulent that nearly all of Braesch's twenty-one men can be identified only by their occasional or intermittent tenure of secretarial or presidential office. Thus, between August 10 and 17, Bourdon signed some documents as a secretary and others as the president of the assembly; however, because the delegates at first remained in almost continuous session, these positions changed hands too often to be indicative of anything more than literacy, prominence, and popularity.

Yet it is also impossible to separate Bourdon from the Commune of the Insurrection. Called at first "the assembly of the commissioners of the majority of the sections united with full powers to save the public weal," this Commune has long been of evil repute. If it did not actually direct the assault on the Tuileries, it certainly came into existence when the armed forces of the sections, together with the *fédérés* and huge crowds of people, were converging on the palace, so it has always been associated with the bloodshed that ensued. In this, as in its intimidation of the National Assembly, its insistence on the close confinement of the royal family, and its repression of all who could be suspected of royalist sympathies, it was essentially a revolutionary body, and the same was true of its less familiar endeavours to organize the security and defence of Paris and of France. Identified with Terror in each of these ways, the Commune also symbolized the advent of direct democracy and social egalitarianism. Composed of constantly changing delegations from the sections, it acknowledged no authority save that of the sovereign people for whom it claimed to speak, yet its dictatorial attitude scarcely concealed the ultimate independence of the sections themselves. Moreover, although its membership included men as diverse as Robespierre and Jacques Roux (as well as Bourdon's younger brother, Bourdon de Vatry), it was broadly made up of shopkeepers, craftsmen, minor journalists, clerks, and petty lawyers. Although there were but few dependent manual workers, there were many men whose obscure origins and illiteracy made them exceedingly resentful of anything smacking of social privileges and pretensions.[25] To such men, the new revolution was indeed the beginning of "the reign of holy equality," and this again was a regime that they were ready to enforce. Consequently Bourdon's brief but obvious identification of himself with the Commune in the terrible days of August 1792 meant, and must mean, that he was then fully committed to militant popular democracy.

Moreover, if Bourdon, as a man of some standing, was somewhat socially distinct in the Commune, he was also, as an educated and articulate believer in freedom and equality, better able to represent that assembly, and in doing so he at least showed that his courage matched his convictions. Thus, early in the morning of August 10, he countersigned as a secretary the Commune's first proclamation, which announced its existence ("Placed between death and slavery, the people has again resumed its rights . . ."[26]), and almost immediately afterward he and four other delegates accompanied Huguenin to the National Assembly, in which the royal family had taken refuge, to tell the deputies that a new authority had been established in Paris. It was on this occasion that Huguenin, openly addressing the deputies as their equal, if not their master, warned them that the people, "your sovereign and ours," would decide the validity of their decisions. Bourdon then theatrically announced that, although his colleagues would return to the Hôtel de Ville, he himself, despairing of freedom, would at once take arms and die fighting in the streets.[27]

Minor matters apart, Bourdon's name was also formally associated at this time with two questions of increasing importance, the fate of the captive king and that of those royalists who survived the assault on the palace and the massacres that followed it. As president of the Commune, it fell to Bourdon to announce on August 10 that Louis had been suspended by the National Assembly until a National Convention could be formed, and two days later, again as president, he signed the order by which the king was transferred from the Luxembourg Palace to the grim tower of the Temple[28]— a move forced on the National Assembly by the Commune. Similarly, and once again as president, on August 17 he signed the order for the election of the judges, jurymen, and officers of the revolutionary court generally known as the Tribunal of August 17.[29] His approval of these retributive measures is implicit, but there is no obvious indication that he was personally inclined to brutal terrorism. Although on August 16 Bourdon was one of those who called on the National Assembly to make immediate provision for the replacement of the existing criminal court,[30] in an earlier address to the same assembly about the state of Paris he apparently reported that the people had already wreaked sufficient vengeance on their enemies.[31] Indeed, on August 17 itself, he endorsed a request from his father that one of the latter's friends be allowed to visit an imprisoned relative,[32] and, when he himself was elected as an assistant clerk to the new tribunal, he immediately resigned that office.[33]

Beyond all these developments, Bourdon's participation in the feverish activities of the Commune soon became concentrated on practical affairs, for the Commune, despite its inflation to 288 delegates, depended heavily on a minority of educated men. Between August 14 and 25, Bourdon was appointed to a committee concerned with the development of a military camp on the northern outskirts of Paris, to one charged with the arrest of suspected persons and the security of the prisons, and to one that had the more familiar task of maintaining the supply of food to Paris.[34] On August 25, however, all these responsibilities were superseded by a still more onerous one, for on that day Danton, now the Minister of Justice, named Bourdon and Prosper Dubail, a judge of the Tribunal of August 17, as commissioners of the national government. In accordance with a decree accepted earlier in the day by the National Assembly, the two men were to go at once to Orléans to inspect its prisons, to ensure their security, and to find out how far the National High Court had advanced toward proceeding against those political prisoners who had previously been sent to Orléans for trial.[35]

Whatever Bourdon may have thought, popular anger in Paris against those who had defended the Tuileries on August 10 was certainly not appeased by the immediate slaughter of many of them. On the contrary, demands for the trial—and execution—of the surviving "criminals of August 10" became increasingly strident. The funerals of Parisians killed in the attack excited cries for vengeance, and the apparently inexorable advance of the Prussian army toward Paris stimulated the fear that imprisoned royalists might break out to seize and surrender the city. Directly threatened by a further insurrection, the National Assembly reluctantly consented to the creation of an extraordinary court, the Tribunal of August 17, in which political prisoners could be tried openly and quickly. This concession, however, led at once to a further demand by the Commune. There were then at Orléans fifty-three political prisoners who had long been awaiting trial for treason by the National High Court, a body always regarded as dilatory and now believed to be entirely composed of counterrevolutionaries; for some time, moreover, reports had been reaching Paris that those imprisoned at Orléans were not only loosely guarded but even living in considerable luxury.[36] The Commune, again threatening the assembly with insurrection, therefore demanded that these prisoners immediately be brought before the new tribunal in Paris "to pay the price of their crimes."[37]

As a half-measure, the assembly responded by authorizing the investigation that Danton then required Bourdon and Dubail to conduct; by that time, however, the Commune had already acted independently. On August 23, two days before Bourdon's appointment, it had authorized Santerre, now the commander of the Parisian National Guard, to despatch an armed force to Orléans.[38] Although the purpose of this force was not specified in writing, some 500 men, *sans-culottes* of the Faubourg Saint-Marcel and *fédérés* from Marseilles, left the capital the next day, being at least nominally under the command of Claude Fournier, generally known as Fournier l'Américain. According to Madame Roland, who detested him, Fournier was a man of sinister and piratical appearance, "gross in language, having long moustaches and three pistol belts around his waist."[39] Despite his sobriquet, he was in fact a Frenchman who had long prospered as a planter in San Domingo. Suddenly and suspiciously impoverished in 1784, he had returned to France, where Marie Antoinette had received him kindly, yet in the Revolution he had quickly become notorious as an agitator and street fighter. He was, in short, at best a truculent and disreputable character, and it was most unfortunate for Bourdon that some association with him at this critical time became unavoidable.

Accompanied by Tallien, who was then secretary-registrar of the Commune, Bourdon and Dubail left Paris on the evening of August 25, immediately after their appointment, and thus overtook Fournier's force in the early morning of August 26 at Longjumeau, where it had spent the night. Of what then occurred, little is known, but much has been alleged: indeed, from at least 1795 on, writers hostile to the Revolution have repeated the story that Bourdon and Fournier secretly agreed to seize, rob, and murder all the prisoners at Orléans. Improbable though it is, the story is naturally difficult to refute, for the most substantial evidence is that of the two men who are supposed to be the guilty parties. In fact, the memoirs of Fournier, in which he is principally concerned to exalt and excuse his conduct, are evidently untrustworthy, but the report of the two commissioners, which is manifestly the work of Bourdon and which is almost overtly an indictment of Fournier, seems to be more restrained and reliable. If read with other evidence that has survived, then these accounts permit a more mundane record of what happened at Longjumeau and, subsequently, at Orléans.[40]

According to Bourdon, Danton had spoken to him and Dubail about Fournier's men, and he had then urged the two commissioners to try to ascertain their purpose and "to do everything in our power to recall them to their duty and to obedience to the law." It was, Bourdon adds, with this injunction in mind that they had asked Tallien to accompany them until they overtook the Parisian column. All accounts agree that Bourdon and Dubail tried at Longjumeau to

Map 4
The abduction from Orléans of the prisoners of the High Court,
September 4, 1792

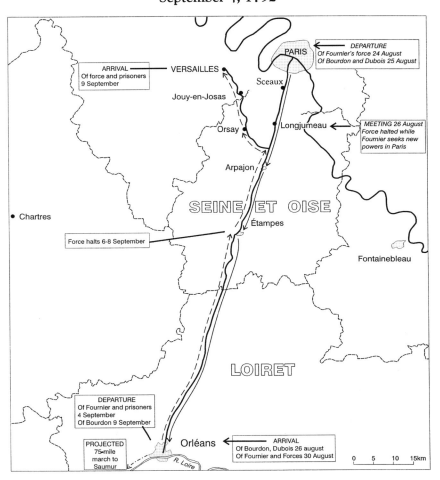

DEPARTURE
Of Fournier's force 24 August
Of Bourdon and Dubois 25 August

ARRIVAL
Of force and prisoners
9 September

VERSAILLES

PARIS

Sceaux

Jouy-en-Josas

Orsay

Longjumeau

MEETING 26 August
Force halted while
Fournier seeks new
powers in Paris

Arpajon

SEINE ET OISE

Chartres

Étampes

Force halts 6-8 September

Fontainebleau

LOIRET

DEPARTURE
Of Fournier and prisoners
4 September
Of Bourdon 9 September

Orléans

ARRIVAL
Of Bourdon, Dubois 26 august
Of Fournier and Forces 30 August

PROJECTED
75-mile
march to
Saumur

R. Loire

0   5   10   15km

convince Fournier and his men that their own mission as national
agents made the Parisians' activities superfluous and that their army
should at once return to Paris. This return, however, proved impossible. According to Fournier, the men suspected the existence of a plot
to save the prisoners and therefore refused to return, even threatening
to kill him if he would not lead them any farther: "We left Paris to go
to Orléans, and to Orléans we will go!"[41] Whether that is true or not,
Fournier certainly agreed to return to Paris to obtain fuller authority
for his expedition, and he then left Longjumeau with Tallien.

Fournier's men remained where they were to await his return, and Bourdon and Dubail went on alone to Orléans. So stated, Bourdon's conduct seems to have been impeccable. Bourdon had nevertheless committed himself further than Dubail had: understandably, if perhaps unwisely, he had joined Tallien in signing numerous chits to cover the board and lodging of the *sans-culottes*, and he seems to have been rather too ready to hobnob with Fournier and his henchmen.[42]

Welcomed at Orléans by the municipal council on the evening of August 26,[43] the two commissioners proceeded the next day to inspect the city's two principal prisons and to check the identities of the prisoners. The majority of these unfortunate inmates were army officers who had made many marches from Perpignan, where their failure to suppress a riot had allegedly been intended to facilitate an occupation of its great fortress by Spain. Among the others were four notable prisoners: the magistrate Larivière, who had dared to issue a summons against three deputies of the extreme left; d'Abrancourt, the Minister of War immediately before August 10; the old Duc de Cossé-Brissac, until late May 1792 the commander of the king's Constitutional Guard, which he was supposed to have packed with ardent royalists; and the man who was the most hated of them all, Delessart, who as Minister of Foreign Affairs in the winter of 1791-92 was believed to have acted more in the royal, and even the Austrian, interest than in that of France.[44] To all these prisoners, Bourdon and Dubail apparently promised a prompt trial—or, as some later accounts say, speedy "liberation."[45]

During this time, Fournier had won the support of the Commune, which in its turn appealed to the National Assembly, a body by now effectively reduced to its previous "patriotic" minority, and in response to the assembly's order the restored Minister of the Interior, Roland, instructed Fournier "to go at once to Orléans with 1,000 men of the National Guard to guarantee the security of the prisons in that city."[46] Thus, as one official in Orléans later wrote, "The assembly had to sanction what it could not forbid."[47] Fournier then returned to his men, whom he led to Étampes, where he received from the Commune an advance of 6,000 livres, the brevet of a general, and, as reinforcements, two more battalions of *sans-culottes* led by Bécart and Lazowski.[48] This force, which left behind it a long trail of what Fournier himself called "thefts described as requisitions," entered Orléans on August 30 as if it were enemy territory. Bourdon, who had assured the local authorities that the Parisians were coming as their brothers, prompted the city to offer the force a campsite and a civic reception, but that offer was rejected in favour of "a frugal repast."

Both prisons were seized, and something very like an armed camp was established at the great central square, the Place Matroy—where, as the result of pressure already exerted by Bourdon, the first man to be condemned by the High Court was being executed as a recruiting agent of the *émigrés*.[49]

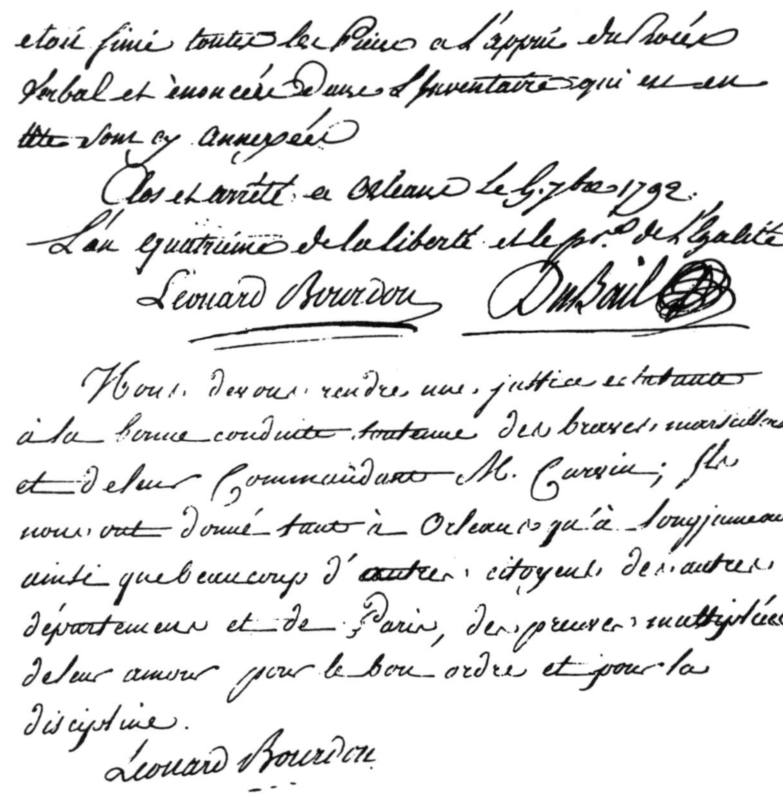

Fig. 3. The Mission to Orléans (I). Final page of the Report submitted to the Legislative Assembly in September 1792 by the two Commissioners of the Executive, Dubail and Bourdon, with Bourdon's postscript praising the patriotic conduct of the *sans-culottes* of Orléans and Paris. Courtesy of the Archives nationales de France.

Accurate assessment of the situation that then developed is difficult because the local records, save for those reports that were soon submitted to Paris, and a few others that later appeared in print, were destroyed in Orléans in 1940.[50] In effect, however, the national government, such as it was, had simultaneously sent two different missions to Orléans for ill-defined and potentially conflicting purposes, and one of these missions had the backing of substantial military power. Moreover, because Parisians generally regarded Orléans as a stronghold of aristocracy, the possibility of a clash between them and the local forces was considerable. In his account, Bourdon was careful to distinguish between the majority of Fournier's men and an intransigent minority, but some of them were certainly ill disciplined and truculent. They terrorized the people, abusing shopkeepers and releasing "patriotic" soldiers, who had been arrested as deserters, from the civil prisons. On August 31, Fournier and some forty of his followers once again inspected the prisons of the High Court, so intimidating the prisoners that one poor man leapt from a window, breaking a leg in his fall. At this point, the prisoners were deprived of their papers, money, and jewels, nearly all of which were lost forever.[51]

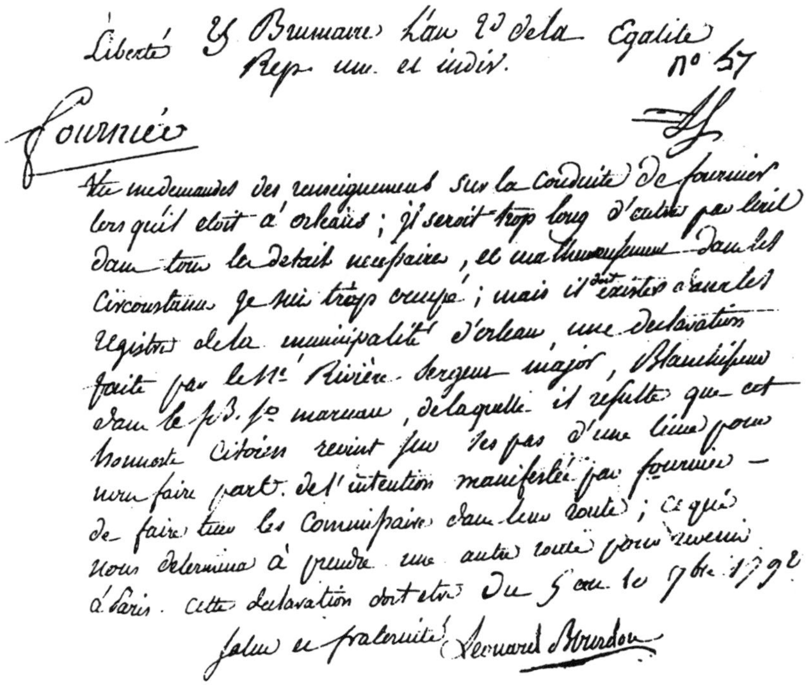

Liberté 19 Brumaire l'an 2d dela Egalité
Rep. un. et indiv. N° 57

Fournier

Vu vos demandes des renseignements sur la conduite de fournier lors quil etoit a orleans; il seroit trop long d'entrer par le detail dans tous les details necessaires, et malheureusement dans les circonstances je suis trop occupé; mais il doit exister dans les registres dela municipalité d'orleans, une declaration faite par le Mr Riviere sergent major, Blanchisseur dans le p.3. f. marceau, delaquelle il resulte que cet honnete citoien revint sur ses pas d'une lieue pour nous faire part de l'intention manifestée par fournier de faire tuer les Commissaires dans leur route; ce qui nous determina à prendre une autre route pour revenir à Paris. cette declaration doit etre du 5 au 10 7bre 1792

salut et fraternité Leonard Bourdon

Fig. 4. The Mission to Orléans (II). In October 1793, Bourdon replies evasively to a request for information regarding the conduct of Fournier—but says that he and Dubail avoided returning from Orléans to Paris with Fournier since they were told that he meant to have them both killed. Private collection: copy, Charavay Sale, May 12, 1990, 71(1).

Because Bourdon appeared in the prisoners' rooms on this occasion, some accounts say that he sanctioned outright robbery, making sure that the proceeds were taken directly to his lodgings.[52] He, however, asserts that he arrived to find the looting in progress and that he sought to restore some semblance of order, so that many of the valuables were returned. He also says that he gathered up the prisoners' personal papers, which were first taken to his inn and then deposited with the registrar of the High Court.[53] Because some of those who later marched away from Orléans, including Fournier,[54] apparently had their horses adorned with prized royalist decorations, extensive petty pilfering seems to have been more likely than official theft on a grand scale, and later Fournier even convinced Roland, who was nothing if not meticulous, that his official accounts were substantially correct. On his return to Paris, moreover, Fournier deposited at the Hôtel de Ville a big box of valuables that mysteriously disappeared at some later date.[55] As for Bourdon, despite his recurrent financial difficulties and all the later vilification of him, he does not seem likely to have sunk to outright and premeditated robbery. In this matter, his only proven fault is that of acquiescing in an outbreak of violence that he could not have prevented.

The same may also be said of the still sorrier sequel. After pillaging the prisoners on August 31, the Parisians remained on guard; by then, however, the municipality had become so alarmed by their conduct and by the possibility of conflict between them and the National Guard of Orléans that it sent an urgent appeal to Paris for instructions. In response, the National Assembly decreed on September 2—the day that the massacre of prisoners began in Paris—that the prisoners at Orléans should be transferred immediately to Saumur, some seventy miles farther west. More particularly, Bourdon, Dubail, and the two deputies who were permanently assigned to the High Court as state prosecutors, the Grand Procurators Garran-Coulon and Pellicot, were to effect an arrangement by which Orléans would finance the journey and supply an armed escort, whereas Fournier was to provide any necessary reinforcement but to bring most of his men back to Paris to help in its defence. This decree, rushed to Orléans by Danton's personal order, arrived on September 3 and was promptly implemented by the city, wagons being requisitioned and 500 men made ready to march.[56]

At this point, some deliberate deception was undoubtedly practised, and uncertainty about the extent to which Bourdon was privy to it has always enabled his detractors to assume the worst about him. According to Fournier, the *sans-culottes* once again refused to obey the order from Paris, crying that they would not be divided and that they meant to return to Paris with the prisoners. The municipality, however, was somehow convinced that all was well. Reluctantly, but in the belief that its own men were to march with some of the Parisians to Saumur, it accepted Fournier's outrageous demand for 15,000 livres for expenses, and at dawn on September 4 the prisoners were roughly hustled into the waiting wagons. However, when Fournier and his force moved off the Place Matroy, they took the road leading to Paris, leaving most of the guardsmen from Orléans standing fast.[57]

Happily there is no need here to follow the prisoners on their journey to the horrible fate that overtook them five days later, when nearly all of them were slaughtered in the streets of Versailles. They were killed not by their escorts but by countrymen who had assembled there in response to the general call for recruits and who may have been incited to kill by a few agitators from Paris.[58] The supposed presence of the latter has long provided popular and right-wing historians with material from which a plot, hatched either by Danton or by the Commune and effected by Fournier and Bourdon, may be postulated. More detached scholars, however, now accept the conclusion of Pierre Caron, the principal modern authority on the subject, that this and all the other September massacres were marked "by common features of a general order," being essentially the spontaneous outcome of intense public alarm.[59] More particularly, much may be learned from the instructions that were sent to Fournier when he halted his men for two days at Étampes. Roland, the minister to whom he was responsible, then wrote: "I hear the prisoners are at Étampes. Do all you can to keep them there"; simultaneously the National Assembly explicitly authorized him to march to wherever he wished *outside Paris*.[60] The fact is that at this time all authority was in abeyance, and this in itself may be an adequate ground for rejecting the hypothesis that the robbery and the murder of the prisoners of the High Court were the calculated consequences of a complicated conspiracy.

Nonetheless, Bourdon cannot be cleared of all responsibility for the initial abduction of these unfortunate men from Orléans. According to a statement made by one of Fournier's followers, a man who remained in the city after the others had left, the refusal of the Parisians to go to Saumur had been a farce, something arranged in advance by Fournier;[61] if that was so, then Bourdon was possibly aware of it but kept his knowledge from the municipal authorities. Although the truth of this affair is now beyond reach, one obvious fact is that the Parisians would certainly have been reluctant to march down the Loire when their homes and families were in danger in Paris—to which, indeed, the majority of them had been explicitly recalled both by the National Assembly and by an urgent message from the Faubourg Saint-Marcel.[62]

Even so, Bourdon may have had some idea of what was in the wind, for there seems to have been a working arrangement by which his colleague Dubail generally dealt with the local councillors while Bourdon kept in touch with the Parisians. Thus, although both commissioners were in the difficult position of having responsibility without power, Bourdon's situation was particularly invidious: answerable to government for the fulfilment of his mission, and perhaps particularly for maintaining the peace, Bourdon was also an avowed revolutionary who could hardly have repudiated decisions endorsed by a force of Parisian revolutionaries. Furthermore, he was probably anxious above all to avoid the real danger that the National Guard of Orléans might oppose the prisoners' abduction. Thus, he may indeed have condoned some part of Fournier's deception of the local authorities. Yet his conduct on September 4, however understandable, cannot be commended. Like Dubail, he easily accepted the argument that the departure of the prisoners meant that his mission was complete, and, although he joined Grand Procurator Garran-Coulon in reproaching Fournier as the column left the Place Matroy, he certainly did not follow Garran-Coulon to the point of deliberately placing himself in the path of the leading horsemen and being brutally knocked aside in consequence.[63] Few, however, could then have afforded to criticize Bourdon for this failure to oppose the will of the *sans-culottes*.

In truth, Bourdon's sympathies were probably more with Fournier's men than with the prisoners, indicted traitors for whose well-being Bourdon was not greatly concerned.[64] Still more certainly, his real interest was in the city in which he remained. It was generally held to be "aristocratic"—that is, that it had long been a peaceful place administered by moderate men of good social standing and royalist inclinations. It was nonetheless a deeply divided city, its working people far removed from the influential merchants who controlled the area's extensive trade in textiles.[65] The latter were openly hostile to the Revolution; the ever-increasing price and the recurrent scarcity of grain constantly increased social tension; and in August the news from Paris had roused the minority of more extreme democrats to intense activity.

In this situation, Bourdon made it his business to stimulate patriotic recruitment and to encourage the local Jacobins.[66] That he habitually met and ate with such commoners was for many respectable people almost criminal in itself,[67] and his speeches in the Popular Society, which he described as his "daily instruction" of the citizens, were so fiery that his staider colleague Dubail felt compelled to protest. Indeed, several later stories say that Dubail disapproved strongly of Bourdon's attitudes and activities.[68] By the latter's own account,[69] before he left Orléans he promoted the destruction of "feudal" monuments (including the treasured statue of Joan of Arc) and initiated the evaluation of religious houses, the distribution of pikes, and house-to-house searches for weapons and suspects. Moreover, he instigated the formation of a central committee of the sections, a crucial step toward popular control of the city. Thus, while in Orléans he acted as an ardent revolutionary who did all that he could to revolutionize the city, and he therefore became identified by the more moderate citizens with all that was obnoxious in the Revolution. That he actually incited violence is unlikely: indeed, he seems always to have urged the people to respect the law, and on at least two occasions he and Dubail succeeded in averting food riots. Nonetheless, it is hardly surprising that serious rioting occurred soon after his departure.[70]

Bourdon's return to Paris was approximately coincident with his appointment on September 9 as second assistant to the *procureur* of the Commune, and soon after he was ordered to report on the security of the Temple, where the king and his family were being ever more rigorously confined.[71] His first care, however, was to join Dubail in presenting to the National Assembly what was effectively his own report on their mission. Characteristically the assembly declined to hear or even accept this report on September 11, ruling it a matter for the executive.[72] Bourdon nonetheless had it published, with an additional passage indicating his success in awakening enthusiasm in Orléans and explaining explicitly that he was not prepared to order the use of force for the sake of conspirators.[73] Thus, he contributed directly to the passionate disputes that soon began about the massacre at Versailles, as about the still bloodier killings in Paris itself. More immediately, however, controversies arose about the possibility that he might become a deputy in the National Convention, which was then being elected.

One interesting feature of the attacks to which Bourdon was subjected at this time is their implication that he was then thought of in Paris more as a moderate revolutionary than as an extremist. Presumably because voices on the right were effectively silenced, challenges to his position emanated either from the left or "from below," and, when he himself demanded written copies of oral denunciations of him, he referred to men such as Lullier, Lazowski, and Hébert.[74] Moreover, one of these episodes may serve in a minor manner to strengthen the argument that the division between "the Girondins" and "the Montagnards" was not at this time so clear-cut and extensive as is usually supposed. Toward the end of August, Louvet, whose paper La Sentinelle was subsidized by Roland and was immensely influential both in the provinces and among the sans-culottes of Paris, listed the names of those whom he recommended for election to the National Convention, and this list included Bourdon's name. Apparently Louvet was then afraid that the new assembly would be won by moderate royalists who would reinstate the king, and his list, which included future Girondins such as Buzot as well as future Montagnards such as Robespierre, was meant to ensure that the democratic and republican cause would be strongly represented.[75] Evidently, however, there were some in whom suspicion outweighed all other considerations. On September 5, Marat's L'Ami du peuple damned Louvet's list as the work of a faction (i.e., the Rolandist or Girondin coterie), and Marat most improbably dismissed Bourdon as a man wholly unknown.

In the reply that Bourdon then published,[76] he rightly reproached Marat for assailing him while he was engaged in a "delicate mission" at Orléans, where he was "urging the people to rise to the same heights as the Parisians." The appropriately embellished review of his earlier record that followed is of interest in its implication that he had been one of those whose support the court party had sought to purchase earlier in the summer of 1792. Substantially, however, Bourdon's claims, sufficiently noticed here in previous pages, may serve to introduce the lengthier attacks made on him at this time by the men of the Section Finistère, that part of the Faubourg Saint-Marcel in which he had first attempted to establish his school in 1788-89.

The first of these attacks is now known only from the consideration given to it by the Commune on August 23.[77] On August 20, apparently, the section had formally accused Bourdon of appropriating in 1789 the sum of 15,000 livres, which had been entrusted to him, it had said, for the purchase of flour and grain. Both the Commune and the Section des Gravilliers had then appointed commissioners to investigate the matter, and both bodies had reported that no one could be found to take responsibility for what were essentially vague charges. The men of Gravilliers, indeed, had gone further, reporting that Bourdon had assured them on his honour that he had never received any sum for purchases for Paris and that in his various missions in 1789 he had had to depend entirely on the persuasion of farmers and local councils. Affirming that Bourdon had been instrumental in effecting

the Revolution both in 1789 and in 1792, the Gravilliers commissioners had concluded that the denunciation of him had simply been an
attempt to undermine public confidence in enlightened republicans on
the eve of the impending elections. Having heard both of these
reports, the Commune declared that the charges were unfounded, and
it ordered that the scarf of office, of which Bourdon had been temporarily deprived, should be returned to him immediately.

This action, however, did not end the matter. On August 26, Bourdon was chosen as an elector of Gravilliers, being the third of the
thirty-three that the section was entitled to send to the new Electoral
Assembly of Paris,[78] and on September 10, when the tenth of the city's
twenty-four deputies was being chosen by that assembly, his name
appeared for the first time among those who were in the running.[79] On
September 13, however, twenty-four delegates of the Section Finistère
appeared in the hall to renew its denunciation and to give notice that,
if Bourdon remained an elector, all of its own representatives would be
recalled immediately.[80] The electors thereon decided to suspend Bourdon until he was heard. Then, on September 14, a counterblast to
Finistère's attack was presented by thirty-two delegates of Gravilliers;
Bourdon spoke in his own defence, and long, inconclusive, and
unrecorded discussion ensued, until the electors resolved to maintain
his suspension pending further investigation.[81]

In a passing reference to this tangled web of denunciation and justification, Braesch remarked that the eulogy from Gravilliers was much
more concerned with Bourdon's patriotism than with his probity. That
it was more general than particular is true; however, as far as the allegations made by the Finistère delegation were specific, they varied
between the trivial and the hysterical. Thus, it is manifestly false that
Bourdon had allied himself with the aristocrats of Orléans, giving his
time there simply to feasting and debauchery, and this obvious falsehood makes it still more improbable that he had spent public money
freely on sumptuous feasts and splendid balls and festivals at Provins in
1789. On the other hand, the assertion that he had failed to fulfil a
widely advertised promise to accommodate four (*sic*) of the children
orphaned on July 14, 1789, has verisimilitude but ignores the point
that the Royal Society of Emulation had probably never materialized
anyway. If the general wildness of the charges is granted, then the most
valid of them all may be the allegation that Bourdon left his lodgings
in rue Mouffetard surreptiously, so that his landlord had to seize his
furniture and pay watchmen thirty-three livres for keeping it under
observation. Yet even here we have an explicit denial by Bourdon in

October 1790 that he owed anything to anyone in the Gobelins area: on the contrary, he then asserted that he had spent money freely there on the strength of royal promises that had never been fulfilled.[82] Because the truth of the matter is now beyond discovery, two points alone emerge as worthy of note: Bourdon was probably apt to take promises literally but to give them freely, and those who believed that they had been deceived were so intensely hostile to him that they did not hesitate to call him a liar, an intriguer, a traitor, and a man whose sole merit lay in the arts of seduction and deceit.

All these various difficulties were resolved by chance. During his last days at Orléans, Bourdon was invited to take the chair at a meeting of the Jacobins, and one of the members, who particularly praised him for his profound understanding of current educational and economic problems, commended both him and his colleague Dubail for their insistence on the observance of the law. This insistence, he said, had effectively prevented bloodshed in Orléans, and he thought that the two commissioners' patriotism and devotion to freedom and equality entitled them to nomination as candidates for election to the National Convention. Approved unanimously, this resolution was despatched at once to the Electoral Assembly of the Department of the Loiret, which was then in session at Beaugency. At first, it seemed that the proposal had been made too late, for those who took it reported that the elections were completed by the time of their arrival.[83] As it happened, however, two of those elected, Brissot and Condorcet, had also been chosen by other departments, and these two vacancies were at once filled, not from the assembly's list of elected alternatives, but by agreement to name Louvet and Bourdon.[84] This news was first announced in Paris by some of those men of Orléans who had left the city with Fournier's force, who told the electors in the capital that Bourdon had done much to arouse patriotism in Orléans and had shown "wisdom in reconciling his duties as a magistrate and man of the law with those of a friend and a man of the people."[85]

A final bitter dispute occurred between Bourdon and his unrelated namesake, François-Louis Bourdon, who disputed the former's claim that Léonard had also been chosen by the *département* of the Oise (as, in fact, he had), but this argument was at least superficially assuaged when François-Louis was able to opt for the Oise, thus becoming— usually—identifiable as Bourdon de l'Oise.[86] Thus, in the summer of 1792, Léonard Bourdon, no longer termed M. Bourdon de la Crosnière, became not only the principal of a state-supported experimental school but also a deputy in what would be the most powerful assembly ever to preside over the fortunes of France. In rising so far, he had identified himself both in Orléans and in Paris with "the Revolution of Equality," and in desperate circumstances he had thus alienated many local people, who became his implacable enemies. He can nevertheless confidently be cleared of the heinous crimes that he was later charged with but that really reflected the bitterness aroused by the Revolution. Indeed, even his identification with extremism may be questioned, for there are several indications that his devotion to the ideals of the Revolution was combined with a determination to do all that was possible to reconcile the will of the people with the maintenance of law and order.

5

Regicide (September 1792 to January 1793)

$\mathcal{T}$he name of the National Convention, the assembly of which Léonard Bourdon became a member on September 20, 1792, is fraught with significance. Confronted by insurrection, the Legislative Assembly had ordered the formation of this new body so that men fully representative of the sovereignty of the people might determine whether France should be monarchical or republican. The Convention, supposedly an august and austere senate, consequently always had something of the sanctity of a constituent assembly, and at least some of the deputies presumed that a few weeks would be sufficient for them to complete an appropriate revision of the Constitution of 1791.[1]

In reality, however, the new assembly lasted for three full and fearful years. For much of that time, it was divided by bitter political conflicts that were in part the legacy of previous quarrels and in part the outcome of deep differences of view about the point at which the Revolution should be regarded as complete. Moreover, because the country long remained perilously close to internal chaos and disastrous military defeat, the deputies were constantly involved not only in constitutional and legal problems but also in herculean endeavours to cope with the exigencies of recurrent crises. Only when the most resolute men had silenced their critics and taken direct and dictatorial control of every aspect of life, and in turn had been destroyed, was some measure of stability restored. Thus, the Convention, elected when the Prussian army was approaching Paris in the summer of 1792, was not dissolved until the autumn of 1795, when the apparently invincible armies of France seemed to be on the verge of dominating all of Europe. By that time, its name had become synonymous with ruthless repression as well as with national unity and military victory.

Notes to Chapter 5 are on pp. 361-63.

This three-year period, during which the Revolution attained and passed its climax, is commonly and conveniently considered in successive stages. Initially the assembly was constantly distracted by political strife between the Girondins (because several of their leading deputies, such as Vergniaud, came from Bordeaux) and the Montagnards (those who occupied the highest tiers of seats, "the Mountain," in the chamber). The national crisis was indeed relieved by temporary military success, for after the battle of Valmy on September 20 the Prussian forces fell back, and the French armies advanced triumphantly into Belgium, the Rhineland, and Savoy. In the aftermath of the August revolution and the September massacres, there was nevertheless fierce dispute about the power of the Commune and the sections of Paris. This antagonism also permeated the assembly's debates about its most immediate problem, that of deciding on the fate of the imprisoned king, for the deputies of Paris, who formed the core of the Montagnard minority, were naturally particularly identified both with the capital and with a total repudiation of the monarchy.

According to the entries about Bourdon in most historical dictionaries, he was notable in this new assembly as a Montagnard who was a violent revolutionary extremist. Certainly his debut was swift, for on September 22 he spoke in support of the general demand for the renewal of all local administrative authorities,[2] which were commonly agreed to have become corrupted by their previous dependence on the monarchy. On that day, too, Bourdon was named as one of four deputies required to draft proposals for the regulation of the Convention's daily meetings, and as the spokesman of this commission he subsequently succeeded in winning approval for its proposals.[3] The assumptions underlying this *projet de règlement* nevertheless proved highly unrealistic: rare indeed, for example, were occasions when the public galleries remained respectfully silent while the deputies spoke in due succession about great affairs of state.

This beginning should not, however, suggest that Bourdon was particularly prominent, or even very active, in the Convention in 1792. He was an occasional rather than a frequent speaker, and his interventions in debate, though forceful, were usually brief and concerned more with specific matters than with generalities. Thus, he seems to have been a recognized but not a considerable figure, and his relative obscurity proves more striking than the unrestrained violence ascribed to him in historical literature. Strangely, too, no single satisfactory explanation of this obscurity can be easily substantiated. Always a somewhat isolated figure, and now a newcomer to the nation's parliament, Bourdon may simply have felt overshadowed in so large an assembly. He was, moreover, identified with the minority, for most of the other deputies were deeply suspicious of Paris as a place of popular violence, and although Bourdon had been elected by Loiret he had also recently been an active Parisian revolutionary. Such suspicions probably explain the fact that, when he was first elected on October 13 as a member of the new Committee of Public Instruction, he was the last of twenty-four members chosen.[4] Indeed, that he was chosen at all still seems shameful to those who believe that he had played some sinister part in the massacre of prisoners at Versailles.

It is, of course, possible that at this time Bourdon was primarily concerned with the development of his school. This concern, however, remains speculative, for the most pertinent (and controversial) records are illustrative of the situation of the school in 1795, when official inquiries were made. Bourdon himself, however, had anticipated that a trial period of at least twelve months would be necessary before any proper assessment of his experiment could be made,[5] and in 1792-93 la Société des Jeunes Français was in fact established gradually. The Ministry of War's undertaking to send Bourdon fifty pupils was apparently implemented piecemeal: in June 1792, immediately before the summer vacation, he had only six enrolments, and even at the end of that year there were but thirty.[6] By the end of February 1793, however, he was able to advertise an "open day" on which his pupils would demonstrate their activities to the Committee of Public Instruction, and in this announcement he said that the school had a total of seventy young republicans, either "élèves de la nation" or pupils privately maintained.[7] Bourdon also specified the subjects in which tuition was available, and his curriculum implied the existence of an appreciable staff, even though many of the teachers probably came in as visitors. In February and March 1793, too, he approached the committee, the Convention, and the Minister of War with the request that the number of pupils allocated to him should be increased from fifty to sixty.[8]

Yet this expansion provides no indication of how far Bourdon was personally engaged either in teaching or in supervision. Indeed, Armand Le Corbeiller, who regards him as a charlatan, presumes that he simply left the daily management of the establishment to his wife and daughter.[9] By contrast, Mlle. Thibal, whose assessment is both more sympathetic and better established, suggests that, despite his reiteration of the importance of practical experiment, Bourdon himself was always primarily concerned with promoting the growth of his school by advertisement and by a constant search for more pupils and more varied equipment.[10] Even in this, however, the period 1792-93 appears to have been one of consolidation, for his next brochures about les Jeunes Français, which bear no date, seem to belong to a somewhat later period.

A further possibility, that Bourdon had much to do as a member of the Committee of Public Instruction, is still more speculative. The organization of that committee proved difficult; it was not until late December 1792 that Bourdon was eventually attached to its second, economic, section, and even then no action followed in any of the minor matters with which he was charged in February and March 1793.[11] Nor did he take part in presenting the committee's first proposals to the Convention in December 1792. No doubt his silence was partly a consequence of the fact that these plans—those proposed by Lanthenas for the organization of primary education and by Romme for that of education in general[12]— were received without serious discussion. As in so much else, matters of more pressing political importance had priority. Moreover, at this time Bourdon was probably not greatly interested in theoretical plans for the organization of national education: what concerned him more was his hope that his own school would become the model for a form of education that would be copied throughout France.

In all likelihood, too, Bourdon was out of sympathy with most of the other committee members. Apparently the committee's first reaction to its responsibilities was to produce modified versions of the seminal report on national education that had been laid before the Legislative Assembly by Condorcet on April 20, 1792, and that still had to be debated. Matters of national organization apart, the proposals of Lanthenas and Romme reflected Condorcet's conviction that education is primarily a matter of instruction in which the teacher's ultimate objective ought to be the fullest possible development of each student's ability to use reason.[13] If this view indeed prevailed in the committee, then Bourdon's silence is not surprising, for it was the antithesis of all that he ever said or wrote about education.

On the other hand, he would certainly have been sympathetic to a very different proposal made independently on December 21 by Rabaut Saint-Étienne,[14] who had been prepared in March 1791 to promote Bourdon's plans in the Constituent Assembly. Rabaut did not deny the importance of knowledge, nor did he explicitly question Condorcet's assumption that people accustomed to reasoning would naturally become virtuous. Like Bourdon, however, Rabaut drew a sharp distinction between instruction, which at best could only gradually be socially beneficial, and education, by which he meant a direct appeal to the hearts of young and old through all their senses and in every type of communal institution. Only this approach, he maintained, could effect that immediate elevation of outlook and behaviour imperative to the survival of France's new institutions of freedom, equality, and justice. The sequel to this address is interesting because Rabaut's thesis won enthusiastic applause, and Rabaut himself was immediately nominated from the floor as an additional member of the Committee of Public Instruction. Here again there is the implication that Bourdon's reticence may well have been due to a fundamental difference between his own approach to education and that of the majority of the committee as it was at first constituted.

In some respects, Bourdon's particular situation indeed reflected the difficulties of the whole Convention in the period between September 1792 and June 1793. In the first place, the problems and the perils of the country constantly demanded the deputies' immediate attention. Not without reason did Marat interrupt those speaking about education, comparing them with a general who made his starving soldiers plant fruit trees for their future nourishment.[15] Moreover, people became increasingly alarmed as it became ever more obvious that almost every problem confronting them was aggravated by division in the Convention itself. Only initially, when the deputies enthusiastically abolished the monarchy, was there unanimity. After that brief truce, they were perpetually plagued by the political strife that prevented either the Girondins or the Montagnards from governing France effectively.

In late 1792, when the Girondin coterie was the most influential, Bourdon's role was really that of a minor critic or backbencher. However, some indication of his interests and general attitudes appears in the various comments that he made at this time in the Convention or in the Jacobin Club. Evidently he shared the general enthusiasm for the extension of the Revolution beyond the frontiers of France, for he complimented the patriots in Belgium on their recognition of the dawn of a new era of freedom, and he even accepted some responsibility for organizing the translation of the Convention's decrees into German. He was nevertheless insistent that no decisions should be made about the future of Savoy without reference to the wishes of its people.[16] Similarly, although Bourdon sometimes commented on military commanders such as Dillon, Dumouriez, and Kellermann, it was their political reliability rather than their professional competence that concerned him.[17] Here again his strongest interest was in the rights and welfare of groups of people who were being adversely affected by the war. France, he said, should avow its intention to ensure that prisoners of war were well treated; men who made arms should be allowed, but not compelled, to leave the army and resume their trade; and inquiry about the soldiers' lack of proper clothing should be pressed to the highest level of administrative responsibility.[18]

The same concern for the unfortunate is also evident in Bourdon's interventions in matters more directly related to civil affairs, so far as they are distinguishable in a time of revolutionary war. For example, Bourdon agreed that the costs incurred in the renovation of the Ministry of Foreign Affairs during Delessart's period of office should be charged to Delessart's estate, but he also urged that the men who had done the work should be paid by the nation in the first instance.[19] On other occasions, having praised the patriotism of the Jacobins and the municipality of Orléans, he tried to obtain a substantial subsidy for the support of the indigent in that city.[20]

Such interventions may suggest that in some respects Bourdon was an individualist who invariably, if somewhat haphazardly, championed the underdog. Yet his liberalism had its limits. In his view, recaptured émigrés should not be eligible for the compassionate treatment that he recommended for other prisoners of war.[21] A further episode is equally revealing: when a financial house that backed municipal poor-relief in Paris went bankrupt, he shared the political anxiety of the Jacobin Club lest disorders should occur and be exploited to discredit the capital, but he was principally concerned to ensure that the immediate needs of the poor were met by draconian taxation of wealthy capitalists.[22] Ultimately he remained a revolutionary whose humanitarianism was sincere but selective.

Bourdon was also indisputably a Montagnard. Although his outlook alone would doubtless have drawn him to support the more extreme group in any sustained parliamentary conflict, in and after September 1792 his previous associations certainly did so. That is not to say, however, that he was—from the opening of the Convention— simply one of a Robespierrist party. Indeed, Bourdon did not speak specifically in Robespierre's support before the middle of December,[23] in itself an interesting indication that parties then grew gradually, as apparently personal conflicts clarified underlying issues. Bourdon was nonetheless one whose position was determined by his past. As a staunch Parisian Jacobin, he shared the conviction of the Jacobin Club that in the Legislative Assembly Brissot and the deputies of the Gironde had constantly sought to turn the Revolution to their own advantage. The Jacobins were sure that these men, variously called "the Brissotins," "the Girondins," and "the Rolandins," had tried to avert the insurrection of August 10, condemning republicanism even while they negotiated with the court. The Jacobins, the "true revolutionaries," were also sure that these men had thwarted the nation on August 10 by suspending instead of deposing the king and by immediately reinstating their own friends, particularly Roland, as ministers. Worst of all, perhaps, once the Convention had been summoned, they seemed to the Jacobins to have sought to consolidate their position by repudiating Parisian violence and by persuading France that they alone had averted counterrevolution.

However misleading this interpretation may have been (and even now it is easier to sympathize with the Girondins' motives than it is to justify their conduct), Roland had certainly employed the considerable resources of the Ministry of the Interior to exalt his friends' role in the insurrection. Throughout the crisis, on the other hand, the Jacobins had allowed their own correspondence with their affiliates to lapse. Consequently most of the new deputies in the Convention regarded Roland and the Girondin-Brissotin coterie as their saviours, and Bourdon had no doubt that the Jacobins' part in effecting the destruction of the monarchy had been grossly misrepresented. As early as September 23, he told the Club that he was having great difficulty in convincing his colleagues in the Convention that they had been deluded, and he protested against the attempt then being made to attract the newcomers to a different political society (the "Reunion"), which did not meet in public.[24]

That particular danger proved short-lived. A week later, immediately after Bourdon had warned the Jacobins not to tolerate discreditable disorders in their meetings, another member reported that all those in the "Reunion" had resolved to join the Jacobins immediately.[25] On October 12, too, Brissot's name was formally struck from the Jacobins' list of members. Even so, in mid-November Bourdon, now again a member of the Correspondence Committee, emphasized the extent to which the Club's affiliated societies had been misled by "the placards profusely distributed in the departments" by Roland.[26] It was, Bourdon said, important to explain that the Girondins were certainly not responsible for the rising of August 10, and it was still more essential to make it known that that day was due to the true Jacobins, the very men who, as deputies, were now being abused in the Convention.

His political position was also governed by the fact that he had briefly been prominent in the Commune of the Insurrection. That body had dictated its will to the Legislative Assembly, and for more than two months it continued to exist in defiance of the Convention's decree calling for prompt municipal elections. It was consequently repeatedly attacked by the Girondins and their sympathizers, many of whom held that the Commune had deliberately instigated the September massacres in Paris. Although Bourdon was not, and indeed could not have been, personally culpable on that account, as were Robespierre, Danton, and Marat,[27] he did sometimes try to plead the Commune's cause. On October 10, for example, he spoke boldly against the proposal that a commission be created to find out how much of the property deposited at the Hôtel de Ville during the insurrection was still available to the nation.[28] Calling for a less odious procedure, by which the Commune would be given adequate time to prepare and post accounts for all to see, he alleged in typically Montagnard terms that those who had made the proposal really wished to call the Revolution of August 10 into question by discrediting the very men whose patriotism had saved the whole country.

In other circumstances, Bourdon's readiness to defend the Commune might well have proved embarrassing for one who was not only a deputy but also a prominent person in the Section des Gravilliers. The sections of Paris had rapidly become virtually autonomous republics, and as such they were initially as resentful as the Convention of the pretensions of the Commune. Indeed, Bourdon's earliest defence of the Commune in the Convention was evoked by a denunciation of its despotism by the Quinze-Vingts Section, an attack that Bourdon tried to answer by explaining the complexities involved in organizing municipal elections.[29] That he was able to avoid a more serious conflict of loyalties was due in part to his belief in popular democracy, a belief that enabled him on at least one occasion to urge the Convention to order open voting in those elections.[30] Voting aloud and by name ("par appel nominal et à l'haute voix") was the established procedure in primary assemblies at that time, and in the sections of Paris, the archetypes of direct democracy, it was regarded as the only method worthy of free people. Certainly the futile attempt of the majority of the deputies to enforce a form of secret ballot did much to swing the sections to the support of the Commune and the Montagnards.[31]

Somewhat surprisingly, however, Bourdon did not openly champion the sections' growing demands for more effective measures of price control. In the autumn of 1792, some local control of the distribution of grain was permissible, for in September, before the Legislative Assembly was dissolved, it had approved legislation that authorized local administrations to take stock of the grain available in their areas and, where appropriate, to requisition surplus supplies for sale in their markets. Limited as it was, this legislation, meant to meet the immediate difficulties caused by the demands of the armies in northeastern France, was too much for the Minister of the Interior. Roland, a fervent believer in complete economic freedom, told the Convention on October 7 that all that it could allow itself to do about food supplies was to declare that it could do nothing,[32] and, as he advised, rioting in the countryside was then rigorously repressed. By late October, however, rising prices, the result of issuing too much paper money too quickly, were a more serious problem than that of supply. Although inflation was only in its infancy, its effects were soon evident in Paris, especially among the small shopkeepers and working people of sections like that of Gravilliers. A newly formed central committee of delegates of the sections, including Gravilliers, then drew up proposals for a law to subject all grain producers and merchants to strict supervision;[33] however, when the Convention considered the question in early December, it simply restored complete economic freedom by abolishing the legislation of September. At this time, the Montagnards were indeed as averse to regulation as were other deputies, although they were more sympathetic to the poor and correspondingly hostile to reliance on repression alone.

Bourdon, who took no part in this debate, presumably remained silent because he had already twice pressed the Convention's Committee of Agriculture and Commerce to adopt his own—and his father's—proposals for the nationwide organization of granaries. Moreover, the outcome of that approach had been discouraging, for his plan proved to be but one of forty-six submitted to the committee by deputies, and on the second occasion "plusieurs objections" had led to the adjournment of any further consideration of it.[34] Beyond this, Bourdon had apparently become convinced that the great political question of the day, the trial of Louis XVI, was of more immediate importance than any other problem. On November 23, he indeed demanded that the order of business in the Jacobins be changed to give consideration of this question priority over matters of subsistence and finance, for he believed that the trial had become so great a cause of discord in the Convention that the republic itself might well be torn apart by factions.[35] However comprehensible, this preoccupation with one problem was perilous, for many of the poor in Gravilliers soon found the social and political extremism of Bourdon's principal rival in the section, the *enragé* Jacques Roux, more pertinent to their immediate needs.

In all these matters, Bourdon's reticence belies his later reputation, so that he seems to have been a surprisingly quiet and moderate revolutionary. In his uncompromising attitude toward the deposed king, however, he was very different. Because this aspect of his record has been most commonly emphasized in the little that has been written about Bourdon, some preliminary restoration of perspective is appropriate. Thus, it would not now be possible to maintain, as did some authors in the time of Louis XVIII, that Bourdon played a great part in the process by which Louis XVI was sentenced to death. His influence may indeed have been more considerable than is now supposed, but the truth is that even on this matter he was neither a prominent nor a frequent speaker. Recent authorities on the trial do not in fact regard either his views or his fervour in promoting them as unusual enough to warrant particular notice.[36] Similarly, nineteenth-century condemnations of him as barbarously inhumane, as "one of the most ferocious enemies of Louis XVI,"[37] need not be accepted uncritically: although his own rhetoric invites extravagance in assessments of him, his opinions about Louis were consistent and comprehensible.

On January 21, 1793, the day of Louis's execution, Bourdon told the Jacobins that ever since the flight to Varennes he had believed that the king should suffer the punishment he deserved.[38] Certainly he had demanded in 1791 that Louis be put on trial, and all that had happened since then must have strengthened his conviction that condemnation of "the tyrant" was imperative. More particularly, his position at the opening of the Convention is implicit in his first recorded intervention in its debates: on September 22, as we have seen, he called for the renewal of all administrative bodies, saying that they were certainly corrupted by their earlier dependence on "le premier fonctionnaire."[39] That demand is one of many indications that republicans, particularly those who were the most ardent revolutionaries, were then extremely conscious of the insecurity of their newborn republic. Despite the retreat of the Prussians, despite the apparently triumphant progress of French arms, this anxiety was constant. Beyond the real or supposed activities of recognizable counterrevolutionaries such as *émigrés* and nonjuring priests, there lay the frightening fact that none could know which officials, from the ministers and the generals down to minor local officers, had really accepted the republic wholeheartedly; worst of all, the same doubt existed about the deputies in the Convention itself. The Girondins' perpetual attacks on Paris and on men such as Robespierre, Danton, and Marat, whose association with the Revolution of August 10 was obvious, were thus increasingly seen by the Montagnards as manifestations of royalism and proof that a repudiation of the republic and of republican democracy was imminent.

That Bourdon fully shared such anxiety is not surprising, for he was not only a Parisian revolutionary but also a man who had become closely associated with Orléans, a city far from being fully converted to republicanism. Apparent from the first meetings of the Convention, his fears are implicit in his reassertions of the rights of the Commune of Paris as the body primarily responsible for Louis's imprisonment. On September 24, the day on which the Girondins first advanced their policy of raising an armed force from the departments to guard the Convention, he called for the immediate suppression of the allowance of 500,000 livres for the king.[40] Saying that no captive had ever been so well treated, Bourdon demanded that the municipality alone should be responsible for meeting all Louis's needs. More dramatically, on December 15, when the Convention had finally decided on the procedure that would be followed for Louis's defence, he joined Tallien in demanding that the assembly repeal its decision to allow the king to be visited by his family.[41] This apparent harshness has repeatedly been cited as a flagrant instance of his inhumanity, but both Bourdon and Tallien were again primarily concerned to assert the independence of the Commune in a matter of security. The uproar that their demand occasioned arose because Bourdon explicitly denied that the Convention had any competence in the matter, and Tallien dared to say that the Commune would act as it thought fit regardless of the deputies' ruling.

Similarly, Bourdon was always impatient about the Convention's refusal to resolve the king's trial quickly and decisively. As early as October 16, he called on the deputies at least to decide that there would be a trial.[42] Even on November 7, when Mailhe reported on behalf of the Committee of Legislation that Louis could properly be tried despite his constitutional inviolability, Bourdon tried to have the recommendation formally accepted rather than embodied in a decree, for in his view the people had already decided the issue by appointing the Convention to act for them.[43] Moreover, as the apparently endless debates continued, he became convinced that the real cause of delay was the presence in the hall of a considerable number of deputies who secretly hoped to save the king and restore the monarchy. In this he was wrong. That many deputies were reluctant to condemn Louis to death means not that their acceptance of the republic was superficial but that they were deeply troubled by the legal problems involved in judging a deposed king and thus by the possibility of basing the republic itself on some abuse of legality. Again, many deputies were reluctant to identify themselves either with the Girondins or with the Montagnards, a choice that was implicit in a trial in which the two groups would surely contend for predominance.

Bourdon, whose constant commitment to the Mountain is indisputable, presented his own justification of the trial to the Convention on December 3. However, because his nineteen-page *Opinion . . . sur le jugement de Louis Capet, dit Louis XVI*[44] was one of many that were officially printed by order of the assembly in an attempt to save time, it was actually written before November 18, the date of its printing, and thus before suspicions were intensified by the discovery of further evidence of Louis's duplicity in his secret safe, the notorious *armoire de fer*. Even so, Bourdon began his address by saying that sophistry and a false sort of sentimental humanity had combined with established royalist habits of thought to produce opposition to a trial that the Convention had at first expected as a matter of course. Similarly, he concluded by appealing to the deputies to beware lest their prolonged discussion of an essentially simple matter should make people suppose that there were still partisans of monarchy among them.

Bourdon's main concern, however, was to refute the argument that Louis could not be placed on trial for acts that he had committed while king because, although his ministers were responsible at law for all that they had done in his name, he was constitutionally inviolable. Only for specific offences, the argument ran, was the immunity invalid, and, because the prescribed penalty for those offences was loss of the throne, Louis had already suffered all the punishment that could legally be imposed on him. But for Bourdon the Constitution of 1789/1791, far from being a contract made between equal partners, had never been anything more than the conditions imposed by a victorious nation on a vanquished and suppliant monarch. Because the interest of the nation had been the prime consideration from the outset, to Bourdon it was inconceivable that those who had made the Constitution would have tacitly authorized their principal official to do anything contrary to that interest. The inviolability of the king, like that of his ministers, thus existed only insofar as it was in the public interest. In Bourdon's eyes, the case was essentially one in which natural law, from which sprang the imprescriptible rights of the sovereign people, was infinitely superior to the legal fiction by which the people afforded inviolability to its own appointed agents.

At least by implication, Bourdon also dismissed an anxiety that troubled many of the deputies, the fear that they might condemn the king for actions that were not originally illegal but that were being made so retrospectively. He could not believe that the men who had made the Constitution would have had any intention of affording Louis freedom to commit every imaginable crime. Even granted that their judgment had been weakened by their inability to understand that free people are perfectly capable of managing their own affairs, Bourdon did not think that they could ever have countenanced any such absurdity. On the contrary, the very immunity granted to the king in constitutional matters implied that he was as liable as any other official or private person to prosecution and punishment for offences against the penal code.

Bourdon consequently asserted that the king's constitutional inviolability applied only to his official actions, those for which his ministers could be called to account. There would thus, for example, be no question of trying Louis for his refusal to sanction crucial decrees. Yet, according to Bourdon, Louis could and should be held legally responsible for everything that he had done unofficially and in his personal capacity, such as writing secretly to foreign rulers, the open or potential enemies of France, or (as Bourdon believed) giving orders that led directly to massacres. Moreover, Louis's abdication, and the indisputable loss of all immunity, was to be dated not from his deposition in August 1792, which should be seen as the imposition of a constitutional penalty, but from the first moment that Louis had acted, or even had conceived the idea of acting, personally and in his own interest as opposed to that of the nation.

From this basis, Bourdon proceeded in impassioned passages to survey the history of the Revolution since July 14, 1789, every episode of which was presented as irrefutable proof of Louis's perpetual perfidy. The details of this demonstration need not now be recapitulated. The point of view, however, is of interest as illustrating popular belief, and despite all exaggerations that belief was rooted in the fact that Louis had repeatedly sought to check and reverse the Revolution, his last wholehearted commitment having been to the proposals that he had put forward in the "Royal Session" of June 23, 1789. No doubt, too, the bitter hostility with which almost all the revolutionaries regarded him in 1792 was the outcome of their conviction that he had repeatedly betrayed not only them but also the exalted revolutionary vision that has been called "the sublimity of the nation."[45] More particularly, Bourdon's *Opinion* is of interest here in its revelation of his complete inability to think of a king as anything more than a *premier fonctionnaire*, a mere agent of the nation. He evidently had no conception either of "the divinity that doth hedge about a king," entitling him to honour, loyalty, and obedience whatever his faults, or of the possibility that a king might be the personification of his people, not simply a notable representative of a nation. In this attitude, he was indeed a real republican, a pole apart from those *émigrés* who believed France to be "where the lilies were."

Bourdon's *Opinion* must therefore be seen as the product of a convinced partisan of a particular position. As an exposition of that point of view, it bears the stamp of sincerity, but it is repetitive in form and somewhat specious in argument. Robespierre, who made one of his most remarkable speeches on the same day, December 3, icily maintained that the deputies could act only as men of state whose sole concern must be public safety and that any trial must inevitably call the Revolution itself into question. For many Montagnards, reasons of state ultimately made the existence of the king incompatible with that of the Revolution; however, beyond a brief identification of national justice with national interest, Bourdon did not explicitly argue in such terms. Moreover, although he had begun his address by reminding the Convention that the question of inviolability must be considered calmly and dispassionately, he himself became increasingly pejorative in his references to Louis, whom he described, for example, as a cruel and cowardly despot, a tyrant who had committed crime after crime in his efforts to subjugate a great nation. Even the king's habitually impassive appearance and his stoicism in adversity were ascribed to his heartless indifference to the sufferings of the people. Similarly, although Bourdon began by avowing that his concern was not with the question of the king's punishment, but only with that of whether the king could be tried at all, his concluding call for a trial came as an anticlimax to his fervent demand that Louis be sent to the scaffold: "La loi, la raison, la justice exigent hautement le jugement de Louis, et son jugement, c'est la mort."

On December 3, it was finally decided that the king would be tried by the Convention, and Bourdon was anxious to ensure that the whole process would be as simple and as swift as possible. As he indicated in a note printed as an appendix to his *Opinion*, he feared that formal indictment and interrogation of the prisoner, to say nothing of his counsels' presentation of his defence, would open the way for endless evasions of responsibility—and the extremely dangerous political exploitation of such procrastination by enemies of the republic. Although, as Bourdon told the Jacobins that night,[46] the rejection of inviolability was indeed "a sort of victory," he believed that the deputies ought to accept the fact that "the cannon of Paris" (i.e., the insurrection of August 10 and hence the will of the people) effectively constituted a jury of accusation. The Convention was consequently bound to act simply as a tribunal charged with the application of the law; moreover, because Louis should be regarded as a conspirator caught red-handed, it would suffice for the assembly to hear all that could be said in his defence and then proceed immediately to decide on his sentence.

In all likelihood, it is not, as has been alleged, sheer savagery but the same simple desire to see a wretched and potentially perilous situation resolved quickly that explains Bourdon's two consecutive motions in the Convention on December 13.[47] With the first motion, accepted without protest, Bourdon proposed that Louis be told that the counsel whom he had chosen for his defence, Target, had declared himself too infirm to appear and that he then be required to make an immediate choice between others (notably Lamaignon de Malesherbes) who had offered their services. The second motion, that all the evidence against Louis be made available to him and his counsel within twenty-four hours, evoked a minor uproar. Perhaps some found Bourdon's precipitation offensive, but those who protested did so because they thought it impossible to have the mass of material transcribed so soon, and the Convention in fact adopted Bourdon's plan after ordering the employment of every available clerk.

Thus far, Bourdon has appeared here as a somewhat isolated individual, a man whose background and convictions were those of the Montagnards but who was not obviously an active supporter of the Mountain as a political party. However, during the last four to five weeks of Louis's trial, he seems to have participated in the political conflict more often and to have been much readier to support an agreed position. Insofar as this difference was real, it may be seen simply as another example of his tendency to respond vigorously to a critical situation. Probably, however, his response illustrates a general hardening of attitudes and party alignments, for as the trial developed it became increasingly apparent that the verdict would affect both the balance of political power in the Convention and the position of France in Europe. Certainly, if then less obviously, it would also commit the revolutionaries either to a relatively mundane or to an extremely doctrinaire interpretation of the rights and powers of the revolutionary state.

Something of all this appears in Bourdon's *Réponse à Charles Villette*, a letter printed by the Jacobins' order of December 17.[48] According to Bourdon, Villette had expressed serious disquiet about a trial in which a large assembly would act as prosecutor, jury, and judge of one man; in which the fate of the accused would be decided by a simple majority of deputies; and in which each deputy would be compelled to vote individually and aloud. "Where, then," asked Villette, "is liberty?" Bourdon's reply has been described as an abusive diatribe,[49] and he did imply that those who had such doubts were either weaklings or hack writers paid to confuse public opinion. Nevertheless, he agreed that all such doubts ought to be raised and resolved before the trial took place. More particularly, he averred that, because publicity was the people's safeguard, all deputies ought to state their views explicitly at the trial instead of being able to publish whatever they chose afterward. As for the legitimacy of the procedure, he again asserted that, although the Convention had made the mistake of approving an indictment, an interrogation, and a defence, it was not really either prosecuting or trying Louis but simply acting as the judge in a case predetermined by public opinion. Dubiously alleging that the primary assemblies had authorized their deputies to condemn an oppressor, Bourdon claimed that the assembly, the representation of the nation, had no need to do more than pronounce the penalty, just as the courts commonly did when known and armed *émigrés* were brought before them. Now, however, his constant conviction that the king be condemned to death was principally justified by expediency: "Sa morte importe à la tranquillité publique." As for liberty, he frankly avowed that what interested him was not individual liberty but "liberté publique."

By this time, the debates in the Convention were inevitably becoming both more repetitive and more acrimonious. On December 25, two weeks after Louis had been interrogated before the assembly on December 11, and immediately before his lawyers were due to present his defence, Bourdon again obtained the rostrum in an attempt to anticipate their arguments.[50] This relatively short address, much of which was a reassertion of points that he had made previously, is perhaps most notable for his denial that Louis could be absolved of all guilt for the "massacres" of August 10 by a plea of self-defence. Comparing the king with a brigand chief whose followers resisted the gendarmes even when their last stronghold was surrounded, he claimed that the deaths that had occurred when the Tuileries had been invested were simply additional crimes and that Louis was ultimately responsible for all of them. The Convention nonetheless brushed aside his proposal that the defence be told that the assembly would only take cognizance of indisputable crimes, such as Louis's correspondence with external enemies, and that no consideration would be given to formal acts that he had explicitly disavowed or that had been endorsed by his ministers. Presumably the deputies agreed that, as one of them exclaimed, it was ridiculous to expect the lawyers to change their entire defence on the eve of its presentation.

All this argument, to say nothing of the still more embittered partisan allegations of royalism and Orléanism, of federalism and dictatorship (aspects of the controversy in which Bourdon took surprisingly little part), acquired a new dimension on December 27. Jean-Baptiste Salle, a deputy of the right, then proposed that the Convention limit itself to pronouncing its verdict and that, if it declared Louis guilty, the question of which sentence to impose be referred to the people in their primary assemblies. This proposal, notorious as *l'appel au peuple*, was certainly a political move. If not an attempt to save the king, as was immediately alleged, it was apparently a shrewd response to the Montagnards' exploitation of addresses from Paris: if their claim to be the only true representatives of the people could be annexed, then their growing influence in the assembly might well be curtailed. Nor was it easy to refute the assertion that the only sovereign people as a whole could determine so irrevocable a matter as the fate of a king. As always, however, the proposal of a referendum raised far-reaching questions about the nature of representative government.

Bourdon, whose views on this new question appeared as his *Seconde opinion . . . sur le jugement de Louis Capet,*[51] was of course no more than a secondary speaker in a sequence of debates to which both sides sent their principal orators and in which the most telling speeches were made by Vergniaud on the one hand and by Robespierre on the other. Of these debates, it is sufficient here to say that the decisive argument was that an appeal to the people would be nationally disruptive, possibly to the point of causing civil war. Perception of this problem was widespread, but Bourdon was probably unusual in openly recognizing that the people of the countryside were more numerous but less enlightened ("éclairée") than the townspeople and that they were at least still liable to be swayed by royalist influences. The Revolution had in fact long become that of an urban minority, and a real referendum would probably have favoured a restoration of the monarchy.

Needless to say, Bourdon opposed the *appel*. He condemned it in advance at the Jacobins on December 25,[52] when he supported the younger Robespierre's demand that the Club give it continuous attention as one of the ways in which the friends of the tyrant would seek to save his life. His *Seconde opinion*, which began with a brief summary of his previous arguments for condemning the king, was in part a refutation of the points made by Louis's counsel in the king's defence. Bourdon passionately denied the claim that Louis had constantly been a liberal monarch. Like Robespierre, he repudiated the word agitators as appropriate for those who had opposed the king, those "généreux citoyens qui cherchaient à allumer le feu sacré de la liberté dans le coeur de cette grande cité." His main concern, however, was now with the *appel*, which he damned as being at best a manifestation of feebleness and folly.

In saying this, Bourdon was saying no more than others. It was not difficult to point to the absurdity and the danger of supposing that a matter about which the Convention was deeply divided would be resolved if it were referred to the 44,000 primary assemblies of France. More interesting is his analysis of the relationship that he believed to exist between representative government and the sovereignty of the people. As Bourdon saw it, because the mass of the people could not possibly govern themselves constantly and in all matters, government was essentially a matter for their chosen representatives. Although it was that word, not *mandataire* or delegate, that he used, his conception of it was not one in which free choice is allied to responsibility, for it was evidently the duty of the representative to express the general will rather than his own opinion. Moreover, he believed that the people retained a reserve of sovereign authority, which they were entitled to use in three specific ways: the election of their representatives, the approval or rejection of constitutional laws, and insurrection against oppression. From this analysis, Bourdon concluded that consideration of the punishment of the king, far from being a matter to be referred to the people, was indisputably the responsibility of the chosen representatives, and he again asserted that by electing the Convention the people had expressly charged the deputies with abolishing the monarchy and punishing the oppressor. To evade that obligation would, he believed, be infamous; to do so by exposing the republic to faction, even perhaps to the foundation of some new tyranny, would amount to criminal negligence. Provided that the deputies could in good conscience condemn Louis as their mandate directed, their own reputations and security were of no account: "si je n'ai éxprimé que ce que j'ai cru être la volonté générale, que m'importe, si un jour le sang du tyran de ma patrie devait s'élever contre moi?"

No doubt the great tension of this time, which is said to have caused some deputies to secrete arms about them when they attended debates,[53] explains the fact that Bourdon's convictions were now being advanced more dramatically and with less regard for consistency. Thus, in this *Seconde opinion*, Bourdon postulated a united national will, even affirming that the king's crimes had not left a single inhabitant of France without someone to mourn; however, he identified an appeal to the people with division and even civil war. Beyond indicating differing degrees of enlightenment, he did not, however, attempt to resolve the fundamental question, that of the identification of the nation itself. His tendency toward theatrical hyperbole may also have been intensified when he was addressing the Jacobin Club. It was there that the *Seconde opinion* was heard on December 28[54] as one of the many addresses that were simply printed for circulation by order of the Convention. Similarly it was in the Jacobins that on December 30 Bourdon eventually said that there was no need to be afraid of an appeal to the people, for even if it were approved new soldiers of liberty would dispose of the aristocats just as their predecessors had done in Paris the previous September, so consolidating freedom by killing its enemies.[55]

Less extravagantly, if perhaps more characteristically, Bourdon drew the attention of the Club earlier that evening to the fact that a great many people had been waiting for hours in the rain in the hope of getting a place in the public galleries, and by his proposal the doors were opened so that they could enter the hall.[56] He then successfully proposed that all those present hear a reading by Robespierre of the "discours sublime" that this "patriote éclairé" had delivered in the Convention on December 28 and that Bourdon said would open everybody's eyes to the manoeuvres of the Brissotin faction. The trial of the king was indeed compelling many deputies not only to choose a side but also to declare their allegiance. Inevitably such commitments also meant that many old associations were severed. According to the Rolandist journal the *Bulletin des amis de la verité*, it was "the frenzied Bourdon" who led a chorus of applause by the Montagnards when "the venerable Dusaulx" (with whom he had worked closely in 1789-90) offered to resign his seat in protest against the "scandalous disorders" in the Convention.[57] To Bourdon, the situation seemed so dangerous that on January 11, just before the final voting took place, he presented the Jacobin Club with the draft of an address to the people of Paris.[58] Warning the citizens that any demonstration would give their enemies an excuse to say that Paris was usurping the sovereignty of the nation, and thus to call for armed intervention by forces from the departments, he implored them to remain calm. In effect, however, even the Jacobins shelved this proposal as praiseworthy but premature.

In the voting that finally ended these prolonged debates about the king, Bourdon consistently cast his vote against all moderation, therefore being at one with the Montagnards and, as it turned out, with the majority. As he and other Montagnards had repeatedly demanded, the voting was by *appel nominal*, so that as constituencies and names were called in rotation each deputy took the rostrum and gave his opinion aloud. Although some, generally those who wished to justify a qualified decision, then spoke at length, Bourdon's explanatory comments were bitingly brief.

Initially, in the vote taken on January 15, Bourdon was one of the overwhelming majority (by the most careful analysis, 707 of the 721 present, with fourteen abstentions) who declared Louis guilty.[59] On this occasion, too, the deputies from his constituency, the Loiret, and from his home town, Paris, were unanimous. The process of voting being continued without interruption, the question of the *appel au peuple*, whether or not whatever sentence the Convention passed should be referred to the primary assemblies for ratification, was then opened, and this proposal was eventually rejected by 425 to 286 voices, with ten abstentions. The question, so contentious that the minority, *les appellants*, became in effect men marked as royalist sympathizers, significantly reflected the division in the deputation of the Loiret. Four of its nine deputies favoured the *appel*, and they included Louvet, who had been belatedly elected alongside Bourdon in September, and Garran-Coulon, who had then been more courageous than Bourdon in resisting Fournier's abduction of the prisoners of the High Court. On the other hand, Bourdon, like all but two (Manuel and Dusaulx) of the twenty-two deputies of Paris who were present, rejected the *appel* outright ("Je dis non"), simply stating that Louis was already in irons when the electors had appointed him with full powers to act for them.

Because whatever sentence the Convention imposed would now be final, the third question, that of what the sentence should be, naturally became crucial. As the voting on this question proceeded during January 16 and 17, tensions were further increased by the realization that there would be little difference between the number of votes cast for a sentence of death and those in favour of some lesser penalty. Moreover, matters were complicated because some deputies followed the example of Jean Mailhe, who coupled his vote for death with the recommendation that the Convention should also consider a stay of execution. In this situation, Bourdon voted for death and execution within twenty-four hours, stating that he did so for reasons of general security and humanity. All but three (Manuel, Dusaulx, and Thomas) of the twenty-four deputies of Paris also voted for death, and four of them (Billaud-Varenne, Marat, Raffron, and Fréron) similarly called for execution in twenty-four hours; however, of the nine deputies of the Loiret, only two now joined Bourdon in demanding capital punishment. That was nonetheless the sentence approved by the majority, the official figures being 387 unreservedly for death (including Mailhe and twenty-five others like him) as opposed to 334 for some lesser penalty.

A fourth vote, which took place on January 19 to determine whether or not a reprieve should be granted, was less in doubt, and the Convention finally decided by 380 to 310 votes that Louis should be executed immediately. Because the deputies agreed on this occasion that no response save a simple "Yes" or "No" would be permitted, Bourdon's vote against a reprieve stands without comment. Although again in accord with all the deputies of Paris save two (Manuel having resigned his seat), he was now one of a minority of two among the nine deputies of the Loiret (for Lombard-Lachaux, who had been mayor of Orléans in August, when Bourdon had been there, and who may indeed have arranged his election,[60] had favoured moderation at the eleventh hour).

On January 21, 1793, the day on which the king was guillotined, Bourdon simply said in the Jacobin Club that this action was what he had demanded since 1791; now that Louis had paid his debt, all resentment should die with him.[61] In Bourdon's eyes, it was equally important to extol the merit of Michel Le Peletier, a deputy whose assassination by a royalist the previous evening was immediately extolled as martyrdom for the cause of freedom. Anticipating further triumphs for that cause, Bourdon also urged the Club to rejoice because the Girondins' principal agency of propaganda, the Bureau de l'Ésprit Publique, had at last been suppressed.

All these debates were in reality much more complex than the record of voting may suggest. Very little, for example, has been said here about the effects that the deputies' decisions would have on the situation of France in Europe, a matter that Bourdon tended to dismiss by bellicose asides but one that seriously concerned many others. Indeed, the variations in opinion about many aspects of the trial contributed considerably to the successes of the Montagnards in securing the majorities that they won for severity toward Louis. Justifiable or not, the policy of ruthlessness had the merit of simplicity. It was also one that Bourdon supported wholeheartedly. As an unreserved regicide, he was at odds with most of the deputies of the Loiret but constantly at one with the hard core of the Montagnards and, more particularly, with the overwhelming majority of the delegation of Paris.

Bourdon was also constant in his implacable opposition to Louis and to the monarchy. When feelings ran highest, and particularly when he addressed the Jacobins, his language sometimes approached the hysterical. In general, however, it does not seem, as has been alleged, to have been exceptionally ferocious and even barbaric. Whatever may be thought about the validity of his arguments and his analysis of the situation, his views were generally logical expositions of his point of view, and even his insistence on the immediate execution of the king appears to have been at least partly prompted by a creditable desire to spare the victim protracted anguish.

More remarkable, and more revealing, than his extravagance in expression is his consistency in demanding the death of one whom Bourdon believed to be the principal enemy of the people. His sincerity in this uncompromising belief is sufficiently evident, but the belief itself is less easily comprehended, for it presumes of course that throughout the Revolution all that was right and good was on one side whereas all those who opposed that side were utterly wrong and ultimately evil. This attitude was certainly largely emotional: in critical circumstances, people easily assume that those who are not with them are against them. Moreover, those who were fully committed to the Revolution were also intellectually convinced that a vastly better world had come within the reach of all people everywhere. Exalted by their achievements and by all that became possible once the complexities of a hierarchical and pluralistic society had been swept aside, they were correspondingly embittered by the reappearance of opposition. Realizing that all that had been, and might still be, won could well be lost, they held Louis primarily responsible for all their frustrations, regarding him as one who had deliberately betrayed them and thus imperilled the future happiness of all humankind.

Unlike those deputies who emphasized the ideological aspects of this attitude, Bourdon generally spoke in more mundane terms. Although he sometimes referred to the political necessity of executing the king, he was usually concerned simply with Louis's conduct and with maintaining that the king could legally be punished as a criminal hardened in crime. Nevertheless, Bourdon was as thoroughly revolutionary as anyone. For example, his conviction that he was fully entitled to speak for the nation was impregnable. In fact, as we have seen, he was a man whom the Jacobin minority in Orléans had imposed on the Electoral Assembly of the Loiret at the last moment.

For him, as for the Montagnards, however, the Jacobins *were* the nation, entitled by enlightenment to speak for an inarticulate people whose future happiness was imperilled by the weakness and self-interest of some supposed friends as well as by the open hostility of avowed enemies.

6

The Representative on Mission (January to May 1793)

$\mathcal{F}$or France, the first half of 1793 was a particularly momentous period. Within a few weeks of the king's execution, political passions were revived by new dangers, and within a few months the constant interaction of military disasters and civil strife compelled the Convention to condone yet another popular insurrection, "the Revolution of May 31." That event, by which the assembly was purged of its most prominent "Girondin" deputies, may be seen either as "the triumph of the Mountain" and the beginning of the process by which the nation wrested victory from defeat, or as a catastrophe that long proved fatal to the growth of freedom and parliamentary democracy in France. Similarly, for Léonard Bourdon the time was one of great personal consequence. Although he was only a minor participant in the Parisian rising, for almost two of these months he was able to exercise considerable authority in eastern France as a commissioner of the Convention, a representative of the people "on mission." His involvement in March in a dramatic episode at Orléans then won him both transient fame and enduring infamy.

One central feature of the general situation at this time was the ever-growing danger that revolutionary France would be overwhelmed by foreign enemies. In the euphoria of its first easy victories, the republicans almost blithely committed themselves to campaigns to "liberate" adjacent states; moreover, because the advance of the Revolution was accompanied by annexations and ruthless economic exploitation, France was soon confronted by a powerful European counterrevolutionary coalition. Blockaded by the British and forced to defend their own frontiers in the Pyrénées, the Alps, and the Rhineland, the French were now again particularly threatened from the northeast.

Notes to Chapter 6 are on pp. 363-67.

There General Dumouriez, who advanced into Holland even though Belgium was already in revolt against the French, was decisively defeated by the Austrians at Neerwinden (March 18) and at Louvain (March 21). Hastily evacuating both Holland and Belgium, the French forces then retreated in disorder until they again stood on French soil, and, like Lafayette before him, Dumouriez first sought to turn his men against the revolutionaries in Paris and then abandoned the army by defecting to the Austrian camp (April 5). Although the allies, distracted by the problem of partitioning Poland, did not take full advantage of this time of opportunity, the French frontier towns and fortresses were henceforth systematically and successfully besieged.

This increasingly critical situation naturally intensified the bitter disputes that divided the deputies in the Convention and effectively prevented either the amorphous Girondin mass or the more solid Montagnard bloc from establishing a generally acceptable government. Each successive calamity caused more recrimination, and every step taken to strengthen authority—such as the creation of the Revolutionary Tribunal (March 10) and the Committee of Public Safety (April 6)—was approved amid angry allegations about anarchy, dictatorship, and counterrevolution. Not surprisingly, the complex and rationalist constitution proposed by Condorcet in mid-February, and damned by the Montagnards as a decentralizing device, received scant consideration.

All these difficulties were aggravated by the constant deterioration of the economic situation and by rising social unrest. Like earlier assemblies, the Convention repeatedly sought to meet all its financial needs by authorizing the issue of more paper money, and the inexorable depreciation of this currency was accompanied by sharp rises in the costs of essential commodities.[1] Shortages of supply, too, were endemic, for farmers were understandably reluctant to exchange good grain for unreliable paper. Resentment of increasing hardship consequently combined with the belief that the nation was being betrayed, and in Paris the work of the Convention was perpetually interrupted by angry delegations and noisy demonstrations in support of the Montagnards. In the provinces, however, many local authorities[2] became convinced that the prime cause of all the ills was the intimidation of the national parliament by the Montagnard deputies, the Commune, and the *sans-culottes* of Paris, so they sent in angry protests, contingents of guardsmen, and even offers of more substantial intervention.[3]

More particularly, the exasperation of the Parisian poor was now expressed by extremists whose principal demands were for an immediate reimposition of price control (the *maximum*) and the ruthless repression of all those supposedly profiting from the sufferings of the people by hoarding and speculation. Of these extremists, who became known as the *enragés*, the most influential was Jacques Roux, a curate of the Church of Saint-Nicolas-des-Champs in the Section des Gravilliers.[4] This man organized practical aid for the impoverished and the destitute, pleading their cause with passionate sincerity, yet he was also an advocate of extreme violence, a rabid demagogue who preached and even promoted direct action in the streets to enforce popular prices. In the circumstances that prevailed in 1793, his virtues and his violence alike won him at least as strong a following in Gravilliers as that of Léonard Bourdon, whose educational and economic objectives were less immediately attractive and who, as a Jacobin and a Montagnard, was then a more orthodox type of political democrat.

Moreover, between September 1792 and March 1793, Bourdon was probably as much concerned with his school as with public affairs: in this respect, even his part in the debates about the king's trial seems somewhat exceptional. Between January 21 and March 14, when he left Paris *en mission*, he spoke in the Jacobin Club on only six occasions,[5] none of sufficient importance to merit more than some short notice in the records. Although on February 18 he joined in the general criticism of Condorcet's constitution, his remarks in the Club at this time were usually about matters such as the welfare of disabled soldiers and the problems of recruitment, questions in which he could claim enduring interest. Similarly he did not speak again in the Convention until March 5, when he urged the dismissal of army officers who were illegitimately absent from their duties.[6]

As had happened before, however, Bourdon became somewhat more prominent when a new crisis loomed. Although the general situation early in March was not as serious as it was soon to become, reports of the revolt in Belgium and of sporadic disorders throughout France were alarming. Deputies of all shades of opinion were also deeply disturbed by the food riots that occurred in Paris in late February and by what became known as "the Conspiracy of March 9." An attempt by an *énragé*, Jean-François Varlet, and other extremists to effect an insurrection, this "conspiracy" ended in nothing more than an ugly demonstration, but many of the deputies became convinced that massacres such as those of September 1792 were imminent. It was to anticipate that possibility that the Revolutionary Tribunal was created by the decrees of March 9 and 10. As Danton then said of 1792, "if a tribunal had then existed, the people . . . would not have stained those days with blood."[7] Speaking in support of initial proposals by Montagnards such as Jeanbon Saint-André and Jean-Baptiste Carrier, Bourdon also demanded immediate action in this matter, "so that the men of our armies should not be distracted by anxiety about the activities of conspirators at home."[8]

On March 9, the Convention also decided to send eighty-two of its deputies out to the provinces "on mission," and Bourdon was one of those named as commissioners.[9] Although the appointment of one or two deputies to investigate particular problems in the field was not unusual, this general mission, in which forty-one pairs of commissioners were each assigned to two adjacent departments, was an innovation, in itself indicative of the gravity of the national situation. More particularly, the commissioners' primary purpose was to stimulate recruiting, for many of the men who had volunteered to defend the frontiers in 1792 had returned to their homes when the French forces first moved into enemy territory.[10] Bourdon's inclusion in the mission may therefore have been due in part to his interest in recruitment and the treatment afforded to civilian soldiers.

More than this, however, was involved. Because no record has ever been found of the process by which the commissioners were selected, it was soon presumed that deputies of the Girondin coterie had contrived to name many of their most obdurate opponents, thereby removing them temporarily from Paris.[11] Certainly many of the commissioners were Montagnards, and, if the selection had indeed been prearranged, then the appointment of Bourdon would be sufficiently explained. There is nonetheless the further possibility that those appointed had been chosen as particularly vigorous men, as Bourdon was in times of crisis, for their task was arduous and perhaps even perilous. Specifically they were expected to ensure that local authorities fulfilled their obligations under a recent law, that of February 24, by which the departments were required to raise a total of 300,000 men, a call for volunteers being followed by compulsion. This measure immediately proved extremely unpopular as one of partial conscription. Moreover, it was manifestly inequitable, for all officeholders, including members of the National Guard, were exempt; some men could pay others to replace them; and local councils were left to decide how the conscripts should be chosen from among those eligible. If in some communes selection was made by public drawing of lots, in others it provided a fine opportunity for personal, political, or social discrimination.[12] Complaints and angry demonstrations were consequently commonplace. In central Brittany rioting led to serious disorder, and in the

Vendée the attempt to enforce conscription occasioned the outbreak of a long and singularly savage civil war.

The commissioners of the Convention were consequently expected not only to ensure that recruits were duly enlisted, clothed, armed, and equipped, but also to conduct a searching investigation of all local administrative bodies, suspending or even arresting those officials whose conduct seemed suspicious. On March 10, moreover, an additional general instruction required them to make particular inquiries about food supplies and shortages.[13] Although in all this they were obviously expected to act jointly and in accordance with local advice, their authority as delegates of the Convention, itself the embodiment of the sovereignty of the people, was subject only to the necessity of submitting regular reports of their activities. Although the different commissioners' use of this almost unlimited discretionary power naturally varied according to their abilities and the situations that they encountered, many of them, including Bourdon, certainly set out from Paris believing that resistance to recruitment was rooted in royalist conspiracy, that shortages of food were the artificial outcome of hoarding and speculation, and that the countryside was politically apathetic because the departmental and district authorities were at best composed of well-to-do conservatives. For men of this mind, the true purpose of their mission was to invigorate and revolutionize provincial France.

The necessity of some such stimulation was indisputable. Much of France had long been left to govern itself as best it could in accordance with correspondence with the capital. The indirectly elected district and departmental administrations, too, were generally more conservative in composition than the directly elected municipal ones, and they were probably more inclined to keep to the letter of each law, if only because they had to interpret decrees and apply them to wider and more disparate areas. These factors naturally affected the attitudes of the departmental officials to the larger local municipalities, to Paris, and to the commissioners of the Convention. Nevertheless, they did not dictate either their patriotism or their political position. In practice, much often depended on local considerations, such as the rivalry between one town and another, and on the influence of each department's deputies to the Convention.

More particularly, the administrators of both of the departments to which Bourdon was assigned, the Côte-d'Or and the Jura, have been disparagingly described by local historians. The former has been called a "milieu d'anciens robins . . . dominé par les notables,"[14] and the latter (by derivation from a work written in 1846) is said to have been "très nettement composé de bourgeois notables, gens de robes, employés, riches propriétaires, commerçants et industriels."[15] However exaggerated, this factor must be recognized as one that Bourdon would have encountered. Yet the two areas were by no means identical. Local antagonisms in the Jura were more serious than in the Côte-d'Or. Moreover, whereas all but one of the eight deputies of the Jura were *appellants*, and at least six of them may best be described as minor men of the centre with some sympathies for the Girondins, there were only two *appellants* among the ten deputies of the Côte-d'Or, a delegation that was predominantly Montagnard and included men of the repute of Basire and the calibre of C.-A. Prieur and Guyton-Morveau.[16]

Bourdon's companion in his mission was Claude Prost,[17] a man his senior by twelve years. The sensible practice being that one of each pair of commissioners should be acquainted with the area to which they were assigned, Prost was also a man of the Jura. Born in Dole, he was a moderately successful lawyer in the *parlement* at Besançon before the Revolution, during which he became a justice of the peace and *procureur* of the Commune of Dole. As president of the Jacobin Society there in June 1791, he was ardent for the republic, and in the Convention he was one of the two regicides among the eight deputies of the Jura. He seems nonetheless to have been less vigorous and of weaker character than Bourdon. Certainly other commissioners who were subsequently with him in the Jura came to regard him as a sound republican but a dangerously inconsistent busybody.

On March 14, as soon as their credentials were available, the two commissioners left Paris. They did not, however, take the most direct route to Dijon, the administrative centre of the Côte-d'Or, but went instead by way of Orléans.[18] This they did because Bourdon, always the dominant partner, saw their journey as an opportunity to encourage his particular protégés, the Jacobin minority in that city; indeed, he later claimed that the Jacobins in Orléans had begged him to visit them. As it happened, however, the decision was—to say the least—unfortunate. After arriving in Orléans on March 15, the commissioners were on the point of departing late on the following night when Bourdon became embroiled in a fracas between his Jacobin friends and a body of armed men assembled outside the town hall. Because this conflict, the furore that it caused, and the trial that eventually ensued may be more appropriately considered together,[19] it is sufficient here to say that Bourdon, bruised by muskets and cut by bayonets, had to remain for ten days under medical care in Orléans. Then, with his arm swathed in an enormous sling, he followed Prost to Dijon, being hailed everywhere as one "assassinated," a martyr of the republic.

From the evening of March 26 until the morning of April 6, the two commissioners remained in Dijon, once the principal seat of the dukes of Burgundy and still, as a commercial, ecclesiastical, legal, and administrative centre, one of the greater cities of France. Regrettably, the most easily accessible account of Bourdon's activities during these ten days is a vitriolic denunciation published in 1795 in the name of the six sections of Dijon,[20] bodies dominated by that time by *gens de bien*, substantial citizens who had—at best—been deprived of all political influence during the Terror. According to this account, Robespierre had then sent a swarm of perjured assassins to exhaust and corrupt France so that he could subjugate it, and two of these assassins, Léonard Bourdon and Bernard de Saintes, had particularly afflicted the Côte d'Or. Insofar as this retrospective account distinguishes between the two men—and Bernard, who identified himself as *Piochefer* ("Pickaxe") Bernard, later terrorized much of eastern France—by 1795 Bourdon's great crime was seen as that of stimulating the *sans-culottes*, "the dregs of the nation," to usurp the place previously held in society by worthy, decent, and well-educated men. Not content with instigating innumerable arrests and "slaking his thirst for blood" by ordering a shocking execution, Bourdon, "the best friend of all that is most vile in Dijon," allegedly began the process of destroying public morality by instigating and indulging in every sort of dissolute and sacrilegious debauchery.

Although such details as appear in this *dénunciation* command little credence, the beginning of Bourdon's visit in 1793 indicates that he was indeed more concerned to encourage the Jacobins than to propitiate the establishment in Dijon. On March 24, in expectation of his arrival, the executive directory of the department convened a general meeting of the departmental, district, and municipal authorities, and it was then resolved that all these bodies should go out to meet him, escort him to a banquet, and enable him to hear representative citizens express their satisfaction with the local administration.[21] By accident or intent, however, Bourdon arrived after dark on March 25, thus eluding a sentinel and going directly to an inn. When a deputation waited on him the next morning, he agreed to attend the directors' regular meeting, and there, at his request, a general assembly of the three authorities was arranged for the following day. He then again anticipated proper procedure by going late at night to the Popular Society or Jacobin Club, which apparently marked the occasion by excluding its more moderate members and the general public.[22] Whether or not, as was later alleged, Bourdon was then initiated into the Club's "scandalous and bacchanalian ceremonies," he certainly aroused such patriotic ardour that the process of arresting suspects began that night, presumably with some sanction by the Commune of Dijon.

His attitudes and intentions became still clearer when he and Prost—who seems, inexplicably, to have reached Dijon later than Bourdon—met the three administrative bodies in the ducal palace on March 27. In effect, Bourdon then said that their purposes were to stimulate enlistment, to frustrate counterrevolutionary activity, and to investigate matters concerning food supplies. References in this address to particular popular grievances, such as the shortage of firewood and the neglect of serving soldiers' farms, show that he had already learned much from the Jacobins of Dijon, and this aspect of his speech was strikingly different from the points made in the administrators' replies. In expressing the hope that the commissioners' visit would prove beneficial, the various local officials coupled their concern about the soaring cost of food with their anxiety about arrears in the payment of taxes, the lack of state support for the development of a canal, and the country's enduring need for public education and an established constitution. Bourdon nonetheless pursued his own course, announcing that he and his colleague would begin work at once: after meeting the justices of the peace at five o'clock to discover how many of those who had opposed recruitment were actually in prison, they would meet representatives of the administrative bodies about food supplies at seven o'clock. Shortly, too, they would inspect all prisons and afford all the citizens of Dijon an opportunity to voice complaints about local officials, whose conduct would then be considered in consultation with the appropriate authorities and popular societies.

More specific emergency measures soon followed. On April 2, a proclamation and an instruction (*arrêté*), both signed by Bourdon and Prost but probably composed in the main by Bourdon, were issued for circulation throughout the Côte-d'Or.[23] The proclamation called on all patriots to unite in making war, either by personal service or by financial sacrifice. Correspondingly strict security was to be enforced against internal enemies, particularly those speculators, aristocrats, and priests who held "a cross in one hand and a dagger in the other." The instruction then authorized and required all district authorities to initiate domiciliary visits, using force if necessary to search out suspects, arms, and incriminating papers. Furthermore, the districts were ordered to control travel permits rigorously, to ensure that all those in the National Guard performed their duties in person, and to submit immediate returns showing how many pikes were available and which residents were absent from their homes.

How far these measures were actually effected, either by the commissioners themselves or by the local authorities after their departure, is uncertain. Bourdon certainly did all he could to promote enlistment, particularly by initiating a new recruiting drive in a civic ceremony at the Church of St. Jean on April 1.[24] When only two more volunteers came forward, he let it be known that the register for enlistment would remain open for four more days, after which time suitable men would be conscripted, and on April 5, the day before his departure, he did authorize the directory to resort to further conscription.[25] Moreover, from March 30 on, his daily schedule apparently included a session with the directors to hear and consider people's complaints,[26] and the proclamation of April 2 included the statement that several unworthy officials had already been suspended. His frequent execration of seigneurs and priests also had some effect, for a contemporary diarist noted that the arrest of priests had become a daily occurrence.[27] More precision about these arrests is probably impossible, for the immediate consequences of the commissioners' brief visit are lost in the records of a longer period of repression. Thus, the research of Nelly Bazin[28] shows that between March 10 and mid-May 224 men and women were arrested as suspects in Dijon and its district, but it also indicates that the incidence of arrests only rose sharply in early May, when the departmental council finally clarified its definition of the term "suspect," and that most of those arrested were in fact released after about two months in confinement.

Still more speculative is the extent of Bourdon's responsibility for the death of Lazare Fondard, whose public execution on April 3 was an event without precedent in the Côte-d'Or. A somewhat mentally handicapped servant employed by a lady of rank, Fondard was one of sixteen young men arrested before the commissioners' arrival for their part in the disturbances in Dijon and its vicinity when those eligible for military service were mustered early in March for the selection of conscripts. Scholarly study of these riots[29] has shown that the principal grievance of those involved was the immunity enjoyed by all holding official positions, which commonly meant the local Jacobins. At the time, however, it was generally believed that royalist agitators had been at work, and Fondard had apparently tried to prevent others from accepting conscription, saying that, although it was good to fight for a king, there was no need to put oneself out for the nation. In all probability, Bourdon's presence in Dijon, and particularly his inspection of the prisons and his meetings with the judicial authorities, then moved a dilatory tribunal to action, and Fondard was condemned.[30] The decision was a hard one, for he had apparently been incited to stupidities by his own associates; but the oft-repeated allegation that Bourdon "had him executed" is as unwarrantable as the similar charge that Bourdon "had the chateaux ransacked."[31] The commissioners of the Convention were not sent out either to condone inertia or to encourage civil crimes.

Map 5
The area of the mission of Bourdon and Prost
(March to May 1793)

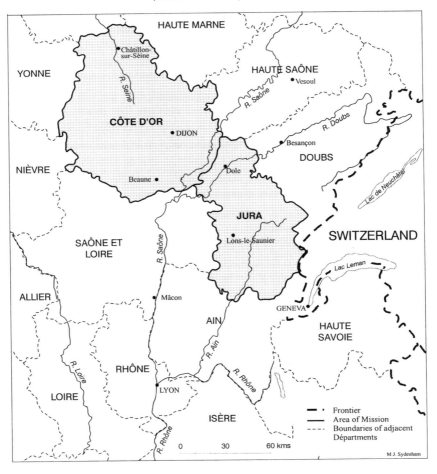

The proclamation of April 2 had included notice that, although Bourdon and Prost were about to leave Dijon, they would return and visit other towns in the vicinity. Even so, their departure was probably followed by general relaxation. There was, for example, no other political execution in the Côte-d'Or until "Pickaxe" Bernard arrived ten months later, and the other young men arrested with Fondard were all free by mid-August.[32] Certainly the authorities in Dijon were slow to effect the commissioners' wishes, if only because they thought it necessary to reconcile these wishes with normal legal procedure.[33] Although there was greater tension than before between the city and the more cautious district and departmental authorities, the latter seem to have been sufficiently well established to absorb the shock of this first visitation from Paris.

Because Bourdon and Prost were anxious to reach the Jura, a frontier department, their visit to Dijon was short. On April 5, they nonetheless concluded it by participating in a revolutionary festival. Meant both to demonstrate and to stimulate popular patriotism and enthusiasm for the Revolution, such festivals were typical of the time, and Bourdon apparently enjoyed them to the full. Although this particular occasion was later damned in the six sections' *Denunciation* as one in which intoxication and impiety led to "crapulous debauchery," it was probably more popular than pernicious. Certainly both commissioners joined in dances around the Tree of Liberty that stood in the forecourt of the palace fronting the Place d'Armes, and the local diarist noted the story that Bourdon, who was invariably accompanied by four bodyguards, so far forgot his sling and his role of martyr that he waved to the people with his injured arm.[34]

Doubtless convinced that they had done something to raise people's eyes above parochial concerns, the commissioners left the next morning for Dole, Prost's native town. Situated on the edge of the Jura, it was a place of considerable importance. On the crossing of one main road to Paris from southern France with that coming from Besançon, it was the first place in the Jura to know of events in the capital, and as it was a substantial port for river traffic on the Doubs it was by far the most flourishing commercial town in a predominantly agricultural area. In the past, moreover, it had been a major administrative centre in Franche Comté, the province of which it had even on occasion been the capital. Yet when the departments were created in 1790 a much smaller and more remote town, Lons-le-Saunier, was selected as the *chef-lieu* of the Jura—because it was more central and, as the Dolois believed, by the machinations of the deputy Théodore

Vernier, a man of Lons.[35] Thus, Dole was more in the Jura than of it. Almost inevitably it became a Jacobin stronghold, for while the more sedate district and the departmental councils[36] constantly strove for administrative uniformity, speaking repeatedly of respect for the law and duly constituted authority, the Commune of Dole jealously guarded its municipal independence and replied in terms of the sovereignty of the people.[37] Bourdon and Prost were consequently in congenial company, and it is unlikely that they ever grasped the fact that the situation in the Jura was far more delicate than that in the Côte-d'Or.[38]

Certainly they began their visit just as they had done before. Again a general proclamation and a more specific instruction were issued, and Jean-François Dumas, the vice-president of the department, was curtly ordered by courier to ensure that copies of them were distributed immediately.[39] This proclamation,[40] now an elusive document, was apparently even more fiery than its predecessor: danger was imminent, and, unless hidden enemies at home were effectively repressed, furious foreign foes would soon spread rape, slaughter, and devastation throughout the area. More succinctly, the instruction[41] announced that "a crisis demands violent remedies" and ordered the imposition of the same stringent measures of security already prescribed in the Côte-d'Or. It seems, too, that on April 7 Bourdon addressed a general assembly of the people of Dole, whom he invited to voice complaints against public officials; although this appeal evoked little or no response, he told another such assembly the next day that five members of the district administration, including its president, vice-president, and secretary, had been deprived of office as insufficiently energetic.[42]

Because this measure became one of some importance in the Jura, the question of responsibility for it merits consideration. Here, as in much else, the principal difficulty is that, because the order was signed by both Bourdon and Prost, the extent of each individual's contribution remains speculative. Evidently Bourdon, a Jacobin who had long since decried departmental administrations, was fully prepared to support the order and even, as the principal public speaker, to be identified with it. It is nonetheless more probable that the move was made at the instigation of the Commune of Dole and its former *procureur*, Claude Prost himself. If that view, which was the opinion forcibly expressed by the departmental council in May,[43] is correct, then the evidence suggests that the advantages of local knowledge might well have been outweighed by prejudice. Whatever the truth, Prost must be held responsible for a considerable failure, for he certainly did not make the realities of the general situation sufficiently clear to Bourdon.

At once intensely patriotic and politically divided, the Jura indeed needed unification rather than stimulation. On the one hand, its authorities had good reason to be proud of its record.[44] Having many men in the regular army, the department had responded to previous calls for volunteers by raising twelve battalions, four more than its allotted quota,[45] and, as the commissioners would soon discover, most of the 1,760 men called for in the latest levy had already been armed, equipped, and sent to join the forces on the frontier.[46] On April 6, the day of Bourdon and Prost's arrival in Dole, the National Convention had consequently recognized that the Jura "a bien merité de la patrie."[47] Nor was this all, for on March 29 the departmental council, convinced that some 20,000 royalist "brigands" were advancing across France from the west in order to meet the armies of Austria and Sardinia at Lyon, had ordered the formation of a further force for local defence. In each of the six districts, a battalion of 833 men was to be available, and each of these battalions in rotation, as well as an auxiliary battalion and a cavalry company, was to be constantly on call at Lons-le-Saunier.[48]

On the other hand, the formation of this force was in itself an indication that the departmental administration was inclined to act independently. Although the measure was explicitly subject to the approval of the Convention, it was also openly justified on the ground that in an emergency no immediate help could be expected from a far-off central authority. As the order explained, "le respect même pour les lois commande d'y suppléer au delà de leur prévoyance." Furthermore, the final clause of the same order shows that the department was committed to a particular political position. Like the rest of France, it had long been deeply disturbed by the paralysis of the Convention,[49] and, like many other departmental councils, it attributed all the divisions and disorders in that assembly to the influence of the populace of Paris and to the determination of the Commune and Montagnard deputies of Paris to control the whole of France. All those holding public office in the Jura were therefore required to swear to defend liberty until death and to repudiate every sort of government save that of "la République démocratique, une et indivisible, sans Roi, Dictateur, Triumvir, Protecteur, Supériorité Municipale, ou tout autre chef étranger à la souveraineté ou représentation nationale directe." Evidently the departmental administrators shared the fears of the Girondins in Paris and were liable to react sharply if their anxieties were aggravated.

Fig. 5. Lons-le-Saunier, Département du Jura: The arcades of the rue du Commerce. Private collection. From G. Girod and J. Brevent, *Lons-le-Saunier, Jura* 39 (Colmar-Ingersheim: Éditions S.A.E.P., 1972).

In this situation, much depended on the conduct of the Jacobins at Dole and Lons-le-Saunier. In the critical spring of 1793, the Popular Society of Lons, long concerned primarily with local affairs, became more anxious about the position of France in general. Swayed by Réné-François Dumas, the younger brother and bitter opponent of the vice-president of the department,[50] and constantly told from Paris that the Revolution was being imperilled by a self-interested Girondin clique and innumerable apathetic rural authorities, the members became more aggressive. Thus, on April 2, the departmental council felt compelled to condemn the conduct of one delegate of the Society who had burst into its bureau late the previous evening, imperiously demanding certain information and alleging that the council was always quicker to publish repressive laws than beneficial ones. On this occasion, peace was restored, for the Society itself censured its delegate, but the danger of confrontation and defiance was evident.[51] Similarly, in mid-April, the Society committed itself to extremism at the national level. In response to Marat's inflammatory call for a nation-wide demand for the recall of all "unworthy deputies," the Society condemned such "impure reptiles" and informed the Convention that it was in full accord with the people of Paris.[52]

In these circumstances, the behaviour of Bourdon and Prost was at best unwise. Initially it was even more provocative than it had been at Dijon. After spending three days at Dole, they reached Lons-le-Saunier on April 9 accompanied by Dumas *cadet*, who had gone to Dole to greet them. They then began work the next day by visiting the Popular Society, where Bourdon, hailed as "the illustrious and estimable martyr of liberty," reiterated their readiness to receive complaints about local officials.[53] The Society happily responded to this and to the earlier instruction by appointing a committee, which soon produced a long list of the suspect and the feeble, those named first being Bouveret, the president of the department, and Ebrard, the *procureur-général-syndic*.[54] Nor was this all, for someone had ordered a call for denunciations to be publicly proclaimed in the streets, and the Commune of Lons had already approved the imprisonment of seventy-seven suspects.[55]

The department, meanwhile, had resolved to receive the commissioners with all due respect. Ebrard and eight council members were to meet them outside, and all were to stand until they were seated, when the president would say that all were ready to receive their orders.[56] It was not, however, until noon on April 11, the fifth day after their arrival in the Jura and their second in Lons-le-Saunier, that Bourdon and Prost appeared, and to say that they entered under escort is to evade the allegation that they were surrounded by men with drawn swords.[57] Although this deliberate disdain caused the councillors intense irritation, formality was preserved, and the president's summary of the situation of the Jura was reinforced by the presentation of returns of recruitment, taxation, and emigration and of the administration of roads and nationalized properties.[58]

After this inauspicious beginning, the commissioners seem to have become more moderate and conciliatory. On April 13, Prost returned to the council to request that the reports be abbreviated, and the next day both men arrived, again considerably later than had been announced, to accept them and to discuss food supplies.[59] A new note was similarly heard in the Popular Society, which Bourdon attended frequently, when he urged members to be present at a meeting at which a constitutional priest would demonstrate the compatibility of the Revolution with the Gospels.[60] The change of attitude may have been due in part to the alarming success of the calls for complaints, for on April 19 and 29 Bourdon warned the Society not to countenance vague and ill-considered denunciations.[61] It is probable, however, that he was also influenced by the evidence of administrative efficiency and by the *procureur-général-syndic*, who was mainly responsible for it. Pierre-Gabriel Ebrard, who became known as "the Themistocles of the Jura," had long sought to keep abreast of the Revolution while upholding his firm belief that no government can survive without public order.[62] Repeatedly harassed by the Jacobins, he had so far succeeded in keeping the peace by combining firmness with humanity. Yet he was soon to write that only he and his colleagues could ever know what it had cost them to moderate the intemperance of Bourdon and Prost.[63]

Whatever the explanation, on April 15 the commissioners issued statements that together amounted to something very like a change of policy. One was a formal, if private, denial that they had ever authorized any call in the streets for denunciations, a step that they condemned as indecent; at the same time, they complimented the department on its administrative record and on the measures that it had taken to maintain peace.[64]

Another measure, an *Instruction Concerning Subsistence*,[65] was taken after consultation with representatives of local administrations. Although in February grain had become so scarce that Ebrard had been compelled to purchase 150,000 livres of rice, the department shared the general conviction that "frightening" prices and scarcity must be artificial, particularly in an area as fertile as the Jura.[66] It, and indeed the Popular Society, therefore wished to revert to the position of September 1792, when local councils had been authorized to regulate the distribution and sale of grain in times of difficulty. Many departments had in fact maintained such limited controls despite the Convention's re-establishment in December of complete economic freedom in France, but it was not until April 4 that the Department of the Jura ordered a general census of the quantity of grain and the number of households in each of its six districts.[67] The commissioners' instruction of April 15 was consequently an attempt to reconcile two incompatible laws, both of which were cited directly or by implication. Reasonably enough, their initiative was justified by the necessity of providing more and cheaper grain for the poor without diminishing popular respect for the law. The instruction, reminiscent of the economic thought of Bourdon and his father, tacitly sanctioned the census and authorized the department to compel farmers to take all their surplus grain to the nearest market. It also banned all sales outside the department save for those approved for the armies, and it ended with an emphatic reminder that the law particularly prohibited any trade in grain with foreigners. Although such measures, commonly taken by other commissioners, were soon to be superseded by the Convention's first attempt to control prices, the *maximum* of May 4, they were in their own context sensible enough.

Still more striking is the commissioners' *Second Proclamation*,[68] which differed so considerably from that first published in Dijon that the directors of the Côte-d'Or only reluctantly circulated the copies sent from Lons, finally doing so without their own endorsement.[69] The new statement might well have caused confusion: although it began by reiterating the necessity of rigorously pursuing those priests and once-privileged persons who conspired against the republic, its substance was a call for discrimination, tolerance, and humanity. Explaining that they particularly hoped to curb religious fanaticism, the commissioners urged all in authority to recognize and esteem those priests and seigneurs who had sincerely accepted the new order and, wherever possible, to supervise women and children, the elderly and the infirm, instead of imprisoning them. Similarly all popular societies were advised to send emissaries into the countryside to enlighten the people by explaining that no one had any intention of attacking religion as such.

This change of emphasis, which was widely regarded as reassuring, has on occasion been attributed to the influence of Prost on Bourdon,[70] but the contrary view seems to be more likely. By mid-April, no doubt, both men had become aware of the nature of the revolt in the Vendée and thus of the danger in persecuting Catholics. Yet Bourdon's insistence on the importance of the priest's address to the Popular Society of Lons on April 14 suggests that he was still the dominant partner. Moreover, the recommendations of the *Second Proclamation* were based on an exposition of the belief that the Revolution was itself a religion, being indeed "the wisest of all religions" because its central tenet, the brotherhood of men, made it one in which every other faith could be included. This view, remarkable as an anticipation of the policy pursued by Robespierre later in the year, is also sufficiently consistent with the opinions expressed by Bourdon throughout the Revolution to warrant the conclusion that he, not Prost, was the principal author of it.

Save for one final decision, these pronouncements ended the commissioners' attempts to regulate the affairs of the Jura in general. On April 19, in the last of three reports that Bourdon wrote personally to the newly established Committee of Public Safety, he said that he was about to go to St. Claude and that he expected to return to Paris fairly soon.[71] Because he appeared in the Popular Society at Lons only twice in the next ten days, on April 23 and 29, he presumably made at least two tours in the Jura's mountainous frontier with Switzerland.[72] Prost, meanwhile, probably remained at Lons, for it was from there that he in turn wrote to Paris, noting inter alia that his "worthy colleague" was "tireless" in scouring the area for armed men.[73] The Society, too, heard an account of these travels on April 29, when Bourdon—accompanied by his wife—made his last visit before the commissioners' departure. No doubt he then repeated his earlier exhortation that members should go out to the smaller towns as missionaries, and he certainly made his final appeal to them to eschew all denunciations that were not based on positive proof.[74]

Unfortunately all did not end on this comparatively happy note. Earlier that evening Bourdon had also visited the departmental council, and according to one account he had made inquiries about those officials of the District of Dole who had been suspended "because the Commune of Dole had accused them of denigrating the Convention's commissioners."[75] He was then told that the men had so far eluded a rigorous search, being sheltered by those who thought that they had been dismissed without being heard. Apparently he was also told that the Commune of Dole had ignored the proclamation of April 15 and that, because it affected superiority over its district and independence of the department, it ought to be recalled to its proper place in the hierarchy of authority. Bourdon's reaction to this request is not recorded, but on May 1, when Bourdon and Prost were again together in Dole, they authorized its commune "to account directly to the Committee of Public Safety of the National Convention for all the measures of general security indicated by the commissioners' proclamation of the 4th of this month [*sic*] . . . without doing so to any other authority."[76]

This was a mistake. Far from preventing further conflicts in the Jura, it precipitated a crisis there and thus contributed to the growth of the wider movement known as the Federalist Revolt. It need not, however, be seen as ill intentioned. Because the commune and the department were both deeply dissatisfied with existing arrangements, some transfer of jurisdiction, a possibility recently mooted by Théodore Vernier, probably seemed desirable.[77] Probably, too, Bourdon had again been content to follow Prost's lead when Dole was in question. In a letter that Prost wrote to Paris from Dole on May 3,[78] he explained that, whereas Bourdon had again gone off to the frontier, his own ill health compelled him to spend some time in Dole with his family. But if, as it seems, Bourdon was primarily interested in the Jura's defences, Prost shows that his own concern was still with the "aristocracy and moderatism" by which he believed Dole to be surrounded. Having had to calm an angry crowd in the street on April 28, he had become convinced that agitators working on behalf of the suspended officials of the district were responsible for the troubles in the town and that some greater concentration of authority was essential to its peace. To conclude that Prost took the initiative is not to absolve Bourdon from all responsibility, for he was probably never more of a Jacobin than when he was in Jacobin company. Furthermore, neither man seems to have had any idea of the possible consequences of approving independent local action. In the second proclamation, significantly, they almost incidentally approved the Jura's formation of its own defence force, and on April 23 Prost reported that he had been helping to organize it: but within a few weeks the existence of that force would be regarded as proof of the Jura's criminal character.

By contrast, the commissioners' return to Dijon, where Bourdon met the departmental directory on May 6 and where both men visited the council, was little more than a formality.[79] Certainly there was now no question of touring the Côte-d'Or, for on April 30 the Convention had recalled all its commissioners. Because it was generally assumed that this recall implied the revocation of their authority, Bourdon and Prost may be supposed to have been ignorant of it when they were in Dole on May 1. The remainder of their journey back to Paris is nevertheless notable for their final joint report, which they wrote at Châtillon on May 7, a letter that they concluded by saying they were "congratulating themselves on the success of their mission, which was ended."[80]

Now, however, consideration of the men and their mission can hardly be so brief or so satisfactory. Certainly something had been accomplished. As they claimed in their various letters—most of which were written by Bourdon—their primary purpose, the completion of recruitment in their two departments, was achieved. Even if due allowance is made for their natural tendency to credit themselves for much that had been done by others, if not before their arrival, their presence and exhortations must have expedited the process of finding not only the additional men but also the gifts in cash and kind necessary for their clothing, arms, and equipment. Indeed, all that they did had some measure of approbation from the Committee of Public Safety, which had briefly acknowledged their reports and commanded them to continue their work.

They may also be credited with supplying Paris with some positive information about their area. Here Bourdon's assiduous tours may have been of more value than appears in his blunt assertion that the frontier was "absolutely defenceless,"[81] for more details were probably reported confidentially in Paris. Copies of their proclamations and orders were also sent to Paris regularly, as were the detailed returns given to them in the Jura. Conversely, too, Bourdon's letters indicate that one or two measures approved by the Convention in their absence were made known locally.[82] More important, both commissioners emphasized the principal impression that they had gained from their travels, and this impression remains of considerable interest. Much to their surprise, they found "fanaticism" (i.e., Catholicism) allied with the love of liberty: "What is most remarkable is that the Communes most infected with this virus are those most assiduous in observing decrees, and that it is among them that recruitment is most zealously completed."[83]

As that comment implies, however, both deputies were men whose judgments were severely limited by their preconceptions. Thus, Bourdon repeatedly reported the predominance of patriotic ardour, of enthusiasm for the republic one and indivisible,[84] but these reports were constantly offset by references to "aristocratic" disturbances and even to the allegation that civil war was imminent in the Côte-d'Or before the commissioners' arrival.[85] Evidently the situation was seen almost entirely as the popular societies in Dijon, Dole, and Lons-le-Saunier saw it. Moreover, despite his praise for, and cooperation with, the Department of the Jura in mid-April, all his urban and Jacobin prejudices became manifest as soon as he was back in Paris. According to the account of his mission that Bourdon gave to the Jacobin Society in Paris on May 10, aristocratic propaganda was spreading like the plague throughout the departments, and people everywhere were demanding that the pretentious and overgrown departmental administrations should be promptly replaced by those of the larger communes.[86] Once again the conclusion that he habitually matched his mood to his audience is inescapable.

Nor can the activity of the two commissioners be adequately assessed without regard for its consequences. Despite their final complacent conviction that they had calmed all unrest, their departure was in fact followed by so considerable a disturbance in the Jura that the department has been branded as a principal instigator of the so-called Federalist Revolt of 1793.[87] In political terms, that complex and extensive movement of protest may be said to have been the outcome of instability and inconsistency in central government and the lack of continuously effective centralizing agencies in the provinces; however, Bourdon and Prost certainly did much to precipitate trouble in the Jura.

For all the ridiculous nineteenth-century identification of Bourdon as "the bloodiest proconsul of the Terror,"[88] conflict did not arise because he was exceptionally repressive. In the Jura, there were as yet no executions, and the only one in the Côte-d'Or, that of Fondard, seems to have been more the result of his presence than the outcome of any command. Nor were the measures of security that Bourdon ordained unusually harsh or extensive. Certainly they were not resented as much as those of Amar and Merlino in the adjacent department of the Ain.[89] Indeed, it was not those who were victimized as suspects who shattered the balance so long and so carefully maintained by Ebrard. If latent problems suddenly became too serious to be contained, then it was because the commissioners, particularly Bourdon, identified themselves almost exclusively with one position alone, that of the Jacobins in the popular societies.

The results of this partisanship were soon obvious. At Lons-le-Saunier, the Commune, ever divided between its Jacobin inclinations and its jealousy of Dole, was outraged by a decision made by Bourdon on the eve of his departure: suddenly and arbitrarily he named a minor Jacobin extremist, Louis Ragmey, as the *procureur* of the town.[90] The Commune, slighted and resentful, consequently stood aside while the Society, exalted by Bourdon's patronage, hardly allowed the commissioner to depart before harrying the department mercilessly. Of the various matters in question, that of most immediate consequence proved to be the department's reluctance to order the deportation of a nonjuring priest whom local doctors had declared to be infirm.[91] On May 9, the Society called for a further examination by doctors at Dole. Affronted by the allegation that it had deliberately consulted politically unreliable experts, the department maintained its decision to keep the priest in prison, and the Society's delegates were told that "the dignity of the law does not permit the sort of correctional war that the Popular Society of Lons-le-Saunier permitted itself to wage against its ministers." The delegates nonetheless returned later at the head of a crowd so large and so noisy that the council had to adjourn until the next day. Relationships then broke down completely. The council resolved that it would no longer receive any requests not presented in writing, and the Popular Society determined that it would henceforth denounce every departmental infringement of popular rights directly to the Convention—by which, in effect, it meant the Montagnards.

Similarly, and still more seriously, the department was soon in open conflict with Dole as well. Being under constant pressure from the friends of those district officials whom the commissioners had suspended early in April, the department heard, and apparently believed, alarming reports about the number of persons imprisoned in Dole. On May 10, it therefore formally requested the Commune of Dole to furnish full information about these people, but the only reply from the Commune was that, because it had been authorized to account directly to the Committee of Public Safety, it was under no obligation to explain its actions to any other body.[92] The department, apparently at the instigation of the District of Dole, then resolved on May 20 to denounce both the Commune and the commissioners to the Convention because Bourdon and Prost, by attacking the hierarchy of constituted administrative authority, had exceeded their powers, which in any case had become invalid on April 30.[93]

The rhetorical document of denunciation[94] that followed on May 21 was then a catalogue of the crimes of Dole and the two commissioners. The situation at Dole was attributed particularly to Prost's desire to replace his personal enemies by his personal friends, and Bourdon was held generally responsible for provoking licence and disorder. More interestingly, the document deplored the fact that both men had assumed that the popular societies had a monopoly of patriotism, accusing as royalists all those who wished to reconcile law and democracy. Its final and almost hysterical call for "Justice, Justice!" was, indeed, fundamentally a denial of the legitimacy of minority government and the delegation of power: the sovereign people, it asserted, had delegated its power only to its chosen representatives acting by majority vote in a national assembly: "Là seulement est le pouvoir légitime."

This appeal by the department to the Convention inexorably evoked furious denunciations of the department by the popular societies of Dole on May 26 and of Lons-le-Saunier on May 24 (although the latter was not finally drafted and despatched until June 8).[95] Something of what this all meant in personal terms may be seen by the fact that J.-F. Dumas, the vice-president of the department, was struck off the membership list of the Popular Society of Lons on May 10 but formally recognized as a meritorious citizen by the department on May 12, and soon afterward he informed his colleagues that he wished to repudiate his name and adopt that of d'Hustâche. Meanwhile, his younger brother, R.-F. Dumas, better known as Dumas le Rouge, carried the Popular Society's denunciation to Paris, where he was soon noted by Robespierre as a good citizen and where he subsequently became notorious as the president of the Revolutionary Tribunal.[96] At another level, two of the letters that the deputy Théodore Vernier had written to the Commune of Lons arraigning that of Paris reached the Popular Society; Bourdon, to whom they were forwarded, then reported them to the Jacobins in Paris on May 20 and duly passed them to the Commune of Paris for information.[97]

Such illustrations of the constant interaction of local and national antagonisms are overshadowed by a more obvious consideration. The denunciations and appeals of the popular societies and of the department were meant for the Montagnards and the Girondins respectively, as were the calls that they also made for the Convention to put an end to its strife by silencing its dissidents; and, in the same way, the Girondins' appeals to the departments were matched by the Montagnards' calls for support from the popular societies. The future of each partner thus became dependent on the success of the other. More particularly, Ebrard and the department were well aware that the situation confronting them in Dole, which has been well described as a little Paris, was not new. In September 1792, agents of the Commune of Paris, claiming national authority, had encouraged Dole to assert its independence from the department, and the town had been severely reprimanded and recalled to order by Roland,[98] then Minister of the Interior. No such support, however, was to be expected of Roland's successor, Garat, or of any other minister acceptable to the Montagnards. This consideration probably weighed heavily in the department's momentous decision on May 24 to order its substitute deputies to go with an armed guard to Bourges.[99] If, as Guadet of the Gironde had urged in the Convention on May 18,[100] other departments also sent their substitutes there, the nucleus of an alternative national assembly would stand ready in a safe city to take control of France should the Convention be subjugated by Paris.

That this bold step was taken a week before the Montagnards effected their purge of the Convention by the Revolution of May 31 would here be incidental were it not for the reaction of the Côte-d'Or, which proved fatal to it. Attempting to rally support for its policy, the Jura sent its own commissioners to the five departments adjacent to it. These commissioners were welcomed enthusiastically in the Ain but received more dubiously in the Saône-et-Loire, the Doubs, and the Haute-Saône, and on May 29 delegates of all these departments, as well as of the Jura itself, were persuaded at Dijon to jettison the Jura's plan in favour of yet another verbal exhortation to the Convention.[101] This appeal, it was fondly hoped, would be something that the whole of France would support, and the new address, wrongly called "the Program of the Jura," in fact circulated widely but uselessly during the following weeks. Although such dependence on unanimity was to prove the fatal weakness of all who sought to sustain representative government in France in 1793, the caution—not to say pusillanimity—of the Côte-d'Or on this occasion meant that the Jura's initial attempt to prevent a coup in Paris was a failure, and it is likely that one contributory cause of this failure was the brief and inconclusive nature of Bourdon's visit to Dijon.[102]

This is not to suggest, of course, that Bourdon and Prost can be blamed for all that happened in the Jura and thus for all its repercussions. The Federalist Revolt, the culmination in different places and at different times of various protracted processes of confrontation, began independently elsewhere even earlier. At the end of April, for example, the insurgent sections of Marseille had forced several prominent Jacobins and the commissioners sent to the Bouches-du-Rhône, Boisset and Moïse Bayle, to fly from the city. Nevertheless, within three weeks of Bourdon's departure, the Jura, which Bourdon had reported to be calm, had taken the initiative in trying to implement a national program of resistance to the Montagnards.

Although three months were to pass before the Jura's further resistance to the Montagnards' fait accompli in Paris was broken, that sad story of misconceptions, of courage, obstinacy, and implacability, has little bearing on Bourdon's original mission. In that mission, Bourdon can only be said to have failed almost completely; nor, for whatever reason, was he again to be employed as a commissioner of the Convention. If he succeeded in stimulating patriotism, in mustering men for the army, and in energetically inspecting half-forgotten frontier defences, he failed to assess the realities of the situation in the Jura and to anticipate the possibility of serious republican resistance to local and Parisian Jacobinism. Neither consistently moderate nor ruthlessly repressive, Bourdon and Prost simply aggravated existing antagonisms so much that their departure was marked by the outbreak of conflicts bitter enough to acquire some national significance. Not without reason did the department denounce them for having thrown "the torch of the furies into this peaceful countryside."[103]

Granted that it was not in his nature to compromise the Jacobin ideals by which he lived, Bourdon emerges in this mission as a man devoid of the political perception that enabled Jeanbon Saint-André to be severe in repressing opposition in the Lot and yet to recommend a positive policy to Paris.[104] By comparison, Bourdon appears as a man of small stature. For all his posturing, he seems in these weeks of sustained responsibility to have been an unusually active idealist but not a relentlessly realistic revolutionary.

7

"The Martyr of Liberty"
(March to July 1793)

W hen Bourdon returned to the Convention on or about May 10, 1793, the conflict between the Girondins and the Montagnards was more intense than ever. Although evidence of his activity at this time is sparse, it suffices to show that he then gave wholehearted support to the Montagnard and *sans-culotte* campaign that culminated in the Revolution of May 31 to June 2, 1793, when the Girondins were overthrown. Moreover, although he was no more than a minor participant in these final struggles for predominance, he was directly affected by them. Initially the attack on Bourdon in Orléans on March 16, and the repression of the city that had ensued while he was in eastern France, became an additional subject of party dispute, and then "the triumph of the Mountain" led inexorably to the public trial, and eventual execution, of his alleged "assassins." Thus, for many his name became identified with the first manifestations of Terror.

During Bourdon's absence, the impasse in the Convention had become more dangerous than ever. It obviously delayed the adoption and implementation of effective measures to control the economy, to repress royalism in the Vendée, and to repel the enemy armies that threatened France on all sides. What is more, the two parties had become representative of divergent attitudes throughout republican France, and the antagonisms that these divergences bred were constantly stimulated by the conflicts in the Convention. Whereas the Girondins and their sympathizers saw every departure from legality as a violation of all that had been achieved for freedom since the beginning of 1789, the Montagnards and the Jacobins believed that national peril made emergency measures imperative. There was thus a real possibility that local zealots, acquiring power as patriots, might so abuse it that

---

Notes to Chapter 7 are on pp. 367-72.

resistance would lead to violence and even a general civil war. Inevitably, too, each side attracted, and indeed appealed to, different social groups, so that to some extent their hostility acquired the character of a conflict between the relatively rich and the poor.[1]

During April and May, moreover, there was a growing danger that the attempt to establish representative government in France might culminate not in a new republican constitution but in the dissolution of the Convention itself. At this time, the Girondins became convinced, not without reason, that some secret committee of *enragés* and *sectionnaires* was preparing another bloody insurrection in Paris; they also believed, or affected to believe, that this preparation was occurring with the connivance of the Commune and the Mountain, each of which was said to be developing a dictatorship. On April 13, they therefore sought to discredit all their opponents by sending Marat to the new Revolutionary Tribunal for advocating the destruction of the National Convention. The "Friend of the People," however, was promptly acquitted, being borne back to the assembly by a triumphant crowd, and the Girondins had to revert to cries for more rigorous control of the sections and the Commune and to increasingly frenzied appeals for armed intervention by forces from the departments.

On the other hand, in April the Montagnards similarly tried to deprive the principal Girondins of their seats. Probably in the hope that these men would retire voluntarily, they encouraged, if not actually stimulated,[2] the demand by most of the sections of Paris and many Jacobin Clubs for the expulsion of all "unfaithful deputies"—variously identified as the *appellants*, as that "sain parti" of the Convention that Dumouriez had hoped to rescue, or simply as the "bad blood" in the assembly. This campaign, however, failed to intimidate the Girondins, who responded to threats by becoming still more intransigent. Moreover, the more responsible Montagnards, particularly Robespierre, became alarmed lest provincial opinion be irrevocably alienated by some premature act of violence in the capital, if indeed that act did not end in the whole assembly being forcibly dispersed. The Montagnards consequently seem to have fallen back on the saner, if slower, course of associating themselves still more closely with "the people" by supporting the universal popular demand for some measure of price control. This position became apparent on April 20, when the Montagnards responded to Girondin denunciations of the Commune by vociferously identifying themselves with that body's sworn intent to remain "in insurrection"[3] until food supplies had been assured. There may then even have been some tacit understanding by which the

Montagnards' backing of price control was matched by municipal acceptance of the view that a purge of the Convention should be restricted to the elimination of the most prominent Girondins.[4]

Although Bourdon was still *en mission* in eastern France from April 25 to May 2, when the Convention debated the question of food supplies, he is sometimes supposed to have been the author of one of the proposals under consideration. In fact, however, it was his father, now aged seventy, who submitted to the Committee of Agriculture the *Projet nouveau* that he had first proposed in 1785, together with a supplementary measure to meet the immediate emergency:[5] all grain remaining from the previous harvest was to be sold for public consumption within three months, after which time it would be confiscated for distribution to the poor. Moreover, the principal proposal, that for the establishment of a network of granaries through which grain would be bought and sold at prices determined by national authority, is manifestly that of Bourdon *père*.[6] This attribution is further reinforced by the fact that on May 7, when Léonard Bourdon reached Châtillon on his way back to Paris, the elder Bourdon asked the Convention's Committee of Agriculture to name a member to present his own proposals formally to the assembly.[7]

As that request implies, his plan had again been lost amid many others, and the committee's only reaction was its resolve to ask the Convention to afford it an additional member. The committee had indeed initially favoured a proposal by Fabre of the Hérault, whose plan was similar to that of Bourdon's *père* but more modest; even that proposal, however, was rejected by the Convention as costly, time-consuming, and generally inappropriate to the immediate emergency.[8] No doubt, too, the deputies' final decision was swayed, if not determined, by the investment of their chamber by some 8,000 men of the Faubourg Saint-Antoine, who would let no one leave until they were sure that a measure of price control would be enacted. Their demand, the longed-for *maximum*, was approved the next day, May 2, with Montagnard support.

This new law, by which the departments were required to take a census of all grain and flour in their areas, to enforce the sale of grain, and to determine its price by averaging market prices since the beginning of the year, did not in fact prove a panacea for all the ills of the poor. Nor did either Léonard Bourdon or his father regard it as entirely incompatible with the latter's plan, to the promotion of which they would return. The Convention's acceptance of this first *maximum* was nonetheless symbolic. Almost all the deputies recognized that the principle of economic freedom, to them an essential attribute of the liberty won in 1789, must be set aside in a time of crisis. Moreover, if some Montagnards saw the return to controls as the beginning of social democracy,[9] it was for most of them not only a necessary evil but also a long stride toward political power.

The revolution by which the principal Girondins were expelled from the Convention followed within four weeks, but Léonard Bourdon, who had been a prominent participant in the events of August 1792, at first glance seems to have been singularly inactive in May 1793. Confronted by a perpetually rising tide of provincial threats and protests, by violent conflicts between the "moderates" and the "patriots" in the sections of Paris, and by recurrent tumult in the Convention itself, the deputies on May 18 rejected Guadet's demand that they authorize the formation of a shadow parliament at Bourges, falling back instead on that great stand-by of democracy, the appointment of a commission of inquiry. Exceptionally, however, the Commission of Twelve, a body composed of men acceptable to the Girondins, acted vigorously.[10] Expected to expose the complicity of the Commune and the sections of Paris in a conspiracy against the Convention, they in fact precipitated a general insurrection, particularly by effecting the arrest of popular militants such as Hébert, deputy *procureur* of the Commune and author of the scurrilous journal *Père Duschesne*; the *enragé* Varlet; and Dobsent, the president of the Section de la Cité. The first result of these arrests was an invasion of the Convention on May 27 by a crowd that mingled with the deputies of the Mountain and eventually enabled them to pass a decree abolishing the commission and releasing those who had been arrested.

To all these developments, the record of Bourdon's activities is no more than incidental. After reporting in the Jacobin Society on his mission to the Côte-d'Or and the Jura, Bourdon apparently spoke there only twice during May and June. On May 20, when the Society's proceedings were interrupted for fifteen minutes by rejoicing at the news that a forced loan of a thousand million, repayable after the war, was to be imposed on the rich, he cynically remarked that this money would give the wealthy good reason to hope for peace.[11] On that occasion, too, he urged all patriots to attend their sectional assemblies because "aristocrats" and intriguers, seeing that they had support in the Convention, supposed that they could assert themselves everywhere with impunity; however, he brazenly added, there were no such people in the assembly of Gravilliers, because the patriots had driven out all those who dared to appear. Beyond these remarks, Bourdon seems only to have given the Society an account of what had occurred in the Convention on May 27, when the Commission of Twelve was first abolished.[12] Similarly, as the crisis developed, he attracted the attention of the parliamentary reporters only once, when on May 18 he was one of those Montagnards who sought amid general tumult to win for a minority of deputies the right to force voting by *appel nominal* (i.e., individually and aloud) on any controversial matter.[13]

In these critical circumstances, however, much political activity necessarily went unrecorded. If in May Bourdon again gave attention to his school, he was probably constant in supporting the Montagnard cause in the Convention and in the sections. Certainly he was one of those who on May 28 voted vainly with the Montagnards in the *appel nominal* by which the Commission of Twelve was reinstated by a small majority.[14] That was also the last success of the Girondins and their sympathizers. Even so, Rabaut Saint-Étienne, the spokesman of the commission, was shouted down when he tried to present its report, and those who had been arrested as conspirators remained at liberty. Indeed, the reinstatement of the commission precipitated the insurrection that followed. For two days, political initiative passed to the sections, whose Central Committee had a small and nominally secret Revolutionary Committee. There Varlet, Dobsent, and a few others determined the procedure to be followed, and they did so with the sanction of the Jacobin Society, the Department of Paris, and the Commune, for on May 29 Robespierre himself had finally approved direct action: "Je dis que, si le peuple ne se lève tout entière, la liberté est perdue. . . . Je suis incapable de prescrire au peuple les moyens de se sauver; cela n'est pas donné à moi . . . il ne me reste plus d'autre devoir à remplir."[15]

Unfortunately evidence of Bourdon's part in the sections' activities before and during the Revolution of May 31 is scanty and of dubious value. Bergoeing of the Gironde, a member of the Commission of Twelve who subsequently—and from concealment—wrote a bitter denunciation of the insurrection, tells us that on May 22 Bourdon ("on voit quel sont les chefs de l'insurrection") was present in the Section du Temple.[16] Apparently he had then said that the Mountain could not save the republic unless the people rose in a body as they had done on August 10. That statement is not unlikely, for by that time this attitude was acceptable to many Montagnards. In reality, their principal problem had become that of ensuring that the Girondins were silenced without indiscriminate bloodshed. Thus, in the very different circumstances of March 1794, it was alleged at the

Cordeliers Club that Bourdon and Chabot had tried to prevent the rising in May 1793 by visiting the Central Revolutionary Committee, saying that those whom the people accused would resign their seats and that the departments would avenge any injury to any deputy. However, if there was indeed such a visit, then its purpose was almost certainly to restrain, not to prevent, popular action.[17]

Surprisingly, too, Bourdon's part in the activity of his own section, Gravilliers, is now more obscure than in August 1792.[18] This obscurity is not because Gravilliers had become less militant than before. On the contrary, from mid-April onward, it was prominent in the campaign by which the sections, singly or collectively, beset the Convention with demands for a purge of the Girondins and, in May, for the abolition of the Commission of Twelve and the release of its prisoners.[19] But even before Bourdon went away *en mission*, his influence in Gravilliers had diminished as the popularity of Jacques Roux had grown, and during his absence Roux's influence presumably increased still more, even though one of Bourdon's more unsavoury associates, Truchon "of the Black Beard," seems sometimes to have opposed it.[20] At the end of May, however, both Roux and Bourdon would certainly have seen insurrection as imperative and done all they could to encourage Gravilliers to participate in it. Nor was much encouragement really needed, for the section ultimately remained its own master. If it contributed a force of at least 1,457 armed men to the popular army that invested the Convention on May 31 and June 2,[21] then it did so both freely and deliberately.

In sum, therefore, Bourdon may be seen as a strong supporter of the insurrection, in the preparation of which he was probably active but not particularly prominent. Certainly he was enthusiastic in welcoming the events of May 31, when the Convention was compelled to renew its abolition of the Commission of Twelve. Typically he promptly proposed that the deputies should assemble the next day at the nearby Tree of Liberty and that a festival of federation should be arranged for the approaching anniversary of the fall of the monarchy on August 10.[22] No doubt Bourdon then supposed, as did many others, that the Girondins had finally been frustrated and that the insurrection was over. Some, notably Marat and Varlet, nevertheless took steps to secure a more decisive result, so that it was on June 2 that a still more massive manifestation of popular power forced the Convention to order the arrest of twenty-nine deputies who were identified as notable opponents of the Mountain, the number including ten members of the Commission of Twelve.[23]

Whatever his immediate feelings on this more ominous occasion, which deputies such as Danton had constantly hoped to avert, Bourdon was soon able to identify himself with it in an open letter to his constituents[24] (whoever they may have been). He asserted that from the opening of the Convention the men who had upheld the cause of liberty and equality since 1789 had constantly been thwarted and discredited by a faction avid for power and adept at deceiving the naïve. Knowing that they could never attain their ends while republican Paris guarded the Convention, these men had perpetually maligned the city in the hope of provoking civil war. To gain time, too, they had first prolonged the trial of the king and then obstructed the passage of essential legislation, and all the while the treacherous generals whom they had appointed were betraying the republic. The assassination of Lepeletier, the honourable wounds that Bourdon himself had received at Orléans, and the ever-increasing support of the faction by aristocrats and counterrevolutionaries had nevertheless revealed the truth, and in four days 200,000 Parisians had effected without bloodshed the arrest of the very men whom Dumouriez had tried to rescue.

Shorn of details, this version of events seems to be commonplace enough. It is nonetheless representative of the Montagnards' point of view, and Bourdon's conclusion is notably effective. While warning his readers against the machinations of wicked or misguided local administrators, Bourdon assured them that in the two weeks since the insurrection much had been quickly and calmly achieved. In particular, the complex constitutional proposals drawn up by the faction were rapidly being replaced by far better ones, which would soon be made public. Therefore, with "a little courage," all efforts would be rewarded, and French citizens could assemble "in holy federation" to celebrate the anniversary of August 10 and place liberty securely on an immutable base.

Characteristically confident, as all real revolutionaries must be, of full and final success, Bourdon was right in assuming that the insurrection of May 31 had ended an impossible situation. Whichever side is thought ultimately responsible for the deadlock in the Convention, that deadlock had indisputably become incompatible with the effective government of France. On the other hand, the Montagnards had undoubtedly condoned and encouraged the use of force to silence those who opposed them. Bloodshed had been averted; three months were to elapse before Terror was formally recognized as being "the order of the day"; after June 2, however, force would remain the basis of the Montagnards' revolution.

Bourdon's own hopes of immediate harmony were in fact rapidly belied. If in the Convention the friends of those who had been arrested (and others who deplored the use of force) were reduced to public silence and surreptitious protests,[25] provincial France was far from being so subservient. Strident denunciations of Paris, rejections of illegal government, and threats of armed intervention to restore proper representation of the whole nation became almost commonplace. Moreover, Marseille, which had previously repudiated Jacobinism, and Lyon, which did so by a bloody municipal revolution on May 29, were soon in open revolt; moreover, closer to Paris, Breton and Norman forces combined in readiness for a march on the capital. At first, the Montagnards met all this opposition by cautious moderation, relying on time and their constitutional proposals as well as on reassurances such as Bourdon's letter and some immediate measures (such as the final abolition of all remaining manorial dues) to reconcile the country to their rule. Even so, Bourdon was one of those who pressed for more stringent legislation. On June 5, for example, his demand that all the departmental administrations be abolished outright was rebuffed by Jeanbon Saint-André, who sensibly said that it was more important to establish an executive that would make local government effective.[26] Again, later in the month, he opposed a proposal to arrest all those deputies of the Aisne who had signed a letter in which they deplored the intimidation of the Convention, demanding instead that a general law be drafted to penalize all who wrote or signed such letters.[27]

More important than such occasional interventions in debate was the part that Bourdon played in thwarting a serious challenge to the Montagnards from an unexpected quarter. Almost the first, and certainly the most prominent, of their proposals for the future happiness of France was that soon to be known as the Constitution of 1793. It was exceptionally democratic, and it was accompanied by a Declaration of Rights that began by proclaiming that "The aim of society is the general welfare." Whether or not the Montagnards ever seriously intended to put this code into effect, it was unveiled in the Convention on June 10 as the foundation of an entirely new era: "In a few days," announced Barère, "we have reaped the enlightenment of all the ages," and Robespierre described the outcome of those days as something "infinitely superior to all moral and political institutions."[28] Enthusiastically endorsed by the Convention of June 24, the plan was referred to the people of France for ratification by a plebiscite to be held on July 14; however, on June 25, a day set aside for triumphant rejoicing, the Montagnards were suddenly attacked by the *enragé*

Jacques Roux as timid and moderate men whose constitution failed miserably to provide any remedy for the real ills of a starving people.

Roux's address,[29] presented in the name of the popular Cordeliers Club and the sections of Bonne Nouvelle and Gravilliers, still remains remarkably moving. "Deputies of the Mountain," he demanded,

> why have you not climbed from the third to the ninth floor of the houses in this revolutionary city? You would have been touched by the tears and sighs of an immense population without food and clothing, brought to such distress by speculation and hoarding, because the laws have been cruel to the poor, because they have been made only by the rich and for the rich.

Whatever sympathies these words evoked, the deputies were alienated by Roux's condemnation of their failure to impose still more economic controls and to terrorize hoarders and speculators by savage punishment. Moreover, the menacing tone of the address was seen as an expression of dangerous discontent among the *sans-culottes*, whose leaders had been superseded during the insurrection, when their demands for far-reaching social and political changes had been set aside. Roux was therefore interrupted by shouts of disapproval; Robespierre intervened to condemn his address as inflammatory; one of those in the delegation of Gravilliers disavowed it as differing from that which the section had approved; and Bourdon, too, repudiated it on behalf of the men of Gravilliers.[30] Their true purpose, he claimed, had been to thank the Convention for the new constitution, and, although they did indeed seek more consideration of the continued high price of food, they would never have sanctioned the authoritarian principles underlying the petition just presented in their name. At this point, Roux's address was formally dismissed, and Roux himself was driven from the chamber.

The principal Montagnards and Jacobins then began a sustained campaign to destroy Roux's popularity and possible sources of power. The popular Cordeliers Club was induced to expel Roux; Marat attacked him in *L'Ami du peuple*, and on July 4 Bourdon succeeded, at least temporarily, in persuading the Section des Gravilliers to disown him.[31] On July 7, indeed, the revolutionary committee of the section opened proceedings against Roux for misusing money that he had collected for charity. Evidently Bourdon could still sway Gravilliers. Yet his influence there was by no means dominant: Roux in fact retained a substantial following in the section, and to these men Bourdon probably now seemed more a man of government than a genuine *sans-culotte*.

Ironically, however, Bourdon's detractors have always turned to this period to demonstrate the belief that he was a particularly cruel and vindictive revolutionary. This belief is a consequence of the assault on him in Orléans on March 16. Immediately after that fracas, he was widely hailed as a hero of the republic: wounded while on mission, he seemed to be proof that patriots would survive every peril and see the ultimate triumph of the Revolution. Yet those who opposed the Montagnards soon challenged the truth of his story, and when the reactionaries prevailed in 1795 he was reviled as the man primarily responsible for the judicial murder of some of the noblest citizens of Orléans. Thus, Bourdon, "assassinated" in Orléans in 1793, became "the assassin of Orléans" in 1795.

Of these two views of the same man and the same sequence of events, it is the second that has become commonly accepted. References to "the Orléans Affair" in the nineteenth century, and the accounts given by some later popular writers,[32] are at least strongly influenced by the productions of the period between 1794-95 and 1800, when journalists prospered by exaggerating the horrors of the Terror.[33] A highly prejudiced interpretation of what occurred has thus become embedded in historical writing, and, although some twentieth-century scholars—notably Georges Lefebvre[34]— have shown that there is a different side to the story, the older assumptions are still current. The matter consequently calls for reconsideration, particularly because the contrast between the apologia of Bourdon and the allegations of his enemies is so sharp.

In general terms, the indictment against Bourdon asserts that he arrived in Orléans unofficially on March 15, 1793, and spent the next day inciting disreputable extremists to flout all established authority. Then, after dinner on the evening of March 16, when he was the worse for drink, he and some of his associates marched along the streets until they were brought to a halt by men of the National Guard on duty before the town hall. Slightly injured in the ensuing scuffle, a conflict that Bourdon himself had provoked, he swore that he would be terribly avenged, and he so magnified the affair that Orléans, a loyal, well-governed, and peaceful city, was subjected to all the miseries of prolonged repression. Worst of all, he personally attended the Revolutionary Tribunal to bear witness against those who were supposed to have assassinated him, and, even after nine of them had been condemned to die ignominiously as parricides, he sat silently in the Convention while the deputies refused to hear appeals for mercy by the victims' distraught relatives.

So stated, the accusations levelled at Bourdon evidently distort the truth, if only because they take no account of the circumstances in which he acted. Consideration of them may therefore help to explain his conduct. To go further and determine precisely what happened is more difficult, for the records at Orléans have been destroyed,[35] and the accounts that accumulated in Paris are almost all retrospective and partial. However, if much must remain controversial, his behaviour can be established well enough to validate some conclusions about him.

Initially the suggestion that Bourdon had no business being in Orléans,[36] and that consequently whatever injury he suffered was something that he had incurred as a private person, may be set aside. It is true that Bourdon and Prost had been assigned as representatives on mission to the Côte-d'Or and the Jura and that, instead of travelling directly to Dijon through Auxerre or Troyes, they had made an appreciable detour to reach Orléans. The deviation is nevertheless understandable and even legitimate, for Orléans was the seat of the departmental administration of the Loiret, the department of which Bourdon was an elected deputy, and according to his own account his correspondents in the city had begged him to visit them because counterrevolutionary activity in the city was daily becoming more dangerous.[37] Moreover, although he seems to have acted in Orléans simply as a deputy visiting his constituency, without asserting the authority vested in him for his mission, he remained fully entitled to all the respect due to his position as a representative of the people, and this respect was unhesitatingly afforded to him by all in official positions.[38]

Similarly, the suggestion that all was calm in Orléans before Bourdon arrived in mid-March 1793 must be discounted. That is not to say, as was widely assumed, that the city was a royalist stronghold. No doubt many people would have welcomed a restoration, but it was not until mid-May, when republican repression had been in effect for two months, that some small but indisputably royalist activity was exposed.[39] By Bourdon's own account (the *Exposé des faits*, written in late May 1793), the population of Orléans included "a multitude of excellent patriots," and Bourdon was probably right in supposing that their employers, wealthy men "with no great love for the Revolution," were principally concerned to keep them firmly under control.[40] Since Bourdon's previous visit, however, the position of the democrats in the Popular Society and the various sections had deteriorated.[41] In September 1792, popular anxiety about food supplies had led to extensive disorder, in which one official had been decapitated and a warehouse and two houses burned, and this outbreak of violence had divided the more moderate democrats from the extremists. Together with the threat of a rising in the countryside, it had also so alienated public opinion that the elections held in December had brought in a municipality markedly bourgeois and conservative in character. Whatever their feelings about the republic, these new officials seem to have been at one with the employers in their anxiety to prevent any resurgence of popular democracy. Their general attitude is apparent in the letter that the new mayor, the *ci-devant* Marquis de Sailly, wrote on December 16 to Roland, then still the Minister of the Interior: "Let us," he said, "ensure above all else that the sectional assemblies no longer meet continuously."[42]

In this situation, in which the local authorities believed that they had the full support of the Girondins in the National Convention, tensions increased considerably as food again became scarce and increasingly expensive in the spring of 1793. Then, too, popular agitation was stimulated by reports of the rioting in Paris in late February, and it seems probable that news of the demonstration against the Girondins on March 10 similarly contributed to the unrest and alarm in Orléans that coincided with Bourdon's arrival there on March 15. Thus far, the authorities had sought to contain the situation without regulation. On the one hand, while some employers had raised their workers' wages, the municipality had tried to alleviate hardship by distributing alms; on the other hand, on March 10 it had acquiesced in the demand of the bourgeois National Guard that voluntary recruiting should be continued even though it had then produced less than half the city's quota.[43] On March 15-16, however, news that crowds were everywhere besieging the bakeries moved the municipality to more positive action: bread was to be sold at a fixed price; all available flour was to be brought for baking to one central bakery, from which, "to avoid a rising," it would be sold still more cheaply; and the regular market day, on Saturday, March 16, was abruptly cancelled.

Even more menacing than these alarms was a reaction, to which the authorities had apparently closed their eyes. Whereas in Paris, and in other great towns such as Lyon and Marseille, "moderates" were trying to win control of the sectional assemblies from the more extreme "patriots," in Orléans the bourgeoisie and the municipality had come to rely increasingly on the possibility of suppressing popular or "patriotic" disorder by force of arms. Apparently some of the more prosperous citizens had long voluntarily patrolled the streets whenever a disturbance had seemed likely,[44] and by March 1793 it had become normal for the National Guard, with any available detachments of gendarmes or regular cavalrymen, to be concentrated at the town hall. Worse still, the municipality had at least condoned the practice by which this heterogeneous force was spontaneously supplemented by self-styled "honnêtes gens," armed men who may be better described as young hooligans in search of trouble.[45] Thus, when Bourdon reached Orléans, the danger of confrontation and conflict between hungry people and a miscellaneous and undisciplined military force was considerable. In short, a protracted period of weak and one-sided municipal government had led to a potentially explosive situation.

In these circumstances, Bourdon's behaviour on March 15 and 16 seems less provocative than might be expected. Broadly it appears that as he was principally concerned to revive the confidence and resolution of the Jacobins in Orléans, he remained constantly in the company of members of the Popular Society and their friends. On his arrival, he was visited by the president of the department, and, on discovering that this gentleman, Benoist des Haut-Champs, seldom attended the society because he disliked divisive debates, Bourdon persuaded him to join him there that evening.[46] According to Bourdon himself, both he and Prost then spoke to the society about the importance of recruitment and of pressing the municipality to provide all citizens with arms; he adds that they did all they could to raise the members' morale, "which had been paralyzed by aristocracy and *feuillantisme*."[47] In contrast, an *adresse* issued three days later by some National Guardsmen asserted that Bourdon had maligned the guard, the city's administrators, and all who possessed property; however, beyond indicating that his speech had been powerful, the paper really said no more than that it had included a denunciation of "a part of the Convention," which is likely enough.[48] The evening nevertheless ended peacefully with a supper at which the deputies, President Benoist, Dulac (the commander of the National Guard), and various other officials were entertained by one of Bourdon's pupils, a lad who sang the "Marseillaise" for them.[49]

But even if Bourdon's conduct was restrained, his very presence in Orléans was disturbing. Whatever Bourdon did, he was seen by many as an extremist from Paris, the principal source of all unrest. Furthermore, he was particularly associated with the abduction of the prisoners of the High Court in September 1792, and probably—for this does not appear in the records—with his stimulation of the sections immediately afterward, and so with the rioting that followed his departure. Being thus to the rowdies of the right practically the personification of revolutionary disorder, he was particularly liable to insult and abuse, if not worse.

Again according to Bourdon's own account, this aspect of the situation became apparent on the first evening of his visit, when someone warned him to be on his guard because certain scoundrels had been ready to assault him if he had gone to the recruiting assembly held two days previously.[50] The reality of some such danger became much more obvious the next day, March 16, when Bourdon and Prost, as well as two other deputies, Bernard de Saintes and Guimberteau, who were on mission to the Charente, attended a dinner given in their honour by the Popular Society. They learned of an ugly incident on the previous evening,[51] when the carriage of Jeanbon Saint-André and Élie Lacoste, deputies on mission to the Lot and the Dordogne, had been brought to a halt in Orléans by a few men who had threatened to throw them in the Loire. Furthermore, two young men had then thrust their heads into the vehicle and spat into the deputies' faces before running away. In what seems to have been the only formal act of his visit, Bourdon then took the initiative in instructing a magistrate who was present to begin an immediate search for the culprits.

Because Bourdon was later concerned to refute the charge that this dinner had been bacchanalian ("il fit dans une taverne une orgie"[52]) and that he had consequently been intoxicated when he had encountered the National Guard, his narrative emphasizes the difference in time between the meal and the conflict.[53] This, he said, was about six hours, and that estimate is confirmed by other accounts of the evening. Still more to the point, however, is the description of the dinner written by President Benoist,[54] who tells us that when Bourdon was first invited, and understood that the occasion was to be at the Society's sole expense, he insisted that it should be "spartan." Such, he adds, it was, there being but a niggardly provision of about twenty bottles of mediocre wine for some forty people, and, although he heard some talk of four bottles of champagne, he saw none of it himself.

Nevertheless, it was after the dinner that difficulties began to arise. About twenty of the more prominent members of the party, including notable men of Jacobin sympathies such as the Bishop of Orléans, as well as some more radical democrats such as Élie Vinson, the tailor Nicole, and the apothecary Besserve,[55] moved to a café near the town hall, and there Bourdon and Prost tried to order a carriage and horses so that they could continue their journey to Dijon. By what Bourdon seems to have regarded as deliberate obstruction,[56] the postmaster refused this request, alleging that the first cross-country part of the route was unfit for travel. Prost then went to the town hall, where he succeeded in obtaining an official order for the provision of transport, and in the meantime Bourdon, Bernard, and Guimberteau agreed to defer their separate departures until the early hours of the morning.

Although Bourdon did not instigate this visit to the café, he was certainly imprudent to take part in it. Apparently someone of the party at dinner had said that members of the Society ought to assert their republicanism by going where they would be noticed and that the café where the *tricolore* had once been destroyed was such a place.[57] Because neither Bourdon nor Bernard de Saintes, to say nothing of their companions, were men to shirk such a challenge, the idea was adopted. The visit of the Montagnard deputies and their Jacobin friends to the café, evidently a rendezvous for guardsmen and others from the courtyards of the town hall, was nonetheless a provocative one, which could easily have led to violence. No sooner had they arrived than the place became crowded with people whom Bourdon later described as "Young men wearing great cravats, mostly in uniform,"[58] and for the three-quarters of an hour that they remained there they were constantly jostled and subjected to the muttered menaces of such men. The behaviour that he ascribed to one peripheral group also seems typical of street-corner boys: as the party left, audible remarks were made by about seven or eight youths standing outside; when Bourdon heard his own name mentioned, he addressed them directly, demanding to know who had paid them to insult him; then all but one, who managed a stuttered apology, either stood silent or moved away.

After this metaphorical crossing of swords, about fifteen members of the party went on to the Popular Society's nightly meeting, which lasted for at least three hours. There Bourdon presided while his colleagues addressed the meeting, and he himself spoke for an hour about the general situation of the republic and of Orléans.[59] According to his own account, he said that the municipality should uphold the laws that ensured public freedom as well as those that secured the tranquility of the rich; and, remarking that the horses of the town's cavaliers were probably more reliable than their riders, he again emphasized the necessity of arming all able-bodied men with pikes.[60] Because he was probably correct in supposing that his every word and action was noted by observers, no doubt his comments were duly bruited about in the vicinity of the town hall.

To conclude their stay in Orléans, the four deputies next paid a final visit to their friend the bishop, at whose residence they stayed for some fifteen minutes. By then, it was shortly after nine o'clock, and Bourdon and Prost—still accompanied by Bernard de Saintes and Guimberteau, as well as by about twelve members of the Society—set out on foot for their inn and the carriage in which they expected to travel overnight to Dijon. Walking in groups of two or three, each group several paces apart, they approached the town hall, past which they had to go. Again according to Bourdon, his companions left him in no doubt that they were accompanying him not only because of courtesy but also because they had heard that some attack on him impended.[61] In fact, the fracas that broke out at the town hall, and in which Bourdon was "assassinated," seems to have been spontaneous. Yet in visiting Orléans Bourdon had deliberately set out to encourage the Jacobins, and that encouragement implied both criticism of the municipality and some overt defiance of the strong-arm men who assembled around it. To that extent, he and those with him had been provoking trouble.

What happened next is sufficiently clear from the formal and detailed *Déclaration* that Bourdon made to commissioners of the department, the district, and the municipality in the early hours of the following morning.[62] Somewhat surprisingly, despite all the controversy that ensued about the responsibility of authorities and individuals, the substance of this statement was not seriously challenged. Apparently the deputies and their companions were insulted on the road outside the town hall, and, when one leading member of the party found himself impeded by men standing in his way, he seized one of them and demanded that they should both present themselves at once to the municipal officials. Bourdon, fearing, as he said, conflict between armed and unarmed men, then hurried forward to support that demand. Seeing that the danger of serious violence was increasing, he identified himself as a deputy of the Convention *en mission*, but this statement only evoked cries of "Qu'est-ce que c'est la convention? Nous le connaissons bien!"

Two men, one of whom was a noncommissioned officer, then stepped between Bourdon and his friends, seized him by the collar, and shook him violently while one exclaimed, "Gueux! Nous allons te donner ton fait!" About a dozen men then hustled him with kicks and blows across the courtyard to the foot of the steps of the town hall, where he was hurled to the ground and assailed repeatedly by musket blows and bayonet thrusts. As he recalled, at least one pistol shot was fired, and one of those who stabbed at him exclaimed, "Va rejoindre Lepeletier!" By strength and agility, Bourdon nevertheless succeeded

in escaping: flailing his arms to ward off the bayonet thrusts, he contrived to regain his feet and struggle up the steps to the doors of the
town hall. They were immediately closed against him; however, while
Dulac, the commander of the National Guard, held his assailants off,
Bourdon forced his way in and burst through the bayonets of the
guardsmen on duty—whom he apparently regarded as still more
would-be murderers. Thus, when the municipal officials, alarmed by
the noise as they ended a long meeting about the supply of bread,
came hurrying from their chamber, they were appalled to see Bourdon,
whom they had supposed to be well on his way to Dijon, streaming
with blood as he staggered toward them.[63]

The truth of Bourdon's statement, taken as soon as a surgeon
allowed officials to enter the room found for him in the town hall, was
substantiated by his wounds and the rents in his clothing. Evidently
Bourdon had one cut on the side of his head, one in his side, and several, of which one was a severe slash, about his arms. Testimony subsequently written for him by Bernard and Guimberteau also confirms his
account, although these two deputies, held back at bayonet point, had
lost sight of Bourdon once he had been separated from them.[64] Moreover, one important feature of the affair became evident in the immediate inquiry begun by the departmental, district, and municipal
authorities in Orléans, all of whom were much concerned to ensure
that the town remained quiet and that satisfactory information was
sent promptly to Paris. Called on to identify all those on guard at the
town hall the previous evening, Dulac replied that, as popular unrest
about food had made additional reinforcement of the guard imperative, "ce sont les citoyens de bonne volonté qui se présentent, et qu'il
n'en est tenu aucun contrôle."[65] Although Dulac was no doubt
anxious to absolve his own force, those who had set on and severely
injured Bourdon were probably men of this unofficial militia, and
whatever their first intentions some of them had become so enraged
that they might well have killed him.

In one major respect, the sequel to this "assassination" is akin to its
prologue: just as Bourdon almost accidently precipitated an outbreak
of the violence implicit in the situation in Orléans, so too the assault
on him seems to have been more the occasion than the cause of the
repression that ensued. No doubt his own initial reactions contributed
to the severity of this repression: if he did not magnify the attack on
him, he certainly dramatized it. Writing briefly to the Convention the
next day, March 17, he announced: "Et moi aussi, j'ai payé mon tribut
à ma patrie; et moi aussi, j'ai versé mon sang pour elle."[66] Similarly, in

a note written on March 19 to accompany a copy of his detailed declaration of what had occurred, he exultantly explained that he owed his life to the fact that the bayonet thrust meant to kill him had been turned aside by a coin in his pocket, a coin bearing the figure of Liberty.[67] In both letters, he also contrived to mention Lepeletier, the deputy who had been assassinated on the day of the king's execution.

Furthermore, his appreciation of the care given to him by the authorities in Orléans rapidly changed to open hostility. Established in the town hall on the night of Saturday, March 16, Bourdon was only with difficulty dissuaded from returning to his auberge the next day, and on the morning of Monday, March 18, he insisted on doing so despite the mayor's offer to accommodate him in his own home. The exchanges involved on these occasions, which were carefully recorded by the Commune, include his effusive thanks for the attentions that he had received: "Léonard Bourdon," he wrote on leaving, "est pénetré de sensibilité pour tous les bons procèdes qu'il a éprouvés des citoyens des trois corps administratifs et, en particulier, du citoyen maire et des officiers municipaux."[68] Nonetheless, his wounds probably affected his outlook and made him suspicious of all who were around him. Certainly he later alleged in his *Exposé des faits* that he had found himself guarded by those who had struck him down and that he had been kept alive simply as a hostage in case the people of Orléans should attack the building. Similarly, although Bourdon simply informed the Convention on March 19 that he was then with the *sans-culottes* of Orléans, he said in the *Exposé* that his first thanks to the municipality could not offset the facts that he had then learned and others "dont j'ai été instruits depuis." These facts, he explained, confirmed the impressions that he had formed from what he had overheard in the town hall and convinced him that this "assassination" had been premeditated and that the city authorities had been privy to the plot.[69]

As far as this attitude can be ascribed to Bourdon while he remained in Orléans, it may have been of some consequence, for in his letter of March 19 he told the Convention that he would stay in the town until its commissioners, for whom he had important information, arrived. No record of any such interview exists, but some continuity in reporting may be presumed. Having hastened back from Nevers to take charge in Orléans, Collot d'Herbois and Laplanche, the two deputies assigned to the Departments of the Loiret and the Nièvre for recruitment, told the Convention on March 22 that Bourdon was reasonably well and would soon continue his journey.[70] Moreover, although Bourdon himself was in Dijon on March 25, Collot and

Laplanche remained in Orléans until April 1, when other commissioners went there directly from Paris to replace them.

The most remarkable, and perhaps the most damning, evidence of Bourdon's supposedly nefarious influence, however, is that which occurs at the end of the declaration of Benoist, the president of the department. He explains that he became aware that neither Bourdon nor his wife—who had joined him from Paris—was well disposed toward Orléans and that his own fears for the future led him to visit Bourdon in his lodgings. At Benoist's behest, his companions, one of whom was Bourdon's acknowledged saviour, Dulac, then joined Benoist in imploring the deputy to restrain his anger. According to this account, Bourdon nevertheless remained untouched by all that was said about justice, truth, humanity, and even his own best interests. On the contrary, with one hand on Benoist's shoulder while he bathed his arm with oil, Bourdon made a terrible prediction: "Président, tu vois cette petite saignée? Elle ne sera guérie que par une grande. Je veux que vingt-cinq têtes orléanaises roulent sur l'échafaud, ou je perds mon nom, foi de Léonard Bourdon!"[71]

If this story is true, then the episode must be recognized as the most specific contemporary evidence of Bourdon's evil nature encountered so far in these pages; moreover, Benoist's account of what occurred before Bourdon was attacked has here been accepted as valuable first-hand testimony. On the other hand, the authenticity of this particular tale seems to be questionable. The manuscript in which it occurs, *Notes relatives à l'histoire d'Orléans* compiled by the *abbé* Pataud, is marked "commencé le 1er juillet 1805," and the duplication of occasional lines shows that the *abbé* was in fact copying an earlier document. Furthermore, the final lines of the paper, those immediately following the story of Benoist's failure, include the comment "as we know, the monster kept his word," which suggests the possibility that the story may be a later addition, either by Benoist himself (whose account seems to show a concern to stand well with all parties) or by his copyist. Nor is it irrelevant to add that the story itself looks like a typical royalist tale.

However that may be, the important fact is that Bourdon's influence in the repression of Orléans could not have been more than peripheral. Travelling in a handsome berline—for which the municipal officers were never reimbursed by anyone[72]— Bourdon left the city for eastern France a week after he had been injured, and thereafter he was not concerned with its affairs until two months later. Moreover, even before his departure, the fate of Orléans had been determined in Paris by the National Convention, at that time singularly united in its initial response to a great national emergency.

On March 18, when the Convention heard of the attack on Bourdon, the news followed the first reliable reports of the threat posed by the rising in the Vendée, and it was immediately succeeded by information indicating that Brittany, where protracted resistance to recruiting had barely been controlled, was still being disturbed by riots and royalist demonstrations. Within two days, too, the assembly heard of Dumouriez's disastrous defeat at Neerwinden.[73] Naturally enough, the deputies regarded all these ill tidings as proof of the menacing reality of one great counterrevolutionary conspiracy, and their reaction to this threat was determined by a remarkable speech made by Barère.[74] Speaking for the Committee of General Defence, he told the assembly that it was essentially a revolutionary body and that it should act accordingly. Because the counterrevolution had begun, deputies could no longer afford to deliberate after disasters that they ought to have anticipated and prevented. So stimulated, the Convention enacted a considerable number of emergency measures, one of which was designed to repress royalism in Orléans.

More particularly, the deputies' attitude toward Orléans was governed by the reports that they received about it on and immediately after that day, March 18. Among these reports, the two short letters written by Bourdon on March 17 and 19 seem to be more personal and flamboyant than incriminating: perhaps because he was a deputy of the Loiret, he was indeed surprisingly restrained. Others, however, had no hesitations. Thus, Bernard and Guimberteau, whose letter of March 16 was the first to be heard from Orléans, said that Bourdon had been massacred, that the attack had been premeditated, and that the municipal body was culpable because it had failed to prevent violence and then begun a biased inquiry: in short, "tout ici est en contre-révolution."[75] That view, moreover, was confirmed by other deputies who had passed through Orléans, notably Jeanbon Saint-André, and even by the first letters of the local authorities themselves, in which they were rash enough to refer to the attack on Bourdon as a scuffle (rixe).[76] The Convention consequently had no hesitation in approving the decree of March 18 by which Orléans was "reputed" to be in rebellion.[77]

In consequence of this decree, three commissioners of the Ministry of Justice—Codet, Duvelleray, and Perdy—were sent to Orléans to investigate the attack on Bourdon and the insulting of Jeanbon Saint-André and Lacoste and to ensure that all those charged as participants or accomplices in these affairs were sent before the Revolutionary Tribunal. At the same time, three other commissioners—the deputies Bourbotte and, after some initial changes, Julien of Toulouse and Prieur of the Marne—were sent with full powers to enforce the other provisions of the decree. The mayor, the *procureur*, and the municipal officers were to be suspended, arrested, and sent to the bar of the Convention; the entire National Guard (with the exception of Dulac) was to be disarmed, and the guardsmen who had been on duty at the town hall on March 16 were to be arrested; and all available arms were to be distributed to citizens of good repute. Only when the city had surrendered those charged with the outrage of March 16 would the decree be rescinded.

Thus, Orléans was subjected to rigorous and prolonged repression. While the agents of the Ministry of Justice sought out those to be judged in Paris, Julien, Bourbotte, and Prieur continued the work begun by Collot d'Herbois and Laplanche to ensure that the city was completely controlled by reliable republican revolutionaries. In all, twenty-six men were named for despatch to the tribunal, of whom thirteen eventually appeared before it, and at least fifty-nine others were imprisoned in Orléans.[78] Beyond the hardships consequently suffered by these men and their families, the well-established bourgeoisie was also afflicted by the wholesale replacement of the municipal administration and its officials by Jacobins such as Bourdon's friend Nicole, who became the new postmaster, and by more obscure *sans-culottes*. Although some of these democrats were probably incompetent and even vindictive, so that stories of abuse soon became commonplace, their party remained firmly in power until the Terror ended in 1794.[79]

Although this repression pales almost into insignificance in comparison with the savagery of the punishments later inflicted on other dissident or rebellious cities, it was singularly shocking in the early summer of 1793. Resentment and revulsion against it no doubt contributed considerably to the abhorrence in which Léonard Bourdon came to be held. Apart from any influence that he may have had on Collot d'Herbois, however, he does not seem to have been in any way involved in the repression before the final days of May, when the question of its continuation was raised in the Convention.

That question had indeed been recurrent during his absence in the Jura, for the unity with which the deputies had responded to national needs in March had soon been lost amid conflicts over responsibility for the crisis and over the rigour necessary to overcome it. Thus, the repression of Orléans soon became a matter of dispute between the

Girondins and the Montagnards. Whereas on March 19 Brissot, like Marat, had seen the attack on Bourdon as a disaster, "to be mourned by all the friends of freedom," by March 28 he had come to think of it as no more than a scuffle in the street, and by May he was publishing letters from Orléans purporting to prove that Bourdon had deliberately provoked the assault so that Montagnard commissioners could oppress innocent people just as they pleased.[80] Twice, on March 23 and April 26, the decree of March 18 was rescinded, and on each occasion it was reimposed after furious protests from Montagnards.[81] On May 19, the Girondins nevertheless again began an attempt to emancipate the city, and to this attempt Bourdon, who had returned to Paris from Dijon ten days previously, felt compelled to respond.

This phase of the affair was so overshadowed by the Girondins' last efforts to check impending insurrection in Paris that it might easily be dismissed as another minor episode in a party conflict. It nevertheless merits attention as an illustration of one of the essential issues involved in that conflict. In the first instance, a spokesman for the Convention's Legislative Committee presented a report on May 19 on a petition that had been brought before the assembly on May 12 by forty women from Orléans. These ladies had made a moving appeal for justice because their husbands or male relatives had been arbitrarily arrested regardless of their age or health, and the committee recommended that new commissioners, deputies who had already gone to Orléans to try to discover some trace of the fugitive Duc d'Orléans, should be authorized to release all those imprisoned without cause shown.[82] If Bourdon was present on this occasion, he remained silent; however, Laplanche and Collot angrily protested that Orléans had been the headquarters of the royalist revolt in the Vendée and that the proposed liberation of prisoners would undermine all that the Convention's appointed agents had achieved.[83] Two Girondins—Louvet, who gave the assembly a vivid description of the way in which the women of Orléans had been humiliated when they had begged for mercy there, and Lehardy, who condemned the proscription of men by political labels alone—nevertheless spoke so effectively that the proposal was approved.[84] That any attempt to implement it was prevented by the victory of the Montagnards on May 31 to June 2 is less important here than its acceptance, for that implied that repression in Orléans should be restricted to the punishment of those directly involved in the attack on Bourdon.

The same argument was advanced explicitly on May 30 by Noel, an elderly deputy who also spoke for the Girondin-dominated Legislative

Committee.[85] On this occasion, the committee's report was concerned with the mayor and municipal officers of Orléans, who had been provisionally released when they had duly appeared at the bar of the house on April 30. Citing Bourdon's own letters of appreciation to these officials, Noel argued that the whole story of their participation in a premeditated plot was a later fabrication. By this cold analysis, they had administered their city well until they had been suspended after an affray of which they could have known nothing. Furthermore, although Noel conceded that those who had actually injured Bourdon should be punished, he maintained that Bourdon had brought his injuries on himself by going to Orléans, by making inflammatory speeches there, and by intervening in a dispute from which he, like his colleagues, could well have stood aside. The report, which amounted to a proposal to reinstate the officials who had been supplanted, was thus an exposition of the general Girondin belief that established law and properly ordered conduct ought always to prevail.

Seemingly surprised by this criticism of his conduct, Bourdon immediately and successfully demanded a delay.[86] Exclaiming that he had been attacked precisely because he was known to be a regicide, he promised to prove that he had acted correctly and that approval of the report would amount to the reinstatement of counterrevolutionary authority in Orléans. Although the insurrection that began in Paris the next day effectively ended this matter, the fact that Bourdon prepared a lengthy apologia, later published as the *Exposé des faits*, is an indication of the uncertainties of each hour. Similarly the first point that Bourdon made in this statement reflects the Montagnards' belief that critical situations must be met and mastered by vigorous action: where the committee had castigated him for acting imprudently on March 16, Bourdon replied that "le courage et le zèle d'un républicain" could only be intensified by obstacles and threats.[87]

In part a recapitulation of Bourdon's original *Déclaration* of March 17, the *Exposé* is also an indictment of the municipality of Orléans, here portrayed as guilty of the blackest perfidy. Supposedly privy to a plot to kill Bourdon, the administrative officers are also accused of doing everything possible to conceal the crime and to protect those most directly involved in it.[88] According to Armand Le Corbeiller, the only recent writer on this subject, all this is explained simply by Bourdon's own lust for blood, which was inflamed by his realization that the fate of those awaiting trial by the Revolutionary Tribunal depended on the Convention's decision about the municipality.[89] This strange hypothesis rests on the fact that on March 17

Bourdon, far from criticizing the municipality, had offered it profuse thanks: from this offer, Corbeiller argues that all his subsequent allegations must have been hypocritical fabrications.

This example of the way in which Bourdon has been condemned may be thought, at best, a considerable exaggeration. Even if all other indications that he was suspicious of the municipality immediately after he was wounded are set aside, contemporary evidence shows that he was remarkably anxious to move out of the town hall and that he insisted on dismissing the guards provided for him by the municipality. Moreover, his indictment of the municipality in May can be explained without postulating a thirst for blood. No doubt his distrust was confirmed and strengthened by what he was told while he stayed in Orléans, and thereafter his view was that of the Montagnards, for whom the establishment and the municipality of Orléans, as well as the Legislative Committee and the Girondins in the Convention, were all alike. If not overtly counterrevolutionary, such people were believed to be imperilling revolutionary France by resisting the drastic steps necessary to save it.

Moreover, although the "assassination" of Bourdon may well be seen as an illustration of the way in which reactionary violence was fostered by municipal apathy, the Montagnards saw it in terms of a conspiracy and a resurgence of aristocracy and royalism. Their triumph in the Revolution of May 31 consequently ended all hope that those who had been sent to the Revolutionary Tribunal might be released by legislative decree. Inevitably, too, the trial of these men between June 28 and July 12 was something of a sensation, for the tribunal was still relatively new, and only once before had it had to consider a collective case.[90] Bourdon himself thus again attracted attention, and, just as the trial is often cited as an early example of the arbitrary character of Revolutionary Justice, so is he condemned for what he did and what he did not do at this time.

What Bourdon did, willingly or otherwise, was to give evidence as the first witness for the prosecution. This appearance of the victim at the trial of those supposedly his assassins is so obviously ironic that the temptation to identify Bourdon with the whole trial is strong, but that identification is, at best, an oversimplification of the situation. After considerable inquiries, the three commissioners of the Ministry of Justice had named twenty-six men as being in one way or another involved in the disorder in Orléans. Of that number, twelve had been secured, and one, the wealthiest and noblest, Tassin de Montcourt, had surrendered himself as a matter of honour.[91] All thirteen were generally charged by Fouquier-Tinville, the dreaded public prosecutor, with participation in a conspiracy against liberty and equality,[92] one of the forms of counterrevolutionary activity that the tribunal had been created to suppress; moreover, because this conspiracy was presumed to have existed since September 1792, each prisoner's guilt might be established regardless of whether or not the man could be shown as one of Bourdon's assailants. Further, although the attack on Bourdon was seen as the principal manifestation of the alleged conspiracy, the relevant charge related to an offence against the state: "Ils ont outragé la représentation nationale en la personne de ses commissaires."

Bourdon's appearance in court thus seems to have been something of a formality, for the first necessity was to establish the fact that an assault had occurred. Beyond that fact, the evidence that Bourdon gave does not seem to have been particularly incriminating.[93] Although he recapitulated the substance of his original *Déclaration*, already embodied in Fouquier-Tinville's formal indictment of the accused, he was unable or unwilling to identify any of the prisoners as his assailants. In reply to questions, he also affirmed that the municipal officers had treated him well and that they could not have heard the disturbance in the courtyard outside the town hall. On the other hand, by stating in his evidence that he had been warned of danger as soon as he had arrived in Orléans, and that the men assigned to guard him after he had left the building were "soldats de l'ancien régime," he gave by implication some endorsement to the allegation of conspiracy.

The trial then continued for two weeks, during which time more than 200 people bore witness for or against the accused men. When it ended on July 12, four of the prisoners were acquitted and, as the law required, the nine found guilty were condemned to death.[94] This verdict occasioned great anguish to all in the court, for it is doubtful whether the mass of conflicting evidence contains conclusive proof that any one of the accused had actually struck Bourdon. On the other hand, it is likely that all the condemned were implicated either in the attack or in some attempt to protect those who had defied national authority. Indeed, the allegation made by some, that Bourdon and his friends in Orléans had agreed on a list of victims before he had left the city in March, seems to be wholly hypothetical. Rather, the whole process of inquiry, by the ministry's commissioners in Orléans as well as by the judges and jury in Paris, appears to have been more discriminating than might be expected. Nevertheless, the trial can only be seen as a political one, an affair of state in which the essential issue was whether an accused man had been wholeheartedly loyal to the Revolution.

From this perspective, Bourdon's appearance in court seems to have been formal and obligatory rather than reprehensible.

Substantially the same conclusion may be reached about Bourdon's silence on July 13, for some writers his worst offence in this sorry story. On that day, the business of the Convention was interrupted by the announcement of its president, then Jeanbon Saint-André, that the relatives of the condemned men wished to present a petition.[95] Even if later descriptions of the scene that ensued are rejected as unreliable, the moment remains as one of much emotion. Amid the cries and appeals of women and children, the petitioners begged that their husbands, sons, fathers, or brothers be reprieved long enough for their innocence to be established. One man offered to take his cousin's place on the scaffold, and the principal petitioner—perhaps Mme. Tassin de Montcourt—appealed for support directly to the generosity of Léonard Bourdon. But he said nothing, and, although some of the deputies were moved to tears, others demanded that regular business be resumed. As one of the latter said, "We are legislators, not judges." This unidentified speaker argued that the accused had been judged and sentenced after the most careful consideration and that, although the deputies might groan as men, their duty as legislators was to give first consideration to the welfare of the entire nation, which was perpetually exposed to upheavals arising from internal conspiracies. Moving that the business of the day be resumed, the speaker concluded: "Nous ne devons pas oublier ce que nous devons à la justice, et à la représentation nationale, indignement violée dans la personne d'un de nos collègues, exerçant la fonction auguste de commissaire représentant du peuple français." Upon this statement, the petitioners were ushered out of the chamber.[96]

That Bourdon was not peculiar in being inexorable at this time is also apparent in what seems to be a separate final episode. Although evidence of it is scanty, it seems that as the hour of execution approached some of the relatives of the condemned men succeeded in persuading Bourdon's sisters to plead their cause before the Convention. On this occasion, however, Jeanbon's announcement of their request for admission evoked only hostility.[97] If Bourdon was present, he said nothing; Robespierre, who remarked that they had come to solicit mercy for conspirators, moved that the day's agenda be continued; and in seconding this motion another deputy, probably Gaston of the Ariège, damned the approach as yet another right-wing intrigue: "Point de humanité, point de grâce pour les assassins des patriots!" The day's business was then resumed, and the men of Orléans went to their deaths wearing the red shirts that marked them as parricides. Remarkably it was on this day that Charlotte de Corday killed Marat and, as she believed, brought the Terror to an end.

Although Gaston's brutal comments may make even silence seem commendable, Bourdon was subsequently savagely attacked for not having intervened to save those who were then represented as the victims of his personal vengeance. To this charge, he replied[98] in 1795 by making two points, one of which was that there was not the slightest chance that any such intervention would have been successful. If that was his opinion, then it does more to explain than to justify his silence, for he was probably the one deputy who might have swayed the assembly. Nor, ideally, should the behaviour of public figures be determined solely by their estimates of failure or success. Much more telling is his further assertion that in July 1793 "Il ne s'agissait pas d'une injure personelle, mais d'un représentant du peuple lâchement et traîtrement assassiné." This conviction that any attack on a deputy, particularly a deputy to whom the authority of the Convention had been delegated, was tantamount to an attack on the Convention, and thus ultimately on the sovereignty of the people embodied in it, is indeed the salient feature of the whole affair. As Bernard and Guimberteau, the two deputies accompanying Bourdon on March 16, said in the letter that they wrote to the Convention that night, "La représentation nationale a été violée par ceux-la même qui sont chargés de la défendre."[99] Moreover, for all true revolutionaries, it was an article of faith that the Revolutionary Tribunal, which expressed the justice of the sovereign people, was infallible.

8

Further Frustration (July to September 1793)

*I*n the high summer of 1793, Léonard Bourdon may well have believed that his future was assured. As we have seen, in February his school was so well established that he could invite the public to a demonstration of his pupils' progress in studies ranging from the rights of humans to instrumental music and horsemanship.[1] Already, too, these youngsters had made their presence felt. In March (and in Bourdon's absence), they had gone to the Convention to present a civic crown for Dulac, the man believed to have saved Bourdon, "their father," from death in Orléans,[2] and, early in July, they told the assembly that, young as they were, they stood ready to fight for the republican constitution.[3] Moreover, Bourdon himself was a "patriot of '89," an ardent Jacobin, a regicide, and a Montagnard "martyr" with no small influence in Paris. Known as a man whose views on education and on the economy merited serious attention, he could confidently expect to play some substantial part in effecting the long-awaited triumph of true political liberty and social equality. Indeed, between late July and early September 1793, he was politically more active and more prominent than at any other time. Yet in retrospect new opportunities do not seem to have opened up for Bourdon in this period. Rather, it seems to have been the climax of his career, perhaps because he remained essentially a radical and an individualist. The more general assumption, that he was no more than an irresponsible associate of Hébert and other extremists, is much more questionable.

Silent when the relatives of his "assassins" appealed to the Convention in mid-July, Bourdon seldom spoke of the dangers of disruption that then threatened France. The royalists in the Vendée remained formidable, and, while frontier towns and fortresses were

---

Notes to Chapter 8 are on pp. 373-75.

compelled to capitulate to the allied armies, Bordeaux, Marseille, Lyon, and Toulon openly defied the Convention. It was, indeed, long impossible to be certain which departments had really accepted the coup of June 2,[4] and it was not until mid-July, when the relatively moderate members of the Committee of Public Safety were replaced by more ruthless men,[5] that the government ceased to tolerate possible disloyalty. In these circumstances, Bourdon's patriotic and revolutionary zeal was implicit rather than explicit, for he was seldom concerned with the generalities of policy. His acceptance of repression nevertheless became obvious when he spoke briefly about the Jura on July 27.

Shortly before that date, on July 19, the Convention had approved a decree, typical of the time, by which the *procureur-général-syndic* and the vice-president of the Jura, Ebrard and J-.F. Dumas, were ordered to appear at the bar of the Convention, and it had at the same time authorized the deputies then *en mission* in the area to treat all administrative opposition as rebellion.[6] The department, citing "the sacred right of resistance to oppression,"[7] had nonetheless remained intransigent: as Ebrard later wrote, there were already "too many examples of the injustice of the Revolutionary Tribunal."[8] On July 27, the Convention's Committee of General Security, almost certainly influenced by Claude Prost and by tales put about by Dumas le Rouge, proposed a more far-reaching measure of repression, which the assembly promptly approved, apparently in the mistaken belief that the men of the Jura were militarily allied with those of Lyon.[9] Supporting the proposal, Bourdon asserted that the administrators of the Jura should be punished most severely, for he alleged that they had initiated counter-revolution on May 24 (when they had invited others to join them in forming a shadow parliament under armed guard at Bourges).[10] In this, Bourdon indeed went beyond the committee, which had been concerned only with the Jura's response to the Montagnard's seizure of power on June 2 and which was still primarily interested in replacing obdurate officials by men on whom it could rely.[11]

Despite the intensity of the national crisis, however, the Convention gave much time in July and early August 1793 to educational affairs, with which Bourdon was deeply involved. Some such commitment was probably more normal for him than is now apparent in the records. One of the original twenty-four members of the Convention's Committee of Public Instruction, he had kept his position on June 6, when some members had been retired by lot, and J. Guillaume, the authority on the committee's work, notes that Bourdon was constant in his attendance at its meetings.[12] On occasion, this attendance also entailed specific duties, one example of which is his attempt on July 8 to obtain exemption from military service for those who taught deaf and mute pupils.[13] On July 10, however, his responsibilities were considerably increased, for he then also became one of a new Commission of Six, a body created at Robespierre's instigation to draft within eight days a single agreed proposal for national education.[14]

Because Robespierre himself was also one of the six until he joined the Committee of Public Safety on July 27, this period may be seen as one of considerable importance for Bourdon. Presumably Robespierre, who had supported Bourdon's own campaign to establish an experimental school, now expected to find Bourdon a staunch ally. Moreover, Bourdon was evidently included in the six as an enthusiastic advocate of residential education, and Robespierre, who had proposed the clause in the new constitution that stipulated that "Society must . . . place education within the reach of all citizens,"[15] was at this time convinced that the only way to honour that obligation was to ensure that all children attended boarding schools. Bourdon was thus compelled to define his attitude to the organization of universal education more precisely than in the past and to do so at the risk of alienating the most influential of all the revolutionaries.

His position was also made difficult by Robespierre's precipitate activity in promoting an extremely radical proposal. That haste is understandable, for from December 1792 onward a succession of reports and proposals about education had been presented to the Convention, and almost all the debates about them had been inconclusive. Similarly the appointment of a small commission of like-minded men is comprehensible, for such a group had already been successful in rapidly producing the new Montagnard constitution. Nonetheless, the methods that Robespierre adopted in his attempt to advance education seem dubious. Having proposed the formation of a select committee, he not only accepted an inevitably predominant place within it but also proceeded almost immediately, on July 13, to unveil and endorse in the Convention a ready-made plan for the future education of French children.[16] What is more, he apparently acquired and revealed this plan, known as the Lepeletier Plan, with little or no regard for the wishes of its true owner.[17] If in all this his behaviour was as high-handed as it now seems, then it may have been prejudicial to the success of the project as well as embarrassing to his colleagues.

Moreover, even in mid-1793, when ardour for the Revolution was most intense, the plan itself[18] was one that few deputies could accept whole-heartedly. Originally written by Michel Lepeletier, the Montagnard deputy assassinated on the eve of Louis XVI's execution, it was both hallowed by his "martyrdom" and permeated by his belief that nothing less than social revolution could make the French a truly united people. In particular, he was convinced that only drastic action could close the abyss dividing the children of prosperous people from those of the labouring poor. Asserting that every child really belonged to the republic, he proposed that all parents should be compelled to send their children at the age of five to boarding schools, which he called "maisons d'égalité." In these establishments, girls and boys would then be brought up separately for six and seven years respectively, and in them all alike would be adequately fed, clothed, and lodged. Their treatment, however, would be spartan, the food being frugal, the clothing coarse, and the bedding hard, and, although they would receive some rudimentary instruction, above all they would be acclimatized to manual labour, either on the land or in some form of domestic industry. Thus, the process of social levelling would also establish the foundation of national prosperity, a population inured to work. To this system, which Lepeletier believed could be enforced by depriving recalcitrant parents of their civic rights and subjecting unproductive children to some form of public humiliation, he almost casually appended various levels of more advanced instruction. For him, however, it was primary education that was of the first importance, and he presumed that even the first of the secondary levels would be appropriate only for one young person in fifty.

Draconian as this scheme was, Robespierre again gave it his enthusiastic support on July 29.[19] As spokesman for the Commission of Six, he then put the plan before the Convention as a draft decree, and in doing so he maintained that the vicious social system of the past had been so degrading that it had become imperative "to create a new people." The only substantial change he suggested was that participation in the new system should be optional for parents for the first four years of its operation. Yet even this suggestion, apparently a concession to criticism within the commission, was one that Robespierre avowedly made reluctantly and in the hope that it would be rejected. After this date, however, his commitment to the Committee of Public Safety meant that the task of promoting the plan, or something similar to it, fell to Bourdon as the commission's expert on communal education.

Bourdon's position was now indeed invidious. Whatever his own beliefs, he was charged with advancing a project so sanctified by Lepeletier's death and Robespierre's prestige that it seemed to be an integral part of the Revolution. Indeed, in the first debate,[20] on July 29, the deputy Lequino virtually equated opposition to the plan with deviationist disloyalty. Yet the proposal was manifestly unpopular: although few went so far as Piette, who said that the new schools would present "a hideous and disgusting spectacle," many deputies were anxious about the costs involved in creating and maintaining them. No doubt many also secretly shared the belief boldly expressed by the *abbé* Grégoire, himself a member of the Commission of Six, that family life (which was then commonly condemned for perpetuating the prejudices of the past) was essentially beneficial: "Nothing can replace the kindness of a father, the caresses of a mother." In this situation, Bourdon naturally sought some acceptable compromise, and in the process his name became so closely associated with the Lepeletier Plan that he is sometimes thought of as its champion. That view, however, is untenable.

Insofar as Bourdon spoke in favour of the plan, he no doubt did so partly by necessity and still more because he saw its appearance as a splendid opportunity to realize his own dream of nationwide residential education. To achieve that goal, however, he had to recommend the plan in principle yet promote major changes to it in accordance with his own ideas. Formulated long before, these ideas now reappeared as his *Projet de décret sur l'éducation nationale*,[21] written shortly before Robespierre's advocacy of the Lepeletier Plan on July 29.

The *Projet*, of course, shows that Bourdon was still an ardent advocate of residential schooling: it alone, his opening lines assert, could completely fulfil the purpose of education, the development of the physical, intellectual, and moral faculties. No matter how many day schools there might be, the distance that children would have to travel, and the help that their parents expected of them on the farms, would make their attendance irregular. Residence, however, would ensure that young people benefited by sustained full-time education, which, if freely available to all, would, as Lepeletier maintained, foster social equality while providing simple but sensible clothing, food, and accommodation for all alike. Unlike Lepeletier and Robespierre, however, Bourdon proposed that the new *maisons d'égalité* be established alongside the primary day schools previously proposed by the Committee of Public Instruction (in the Sieyès-Daunou-Lakanal Report of June 26, 1793).[22] Parents would then be able to choose which type of education they preferred or even to educate their children at home so long as periodic examination[23] proved satisfactory. Although Bourdon suggested a modest initial ratio of one boarding school to every thirty day schools, he anticipated that the superiority of the former would so increase public demand for places in them that the day schools would disappear altogether within fifteen years.

Nor, despite Bourdon's statement to the contrary, was this option the only difference between his project and that of Lepeletier. True, both men accepted child labour as a natural, desirable, and productive part of education, this indeed being for Bourdon the basis of his calculation that the new boarding schools would be financially self-supporting after ten years. On the other hand, although he was now (in 1793) more concerned than before with primary education,[24] he believed that it should begin at the age of seven, not five, and continue until fourteen, not twelve. Correspondingly he was less concerned than Lepeletier with manual labour alone, seeing instead the possibility of training adolescents in appropriate crafts. The curriculum that he proposed was also somewhat wider than Lepeletier's, and he went considerably further in showing how advanced technical and intellectual instruction could be made available to exceptionally proficient pupils in higher *maisons d'égalité*. More important still, he saw the new boarding schools as replicas of his own Société des Jeunes Français: each would have at least eight teachers so that the pupils could in some measure concentrate on congenial work; each would foster activity in learning, thus promoting general happiness; and all children above the age of ten would become members of a self-governing community, thereby fitting themselves morally and socially for free and responsible citizenship.

In sum, therefore, Bourdon's proposal may fairly be described as far more enlightened and humane than that inherited from Lepeletier and favoured by Robespierre. Significantly, where Lepeletier indicated penalties for those who were backward, Bourdon visualized prizes and bursaries for youngsters of promise. Moreover, Bourdon's whole approach was essentially empirical. Convinced that the best way to foster civic virtue was by promoting practical participation in communal life, Bourdon was confident that schools of the type he proposed would gradually prevail by virtue of their merits. In short, his attitude was very different from Lepeletier's belief that a far-reaching social revolution could be effected quickly by compulsory education and the rigid regulation of every child's life.

Bourdon's expectations were nevertheless soon to end in disappointment. Apparently his hopes were still high on July 30, for the *Discours* that Bourdon then delivered to the Convention combined praise for Lepeletier's proposals with the assurance that modifications to it, to be announced by the Commission of Six, would allay all anxieties. On this occasion, his speech, which incorporated much of the substance of his printed *Projet*, ended with a remarkably eloquent appeal for the acceptance in principle of residential education.[25] That step, he contended, would crown the deputies' endeavours by promoting the skill and industry of French people, and the whole world would soon be enviously emulating their freedom and good fortune.

In hard fact, however, the formal report[26] that Bourdon presented two days later on behalf of the Commission of Six was for him a hollow victory. It included many of the modifications that he desired, notably that general education should begin at the age of seven and finish at fourteen. Furthermore, the commissioners advised that attendance at boarding schools be optional, not compulsory. Yet this second departure from the Lepeletier Plan opened the way for the neglect and ultimate abandonment of Bourdon's more liberal project. Because the existence of an option implies that of an alternative, the commission proposed that primary day schools be established immediately. Nominally an interim measure, covered by the assumption that the day schools would be absorbed as the *maisons d'égalité* developed, this alternative to boarding schools was actually the more attractive to some of the six and to many, perhaps most, of the deputies. Seemingly less expensive and far less contentious, it might also be more easily reconciled with the eventual growth of a sophisticated system of secondary instruction. The trend of opinion is apparent in the ironic fact that Bourdon himself had to present in this report the recommendation that the first residential schools should initially house homeless orphans, "les enfants adoptifs de la patrie."

From this point onward, not surprisingly, Bourdon's interest in the establishment by decree of a network of residential schools diminished rapidly. After desultory discussions, which tended to focus on every farmer's need for the help of his whole family at harvest and in the vintage, the whole matter was again debated on August 13. Robespierre again supported the Lepeletier Plan ("Je n'hésite plus; elle doit être adoptée"),[27] but Bourdon intervened only briefly, now apparently to press for the creation of boarding schools in which there would be some real instruction of the children.[28] Danton then brought debate to a conclusion by moving the crucial compromise.[29] He praised Lepeletier, and he avowed that his own son really belonged to the republic; however, recognizing that principles had to be reconciled with circumstances, he proposed that the Convention should simply authorize the establishment of both day and boarding schools, between which parents could choose. The substance of this motion, occasionally and not unjustly called the Bourdon-Danton amendment, was then approved as a decree amid general applause. Nonetheless, on October 19 similar applause and approval marked Bourdon's notable proposal that the decree establishing "maisons communes d'éducation" be repealed.[30] In Guillaume's view, Bourdon's apparently inconsistent conduct was mainly due to his perception that the deputies' opinions had evolved,[31] but it is more likely that Bourdon was glad to be rid both of Lepeletier's compulsion and of a compromise by which boarding schools would become more like hostels than schools.

Whether or not all the consideration given at this time to residential schooling was, as Professor Palmer has concluded, an aberration from the mainstream of development in French educational thought,[32] it was certainly detrimental to Bourdon's interest. Bourdon had in fact been fortuitously associated with an extremely rigid revolutionary proposal, and just as this association damaged his reputation, so too it effectively ended any possibility that his more enlightened ideas might be systematically applied beyond the confines of his own school. Nor is it unlikely that his attempt at once to praise and to modify the Lepeletier Plan marked the beginning of Robespierre's hostility toward him. Although their opposition at this time was not overt, each man had some reason to suppose himself thwarted by the other, and Robespierre was certainly not one to forget any suspicion of disloyalty to his own vision of the Revolution.

Nor was Bourdon thwarted only in his hopes for a new form of national education. At Arcis-sur-Aube, Danton's birthplace, a statue bears words taken from that great orator's speech to the deputies on August 13, 1793[33] ("Après le pain, l'éducation est le besoin suprême du peuple"), and Bourdon was constantly concerned with both of these needs. Remarkably, even while he was striving to establish a national system of liberal residential education, he was also making a fresh attempt to end France's economic ills without resorting either to complete freedom or to unlimited regulation of trade. Once again, however, disappointment was to follow.

As we have seen,[34] since 1789 Bourdon and his father had singly or jointly submitted varying versions of the latter's proposal, the *Projet nouveau* of 1788, to a succession of municipal and national committees, and on all these occasions the plan had been set aside. Yet even after May 2, 1793, when popular pressure had compelled the Convention to impose a measure of price control, the first *maximum*, the Bourdon plan remained in being, and in August there was good reason to expect that it might be brought forward successfully. By then, the

Convention was constantly confronted with the fearful problem of ensuring that bread and other essential commodities were reasonably priced and actually available to the population. Ever-increasing prices, shortages that in some areas almost amounted to famine,[35] and the concomitant danger of further revolutionary violence were fast making new legislation imperative.

Although the harvest of 1793 was a good one, dry and windless weather so delayed milling and river traffic that, just as in 1789, the normal period of shortage in early summer was unusually prolonged. By midsummer, moreover, it was obvious that the first *maximum* had been a failure. Ignored in some areas, it was applied only half-heartedly in others. At best, the maximum price of wheat was determined by local authorities, and this price varied so considerably between *départements* that many producers either kept their grain in their barns or moved it to some distant market to obtain the highest price possible. Local scarcities then led directly to further dislocation of distribution, for the wagon trains and barges carrying grain were often halted and ransacked by hungry people. Other factors, notably extensive requisitioning by commissioners from the armies and the principal towns, and above all the devastating fall of the *assignat* to 20 percent of its face value, also contributed considerably to the critical situation in August.[36] By then, most of the deputies in Paris, men who had accepted price control in May only as a temporary expedient, were hoping either to restore freedom to the grain trade or at least to avoid still more regulation of it.

Speaking in the Convention on August 6, Bourdon asserted that reorganization of the trade had become all the more urgent because speculators were already buying up stocks of newly harvested corn.[37] Whatever the truth of that, the time was certainly propitious for his attempt to convince the assembly that the creation of a nationwide network of public granaries (*greniers d'abondance*) would both relieve the immediate crisis in subsistence and give the grain trade an enduringly effective structure. In all probability, too, this attempt was the result of his own initiative. On July 31, Robespierre, resisting a call for the repeal of the *maximum*, had said that the first step must be the adoption of "des dispositions plus sages," and he added that the Committee of Public Safety was currently considering a proposal that would both frustrate conspirators and assure abundance and public prosperity.[38] This phraseology suggests that the proposal was Bourdon's, and on August 6, when the plan was presented as a *rapport*[39] to the Convention, Bourdon said explicitly that he had submitted it to the Committees of Agriculture and of Public Safety and that it was by their wish that he was reporting it to the deputies for fuller discussion.

Bourdon's address on this occasion was particularly confident. Although the attitude of the committees may now seem to have been somewhat reserved, Bourdon could claim that he was speaking on their behalf, and many who heard him would have known that his proposals had been warmly applauded at the Jacobin Club the previous evening.[40] He could also clothe them in the mantle of revolutionary respectability as the outcome of twenty years of research and reflection by his father, "a republican septuagenarian who had been imprisoned in the Bastille before becoming an Elector of Paris in 1789."[41] Moreover, in 1793 Bourdon could legitimately appeal to recent experience as proof of his contention that France had vacillated too long between freedom and regulation of trade and that neither of these positions had ever led to anything more than high prices, costly subsidies, continual shortages, and perpetual economic and political instability.

Bourdon then argued that the taproot of all these ills was acceptance of the pernicious teaching of those economic theorists who had advocated absolute freedom of trade. Blinded by their devotion to dogma, these "sophistes modernes" had failed to appreciate that in the real world every absolute principle must be subject to modification: in practice, their chimerical freedom had afforded unlimited opportunities for abuse by speculators, monopolists, and hoarders, whose activities had constantly to be curbed by new controls and increasingly savage penalties.[42] Such ad hoc legislation had nevertheless proved utterly inadequate. Even in times of abundance, exploitation of the freedom to export grain had led directly to scarcities in France, which sudden embargoes had come too late to correct; moreover, no particular expedient could ever overcome the widely varying needs of different *départements* or reconcile the generally conflicting interests of rural producers and urban consumers. Because the latter, above all, had to eat thrice a day, it was high time to recognize that property right must yield to people's right to life and that economic freedom, like any other freedom, must always be corrected by laws dictated by the general interest.

The plan that Bourdon then put to the Convention was substantially that previously noted here as his father's *Projet nouveau*. His exposition of it, however, suggests that the experience of the years 1789-93 had given him greater appreciation of social realities, and he wisely discarded statistics in order to secure acceptance of the plan in principle. Asserting that simple ideas were preferable to abstract theories, he declared that, because people live naturally in society, there must be some natural way in which the subsistence of society can be assured. As the Revolution had made the people of France one family, the natural path for the nation to follow was that of the thrifty farmer, who would set aside sufficient grain for the needs of his household and his farm before selling his surplus produce. All that need be done, therefore, was to appoint a representative body, the national equivalent of the husbandman, and afford it both a monopoly of foreign trade in grain and the authority to establish and supervise public granaries in every district and military headquarters throughout the country. As in the *Projet nouveau*, the central body could then so regulate sales and purchases abroad that all the granaries would always be open and well stocked; moreover, because it would determine fixed and fair prices for local purchases and sales at the granaries, the price of grain at the public markets would necessarily become approximately the same. In short, monopoly control of foreign trading would enable the nation to ensure that an adequate supply of grain was always available to everyone, and national participation in free trade within France would act as a constant corrective to abuses.

Despite his conviction that the adoption of these measures, and the accompanying abolition of all existing military and local commissions of requisition, would rapidly restore national prosperity by reducing prices and stimulating trade,[43] Bourdon was well aware that they could not be implemented quickly enough to avert the crisis that he believed to be imminent. He therefore followed his principal draft decree with a subsidiary emergency proposal, which he described as a revolutionary step. To expedite the establishment of stocks in the granaries, the new national body must at once resort to compulsory purchase. Excepting only sufficient grain for each farmer's needs for his household and for seeding, all that remained of the harvest of 1792, and two-thirds of that of 1793 itself, should be acquired in that way. Granting that even this approach would not make the new system fully effective for three months, Bourdon claimed that the decrees he was suggesting would be immediately beneficial, because all who held grain in store would naturally hasten to sell a commodity no longer likely to rise in value.

Whatever merits there may have been in these various proposals, Bourdon's recipe for the immediate relief of popular hardship and the speedy restoration of general prosperity was soon forgotten. Apparently most of the deputies were unwilling either to accept it or to reject it outright, and those historians who have given it attention have regarded it as impractical. Bourdon's confidence in the integrity of local farmers and administrators, and in the ability of a few central commissioners to assess the resources and needs of every part of France, has indeed been dismissed as naïve.[44] In Mathiez's view, too, the Convention was more devoted than the Jacobin Club to the doctrine of free trade,[45] and despite all Bourdon's disclaimers his plan undoubtedly involved a substantial increase in intervention in the economy by the state. Certainly the Convention procrastinated. On August 6, it authorized the printing of Bourdon's *rapport* but adjourned any consideration of it, and the next day it similarly avoided approving an alternative plan, proposed by Chabot for the Committee of Agriculture, by which prices would be reduced by subsidies financed through further taxation of the rich.[46] Then on August 9—ironically just when Bourdon was beginning a two-week term as one of the Convention's secretaries—it accepted without debate a decree, proposed by Barère for the Committee of Public Safety, that effectively stripped Bourdon's plan of all substance.[47]

Among other things, this decree, a composite measure, sanctioned the creation of *greniers d'abondance* but failed to provide for their organization. In effect, local authorities were authorized to establish public granaries in every administrative district of France, and the committee was afforded an extraordinary credit of 100 million livres to purchase grain for them. Nothing, however, was said about the way in which supplies were actually to be acquired, about the regulation of exports and imports, or about the creation of a central directing commission. On August 21, Bourdon indeed made one further attempt to remedy these deficiencies by presenting the Committee of Agriculture's more detailed proposals for the organization of the granaries,[48] but this effort was also futile; although a central commission of twelve now appeared (Bourdon had originally suggested twenty-four), hostility to the existence of any such body immediately led to the adjournment of debate. All was consequently left to the initiative of the Committee of Public Safety, which in fact made no use of its new credit, and to the local districts, which were generally unable to acquire grain for storage and unwilling to trust anyone with control of what little they had.[49]

Substantial parts of Bourdon's plan for the effective organization of the grain trade, then the most vital factor of the French economy, were in fact implemented piecemeal in response to the exigencies with which the committee and the Convention were daily confronted. On September 11, for example, the harvest of 1793 was requisitioned, and, most remarkably of all, October 22 saw the establishment of the Subsistence Committee. That body was created to impose national control of the distribution of supplies as well as to supervise the operation of price controls, and in time it became one of the largest and most effective of the institutions of the Revolutionary Government of 1793-94. In none of this, however, was free trade tempered by the adoption of a coherent overall plan. Rather, it was whittled away, haphazardly and under popular pressure, by a combination of price controls and requisitioning. In this process, Bourdon's vision of a national network of well-stocked granaries vanished just as had his hopes for nationwide residential education: where the latter probably led only to the expansion of a few orphanages, the former apparently produced no more than a handful of isolated and neglected barns.[50]

* * *

Preoccupied though Bourdon was for much of August 1793 with these economic and educational plans, he was also involved in the political crisis that developed in Paris as the month progressed. Angered by the failure of the Montagnards and the Committee of Public Safety to effect any obvious change in the situation of France, people in the capital were constantly urged to further action by inflammatory journals such as Hébert's *Père Duschesne*. By the end of the month, moreover, bread was so scarce that, as one observer reported, it could sometimes be obtained only after seven hours of waiting in line.[51] News of the surrender of Toulon, which reached Paris on September 2, then precipitated the *journée* of September 5, when the Montagnard government was almost overthrown by angry demonstrators.

As a Montagnard and a Jacobin who still had some substantial following in the heart of revolutionary Paris, Bourdon's position was certainly ambiguous at this time. Indeed, even Robespierre, by now the most outstandingly effective defender of the Committee of Public Safety, had at times to bow before the storm in the Jacobin Club and give some sanction to the demands of extremists. It is consequently easy to assume that Bourdon was now becoming not simply a terrorist (i.e., a supporter of very strong government by the Montagnards) but also a Hébertist (i.e., an associate of Hébert and an agitator intent on replacing the existing government by one willing to condone extensive repression by popular violence). As always, however, such assumptions are more easily made than substantiated, particularly when they refer to a man like Bourdon, about whom the evidence is slight.

His position seems to have been more significant than any presumption of affiliation can suggest. It is, for example, interesting that from August 8 to 21 Bourdon was one of the Convention's secretaries and that from September 4 to 18 he was president of the Jacobin Club.[52] Although these offices, regularly renewed by election, were not positions of power, tenure of them is an indication of the balance of forces at any particular time. Thus, because Bourdon was at least a notable radical in the Convention, his secretaryship may be a measure of the growth of dissatisfaction among the rank and file of the Montagnards; his presidency of the Jacobins at a critical hour is indicative of the swing to extremism in the society; and his election to both of these offices probably marks the acceptability at that time of a man known to have ties both to the Montagnards and to the *sans-culottes*.

Further assessment of the nature of Bourdon's participation in political life in August depends on brief entries in the records of public proceedings about many miscellaneous matters. Although these entries once again usually relate more to individuals than to generalities, they show that as a revolutionary Bourdon remained inflexibly hostile to those whom he regarded as actual or potential enemies of the people. This hostility was apparent on August 2, when Chabot, speaking for the Committee of General Security, denounced Rouyer and Brunel, two deputies who had improperly prolonged the period of their mission to southern France.[53] Chabot cited letters to show that these men had, at best, been too sympathetic to the rebellious authorities in Bordeaux and Lyon; some deputies then asked that the accused be allowed to speak, but Bourdon declared that their correspondence was sufficiently incriminating and demanded their arrest, which was immediately effected. In mid-August, similarly, he was one of many witnesses in the protracted trial of General Custine by the Revolutionary Tribunal.[54] Spectacularly successful in the conquest of the Rhineland in 1792, Custine (a *ci-devant* count) had been forced to surrender Mayence to the Prussians in July 1793, and he was soon accused of connivance with the enemy. Because he was also suspected of despising civil authority and aspiring to dictatorship, his trial reflected the revolutionaries' distrust of noble officers and their determination to subordinate military to civil power. Bourdon, who disclaimed all knowledge of the principal charges against the general, simply told the court that in the Jura he had seen a letter that a young volunteer serving with the army of the Rhine had written to his mother. According to that letter, Custine had addressed his men just before the loss of Wissembourg, telling them that he was not to blame if they were short of everything they needed, for the fault was that of "la foutre Convention." Second-hand as this story was, the incident was not improbable, and Bourdon's account of it was neither irrelevant to the trial nor discreditable to him personally.

Characteristically, too, his most constant concern was with those who had been wounded, widowed, or orphaned in the course of the war but who had been neither recognized nor granted any financial aid. In one such instance, Bourdon drew the Convention's attention to the plight of a boy aged ten, "a soldier of the republic" who had accompanied his father on two campaigns and been wounded when his father was killed. At Bourdon's request (a precursor of many others), this lad was presented with a sword by the Convention's president, Hérault de Séchelles, and afforded admission as a subsidized pupil to la Société des Jeunes Français.[55] Another illustrative episode is Bourdon's success in securing a place in the Invalides for an elderly captain, Jean Cécire, who had commanded a detachment of the National Guard at Lons-le-Saunier until he was imprisoned by the "federalist" administrators there. Wounded while escaping from captivity, this man had apparently sold his watch, his last possession, to pay his way to Paris, which he had finally reached in a state of destitution.[56]

Presumably because he had been approached personally, Bourdon presented a succession of cases of this sort,[57] supporting each one on its own merits. Naturally he was not always successful: for example, he failed in his attempt to ensure that the property of French refugees from Spain be exempted from the law by which the property of France's enemies was subject to confiscation.[58] Sometimes, too, he was probably at fault, as when he tried to obtain a reprieve for a supposedly innocent man who had been condemned to death for complicity in the forging of *assignats* and whose case, as Bourdon was soon told, had been irrevocably decided by the verdict of a jury.[59] Nonetheless, he was undoubtedly sympathetic to the sufferings of ordinary people, and this sympathy must certainly have made him increasingly aware of deficiencies in the administration of the law.

These defects Bourdon apparently hoped to rectify, at least in some areas, by clarifying the responsibilities and emphasizing the accountability of ministers. Thus, on August 6, when it was reported that a reactionary group had intimidated patriotic people in a township in the Drôme, Bourdon demanded that the Committee of Public Safety investigate the affair and that the Minister of the Interior be required to give a report about how certificates of citizenship were issued and what he had done to replace officials who had handed them out too freely.[60] Again, on August 27, he secured the Convention's approval of an order by which requests for relief from widows and orphans were transferred from the assembly's committee to the Ministry of the Interior.[61] For him, however, such steps were certainly subordinate to effective supervision of the ministers and all other officials by the patriots in the popular societies. As Bourdon asserted in the Jacobin Club on August 5, its members were interested not in obtaining office for themselves or their friends but only in maintaining surveillance of officials; the Society, he added, must always reserve its right to scrutinize the selection of ministers.[62] This, of course, was both orthodox Jacobinism and an opinion closely akin to the *sans-culottes'* attitude toward all officeholders.

By mid-August 1793, there was indeed a general conviction that much more vigorous and effective government was necessary for France. In Paris itself, the *sans-culottes* were deeply disappointed by the failure of the Revolution of May 31 to June 2 to effect anything more than the expulsion of the Girondins from the Convention, a purge that seemed to have led only to extensive provincial revolts.[63] They also knew that in early June their committees had been superseded and their own demands evaded. Those demands had included more taxation of wealth and correspondingly more measures of relief for the poor; more price controls (the "general maximum") and severer punishments for hoarders and speculators; and, to ensure that such measures were effective, the general replacement of unreliable officers and officials by *sans-culottes*. Furthermore, they had hoped to see the establishment of popular militias or revolutionary armies, so that patriotic townsmen might scour the countryside in search of concealed enemies and hidden stores of grain.

By the end of July, however, very little had been won. The Constitution, although acclaimed, had still to be approved; price control remained restricted and ineffectual; the Law of July 26, by which hoarding became a capital offence, was in fact inoperative; and a Parisian revolutionary army had no more than nominal approval. Not surprisingly, therefore, the populace's demands were voiced ever more stridently as the national situation deteriorated during the summer. Moreover, the official repudiation of Jacques Roux and the death of Marat opened the way for ambitious and unscrupulous agitators such as Hébert, so that still more violent courses became accepted in the streets as panaceas. To overwhelm rebels, royalists, and foreign foes, there needed to be a *levée en masse*, a measure of universal conscription equated with a general rising of all patriots against their enemies. To intimidate all traitors, many urban revolutionary armies must be created and accompanied by tribunals and portable guillotines; the

Revolutionary Tribunal itself must be greatly expanded so that more conspirators might be condemned more quickly; and in the first instance notable prisoners of state such as Marie Antoinette and the Girondins, "J.-P. Brissot et ses complices," must be speedily tried and executed. There also developed an undercurrent of demands for the reorganization of the executive ministries, if not of the Committee of Public Safety itself, and even for some further purge of moderate deputies in the Convention. The implication in all this was that even the rump of a representative form of government should be subject to the dictates of direct popular democracy.

Bourdon, however, does not appear now as he did twelve months earlier, as a prominent spokesman for the Section des Gravilliers and for the *sans-culottes* in general. On the contrary, there is no obvious evidence by which he might be related to any organized activity by the sections. No doubt this relative obscurity is due in part to the difference in his own situation. Unlike Hébert, who, as a popular journalist and the deputy *procureur* of the Commune, could pose as a champion of the people, Bourdon was a deputy and a Montagnard, one of those whose government was being criticized and jeopardized. Similarly the sections could not now concentrate all their anger on one unfortunate king, and those who participated actively in their meetings and work— as distinct from the poorer people of Paris in general—were usually more concerned to goad the Commune about the shortage of food than to press the Convention to adopt one or another of several extreme measures.

Moreover, the Section des Gravilliers was now so rent by internal dissension that it could hardly have coordinated projects with others. Although Jacques Roux had been disowned by the Jacobins, the Commune, and the Cordeliers Club, he continued to represent himself as Marat's natural successor and to assail authority in his journal, the *Publiciste de la République Française.* He also remained potentially powerful in Gravilliers, where his adherents, strongly entrenched in the general assembly, were at odds with those whom historians commonly call the party (or henchmen) of Bourdon, men who controlled the bureau of the assembly and its crucial Civil and Revolutionary Committees until mid-August. There was then, on August 18, "une véritable révolution sectionnaire."[64] Amid prolonged tumult, those still present in the assembly succeeded in electing Roux as its president, in appointing new secretaries, and in arresting some subordinate figures. This elevation of a man recently denounced by Robespierre[65] as a paid agent of France's enemies evoked a swift reaction. Responding to protests from the section's committees, the Commune ordered the arrest of Roux, who remained in prison until August 27: even so, his following in Gravilliers remained strong, and he continually added his voice to those attacking the government. In none of this does Bourdon appear in person; however, if those who opposed Roux in Gravilliers, notably Truchon "la Grande Barbe," were indeed "of Bourdon's party," then he and they were also making common cause with what may be called the establishment of the day, the Jacobin Club and ultimately the Montagnards and the Committee of Public Safety. Far from being an extremist, he seems in Gravilliers to have become the mentor of those who opposed extremism.

In early August, Bourdon also appears as one of the government's supporters in the Jacobin Club, which for some time had been deeply divided. Some members then thought it vital to sustain the Convention and its Committee of Public Safety in the immense tasks involved in overcoming all the perils that threatened the Revolution. In increasing numbers, however, others shared the popular conviction that more extreme social and political measures were imperative and that the Convention must be made to adopt and implement some or all of the *sans-culottes'* demands.[66] In this complex and inconstant situation, at least Bourdon's initial position is clear. As already noted, on August 5—the day on which Bourdon presented the society with his plan for the development of *greniers d'abondance*—he emphasized that members must be concerned with the supervision of ministers, not with securing office for themselves.[67] Three days later, when the formal announcement of the ratification of the new constitution was imminent, he made his views much more explicit. The Society being deeply involved then in a discursive debate about the best means of saving the country, Bourdon declared that those who challenged the Convention to prove its purity by dispersing in favour of a new legislature were enemies of the republic. "Maintenant," he said, "il ne faut que redoubler de courage, travailler sans relâche à affermir la Constitution, et, au mois de mai prochain, il nous sera permis de penser à la législature prochaine."[68] Evidently believing that the nation's most urgent need was for much more efficient and reliable administration, he proposed that the Convention be presented with an address calling for the exclusion from office of all nobles, the renewal of all departmental administrations, and the restriction of eligibility for bishoprics to priests whose patriotism was proven by marriage.

On this occasion, Bourdon's specific proposal was that the address be presented by "tous les envoyés," these being the commissioners of the primary assemblies who were then assembled in Paris. These men, who came from all loyal parts of France, had been chosen by their assemblies to report the acceptance of the new constitution by the plebiscite held in July, and—like the *fédérés* of 1792—they were almost by definition the most notable revolutionaries in provincial France. Certainly their presence in Paris throughout August revived ardour for the Revolution, and when they marched on August 10 in the great Festival of Unity and Indivisibility, encircling the entire Convention and linked together by a tri-coloured ribbon, their participation demonstrated the potential invincibility of a reunified nation.[69] Moreover, they soon made it clear that they expected far stronger direction from the capital. The pressure that they exerted certainly contributed to the Convention's acceptance on August 16 of the concept of the *levée-en-masse*,[70] and it was indeed their principal spokesman, Royer, a delegate from Châlons-sur-Saône, who first voiced the demand on August 30 that Terror be made the nation's highest priority: "Qu'on place la terreur à l'ordre du jour! C'est le seul moyen de donner l'eveil au peuple et le forcer à se sauver lui-même."[71]

Although there is no firm evidence to show that Bourdon was in direct personal contact with these men, such a development would not have been uncharacteristic of him. He certainly seems to have been interested in them and to have seen in them a force by which the Convention might be moved to act more effectively. When petitioners went to the Convention on August 6 to ask for aid in obtaining a meeting place for the commissioners, he was quick to support Danton's friend Delacroix in questioning the supposed delegates' credentials.[72] Because the Jacobins had already made their hall available to the men from the primary assemblies, he suggested that the newcomers, one of whom he recognized, were really seeking to establish a rival assembly, and these men were in fact repudiated by those in the Jacobins the next day. In mid-August, more interestingly, he seems to have encouraged, if not instigated, an attempt to convene a meeting of the provincial commissioners with the Jacobins and the delegates of the sections of Paris in order to determine the best means of national salvation. When Robespierre, who was then presiding, opened a discussion in the Society on August 14 to decide how such a meeting might be arranged, Bourdon promptly pointed out that action was urgent because many of the commissioners were preparing to return home.[73] He also made several practical suggestions about how word of the meeting could be conveyed to the sections by dawn the next morning.

This episode, which may be compared with an earlier speaker's hysterical suggestion that the people should rush on the enemy while sheltered behind screens of chained aristocrats,[74] had no immediate sequel. Indeed, it seems to have been the last occasion before September 4 on which Bourdon took any public part in the increasing popular agitation. Even supposing that he may then have been working quietly in Gravilliers to stiffen the resistance to Jacques Roux, his reserve is remarkable for one whose high hopes of extensive educational and economic reform were then being brusquely set aside by the Convention. Moreover, these last two weeks of August were ones in which all but a few of the Jacobins temporarily accepted the necessity of extreme measures.[75] Beset by delegations from the Cordeliers Club and the *enragé* Society of Revolutionary Women, the Jacobin Club was also inflamed by Hébert, who sometimes rallied to Robespierre in order to crush Jacques Roux but more often sought to outbid Roux in attacks on the government. Such attacks could now be masked as demands that the new constitution be put into effect, and such was their force that on August 30 even Robespierre was compelled to avow that the people's call for vengeance could not be disregarded.[76]

It was in these circumstances that from August 28 onward the Jacobin Club renewed its attempt to rally the sections, and those provincial commissioners who (like the militant *fédérés* of 1792) remained in Paris, so that all could act together in presenting their demands to the Convention. A central committee was in fact formed, but the problem of drafting proposals that all could accept delayed agreement from day to day.[77] Whether or not all this amounted to the preparation of a new revolution, it is now generally agreed that on September 4 the poor of Paris, angered and alarmed by the evil tidings from Toulon, and driven to desperation by the shortage of food, took matters into their own hands. Strike action soon led to the appearance of considerable crowds in the streets adjacent to the Section des Gravilliers (rue du Temple, Saint Avoie) and thus to a great concentration of people on the Place de Grève.[78] The Commune, the Jacobins, and all their allies had then no alternative but to follow the tide and hope to turn it to some political purpose or personal advantage.

Bourdon's reappearance at this critical hour is not surprising, for he was invariably responsive to a political emergency. His election as president of the Jacobin Club on the same day does not, however, serve to identify him as an irresponsible extremist. On the contrary, he may well have been the man most generally acceptable, being one known to want much more vigorous government but not a change of government. Nor is his conduct on September 4-5 inconsistent with that position.

Initially, and presumably as president, Bourdon led[79] a delegation of some twenty members of the Society to the Maison Commune (as the Hôtel de Ville was now called) on the evening of September 4. By that time, the people, who had long been repeatedly demanding bread ("Du pain! Du Pain!"), had made it clear that they were not satisfied by the news that the Convention had already approved the principle of general price controls and was even then discussing the question of supplies. Both the *procureur*, Chaumette, and his deputy, Hébert, had then made fiery speeches, the effect of which was to identify the Commune with the movement and to direct it toward the attainment of an immediate political objective: the people must march the next day to the Convention and demand the creation of a revolutionary army. If Hébert had his way, then each section of this army would be accompanied by a portable guillotine. Typically the Jacobin delegation then arrived in time for Bourdon to give an assurance of Montagnard support and to associate the Jacobin Club "with all the measures ordered by the people in association with their magistrates."[80] The demonstration was also endorsed by all the more radical sections, but Jacques Roux, one of those initially delegated by Gravilliers to the central committee, had been replaced.[81]

According to Barère, the scene in the Convention the next day, September 5, was one of prolonged delirium. In this scene, Bourdon— now present as a Montagnard deputy—was certainly an active participant. Indeed, he had previously urged the assembly to complete the process of reorganizing the Revolutionary Tribunal so that the prisons could be cleared of the guilty and space could be made for others who were still at liberty.[82] The reorganization of the tribunal (to ensure that two of its sections could be constantly and simultaneously at work) had just been completed when Pache, the mayor of Paris, arrived at the head of an immense procession. The deputies then heard a powerful address by Chaumette, whose call for the immediate creation of a revolutionary army with its own guillotine concluded with his oft-quoted summary of the people's demand: "Des subsistences, et, pour en avoir, force à la loi!"[83] That demand was then championed by one of the most fierce Montagnards, Billaud-Varenne, and in this, as in his later call for an immediate purge of all sectional security committees, he was strongly seconded by Bourdon. The latter declared that a report about local authorities was urgent because good patriots had been wrongfully arrested in many parts of France, and he unhesitatingly insisted that the revolutionary army be paid for by the rich and empowered not only to seek hidden grain but also to expose and punish public enemies.[84] He did not, however, follow Billaud-Varenne in calling for a new governing Committee of Public Safety.

Although no further interventions by Bourdon are recorded, his presence amid the turmoil that prevailed for the remainder of the day's proceedings[85] may be assumed. All had then to be done amid the people, who had soon flooded into the chamber, mingling freely with the deputies. After Jeanbon Saint-André had done his best to gain time for the committee, Danton evoked renewed enthusiasm by calling for the revolutionary army, for the making of munitions in sufficient quantity to provide every citizen with a musket, and for the limitation of the assemblies of the sections to two evenings in each week, for which those who attended should be paid. The climax of the day then came with the arrival of delegates speaking in the name of the Jacobin Club and the sections of Paris (again including Gravilliers). Renewing the demand for a revolutionary army with punitive powers, these delegates also called for the exclusion and internment of all those nobles who held military or civil office. The extent of Hébert's influence on the society is still more apparent in the demands for the establishment of twelve revolutionary tribunals in Paris, for the immediate trial—and blood—of Marie Antoinette and the Girondins, and for the recognition of Terror as the order of the day.[86]

Of all these various demands, only that for the creation of a Parisian revolutionary army (of 6,000 men and 1,200 gunners) was formally enacted at the end of the day, when Barère finally succeeded in placating the crowds by announcing it and promising that further decrees would soon follow. But if Terror was not officially adopted on September 5, acceptance of it was implicit. It is, for example, significant that the Commune had Jacques Roux arrested again that night. Many of the measures called for during the day had indeed been previously adopted by the Convention in principle, so that they were soon decreed in detail. Thus, the arrests of suspects, sanctioned on August 11 and (as Bourdon's anxieties about the arrest of patriots indicate) immediately and indiscriminately effected at the local level, became the notorious Law of Suspects on September 17. Again, nationwide price control, approved in principle on September 4, became the general maximum on September 29. The *journée* of September 5 nevertheless did more than impart a new urgency to the legislative process. It amounted, in fact, to a partial defeat for the Committee of Public Safety and more particularly for Robespierre, who had opposed the movement in the Jacobins until the last moment. The concessions that the committee made enabled it to survive, but its insecurity compelled it to accept Billaud-Varenne and Collot d'Herbois, deputies who personified violent courses, as new members. Although in practice both men proved to be able administrators, their presence on the Committee symbolizes the fact that intimidation, latent in the Montagnard government since the Revolution of May 31, was henceforth openly accepted as the legitimate means of Revolutionary Government.

For this development, Bourdon, a minor but not an insignificant figure, must bear a share of the common responsibility. More particularly, his fervour for the creation of the revolutionary army, a force that soon became the terror of the countryside, mars his record. Explicable by his determination to ensure that the people of Paris were fed, this zeal still identifies him as a revolutionary and a man implacably hostile to all who were supposed to be the people's enemies. There is, however, no reason to regard Bourdon at this time as an associate of Hébert, for he was neither an advocate of unrestricted violence nor an irresponsible assailant of the Montagnard government. Indeed, although he often tried to remedy abuses and inefficiencies in day-to-day administration between late July and early September, he continued in increasingly difficult circumstances to sustain that government. Even on September 5, when he took some part in forcing it to implement popular policies, he did not challenge its existence or question its composition. Moreover, despite the frustration of his hopes for enduring economic and educational change, he apparently remained unaffected by personal ambition, and, if he was something of an exhibitionist, his interest in the welfare of individuals afflicted by misfortune is no less commendable for that. Overall Bourdon seems in mid-1793 to have been a man much more restrained and responsible than has been supposed.

9

The Approach to Extremism
(September to December 1793)

$\mathcal{J}$f Bourdon's position in the summer of 1793 as a Jacobin with strong but potentially conflicting ties both to the Montagnard government and to the *sans-culottes* of central Paris was ambiguous, it became still more delicate in the months that followed. Nor did Bourdon survive that time unscathed. Forward in the development of "dechristianization," the revolutionary assault on organized religion, he had certainly incurred Robespierre's displeasure by the end of December, and it is often assumed that he either was or soon became one of the extremist faction known as the "ultras" or Hébertists.

The difficulty in determining the validity of that assumption is a measure of the complexity of a situation in which it was almost impossible for any politically active person *not* to incur suspicion. Recognition of the legitimacy of Terror necessarily implied a still sharper definition of the familiar distinction between "the people" and "the enemies of the people," so that any departure from an acceptable revolutionary attitude became more dangerous than ever. Indeed, even a record of strict conformity scarcely ensured security, for positive and successful activity in promoting the Revolution was also expected of all true patriots. As Bourdon himself put it when speaking in the Jacobins on September 27 about the composition of the staff of the revolutionary army, "ce n'est pas assez de n'être pas connu pour un mauvais patriote, il faut encore que de bonnes raisons fassent présumer qu'on est capable et digne d'occuper une semblable place, et de remplir toutes les conditions qui y sont attachées."[1]

After September 5, furthermore, the path of those who, like Bourdon, sought to sustain both the Revolutionary Government and popular democracy became ever more precarious. Initially activists in the

---

Notes to Chapter 9 are on pp. 375-79.

Jacobins, in the Commune, and in the sections strove to reinvigorate all administrative and deliberative bodies by pressing them to purge themselves of everyone whose conduct was questionable. This "purification" was at first in the interest of the government, which was presumed to have sanctioned it on September 5, but those who encouraged it for too long were themselves in peril, for the process soon threatened the very bodies through which the Committee of Public Safety was slowly consolidating its control of France. Nor could the possibility that the popular purge might be extended to the Convention and to the Committee itself be forgotten.

Misdirected zeal, no matter how well intentioned, also became increasingly dangerous because the emergency measures forced on the Committee on September 5 actually served to increase its power enormously. While a vast bureaucracy grew up to organize the national economy and the national war effort, the Law of Suspects (decreed on September 17) afforded the Revolutionary Government and its agencies, notably the local security committees (*comités de surveillance*), the ability to treat all criticism as counterrevolutionary. Nor was this opportunity neglected. When Danton's friend Thuriot called on the Convention on September 25 to end the growth of regulation and repression, Robespierre made it clear that the Committee would not tolerate such challenges: "Whoever seeks to debase, divide or paralyze the Convention is an enemy of the country, whether he sits in this hall or not. Whether he acts from stupidity or from perversity, he is of the party of the tyrants who make war on us."[2] Soon afterward, too, the Law of October 10 not only increased the Committee's power to act independently but also declared the government of France to be "revolutionary until peace."[3] Thus, the Constitution of 1793 was formally set aside, and any consideration of the possibility of replacing the Convention with a newly elected legislature became illegal.

That this situation, in which political power was monopolized first by one party and then by some members of that party, promoted the growth of factions is not surprising. Despite the almost hysterical fervour with which people expressed their hopes and fears, politics naturally became increasingly artificial when the questions that really mattered most were administrative. Because the revolutionaries' security demanded the elimination of all potential threats, and the organization of victory demanded the effective employment of reliable men, considerations of detail and conflicts about personalities overshadowed issues, on which all were at least nominally united.

This is not to say that the groups that emerged to the right and the left of the Committee of Public Safety were devoid of all principle. On the one side, the "cintras" or Dantonists gradually came to represent the view that the Terror, which the Committee was determined to maintain under its own control, ought at least to be relaxed. Conversely the "ultras" or Hébertists became identified with the belief that the Terror should be intensified and enforced by the people themselves as part of the all-out war that had to be waged against supposed oppressors. Today the second opinion seems to be artificial, for hindsight suggests that by mid-October the French armies had begun to win the war actually being fought. Defeated at Hondeschoote on September 8, the British were forced to abandon Dunkirk; besieged and bombarded, Lyon was compelled to capitulate on October 9; and, after beating the Austrians at Wattignies on October 16, the French were able to reoccupy Maubeuge. At the time, however, the Hébertist attitude was no doubt more defensible than it seems in retrospect. Yet, whatever their justification, both the moderate and the extremist positions were compromised by the self-interest of many of those who espoused them. As responsible participation in public life became more hazardous, many men became increasingly involved in personal feuds and competition for the offices that might give them and their friends security, influence, and even illicit personal profit. Political affairs, confused by the obscure activities of such interest groups, were then complicated by belief in the "foreign plot": foreign agents, it was alleged, had successfully corrupted a number of notable deputies and popular leaders, involving them in an extensive conspiracy to discredit and destroy the Revolution.

The situation thus became one in which almost anyone might be supposed to belong to one faction or another. Such identifications have also proved convenient for historians. They are nonetheless suspect, for even when unanimity was becoming imperative the revolutionaries still believed that it was attainable only through the free expression of sincerely patriotic opinion. Moreover, the presumption of affiliation with a faction, which implies predetermination in attitude, obscures the true colour of political life at the time. In reality, the record of public debates reveals more of fragmentation than of faction: although small groupings appear, individuals abound, and it is in the exchange of views and recrimination between individuals that their characters and actual reactions to events appear most clearly.

It is in fact in the immediate aftermath of the excitement of September 4-5 that Léonard Bourdon seems to have been most inclined to extremism. That is probably also true of the whole Jacobin Club, where sympathy for militant radicalism remained strong until the measures forced on the Convention on September 5 were actually implemented.[4] Bourdon himself was particularly interested in the protracted process by which revolutionary bodies of all sorts were purged of those considered inefficient or politically unreliable. Indeed, as early as September 6, when discussion in the Jacobins was interrupted by a minor disturbance, he remarked as president that it was time for the Club to purify itself by scrutinizing members' conduct,[5] an inquisition that did not actually begin until November 26.[6] The next day, in the Convention, he sought assurance that the purge would extend to all the departmental administrations throughout France,[7] and in the Club on September 9 he supported Hébert's attack on some of the Convention's committees.[8] On that occasion, Bourdon even demanded that the Convention be pressed to expel all those deputies who had voted for a referendum about the decision to execute the king. Declaring that these men's influence had increased because many committed Montagnards were away on missions, he urged that the *appelants* be replaced by those elected as their substitutes. This proposal, as well as his still more extreme suggestion that every department in France should have its own revolutionary army, were rightly rejected by the Club as apt to increase existing dangers, even though "Le martyr de la liberté ne doit pas être soupçonné de vouloir causer sa chute."[9]

Nevertheless, nothing here indicates association, as distinct from similarity of view, between Bourdon and Hébert; as has well been said, "Hébertism was only an extreme form of Jacobin orthodoxy."[10] Indeed, although Robespierre had done all that he could to block Hébert's extremism at the end of August, it was not until early November that a breach between the two became obvious.[11] Even in September, Bourdon's militancy was tempered by his respect for Montagnard authority. Although he certainly wanted the departmental administrations— which he had always distrusted—to be purged, his immediate purpose on September 7 was to ensure that information about what the deputies *en mission* were doing, and about the guidance given to departing delegates from the provincial primary assemblies, was made available to the Convention.[12] In this, as in his opposition to the further demand that the deputies *en mission* should themselves be purged, he seems at bottom to have been trying to help the government to thwart counterrevolutionary activity. Similarly he was unusually tentative in suggesting some relaxation of the limitation imposed on September 5 on sectional assemblies,[13] and, whereas the most militant *sans-culottes* disliked the government's inauguration of system-atic conscription, Bourdon was obviously pleased to tell the Conven-tion that one of the petitioners who had objected to this conscription, as less egalitarian than the *levée en masse*, had subsequently acknowl-edged his mistake.[14]

It was, however, in the Jacobin Club that Bourdon spoke most fre-quently and forcefully. Like many other members, he apparently became less militantly radical as measures such as the general maxi-mum and the Law of Suspects were enacted and enforced. He nonetheless seems to have been convinced that the establishment of stronger government had made the role of the Jacobins in the Revolu-tion more important than ever. Thus, on September 27, he was promi-nent in insisting that all those who might lead the Parisian revolutionary army should appear in person before the Club, and, as we have seen, he then expressed strong views about the qualities expected of them.[15] In practice, when the choice of Mazuel as an adjutant-general was in question, he proved more revolutionary, main-taining that "c'est moins les talents que le patriotisme qui sont néces-saires aux chefs de cette armée";[16] moreover, when Mazuel subsequently declined to accept the office, Bourdon may have tried to secure the appointment for a man from the Faubourg-du-Nord, a protégé of his brother, Marc-Antoine Bourdon de Vatry.[17] Still, Léonard certainly believed that the Club, and indeed its affiliates throughout France, should scrutinize and approve all who held or aspired to hold any public office. As he said on November 3, decrees authorized the Jacobins to do so, and he even reproached the members for not being sufficiently assiduous in fulfilling their duty.[18]

As certainly, Bourdon shared the general Jacobin conviction that the Club should aid both the government and the people by exposing abuses. Complaints by individuals frequently led to the appointment of commissions of inquiry, such as that created at Bourdon's behest on October 5, when it was asserted that many officials at the Ministry of Marine did not hold *certificates de civisme*, which were then required of all citizens as proof of their identity and patriotism.[19] Equally alert to allegations that real patriots were being arrested as suspects, Bourdon also called on October 9 for the appointment of commissioners to investigate these reports by visiting the prisons.[20] He then said that his own doctor, who had treated his family for thirty years, had recently been imprisoned for three weeks, this apparently being one of many instances in which local revolutionary committees had arrested men who owed money to one or more of their members. Furthermore, as the head of the commission in question, he reported its recommendations early in November. Whenever the commission, which would be permanent, was satisfied that a man of sure patriotism was being held in prison, the commissioners would personally visit the Committee of General Security and remain there until a decision was reached. They would also welcome information about "aristocrats libres," and the Jacobin Club was assured that "la commission montrera autant d'activité pour les faire arrêter que d'ardeur à faire relâcher les patriotes victimes de l'oppression."[21]

On the same day, November 3, Bourdon was angered by the revelation that senior officials of the National Treasury were required to deposit sums said to be as much as 500,000 livres as cautionary money. That practice, which would of course prevent any impecunious patriot from holding an important position, roused him to an impassioned plea for equality of opportunity. Cautionary money, he said, was a relic of the past, when it was supposed "que sans argent on ne pouvait avoir de vertu, et qu'il n'y a que des riches qui en aient." In the republic, however, "La véritable cautionnement, c'est la guillotine; il faut qu'un homme réponde sur sa tête de la fidelité de ses opérations." Here again Bourdon secured the appointment of a commission to draft a petition to the Convention to ensure that henceforth there should be only "cautionnements de patriotisme."[22]

Several of the various minor matters that Bourdon raised or remarked on in these earlier autumnal weeks similarly reflect his concern for equality. Thus, he deplored the apparent tendency of the Revolutionary Tribunal to allow notable persons to brief abler and more experienced lawyers than any poor and obscure prisoner could employ.[23] That complaint was unhappily evoked by Collot d'Herbois's sneers about those who defended Marie Antoinette ("cette femme"), but Bourdon's sudden indignation about an order made in the Meurthe for the deportation of Jews seems to have been both spontaneous and disinterested.[24] More revolutionary, if still essentially egalitarian, was his demand that young men who evaded conscription be imprisoned,[25] and so was his support for the Jacobins' drive to expel supposed royalists from the transport office (*l'administration des charrois*), where employment meant exemption from military service.[26]

Although there is no doubt about where Bourdon's sympathies lay, none of his interventions in debate suggests that he ceased to be independent. As president of the Jacobins, he indeed wrote the letter that on September 13 expressed the Club's complete confidence in Rossignol,[27] the *sans-culotte* goldsmith who had become the commander of

all the republican forces in western France—and who had been summarily dismissed on August 18 by one of the deputies on mission there,
François Bourdon de l'Oise.[28] That dismissal provoked much recrimination in Paris, for it crystallized dispute about the relative virtue of
revolutionary zeal and professional competence. François Bourdon,
who was recalled to Paris, even dared to assert that, had it not been for
the presence of people such as Rossignol, the war in the Vendée would
have been concluded long beforehand.[29] He drew closer to the Dantonists, and Léonard Bourdon, who certainly remembered the quarrel
with François about his own election in 1792, probably wrote his letter
in support of Rossignol with enthusiasm. He does not, however, seem
to have taken part in the attacks made on his namesake, and the letter
itself was written for, and accepted by, the Jacobin Club, then particularly radical in temper.

More illustrative of his own outlook and political position are the
comments that Bourdon made on the activities of the attractive
actress Claire Lacombe and la Société des Femmes Révolutionnaires,
of which she had become the moving spirit.[30] By September 1793, that
society, composed of women who were nothing if not revolutionary,
had adopted policies closely akin to those of Jacques Roux, and it was
consequently fast falling from favour among the Jacobins. On
September 13, as president of the Club, Bourdon assured a deputation
from the *société* that they could rely on the Club's support in calling on
the Convention to order the arrest of prostitutes and other "aristocratic" women;[31] his assurance, however, applied only to occasions
"quand il s'agira de coopérer au rétablissement des moeurs at à l'affer-
missement de la liberté." Three days later, Lacombe, no mean orator,
attempted to respond from the public gallery to attacks on her and
another *enragé*, the journalist Théophile Leclerc, and Bourdon then
rebuked her from the chair.[32] Her behaviour, he declared, substantiated the charges just made against her, for it was criminally unpatriotic
to trouble the peace of "une assemblée de gens qui ont besoin de
délibérer froidment sur les intérêts du peuple." Although (illegally)
arrested on this occasion, Lacombe continued to campaign until
October 28, when her society was disrupted and she herself was publicly thrashed and humiliated by the market women of Les Halles,
whose dislike of the revolutionary women's attempts to force all
women to wear a *tricolore* cockade was matched only by their resentment of exposures of their own petty infringements of price control.
Being that evening at the Commune (where he was seeking support
for a plan to improve the distribution of bread to the poor), Bourdon

was at best unsympathetic to the victims of this violence.[33] Although he conceded that the revolutionary women meant well, he thought that the Jacobins should warn them to observe the law and to avoid causing disturbances by forcing others to adopt distinctions in dress. That women's societies in general were officially banned two days later was part of the repression of all *enragés*;[34] that Lacombe and Bourdon really seem to have had much in common was probably coincidental; but that her activities were feminist only by implication, whereas his remarks constantly presupposed masculine superiority, was typical of the time.

Probably the most reprehensible of Bourdon's activities during these weeks was his appearance on October 29 as one of the witnesses in the trial of the Girondins by the Revolutionary Tribunal. Their trial, and that of Marie Antoinette, had been one of the principal demands made by the Jacobins on September 5, but it was also a step that the government was most reluctant to take. Apart from humanitarian considerations, which need not be discounted,[35] such reluctance is readily understandable, for a trial of those whom the Montagnards had forcibly supplanted could easily have become one in which their own conduct and power were called into question. However, because extremists represented the condemnation of the Girondins as a crucial test of the government's resolution, public proceedings eventually became unavoidable. The conviction of the accused then being imperative, the prosecution adopted a course that was fast becoming familiar: as Hébert had been urging,[36] the prisoners were charged with participation in a conspiracy.[37] This presumption meant that, if anything said or done by any one of them could be regarded as contrary to the actual course of the popular revolution, the offence could be imputed to all who had been associated with him, however indirectly. The exploitation of this device was indeed particularly necessary because the accused really had little in common: of the twenty-one deputies in court, only nine had been expelled from the Convention on June 2, 1793.[38] The others, who had been arrested subsequently for various offences against the regime, were simply the most obvious offenders who could be produced.

Once the indictment of "J.-P. Brissot et ses complices" had been read, the tribunal heard a succession of witnesses for the prosecution.[39] Like Bourdon, most of these men were, or had been, members of the Commune of Paris. None of them was a revolutionary of the first rank, and none of the others' names inspires confidence or enhances Bourdon's reputation. His evidence,[40] given on the sixth day of the trial, was nevertheless much briefer than the long diatribes pronounced by men such as Hébert and Chabot. It was also a singular amalgam of general allegations about "the faction" and more specific charges against deputies who had so far succeeded in evading arrest.[41] According to Bourdon, in 1792 "the faction" had first sought to prevent the insurrection of August 10 and had then tried to thwart the people by delaying recognition of Louis's deposition. Similarly, on the eve of the Revolution of May 31, 1793, when the Commission of Twelve had attempted to post armed guards around the Convention, the guards had been drawn from the most reactionary sections of Paris. More generally still, Bourdon apparently[42] asserted that discreditable (or unsuccessful) occasions in the calendar of the Revolution—the September Massacres, the investment of the Tuileries on June 20, 1792, and the disorders of March 10, 1793—had all been deliberately provoked by the conspirators so that the people might be more plausibly maligned.

To substantiate these charges, Bourdon related his own meetings with Pétion, a proscribed fugitive in October 1793. To Bourdon, Pétion's pusillanimous behaviour as the mayor of Paris on August 10-11, 1792, had later seemed explicable only as proof that Pétion was responsible for ordering the National Guard to fire on the people and that he had even been privy to the murder of Mandat, its commander, who might have revealed his wickedness. Bourdon also spoke forcefully of the hostility that he had encountered when he had met the Legislative Assembly's emergency Committee of Twenty-One in mid-August 1792 and the National Convention's Commission of Twelve in May 1793. Specifically, however, he supported one of his allegations, that "the faction" had tried to pack the Convention with men of its own choice, only by reference to Brissot's recommendation of Louvet to the Electoral Assembly of the Loiret. Furthermore, he even declared that Vigée, the only one present in court among those whom he named when he referred to the Commission of Twelve, had ordered the dispersal of the conservative force as soon as he had heard about it. Although the accused had little opportunity to reply to any of these assertions, Brissot acknowledged his recommendation of Louvet but claimed that it had been made only in private correspondence, and Vigée agreed that as far as he was concerned Bourdon's account of the episode in May was correct.

Apparently, therefore, Bourdon's participation in this trial, which was abruptly closed by the condemnation of all the accused the next day, "the jury being sufficiently enlightened,"[43] was more restrained and less discreditable than might be expected. As a convinced revolutionary, Bourdon doubtless believed that all political differences, and all the difficulties that he and like-minded men had experienced, were the outcome of malevolence. His reluctance to identify those actually present with such iniquity is thus notable. Moreover, he presented the court with a letter that one of the accused, Jacques Boilleau, had written to him asking him to speak in his defence.[44] In that letter, Boilleau avowed that he had finally recognized the reality of a conspiracy, to which he, a true Montagnard, had long been blind. Whether or not Boilleau had intended this feeble plea, promptly treated as a damning admission, to be made public, it is remarkable that his letter was sent to Bourdon. Presumably he had seen in him a revolutionary of some repute who even in poor company still retained some standing and integrity.

Nevertheless, on November 14, when P.-L. Manuel was similarly tried and condemned by the tribunal as one of the same "faction liberticide," the evidence that Bourdon gave for the prosecution was obviously hostile.[45] In this instance, he was no doubt more personally resentful of what he saw as a betrayal, for in July 1792 he had been prominent in demanding that Pétion and Manuel, then suspended from their offices as mayor and *procureur* of Paris, should be reinstated.[46] Manuel, successful in saving the lives of several notable people during the prison massacres in September 1792, had subsequently condemned those murders, openly avowing that he had ever since been tormented by the question "la liberté serait-elle meilleure à espérer qu'à posséder?"[47] So far had Revolutionary Justice sunk, however, that the principal charge against him in November 1793 was that he and Pétion had incited the massacres in order to intensify provincial hatred of Paris.[48] Trivial in itself, Bourdon's evidence lent some colour to this charge, for Bourdon alleged that before the massacres began Manuel had ignored, if not concealed, proof that the royalists were about to break out of the prisons. Another of Bourdon's assertions was at least more politically realistic, for it related to the rioting and repression that had occurred in Orléans that September, soon after Bourdon had done all he could to organize and stimulate popular activity there. Sent to investigate the situation, Manuel and other deputies had sought to restore stability by supporting the local administration. Although they had condemned the selfishness of the very rich, they had ascribed all disorder to agitators in the pay of royalist agents.[49] To Bourdon, however, the essential point was that Manuel had failed miserably to respond to the appeals of patriotic people who had been penalized and imprisoned after the riots.

Although these court appearances show that Bourdon remained fully committed to the Revolution, his activities for some time after the *journée* of September 5 generally seem to have been more miscellaneous but less purposeful than usual. No doubt many ardent revolutionaries found it difficult to adjust to a situation in which their own government was taking more and more control of the life of the nation, and Bourdon himself also had to accept the emasculation of his own cherished projects for reform. Even in educational affairs, those ever closest to his heart, he seems to have been temporarily at a loss.

Thus, some inconsistency is apparent in his comments about colleges, on which he presented a report early in September. As the opening of the new academic year approached, various urgent appeals for financial help had reached the Committee of Public Instruction, and these appeals had almost automatically been passed to Bourdon.[50] Speaking for the committee,[51] he recommended that the payment of professors and the bursaries of students be subsidized until the Minister of the Interior could act on more comprehensive information from local administrations generally. The only proviso was that the Declaration of Rights and the Constitution be included in the curriculum at each college. Almost simultaneously, however, a different note appears in Bourdon's indictment on September 6 of the principal of the Irish College in Paris, a man who had already been arrested as *incivique* and whom Bourdon accused of corrupting the students.[52] This college had indeed long occasioned strife in Paris: because its priests and its property were exempt from the laws that afflicted the Church of France, it had become a haven for nonjurors.[53] On the other hand, many of the seminarists who remained within this supposed centre of conspiracy had adopted revolutionary ideas: one of them, William Duckett, indeed appears at intervals as Bourdon's personal secretary.[54] Certainly Bourdon's sympathies were with the students whenever they came into conflict with their superiors, and he now secured approval for his proposal that the Convention should confirm the arrest of the principal and revive an old regulation by which the students were entitled to elect their own directors. Still more strikingly, when the general question of providing higher education again came before the Convention on September 15, he abruptly declared that what was needed was not some master plan but practical steps to cleanse existing colleges of the "aristocracy and barbarity" that still predominated within them.[55]

Although Bourdon spoke only briefly in this particular debate, his participation reinforces the impression that he was at this time a man in search of some new raison d'être. As J.-M. Couppé (of the Oise) told the Convention on September 16, the extraordinary Commission of Six had split into two groups of three, and neither group was prepared to modify its views about national education above the primary level.[56] That the commission was then increased in size and finally abolished altogether on October 6 is here incidental to the fact that one of the two obdurate groups consisted of Bourdon, Lakanal, and the *abbé* Grégoire.[57] These three men advocated the adoption of an organized and graduated system of national secondary and higher education, their plan being akin to that once proposed by Condorcet; however, the other group, which included Couppé, feared the creation of a new form of aristocracy, an intellectual elite, and thus maintained that national education should be restricted to the primary level. In this situation, Bourdon's group certainly encouraged, and probably contributed directly to, the development by the Department of Paris of a plan similar to their own.[58] This "Paris Plan," presented to the Convention on September 15 in the name of the Department, the rural districts, the Commune, the sections, and the popular societies of Paris, is indeed striking. Assuming that agreement about universal primary education had been reached, the delegates asserted that the provision of more advanced education was a matter of great urgency. Specifically they called for the creation of a three-tiered system in which the lowest level would provide instruction "indispensable for artists, artisans and workmen of every sort,"[59] and, as the corollary of this system, they called for the immediate suppression of all colleges and university faculties throughout France.

These proposals were twice debated: the Convention, almost as deeply divided as the commission, accepted them with enthusiasm on September 15 and then suspended its decree on the following day. Lakanal and Grégoire both spoke in favour of the plan, but the only intervention by Bourdon was his brief condemnation of the barbarity that he saw in the colleges.[60] Although he has been called the leader of his group in the Commission of Six,[61] it is unlikely that he was entirely in favour of a plan completely concerned with the practical and intellectual aspects of human development, and (as noticed above) he generally preferred practical action to theoretical planning. On the other hand, the proposals that Bourdon had put forward in July for residential schools had foreshadowed the growth of secondary education and had even provided for the development of departmental *lycées* and a national *lycée* of advanced learning in the château of Versailles.[62] What is more, because he had long believed that practical training should be an integral part of education, it is not surprising that his condemnation of the colleges concluded with a call for their replacement by schools of arts and crafts. Although it was not until October 19 that he proposed a repeal of the decree that had authorized the establishment of "maisons communes d'éducation," by mid-September he seems to have accepted technical rather than residential schooling as the most feasible way to develop national education. Such a change of emphasis would indeed have been natural at a time when immense efforts were being made to mobilize the material resources as well as the manpower of France for war.

More immediately, Bourdon apparently found some satisfaction in renewed concern for his own school. On November 8, in an episode typical of the time, the Commune of Paris welcomed a deputation from la Société des Jeunes Français and granted the request of its orator, a child of seven, that the society be given the flag that it had long been promised.[63] Coming forward, Bourdon then declared that "il mettra tous ses soins à former le coeur de ses élèves, et que ce devoir lui est plus cher que la vie." The next day, too, the Convention, which had just suppressed many military schools (but not those of Bourdon, Liancourt, and Pawlet), decided that the Jeunes Français should receive the orphaned children of men killed in the defence of France, regardless of rank.[64] Although this new recruitment involved a process of recommendation by the sections,[65] it gradually led to a substantial increase in the number of those for whom Bourdon was responsible. If the size of the school remained constant in the meantime, at about sixty bursaried pupils and "a few" private *pensionnaires* between March and December 1793,[66] its composition was clearly becoming very different from that of the select establishment that Bourdon had tried to found in 1789. From time to time, too, he still took advantage of opportunities to add particularly "patriotic" youngsters,[67] and in all probability his pupils, who had long successfully run their own printing press, now had access to still more workshops, so that instruction in a growing variety of trades was becoming available to them.[68]

In the autumn of 1793, moreover, Bourdon, who was probably finding political activity frustrating, discovered a new and increasingly absorbing outlet for his energies. On September 19, the Convention heard an account of how eight men of Marseille, condemned to death by the rebellious authorities there, had extolled the republic and sung the Marseillaise as they went to the guillotine. Bourdon then promptly proposed a decree[69] by which their courage would be commemorated by the erection of a monument in the Tuileries gardens, and the

Committee of Public Instruction would take all the necessary steps to collect and record acts "de patriotisme héroïque qui caractérisent les Français républicains, afin qu'aucun d'eux ne soit perdu pour l'instruction de la jeunesse." According to the *Moniteur*, Bourdon had called still more specifically for the recording of heroic deeds "pour servir à la composition d'un livre élémentaire d'instruction publique."

Soon after, when the Commission of Six had been abolished and the Committee of Public Instruction reconstituted, Bourdon became a member of that section of the committee to which supervision of the compilation was assigned.[70] At first, however, progress was slow. As spokesman for the section, the *abbé* Grégoire secured the Convention's approval on September 28 of a proposed approach,[71] but it was not until November 13 that the Jacobin Club heard a letter from him requesting that he be given appropriate details of the Society's activities in the Revolution ("les traits éclatants de l'amour de la patrie qu'a produits cette société").[72] Nor was this letter well received. The request itself was welcomed, but Grégoire's participation was not. One member remarked that Grégoire had ceased to be a Jacobin, and Bourdon (who may well have thought that Grégoire was at fault in concerning himself with collective actions) nastily remarked that the committee had asked the Society to recommend for this work a man well known for both *civisme* and ability. It was, however, François Bourdon of the Oise, not, as is sometimes supposed,[73] Léonard Bourdon, who declared that Grégoire "voulut christianizer la révolution" and "prétendit que Jésu-Christ avait prophétisé qu'il y aurait des Jacobins." Furthermore, when Grégoire eventually presented a draft of the first number of the *Annales Héroïques* to the committee on December 7, it was rejected as being insufficiently simple in expression, and he was then replaced by Bourdon, who no doubt had been his principal critic.[74]

The preparation of successive issues of this publication (renamed and remarkably successful as the *Recueil des actions héroïques et civiques des républicains français*) occupied much of Bourdon's time in the first four months of 1794. Here, however, François Bourdon's mockery of Grégoire is more immediately pertinent, for it was in November 1793 that the revolutionaries attempted to destroy all established religion in Paris. In this movement, rather misleadingly called dechristianization, Léonard Bourdon was actively involved for a time. He has consequently been regarded as one of those "adventurers on the margins of power"[75] who were most zealous in promoting it in their own interests. The speech that he made in the Jacobin Club on November 6 has indeed been seen as the signal for a preconcerted assault on the church, and he is sometimes said to have been one of those who visited Gobel, the metropolitan bishop of Paris, later that night, terrifying him so much that he abdicated the next day.

His participation in some secret scheme nevertheless seems intrinsically improbable. In general, dechristianization, which developed almost simultaneously in different parts of France, is now seen as neither "truly spontaneous" nor "imposed from above" but as a "collective reaction . . . which arose directly from the development of the French Revolution"[76] in the winter of 1793-94. Already "highly politicized," this movement became organized to some extent, but it is now thought futile to attempt to establish any precise chronological sequence of cause and effect for it.[77] More particularly, however, some specific stimuli to the growth of the movement in Paris are apparent. Early in October, the Commune followed the Convention in approving the introduction of the new revolutionary calendar, which has well been called the most anti-Christian act of the whole Revolution,[78] and the procureur, Chaumette, welcomed it because its festivals would eliminate "the least trace of fanaticism."[79] Later that month, after his collaboration with Fouché in Nevers, Chaumette ensured that news of events there became known in the capital, and, although he sought to suppress social evils such as prostitution, he also introduced measures meant to curtail the civil activities of the clergy and to confine all religious worship to the interior of churches.[80] Nor did he hesitate to describe priests as "hypocrites qui s'emparent de l'homme à sa naissance et ne le quittent qu'au tombeau."[81]

Coincidentally or otherwise, Bourdon thus had good grounds for declaring on November 6 that each day brought new reports of renunciations of office by priests who sincerely wished to return to the "principes éternals de la raison et de l'amour du peuple."[82] He also claimed that towns and even whole districts were daily repudiating their acceptance of antiquated superstitions. Although in this matter he probably exaggerated, it is true that Paris followed rather than anticipated the development of dechristianization in some other departments, and it is particularly significant that earlier on November 6 the Convention had explicitly approved the action of one commune, Mennecy, in the Seine-et-Oise, in dismissing its curé. Barère and the Dantonist Thuriot had then moved decrees by which any commune was authorized to adopt or renounce whatever cult it wished,[83] measures that effectively destroyed the Civil Constitution of the Clergy of 1790.

In this context, it seems superfluous to suppose that Bourdon's address to the Jacobins that evening was part of some prearranged plot. Bourdon spoke, or at least claimed to speak, in support of petitioners from the Section des Gravilliers, who apparently hoped that the Jacobins would endorse a call on the Convention to end the payment of priests' stipends by the state. Distinguishing constant and courageous patriots from those people so blinded by the beliefs of their upbringing that their prejudices must be respected, he condemned some priests as counterrevolutionaries, declaring that these "soldiers of Lafayette" must be struck down. Others, however, he merely mocked, maintaining that they must be either imbeciles, who alone could accept such absurdities as the Immaculate Conception, or rogues who deliberately propagated nonsense in order to perpetuate their own privileges. Paris should therefore follow the example of smaller communes by giving the baubles of the churches to the National Treasury; the Jacobins should press the Convention to stop subsidizing men who were either dangerous or useless; and people who were not prepared to honour the divinity simply by being happy, as natural law commanded, should content themselves by hiring halls in which they could worship as they wished.

This speech may have served to solidify opinion; it may even have provided men more hypocritical than Bourdon with an opportunity to launch a campaign as spectacularly as possible; however, in itself it seems to be sufficiently explicable as the spontaneous reaction of a naturally impulsive man to a rapidly evolving situation. Moreover, the views that Bourdon expressed were those that he had long openly avowed. In Orléans in 1792, he had rejoiced to see the destruction of the statue of Joan of Arc, "a grotesque and ridiculous representation of a virgin at the knees of an imbecile king," both of whom looked toward "a crucified man indecently stretched across a woman's lap."[84] In Dijon in March and in Lons-le-Saunier in April 1793, he had unhesitatingly demanded the pursuit of recalcitrant priests as public enemies and agents of Austria.[85] On the other hand, while publicizing his school he had constantly emphasized the supreme importance of fostering civic morality, he had also recognized his pupils' right to freedom in religion.[86] Still more strikingly, in the proclamation that he had issued in Lons-le-Saunier in mid-April,[87] he had explained that "la révolution est de toutes les religions sages" because it was concerned with the happiness and camaraderie of all people, whose equality was implicit in its principles. All true patriots were then told to remember that persecution augmented misunderstanding and thus promoted religious fanaticism. Rather, they must prove by their conduct that they had no wish to destroy religion: although those priests who incited disorder and even civil war must be dealt with severely, religious opinions in themselves "ne peuvent jamais être le prétexte d'aucune arrestation; chacun est libre dans son opinion ... et ceux qui, à raison de ce, voudrait inquiéter un citoyen, seraient eux-mêmes dans le cas d'être poursuivis commes des perturbeurs du repos publique."

It is understandable that Bourdon's attitude should have become more vehement and impassioned at the end of 1793, when the strictest conformity with the observance of equality was obligatory, and when the strength of resurgent Catholicism in the Vendée was still manifest even as the republican armies overwhelmed the area. Essentially, however, nothing in the views that Bourdon voiced on November 6 suggests that they were adopted to promote the manoeuvres of a political faction. Specifically the allegation in question is that he was acting in the interest of various minor militants (the German baron "Anacharsis" Cloots, Desfieux and Dubuisson, Pereira and Proli), most of whom were of foreign origin. These men claimed to speak for a shadowy "Central Committee of the Popular Societies" of the sections of Paris, bodies that had been created to circumvent the restriction of sectional assemblies to two meetings a week, and it is true that a deputation from this committee also presented a petition to the Jacobins on November 6.[88] Moreover, like the Section des Gravilliers, these men apparently called, as did Bourdon, for an end to the payment of priests. Although this coincidence is striking, it is not conclusive proof of connivance, for in the course of his speech Bourdon spoke of the Gravilliers petition as one that had just ("vient de") been heard,[89] whereas that of the committee was read slightly later. All that can really be said of this obscure matter is that, insofar as the popular societies, which the Revolutionary Government regarded with suspicion, really represented popular democracy, Bourdon was probably sympathetic to them and may have been prepared to collaborate with their spokesmen on this occasion.

This is not to say, however, that Bourdon had no personal interest in discrediting priests. Speculative as it is, there is some possibility that he was then at odds with Grégoire, the bishop of Blois and the personification of the constitutional church, about the preparation of the Annales héroïques. More obviously, he still had to re-establish his own and the Jacobins' influence in the Section des Gravilliers. Although Jacques Roux, who never renounced his priesthood, remained in prison, he contrived to publish his journal until sometime in November, and until then his followers in the section, the "jacquesroutins," continued to distribute his writings and to agitate for his release.[90] Although Albert Soboul, the leading authority on developments in the sections, does not substantiate his statement that dechristianization in Gravilliers "was the work of Léonard Bourdon,"[91] it is surely not by chance that the nine leading "jacquesroutins" were arrested on November 26, when the campaign against the priests of Paris was at its height.

More positively, Bourdon can be exculpated from the most damning of the charges about dechristianization that have been levelled against him, even though it was accepted by a great historian, Albert Mathiez.[92] This is the allegation that he was one of those sinister figures who, in the dead of night, visited Gobel, the bishop of Paris, and forced him to agree to abdicate the next day, November 7. Grégoire, warned of a similar visitation, may have been correct in supposing that Bourdon's speech at the Jacobins foreshadowed Gobel's surrender, but he adds only that "people say" ("on prétend") that the bishop yielded to the threats and promises of Anacharsis Cloots, Léonard Bourdon, and Chaumette.[93] Soboul takes us to safer ground by accepting the account of Gobel himself, who should surely have known: he subsequently told the Revolutionary Tribunal that he had been roused from sleep by Cloots and Pereira (the one an avowed atheist, the other a Jew of Portuguese origin).[94] There are complications, however, for it seems that earlier that night the bishop was openly visited by at least one larger delegation, the principal members of which were later identified by one of Gobel's vicars, the *abbé* Lambert, as Chaumette, Hébert, Momoro (a member of the Directory of the Department of Paris and prominent in the Cordeliers Club), Cloots, and François Bourdon of the Oise.[95] There are also more dubious indications that the final visit by Pereira and Cloots was preceded by an initial warning to Gobel on October 31 by Hébert, Chaumette, and others. This warning is said to have followed a private conference between members of the Commune and of the Department (including Lhullier, its *procureur-général*) with some notable Jacobins and deputies (among whom both Collot d'Herbois and J.-Julien of Toulouse are named).[96] Despite differences in reliability, all this evidence suggests that the intensification of dechristianization in Paris was brought about by collaboration between the Department and the Commune, together with some extreme revolutionaries and some of those who became known as "les Pourris," corrupt men who associated themselves with Danton.

It also strongly suggests, of course, that Léonard Bourdon, whose name occurs only in the hearsay reported by Grégoire, was not involved in the intimidation of Gobel and that he has become associated with it only by a false identification with his namesake, François Bourdon.

To acquit Léonard Bourdon of complicity in a reprehensible political conspiracy is not to deny that he was enthusiastically in favour of the destruction of the Christian church in France. For him, as for many others, the continued existence of the church seemed to symbolize the survival of a deplorable past, and its elimination seemed certain to carry the Revolution forward to a final triumphant conclusion. Curiously, however, his contempt for all things ecclesiastical was combined with a measure of tolerance. On November 7, soon after Gobel had gone to the Convention to renounce his office and his priesthood, David proposed that a huge statue of Hercules be erected on the Pont-Neuf as a symbol of the strength of the French people, and Bourdon moved an amendment[97] by which the pedestal would be composed not only of the débris of monarchy but also of that of superstition. Yet immediately before Gobel entered, he had supported the claim of a *curé* for a pension to enable him to cease deceiving his parishioners: according to Bourdon, the strong tide of public opinion was at last opening the eyes of many such men, who had been fed on prejudices since their infancy.[98] In the circumstances, it was no light thing to speak in this way, for the abjuration of Gobel and his vicars was greeted with prolonged applause, as was that of many deputies who were, or had been, either Catholic priests or Protestant ministers. By contrast, Grégoire, who later went into the assembly in full canonical dress and bluntly told the deputies that religion was no concern of theirs, subsequently wrote that he felt every word that he had uttered to be the equivalent of a sentence of death.[99]

However, despite fundamental sincerity and even tolerance, Bourdon remained responsive to excitement, a lover of flamboyant gestures who was always ready to draw attention to his school. Now, if briefly, he took part in the popular demonstrations that occurred in Paris. On November 8, when his pupils received their flag, he proposed that the Commune should organize a procession, representative of the whole city, to take "the bagatelles" of the churches to the Convention.[100] This proposal, however, was rejected as "a useless masquerade," probably because the Commune was reluctant to commit itself so far. Similarly inconclusive is the appearance of some "orphans of the defenders of the patrie" at the Convention on November 10, when Chaumette introduced the Goddess of Liberty (Claire Lacombe) and invited the deputies to return with the people to Notre Dame, newly reconsecrated as the Temple of Reason.[101] These boys, who came amid the leading contingents of the marchers, sang a patriotic song in which all joined; however, because responsibility for them had only just been assigned to Bourdon, the episode may not have occurred at his instigation. On the other hand, he must certainly have had a hand in preparing the demonstration that took place on November 12, when the Section des Gravilliers went in strength to the Convention to announce that its churches had been closed and that an immense quantity of silver had been taken to the National Treasury.[102] Although such processions were becoming commonplace, this one was notably spectacular. Behind a splendid canopy surmounting a bust of Marat marched the section's companies of the National Guard, some grotesquely clad in clerical costume and some carrying ornaments taken from the churches, while the musicians of la Société des Jeunes Français played appropriately lugubrious airs. The Convention was then addressed by one of Bourdon's pupils, the seven-year-old Paulin, "whose ears have not yet been polluted by lies." Raised aloft, the child explained that by closing its churches the section had destroyed "the lairs of foul beasts, dens built and maintained by the blood and subsistence of the people."[103]

Although dechristianization continued to erupt elsewhere in France, often at the instigation of particularly fanatical commissioners of the Convention,[104] its climax in Paris was marked by the Commune's order of November 22 for the closure of all churches in the city. Bourdon, who had urged the Convention on November 16 to authorize communes to give linen taken from the churches to the poor,[105] took no further political part in the movement at this time. As usual, his record for the remainder of the year reflects his concern for various matters, to some of which we will return. Shorn of suppositions, his share in dechristianization thus seems comparatively slight. As one among many assailants of the clergy, he attracts attention principally by his success in dramatizing the attack on them. Nor does that type of activity seem inappropriate to the man. Believing that organized religion was an impediment to the forward march of people and society, he probably also welcomed dechristianization as a resurgence of revolutionary fervour and a new opportunity for purposeful activity.

That opportunity, however, was brief, for in the Jacobin Club on November 21 Robespierre made one of his greatest speeches to reaffirm religious freedom.[106] Fearing that the assault on the church would alienate opinion in those countries still sympathetic to France, he had foreseen for some time that it would also antagonize the great majority of France's predominantly rural population.[107] Now, in words reminiscent of those proclaimed by Bourdon in the Jura in April, he declared that those who would prevent priests from saying the Mass were more fanatical than the priests themselves. Furthermore, although he recognized that everyone had the right to hold any belief, he particularly condemned the attempt to impose atheism on all citizens. In saying "L'athéisme est aristocratique," Robespierre damned it both as contrary to his own convictions and as a manifestation of a counterrevolutionary conspiracy to discredit and destroy the Revolution from within.

Because few of the revolutionaries were willing to be as frank as Robespierre in avowing their personal religious convictions, it is not clear how far Bourdon differed from him and from others in this respect. Almost certainly, however, Robespierre was exceptional in his belief in the existence of a deity vitally concerned with the immediate welfare of France and the ultimate success of the revolutionaries' mission to all people. Although many no doubt endorsed his concession to expediency ("Si Dieu n'existait pas, il faudrait l'inventer"),[108] few could have been so passionate as he in seeing the Revolution as nothing less than the manifestation of the will of the supreme being.[109] Less exceptionally, Bourdon seems always to have thought in terms of human progress through human endeavour, and many certainly shared his opinion that the use of reason was but one contributory factor to such endeavour. Like that of Robespierre, his belief was ultimately one that sprang more from the heart than from the mind: unlike Robespierre, and in this he, too, was probably unusual, he sometimes seems to have seen the Revolution itself as almost divine.

Of more immediate consequence to Bourdon and many others was Robespierre's belief in the reality of an extensive conspiracy to defile and debase the Revolution so much that it would collapse. This belief in what became known as the "foreign plot," because those supposed to be promoting it were either foreigners or men alleged to be foreign agents, henceforth dominated his attitude toward all who criticized or opposed the Revolutionary Government.[110] Broadly the "Indulgents," those like Danton, who advocated some moderation of the Terror, were seen as the fountainhead of corruption, a judgment derived from growing appreciation of the malversations and fraud that had accompanied the dissolution of the East India Company; and those like Hébert, who called for more controls and still more repression, were thought to be deliberately inciting popular violence. But to Robespierre this distinction was blurred, for to him corruption and extremism, of which he saw dechristianization as one facet, were but different forms of political immorality. Moreover, however real or imaginary the "foreign plot" may have been, most of the members of the Committee of Public Safety regarded the attacks on the churches as a dangerous recrudescence of the public anger that had so nearly destroyed the government in September.

The dechristianization campaign consequently contributed to the development of a reaction and the advent of the still more authoritarian regime established on December 4 (Frimaire 14) by the Law on Revolutionary Government, sometimes called the "Constitution of the Terror." At the conclusion of his speech on November 21, Robespierre called for the immediate expulsion from the Jacobins of Dubuisson, Proly, and Pereira and for the initiation of a *scrutin épuratoire* by which the Jacobin Club could publicly review its membership and cleanse itself of all those whose views and conduct were suspect. Two days later, the Club[111] decided that the Central Committee of Popular Societies should be dissolved; on November 25, Chaumette hastened to exculpate himself and the Commune;[112] and, on December 6, the Convention formally reaffirmed people's freedom to worship as they chose.

Bourdon apparently escaped unscathed from all this. On December 12, he was one of those who succeeded in passing the Jacobin Club's self-scrutiny, "sortent purs du creuset des épreuves,"[113] whereas Cloots—who had been the society's president until a few days before—was ignominiously expelled at Robespierre's instigation.[114] Even so, it is most unlikely that his denigration of priests had failed to attract unfavourable attention, and doubts about his integrity would certainly have been increased by his association in December with a dramatic production entitled *Le Tombeau des imposteurs ou l'inauguration du Temple de la Vérité*.[115] As ephemeral as it was theatrical, this play contrasts the conduct of those who cling to superstition with that of the sturdier *sans-culottes*. The former are mostly old women, who mumble prayers for the success of counterrevolution while their priest, sneaking off with silver filched from the church, pauses to try to seduce a girl under cover of the confessional. Tolerant though they are of the women's weakness, the *sans-culottes* have the priest arrested for theft before they transform the church into a Temple of Truth and Reason. As a prelude to all this, it is explained that Jesus was a just man but that he was not God.

Incredible as it may now seem, this drivel was actually performed in Paris. Presumably its puerility was masked by melodrama such as the appearance of the Shade of Marat in the cavern of the Furies of (religious) Fanaticism, and it was enlivened by songs and music, which culminated in appropriately patriotic hymns. On the whole, however, it is perhaps just as well that there is no telling how far Bourdon was responsible for the script of Le *Tombeau*, on which his name appears as the first of three, his associates being identified only as Moline and Valcour. It is therefore possible that he simply sponsored the production, as is suggested by Kuscinski in the *Dictionnaire des conventionnels*: "L. Bourdon avait fait recevoir par un des théâtres une pièce intitulée 'Le Tombeau. . . .'" For him, furthermore, the venture may have been no more than another way of advertising his school, for in the final scene boys and girls, the orphans of the defenders of the patrie, appear, and they may have been among those of the cast who were practising "the mechanical arts" before they paused to rout a surprise attack by Austrians and *émigrés*. However great or small his participation may have been, the play was identified with Bourdon, and it was certainly repugnant to Robespierre, who, Kuscinski notes, detested Bourdon at this time. On December 22, the play was in fact banned by the Committee of Public Safety as contrary to the decree reaffirming freedom of worship, and that order was in Robespierre's own writing.[116] The demise of Le *Tombeau* thus marks a parting of the ways and the beginning of Bourdon's descent into disgrace. Like all else at that time, his fault was seen as political, but there seems to be no real reason to suppose that his "extremism" had ceased to reflect the personal convictions of one who had always acted independently.

10

Under Suspicion (December 1793 to July 1794)

*I*n the course of 1792-94, a young man named Gabriel, of whom little is known beyond his love of observing the events of the Revolution, made a number of lightning sketches of those political figures whose appearance struck him most forcefully.[1] Some of these drawings, which are best described as cruel caricatures, can usefully be compared with other and more orthodox portraits. Unhappily, however, that identified simply by the name Léonard Bourdon remains the only known contemporary illustration of him (see frontispiece).

What is more, in the early 1840s, when the comfortable French bourgeoisie regarded all revolutionary agitators with revulsion, several of Gabriel's sketches were reproduced as engravings, and in this process the representation of Bourdon became still more grotesque (see p. 215 below).[2] True, both the sketch and the engraving present the profile of an ill-favoured and disreputable man whose lank dark hair falls loosely about the collar of his coat; however, although the engraving is inscribed "Drawn from life by Gabriel," it has evidently been subtly modified. Now the brow has become more beetling and the jowls heavier; the lower lip and the nose are so accentuated that they seem obtrusive; and, most obviously, the replacement of an open eye by a sinister slit deprives Bourdon of every sign of animation and intelligence. Still occasionally reproduced,[3] this picture has no doubt contributed considerably to the general belief that he was a man of formidable appearance and brutal disposition.

Whatever his faults, the real Bourdon was certainly a more civilized man than this crude portrayal of him suggests. That is not to say, however, that Gabriel's representation of him can be entirely disregarded. Historians now recognize that the behaviour of the "revolutionary

---

Notes to Chapter 10 are on pp. 379-84.

man" of Year II was abnormally exalted, and exaggeration in the outward manners of men like Bourdon may well have been particularly apparent in the middle of the winter of 1793-94, when people in general were becoming increasingly disillusioned about their future. If, as seems most likely, it was at that time that the sketch of Bourdon was drawn, he is probably rightly represented as a man striving to identify himself with the *sans-culottes*.

Some confirmation of this view appears in the private notes in which Robespierre later recorded his opinions about some of the deputies whom he particularly disliked. Bourdon, he alleged, was "one of the first of those who tried to debase the Convention by instigating indecent behaviour, like speaking while wearing a hat, and wearing ridiculous clothing."[4] Here again allowance must be made for prejudice, for when these notes were written Robespierre (uncommonly meticulous about his own appearance) was living under such intense stress that his suspicion of others almost amounted to paranoia. By contrast, a more detached comment by Bourdon's brother, Bourdon de Vatry, is revealing. Being involved from January 1794 onward in a protracted dispute about the civic virtue of a colleague in the Ministry of Marine, de Vatry felt bound to defend his own record, and in the course of this apologia he asserted that he had constantly combined the appearance of a man dressed *comme il faut* with the conduct of a true *sans-culotte*.[5] No doubt Léonard, a public figure and a man more theatrically inclined, was less hesitant about showing his sympathies by his manners and his mode of dress.

However far Bourdon went in adopting the style of the *sans-culottes*, his concern for the sufferings of the poor during the winter of 1793-94 need not be doubted. On November 19, for example, he succeeded in persuading the Convention that the clothing and bedding that had accumulated in the National Pawnshop (*le Mont de Piété*) in Paris should be distributed freely to those in need, and on December 6 he again urged the deputies to spare time to alleviate the hardship of those who were making the greatest sacrifices for the Revolution.[6] On this occasion, Bourdon proposed that soldiers' dependents, and all who could show a valid certificate of impoverishment, should be allowed to redeem up to fifty livres worth of their household goods without payment. Nor did he abandon this idea when the Convention referred it to a committee: in mid-January 1794, he demanded that the committee's report be presented, and on January 23 his efforts were rewarded when the proposal was approved as a decree.[7] Moreover, he continued to draw the assembly's attention to particular instances of individual adversity or

Fig. 6. J.-J. Léonard Bourdon. An engraving made and published between 1842 and 1846 by Vignières, Paris, probably with the approval of Gabriel and from his original sketch in 1794. (See J.-M.-B. Renouvier, *Histoire de l'art pendant la Révolution* [Paris, 1863], vol. 2, p. 371.) Readers should notice that the caption to this engraving is only partially correct, and that in the early 1840s middle-class hostility to all past and prospective revolutionaries was intense. Courtesy of Collection iconographiques, archives départementales du Loiret.

courage. Thus, on December 20, he secured an interim grant for a mutilated soldier whose application for a pension had still to be approved, and a week later, having heard that some convicts at Toulon had worked strenuously to extinguish fires and save shipping when the republican forces recaptured the port on December 19, he did all he could to ensure that the release of these men would be considered.[8]

By this time, however, even activities like these had political significance. Whatever his dress, Bourdon's readiness to champion the poor implied some criticism of the Revolutionary Government, and it may still suggest that Bourdon can be put in the same category as ambitious agitators such as Hébert. More weight might nevertheless be given to the fact that, while his own behaviour really remained remarkably consistent, the situation in which he stood was changing. The salient feature of this change was the ever-increasing strength of the Revolutionary Government, particularly that of the Committee of Public Safety. The powers that government had acquired by the Law of Frimaire 14 (December 4, 1793), a major measure of centralization, soon seemed to be justified by military success, for in December the armies of the revolutionary republic had crushed the royalists and peasantry in the Vendée; moreover, the recapture of Toulon symbolized the suppression of the "federalist" rebellion throughout France. And, as the government organized the nation for the wider war against foreign enemies, it both tightened its grip on daily life and began to move toward long-term measures of economic and social reorganization. In February 1794, price control was modified in an attempt to revive regular commercial life, and in the Laws of Ventôse (February 26 and March 3) Saint-Just unveiled far-reaching proposals for the redistribution to the poor of the property of all those identified as enemies of the Revolution.

This growing power of government was nonetheless masked by apparent weakness. The members of the Committee of Public Safety in fact lived precariously, constantly coping with an endless stream of particular problems and frequently encountering major crises.[9] Moreover, because they themselves came from the left as well as from the centre of the Montagnard Convention, they had great difficulty in remaining united and independent when their authority was challenged. More particularly, their position was imperilled in December 1793 by the emergence of open public controversy about whether the Terror should be relaxed, maintained, or intensified. Vitally important in itself, this issue was all the more crucial because at root the question was how, and by whom, Terror of any degree would henceforth be imposed.

The political conflict that ensued was thus really a triangular struggle for supremacy. While the Dantonist "Indulgents" and the Hébertist extremists, particularly those at the Cordeliers Club, sought to discredit and destroy each other, both factions also sought to control, if not to supplant, the Revolutionary Government. Ultimately even the machinations of men such as Chabot and Fabre d'Eglantine, who tried to conceal their own malversations by "revelations" about the involvement of others in an all-embracing "foreign plot," only aggravated this situation by fostering an atmosphere of universal distrust. Such suspicion certainly affected Bourdon, yet his participation in these conflicts, at least so far as it is recorded, was so slight that it can hardly be called even peripheral. Although his sympathies were clearly with the extremists, he seems to have been less interested in opposing the Revolutionary Government than in trying to ensure that it did not isolate itself entirely from the *sans-culottes* and the people.

Long latent, the fight between the factions became fully apparent on December 17, two days after Camille Desmoulins published his damning indictment of Terror in the third number of his *Vieux Cordelier*. On that day, Ronsin, the field commander of the revolutionary army of Paris, returned to the capital from Lyon. Sent back by Collot d'Herbois, who was then representing the government in that area, Ronsin came to rally Parisian opinion against any condemnation of the slaughter that had marked the repression of "federalism" in Lyon. In the event, however, Ronsin's arrival enabled the more moderate Dantonists to take the offensive, and Ronsin was at once arrested by order of the Convention. So, too, was another Cordelier, François Vincent, an advocate of popular terrorism who had long used his key post at the Ministry of War to fill its offices with his own henchmen, and so, too, were various strong-arm men such as Héron, the agents of the security police who habitually terrorized peaceful people in the streets of Paris.[10]

The fact that François Bourdon of the Oise, the fiery and vindictive toper who had quarrelled with Léonard Bourdon in 1792, was prominent in this Dantonist assault on the extremists probably helps to explain Léonard's own participation in one of the incidents that ensued. Collot d'Herbois, recalled to Paris by his colleagues on the Committee of Public Safety, rushed back from Lyon to justify his ruthlessness there and to counteract the effect on opinion of petitions for mercy from the people of the city. His arrival, however, was presaged by the delivery at the doors of the Convention of the head and ashes of Châlier, a "martyred" terrorist whom the moderates of Lyon had guillotined during their time of triumph. Whether by accident or design, it was Léonard Bourdon who received these remains on December 20 and arranged their temporary removal to the assembly's archives. He also reported the arrival of the cortège to the Convention and secured an annual pension for those who had disinterred the body and brought its relics to Paris.[11] That Collot d'Herbois subsequently arranged a grand funeral procession to mark Châlier's final removal to the Panthéon is symbolic of his own success in winning the Convention's approval of his conduct at Lyon and thus virtually forcing the Committee of Public Safety to continue to sanction the Terror.

The Committee, however, was less ready to yield to the Cordeliers Club's organization of popular pressure for the release of Ronsin and Vincent. They were lesser men, and there was probably much to be said for weakening the Parisian revolutionary army by the incarceration of its most prominent officer. That army was indeed the only such force allowed to exist after the Law of Frimaire 14, and on at least one occasion its adjutant, uneasily aware of hostile opinion, sought Bourdon's support, seemingly without result.[12] Bourdon's first intervention in debate in support of the Cordeliers' campaign is similarly no more than a pointer to his sympathies. When a deputation from the Cordeliers sought admission to the Convention on December 23, Bourdon called for its admission and joined other deputies in asking for the allocation of more time to the reception of petitions from the public.[13]

Not until a month later did Bourdon go further. On January 28, 1794, he informed the Jacobins, no doubt with relish, that the Committee of General Security had ordered the release of a popular zealot of Orléans and initiated proceedings against certain administrators of Loiret; he then invited the Club to use its influence at the Convention to restore freedom to Ronsin and Vincent, against whom he said there was no written evidence.[14] In this context, the fact that on February 2 the two men were released from imprisonment (which had never prevented them from inundating Paris with placards) is incidental, for Bourdon's proposal was promptly repudiated by Robespierre. Sensibly enough, Robespierre maintained that the Committee of General Security should be allowed to make its own decisions, it being undesirable from every point of view that it should seem to be subject to external pressure.

Mild though it was, this public rebuff by Robespierre seems to have had a remarkable effect on Bourdon. For the next five weeks, the period in which Hébert, Ronsin, and other Cordeliers compromised themselves irretrievably by their endless agitation, he spoke only occasionally in the Convention, and even these speeches were about education. Rare and equally innocuous was his participation in the proceedings of the Jacobin Club. Characteristically he called on February 26 for the provision of pensions for unmarried women whose male relatives were away on military service, and on the same day he tried to initiate a fête in recognition of the patriotism of people from the provinces who had come to Paris to learn how to make munitions.[15] Early in March, too, he reported that as a commissioner for the society he had visited the military hospital at the Invalides and found that the men living there were deplorably neglected, not to say ill treated.[16] At this time, Bourdon was indeed heavily engaged in some aspects of the work of the Committee of Public Instruction, but so he had been before he was rebuked by Robespierre on January 28. Obviously any political initiative was becoming highly dangerous, yet Bourdon's avoidance of controversy during this critical period may also be due to the reluctance of an independently minded Montagnard and Jacobin to countenance any serious challenge to the government by extremists posing as champions of the people.

In fact, the perilous nature of his position was soon to be still more forcefully impressed on Bourdon. Before that happened, however, he was on one occasion prominent in the Section des Gravilliers. On March 10, a police agent (one of many who regularly submitted reports on public opinions and conditions in Paris) noted that some 2,000 people had assembled in the Temple of Reason, previously the Church of Saint-Nicolas-des-Champs, in Gravilliers and heard various patriotic addresses.[17] The meeting, evidently an unusually well-attended celebration of the ceremonies prescribed for every tenth day by the revolutionary calendar, was then enlivened by the appearance of Léonard Bourdon's pupils, whose singing of patriotic songs moved the people to "un enthousiasme . . . vraiment civique." Bourdon himself next entered the pulpit, from which he spoke so passionately of the miseries of the old order, of the blessings of republican government, and of the vital importance of civic virtue that many of the women were moved to tears. To end the morning, two trees of liberty were then carried around the church to the accompaniment of cries of "Vive la République!" and "Vive la Montagne!"

There is nothing unusual, of course, in Bourdon's readiness to promote patriotic demonstrations of this kind. Equally familiar is his willingness to encourage, if not to stimulate, his pupils' eagerness to participate in them. At the end of January, indeed, Bourdon had succeeded in organizing a ceremony in the Tuileries Gardens to mark the first anniversary of the execution of Louis XVI. His first proposal of this ceremony in the Jacobins on January 21 was followed the next day by the appearance before the Convention of a deputation of the *orphelins des défenseurs de la patrie*,[18] the youngsters for whom Bourdon had become responsible. Their speaker, a boy wounded while campaigning with his father, won warm approval for his request for permission to uproot and replace the tree of liberty once planted by the hand of Louis ("O comble de tous les crimes!"). It is nonetheless remarkable to find Bourdon prominent in similar activity at the Church of Saint-Nicolas on March 10, only three days before the Revolutionary Government ordered the rearrest of Ronsin and Vincent, a move that was immediately followed by the arrest of Hébert and other alleged conspirators. Whether Bourdon wrongly supposed that the political crisis was over, or whether he was anxious both to re-establish himself and to revive popular enthusiasm for the Revolution and the Revolutionary Government, can only be surmised.

A further possibility, that Bourdon had actually become an agent of the government, can be confidently discounted, for he was soon to incur a second and still more devastating rebuke by Robespierre. The arrest, trial, and eventual execution of the Hébertists were precipitated by their folly in calling openly for an insurrection like that of May 31, 1793. However, despite all their ranting about the miseries of the poor, their real interests were always political, whereas the hardships of the winter had made the sections of Paris more concerned than ever about the cost and scarcity of the necessities of daily life.[19] By this time, too, many of the most militant *sans-culottes* had become serving soldiers, and others had accepted so many patriotic responsibilities that they had virtually become local servants of the state. Consequently only one of the forty-eight sections—the section Marat, once the Théâtre-Français, where the Cordeliers Club was located—answered the call of that club by marching to the Commune, which in its turn responded only with cold assurances that the city and the government could be trusted to do everything possible for the welfare of the people. The indictment of the extremist faction, together with more revelations about the fraudulent financial dealings of deputies such as Fabre d'Eglantine and Chabot, nevertheless seemed to be conclusive proof of the reality of the "foreign plot" to discredit and destroy the republic, and it inevitably involved yet another purge of administrative officials at all levels. As Billaud-Varenne told the Jacobin Club on March 14, "Cette conjuration avait des ramifications étendues."[20]

At the next meeting of the Club, on March 16, Bourdon agreed with the previous speaker, Couthon (like Billaud, a member of the

Committee of Public Safety), that unreliable men must be excluded from the public service. However, whereas Couthon had indicated that investigations would be made by the revolutionary committees of the sections (bodies now directly subject to government control), Bourdon proposed that members of the Club should personally visit their own sections to obtain the names of all those holding offices in them, as well as in the Municipality and the Department of Paris. Brought to the Jacobins, these lists could then be publicly scrutinized and purified by the elimination of all about whom reservations were voiced. In short, he asserted that "Il est de l'intérêt général que les Jacobins remplissent la carrière de sentinelles du peuple."[21]

That principle, which Bourdon had upheld on various occasions during the Revolution, may be thought a simple statement of Jacobin orthodoxy. Robespierre, however, now took immediate exception to it.[22] As a member of the national government, he assumed that it was intended to apply to all the Jacobin Clubs throughout France, and he asserted that it would simply stimulate selfish ambitions and turn all the Clubs into hotbeds of intrigue. More pointedly, he condemned Bourdon's plan as one certain to ruin the Revolutionary Government by depriving it of all control of public officials,[23] and he even alleged that it had been proposed for that purpose. Akin to "la système de Pitt," it seemed to him to be yet another insidious attempt to destroy liberty in the name of patriotism; nor did he find that surprising, for experience showed that, as soon as one scoundrel was executed, others appeared at the foot of the scaffold. After dealing in similar terms with a different topic, Robespierre concluded by proposing that Bourdon's motion be denied further consideration, remarking that, although he was reluctant to denounce anyone without proof, "il n'est pas encore prouvé à mes yeux que Léonard Bourdon n'appartient pas à la conjuration."[24]

Shattering at the time, Robespierre's uncertainty about Bourdon's position may now be seen as adequate evidence in itself that Bourdon was not in fact associated with the Hébertists. Indeed, just as his earlier record suggests that his proposal on March 16 was his nearest approach to overt opposition to the Revolutionary Government, so does his subsequent immunity from prosecution imply that no indication of his alleged involvement either with the Hébertists or the Dantonists[25] was ever found. Yet even as an independent Jacobin Bourdon was in grave danger. In indicting the Hébertists on March 13, Saint-Just had made the revolutionary doctrine crystal clear by defining all faction as a criminal attack on sovereignty: "Every party is criminal because it is a form of isolation from the people . . . , a form of independence from the government."[26] One consequence of that speech was the voting of a decree by which resistance to the Revolutionary Government became a capital crime. Certainly the tides of change were running strongly against any initiative, no matter how well intentioned, and from mid-March until the end of July Bourdon probably preserved his life only by withdrawing almost completely from political activity.

There is consequently no means of knowing his reactions to the momentous events that marked the final months of the Terror. The arrest and execution of the Dantonists (from whom Bourdon of the Oise contrived to separate himself), and the carnage caused by the concentration of repression and the acceleration of Revolutionary Justice in Paris, must here be set aside. So, too, must other aspects of the time, such as the gradual restriction of the *sans-culottes*, the inauguration of Robespierre's Cult of the Supreme Being, and the military victories by which the republic inaugurated its conquests in Europe. On the other hand, the hiatus in political life enabled Bourdon for a while to give more attention to those aspects of education with which he had been increasingly concerned since the beginning of 1794. In one of these aspects he achieved remarkable success before he was again frustrated.

This distinction between political and educational activities must nonetheless be recognized as singularly inappropriate to the first half of 1794, when the revolutionary state so strove to transform the beliefs and attitudes of the entire population that the courage and virtue supposedly peculiar to republicans would become habitual for succeeding generations. As Robespierre, the supreme exponent of this policy, put it in his great speech on May 7, "L'art de gouverner a été jusqu'à nos jours l'art de tromper et corrompre les hommes; il ne doit être que celui de les éclairer et de les rendre meilleurs."[27] To that end, every possible means of arousing—yet controlling—immediate and enduring love for the republic was employed as a matter of urgency. Of this all-embracing political campaign, education in the sense of formal schooling was but a minor part.

A new law about education, decreed on December 19, 1793, exemplifies this relationship. Generally known as the Bouquier Law because it was proposed by a comparatively unknown deputy of that name, it is notable as the only educational law actually enacted and sustained by the Convention before the end of the Terror.[28] That may have been because it represented the minimum on which all the deputies could easily agree: as Bouquier, with rare lightness of touch, described it, it had the merits of "liberty, equality, and brevity." It is also probable that Bouquier was persuaded by one or more members of the Committee of Public Safety to put forward a plan that actually emanated from the committee itself. Significantly his initial proposal dealt simply with "a first stage" and "a last stage" in education: that is, with what would now be called primary or elementary education and with higher technical studies. There was thus no provision for any intermediate or secondary education, it being thought sufficient for older children and adolescents to participate in "the meeting of citizens in popular societies, theatres, civic games, military evolutions and local and national festivals."[29] Significantly again, the Convention enacted only that part of the plan which related to the "first stage," thus making three years of education compulsory for all children between six and eight years of age. Nevertheless, the most immediate educational objective of this stage was the inculcation of republican laws and morality. Anyone who could furnish proof of patriotism and proper behaviour was free to open a school and would be paid by the republic according to the number of pupils enrolled. All, however, were to be under constant public surveillance, so that the teaching of "precepts and maxims contrary to republican law and morality," or any personal violation of moral conduct, exposed the teacher to denunciation, trial, and possible punishment. Furthermore, the law required the Committee of Public Instruction to present the Convention with its selection of "elementary books of the knowledge absolutely necessary for the training of citizens."

In this situation, Léonard Bourdon came into his own for some months. As a member of the Committee of Public Instruction, he was involved in February 1794 in preparing and presenting the financial measures necessary for the payment of teachers,[30] a tedious task but one presumably congenial to a man who had long sought to secure adequate remuneration for them. Bourdon had also constantly emphasized the importance of ensuring that children were educated to become morally responsible citizens, his own school being dedicated to that end, and he had seized every opportunity to stimulate and organize festivals in which young and old alike could rejoice in their new freedom. Although by 1794 many people shared these convictions, which were characteristic of the final period of Montagnard supremacy, Bourdon could fairly have claimed that he had been one of the first to formulate them and to make a serious attempt to implement them in practice.

It is true that the Bouquier Law, which relied almost entirely on local initiatives, was neither immediately nor universally operative.[31] Nor did elementary teaching of reading, writing, and arithmetic, together with civic instruction by "precepts and maxims," come close to Bourdon's conception of the school as a self-governing republic in miniature. Nevertheless, the new law contained two clauses that afforded Bourdon a unique opportunity to participate in the national propaganda campaign and to influence the content and method of primary education. One of the clauses required all teachers to use the textbooks that were to be published with the Convention's approval, and the other defined the texts "absolutely necessary for the training of citizens," these being "the Rights of Man, the Constitution, and the list of heroic or virtuous acts."[32] Thus, the use of the *Recueil des actions héroïques et civiques des républicains français*, the journal that Bourdon had been actively promoting since September 1793,[33] became compulsory in all elementary schools throughout France. Moreover, on December 30, 1793, three days before the Convention gave its final sanction to Bourdon's first number of the *Recueil*,[34] it decreed that copies of each issue, which were to be printed as both posters and booklets, should also be distributed to the armies, the municipalities, and the popular societies of the entire republic.[35]

As that decree suggests, Bourdon's work in this field was astonishingly successful. In January 1794, when the first of the monthly numbers was circulated, 100,000 copies were printed by order of the Committee of Public Instruction.[36] In February, the Committee of Public Safety intervened directly by ordering the publication of 150,000 copies of every issue and authorizing local authorities to reprint others if need arose.[37] Yet requests for still more copies continued to reach Paris.

Bourdon was not unusual, of course, in appreciating the urgent necessity of supplying the schools with some standard textbooks. That need had been stressed in all the major reports about education since 1791. Indeed, in January 1794, Grégoire took the lead in organizing a national competition in which scholars in different fields were invited to submit scripts for basic books in their own subjects.[38] Nor was Bourdon peculiar in believing that the paramount need of the day was for a book that would inspire everyone to emulate the courage and self-sacrifice of proven patriots, an objective repeatedly and enthusiastically endorsed by the decrees of the whole Convention. Even the method that he adopted, that of presenting a succession of *traits* (i.e., illustrative actions), was common in the literature of the eighteenth century.[39]

On the other hand, Bourdon's belief in the importance of recording military valour and civic fortitude was probably unusually personal, for he had long been familiar with youngsters orphaned by war, and he had repeatedly sought to help wounded and impoverished men. He was, moreover, skilful in selecting appropriate material and in varying the length and the subject matter of the episodes that he chose. As he explained, these "seront variés de manière à éviter l'uniformité: tantôt ce sera un trait de désintéressement; une action héroïque lui succédera, et sera suivie d'un sentiment de piété filiale."[40] Bourdon was also rigorous in the exclusion of explanatory comment ("l'acteur seul doit être vu"). Although the various episodes opened possibilities for elaboration and discussion in the classroom, each was meant to be sufficient in itself as an example of republican virtue. Above all, Bourdon was commendably determined that all should be expressed in vivid but simple language: the style, he insisted, must be one in which "la pureté, la simplicité et le choix des mots sont les qualités principales."

Responsibility for the first four issues of the *Recueil*, which appeared from January to April 1794, was allocated by the Committee of Public Instruction to a subcommittee of three—Bourdon and two self-effacing men, Thomas Lindet and an ex-noble, Aoust.[41] As the most, if not the only, active editor, Bourdon was much concerned to ensure that whenever possible the people involved should be identified by name and that the episodes selected for publication should be precisely dated.[42] Each of the *traits* nevertheless appeared in its own right, regardless of any geographic or chronological sequence. Their character is sufficiently apparent in the first number published. It consisted of twenty separate episodes, usually of not more than twelve or fifteen lines in length. The first, and one of the longest, tells the story of the courage of those men of the French Guards who refused to obey an order on June 30, 1789, to disperse the people of Paris by force. Imprisoned, they were rapidly released and fêted by the people, who raised a considerable sum of money to sustain them: "Telle fut l'aurore des beaux jours de la liberté."[43] The stories that follow illustrate the bravery and self-sacrifice of civilians and soldiers alike. In one, a poor woman, finding an *assignat* worth twenty-five livres in the street, contrives to identify its owner and return it to him; although this man, whose own children are in need, can do no more than thank her, she returns home well content.[44] In another, a republican soldier, mortally wounded while fighting the brigands in the Vendée, rejects the aid offered by his own brother: "Laisse-moi, lui dit Michau, retourne à ta

CONVENTION NATIONALE.

RECUEIL

DES

ACTIONS HÉROIQUES ET CIVIQUES

DES RÉPUBLICAINS FRANÇAIS.

Nº. Ier.

PRÉSENTÉ

A LA CONVENTION NATIONALE,

AU NOM DE SON COMITÉ D'INSTRUCTION PUBLIQUE;

PAR LÉONARD BOURDON,

DÉPUTÉ PAR LE DÉPARTEMENT DU LOIRET.

IMPRIMÉ PAR ORDRE DE LA CONVENTION NATIONALE.

A PARIS,

DE L'IMPRIMERIE NATIONALE.

L'AN II.

Fig. 7a. The *Recueil des actions héroïques*. Title page (fig. 7a) and first page (fig. 7b) of Bourdon's presentation to the National Convention of the first number of the *Recueil des actions héroïques*, December 1793. Courtesy of Archives nationales de France.

Citoyens,

Changé par votre comité d'instruction publique
de la rédaction du *Recueil des actions héroïques
et civiques des Républicains français*, je ne me
suis déguisé ni la difficulté d'un pareil travail, ni
l'étendue des obligations qu'il m'imposoit, ni les
talens qu'il auroit fallu pour être à sa hauteur.

Cet ouvrage destiné, d'après vos décrets, à être lu
dans les assemblées populaires, les jours de Décade,
et dans les écoles publiques, doit avoir le mérite que
l'on desire dans les livres élémentaires, vulgairement
appelés classiques ; il doit présenter un bon modèle de
narration : le rédacteur doit entièrement disparoître,
l'acteur seul doit être vu. Toutes réflexions doivent
être bannies ; les traits cités doivent être assez bien
choisis pour se louer eux-mêmes. Aucun terme hy-
perbolique, aucune expression triviale ou ampoulée
ne doivent défigurer un style dont la pureté, la simplicité et le choix des mots propres sont les qualités
principales.

Nous aurions pu remplir ce numéro et beaucoup
d'autres ensuite, de récits plus saillans ; nous aurions
pu y réunir un ensemble de traits tous plus héroïques

A 2

Fig. 7b

pièce et venge ma mort."[45] Again, a boy barely aged thirteen, Joseph Barra (who subsequently became one of the cult figures of the time), accompanies the hussars into battle, astonishing the whole army by overpowering two brigands who attack him as well as by taking the lead in cavalry charges. When hopelessly outnumbered, he refuses to the last to surrender horses that have been entrusted to him: "Il est mort en criant VIVE LA RÉPUBLIQUE!"[46]

The preparation of this material undoubtedly involved Bourdon in a great deal of work. In introducing the first number, he remarked that a multitude of stories had already reached him, and subsequently his appeals for further reports evoked an overwhelming response. Almost every day in March and April the minutes of the Committee of Public Instruction recorded the arrival of new instances of heroic or virtuous deeds, and they were always promptly referred to Bourdon.[47] All this, however, was then abruptly changed: on May 12, after unrecorded discussion, the Committee of Public Instruction altered the entire membership of its subcommittee and in effect replaced Bourdon by A.-C. Thibaudeau, a man then relatively unknown.[48]

Whatever the real reasons for this change, they do not seem to have included any criticism of those features of Bourdon's tales that might now be thought objectionable. Because the stories were intended to foster uniformity, their appeal was emotional, and one modern scholar, C. Pancera, has rightly deplored the general tendency of the time to equate adults with children in an attempt to capture "the popular and infantile imagination."[49] Moreover, even if every allowance is made for the exceptional situation of France in 1793-94, Bourdon's stories appear unduly ferocious for children. All the enemies of France appear as rascally poltroons, and many of them "mordent la poussière"; traitors either kill themselves or are shot amid general rejoicing; and, in the first issue alone, we meet a soldier deprived of both hands in a single battle as well as a blacksmith who leaves his forge to join in a fight from which he emerges with his hammer reeking with the blood of the monsters whom he has slain.[50]

According to Thibaudeau, who was probably Bourdon's principal critic, the objection made at the time was that the material in the first four numbers of the *Recueil* was far too scrappy to be either edifying or useful. In explaining the new character adopted for the next number, he argued that "Les traits les plus sublimes ne sont toujours que des débris muets et souvent méconnaissables tant qu'ils restent isolés; ils ne deviennent importants que lorsqu'on a su les réunir et les employer à propos."[51] Thibaudeau therefore produced the fifth number as a far more unified account of the campaign of the armies of the Rhine and the Moselle in the winter of 1793-94, and it is in this setting that various instances of commendable conduct appear. Pancera's description of this fifth and, as it proved, final number of the *Recueil* as "long and singularly boring"[52] is perhaps unduly harsh. Its approach, however, was far more academic than before, a fact sufficient in itself to show that Bourdon knew far more than Thibaudeau about what would interest a class in a primary school.

How far this new format contributed to the sudden demise of the paper after its last appearance on July 1 is uncertain.[53] Although Thibaudeau expected in June to devote future issues to the feats accomplished by other republican armies, and others again to the zeal of civilians, he subsequently noted only that the *Recueil* was abandoned after the fall of Robespierre on Thermidor 9 (July 27, 1794).[54] The whole project, it appears, was then simply allowed to lapse. As Dominique Julia, a notable authority, wrote, "une entente tacite des thermidoriens enterra dans l'indifférence l'une des rares réalisations où la Révolution avait pu mettre ses décisions à la dimension de ses ambitions."[55] In a word, the *Recueil des actions héroïques et civiques des républicains français* proved as ephemeral as the Republic of Virtue itself.

Whether Bourdon's earlier exclusion from control of the paper was simply the outcome of unhappiness about his way of handling a mass of miscellaneous material is also debatable. There may well have been increasing antipathy to blatant proselytizing by an increasingly unpopular government, but there is nothing to show that Bourdon was superseded at Robespierre's instigation. True, Thibaudeau soon reported his new policy to the Committee of Public Safety,[56] but that seems to have been both a routine step and a request for information about the campaigns that he hoped to describe; moreover, he was certainly no tool in the hands of Robespierre. All that can be said is that Robespierre's known suspicion of Bourdon was probably at least one of the factors that affected opinion in the committee.[57]

On the other hand, Bourdon seems at this time to have succeeded in developing la Société des Jeunes Français despite growing doubts about his demands, which seemed to smack of self-aggrandizement—another factor that may have contributed to his loss of control of the *Recueil*. Unease about the cost of the school, evident in January[58] and later much more obvious, was certainly aggravated by his constant efforts to secure more and more facilities for his pupils. As Thibaudeau put it in a disparaging reference to Bourdon in his *Mémoires*, "he was concerned above all else to promote the interests of his school at the cost of others of the same sort."[59]

Matters were further complicated for the Committee of Public Instruction, as indeed they still are for historians, by ill-defined divisions of responsibility for the financing, administration, and educational progress of the school. Insofar as a proportion—by Bourdon's own estimate, about a quarter[60]— of the pupils were *pensionnaires*, the school was at least partially private. It was nevertheless primarily a military school, most of those in residence being paid for by the Ministry of War. After April 1, 1794, however, all ministries were replaced by small commissions directly answerable to the Committee of Public Safety, and it was later agreed that payments to Bourdon should be resumed by the Commission for the Organization and Movement of the Armies of the Land.[61] Beyond that complication, the school was also dependent on the Convention, which had sanctioned its survival when nearly all military schools were abolished on September 9, 1793, and which from time to time approved the admission of individual pupils. Some degree of supervision by the Convention's Committee of Public Instruction consequently continued.

The Convention's most notable intervention in the affairs of the school was its allocation to Bourdon in November 1793 of responsibility for the *orphelins des défenseurs de la patrie*. That allocation eventually meant that on May 20, 1794, the Public Assistance Commission had to contribute a considerable sum for their upkeep.[62] Nor was this all, for various other commissions, committees, and subcommittees, particularly the Commission of Arts, became increasingly involved in aspects of Bourdon's enterprise. Until June 16, 1794, when the Committee of Public Safety finally decided that the Jeunes Français should be governed by the Committee of Public Instruction,[63] this complexity was a cause of irritation to all concerned, particularly because Bourdon could fairly claim that payments due to him were invariably in arrears.[64] It is nonetheless highly probable that he was able to exploit the situation by persuading one committee to approve some proposal that another was reluctant to sanction.

Despite these possibilities of friction, la Société flourished during the months preceding Thermidor. Meticulous research by Agnès Thibal[65] has shown that in July 1794 the number of those enrolled had risen to about 120, of whom ninety-five were subsidized by the state. These boys, mostly between eleven and fourteen years of age, had a total of twenty-four teachers, many of whom offered several different subjects. There was thus a wide variety of instruction available;

however, the curriculum, broadly coincident with that offered by Bourdon in different editions of his prospectus,[66] was primarily practical. Essentially it combined military and physical training with participation in the performing arts and apprenticeship in one or more of at least six crafts. Particular attention was given to music and drama, and printing was a compulsory subject. Beyond this curriculum, elementary classes in reading, writing, and arithmetic could be supplemented by more advanced work in subjects such as mathematics, technical drawing, engineering, geography, and mapmaking. Literature, including the study of both the classical and "the American" languages, was also available, but history, particularly recent history, was taught only informally as "morality in action." Citizenship, the real raison d'être of the school, was not taught at all, it being regarded as implicit in the whole organization of the school as a self-governing community.

This subordination of academic study to technical training accorded well with the attitude then prevalent among the Montagnards. So, too, did Bourdon's readiness to encourage his pupils to participate in public events, as they did in January 1794, when the new tree of liberty was planted in the Tuileries Gardens. At their instigation, that ceremony was accompanied by one in honour of Barra, whose death soon became symbolic of the devotion of the young to the service of the republic. The school also responded well to various demands made on it early in 1794. Of them, the best known is the Committee of Public Safety's order on January 20, by which six of the older boys, named individually, were to be sent in pairs to the workshops in which arms were being made, where their knowledge of technical drawing would enable them to suggest improvements in the designs and the tools in use.[67] According to Bourdon, these boys' work was subsequently commended by two notable scientists, Monge and Hassenfratz,[68] and on February 17 the committee ordered six more of his pupils—again identified by name—to report for instruction to the laboratory in which small arms were tested.[69] Minor examples of the detailed way in which the committee was organizing the national war effort, these orders were similar to that of February 16, which stipulated that a proportion of the printing of the *Recueil des actions* should be done in Bourdon's workshop. This, too, was well done, for 12,000 copies of the second issue, as well as an unknown number of the third, were very satisfactorily printed by the Jeunes Français.[70]

Thus, in various ways, Bourdon's school attracted favourable public attention, and that attention no doubt contributed to his immunity after Robespierre's censures of him on January 18 and March 16.

Remarkably, however, writers who mention his pupils' activities at this time usually cite an adverse report that is wrongly identified as referring to them. On February 19, a police observer noted that "Les jeunes gens appellés enfants de la patrie (ci-devant la Pitié) sont aussi corrompus qu'on puisse imaginer."[71] These boys were said to have offended people strolling in the Jardin des Plantes by singing obscene songs, conduct that their supervisor made no attempt to check. Although the observer also noted that people generally blamed Chaumette, the *procureur* of Paris, as these children's protector, successive editors have assumed that the report referred to Bourdon's Jeunes Français. That assumption, however, seems to be simply a reflection of his success in perpetuating the image of his school: far greater is the probability that the misbehaviour was that of a group of those properly called "les enfants naturels de la patrie," children who had literally been abandoned by their parents and subsequently adopted by the state instead of by the church.[72]

On May 20, nonetheless, the Convention heard some weighty criticism of the school. Speaking for the Public Assistance Committee, the deputy Peyssard explained that new financial regulations had made it necessary for the committee to secure approval of payments to Bourdon for the clothing of the *orphelins de la patrie*. Here he was certainly referring to those properly called the *orphelins des défenseurs de la patrie*—who at this time seem to have been officially "united" with the Jeunes Français but not yet "admitted" to their society. The Convention then accepted his proposal that the requisite payments be made "provisoirement et jusqu'à ce qu'il ait prononcé sur l'existence de la société dite des Jeunes Français." The committee, and probably the Committee of Public Safety, which had been consulted, had obviously been shocked by the sum demanded, which was calculated on the basis of 300 livres for each child over the age of twelve and 250 livres for each of those younger than that. According to Peyssard, the members of the committee were "well aware that the expenditure entailed by the establishment in question was exorbitant and contrary to the principles of economy and equality prescribed by the laws about public education."[73]

Nothing if not resilient, Bourdon seems generally to have responded to criticism by seeking to demonstrate the value of his work. On March 30, soon after he had been silenced by Robespierre in the Jacobin Club, the *orphelins* had gone to the Convention to present evidence of their industry and that of the Jeunes Français.[74] A copy of their address, and specimen copies of the *Recueil des actions héroïques*, illustrated their prowess in printing, and they displayed six pairs of strong shoes suitable for those "qui combattent les assassins de nos pères." In addition, there were copies of the designs prepared for the workshops making arms and the prototype of a new instrument of measurement. Similarly the strictures by the Public Assistance Committee on May 20 soon evoked a positive response from Bourdon, who on several occasions invited the members of the Committee of Public Instruction to attend a public demonstration of the life and work of the school.[75]

These "exercises," as they were called, eventually took place twice in mid-June, and they were highly commended by the *Moniteur*, which concluded its notice about them by praising Bourdon's "assiduous care" for the school and recommending that it be given more support by the government.[76] Still more favourable was the official report submitted to the Committee of Public Instruction by four commissioners from the Commission of Arts.[77] A salient document for the historian of the school, it is a detailed description of the demonstration that they had seen. Initially a general assembly of all pupils had met to approve the application of a new candidate for admission to "a society of free men," and a session of the pupils' court had then "followed republican forms" in considering the penalties appropriate to various minor offences. The boys had then demonstrated their abilities in their different crafts, which included baking, engraving, and printing, as well as the making of shoes and furniture. Some had also played musical instruments, and, after the younger children had solved some simple problems of arithmetic, they had sung an air to words composed by members of the school. Moreover, as an indication that optional academic studies were respected, several boys had spontaneously translated unfamiliar passages of French into English. All had then joined in a mock combat and a military parade held to honour Barra and Viala, the two youngest heroes of the war, and the display had ended in the presentation of prizes to those whom their comrades judged most meritorious.

Because both Bourdon and the school were later described in very different terms, the comments of the four commissioners on their work at this time are particularly important. The visitors approved not only of the practice of self-government but also of the way in which military training was accompanied by the development of physical, technical, musical, and, if to a lesser extent, academic skills. In seeing them all equally honoured, they believed that they saw something really reminiscent of the classical ideal of all-round education. They were also struck by "l'air de propreté, de santé et de contentement qui éclate sur toute la personne de ces jeunes citoyens," and in conclusion they wrote: "Cette École fait honneur à ceux qui enseignent et surtout au Citoyen qui en est le Créateur et que les Élèves regardent tous comme leur père."[78] This was high praise, and, although we need not suppose that all was quite so spontaneous as it seemed, neither need we presume the four commissioners to have been unusually gullible men. The truth is probably that some aspects of Bourdon's conception of education are of enduring validity and that his successful practice of the whole, like his work on the *Recueil*, was particularly appropriate to the exceptional circumstances of the time.

The commissioners' report, directed to the Committee of Public Safety as well as to the Committee of Public Instruction, probably contributed to the decisions of June 16, by which responsibility for the school was finally allocated to Public Instruction, and of June 20, by which the school originally established by Pawlet, and subsequently adopted by the Popincourt Section, was to be incorporated into the Jeunes Français.[79] Bourdon may indeed have survived these final weeks of the Terror because the society attracted public attention and seemed to show that real republicanism was attainable through education. However, as his relationship with the Commission of Fine Arts clearly shows, his unceasing efforts to make his school still more important proved irritating and raised doubts about his wisdom and even his integrity.

Bourdon was naturally concerned to ensure that his pupils were provided with the equipment necessary for their education, and it seems that at least some of the workshops in the school were set up at his own expense.[80] On occasion, too, windfalls came his way: in May or June 1794, for example, the Commission of the Armies offered him seventy muskets from Versailles, and he had only to urge that they be delivered before the display given on June 15.[81] He seems, however, always to have cherished the hope that his school would eventually become a national cultural centre, and this hope long led him to make excessively ambitious demands. Thus, in 1792, when Bourdon first occupied the Priory of Saint-Martin-des-Champs, he had not only tried to take over its library but also had calmly asked the Department of Paris to remove all the books on theology and to restock the shelves with the best books from all the other unused religious buildings in the city, "confiding all to my care."[82] Although this initial demand was unsuccessful, similar ones became frequent after December 1, 1793, when he wrote to the Minister of the Interior to remind him of an

earlier letter. He then suggested that "l'École National de Saint-Mar-
tin- des-Champs, . . . la seule école républicaine que nous ayons,"
should accommodate "des divers materiaux des connaissances
humaines trouvés dans les domaines nationaux ou chez les émigrés."
Thus, he wrote, collections of natural history, mechanics, chemistry, et
cetera, "qui aujourd'hui sont entassées dans les galeries ou ils [*sic*] se
detériorent, seront utilisés dans la Société des Jeunes Français et conservés soigneusement."[83]

Forwarded to the Committee of Public Instruction and then to the
Commission of Fine Arts, this request was at first favourably received,
and by February 9 a subcommittee of three—David, Grégoire, and
Bourdon himself—had been authorized to consider how it might be
effected. According to Bourdon, the Commission was also explicitly
instructed by a decree dated December 20, 1793 (Nivôse 6, Année II),
to ensure that the Jeunes Français received from property confiscated
by the state "all those objects that were appropriate to their
instruction."[84] In consequence, the existence of a wide variety of
material was brought to the attention of the Commission, either by
Bourdon personally or in response to his insistence that inquiries be
made by the sections of Paris.[85] Directly or indirectly, too, several other
committees and subcommittees became involved in the process of
approving proposals for the transference of particular articles to the
school.

Precisely how much material Bourdon acquired in this way remains
indeterminate, for the only known inventory of the building was taken
in 1795, when many items had been dispersed. Nor were all of Bourdon's suggestions sanctioned. There is, for example, no known sequel
to his proposal that a statue of Saint Denis and four black marble
columns be taken from the Church of Montmartre.[86] Moreover, even
the approval of a project did not necessarily mean that the object was
actually removed from a depositary. On the other hand, Bourdon certainly acquired a considerable number of books; a large cupboard that
came from Saint-Sulpice; a collection of engravings; an assortment of
plaster casts of heads, hands, and feet; and various cabinets containing
mathematical and scientific instruments. Most remarkable of all,
however, is his acquisition of a fully equipped theatre from the Petit
Trianon at Versailles.[87]

As time went on, however, the Commission became increasingly
reluctant to accept Bourdon's endless requests. Thus, in May, one
mathematical device was judged too precious to be entrusted to his
pupils, and a scientific collection was said to be too dilapidated to be

moved.[88] Such hesitancy reveals doubts that did not become explicit until later in the year, when the commissioners tried to distinguish between material suitable for advanced studies and that "appropriate to the instruction" of Bourdon's pupils. At that point, in November 1794, they even suspended all deliveries to the school until they could see the decree of Nivôse 6, to which Bourdon so frequently referred.[89] Obviously they did not share his vision of the society of young Frenchmen as a university in embryo and were correspondingly suspicious of his sincerity. Indeed, even Agnès Thibal, a far more sympathetic modern scholar, has been compelled to conclude that he wished to appropriate everything, including much that was well beyond his pupils' comprehension.[90]

Although that conclusion rests in part on developments later in the year, Bourdon's position during the last days of the Terror was certainly precarious. Enterprising and energetic, he had served the government well in promoting and editing the *Recueil des actions héroïques*, but since mid-May he had been excluded from participation in that project. In June, similarly, he had shown that his school was successful, but he had done nothing to meet the criticism that it was inordinately expensive. Moreover, although he may be thought sincere in propagating patriotic and democratic republicanism in both these ways, he had almost certainly offended his more orthodox colleagues on the Committee of Public Instruction by trying to do all by himself and as he thought best. In short, although he may have survived until July 1794 by immersing himself in educational projects, he had neither made himself indispensable nor raised himself above all suspicion.

Speculative as it is, the possibility that Bourdon was conscious of this suspicion is of some importance, for there is a sharp contrast between his silence in political matters after mid-March and his sudden reappearance on July 27 as the deputy principally concerned in the final arrest of Robespierre. That contrast is indeed somewhat illusory, for Bourdon may have attended many of the meetings of the Convention and the Jacobin Club without intervening in them. Nor would such silence be remarkable, for both assemblies had been reduced to endorsing official reports, and many deputies had good reason to suppose that their lives were in danger.[91] Even so, Bourdon's dramatic re-emergence remains sufficiently striking to require consideration.

As long as the Committees of Public Safety and General Security were united, their position was unassailable, but their very success in freeing France from all immediate danger of invasion allowed both personal antagonisms and differences about political measures to appear as open hostility. That dissension meant that the men who won the mastery would eliminate their rivals and all those believed to be their supporters. In this situation, one of three possible proscriptions might have occurred. If the committees could be reunited, then they would certainly strike down men such as Tallien, Fouché, and Fréron, who were rightly believed to be conspiring against the government in order to avoid indictment for their corruption and cruelty in repressing provincial rebellion. However, if these men allied themselves with some of the more extreme members of the committees, particularly Collot d'Herbois, Billaud-Varenne, and several of those on the Committee of General Security, then they might save themselves by destroying Robespierre, Couthon, Saint-Just, and all who supported them; conversely, if these Robespierrists were triumphant, then they would rid themselves at one stroke of all their enemies in the Convention and in the committees. While so much was uncertain, many were afraid, and their fears were intensified when Robespierre in effect appealed to the Convention on July 26 (Thermidor 8) to help him destroy all the heirs of Danton and Hébert, men whose corruption, obstruction, and extremism were preventing the consolidation of a truly virtuous republic.[92] Robespierre, however, explicitly refused to name these alleged conspirators, so he left almost everyone in expectation of imminent arrest and execution.

According to one contemporary report, Bourdon's name was actually one of forty-seven on a Robespierrist proscription list.[93] True or not, Bourdon might well have thought himself marked for the guillotine. Because he seems always to have acted alone, he, unlike Bourdon of the Oise, was probably not involved in any previous plot against Robespierre, nor has that involvement been alleged against him. As we have seen, however, he had incurred Robespierre's anger by thwarting the Lepeletier Plan in August 1793, by supporting the *sans-culottes* that September, and by associating himself with dechristianization at the end of the year; moreover, Robespierre had attacked him as a suspected Hébertist in March 1794. Nor does it seem to be simply coincidental that on July 24 (Thermidor 6) he was suddenly assailed in the Jacobin Club by a woman of the Section des Gravilliers,[94] who alleged that he and others in la Société du Vert-Bois were responsible for the imprisonment of five men whose innocence had eventually been recognized by the Committee of General Security. Bourdon, who then spoke in the Club for the first time for weeks, denied all knowledge of this affair and said that la Société du Vert-Bois was composed of good patriots who would separate if the Jacobins so wished; however, others alleged that the society had been directed by Hébert and his partisans. Moreover, although Bourdon could not have known anything of Robespierre's personal notebook, it contained a damning attack on him as "one of the principal accomplices of Hébert" and "one of those most persistent in propagating the Hébertist doctrine in the Jacobins."[95] These notes, incidentally, also accused Bourdon of "unparalleled perfidy in intrigues to increase the number of his pupils and to acquire control of the *élèves de la patrie*."

Despite all these things, known and unknown, Bourdon does not seem to have taken any notable part in the tumultuous meeting of the Convention on the morning of July 27 (Thermidor 9), when—in accordance with a prearranged plan—Robespierre was kept out of the speaker's rostrum, shouted down, and eventually placed under arrest, together with his brother Augustin, his friend Lebas, and his closest colleagues, Saint-Just and Couthon. Only that evening, when the deputies heard that all five men had been released and established in the Hôtel-de-Ville by the Robespierrist Commune, which was mustering forces to subjugate the Convention, did Bourdon's name appear in the record; and even then his reappearance does not seem to have been a result of his own initiative. At the instigation of the Committee of General Security, the assembly entrusted its defence, and the responsibility for seizing the Robespierrists, who were all outlawed, to Paul Barras. At his request, seven deputies—Féraud, Fréron, Rovère, Delmas, Bollet, Bourdon of the Oise, and Léonard Bourdon—were appointed to assist him.[96]

Unfortunately the composition of this group is no guide to Léonard Bourdon's position, for those selected had no obvious common characteristic. Only Barras, the future director, and Féraud had any substantial military experience. Two of them, Fréron and Rovère, were remarkable for their violence and rapacity as representatives *en mission*: indeed, Fréron and Barras had been responsible for the notorious *fusillades* at Marseille and Toulon, in which hundreds had been slaughtered. These three, as well as Bourdon of the Oise, were certainly among those who had been conspiring against Robespierre, their mortal enemy. Of the others, however, only Léonard Bourdon and Delmas seem to have been prominent enough to have incurred Robespierre's suspicion, and just as Robespierre regarded Léonard as a Hébertist, so too he saw Delmas as a Dantonist. As for Féraud, he had been notable *en mission* for his vigorous participation in the war against Spain, and Bollet was apparently a nonentity. In all probability, therefore, the seven were named simply as representative of a cross-section of opinion in the Convention.[97] Moreover, it seems that only two of them, Barras and Léonard Bourdon, did anything of consequence, whereas other deputies, such as Legendre and Merlin de Thionville, were spontaneously active in the streets.[98]

The relative importance of the activities of Barras and Bourdon that night, Thermidor 9-10, is controversial, if only because neither of the accounts that they gave is wholly reliable. Such credit as the event deserves is usually ascribed to Barras, probably because, as the Convention's principal commander, he took pains to secure its defence, and even its possible retreat, before he allowed the forces that had rallied at the Tuileries to move.[99] He then led these men along the *quais* to the Hôtel-de-Ville, but his account suggests that he deliberately advanced slowly, in the hope of avoiding conflict by a display of force. Thus, when, as he tells us, he eventually followed Merlin de Thionville into the Hôtel-de-Ville, he was confronted by a shambles. At that point, only Saint-Just was upright; Robespierre was horribly wounded by a pistol shot; Lebas was lying dead; Couthon, long sadly crippled, had been severely injured by a fall; and Augustin Robespierre was broken and bloodied after having thrown himself from the balustrade outside the window.

On the other hand, as that account implies, the arrival of Barras followed that of the forces brought by Bourdon from the area of the rue Saint-Martin, to the north of the Hôtel-de-Ville. The account that Bourdon is usually said to have given to the Convention is, however, singularly erroneous. After explaining that he had sought forces in three sections, Lombards, Arcis, and Gravilliers, he asserted that all the defenders of the Commune had fled as his men approached. Some exaggeration apart, this account is acceptable, but he is also reported as saying that both Robespierre and Couthon had been discovered armed with knives and that "a brave gendarme," Méda, whom he presented to the Convention, had struck both men down. That story is so intrinsically unlikely that a different version of it may be nearer the truth. According to one paper, the *Messager du Soir*, Bourdon simply said, "Représentans, nous sommes entrés le pistolet à la main dans la Maison Commune. Robespierre a été saisi au moment où il venait de se frapper. . . ." Beyond that, he is supposed to have announced that the prisoners, including Robespierre, were being taken to the Tuileries (which evoked cries of "No! No!" from all sides) and to have claimed, like Barras, that he had established guards at the Hôtel-de-Ville and initiated a search for other conspirators.[100]

The reality behind this account is difficult to determine; although the records of the sections have been studied by a long succession of historians,[101] these papers relate to the reactions evoked by the crisis at different times and by various bodies—the battalions of the National Guard (now grouped and commanded as legions) and the civil and revolutionary committees of the sections as well as their general assemblies. Moreover, many of them were written or modified retrospectively. It is consequently impossible to be certain of Bourdon's exact route, but it is likely that, as Méda asserted in his generally unreliable account in 1802,[102] Bourdon first went northeast from the Tuileries by way of the section Halle-au-Blé and thus reached the section Amis-de-la-Patrie, adjacent to Gravilliers, shortly before midnight. Accompanied by Camboulas (a deputy often loosely called a Girondin), he then called on the general assembly of the section to march in arms to the defence of the Convention, a call that was "heard with enthusiasm and unanimously approved."[103] Apparently, however, this response was more nominal than real, for the National Guard of this section, as well as that of the Lombards, had previously responded to the Commune's call to assemble on the Place de Grève. The Civil Committee, too, was evasive, and all were distracted by conflicting orders and reports.

In Gravilliers, which Bourdon and Camboulas probably visited next, the Civil Committee was similarly hesitant, but the general assembly, in which he still had a considerable personal following, received him with prolonged applause.[104] He then called on all citizens to destroy those traitors in the Commune and the Jacobin Club who were in open revolt against the National Convention, and the assembly, "levée toute entière," swore to annihilate all such conspirators. Whether or not this response came because, as historians now say, many people of the section held Robespierre responsible for the imprisonment and death of Jacques Roux, Bourdon's force was certainly drawn mainly from Gravilliers. Probably Bourdon also acquired more strength from the Lombards Section as he moved on south along the rue Saint-Martin. There, however, the record of the Civil Committee[105] simply says that two of its delegates, returning from the Place de Grève with the news that the men assembled there were dispersing, had met a strongly armed detachment led by Léonard Bourdon and another deputy, and that in response to his invitation they had accompanied him to the Hôtel-de-Ville. By that time, he had rallied some 3,000 gendarmes and *sectionnaires*, as well as the boys of la Société des Jeunes Français.[106]

Fig. 8. *La Nuit du 9 au 10 Thermidor, An II* (sometimes called *Le coup de pistolet du gendarme Merda*), dessin de Harriet, gravé par Tassaert; "of the period," probably 1795. (See E. Benezit, *Dictionnaire des peintres et graveurs* [Paris, 1976], vol. 5.) Imaginative and dramatic though it is, the engraving is of interest as showing Bourdon—centre background, in the dress of a deputy, with sabre and the Convention's proclamation—as a relatively young and attractive figure. Courtesy of Phototèque des Musées de la ville de Paris.

Fig. 9. Sketches used in preparation for *La Nuit du 9 au 10 Thermidor* (8: Robespierre; 9: Couthon; 10: Saint-Just; 11: Le Bas; 12: Léonard Bourdon). Courtesy of the Bibliothèque nationale de France, estampes.

Although Bourdon apparently advanced more boldly than Barras, both men might well have anticipated serious fighting, for the Commune had previously assembled more than 3,000 guardsmen on the Place de Grève, where there were also seventeen companies of gunners with thirty-two cannon.[107] These men, however, had been kept waiting for hours without orders or even food, and as time wore on some were recalled and others dispersed. Last to leave, at 1:30 a.m. on July 28 (Thermidor 10), were the men of the section Finistère. Thus, as Soboul wrote, "La Commune était vaincue sans avoir combattu."[108] Despite the claims of both Bourdon and Barras that each of them had dispersed all remaining resistance, the Place de Grève was deserted when Bourdon's men arrived.

What happened next has always been highly disputable. It nevertheless seems possible to reach reasonable probability by piecing together separate accounts of variable reliability. One story, that of the gendarme Méda, most improbably alleges that he had organized everything, having been given full freedom by Bourdon, and he claimed that he entered the Hôtel-de-Ville and shot Robespierre before Bourdon entered it.[109] In 1795, however, a police officer, Dulac, explicitly denied Méda's version of the facts. On the Place de Grève when Bourdon's columns arrived, Dulac says, he heard two shots, the sound of which made Bourdon fear an explosion and think of besieging the building. Sure that such caution was not necessary, Dulac, as he tells us,[110] entered the building at the head of a few followers and found Robespierre lying wounded on the floor: "c'est moi qui l'ai vu le premier." Furthermore, a careful modern historian, Sainte-Claire Deville, has concluded that the members of the Commune heard two shots soon after 2:00 a.m., fifteen minutes before Bourdon, "le deputé empanaché," arrived.[111] Taken together, these three accounts suggest that the shots that killed Lebas and ravaged Robespierre were self-inflicted;[112] that they were fired before Bourdon's arrival; and that Bourdon himself entered the room soon after one or more subordinate officials had independently discovered the dead and wounded. If this version is true, then it explains much of the tale that he told to the Convention, for he may be supposed to have believed an initial version of Méda's melodramatic story.

Whatever the truth, neither Bourdon's hyperbole nor his allegedly cautious behaviour on the Place de Grève should diminish appreciation of his energy and resolution in raising a strong force in central Paris and then leading it against the Commune. Nor need it be supposed that in this Bourdon was either a factious extremist or a man solely concerned with saving his own life. If the dictatorship of the Revolutionary Government collapsed so swiftly, that collapse occurred not only because intolerable fear possessed almost everyone but also because much that the government had done was unpopular and by July seemed to be unnecessary. Just as worldly men despised Robespierre's exaltation of virtue and sneered at his Cult of the Supreme Being, so too working people detested the new law that imposed maximum levels on wages.[113] More particularly, Bourdon must have disliked both the subservience to which the Jacobin Club had been reduced and the way in which political freedom was being systematically stifled in Paris. In both respects, the attack on him in the Jacobins on July 24 was doubtless exceptionally galling for him, for he then had to offer to effect the closure of la Société du Vert-Bois, affiliated though it was with the Jacobins, and to deny that it was a "sectional society," one of those by which the *sans-culottes* had tried in vain to evade the limitations imposed on the general assemblies of the sections.[114] In a wider perspective, too, the whole record of his conduct since 1789 suggests that he probably expected the destruction of Robespierre to lead to the restoration of republican freedom in the Convention, in the Jacobins, and in the assemblies of the sections.

11

In Adversity (July to November 1794)

*W*hatever hopes Léonard Bourdon had in July 1794 for himself and for the future of France were soon disappointed. In reality, the death of Robespierre marked the beginning of a period of reaction that eventually proved so fierce and far-reaching that at times a repudiation of the republic itself seemed to be imminent. In this new situation, Bourdon, who had helped to destroy Robespierre, remained a Montagnard and a Jacobin, one of the minority who believed that some degree of Revolutionary Government was still a national necessity. In the summer and autumn of 1794, however, all who held that view became politically isolated, for as the French armies continued to advance, and as the danger of defeat and counterrevolution diminished, most French people became convinced that the laws and institutions of emergency could safely be abandoned. Moreover, even the *sans-culottes* of Paris, whose support had for so long been basic to the Montagnards' strength, were now disunited and disillusioned. Bourdon and others like him, who did not change their colours to suit the times, consequently found themselves exposed to obloquy and even persecution, being damned—whatever their actual records—as the successors of the "tyrant" Robespierre. This period of adversity nevertheless reveals something more of Bourdon's better qualities. In an increasingly impossible situation, he did not seek security by renouncing his beliefs; moreover, although he gradually abandoned regular political activity, he sometimes spoke and acted sensibly and even courageously.

The conspiracy that destroyed the Robespierrists in July 1794 was possible because the French victory at Fleurus in June had effectively ended all immediate danger of foreign conquest and thus broken the principal bond uniting the members of the Committees of Public

---

Notes to Chapter 11 are on pp. 384-86.

Safety and General Security. Similarly the successes of the republican armies later in the year, when the conquest of Belgium was followed by the invasion of Holland, led to continual repudiations of the laws and institutions of the Terror as well as of the men identified with them. This process began immediately after Thermidor, when those who had combined forces against Robespierre—particularly Barère, Billaud-Varenne, and Collot d'Herbois in the Committee of Public Safety, Vadier in the Committee of General Security, and notoriously corrupt and ferocious terrorists such as Barras, Fréron, and Tallien—discovered that they had really revived the importance of the Convention itself. Although political alignments were far from stable, the victors' own survival then depended on the support of the deputies of the centre, the men of "the Plain" whom they had long despised as feeble and irresolute.

That support, originally rallied in secret to destroy Robespierre, now had to be consolidated by substantial concessions.[1] Confronted with a general demand for the reduction of the power of Revolutionary Government, if not for its complete abolition, the Thermidorian group soon accepted changes that left the Committee of Public Safety responsible only for war and diplomacy. All the other powers that it had accumulated in acquiring its virtual monopoly of government were distributed among fifteen other committees, of which the two most immediately important were those of Legislation and General Security. Every committee was also subject now to frequent re-election.[2] At the same time, Revolutionary Justice was correspondingly curtailed. On August 1, the hated Law of Prairial was repealed, and later in the month the Revolutionary Tribunal, which had temporarily ceased to function, was purged and authorized to consider the motives of accused persons, a clause that made acquittals common. Furthermore, Paris was stripped of most of its potential power. The Commune, decimated by the execution of eighty-three of its members as Robespierrists, was simply not re-established. The forty-eight sections, amalgamated for all matters of police and security into twelve *arrondissements* of four sections each, were deprived of their dreaded *comités de surveillance*; moreover, although the general assemblies in each section continued, they were now allowed to meet only on every tenth day, and the payment of forty sous to enable working men to attend was abolished. In sum, these various measures increased the ability of the central government to control popular unrest, but they also shattered the unity and general executive strength of that government.

The Thermidorian group also had to accommodate itself to an almost universal call for the release of people imprisoned during the Terror. This indeed seemed to be the logical consequence of Thermidor: if these prisoners were, as they and their friends promptly asserted, really the victims of the "tyranny" of Robespierre, then they must surely have been exonerated by his execution. Initially, too, almost the whole Convention took the same view, for the survivors of successive purges all had their own partisans in prison. On August 5, therefore, the assembly ordered the release of all those not specifically held according to the provisions of the Law of Suspects of September 1792. Logic and legislation apart, however, the process of liberation continued with increasing momentum. From the last days of July 1794 onward, the prisons, the Committee of General Security, and officials both high and low were besieged by people demanding freedom for their relatives, friends, or allies. Money and influence were freely used to win favourable decisions, and, as those released resumed their places in social and political life, their voices strengthened the calls for the freedom of others.

Unhappily many of them also sought to avenge themselves on those who had persecuted them, so that as a new Thermidorian right in the Convention gained strength, and as more and more substantial citizens, "les honnêtes gens," made their presence felt in the sections, political life at all levels became increasingly impassioned, vindictive, and violent. Still less happily for France, the men who had combined to destroy Robespierre soon became bitterly divided, for some of them, such as Barras and, more obviously, Tallien and Fréron, whose records as terrorists were particularly tainted, deliberately chose to protect themselves by championing this vengeful reaction. Quick to perceive that the fall of Robespierre was generally regarded as the end of the Terror, these men exploited the new, if unofficial, freedom of the press. They first condoned and then actively encouraged the emergence and brutality of those dandified draft dodgers known as *la jeunesse dorée*, who first abused and then assaulted *sans-culottes* as "buveurs du sang." Above all, they constantly played on the general fear that the Montagnards, the Jacobins, and the *sans-culottes* might again combine to renew the Terror. Thus, these men, to whom the name Thermidorians most appropriately applies, and many more, such as Merlin de Thionville, Reubell, Legendre, and Bourdon of the Oise, who for one reason or another rallied to the reaction, gradually became predominant in the final months of 1794. To them, the survival of Montagnards such as Barère, Billaud-Varenne, Collot d'Herbois, Vadier, and, at another level, Léonard Bourdon, who did not abjure their past beliefs and actions, or at least quietly defect to the new majority, naturally became particularly obnoxious, for their existence seemed to be both a potential danger and a perpetual condemnation of their own self-centred apostasy.

Although Bourdon clashed with Fréron as early as August 4, when he objected to the latter's inane proposal to demolish the Hôtel de Ville of Paris,[3] he is not again recorded as addressing the Convention until mid-September. If, as may be presumed, he shared the general attitude of the staunchest Montagnards during these formative weeks, then he would have welcomed the initial reduction of the power of the authoritarian "Robespierrist" regime and the interlude of apparent concord that ensued—a time perhaps symbolized by the repeal of the ban on his own dreadful play, *Le tombeau des imposteurs*.[4] Bourdon would nevertheless have been increasingly concerned by proposals implying not only that abuses of Revolutionary Government should be corrected but also that such government could now be drastically curtailed or even abolished altogether. He would also have been alarmed by the proliferation of right-wing papers and pamphlets,[5] which in late August began to call the men of the Mountain "Robespierre's tail" ("la queue de Robespierre"). Certainly, too, he would have regarded the denunciation by Lecointre on August 29 of seven members of the old Robespierrist committees (notably Billaud-Varenne, Collot d'Herbois, Barère, and Vadier, all of whom either resigned or were retired from office on September 1) as the equivalent of an open declaration of war by the new right. No one, however, could have foreseen the consequences of the Convention's decision that day to censure Lecointre, a deputy who habitually practised denunciation and who was on this occasion speaking for Fréron and Tallien.[6] In fact, this rebuff, together with the Jacobins' decision on September 3 to expel all three men, led the Thermidorian right to seek safety and political predominance by more direct methods.

More specific evidence of Bourdon's position at this time appears in the proceedings of the Jacobin Club, in which Bourdon seems to have acquired a certain standing as a comparatively detached veteran of the Revolution. As always, in August and September he spoke to the Club only occasionally, but it is no less remarkable that he did not then contribute to the members' consideration of controversial matters such as the liberty of the press or the expulsion of Fréron, Tallien, and Lecointre. Indeed, even his participation in the common demand for the liberation of imprisoned "patriots" was more particular than general: although he called for the release of all artisans and agricultural workers held in provincial prisons,[7] he remained primarily concerned about the fate of some radical *sans-culottes* from Orléans. According to Bourdon, these men had been arrested and barbarously treated as *hébertistes* by the national agent in Orléans before being sent to Paris for trial. Indeed, he alleged that he himself was really being indicted, because the prisoners "ont été assassinés en même temps que moi par les chevaliers du poignard."[8] Certainly he was not wise enough to refrain from demanding that the agent, and others like him, should in turn be punished.

More interestingly, Bourdon was concerned about the composition and conduct of the Club itself, for it was common knowledge that many of those present on the night of Thermidor 9 had supported Robespierre until the last moment and had even made desultory attempts to act in concert with the Commune to save him.[9] Because some Jacobins, such as Legendre—who had eventually closed and locked the doors of the Club—and Bourdon himself, had been active in rallying resistance to Robespierre in the streets, it was possible to claim that those who had remained in attendance were not true Jacobins at all. That claim, however, was so artificial that a major effort to clear the Club of all association with Robespierre at Thermidor was imperative. On August 5, Bourdon therefore urged the members to adopt once again the method that had been used to purify and revive the Club in the critical days of July 1791, a process in which he had been an active participant.[10] He consequently became one of fifteen men, all regarded as irreproachably Jacobin, in a committee created to select others whose records were satisfactory and then to act with them until the membership of the Club was entirely approved.

All this was of no avail. Although the selective purge was completed within two weeks, the figure of 600 announced as the new membership seems to be suspiciously large, and some alleged that the whole process had been slipshod.[11] However, even if it had been more rigorous, and not merely used to eliminate some obvious scapegoats as publicly as possible, the Jacobins could never have isolated themselves entirely from Robespierre, the man who had been their idol for so long. Nor, in the early autumn of 1794, could they follow any well-governed pattern of conduct, for by then they were constantly compelled to defend themselves against increasingly devastating attacks from all sides.

Those attacks were probably precipitated because it seemed for a time in early September as if the revolutionary forces in France were reviving. Many provincial clubs sent addresses to the Jacobins in Paris, and one address, that from the Popular Society of Dijon, expressed the Jacobins' views so well that it was circulated and won the support of at least eight sections of Paris.[12] Because the *sans-culottes* were everywhere complaining that the enemies of the Revolution were being released from the prisons, and that they and the well-to-do were dominating the sectional assemblies and committees, Dijon's demand for "Gouvernement révolutionnaire, nécessaire, indispensable dans ce moment"[13] was both encouraging to the Jacobins and alarming to all who dreaded a renewal of the Terror.

These hopes and fears, together with some expectation that civic harmony might yet be restored, help to explain the curious fact that between September 12 and 15 Bourdon secured the Convention's agreement to the pantheonization of Jean-Paul Marat, the revolutionary who in life and death alike was loved, or hated, as the friend of the people par excellence. Almost equally remarkable is this sudden—and, indeed, final—appearance of Bourdon as a prominent figure in the National Assembly.

Exactly how far Bourdon was personally responsible for the proposal is disputable.[14] Certainly the idea was not new, for as far back as November 1793 the Convention had decreed that Mirabeau's coffin be removed from the Panthéon and that Marat be reburied there instead.[15] Furthermore, on September 5, 1794, the assembly decided that the last day of the Year II (the fifth *sans-culottide*, September 21) should be a day of national festival on which all citizens would join "pour reserrer entre eux les liens de la fraternité" and to celebrate the victories won by the republic.[16] The decision was then referred to the Committee of Public Instruction for development in detail, and it was there that "a member" of the committee persuaded it to accept the idea that the festival should honour Marat as well as the armies.[17] That this unnamed member was Bourdon, who had recently been attached to the committee's section of Public Morale,[18] seems to be probable, if only because he was allotted the task of presenting it to the Convention. Another striking fact is that on the night of Thermidor 9, after he had reported the seizure of Robespierre to the Convention, he had visited the section Marat, the home of the Cordeliers, and promised that the decree for Marat's reburial, "held back by Robespierre's jealousy," would soon be put into effect.[19]

There are also several indications that the proposed arrangements for the festival in Paris were at least greatly influenced by Bourdon.[20] Six *orphelins des défenseurs de la patrie* were to be included in the guard of thirty appointed to watch over Marat's body after its arrival in the vestibule of the Convention, and a detachment of the *orphelins*, with its band, would be prominent both in the opening ceremony in the Tuileries Gardens, when the president of the Convention would distribute banners to wounded veterans of each of the armies of the republic, and in the procession to the Panthéon that would follow. Again particular places were allotted to wounded soldiers, for whom Bourdon had long been solicitous, as well as to the authorities of each of the sections and to the popular clubs or societies, all the members of which would be required to wear their cards where they could be seen. The proposals certainly had a distinctly Jacobin flavour, and it is surprising that the deputies rejected only one part of Bourdon's first presentation of the plan, the strange suggestion that, although only half of them should participate, all who did so should wear their distinctive ceremonial dress. After an effective speech by Thibaudeau and succinct guidance from Collot d'Herbois ("point de division, marchons tous ensemble"), the deputies resolved to appear as a body and in their normal dress as citizens.[21]

Questionable though it may be to attribute to Bourdon all the details that he brought forward as the representative of the Committee of Public Instruction, the speech in which he introduced them to the Convention[22] may well be thought his own. Essentially he claimed that the cause of fraternity would be well served if Marat and the armies were honoured simultaneously, for Marat had fought the foes of freedom within France just as heroically as the soldiers of the republic had fought those from abroad: "Ainsi seront en même temps célébrées les victoires nationales sur les ennemis du dedans et sur les ennemis du dehors." Moreover, the contrast that he found between the virtues of Marat and the infamy of Mirabeau enabled him to be sufficiently pointed in rebuking all those who were swayed by "vile calculations of self-interest," men who "for the sake of their personal passions and hatreds constantly fostered discord among the fatherland's most zealous defenders and thus imperilled its greatest interests."

On September 21, the ceremonies took place as arranged, marred only by an initial delay that occurred because the deputies had to return to their hall to consider news of serious conflicts in Marseille,[23] and the day ended amid appropriate theatrical performances, which naturally included one in which Bourdon's pupils demonstrated the contrast between the past and the present in education.[24] Nevertheless, the festival can hardly be called successful. At best, it seems to have been a hastily contrived imitation of the great occasions organized by

David, "the pageant master of the Revolution" (imprisoned at this time as an associate of Robespierre). Apparently, too, it was poorly attended: according to one police observer's report, there were "fewer people, less gaiety, less enthusiasm than usual."[25] Even Bourdon complained the next day that "evil-minded men" had done all in their power to prevent the transference of Marat's remains to "the temple of immortality."[26] Whatever the truth of that complaint, he had been unwise to commit himself so much to a festival that did little or nothing to foster fraternity and that really demonstrated both the Jacobins' weakness and the decline of popular enthusiasm for their sort of revolution.

Bourdon, and all who still clung to that Jacobin conception of the Revolution, which had proved more elitist in practice than it was in theory, were also particularly unfortunate in that their attempt to re-establish themselves coincided with a series of trials that showed how easily Revolutionary Government could degenerate into unrestricted terrorism. From September 8 to 15, the reorganized Revolutionary Tribunal considered the case of ninety-four "federalists" who had been sent to Paris during the Terror by the revolutionary committee of Nantes. In defending themselves, these men revealed horrifying facts about atrocities committed in Nantes when Carrier was the Convention's commissioner there in the winter of 1793-94. Thus, the tribunal and France heard not only about *fusillades* but also about the *noyades*, the brutal drowning in the Loire of several thousand men, women, and children, supposedly all rebels. Furthermore, this evidence was fully confirmed by that of the members of the local revolutionary committee of that time, whom the "federalists" called as witnesses.[27] The acquittal of all those originally accused was then followed by the indictment of the members of the local committee, whose plea of obedience to superior orders led the Convention on November 23 to decide by 498 votes to 2 (Bourdon being one of the majority[28]) that Carrier, a deputy, should be tried with them; and he and his two principal subordinates were eventually condemned and executed on December 16.

Appalling and irrefutable, the facts established during these protracted proceedings seemed to substantiate many other rumours about the real nature of the Terror. In the Convention, increased support for the Thermidorians was evident: on October 3, a new demand for the impeachment of Billaud-Varenne, Collot d'Herbois, and Barère was frustrated only by the intervention of Carnot and Prieur of the Marne, who insisted that all the members of the old Committee of Public Safety had been jointly responsible for all its decisions.[29] The Thermidorian journalists nevertheless had no difficulty in portraying all militant revolutionaries as murderous scoundrels, and, because Carrier had of late been a dominant figure in the Jacobin Club, fact and falsehood alike contributed considerably to a general repudiation of the Club.

In this increasingly hostile atmosphere, Bourdon still tried at intervals to restore the Club's self-confidence. Concerned about the decline in attendance by deputies, he urged the Committee of Public Instruction (in which he was now one of the few remaining Jacobins) to alter its regular evening meetings so that they would not clash with those of the Jacobin Club;[30] for the same reason, he persuaded the Jacobins to accept an earlier opening hour.[31] Moreover, on September 23, when he addressed the Club about the much-discussed question of the freedom of the press,[32] he strove to reassert what he believed to be the Jacobins' true raison d'être. Acknowledging that public opinion was being swayed by a multitude of counterrevolutionary pamphlets, "plus dégoûtants les uns que les autres," he declared that the authors could be overcome, as the Girondin journalists had been, but he was principally concerned to refute the damaging allegation that the Club was some sort of second chamber, superior to the Convention. On the contrary, he said, la Société des Jacobins and other popular societies were originally established both to discuss matters of public welfare and to be vigilant in exposing abuses of power by the agents of the executive. They were concerned not to make laws but simply to ensure that the people would appreciate and uphold the principles underlying decrees approved by the legislature. Sensibly he therefore recommended that the Club restrict its debates to matters due for discussion in the Convention, just as he said the first Jacobins had done in and after 1789.

As far as the press was concerned, Bourdon and the Jacobins were nevertheless fighting in a lost cause. Although they maintained that absolute freedom of printing was impossible while the activities of counterrevolutionaries still made some measure of emergency government imperative, control of the press had in fact been abandoned since Thermidor. By mid-September, right-wing writers were not only free but also financed and coordinated by Tallien, Fréron, and their agents.[33] Moreover, on September 11, while the trial of the Nantes "federalists" was in progress, an intensification of their attacks on all who could be called Jacobins was symbolized by the appearance of the first number of Fréron's own paper, L'Orateur du peuple.[34] A clever combination of scurrilous abuse and incisive ridicule, this paper soon became particularly influential, and at intervals it gave sufficient attention to Bourdon to suggest that, if he was a secondary figure, he could nonetheless be denigrated to advantage.

On October 14, a few days after Bourdon had finally lost his long-held place on the Committee of Public Instruction,[35] the first of these attacks came in the sixth number of *L'Orateur*.[36] This attack concentrated on two particularly sensitive aspects of his record. Initially the paper alleged that all France was horrified by the cold barbarity with which he still pursued certain peaceful citizens of Orléans, people who had happened to witness his "crapuleuse intempérance" when he was in that city in 1793. Because the Terror was then in its infancy, he had had to content himself with dragging his victims before the Revolutionary Tribunal; however, some of them, "buried in the depths of dungeons," had evaded the haggard and hungry glance of the "précurseur et de l'ami de Carrier," and, despite his desire to conceal his first atrocities by new crimes, these men had recently been released by the reorganized tribunal. Thus, "Le tigre a vu échapper sa proie," and all that Bourdon could do was to deplore the Convention's replacement of Terror by justice.

Suitably developed, this presentation of Bourdon as the drunken and ruthless oppressor of Orléans soon became deep-rooted. For a time, however, the second allegation in the *Orateur* was probably equally effective. To console himself for losing his victims, readers were told, Bourdon and his family spent some days in early October at Versailles, and there his "burning love for the welfare of the republic" led him to inspect the various articles stored in the palace. He then decided to take as his fair share all that could be stowed in "six grandes voitures, attelées chacune de quatre vigoreux chevaux de requisition," the lot being taken back to his house in the rue Saint-Martin. As for the custodian at Versailles, who was said to be dissatisfied when Bourdon asserted that he was a deputy, a member of the Committee of Public Instruction, and the teacher of 200 young republicans, his protests were supposedly silenced when Bourdon muttered "Orléans" through clenched teeth. After all this, the *Orateur* promised to publish whatever documentary evidence Bourdon could produce to show that he was authorized to take what he had from the palace (not forgetting "the Turkish carpet and a certain cupboard"). Failing that, however, "I will cry after you, with our colleague Bourdon de l'Oise, 'Au voleur— Arrêtez le voleur!'"

The efficacy of these "Anecdotes sur Léonard Bourdon" is evident in his reaction to them. On October 15, the day after they appeared, he protested in the Convention, offering documents as proof that he was being falsely accused, and over the next few days he did so again in the Jacobin Club and in the assembly of the Section des Gravilliers.

Equally, however, the reception that his complaints received is an indication of the rapidity with which the Jacobins' prestige was disappearing. Hardly had Bourdon begun to speak in the Convention[37] when he was interrupted by repeated cries for the resumption of regular business ("l'ordre du jour!"), and Pelet, a deputy of the right, told him that, because he had no special privileges as a deputy, he should take his proofs to a court of law. On October 24, still more strikingly, he apparently got the same response in the assembly of Gravilliers,[38] where a police observer reported that he had been unable even to reach the speaker's rostrum. If that report is true, then the hostility that Bourdon encountered was probably partly due to Fréron's success in encouraging a popular extremist group, the so-called Société de l'Evêché,[39] to undercut the influence of the Jacobins in the Paris sections by calling for the prompt restoration of the people's right to elect all officials. Certainly the Jacobins had decisively condemned any such restoration as fatal to all true patriots and thus to freedom itself.[40] As it happened, too, on the same day the Committee of General Security, which became controlled by Fréron's friends on October 6,[41] declared the group at the Evêché subversive, a sure sign that Fréron thought his brief alliance with direct democracy had achieved its purpose.

In the Jacobin Club itself, Bourdon's complaint naturally evoked more sympathy: on October 20, a general murmer showed that "La Société ne le regarde point comme inculpé per les calomnies de Fréron."[42] Nonetheless, his attempt to prelude his participation in a discussion of education by reading out his proofs of innocence was unsuccessful, and Bourdon could do no more than associate himself with the educational ideas of the previous speaker, the Montagnard Goujon, and request permission to speak at the next meeting. Moreover, although that request was approved, a week elapsed before Bourdon could speak again,[43] and even then he had to be more general than particular. Ironically, although that course was in accord with his previous advice to the Club to restrict debate to general issues, it was still more a consequence of the fact that on October 19 a new law,[44] approved by the Convention three days earlier, had come into effect. This law ordered all popular societies to submit detailed membership lists to the local authorities immediately and to do so again every three months. More important still, it forbade all collective petitioning and any form of affiliation between such societies. This prohibition, of course, cut at the root of the Jacobins' influence and their means of action. More disoriented than ever, they sought desperately for ways to defend themselves; but they did so with extreme circumspection, and they were certainly not inclined to champion the grievances of Bourdon or anyone else.

In these circumstances, Bourdon, understandably if perhaps unwisely, risked replying to Fréron in a pamphlet entitled *Léonard Bourdon à ses concitoyens*,[45] which was printed on his own press, that of the Jeunes Français. In this pamphlet, he explained that, although he had not deigned to notice an initial innuendo by Fréron, to the effect that he had sought to divide the Convention by promoting the festival in honour of Marat, he now felt bound to reply to the latest charges of being both a thief and an assassin. As far as the latter was concerned, he asserted that the material in the *Orateur* had been lifted almost verbatim from the papers published in 1793 by the Girondins Brissot and Gorsas, who had derived it from the accounts submitted to their Committee of Legislation by the aristocratic municipality of Orléans—"mes propres assassins." Bourdon also maintained, not unreasonably, that the Revolutionary Tribunal that had condemned the men accused of "assassinating" him was very different from the tribunal that had acted in 1794 under the Law of Prairial. He also claimed that he was happy to hear that those who had remained in prison since the trial had finally been acquitted and released. Moreover (as noted here in a previous chapter), he stated that he had been compelled to appear at the trial as a witness, that he had not identified any particular individual, and that he had remained silent in the Convention because the real question at issue was not that of an attack on him but that of an assault on the sovereignty of the people, which he then represented.

This apologia also contained the two proofs of his innocence that Bourdon had tried to produce in the Convention, the Jacobin Club, and the Section des Gravilliers. One (also noted in the previous chapter) was the letter written by the deputies Guimberteau and Bernard on Vendémiaire 26, An III (October 17, 1794),[46] attesting to his sobriety and to the fact that the assault on him in Orléans in 1793 had been unprovoked. The other, written on the previous day (Vendémiaire 25) by Cossard, the custodian at Versailles,[47] stated that Bourdon, accompanied by his wife and four of his pupils, had visited him with letters from the Committee of Public Instruction that authorized him to collect various articles to complete the furnishing of a small theatre, previously supplied. These items had included a large cupboard suitable for storage, but not a Turkish carpet. The custodian also denied that any threats had been made, or indeed that any had been necessary, because the requisition had been in order and a detailed receipt had been duly signed.

Apparently supposing this second certificate to be a sufficient answer to Fréron's charge of theft, Bourdon avoided further detail, confining himself to reproaching Fréron for his derogatory references to the Jeunes Français. These comments Bourdon thought particularly despicable because the whole purpose of his experiment in communal education was to help his pupils become men worthy of the freedom for which their fathers had died. By fostering simplicity of life and habitual happiness in work, by encouraging application to the useful arts, and by inculcating the necessity of consciously loving humanity and being prepared to sacrifice all personal interests for the general good, he was making his boys aware that virtue and happiness are synonymous, thereby inspiring them with love for republican government.

Thus far, Bourdon's reply to Fréron may be thought adequate, reasonably detached, and even dignified. In his conclusion, however, he allowed himself to be more contentious. Asking why his pupils' minds should be troubled by Fréron's horribly bloodthirsty ideas, he also asked why he himself, one who detested all party spirit and was concerned only with his own duties, was being attacked. He surmised that it was because he sincerely believed in the value to freedom of popular societies and because he had been active on every decisive day in the development of the Revolution since July 14, 1789. More particularly, he suggested that people such as Barras and Fréron hated him because he had not followed them to the Faubourg Saint-Germain on the night of Thermidor 9 but had led the men of Gravilliers directly to the seizure of the Robespierrists in the Hôtel de Ville—at which they had arrived hours later.

Some exaggeration apart, this analysis seems to be perceptive, but Bourdon was no match for Fréron in polemics. Referring to Bourdon again on November 9,[48] the *Orateur* ignored his defence of his conduct in Orléans and at the trial that had followed, simply describing him as a Jacobin, an atrocious liar, and a *buveur de sang*. As for Cossard's certification of the legitimacy of the removal of material from Versailles—which here became "les vols de 12 Vendémiaire"—it was dismissed as worthless. Apparently well informed, Fréron pointed out that the validity of the whole transaction ultimately depended on the reality of "the decree of 11 Pluviôse" (i.e., 11 Nivôse), by virtue of which Bourdon alleged that he had acted on behalf of the Committee of Public Instruction but which no one seemed able to find. Until it was produced, if indeed it had ever existed, Bourdon could be seen only as a thief who ought to return his loot immediately, together with a precise inventory of it. For the present, this passage ended with a direct threat:

the deputies charged with the direction of the forces of Paris on the night of Thermidor 9 would reply to "les injures qu'il vomit si gratuitement" against them, and they would do so in "une manière énergique, frappante, et digne de lui."

Although these exchanges no doubt exposed Bourdon as vulnerable, he was not yet in personal peril. His fortunes were nonetheless inextricably tied to those of the Jacobin Club, the destruction of which was by mid-October recognizably Fréron's immediate objective. Speaking in the Club on October 28,[49] Bourdon ascribed this purpose to the wounded pride of certain persons (i.e., Tallien, Fréron, and Lecointre) who had been expelled from it: "parceque qu'on leur a fait l'honneur de les en chasser, ne voilà-t'-il pas que ces messieurs, tout gonflés de colère, trouvent ces Sociétés détestable?" As he saw it, counterrevolutionaries of all shades had consequently rallied to their support, "Parcequ'ils ont tous le même but, celui d'anéantir jusqu'à la moindre trace les Sociétiés populaires."

On this occasion, Bourdon again complained that patriots, particularly those in Orléans, were being arrested or even rearrested for reading his printed reply to Fréron, and he again deplored the Thermidorians' abuse of the press: "On travaille l'opinion publique. Le système des factieux est la calomnie."[50] Alleging that some people were even asserting that calumny was useful in a republic, he emphatically denied it: "Je ne reconnais dans aucune affaire . . . d'autre véritable et sûr guide que la seule verité." In the optimistic belief that the Convention would soon proclaim the imposition of severe penalties for false allegations, particularly about the people's chosen representatives, he urged all those Jacobins who were deputies to redouble their zeal until "ce principe éternel de justice et de raison" had been decreed.

This speech, apparently the last notable one by Bourdon, suggests that his appreciation of the situation was somewhat simplistic. No doubt Fréron and his friends were irritated by their expulsion from the Jacobins, but their principal and almost openly avowed purpose was to maintain their position as the leaders of a reaction against every aspect of the egalitarian and puritanical revolution of 1793, and for that reaction the elimination of the Jacobins was a prerequisite. Moreover, the hopes that Bourdon expressed on October 28 were so unrealistic that he seems to have been deluded by his own ideals. The Jacobins heard him sympathetically enough, but they were primarily concerned to avoid any action that might compromise the Club. Successive speakers sought to distinguish mere calumny, which was best despised, from the more serious offence of false denunciation, and the debate eventually ended on October 30 with the Montagnard Fayau's conclusion that the Jacobins' first duty was to show the people an example of respect for the National Convention.

Nor, as an episode in the Convention on November 3 revealed, was that assembly as detached as Bourdon had implied. Speaking there for the Comité des Secours, the deputy Paganel reported on the situation of war-wounded soldiers at the Invalides,[51] a matter in which Bourdon had long been interested. The committee's conclusion was that the Convention should uphold its earlier decision to dismiss the women who had been charged with the care of the wounded but who had proved themselves to be creatures of Robespierre, as disorderly as they were immoral. Bourdon, who gained the rostrum after the Convention had approved this proposal, then tried to justify the fact that he and two others, together with some of his pupils, had also visited the hospital as commissioners of the Jacobin Club, to which some relatives of the wounded had appealed on behalf of the dismissed women.[52] A derogatory reference to their presence, and particularly to that of Bourdon's boys, in Paganel's report suggests that the Convention now resented the challenge to its authority implicit in any such unofficial investigation, and Bourdon's intervention made matters worse. First, Bourdon asserted that any citizen had the right to find out how wounded soldiers were treated; second, he remarked that he and his companions had been struck by the number of crucifixes and images of the Virgin Mary presently in the hospital. That comment, which implied that the men whom the committee had appointed to replace the women were Catholic "aristocrats," caused an immediate uproar. Bourdon and some who supported him were accused of insulting the assembly, which effectively silenced him by formally reaffirming its decision. In this context, it is worth noting that two days later, on November 5, another Jacobin, Arena, told the Club that the public galleries of the Convention were so filled with people recently released from prison that a Montagnard could hardly open his mouth before he was silenced by their outcries.[53]

Bourdon's constant concern with calumny also suggests that he, and probably many other Jacobins, had failed to recognize that Fréron's campaign against them was no longer simply one of verbal abuse. By this time, the real danger was of open intimidation and physical violence. Ever since August, small bands of young men, predominantly those who had evaded conscription by securing some minor clerical office in the swollen bureaucracy, had been making their presence felt

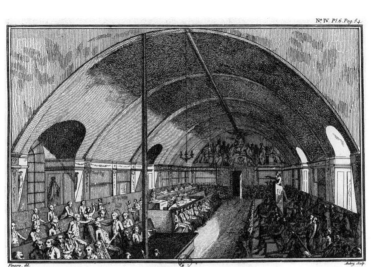

SOCIÉTÉ DES AMIS DE LA CONSTITUTION.

Fig. 10. Interior of the Jacobin Club in Paris. An engraving of a meeting of the Society, probably early in 1791. Courtesy of the Bibliothèque nationale de France, estampes.

CLOTURE DE LA SALLE DES JACOBINS.
dans la nuit du 27 au 28 Juillet 1794. ou du 9 au 10 Thermidor. An 2. de la République.

Fig. 11. Exterior of the Jacobin Club in Paris. An engraving of the closure of the building on July 27, 1794. Courtesy of the Bibliothèque nationale de France, estampes.

in Paris by their increasingly rowdy behaviour. Carrying heavy canes, and so ostentatiously well dressed that they had become known as the Gilded Youth (la Jeunesse Dorée), these toughs congregated each night in the gardens and cafés of the Palais Royal, where they insulted, threatened, and manhandled any obvious *sans-culotte* who came their way.[54] As such brawls became forays in search of victims, the activities of the gangs were gradually coordinated by the agents of Fréron, to whom the ringleaders looked for direction and, ultimately, protection from his Committee of General Security.[55] Thus, by late October, the streets became dangerous for any supporter of the Jacobins, whom these self-styled protectors of the Convention affected to regard as rebels.

Although the attendance even of members of the Club declined appreciably, Bourdon, loyal to the last, continued to contribute to their final efforts to defend themselves. As is well known, the crisis was precipitated by Billaud-Varenne, who of late had seldom spoken in the Jacobins. On November 3, he told the meeting bluntly that all patriots were being attacked because their opponents meant to revise the whole Revolution. Rashly he then warned the reactionaries that it was dangerous to arouse a sleeping lion: "La tranchée est overte; les patriotes vont reprendre leur énergie et engager le peuple à se reveiller."[56] This futile threat caused an uproar at the meeting of the Convention on November 5, when general charges of a Jacobin conspiracy were reinforced by the allegation that some members of the Club were in touch with royalist *émigrés* in Switzerland.[57]

To this attack, the Jacobins responded by a petition, signed individually, to which Bourdon is recorded as contributing.[58] Because it was essentially a simple request for exact information about the alleged correspondence with Switzerland, it is possible that Bourdon had suggested at least one of two accompanying statements. By one of them, the Jacobins were said to be "inseparably bound to the National Convention, the sole centre of government," and the other asserted that, because they were loyal (*purs*), they were entitled to be known as such. Despite these protests, the petitioners were rapidly dismissed the next day, November 6, when Reubell (a future Director) told the Convention that, if the Jacobins were really as loyal as others, then they had no special claim to the deputies' attention.[59]

That rebuff, and the similar one subsequently meted out to a protest by one of the sections of Paris,[60] showed sufficiently clearly that the Club could be attacked with impunity. On November 7, while rumours of such an assault abounded, Bourdon boldly identified himself with the Club by protesting that his name had been omitted from the membership list submitted to the police.[61] On November 9, just before an initial attack began, he even dared to point out that some of those due to give evidence against Carrier had previously been arrested as counterrevolutionaries.[62] He was also notably active during the tumult in the evening, when some 200 to 300 of the Gilded Youth tried to force open the doors of the Jacobins' hall and were only held at bay by sorties of members of the Club.[63] As one of those who went outside, Bourdon heard the cry "Conduis-le devant nous!"; and, when calm was being restored, he displayed a stone that had hit him in the stomach, one of the many that had shattered the windows and that he promised would be taken to the Convention the next day.[64] His final proposal, that the Club's committees should meet at once to prepare a full report about events for the Committee of Public Safety, was nevertheless rejected on the advice of Prieur de la Marne, who said that such activity could be construed as conspiracy and that it would be better to rely on the police and the Convention.[65]

In all probability, no rational proposal would then have altered the situation; certainly Prieur's did not. On November 10 and 11, the Convention became engaged in a furious debate about the Club and the failure of the Committee of General Security to protect it. Although some Montagnards, notably Duhem, persistently struggled to state the facts and win some support for the Jacobins, Bourdon is mentioned only as one of those who tried in vain to secure a chance to speak.[66] In retrospect, the most perceptive comments seem to have been made by Duroy,[67] a Montagnard deputy who was not a Jacobin. After explaining that he had only recently returned to the assembly after missions lasting for eighteen months, he gave an account of the impressions that he had formed and of what he had seen outside the Club on the night of the ninth. He was, as he said, convinced that certain men had acquired power and manipulated public opinion so effectively that a dangerous reaction was developing; one result, obvious when men and women alike were covered with filth and openly thrashed in the street, was that "nous n'avons pas de police, pas de gouvernement." Much more to the general taste was the indictment of the Jacobins pronounced by Reubell: "Où la tyrannie s'est-elle organisée? où a-t-elle ses suppôts, ses satellites? C'est aux Jacobins. . . . Qui regrette le régime affreux sous lequel nous avons vécu? les Jacobins."[68]

When further debate was informally postponed on November 11, violence prevailed. That night, the Jeunesse Dorée, now between 2,000 and 3,000 strong and directed from a distance by Fréron and

Tallien, stormed the Club for a second time.[69] On this occasion, the people in the galleries were driven out, the men being beaten and the women flogged, and many members of the Club escaped only after running the gauntlet between lines of men wielding canes or clubs. Only then, on November 12, did the Convention intervene by approving the order brought forward by its principal committees and thereby suspending all activity by the Society of Jacobins in Paris. Closed and locked that night, its doors were never reopened.[70]

This was certainly a major triumph for the reactionary Thermidorians. Ineffective as the Club had been of late, it had remained potentially the principal link between the Montagnards in the Convention and the "patriot" *sans-culottes* in the sections of Paris. Once it was destroyed, the Montagnards, a small minority in a hostile assembly, were left without any obvious means of access to public support, and the *sans-culottes*, similarly deprived of a common centre, were hopelessly exposed to persecution. As for Bourdon, who had never been as much at home in the Convention as in the Club, the closure was a devastating blow, which at best condemned him to impotent obscurity. Nevertheless, for many of the deputies in the Convention, acquiescence in the destruction of the Jacobins was something more than subservience to Fréron's clique. Despite the Jacobins' reiterated assertions of loyalty to the Convention, by the nature of their society the Jacobins were what they had always been, a watchdog of all authority, a shadow parliament, and the potential rival of any government. As Laignelot, reporting to the Convention as the spokesman of its principal committees, asked, "Dans quel gouvernement bien ordonné . . . a-t-on vu deux pouvoirs rivaux? Dans quelle République a-t-on-vu un gouvernement à côté d'un gouvernement?"[71]

12

Persecution (November 1794 to October 1795)

In 1795, Léonard Bourdon's fortunes sank to their nadir. Initially indications of his existence are so few that Bourdon may be thought to have sought safety in obscurity. Subsequently, however, he appears as a victim of persecution. Abused as a dangerous demagogue, he survived only because he was imprisoned in April, shortly before the reactionaries finally crushed popular democracy completely. Although he regained his liberty in October, when the Convention ended its sessions by a general amnesty, he then found that all his pupils had been dispersed. Of his beloved school, only an open building and few relics remained.

Once Bourdon had lost the place that he had held for so long in the Committee of Public Instruction, he had become, at best, no more than a relatively minor member of the Convention. Moreover, his party, the Montagnards, had been decisively defeated in its attempt to prevent the closure of the Jacobin Club, an endeavour that had seemed to many to be new proof of the identification of the Montagnards with the horrors of the Terror. Consequently it is not surprising that Bourdon is not noted as speaking in the Convention between mid-November 1794 and February 1795. Even then, on February 2, he intervened only to call briefly for the prompt payment of the salaries due to professors who had been employed at the University of Paris.[1]

Apparently, too, he was becoming ever more politically isolated. Certainly the closure of the Jacobin Club, which had always been his favoured forum for the promotion of his ideas, must have severely curtailed his opportunities for association with like-minded men. Nor was support to be found in his constituency, Orléans, for after Thermidor that city was so effectively reorganized by successive commissioners of

---

Notes to Chapter 12 are on pp. 386-89.

the Convention that by the beginning of March 1795 the patricians had completely recovered their traditional control.[2] In February, indeed, all the sections there united in demanding that the Convention cleanse itself of terrorists.[3]

As for the Section des Gravilliers in Paris, of which Bourdon had once been *le grand homme*, it too was increasingly controlled by men of some status and substance, "moderates" who first won a majority in the general assembly of the section on January 29.[4] By that time, moreover, many of the *sans-culottes* in Gravilliers had come to prefer their own direct democracy to the dictatorial elitism of the Jacobins. Significantly la Société du Vert-Bois, which Bourdon himself had founded in Gravilliers as a popular society and an affiliate of the Jacobins, had in September 1794 offered its premises to the extremist Electoral Club, which was soon afterward officially condemned and closed.[5] Bourdon did not then hold any office in la Société du Vert-Bois, nor is there anything to show positively that he remained influential in it during the winter of 1794-95. Although he may have continued to meet his cronies there, he presumably did so quietly: when the government discovered in March 1795 that the Society was still in existence, it too was promptly shut down.[6]

Nevertheless, Bourdon himself was not immediately victimized. Although the closure of the Jacobins certainly opened the way for persecution and revenge on the men of 1793,[7] the vindictive reaction that followed is here seen as a gradual process and one somewhat haphazardly promoted by a minority in the Convention.[8] The core of that assembly was composed of more moderate men determined to replace arbitrary Revolutionary Government and its inflated bureaucracy by some modified republican form of the liberal constitutional regime of 1791. Evidence of this relatively moderate predominance is apparent in the principal measures approved in the winter of 1794-95: the recall of those deputies who had protested in 1793 against the proscription of the Girondins (December 8); the abolition of price controls (December 24); the pacification of the Vendée by the Treaty of La Jaunaye (February 17); the separation of church and state, and the granting of limited toleration to religion (February 21); the recall of the surviving Girondins (March 8); and the creation on March 30 of a constitutional commission.

Because in the nature of the case every such step favoured a conservative as well as a liberal revival, these measures were accompanied by periodic fears of a renewal of royalism. That threat nevertheless remained chimerical, for the armies of the republic had broken into

Holland in December and occupied Amsterdam on January 20, and in exile the brothers of Louis XVI were still intransigently devoted to absolutism. Conversely, however, in 1795 the general fear of a resurgence of popular power and revolutionary terrorism remained of great political importance. The intermittent domination of the Convention by the *sans-culottes* of Paris was then almost as recent a reality as the Terror itself, and early in the year knowledge of the imminence of a crisis in subsistence even worse than that of 1789 was inescapable. Even so, the hope of moderate deputies that both revolutionary and reactionary passions might be assuaged by the passage of time is apparent in the Convention's reluctance to yield to the demand of the extreme Thermidorians that the "principal criminals" ("les grands coupables") of the Terror should be brought to trial. Although Billaud-Varenne, Collot d'Herbois, Barère, and Vadier were openly accused, again by Lecointre, on December 5, 1794, it was not until March 2, 1795, that they were arrested and indicted by the Convention's main committees, and even then debate on the indictment did not begin until March 22.

In this situation, the fate of Bourdon and many others, from *les grands coupables* to *les petites gens* of the sections, was profoundly affected by a renewal of activity by the Jeunesse Dorée. On January 12 (Nivôse 23), Fréron's paper, *L'Orateur du peuple*, openly urged young Frenchmen to shake off the lethargy to which they seemed to have succumbed since mid-November: although they had then forced the closure of the Jacobin Club, the safety of the country still required the extermination of all who could be called Jacobins.[9] Although addressed explicitly to those free from both the ostentatious pride of the rich and the degradation of the poor, this call was nonetheless a blatant invitation to social conflict, which at that time meant the subjugation of all those common people who, since 1792, had allegedly usurped the offices and powers properly exercised by their natural superiors.

Although this murderous appeal certainly brought the Gilded Youth back into the streets, they were content at first to assemble in their chosen cafés and to demonstrate their own brand of patriotism. Indeed, it seems as if the Fréronists in the governing committees were sufficiently alarmed to enforce some restraint—while still continuing to approve the arrest or exclusion from office of the more notable "terrorist" officials in the sections of Paris. From the end of January onward, however, the new reactionary campaign emerged in the guise of a drive to eradicate the principal symbols of popular revolution. Because the people particularly venerated Marat, "l'Ami du Peuple," as the purest martyr of liberty, representations of him naturally attracted the real or simulated fury of the Jeunesse Dorée. In the theatres, and indeed wherever busts of him could be reached, they were destroyed, and on February 8 the Convention weakly, if perhaps not too unwillingly, resolved that Marat's remains, as well as those of other popular heroes such as Michel Lepeletier and Bara, should be removed from the Panthéon.[10] The depantheonization of Marat that followed on February 26 of course amounted to a complete repudiation of the festival promoted by the Jacobins barely five months earlier. Although Bourdon does not seem to have been individually assailed for his prominence in organizing that festival, he doubtless shared the distress and anger that led to street fighting in Gravilliers and is thought to have occasioned unrest in as many as twenty-four of the forty-eight sections of Paris.[11]

Although recollection of Bourdon was probably stirred by this denigration of Marat, he also drew attention to himself by behaving rather rashly on February 6 (Pluviôse 18). The Jeunesse Dorée were by then making a practice of interrupting, if not disrupting, theatrical performances whenever they saw an actor notable in 1793-94 or heard something smacking of revolutionary sentiments. One such affair proved a test of the will, or ability, of the government to control them. On February 5, the presentation of a new comedy, Le concert de la rue Feydeau, a play that ridiculed the loose living of wealthy fops, was halted by an incursion of young rowdies. The next night, no performance was possible because uproar and fighting followed the preliminary reading of a new endorsement of the play by the Committee of General Security. On this second occasion, however, the theatre was surrounded by an armed force, and some 200 young men were rounded up and removed to the nearest local security committee. It was that of the sixth *arrondissement*, which met in the Section des Gravilliers in the precincts of the Priory Saint-Martin, where Bourdon lived and had his school. Not surprisingly, he was soon on the scene.

A highly coloured account of what followed was soon written by a leader of the Jeunesse Dorée and published in the *Moniteur*.[12] This version of the affair asserts that Bourdon was insolent in his behaviour toward those under arrest and even sought to stir the *sans-culottes* to anger against them, so that cries of "À la guillotine!" and "À bas les Jacobins!" were soon intermingled. Later again, the local security committee declined to refute these allegations officially. Noting that Bourdon was not a member of the committee, it merely advised him that false reports deserved only contempt. Nevertheless, the draft of a certificate prepared for the committee still exists,[13] and it affirms that citizen Léonard Bourdon, a representative of the people, entered the room at midnight on the occasion of the disorders at the theatre but took no part, either directly or indirectly, in the committee's proceedings. It adds, however, that he independently walked around and questioned some of those detained, apparently in an attempt to identify certain young men who had previously created a disturbance in the Convention.

Whether the Committee of General Security was privy to the disturbances at the theatre or simply anxious to pacify the Jeunesse Dorée, all those detained were released the next morning, February 7. Remarkable mainly because so many young men were at least nominally arrested, this incident illustrates the immunity enjoyed by ruffians of the right in many more violent episodes. Certainly their constant provocation of all whom they could call monsters and *buveurs du sang* (the Jacobins and *sans-culottes* of 1793-94) contributed considerably to the rise of social and political tensions in Paris. Bourdon, for example, may have responded to misrepresentation by showing himself more openly. By one report in the Thermidorian press later in February,[14] he led his pupils through the streets to their school, all marching to the beat of a drum. On the other hand, the Jeunesse Dorée were bold enough by then to abuse and harass deputies of the Mountain in public, and the same press report may refer to an incident of this sort. Contemptuously referring to Bourdon's ridiculous retinue ("sa meute de polichinelles") of boys whose minds were being poisoned by his pestiferous maxims, it asserts that "some bystanders" openly called him a scoundrel, the man who had caused the deaths of innocent citizens of Orléans. Notably, too, this writer seems to have been the first to refer to him as "Léopard" Bourdon.

Far more ominous for Bourdon and for all the remaining Montagnards was the Convention's readiness to dismiss such episodes. That willingness was apparent, for example, on the evening of March 7 (Ventôse 17), when a band of young men invaded a café on the premises of the Convention, a place well known as a rendezvous for Montagnards and other "patriots."[15] There they encountered Bourdon and another deputy, Armonville, an illiterate man of the working class who habitually wore a red woollen cap. Abused as a blood drinker, Armonville refused to doff his symbol of liberty at the behest of those whom he called counterrevolutionaries, and after something of a scuffle the guards of the building took five of the intruders into custody. Bourdon, meanwhile, succeeded in making his way to the Convention, then engaged in the protracted process of electing a new secretariat. Bursting in, he cried that deputies were being insulted at the very doors of the assembly. Some of those on the left then rose to go to the rescue, but Danton's old friend Legendre brutally rebuffed Bourdon: "Il t'appartient bien, assassin de neuf pères de famille, de neuf citoyens d'Orléans, de te plaindre d'avoir été insulté!"[16] The upshot was that the assembly resumed its regular business, and a later attempt to revert to the alleged insults led only to acceptance of the assumption that Armonville, and by implication Bourdon, had been the worse for drink. As for those taken away by the guards of the building, they were released after a cursory inquiry by the Committee of General Security, and they promptly started planning to waylay Armonville on the Pont National and throw his red cap into the Seine. That a different unpopular deputy was similarly assaulted the next day is not surprising.

Ironically it was at this juncture that Bourdon was officially cleared of a charge that was then circulating about him and that may still occasionally be encountered. It was that he had been one of those informers on whose report thirty people, including the poet André Chénier, had been sent to their deaths just before Thermidor as participants in a supposed conspiracy among the prisoners confined in Saint-Lazare. Like other "prison conspiracies" that were "discovered" late in the Terror, it had really been a device used to justify a mass trial to reduce the number of those in prison. An official inquiry into the whole unsavory business began in December 1794, and in mid-March 1795 its report named Bourdon as one of those involved. In fact, however, he soon secured a certificate acknowledging that a mistake had been made in the identification of handwriting, and a correction was duly entered in the Convention's records.[17]

More generally significant is the appearance on March 15 and 24 of two further savage attacks on him in Fréron's *Orateur du peuple*.[18] Because the situation in Paris was then fast becoming critical, Fréron was probably preparing to strike at Bourdon as soon as the victory that he expected would make general repression possible. Of interest, too, is the fact that both attacks were primarily concerned with discrediting Bourdon's school, which by this time was the last bastion of his reputation. According to the *Orateur* of March 15, however, "Léopard" Bourdon lived in terror lest his pupils ("Les malheureux orphelins qu'il eût plutôt fallu étouffer au berceau que de les confier aux soins des tigres") should yield to the temptation to become true republicans. Alleging that some of them had picked up the strains of "Le reveil du peuple" (the reactionaries' battle hymn), and had even dared to sing it within the precincts of the Priory, the writer claimed that Bourdon, their tyrant, flushed with fury and growling "l'assassin d'Orléans," had at once set up in the school a number of iron rings, to which his pupils were chained whenever he heard the same refrain. Nor, in this article, did Bourdon's wife, the school's matron, escape unscathed: "la signora Léoparda" was said to love her little orphans so well that every one was covered with scabs.

The second article, that of March 24, which purported to be a letter from "a friend of order," was principally concerned to relate a tale about the Bourdons' alleged attempts to cajole or bully some of the pupils and their teachers into writing a reply to L'Orateur. When all else failed, Bourdon was said to have written his own response, claiming, for example, that he allowed some humming of the tune of "Le reveil du peuple" but hoped to make a Jacobin song more popular. This second article, however, has more than the first about the "faction sanguinaire" of the Jacobins. Perhaps few readers would really have believed that Bourdon had been heard repeatedly muttering "Je suis terroriste et homme de sang, je m'en fais gloire," but the assertion that he and other deputies such as Duhem were nightly holding secret meetings, and were sure of their ability to initiate a popular rising, was then both credible and inflammatory. More notable now is the Orateur's assumption, apparent on both March 15 and 24, that for Bourdon and those like him the end was steadily approaching.

That sinister forecast was correct. One week later, on April 1, Bourdon, Duhem, and six other Montagnards were placed under arrest, and in little more than a month the execution of fourteen others marked the extinction of the Montagnard party. By the same process of repression, moreover, popular democracy in France was effectively crushed for the next half-century. It would, on the other hand, be wrong to suppose that the activities of Fréron, his henchmen, and his so-called army of young swells constituted more than one considerable cause of the risings that occurred in Paris in Germinal and Prairial (April and May) 1795. Nor, indeed, should these men be held solely responsible for the repression that ensued; rather, they sought to exploit the almost inevitable outcome of conditions and antagonisms that had passed beyond control. Still less should Bourdon be regarded as having any great importance in the risings; on the contrary, although he had virtually withdrawn from active political life, he was typecast as one of the first victims of reaction.

The situation in Paris at this time was in many respects similar to that of July 1789. Once again a fundamental cause of increasing unrest (and of further writing by Bourdon's father, Bourdon des Planches[19]) was economic. Soaring prices, essentially the result of repeated issues of vast quantities of paper money, were accompanied by appalling shortages.[20] After an indifferent harvest in 1794, the exceptionally severe winter of 1794-95 made the milling of grain difficult, and impassable roads and frozen rivers practically prohibited the transport of essential supplies of flour, meat, and fuel. Furthermore, the dismantling of the hated officialdom of the Terror, and the breakdown and eventual abandonment of price control, meant that the authorities in Paris could do little more than try to ensure that whatever was available was fairly distributed each day among the sections. By March 27 (Germinal 7), a ration per head of one pound of bread a day had to be halved, and by April 1 the amount actually distributed was a quarter-pound at best. A month later, when rice and biscuits were being substituted for bread, famine was fast becoming a reality in the capital, as in much of France.[21]

Once again, too, fear was a pervasive force. For most of the deputies, and for almost all who were not manual workers, fear of popular power now outweighed anxiety about a possible resurgence of royalism. Fed by frequent reports of activity and disturbances in the more turbulent sections, this fear was assiduously fanned by the reactionary press. It was nonetheless founded on vivid memories of the September Massacres and of those occasions in 1792 and 1793 when the people had imposed their will on the Legislative Assembly and the Convention. Nor was it forgotten that until recently poverty and illiteracy had been so far equated with patriotism that daily life had been dominated by a multitude of petty tyrants. On the other hand, men and women who waited for endless hours outside the bakeries naturally blamed the Convention and other authorities for their misery. They also had good reason to suppose that the abolition of the *maximum* had led to hoarding, stockpiling, and speculation, particularly as some foolish people now openly flaunted their affluence in the faces of the poor. Not surprisingly, the needy soon suspected that hunger and even starvation were being used to subdue them. It was certainly not in jest that Boissy d'Anglas, the member of the emasculated Committee of Public Safety responsible for subsistence, was commonly called Boissy "Famine." Similarly the constant arrests of local leaders as "terrorists," and the forays of the Gilded Youth into impoverished districts, where they clashed with the *sans-culottes* and sometimes even dispersed people lining up for bread,[22] were easily seen as presaging massive repression.

At the end of March, all these anxieties combined to intensify political conflict in the Convention and thus to precipitate a new *journée* on April 1 (Germinal 12). On March 22, debate began on the proposed indictment of Billaud-Varenne and the others called the "grands coupables" of the Terror. As the question of their guilt inevitably involved that of the legitimacy of Revolutionary Government and all that had been done in its name, political passions ran high: when the people in one public gallery sang the "Marseillaise," they were answered by "Le reveil du peuple" from the Jeunesse Dorée in another. Furthermore, an even more crucial issue, the nature of France's future as a constitutional republic, suddenly came to the fore. Feeling that Fréron and his associates were going too far, some deputies were moving toward the Mountain, and on March 19 Lecointre, hitherto apparently a rabid Thermidorian, demanded that the long-suspended Constitution of 1793 be put into effect.[23] Recoiling from that prospect, the majority decided on March 30 to appoint yet another commission to report on the drafting of what were evasively called Organic Laws. In effect, therefore, the Convention chose at a particularly critical moment to repudiate the Constitution of 1793, which the people had always seen as the symbol of democracy.[24]

Until recently, historians have generally regarded the events of Germinal 12 (April 1), when a tumultuous crowd occupied the hall of the Convention for some five hours, as the first of two great insurrections by the common people of Paris. It was also usual to say that some of the Montagnards were privy to this rising, one of the few names actually cited being that of Léonard Bourdon, who, as Albert Mathiez has it, "carried with him the section of Les Gravilliers, which was devoted to him."[25] Of late, however, searching examination of the situation "from below" (i.e., of records relating to popular activity) has made much modification to all this imperative.

At the general level, the *journée* itself is now seen not as an insurrection but as a massive spontaneous manifestation of popular anxiety and anger, the culmination of many local demonstrations.[26] The people in the hall may have been asserting their ultimate sovereignty, but their repeated demands were for bread and for the Constitution of 1793, and these demands were so persistent that the deputies could do nothing at all; moreover, the lack of any organization among the crowd is as striking as the absence of any support from the armed forces of the sections. Furthermore, National Guards from the more prosperous parts of Paris, together with some of the Jeunesse Dorée, eventually dispersed the demonstrators so easily that the government is sometimes supposed to have delayed its reaction to make repression seem fully justifiable.[27] As for the Montagnards, some of whom were subsequently said by one of their number, René Levasseur, to have agreed in advance to support the people if doing so became appropriate, it seems that in practice they could only urge the people to leave the hall so that something could be done for them.[28]

More particularly, it seems that Bourdon took little or no part in this *journée*. On and immediately after March 27, there were serious disturbances in Gravilliers, where women went to the Convention to protest about the lack of food and where a considerable crowd tried first to force the Civil Committee of the section to convene a general assembly and then met illegally in an assembly of their own until an armed force was mustered to disperse them.[29] Such records as there are, however, make no specific mention of Bourdon,[30] and la Société du Vert-Bois, in which his influence had probably long diminished, had at least officially ceased to exist. Nor, indeed, does his record suggest that he was a man likely to appear in agitation at the level of the streets. Apparently, too, these episodes, which probably helped to stimulate activity in other districts, so discouraged the people of Gravilliers that they were not prominent in the demonstrations on April 1, which were initiated in the section de la Cité. Nor, again, does anything suggest that Bourdon was particularly active in the Convention itself on the day of the *journée*. Indeed, the Montagnard Levasseur, who later deplored the fact that in the evening of April 1 eight deputies were arrested and condemned to imprisonment without trial, wrote of two of them, Amar and Bourdon, that, although they may have been less honourable than the others, they were also less exposed to blame because they had not spoken in the assembly for the past six months.[31] In short, everything indicates that Bourdon had always been primarily a Jacobin and that the closure of the Jacobin Club had been so devastating that he had virtually withdrawn from political life.

The way in which the arrests were decreed makes that view still more likely. Almost as soon as the hall was cleared of the demonstrators, the Convention ordered the deportation of the *grands coupables* despite the fact that fifty-two deputies, one of whom was Bourdon, vainly demanded a vote by *appel nominal*.[32] Orders for the arrest of eight deputies of the Mountain in succession were then enthusiastically approved, although only four of them (Chasles, Choudieu, Duhem, and Ruamps) had lately been notable as leaders of the Montagnard minority. In this haphazard process, in which Fréron and the despicable André Dumont denounced six of the eight, personal hostility seems to have been the primary consideration.[33] Thus, Fréron named Bourdon as one of the principal instigators of revolt, and he asserted that Bourdon and Choudieu were the main advisors of a secret revolutionary committee in Paris.[34] But he argued only by analogy, alleging that recent events in Gravilliers, "where Léonard Bourdon presides over a so-called popular society in the rue Vertbois," were comparable to those witnessed in the Convention. He added that deputies need not be surprised "that the man who assassinated so many fathers of families of Orléans, weary of his long abstinence from blood, has wanted to go on to assassinate representatives of the people." This mixture of speculation and abuse probably contributed considerably to the growth of Bourdon's notoriety, but it really suggests only that Fréron had nothing of substance to say about any recent political activity on his part.

Still more mythology long obscured the truth about the actual arrest of Bourdon. Whether or not he was, as some say, shouted down while trying to answer Fréron, he evidently left the Convention freely. According to a story current only a few days later, he was nevertheless seized the next morning, April 2, by the citizens of Gravilliers, who took him "bound hand and foot" to the Committee of Public Safety.[35] This improbable tale is contradicted by more mundane documentary evidence. The records[36] show that Bourdon took refuge in the security committee of the sixth *arrondissement*, which met a few yards from his own residence, after a number of "good citizens" had blocked an attempt by some of his friends and his brother, Bourdon de Vatry, to prevent his arrest.[37] The committee then sent one of its members to inform the government of Bourdon's presence, and he eventually returned with an order from General Pichegru, who had just been appointed to command all the armed forces in Paris. This order required the officer commanding the guardsmen of the adjacent Section du Temple to ensure that the deputy was taken under sure guard to the Convention's Committee of General Security.

Consigned to imprisonment in the fortress of Ham, which stands on the Somme near St. Quentin, Bourdon and five of the other deputies arrested with him (Amar, Chasles, Duhem, Foussedoire, and Choudieu) left the Tuileries early on the evening of April 2. By that time, incidentally, a state of emergency had been declared; nine more Montagnards, including Cambon, Lecointre, and Levasseur, had been proscribed; and the police were seeking several of them as well as Ruamps and Huguet, two of the original eight.[38] Escorted by a detachment of mounted gendarmes, the three carriages in which Bourdon and his companions were travelling left Paris by way of the Champs-Elysées, presumably because the western districts were thought safer.

They were nevertheless pursued from the Place de la Révolution (Concorde) by a considerable crowd, and the convoy was eventually brought to a halt at the Neuilly entrance to Paris.[39] There was then a fracas, in the course of which at least one shot was fired, wounding the officer in command, and the deputies were forced to take shelter with the local security committee until a member of the Committee of General Security arrived and managed to placate the crowd. Needless to say, this affair was soon exaggerated,[40] and its significance remains controversial. The most scholarly view[41] is that the real cause of this and allied disturbances was a fundamental fear that all the members of the Convention were secretly leaving Paris, in which starvation and anarchy would be general, and that most of the people neither knew nor cared about any of the deputies as individuals. Yet at least some of those who had followed the carriages from the centre of the city sought to save the deputies, and the latter were certainly in some danger from other people at the Neuilly barrier.

After this episode, the convoy travelled peacefully until it reached Ham on the evening of the next day, April 3. There Bourdon would remain a prisoner for the next six months. Little is known of that period in his life, but there is sufficient evidence to suggest that he was not regarded in Ham as a particularly difficult or dangerous man. By contrast, three of those arrested with him (Choudieu, Chasles, and Duhem) were soon transferred to the stronger citadel at Sedan, even though Choudieu had to be taken from his cell by force.[42] Something more appears in a letter written on June 12 by the deputy Blaux, from whom some hostility might be expected because he is sometimes called a Girondin.[43] In 1795, he was responsible for supervising the distribution of grain grown in the Department of Somme, and his letter says that he visited Ham and spoke to "our colleagues," who all protested their innocence, demanded a trial, and complained that they were almost "hors d'état de vivre" because officials in Paris refused to send them the payments to which they were entitled as deputies. More remarkably, Blaux adds that he was surprised to see among them the twelve-year-old son of "our colleague" Bourdon, and that all were able to come and go freely in the town.

During these months of imprisonment, Bourdon was of course isolated both from some matters that concerned him directly and from changes in the general situation that would eventually affect him. Thus, after Germinal 12-13, when at least sixty more *sans-culottes* were arrested and some 1,600 others "disarmed" (i.e., stripped of all civil rights) in Paris, and when the White Terror began in southeastern

France, the District of Orléans called on the Convention to ensure that "the infamous accomplices of Léonard Bourdon" be tried for their part both in the (judicial) murders of 1793 and in the pillaging of prisoners in Orléans in September 1792.[44] Again, immediately after the failure of the formidable insurrection of Prairial 1-2 (May 20-21)—when the deputy J.B. Féraud was killed in the Convention itself by people who believed him to be Fréron—the formal indictment of thirteen more Montagnards for their supposed support of the insurgents was extended to include the deputies previously arrested in Germinal.[45] It was then fortunate for Bourdon that he was a prisoner in Picardy, for six of the thirteen, the "martyrs of Prairial," were condemned by a military court and died bloodily on the scaffold. Coincidentally, perhaps, it was on Prairial 25 (June 13) that the Convention heard the savage denunciation of Bourdon by the six sections of Dijon, accusations already considered here in the context of his mission in 1793.[46]

For good or ill, the proscriptions of Prairial at least led to some degree of political stability. By executions and suicides, by the flight of some deputies and the imprisonment of others, the Montagnards, the men whose resolution and ruthlessness had saved France from defeat in 1793-94, were virtually eliminated as a political group in the Convention. By further arrests, and still more by the "disarmament" of thousands of "mauvais citoyens" in the sections (men henceforth liable to recurrent preventative imprisonment), the working population was similarly deprived of local leadership. On the other hand, after the initial confrontations on Prairial 1-2, when conflict between the armed forces of eastern and western Paris was imminent, order was imposed on the city by the regular army, now for the first time called in to suppress the people. The auxiliaries of reaction, the Jeunesse Dorée, consequently lost any real raison d'être.

What is more, although the repression of the populace meant that men with money or property became predominant, it also helped to free the liberal centre of the Convention from dependence on the reactionary right. Benefiting by both military and diplomatic successes—between early April and late July, peace was imposed on Holland, and both Prussia and Spain withdrew from the First Coalition—the centre also profited by the frustration of those reactionaries who were secretly royalist in sympathy. Early in June, the death of the unfortunate child called Louis XVII was announced; later that month, his successor, Louis XVI's exiled brother, made his uncompromising devotion to absolutism obvious to all by the Declaration of Verona;

and in July a desperate royalist invasion of Brittany was crushingly defeated by General Hoche. Few on the right could then hope for more than the constitutional republic desired by the centre. The Convention's approval in August of the Constitution of the Year III thus meant that men such as Bourdon might begin to expect their freedom, which was eventually afforded to them by the amnesty that accompanied the final dissolution of the Convention on October 26, 1795.

Yet his return to the Priory of Saint-Martin must surely have been grievous to Bourdon, for he came back not to a flourishing experimental school but to an empty building. That la Société des Jeunes Français, the embodiment of his aspirations and efforts since 1788, had been discredited and destroyed during his absence was probably the heaviest of all the blows he had to bear.

A matter of necessity, his rapid replacement as the director of the school had naturally reflected the prevailing political temper, but the fate of the school had been decided more cautiously. On April 2 (Germinal 13), the day after Bourdon's arrest had been ordered, the deputy Lesage, a newly re-established Girondin and "un des plus acharnés proscripteurs des Montagnards,"[47] said that he had just learned that "l'assassin d'Orléans était à la tête d'une maison d'éducation."[48] At his demand, the Committee of Public Instruction was told to choose in Bourdon's place a man commendable "par son amour de la liberté et la pureté de ses moeurs," and it was further ordered to report on the desirability of preserving or suppressing the school itself.[49] Because the Convention required a response immediately ("séance tenante"), the committee soon advised the provisional appointment of Pierre Crouzet (1753-1811), then the principal of the Collège du Panthéon.[50] That appointment was promptly approved, but the committee evaded the demand for an immediate recommendation about the school, simply saying that two commissioners had been named as investigators and that their findings would be reported as soon as possible.

Although the commissioners did report soon, their inquiry proved but the beginning of an administrative process so protracted that it was not until June 18 (Prairial 30), ten weeks after Bourdon's arrest, that the Convention finally disposed of the school and the problems associated with it. Historians are consequently confronted with a substantial quantity of interim material, the interpretation of which poses a considerable problem. If all the adverse criticisms of the school are accepted without reservation, then Bourdon inevitably appears as a plausible charlatan who had long been imposing on the credulity of the deputies and the general public. On the other hand, it is tempting to suppose that the condemnation of the school was yet another manifestation of Thermidorian vindictiveness, and that view implies that in this matter, as in so much else, Bourdon was simply the victim of misrepresentation and abuse. Carefully considered, however, the evidence suggests that factors fairly creditable to all those most directly concerned were really more important than political prejudice.

The reality of such prejudice should not, of course, be denied. Although the *jeunes français* were not noticeably active in Paris in 1795, Bourdon had long identified them with Jacobin patriotism, and men such as Fréron would certainly remember their participation in the events of Thermidor and in the pantheonization of Marat. After Bourdon's arrest, however, administrative anxieties about the school were more obviously predominant. As we have seen, such worries were evident in 1794, and in 1795 they had undoubtedly been increased by new complications. One was probably the gradual emergence of another foundation, that which ultimately became the new Conservatory of Arts et Métiers. Formally proposed by Grégoire in September 1794, and approved by the Convention on October 10, this plan provided for instruction in the use of a developing collection of technical designs, implements, and machinery.[51] Although the conservatory was not firmly established until 1798 (and then, most ironically, in the buildings of the Priory of Saint-Martin), the plan was clearly in conflict with Bourdon's more nebulous project for advanced technical education, and it may well have contributed to the prolonged opposition of the Commission of Arts to his own more haphazard acquisition of objects of cultural value.

More positive evidence suggests that in 1794-95 the character of Bourdon's establishment changed considerably and that this development aggravated administrative problems that had long been apparent. One obvious feature of the period after Thermidor was a substantial increase in the number of pupils in the school: whereas 69 pupils were subsidized by the state in March 1794, there were 139 at the beginning of October 1794 and 204 on March 26, 1795, a few days before Bourdon was arrested.[52] Inevitably this increase involved greater expenditure and correspondingly greater irritation in the committees responsible for finance: in particular, the Committee of Assistance had much trouble in trying to decide how many of the orphans in the school it had to assist and how much was properly due to each of them.[53]

In this matter, Bourdon may fairly be thought the victim of his own eagerness for publicity in the past: whereas he had once seized every chance of announcing his readiness to welcome the orphaned children of particularly heroic individuals, in Year III the Convention seems to have treated his school as a convenient depository for whole categories of unfortunate youngsters. Thus, in late 1793, eligibility for admission was extended to the "orphelins des défenseurs de la patrie," who were subsequently defined as "les enfants des citoyens blessés ou morts aux armées en faisant un service quelconque"; moreover, in August and November 1794 respectively, eligibility was again extended to include the sons of those killed in an explosion at the Grenelle powder factory, as well as young colonials who had sought refuge in France.[54] And, although at least two of the various reports called for by the Committee of Public Instruction in 1794-95 were not unfavourable to the school, that committee had certainly been considering the idea of developing other schools, similar to Bourdon's but probably superseding it, as orphanages throughout France.[55]

Interestingly, too, references to the school on April 2, 1795, when Crouzet was appointed and an inspection ordered, are to "l'école des Élèves de la Patrie" and "des enfants des défenseurs de la Patrie," not to la Société des Jeunes Français.[56] Still more strikingly, the final listing of pupils, made on June 15 (Prairial 27),[57] shows that at the time 167 pupils were still present, but only 17 remained from the 50 originally allocated to Bourdon by the Ministry of War in 1792. Eight others had come in as replacements, and if eight more, older pupils presented by their parents to learn a trade, are also set apart, then it appears that 134 of the 167, or 80 percent, were in fact orphans. It is therefore a fair conclusion that by the date of Bourdon's arrest his model military school had become little more than a somewhat nondescript state orphanage. Politics apart, those responsible for its administration may well have regarded it as a costly and anomalous administrative nuisance.

A good deal of information about the actual state of affairs in the school, at least insofar as that state could be measured in material terms, is available in the various reports and memoranda drawn up for the Committee of Public Instruction after Crouzet's appointment. The most frequently cited is the report presented on April 20 (Floréal 1) by the two commissioners who had inspected the school on April 3.[58] As Bourdon emphasized in his later claims for compensation, this report was not entirely adverse, for the commissioners found that the children were generally decently dressed and as well nourished as possible under the circumstances. They noted, too, that the dormitories, the workshops, and the infirmary were in good order and that there were few instances of diseases of the skin (a significant sign of the times).

By far the greater part of the report, however, amounted to an out-right condemnation of the school and of what Bourdon had been try-ing to do. The commissioners found that, although there were a considerable number of instructors, the pupils were backward in even the most elementary skills, such as writing and calculation. They noted that some subjects, such as history and political morality, existed only in the school's prospectus and that, although a few pupils had made some progress in music, geometry, and technical drawing, there was no sign of gymnastics, military exercises, or practice in technical work. Worst of all, they reported that "la discipline était presque nulle; qu'au rapport même des instituteurs, la morale était très relàchée." They therefore concluded that "l'éducation, l'objet principal de cet éta-blissement, y était tout à fait negligée."[59]

This assessment may be thought slightly overdrawn: it is, for exam-ple, surprising to see no mention of the work of the school in printing. In its essentials, however, it is a reasonably detached and accurate sur-vey of the state of the school on the morrow of Bourdon's arrest. It should not, however, be accepted without reserve, for in all probability Bourdon had been beset by major difficulties for most of the past year. Economic problems apart, the evidence already considered here sug-gests that in 1795 he had had to accommodate many more pupils than before and that they were probably younger and more heterogeneous than their predecessors.[60] Moreover, the government, to which he once looked for support, had become so hostile to the ideals of 1793 that the school's original raison d'être was no longer relevant to reality. Rightly or wrongly, Bourdon had sought to develop a democracy in miniature, but Crouzet was later to write that he had found the school to be "insurgée en Société populaire."[61]

Consequently the commissioners' report should not be regarded as conclusive proof that Bourdon's methods were pernicious. Rather, their concluding comments[62] show that they equated education with the acquisition of knowledge and had no sympathy at all for his con-ception of it. Bourdon had, they thought, tried to form young men fit for the idealized society imagined in the Constitution of 1793, forget-ting that humanity has to be taken as it is, not as what it ought to be: because people, particularly young people, were far more conscious of their rights than of their duties, their real weakness and dependence ought constantly to be impressed on them.

From this assessment to the outright repudiation of the school by the Committee of Public Instruction was no more than a step. When on May 19 (Floréal 30) the deputy Plaichard eventually presented its report to the Convention, no hint of anything praiseworthy remained. The school, he said, "n'offre que l'affligeant tableau du désordre dans toutes ses parties, presque point de discipline intérieure, peu de moralité, peu de progrès dans les connaissances élémentaires, et nulle base be comptabilité."[63] Because by this time the report had become one drawn up jointly with the Committee of Finance, Plaichard could add that the expenses of the school were still increasing so alarmingly that costs for the current quarter would exceed 100,000 livres—"sans compter le vêtement des élèves, car ils sont aujourd'hui presque nus." Unless something was done, he continued, an establishment that had opened with a great show of luxury would end only as an exhibition of misery and distress, and the two committees had not had a moment's hesitation in recommending its suppression as ruinously expensive for the nation and virtually without any benefit to its pupils.

This committee report, like that of the commissioners from whom it was derived, also has to be read with some reserve, if only because Plaichard was primarily concerned to make a case as strongly as possible. The extent to which the children were really "presque nus," for example, would not be known for another month, when there was a searching inquiry into the ownership of every item of public property in the school.[64] Obviously, too, any fair assessment of expenditures there should have taken some account of the ever-increasing cost of food and the precipitous depreciation of the *assignat*, which had fallen to below 8 percent by May and would soon become worthless.[65] In fact, a particularly moving feature of these weeks is the series of desperate pleas for money made "au nom de l'humanité" by Bourdon's wife, who had been left to cope with the children as best she could: "Je déclare n'avoir pas un sol, je ne les fai vivre qu'avec des dettes [sic]. . . ."[66] That in this endeavour she was fairly soon supported first by Crouzet and then by Plaichard[67] is an indication that for all their rigidity these men were really more concerned with the future of "les élèves" than with passing judgment on Bourdon's record.

That may also be said of the Committee of Public Instruction itself, for by far the greater part of the report made on May 19 was devoted to justifying the proposal that Bourdon's school be amalgamated with that known as l'École de Liancourt. One of the three military schools still extant, Liancourt had survived the emigration of its founder, the Duc de la Rochfoucauld-Liancourt, in 1792, and in 1795 it had 160 pupils, "des enfants de l'armée," who grew much of their own food and were given basic training by their director, Captain Moreux, and his military staff.[68] Although Crouzet, who visited the château with

Plaichard early in May, later said that it had become a place where the sons of infantrymen and drummers learned nothing "à l'exception de la marche militaire,"[69] Plaichard was able to tell the Convention that it was "simple et modeste . . . une école de frugalité, de travail et de bonnes moeurs." The Convention hesitated to approve the proposal only because a deputy suggested that some part of the château at Versailles might be a better location for the combined schools.[70]

The further delays that ensued were inevitably detrimental to all those who remained in Bourdon's school. Three more weeks, during which Crouzet visited Versailles,[71] elapsed before the substance of the committee's original proposal was approved as a decree on June 8 (Prairial 20). Curiously elevating the title, Article 1 then declared that "L'Institut des Jeunes Français est et demeure supprimé."[72] Even that, however, was not quite the end, which was probably postponed in part because the decree had been adapted to extend the process of amalgamation to the third military school, that originally established by the *chevalier* Pawlet.[73] He, too, had become a fugitive in 1792, and his school, one of mixed composition properly called l'École des Orphelins de la Patrie, had long been in distress despite the patronage and protection of the section Popincourt, by the name of which it was commonly known. The more obvious cause of delay in the application of the decree was, however, the insistence of the Committee of Public Instruction that a detailed inventory be made of everything in Bourdon's school that belonged to the republic. Not until June 16 (Prairial 28), when that inventory was done, was the way clear for the removal of the pupils and the formal confirmation on June 18 (Prairial 30) of Crouzet's appointment as director of the combined school at Liancourt.[74]

Although the significance of the inventory,[75] made by Crouzet and an employee of the committee, Mahérault,[76] is disputable, the facts that it reveals cannot be ignored. Initially inquiry on June 15 showed that 18 of the 185 pupils then on the roll were absent, with or without permission. The elimination from the 167 present of those who were not orphans (25), were too young (6 were below the age of six), or were already potentially apprentices (8), reduced the number by 39. It was then further reduced by the temporary exclusion of 15 of the 30 boys in the sick bay, the outright rejection of 11 who were commonly regarded as vicious,[77] and 4 more who were afflicted by ringworm. Because none of the remaining 98 was thought suitable for admission to the army, it was decided for one reason or another that 47 of them would have to be taken to Liancourt (near Chantilly, a distance of some forty kilometres) by carriage, whereas the other 51 were old and fit enough to walk. The inventory also showed that all but 26 of the 167 were either ill shod or habitually went barefoot and that, whereas about half of the boys were either well dressed (43) or at least reasonably so (35), the others were either in makeshift clothing (31) or in rags (58).[78] Furthermore, it appeared that 15 of the 30 in the infirmary were suffering from diseases of the blood or the skin.[79]

On the following day, June 16, Crouzet and Mahérault tried to determine how much of the property in the school really belonged to the republic. They noted a good store of shirts and what was presumably an adequate stock of bedding: 50 mattresses of varied size, 100 sheets, and 100 considerably soiled covers. As far as educational material was concerned, they first noted that there were no books: "il ne s'est point trouvé de livres; tous, a-t-on dit, ayant été usés, sans avoir été remplacés." For design, they recorded a total of thirty items, principally small plaster casts, statuettes, and etchings, said to have come from Versailles, but also including three large pictures (copies of the work of Lebrun), two battered pianos, and two wind instruments. There were also some larger items, notably a big oak cupboard (actually from Saint-Sulpice)[80] and the Salle de Théâtre that had been brought in from the Petit Trianon at Versailles. In all this, and particularly in distinguishing items accepted as being either the personal property of Bourdon or installed in the buildings when he first took occupation, much reliance was necessarily placed on the word of "la citoyenne Bourdon." Whatever records and receipts existed were presumably among Bourdon's papers, which had already been sealed for removal to the Committee of General Security.[81]

Whatever may be thought of this inventory, it cannot be taken as constituting a sound basis for a true evaluation of Bourdon's entire educational experiment. As already indicated, there is ample evidence that the composition of the school had changed appreciably during the previous year, and it is highly probable that Bourdon had been starved of substantial support since Thermidor, if not from the time when he had first been suspected of political extremism by Robespierre. Moreover, Bourdon himself, on whose energy and enthusiasm the school had always depended, had been imprisoned far from Paris for almost three months before the inventory was taken. Still more crucial is the fact that the time was notoriously that of the most devastating hardship in the history of the Revolution. It is consequently not surprising that a number of the pupils were suffering from the effects of malnutrition, and it is likely that, as Thibal has concluded,[82] Madame Bourdon had allowed their clothing to deteriorate so that all available money might be used to purchase food. Nor is the list of equipment particularly helpful, for the items recorded can be traced back to Bourdon's correspondence with the Commission of Arts, and there is no easy means of determining what else might have been in the school. Here again it is safe to assume that at one time there must have been a number of books, if not a small library, and even to suppose that Madame Bourdon, who was evidently no scholar, would have been ready enough to sacrifice them for the sake of subsistence.[83]

Yet the evidence of the inventory remains instructive. At the simplest level, it reflects something of the personal humiliation that "la citoyenne Bourdon" had to endure. Nor was that all, for the president of the Section des Gravilliers subsequently made a second check,[84] even accompanying Madame Bourdon to the extremity of the garden in order to assess the condition and ownership of the three printing presses housed there. There is nonetheless no doubt that the inventory marks the final failure of Bourdon's great experiment and even suggests that Bourdon may previously have lost all hope that it might be resumed.

So sad a conclusion to a substantial chapter in his life naturally demands a measure of explanation, which, it seems, is not to be found in the view that the school was shut down because Bourdon had been branded a murderous terrorist by the extremists of the right. Although dislike, even hatred, of him as a political figure may have been prejudicial to the well-being of the school, it was not closed on that account. Even Fréron had attacked "the tyrant" of the school, not those whom he supposedly victimized. On the other hand, the process by which the school was suppressed is marked by the resurgence of orthodox attitudes in both administrative and educational affairs. Men such as Crouzet understandably wanted to pick up the pieces of a shattered educational system and to reorganize them so that greater advances might gradually be made. Obviously he had no sympathy for any institution that did not fit into an administrative pattern or with educational practices that were neither fundamentally academic nor strictly organized. In this respect, Bourdon's sins were undoubtedly aggravated by his grandiose conception of his school. Whatever the true figures, it was certainly seen as unduly expensive, and his perpetual pursuit of publicity meant that it could never develop in quiet obscurity.

In the last analysis, however, the failure of the school must be ascribed to its essentially political nature. From its inception until its decline in 1794-95, Bourdon's purpose had been to enable his pupils to grow in freedom until they could take their places as responsible citizens of a republic where all would be both free and equal. For Bourdon, political, social, and educational progress would eventually transform the world, and this conception was equated with the triumph of the Jacobins and the Montagnards. The school in which he sought to make his vision a reality was thus fundamentally ephemeral. By definition a republic in miniature, it grew and flourished during the period of the Montagnards' ascendancy but withered and perished in the alien atmosphere of Thermidorian republicanism.

Yet Bourdon's work with la Société des Jeunes Français should not be seen as entirely wasted. Although the results to his pupils cannot be computed, a line of descent, faint but discernible, links his promotion of technical training at the Priory of Saint-Martin with the school at Liancourt and thence, after that school was moved with Crouzet in 1800 to the college at Compiègne, to its final establishment as l'École d'Arts et Métiers at Châlons-sur-Marne in 1806.[85] More definitely, his belief in a freer and happier form of education is one of enduring importance: his vindication ultimately lies not in explanations of his failure but in appreciation of the rigidity and formalism of the methods that Bourdon sought in vain to supplant.

Thus, it seems that in the summer of 1795 Bourdon's whole career was irretrievably ruined. Professionally discredited, Bourdon was also a political outcast, a man never able to free himself from the evil reputation imposed on him by the partisans of both aristocratic and republican reaction. However, although he was apparently destined to complete and permanent obscurity, such evidence as there is shows that he gradually succeeded in re-establishing himself.

13

Starting Anew (October 1795 to July 1798)

*M*eeting for the last time on October 26, 1795, the deputies in
the National Convention resolved to grant a general amnesty
to all accused of political, as distinct from criminal, offences. In the
course of the brief discussion that occurred on this occasion, the
deputies were particularly reminded of the necessity of determining the
fate of "their unfortunate colleagues" who were still imprisoned or in
hiding. Remarkably no one challenged the assertion that, although the
proscription of these deputies had been a measure of public safety, "the
facts for which they were denounced were usually false."[1] Consequently, when Léonard Bourdon, one of those freed by the amnesty,
returned to Paris from Ham, he was at least "le citoyen Bourdon," and
from this time onward it seems that he was treated courteously and
even respectfully by the various officials whom he encountered.

Yet his problem in deciding what to do with his new-found freedom
was probably considerable. Nor is it now easy to keep track of his
career: because all sixty-eight of the Montagnards proscribed since the
spring had already been declared ineligible for election to the new
legislature,[2] Bourdon can no longer be followed in the proceedings of a
national assembly. There are, indeed, several long gaps in the story of
the remainder of his life, and even elsewhere scanty evidence must
often be supplemented by surmise.

It is therefore helpful to glance at the courses followed by some of
those arrested at the same time as Bourdon.[3] When released, some of
these men simply retired from public life: Lecointre, for example,
retired to Versailles, but he did not stop writing letters or even having
placards printed about minor matters. Others were able to resume
their professional careers: René Levasseur and Pierre Duhem returned

---

to medicine and served long and honourably in military hospitals. Whether accidentally or intentionally, however, a few of the rest became involved in dangerous political activities. Some were apparently primarily moved by personal grievances: Chasles, seriously wounded while *en mission* in 1793, thought the honorary military rank awarded to him to be insufficient recognition of his services, and he was briefly imprisoned again in 1796. As for Amar, at one time a spokesman for the great Committee of General Security, he remained so convinced a believer in revolutionary dictatorship that he was one of the few who opposed the new constitutional regime on principle, and he probably even subsidized its most radical enemies from his own considerable fortune.

By no means were all of these options open to Bourdon. He was in no position to retire: for the next four years, on the contrary, he was to spend a great deal of time and effort trying to obtain compensation for the financial losses that he said he had suffered by the abrupt closure of his school. Nor, although he retained his tenancy of a part of the Priory of Saint-Martin,[4] had he any immediate hope of securing support for the foundation of a new experimental school, his most enduring aspiration. In practice, therefore, he had either to re-enter public life as a servant of the new regime or to join those who hoped to persuade or compel that regime to become much more democratic. For a short time, he indeed seems to have followed both courses concurrently, his conduct in this respect being similar to that of another ex-prisoner, Choudieu, who was one of those tried and acquitted as a conspirator in May 1796 but who eventually became a senior administrator in the Ministry of War.

The new regime, established by the Constitution of the Year III (1795), was of course essentially republican, and for that reason alone it was at best only tolerated by all those who hoped for a restoration of the monarchy. Moreover, many ardent republicans were deeply dissatisfied because it was the antithesis of the democratic republic prematurely proclaimed in 1792 and enshrined in the abortive Montagnard Constitution of 1793. The men who had made and approved the new constitution were in fact convinced by their experience of the Revolution that political power could only be entrusted safely to men of property, and that meant that the sociopolitical basis of the new order was remarkably narrow.[5] Nominally all those Frenchmen over the age of twenty-one who were resident taxpayers were entitled to meet annually in the primary assemblies as "active citizens" and electors. In reality, however, a system of indirect election ensured that the effective electorate was reduced to some 30,000 voters for the whole of France, all of them men with considerable property in land.

What is more, in August 1795 the Convention, fearing that monarchists might win a majority in the first elections, had approved supplementary legislation that drastically curtailed the electorate's freedom of choice. To ensure that the new constitutional order was initially entrusted to true and experienced republicans, it was decided that only one-third of the new legislative body should be elected in 1795, the other two-thirds being made up of deputies from the Convention.[6] In theory, this approach meant that the legislature, renewable by one-third annually, could not be entirely composed of newcomers until after two more elections, those scheduled for early 1797 and 1798. In practice, however, it meant that the new regime was constantly confronted by the opposition of all those, whether monarchists or republicans, who had been effectively disenfranchised.

As events were soon to prove, however, opposition was unlikely to be tolerated. The Constitution had in fact been drawn up to reestablish legality and to prevent any concentration of power, either among those in authority or amid potentially dangerous opposition groups. Until 1799, therefore, the republic was bicameral, its legislative body consisting of an initiating Council of 500 and an upper chamber of 250 deputies of forty or more years of age, the Council of the Elders (le Conseil des Anciens), and both were renewable by one-third each year. Strictly separate, the executive power was entrusted to five Directors, men chosen initially by the Elders from a list of fifty drawn up by the 500; and here again every year one of the Directors, chosen by lot, had to retire in favour of a newcomer. However well meant, these provisions, and a great many lesser safeguards, such as those intended to prevent any revival of collective action by political clubs, led to recurrent instability. Legally, however, change was virtually impossible, and in practice the rigidity of the system was aggravated by that of the Directors themselves, men for the most part determined above all to preserve the regime in its entirety. Yet, as many historians have emphasized,[7] the new diffusion of power was ultimately incompatible with the real situation of France, if only because the continuation of the war implied the necessity of unified and arbitrary authority. It is indeed significant that the new constitution included recognition of the annexation of Belgium, an enduring cause of conflict with both Britain and Austria.

Nevertheless, the situation of old Montagnards such as Bourdon was not at first as unfavourable as they probably feared. The new Directors—

Barras, LaRevellière-Lépeaux, Reubell, Carnot, and Letourneur—certainly wished to stabilize the republic, and for that endeavour they needed all the support that could be rallied. All five of these men, too, were regicides, and at least two of them—Carnot, the great "organizer of victory," and Barras, notoriously an unprincipled opportunist—could be expected to favour the left. Moreover, in the first months of their tenure of office, they were profoundly influenced by the fact that their inauguration had been preceded by an unprecedented event, the royalist rising in Paris on Vendémiaire 12-13 (October 4-5, 1795). The most obdurate royalists, those who believed that no monarchy worthy of the name could be restored without outright violence, had stood aside on that occasion; but many others, who had hoped to establish a moderate form of monarchy by victory in the elections for the new legislative body, had been so thwarted by the Two-Thirds Law that they had taken up arms. Crushed by military force, an operation in which the young general Bonaparte had been prominent, this rising had really eliminated the remnants of the Jeunesse Dorée, which had been the instrument of the Thermidorean reaction. It had nonetheless intensified the republicans' abiding fears of royalism. By the Laws of Brumaire, the Convention re-enacted the savage revolutionary code that penalized priests, *émigrés*, and even the relatives of *émigrés*. Thus, the Directors inherited a decree that both deprived it of many potential servants and compromised its claim to real liberalism. Naturally enough, too, for some time they were strongly inclined to seek service and support from the royalists' bitterest enemies, the men so recently persecuted as "Jacobins," "terrorists," or "anarchists."

It was in these circumstances that Bourdon was appointed in mid-November 1795 to supervise the provision of supplies to Paris from the Department of the Seine-et-Marne.[8] That assignment was no doubt most welcome to him, for both the work and the area were known to him from his experiences there in 1789, and in the late autumn of 1795-96 the necessity of supplying Paris with grain was even greater than it had been then. Sown belatedly after a long and bitter winter, the crops had produced little in 1795, and the peasants who had grown them were still understandably unwilling to sell what little they had for *assignats*, which were by now less than half a percentage point of their face value. The people of Paris, to say nothing of others, were in fact confronted with famine conditions for the second year running: as one police agent reported in November, the misery of the people was extreme, with cold and hunger existing alongside the gaiety and luxury of a fortunate few.[9]

One small indication of the way in which Bourdon rose to his responsibility appears in a peremptory letter of his that has survived in the municipal archives in Provins.[10] Written from Melun on November 21 (Brumaire 30, Year IV), it was accompanied by a copy of a schedule agreed to by the departmental administration that showed how much each of its communes had to raise to fulfil a total of 200,000 quintains of grain, of which 82,000 were required from the canton of which Provins was a part. Bourdon then informed the Municipality of Provins that on receipt of this information it should promptly decide how much grain should be required of each individual farmer in its area. It should then proceed actively and zealously to fulfil its responsibilities, reporting daily by post both to Bourdon himself and to a commissioner of the Department of the Seine-et-Marne.

Yet his commitment to this work does not mean that Bourdon had abandoned all participation in political life in Paris, to which he probably often returned from his visits to the countryside.[11] As in other towns throughout France, there were then in the capital many men who had been deeply involved in popular political activity during the most crucial years of the Revolution, and their number was increased by others who, being ostracized or persecuted in their smaller provincial communities, sought anonymity and safety in the city. Initially these men were disoriented, for the reaction of 1794-95 had destroyed all the institutions and associations through which they had acted. It had not, however, destroyed all belief in democracy and in the possibility of a revival of a democratic movement.[12]

That possibility indeed developed as more and more people gradually became aware of the legal limitations imposed on them by the electoral structure and by the Directors' determination to prevent any alteration in the political system or the social order on which it was based. Initially, however, most of the more moderate democrats—as the men of 1793 and their successors will be called here for convenience and because other names, particularly "the Jacobins," became terms of opprobrium[13]— were cautious, for many of them hoped, just as did the royalists, that, by securing appointments or by rallying public support and eventually winning elections, they might make the regime more socially conscious and politically liberal. At the end of 1795, such caution meshed well with the attitude of the government, for in the anxious aftermath of the Vendémiaire rising the Directors were prepared to be accommodating. By appointing men such as Bourdon to administrative posts, by providing generous subsidies to the radical press, and by tolerating a measure of moderate democratic activity, they hoped to rally all republicans to the support of a new national union.[14]

More particularly, the Directors, notably Barras, almost openly sponsored the foundation of a new political society, the Réunion des Amis de la République.[15] Commonly called la Société du Panthéon, it is of some interest here because Kuscinski, in his *Dictionnaire*, states that Bourdon was "l'un des membres le plus actifs" of it. That assertion may seem likely, for the society, established on November 16, 1795, grew so rapidly that it soon became a place of general assembly for many of the democrats in Paris. Moreover, although it was initially remarkably careful to observe the law and to support the government, it became much more radical as winter brought increased hardship for the poor and as the original membership was submerged by an influx of working men and soldiers. Kuscinski's statement must nonetheless be rejected here, for there is no obvious evidence that Bourdon ever took part in the society's proceedings. Although that lack in itself may not be conclusive, the fact that the Society explicitly excluded all ex-deputies who had been released by the amnesty seems to be incontrovertible.[16]

However, if Kuscinki's remark is taken to mean only that Bourdon was at least briefly associated with the activity that led to the growth of the Panthéon Society, then it can be given greater credence. In several centres, predominantly cafés where democrats met, efforts were made to enlist support for the Society, and for a time Bourdon was certainly a *habitué* of one of the most notable of them, the Café Chrétien. Named after its proprietor, an old Jacobin, it was situated on the rue Neuve Saint-Marc, just off the Boulevard des Italiens, and thus within easy walking distance of Bourdon's home in the Priory of Saint-Martin. A number of references to Bourdon in the reports about public opinion compiled by police agents are here informative, even though they are more often derived from hearsay than from direct observation.

These reports suggest that when Bourdon first reappeared in Paris he was seen as a reliable friend by the politically dispossessed. Thus, on November 11, soon after his return from Ham, it was being said that "les sans-culottes du Faubourg Marceau" were ready to propose him as the mayor of their *arrondissement* if he would move back there from the Priory.[17] Three days later, another report noted with reserve ("S'il faut ajouter foi aux bruits") that Bourdon and others were supposed to be going around the most densely populated parts of Paris to rouse the people against the new government;[18] and, on November 26, it was alleged that malcontents gathered in another café, the Bains Chinois, had drawn up a list of those who might lead a better government, that list being headed by Bourdon and Cambon.[19] Conversely that report also struck a note suggesting that this initial popularity may have been short-lived: many people, it said, were surprised to see Bourdon at the head of a sub-sistence commission, and some papers were even saying that the authori-ties should prevent him from denigrating the Directory while hobnob-bing ("indulging in orgies") with other terrorists when he was in Melun.[20]

Behind such tales lies a modicum of certainty. On November 18, Bourdon was reported as having replaced the elderly Vadier in presid-ing at the Café Chrétien over an assembly that was fast becoming much like an illegal Popular Society.[21] The next day, too, he was posi-tively reported as telling everyone—including, remarkably, several of his old pupils who had visited him at the Priory—that the Constitution could not be successful and that, because too few royalists had been killed in Vendémiaire, that work would have to be begun anew.[22]

No doubt much of such talk in the various cafés can fairly be dis-missed as the equivalent of coffeehouse babble. Certainly personal resentments of harsh treatment, and regrets for the greater days of the Year II, were there intermingled with nebulous schemes of arousing the populace or for winning over the Thermidorians in the Councils by disavowing Robespierre while praising Danton. Nonetheless, the cafés were briefly important as potential centres for the renewal of political and even revolutionary agitation. Moreover, the men at the Café Chrétien were straining the new constitutional laws against collective action by encouraging the formation of similar groups in other districts. It is therefore possible that Bourdon was one of those who contributed indirectly to the growth and changing temper of the Panthéon Society.

More significant, however, is that the last date on which any refer-ence to Bourdon occurs in these police reports is December 9, 1795, when an agent noted that he and a few of his cronies had chuckled over the news that Babeuf had evaded those trying to arrest him.[23] Long an extremely intransigent democrat, "Gracchus" Babeuf[24] had been imprisoned so often that he had become practically a professional revolutionary, and, when he was released from prison soon after the suppression of the royalist rising in Vendémiaire, he had promptly resumed the publication of his journal, *Le Tribun du peuple*. In the first of the new issues of this paper (properly number thirty-four, which appeared on November 6), Babeuf had denounced the directorial regime as politically reactionary and socially sterile. Repudiating any idea of general reunion with such people, he had openly praised Robespierre and urged all true democrats to lead "the plebeian masses" in a return to the principles embodied in the Constitution of 1793. Bourdon and his cronies at the Café Chrétien were wrong, however, in supposing that the next issue of the *Tribun* would be a similar attack on the Thermidorians.

Although there is nothing to suggest that Bourdon was in any way involved in the events that ensued, they eventually changed his situation considerably. In this context, the essential fact is that both Babeuf's writing and the Directory's efforts to silence Babeuf precipitated a division in the Panthéon Society. As the Society had grown larger, it had become increasingly representative of popular discontent about the Directors' failure to alter the appalling conditions of life in Paris. At the same time, a few influential men, most notably Robert Lindet[25] and Amar, had done all they could to obstruct the government and thwart the policy of reunion. In this situation, the second of Babeuf's publications (properly number thirty-five of *Le Tribun du peuple*, issued on November 30) proved most alarming to all moderate people by proclaiming the necessity of effecting total social change through unrestricted revolution.[26] On the other hand, the protracted pursuit of Babeuf by the police, and perhaps still more their persecution of his wife, intensified radical hostility to the Directory. Consequently the Directors ordered the closure of the Society, which was summarily effected by Bonaparte, now the commander of the Army of the Interior, on February 27, 1796. Unhappily this action made matters worse again, for opposition inevitably became conspiracy, and the cause of the democrats was long blighted by the eventual arrest in May 1796 of Babeuf and those actually or supposedly associated with him in the "Conspiration des Égaux."[27]

Probably, therefore, what Bourdon did *not* do at the turning of the year 1795-96 is more significant in the context of his life than anything he actually did. He was certainly not implicated in any way in Babeuf's activities: indeed, it seems that in December 1795, when the situation of the democrats began to deteriorate, he abandoned the Café Chrétien and took no further part in politics. What is more, there was no other occasion later on in which he became involved in any comparable activity. It thus seems that after his release from prison he toyed for some weeks with the possibility of further participation in political activity but opted instead to work with and through government.

Bourdon's path, however, was not to prove easy. No doubt moved by his renewed familiarity with the problems involved in providing Paris with food, Bourdon once again put forward a proposal for reorganizing the whole system of supply. Apparently a modified version of the plan that he and his father had long advocated, it was shelved in January 1796 by the Directory on the advice of Bénézech, the Minister of the Interior, as being "too difficult to effect, too costly, and altogether illusory."[28] Moreover, in the same month, his efforts to expedite the flow of grain to the capital from the Seine-et-Marne brought him into conflict with the Municipality of Fontainebleau and thus with the departmental administrators. In two letters to the Directors, dated January 16 and 19 (Nivôse 26 and 29, Year IV), he sought to justify himself by saying that he had found Fontainebleau a centre of royalism in which, even though the people were perishing of hunger, his work had been blocked by "every obstacle of cupidity and ill will."[29] He had therefore authorized agents to supervise the markets, and he had convened a general meeting of "enlightened citizens" to consider possible remedial measures. Accused of exceeding his powers, he had been forced to report to Paris. His request for more explicit instructions and greater authority, however, was merely evaded: the Directors (Lépeaux, Carnot, and Letourneur) did no more than inform him that he was not a commissioner of the government but simply an agent of the Minister of the Interior, whose orders he must follow.[30]

This mission nonetheless seems to have been strikingly successful. In his letter of January 19, Bourdon was indeed able to cite the minister's previous praise: "I can only applaud your energy and zeal in effecting the tasks entrusted to you."[31] Some impression of him and his work also appears in a nearly contemporary account by an English writer, who described him as being "about 40, of strong constitution, middle size and extremely active."[32] According to the same account, Bourdon had finally told the Directors that "The terrorists alone enjoyed the glory of rendering such signal services to their native country," and the author adds that Calonne, once Louis XVI's principal minister, wrote in exile that "the Jacobins were born to achieve miracles." Sadly, however, the conclusion of Bourdon's mission at the end of April 1796 coincided with the Directors' abandonment of their dalliance with the democrats. On April 16, advocacy of the Constitution of 1793 became a capital crime; on May 10, Babeuf was finally captured; and on May 12 the Law of Floréal 23, Year IV, forbade residence in Paris to those ex-deputies of the Convention who were not Parisians by birth.[33] To his disgust, this ban applied to Bourdon, who had in fact lived in Paris since his childhood.

Such expulsion might be thought nominal, but its reality appears in the fact that—with one exception—there are few obvious records of Bourdon's activities for the next twelve months. One exception, slight

in itself, at least affords a glimpse of Bourdon in 1796, when one royalist writer nastily remarked that his flat, greasy hair and his dirty and
disgusting dress sufficed to identify him as one of the most incurable of
terrorists.[34] Rather more revealing is the sequence of events that began
on July 27, 1796, the second anniversary of the fall of Robespierre, a
date that Bourdon wrote as "9 Thermidor, an IV de la République
Française, une, indivisible et Démocratique." On that day, a number of
citizens in Brussels (presumably all good "patriots") were assembled in
the building then called the Temple of the Laws. There they heard an
address by "LÉONARD BOURDON, ex-député de la Convention
Nationale, actuellement défenseur officieux près des Tribunaux des
Départmens réunis."[35] That title is of interest as showing that he had,
or at least claimed to have, official status as one authorized to plead in
the courts of what had been Belgium, particularly on behalf of those
unwilling to plead personally.[36]

As for Bourdon's address on this occasion, all that survives is the
part printed by the Municipality of Brussels at the request of the
audience.[37] Remarkably this part is entirely in verse, the nature of
which may be gauged by its opening lines:

> PEUPLE, dont les vertus égalent le courage,
> À la RAISON enfin tu rends un libre hommage;
> L'auguste VERITÉ, proscrivant tes faux Dieux,
> Par sa vive lumière a dessillé tes yeux;
> Des *Prêtres* et des *Rois* la ligue est confondue,
> De leurs sanglans complots la trame s'est rompue;
> Et la France, sortant d'un pénible sommeil,
> Voit ces spectres hideux disparaître au réveil.

Followed through some ninety more lines, the theme of that first
verse is developed to reveal how grievously the French had suffered
from the unholy alliance of tyranny and superstition; how happily they
had been enlightened by the author of Nature; and how wonderfully
they were now succeeding in bringing the blessings of Reason and
Liberty to the peoples of Europe, "From the Tiber to the Rhine, from
the Moselle to the Po." Nor was Belgium itself forgotten:

> Dejà le Belge, uni par la Fraternité,
> Aux destins du Français a joint sa destinée;
> L'Escaut n'est plus captif, et l'Aigle (Austria), consternée,
> Recule, en frémissant, devant la Liberté.

Whatever may be thought about Bourdon's poetic abilities, his
verses certainly show that, despite all his vicissitudes, in 1796 he was

still a revolutionary. For him, Reason, the Republic of France, and Liberty remained synonymous terms. However, because the only mention of democracy in this extract is that which occurs in the title, it is also probably true that he had come to accept the social and political limitations of the directorial regime as a temporary necessity, one made more palatable by the apparently irreversible successes of the armies of the republic.

On the other hand, his visit to Brussels also led to much defamation of him both personally and as a representative of the French government, which was evidently heartily disliked by a good many people in Belgium. All this ridicule began quietly enough when on August 10 a local journal, *L'Impartial bruxellois*, reprinted a notice dated August 1 from another paper announcing that Léonard Bourdon, "si connu par son proconsulat à Orléans," had been in the city for some days and was seeking to become a judge in one of its courts. The writer hoped that in that quest "ce chef de revoltés de germinal et de prairial" would not be successful.[38] Bourdon then unwisely had the editor of *L'Impartial* summoned to appear before the local justices to answer his allegation of calumny, for which his compensation should be paid to the poor.

Because the editor, A.J. de Braeckenier, refused at an initial hearing to repudiate a statement taken from another paper, the case was referred to a higher court, the Civil Tribunal of the Department of the Dyle, where it was heard on September 4. Although the account of this hearing later published by de Braeckenier relates only to his own defence, it is at least an indication of the hostility that then lay in wait for all real or supposed terrorists. Obviously an able antagonist, de Braeckenier based his defence on the freedom of the press, arguing also that he could not be held responsible for a remark derived directly from a French paper (*L'Éclair*). Furthermore, he held it as his civic duty to warn the public of the presence in Brussels of one regarded by the whole French press as "un monstre altéré de sang humain"—just as a farmer would protect his flock on seeing a wolf emerging from the forest.

The editor's main contention, however, was that a man like Bourdon could not be slandered because he had no reputation to lose. In support of this argument, he cited a considerable number of extracts from denunciations of Bourdon that had been made in the Convention or in the French press since the beginning of 1793, particular play being made with material culled from Fréron's *Orateur du peuple*. The unfortunate Bourdon thus appeared as one of those directly responsible for the Revolution of May 31, 1793, as well as for the risings of both Germinal and Prairial in 1795; he was also represented as a thief, a habitual drunkard, and above all the "assassin of Orléans," where "the bloody spectres of his victims rise from their graves to demand vengeance" on him. In conclusion, de Braeckenier personally protested against the presence of a man "vomi par la France," and he quoted the promise of yet another French paper, *Les Nouvelles politiques*, that this impudent "Amnestié" would be pursued through the liberty of the press until he found safety in obscurity.

This episode, a striking illustration of the process by which Bourdon's traditional reputation was built up by combining all the allegations made by his enemies, is also an indication of the state of opinion in Brussels. According to one of the items from the French press that de Braeckenier appended to his report, Bourdon had been prominent at a festival held in Brussels on August 10 to mark the anniversary of the fall of the monarchy in 1792. There, it was alleged, he had praised the Parisian Commune of the Insurrection ("Nous étions onze alors, et seuls nous avons sauvé la Patrie"), being so provocative that a fracas had ensued between "le peuple" and "ces Brigands." Again according to the *Nouvelles Politiques*, the court in which his case was heard was packed with people, many of whom were so moved by the story of the execution of the nine men of Orléans that the president repeatedly had to call for order, and Bourdon himself intervened to assert that all present were really royalists. Apparently he then withdrew, amid curses and general execration, while the court, charging him with minimal costs, cautiously referred the dispute back to the local justices as merely a matter of verbal injury.

Other material appended by de Braeckenier shows that many of those in Brussels believed that Bourdon was in reality one of a number of democrats who had been sent to Belgium by the French Directory to ensure that they, or men like them, would be successful in the elections scheduled for the early spring of 1797. Although this seems surprisingly soon after the Directors had abandoned their initial toleration of the democrats, there are indications that some such activity may have been begun in the late summer of 1796. By that time, the Directors were no doubt aware that royalism, encouraged by their repression of the democrats, was reviving apace and that even moderate men were disturbed by their failure to effect any obvious improvement in the situation of the country. Moreover, a serious breach was opening between the Directors themselves, for Carnot was in fact a man of government whose sympathies were with the right, and he was followed closely by Letourneur. All five Directors were consequently looking with increasing anxiety toward the elections of 1798, when the advent of a second "new third" was bound to have a profound effect on the balance of opinion in the two legislative councils.

More specifically, it seems that in August 1796 Barras noted that the various commissioners of the government had been charged with giving guidance in the elections,[39] and it may well be supposed that it was particularly important to win support in the nine departments of an occupied and annexed Belgium. If that was so, then perhaps Bourdon was a *defenseur officieux* only in name, his real—and more congenial—function being, or becoming, that of reviving the republican zeal of the democrats in Brussels. There is indeed a little more positive evidence of this function toward the end of 1796, when pressure on Belgium was intensified. At that time, Merlin de Douai, the French Minister of Justice, and Charles Cochon, the Minister of Police, sent circulars to the authorities in Belgium in which they listed the names of those ex-conventionnels whose election "serait agréable" to the Directory,[40] and Thibaudeau's *Mémoires* say that various commissioners, including Léonard Bourdon and another *amnestié*, Mallarmé of the Meurthe, were then sent to the area.[41] Because Mallarmé had been acting as public prosecutor in the Department of the Dyle since December 1795,[42] there is some possibility that both men had been called to Paris for briefing, but the greater probability is surely that both continued with work that they had begun previously. On the other hand, it could hardly have gone on into 1797, for on December 4, 1796, the Councils in Paris approved a measure meant to reassure moderates of the right: by this Law of Frimaire 14, Year V, all the *amnestiés* were excluded from all public offices.[43]

Thus, Bourdon, again a victim of circumstance, was left without any office at all for most of 1797. There is now little trace of his activities at that time. The period, too, was one in which fortune long seemed to be favouring the royalists and the most moderate republicans, whereas those more democratic in sympathy had to struggle to keep their cause alive. It is possible, however, to bridge this gap by surmise. In all likelihood, Bourdon spent some part of the year in modifying his old proposals for economic and educational reform. Although both matters may be more conveniently considered later,[44] it is pertinent to recall here that early in 1796 he had presented the Directors with a plan for improving the supply of food, and in 1798 he would do so again. (Incidentally Bourdon's father, Bourdon des Planches, from whom Léonard had inherited his ideas about economic change, was still in the background in December 1796, when he received a letter from Léonard's brother Bourdon de Vatry.[45]) Similarly it was in October 1797, when (as Isser Woloch, a modern authority on the period, remarks) Bourdon "came out of his retirement,"[46] that he submitted a petition to the Council of Five Hundred in which he again advocated a system of national communal education.

No doubt Bourdon also gave a good deal of attention to the claims that he made on the Directory in 1795-96 for indemnification for the losses that he alleged he had suffered by the closure of his school in 1795. Those claims related in part to payments said to be outstanding after the final months of the school's existence. More, however, were concerned with the losses that he said he had incurred by the dilapidation of his property in the Priory while he was in prison, and others supported his call for compensation for the loss of his means of livelihood. Reviewed at almost annual intervals from April 1796 until 1799, this matter is so involved that even its outlines must be relegated to an appendix;[47] however, some comments, necessarily subjective, are appropriate here. The claims may be, and were, thought exaggerated, but some part of each can be, and was, considered legitimate, and Bourdon himself was certainly passionately convinced that he was both materially and morally entitled to a substantial indemnity. Furthermore, although the amounts in question were reduced through successive recommendations almost to a vanishing point, actual payment appears to have been perpetually deferred. Although that procrastination was doubtless primarily due to the appalling financial instability of the times, of which the repudiation of two-thirds of the state's debts to investors in September 1797 was one manifestation, the treatment that Bourdon received may be seen as declining from consideration to severity and even to shabbiness.

More immediately pertinent to his situation in 1797 is the fact that in his later appeals for justice Bourdon specifically asked for payment in *bons*, the notes that eventually replaced both the *assignat* and its successor, the *mandat*, as bonds valid for the purchase of nationalized land. Indeed, for what they were worth, *bons* could virtually be used only for that purpose.[48] In making that request in 1798, Bourdon explained that he had been in possession for three years of a piece of property purchased from the lands of the nation. If, as seems likely, the purchase was made in anticipation of a substantial payment through the first assessment of his claims in April 1796, then he could indeed have found a haven outside Paris in 1797; however, he would presumably have been considerably in debt, particularly because until April 1798 he continued to hold the tenancy of his part of the Priory, the rental of which was 4,000 francs a year. Certainly he would have been greatly concerned to know the outcome of the second assessment of his claims, which occurred at an unspecified date in July-August 1797 (Thermidor, Year V) and that might explain a well-known reference to his presence in Paris on July 20 (Thermidor 2).

A different explanation, which implies that the democrats were preparing to participate in open conflict with the royalists, is possible but unlikely. True, by midsummer in 1797, a new political crisis was obviously imminent. Thanks in part to subsidies from Britain, the royalists and the more conservative republicans had made great gains in the spring elections of 1797, at the expense of the second third of those ex-deputies of the Convention who had hitherto retained their seats by the Two-Thirds Law of 1795. Although the reinforced right in the legislative councils had not proved intractable, it had insisted on a repeal of the savage laws against the priests and the *émigrés*, and it obviously wanted to conclude the war against Austria and Britain by a moderate peace. That was diametrically opposed to the policies and financial interests of the Directors and the generals, and, although on the one hand royalist extremists prepared to seize power by force, on the other hand the Directors, divided among themselves but urged on by Bonaparte from Italy, at least made sure that they had ample military aid readily available.

It was at this time of tension that on July 20 Boissy d'Anglas, a deputy who had become more and more obviously a royalist, announced his conviction that a return to revolutionary terrorism was imminent. It was, he said, impossible to move a step "sans être éffrayé de l'apparition d'un assassin révolutionnaire: on voit Fournier l'Américain, qui commandait le massacre des prisonniers d'Orléans; Léonard Bourdon; et tant d'autres."[49] Apparitions apart, however, there is nothing to suggest that the democrats, or indeed the people of Paris in general, took any part in the conflict that culminated on September 4 in the coup d'état of Fructidor. On the contrary, the Directors, far from seeking the aid of the "terrorists," as they had done in Vendémiaire, Year III, now relied entirely on using military force to crush the "royalists."

Yet the coup d'état of Fructidor, like that of Vendémiaire, was at least temporarily advantageous to the democrats. Initiated by three of the Directors (Barras, Lépeaux, and Reubell), it was bloodless but drastic. The elections in forty-nine departments were annulled; fifty-three deputies and twelve others, including the other two Directors (Carnot and Barthélemy[50]) were condemned to immediate deportation; the revolutionary laws against priests and *émigrés* were reinstated and ruthlessly enforced; and a sweeping purge of the national and local administrations began. Inevitably such measures implied increased dependence on the loyalty and services of the democrats, who had apparently yet to recognize that, once a minority government had invoked the use of force, even "to save the Constitution,"[51] it might equally well deal arbitrarily with them.

Happily, because Bourdon was one of the beneficiaries of the coup, there is—for once—ample documentary evidence of his experiences in his new employment. According to the account[52] that he submitted in April 1798 to Merlin de Douai,[53] then the Directors' president, he was "in the country" when on Fructidor 18 (September 4, 1797, the day of the coup) he was summoned urgently to Paris. There he had several meetings with the Minister of Police, Pierre Sotin, a man whose sympathies were with the democrats. Told initially that he would be entrusted with an important foreign mission, he was eventually, in November 1797, appointed as commissioner to the neutral city of Hamburg.

This mission is of particular interest because biographical dictionaries generally make conflicting and misleading statements about Bourdon's purpose in visiting Hamburg. Variously described as a financial, commercial, and diplomatic agent of the Directory, Bourdon is said to have been charged with raising a loan of 10 million livres or with completely reorganizing French commerce with the city. Furthermore, almost all writers declare that his principal task was that of expelling the French *émigrés* from the area, and some allege that his brutality in accomplishing this task occasioned his recall. That the truth is very different, and more interesting, is immediately apparent in the instructions that he received on appointment.

These instructions appear in his own account, which was subsequently certified as correct by Sotin, and in an official report made twelve months later to Sotin's successor.[54] Both show that the government had been informed that the Hanseatic towns—Hamburg, Altona, Bremen, and Lubeck—sheltered a nest of conspirators against the republic and that it had decided to anticipate their activities by unobtrusively establishing a perceptive agent in the area. After Sotin, who had met Bourdon among "men known for their attachment to Liberty," had recommended him to the Directory as a well-informed and reliable republican, he had seen both Sotin and Merlin de Douai, and he had been given secret as well as open orders. Ostensibly he was to go to Hamburg and the other Baltic ports to explore the possibility of increasing the supply of goods to France. His real purpose, however, was to observe the activities of the *émigrés* and, if he could not persuade them to return, to keep the government fully informed of their movements and their contacts with the enemies of France, as well as of anything else affecting the internal or external security of the republic.

The myth that grew up about this mission apparently derives from statements printed on February 12, 1798, in the *Moniteur*. The paper noted that at the request of Léonard Bourdon the Directory had ordered the expulsion of the *émigrés* from Hamburg, and it claimed that forty-eight hours after his arrival the Senate of Hamburg had publicly warned all French *émigrés* to quit its territory immediately.[55] This version of the facts, however, seems simply to be propaganda intended to illustrate the Directory's determination to uphold the power and dignity of the republic. Neither in Paris nor in Hamburg do the alleged order and warning seem to exist,[56] and, as his instructions show, Bourdon was not authorized to make any such demand. Indeed, he himself protested against the publication of exaggerated reports that prejudiced the success of his real mission. Furthermore, the Directory had no legal right to issue orders about the internal affairs of a free state, the neutrality of which it had repeatedly recognized. No doubt the Directors would gladly have imposed their will on Hamburg by military force, but at this time that solution was not seriously in question.[57]

However, when Bourdon and his family actually left Paris early in January 1798, he probably believed that he was beginning a new career in the service of a rejuvenated republic. After Fructidor, France was again the principal power in continental Europe, for the elimination of the moderates in France had compelled Austria to accept peace on Bonaparte's terms at Campo-Formio; moreover, although the Directors were apparently unable to agree on any coherent foreign policy, they were at least determined to defeat England and to reassert everywhere the interests and importance of *la Grande Nation*. The realities that Bourdon encountered, which can be reconstructed from his own letters and the records of the Foreign Ministry, nonetheless soon belied all his hopes.

The most obvious of these realities proved to be his inability to effect any real change in the situation of the *émigrés* in Hamburg, the number of whom he not inaccurately estimated at about 8,000. As one of the greatest ports of northern Europe, Hamburg—a name here applied to all four of the Hanseatic ports in the area—had long witnessed the entry and departure of those whose flight from revolutionary France had been the beginning of perpetual wanderings. As a free

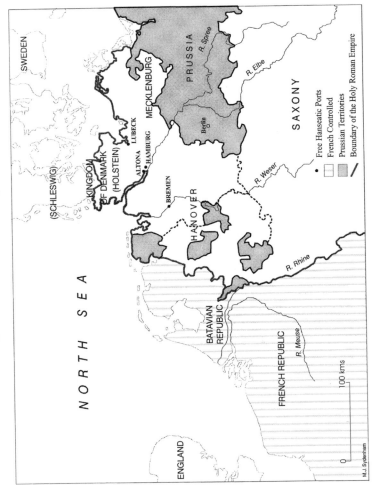

Map 6
The situation of Hamburg, 1798

city within the Holy Roman Empire, and as one seemingly secured by the Line of Demarcation, a buffer zone secretly agreed on in the Franco-Prussian Treaty of Basle in 1795, it had also become a principal place of refuge for the many French exiles who had had to leave Holland and the Rhineland as the republican armies advanced. Some, those of *la haute émigration*, still contrived to maintain the style and standards of the old order, but many more merely survived as best they could, occasionally rejoicing in reunions with relatives and friends and even, as one of them pathetically wrote, "laughing as if we were still happy."[58]

The news of the arrival of Léonard Bourdon, "recently one of the most villainous of terrorists," apparently caused these people "universal alarm."[59] The Senate of the city warned the *chevaliers de Saint Louis* not to wear their crosses, and for some days all anticipated expulsion. Nonetheless, Bourdon soon found that there was little that he could do. Indeed, he had great difficulty in finding either accommodation or servants. Acting with and through C.-F. Reinhard, the (unrecognized) Minister Plenipotentiary of France, he pressed the Senate of Hamburg to furnish a full list of resident *émigrés*, to control a royalist journal, *Le Spectateur du nord*, and to ban the circulation of a royalist pamphlet entitled *Adresse aux souverains de l'Europe*. When all these demands were evaded, he wrote to Paris to suggest that the Senate, which feared either a British blockade or a military occupation by Prussia, might be made more compliant by greater pressure from France. He also asked for authority to make a few arrests himself, as examples, and to expose conspiracies and the forging of passports.[60] But he received no reply, and on his departure in June 1798 one *émigré* noted, "The monster, whom everyone feared, has done no harm to anyone."[61]

Yet Bourdon's activities in Hamburg went much further than his initial requests suggest. If he did not do much to fulfil his nominal role of investigating supplies for France, he soon appreciated that Hamburg was the principal port by which goods coming from Britain, or through British ports, flowed into Europe despite every French embargo. Perhaps optimistically, he advised Paris that such traffic could be made unprofitable if all illicit cargoes, wherever confiscated, were sent for sale to Hamburg, thus flooding the market there.[62] Moreover, if he was at first too ready to report fantastic stories about sinister Englishmen seen carrying chests of gold about at night, he soon knew enough to send back specific, if perhaps somewhat dated, information about the network of royalist agencies that ran from London through Hamburg to Germany, Switzerland, and France itself.[63]

Nor was Bourdon content simply to report the names of the most notable agents of this system. He perceived that just as foreign trade to the Hanseatic ports was being exploited by the enemies of the French republic, who seemed to use the ships "like a ferry service," so too might it also be developed by the agents and friends of France. With this end in view, he first approached Reinhard, from whom he had been assured that he could get funds as soon as he reached Hamburg.[64] In practice, however, all Reinhard could do was to support his efforts to obtain from Paris the money and authority to create in Hamburg a bureau that would concern itself not only with countering espionage but also with subversive activities in Britain. It might, Bourdon believed, thus be possible to rekindle in the Royal Navy the mutiny that had been smothered in 1797. Moreover, an old associate, William Duckett, the Irish exile who acted on occasion as his secretary, put Bourdon in touch with other exiled Irishmen, and he soon realized that a rebellion in Ireland was imminent. It, too, he reported, could be effectively fomented through an agency in Hamburg, where there were already reliable Irishmen who could identify others, expose double agents, and form the core of an Irish Legion.[65]

Some months later, the official report on Bourdon's mission recognized his competence, noting that he had supplied valuable information and that his ideas were well worth the Directors' consideration. The fact remains that all his proposals were ignored, so that he eventually had to return ignominiously to Paris. This failure, which was not due to any brutal behaviour on his part, was to some extent implicit in his ambiguous situation. Because he apparently kept his secret instructions strictly to himself, no one was ever sure of his standing or his purpose. Initially he found a willing collaborator in the Minister Plenipotentiary, but early in March 1798 Reinhard was replaced by a more suspicious newcomer, Roberjot, who was soon shocked by Bourdon's apparent attempts to supervise him. According to the report that Roberjot sent to Paris, Bourdon had been altogether too familiar with Reinhard, even reading his official letters and referring to Reinhard as "a good fellow, but one lacking in energy."[66] This criticism by Roberjot was the more unfortunate for Bourdon because he had just compromised himself by a characteristic intervention in public affairs in Hamburg.

From his arrival onward, Bourdon's anxieties about the freedom enjoyed by French royalists was matched by his concern about the restriction of those French residents who were republicans. Their morale, Bourdon reported, was low: although they were constantly insulted in the royalist press, they had no newspaper of their own. Having few opportunities to meet, they knew little of French affairs or even of Bonaparte's victories. He therefore had no hesitation in accepting an invitation to speak to some of them on February 24, 1798 (Ventôse 6, Year VI). This meeting was sponsored by Lagau, the French consul, who had previously been urged by the Minister of Foreign Affairs to encourage regular reunions of French citizens. Bourdon told the audience[67] that such meetings would serve to educate the young, to promote French commerce, and to prove that republicans were really decent, responsible people. He asserted that members of the French nation had every right to assemble to celebrate national festivals; and, being a natural orator still passionately sure of the ultimate triumph of republican democracy, he spoke boldly of his divinities, Liberty and Equality, which he distinguished sharply from licence and levelling. Those present then resolved to arrange regular meetings open to all registered Frenchmen, and at least one such meeting was soon held.

This second occasion, held to mark the prescribed French festival of the Sovereignty of the People, began with a banquet for forty-four persons. According to an account by Duckett,[68] civic hymns and patriotic toasts then alternated with the composition of couplets—such as "Tremblez royalistes de France / Le peuple souverain s'avance!"—and the company ended the evening in high good humour with singing and dancing. In reporting this festivity to Paris, Duckett emphatically denied the rumour that Bourdon, who had presided, had harangued the people and been hooted by royalists. On the contrary, he asserted that Bourdon had behaved very properly and had contributed greatly to the success of the occasion by his carefree sociability and obvious patriotism.

His behaviour was nevertheless at once represented as an attempt to establish a revolutionary political club in Hamburg. It thus evoked considerable hostility. That reaction is understandable, for at that time the French armies, which had already occupied Rome and supervised a coup d'état in Holland, were in the process of establishing yet another satellite republic in Switzerland, and no one knew which state would be occupied and revolutionized next. The Senate of Hamburg therefore told Roberjot that it could not permit the formation of political clubs, and the king of Denmark, who was particularly worried because Bourdon had visited Altona, in Danish Holstein, similarly expressed anxiety about his activities. Roberjot then informed the Directory that Bourdon's conduct was causing grave disquiet, and the Directors began to ask questions of the Minister of Foreign Affairs, Talleyrand, which neither he nor anyone else seemed able to answer.[69]

At this level, it appears that the Directors, if not averse to extending their resources by revolutionary aggrandizement, were particularly anxious not to prejudice the negotiations that had begun at Rastadt about the reorganization of Germany,[70] negotiations already forced on them by Bonaparte. Although they resented Hamburg's dalliance with Britain and Prussia, they were also well aware of the city's considerable value to France as a neutral centre of banking and commerce. Moreover, the Directors' anxieties of 1797 about royalism in France had by now yielded to new fears of a resurgence of the left, and the coup d'état of Floréal (May 11, 1798), a general purge of democrats, was imminent. It was in these circumstances that on April 24, 1798, Bourdon was curtly informed that his mission was over and that he should return to Paris immediately.[71]

More surprisingly, that order was a welcome one, for by this time Bourdon was feeling completely abandoned. He had regularly sent long and detailed reports to Paris, numbering them in sequence from one to twenty-three. He had asked for more specific authority, and he had made various recommendations, particularly about the importance of adequately funded countermeasures against espionage; however, he had not had a single word in reply. Worst of all, he had received no money except that advanced for his initial travelling expenses, and when his own resources were exhausted he was reduced to living as best he could on what he could borrow.[72] At first he had asked if his letters could have been intercepted; then he had sent his secretary to Paris in quest of an interview; and later his brother, Bourdon de Vatry, tried in vain to deliver a letter personally to Merlin de Douai. Finally Léonard Bourdon himself had to beg the government either to provide him with the means to do useful service or to recall him for employment elsewhere.[73] Yet, even when that recall came, no money came with it, and it was not until June 1798 that he received a sum barely sufficient for his return journey.

Deeply disappointing as this whole affair was for Bourdon personally, it is illuminating. At the general level, it exposes remarkable deficiencies in the government of France. At every stage, from Bourdon's first interview in September 1797 to his eventual reappearance in Paris in June 1798, there were long delays, and it was not until the end of 1798 that repayment of his outstanding expenses was finally recommended. Again, even before he had reached Hamburg in January 1798, he was disowned by the Ministry of Finance, for which he was ostensibly acting but which really knew nothing of his mission.[74] Moreover, Sotin, the Minister of Police for whom he was actually an agent, was abruptly dismissed from office in February 1798. As a police report[75] later admitted, that dismissal meant that Bourdon was simply forgotten: although the arrival of his reports was duly recorded in the "In" register of the ministry, there was only one entry in the "Out" register of replies, that being the order for his recall. Furthermore, much interdepartmental correspondence accumulated when Talleyrand, becoming concerned to maintain the neutrality of Denmark, wanted Bourdon to be told to exercise more restraint. He politely asked Dandrieu, the new Minister of Police, to let him see Bourdon's letters, but they were so difficult to find that they had to be sent to the Foreign Ministry severally or even singly, as they happened to come to light in various police bureaux, each of which was more secretive than the previous one.[76]

In this particular affair, Bourdon's reputation as a brutal and tyrannical terrorist is also decisively belied. If he did not attempt to persuade the *émigrés* to return to France, neither did he try to intimidate them. Indeed, it seems that he soon took pride in ignoring their contemptuous disregard of him. It also seems natural and even creditable that he should have welcomed the possibility of serving France by reviving the courage and confidence of his compatriots. He was, however, mistaken in supposing that he could act politically as if he were a private citizen. By remaining true to a vision of popular democracy that had become obnoxious to the authorities in France itself, he simply embarrassed them and compromised himself. Beyond this, Bourdon was from the beginning of his mission placed in an impossible situation by the inconstancy of his political masters, by the innate secrecy of their police force, and by the penury of France. As his immediate successor sadly reflected, "Zeal can achieve nothing when all means are lacking."[77]

14

A Servant of the State
(July 1798 to May 1807)

*T*hroughout most of the nineteenth century, those who compiled biographical dictionaries wrote vaguely of the conclusion of Léonard Bourdon's career. Some of these authors refer to a period in Toulon, but almost all of them assert that at some point after his visit to Hamburg Bourdon established a primary school in Paris and taught there for the rest of his life. His death was then ascribed to various dates between 1805 and 1825, that most commonly accepted (or transcribed) being in or about 1816.

This tradition was broken in 1889, when Auguste Kuscinski contributed his synopsis of information about Bourdon's birth and death to *La Révolution Française*.[1] It stated authoritatively ("Voici la verité"), but without any specific documentary references, that in November 1800, "un an après le coup d'État du 18 brumaire," Bourdon succeeded in getting himself named ("réussit à se faire nommer") a member of the administrative council of the military hospital in Toulon. Kuscinski then adds that on March 12, 1807, he became a principal director of military hospitals and that in this capacity he then followed the Grand Army into Prussia, where he died: "C'est là qu'il est mort, à Breslau, le 29 mai 1807." Although the older and vaguer version of the facts may still be encountered, Kuscinski's statement, reiterated in his *Dictionnaire des conventionnels* (published posthumously in 1916) is now generally accepted.[2]

With one exception, the date of Bourdon's appointment to Toulon, Kuscinski's pronouncement is also accepted here, for initial research suggests that proper verification of it would be a protracted process. Of Bourdon's final years, which should be informative because he then lived in less turbulent times than during the revolutionary decade,

---

Notes to Chapter 14 are on pp. 392-94.

something more may indeed be said, but here again much must remain speculative. If in this there is some criticism of Kuscinski's work, particularly in his failure to identify his sources, it is accompanied by full recognition of the astonishingly comprehensive nature of his *Dictionnaire*. That volume is indeed "an indispensable source"[3] and a mine of fascinating information about the hundreds of deputies who sat in the National Convention. Neither minor errors nor the absence of precise annotation can weaken appreciation of the achievement of one whom Alphonse Aulard judged "un érudit de première force."[4]

In one sense, Bourdon's life as a man of the Revolution may be said to have ended with his period of employment in Hamburg, for it proved to be his last opportunity to make any substantial political contribution to the cause of democratic republicanism. However, if for Bourdon the Revolution in effect ended eighteen months before Bonaparte and his henchmen created the Provisional Consulate in November 1799, that did not mean that he immediately abandoned all hope of effecting those reforms that he and his father had believed even before 1789 to be fundamental to the welfare of France. On the contrary, being without employment after his return to Paris in June 1798, Bourdon lost no time in attempting to interest the government in either or both of his projects for educational and economic reform. On July 30 (Thermidor 12, Year VI),[5] writing from a new address in the rue Dominique ("près celle de Bourgoyne" and thus conveniently close to the meeting place of the Council of Five Hundred),[6] he sent the Minister of the Interior an outline of his ideas on education and suggested that he should be invited to justify them at a meeting of well-informed men of the minister's choice. Furthermore, on August 28 (Fructidor 11), he submitted a petition to the Council of Five Hundred in which he urged the deputies to consider his plan for legislation to reorganize the grain trade.[7]

This plan was introduced just as its predecessors had been, as the outcome of a lifetime's work by an octogenarian who had once been imprisoned in the Bastille; and, as had happened so often before, it was promptly referred to a commission. A month later, on September 25 (Vendémiaire 4), Bourdon nevertheless returned to the attack,[8] this time attempting to make his scheme more topical by relating it to Article 16 of the Constitution of 1795, by which young men could be enrolled as citizens only if they could prove their literacy and their ability "to carry on a mechanical occupation."[9] Related both to his educational and to his economic ideas, this presentation of his views to the Council of Five Hundred now extolled the plan as a means of stimulating and perfecting French industry, but it was also relegated to the commission. The fate of this whole project is sufficiently apparent in the fact that a full year later, on September 2, 1799 (Fructidor 16, Year VII), when the commission had been reconstituted and Bourdon again called for consideration of his proposal,[10] his plea was simply, and apparently finally, disposed of in the same way.

Beyond the obvious fact that what may be called "the Bourdons' plan" had been repeatedly rejected as impractical ever since 1789, by 1798 it had become even less acceptable than before. At that time, the Minister of the Interior, François de Neufchateau, was indeed making remarkable efforts to promote agricultural and industrial recovery, but even he was representative of prevailing opinion in being averse to any direct intervention by the state in the economy. Moreover, in the aftermath of the coup d'état of Floréal (May 1798), when the democrats' successes in the elections were annulled, no proposal reminiscent of the controls of 1793 was likely to find favour. Nor were the prospects really any better in the late summer of 1799, when substantial gains by the democrats in the elections of April 1799 were offset by the initial military triumphs of the armies of the Second Coalition and by renewed anxieties about a revival of the Terror. Although in all this Bourdon's frustrations are reminiscent of his experiences earlier in the Revolution, his persistence once again suggests that he was strangely insensitive to realities.

Much the same might also be said of his final attempts to reestablish himself as the director of a new school, which Bourdon again visualized as standing at the centre of a nationwide network of similar institutions. On October 16, 1797 (Brumaire 26, Year VI), just before he was appointed to the post at Hamburg, this project was proposed in the *Petition au Conseil des Cinq-Cents sur l'Éducation Commune*.[11] It was taken up again in the letter (noted above) that he wrote to the Minister of the Interior on July 30, 1798, almost immediately after his return to Paris, and in March 1799 (Ventôse, Year VII) it finally appeared as one of Bourdon's most effective works, *Le Voeu de la nature et de la Constitution de l'an III sur l'éducation générale*.[12] In this form, it was presented as a proposal first to the Department of the Seine[13] and then to the Council of Five Hundred. Despite some differences of emphasis, all three of these proposals are so alike, and so closely akin to Bourdon's earlier expositions of his ideas, that they may here be treated together.

As before, Bourdon was forthright in condemning the methods and content of traditional teaching: far too many people, he averred, had been educated in a useless way, so that while agriculture and industry stagnated the country was plagued by hack writers and a multitude of applicants for minor clerical appointments. In place of the old arbitrary imposition of artificialities on unwilling pupils, Bourdon pleaded earnestly for the creation of schools that would really provide an apprenticeship for life. What was required, he maintained, was a combination of physical education and practical experience in craftsmanship, with due attention to the fine arts, and every opportunity should be provided for pupils to follow their natural inclinations to choose and concentrate on whatever they could do best. Furthermore, he again insisted that such schools ought to be communal schools in which the practice of self-government would enable boys to acquire real understanding of their rights and duties and in which their instructors would be regarded, not as tyrants, but as guides and friends. Thus, young people would be fitted morally as well as physically for life as responsible citizens of a republic, and the schools would make a valuable contribution to the growth of a sound national economy. Above all, Bourdon argued that his approach would transform education by making it an enjoyable instead of a corrupting experience, "et le bonheur qui est le but de l'éducation, en deviendra encore le moyen."[14]

In all this, and particularly in *Le Voeu de la nature*, Bourdon placed more emphasis than in the past on the value and importance of manual work. Although perhaps influenced by the ideas advanced in 1793 by Lepeletier, he was no doubt also conscious that such emphasis was likely to appeal to the social minority whose power prevailed in France after 1795. He also repeatedly cited his own experience with la Société des Jeunes Français, an experiment that he evidently believed to have been strikingly successful until it was destroyed by inflation, famine, and the blind hatreds of his political enemies.

More specifically, Bourdon's proposal in its final form was for the establishment in Paris of a free school for fifty orphans aged between nine and sixteen years, these being initially and principally the sons of *les défenseurs de la patrie*. This example, Bourdon believed, would lead to the foundation of similar schools, locally financed and open to voluntary enrolment, in the departments, each of which might be expected to have at least one within five years. Confidently predicting that 90 to 95 percent of an initial overall enrolment of 1,200 pupils would become able workmen and artisans, he anticipated that most of the minority would be well qualified to begin to contribute to the professional and cultural life of France. Moreover, he estimated that the payment of 600 francs per pupil for each of the first five years of the operation of the school in Paris would thereafter be diminished by productivity: the senior classes would become first self-supporting and then profitable, and ultimately no costs at all would be involved.

Despite the political instability of the spring of 1799, this plan seems to have been considered seriously and even to have won a good deal of support.[15] The provision of education, particularly at the primary level, was in fact a perpetual problem for administrators: although the Daunou Law of October 25, 1795[16] (the National Convention's final educational legacy to France) had required every local authority to provide at least one primary school in its locality, by 1798-99 these state schools were still greatly outnumbered by private—and less secular—schools.[17] Moreover, as Bourdon pointed out in his estimate, the expense of providing adequate public care for 100,000 orphans was already considerable but not financially remunerative.

Le Voeu de la nature, too, had, and in some respects still has, particularly attractive qualities. At that time, it conformed closely to the constitutional requirement that all new citizens must be able to read, write, and show proficiency in a "mechanical operation"; it was also fully in accord with the republicans' expectation that their schools would be very different from those of the past. Bourdon's combination of republican morality and technical skills was thus one that merited attention. As in his earlier expositions, too, Bourdon proposed an approach to teaching that transcended the immediate needs of his day, and, although this approach no doubt seemed visionary, it was not to be lightly set aside. In the days when the directorial regime was crumbling, he wrote as persuasively as in 1788 of the possibility that schools, all too often rigidly formal places where abstract information was imposed on passive pupils, could become centres in which practical and constructive activities might be followed freely, naturally, and happily.

Yet in 1799 Bourdon's convictions could not outweigh the costs of his proposal. The *Pétition au Conseil des Cinq-Cents* was referred to a commission; the letter to the minister had no apparent sequel; and *Le Voeu de la nature* was rejected as an unduly expensive luxury by the Department of the Seine and then, on its advice, by the commission of the Council of Five Hundred (May 27, 1799/Prairial 8, Year VII).[18] That commission had indeed previously (on April 13/Germinal 24) reported to the council that Bourdon's claims for the reimbursement of his losses in 1795, as determined by the Minister of the Interior, were justified and should be paid;[19] however, even that was probably a Pyrrhic victory, for the amount in question was but a fraction of that originally requested, and the council had in fact only adjourned its final decision.

The end of the century, whether it be called December 1799 or Nivôse, Year VIII, must therefore have been a time of deep disappointment to Bourdon. Although his reaction to the coup d'état of Brumaire and the emergence of Bonaparte as First Consul is unknown, it is unlikely that so ardent a republican would have welcomed Bonaparte's equation of the sovereignty of the people with the power of government;[20] moreover, to anticipate, the restoration of Catholicism in 1802 must surely have been repugnant to him. His own situation, too, was certainly far from satisfactory. Aged forty-six, active, energetic, and well aware of his abilities, he had already been without employment for eighteen months, and all his recent attempts to initiate reforms had been distressingly unsuccessful. After 1799, he indeed seems to have abandoned all hope of seeing his economic and educational ideas generally adopted.

Nor, as it so happened, was his brother, Bourdon de Vatry, then in a better case.[21] In May 1799, Sieyès, returning to France from Berlin by way of Antwerp in order to take office as a Director, met Bourdon de Vatry, then the agent of the Ministry of Marine in that port. Impressed by de Vatry's ability, Sieyès secured his appointment on July 3, 1799, as Minister of Marine and the Colonies, and in that capacity he worked successfully for a while with the Minister of War, General Bernadotte. Desperately needed supplies were sent to the army of the Alps, and preparations were made for the projected invasion of Britain. The return of Bonaparte from Egypt in October nevertheless led to friction, for he was then averse to the proposed invasion, and he supposed de Vatry to be allied to Sieyès. De Vatry consequently offered to resign in November, when the coup d'état of Brumaire brought Bonaparte to power. Unhappily his offer was refused, and the remainder of his short time in office was marked by serious conflicts with Bonaparte. De Vatry first advised against any attempt to send supplies to the French forces holding Malta and then objected to giving command of the squadron to an officer on parole. Furthermore, he gave great offence by pressing for proceedings against a fraudulent munitions contractor whom Bonaparte favoured. Sent briefly back to Antwerp, he was replaced as minister on November 23, 1799, by a more amenable man, and it seems that he then cut himself off from public affairs throughout 1800.

De Vatry was nonetheless more fortunate than Léonard Bourdon: although Léonard may not have realized it, his name was steadily being made more and more odious. As retrospective and reactionary writing about the Revolution developed, attention was inevitably drawn to its more horrific aspects, and to some writers Bourdon's involvement in particular episodes was sufficient proof of guilty responsibility for them. Thus, in 1797, L.M. Prudhomme, a successful but malicious journalist who had moved from extreme radicalism to its opposite pole, published his *Histoire générale et impartiale des erreurs, des fautes et des crimes pendant la Révolution.*[22] It was a work of six volumes, of which the fourth and fifth each included a chapter about Bourdon's visits to Orléans. In the one, Bourdon is the personification of perfidy, the man who first robbed the royalist prisoners there and then personally ordered the massacre that took place at Versailles in 1792. The other, called Bourdon's "Deuxième voyage sanguinaire à Orléans," is an account of his "assassination" in March 1793, and here Bourdon is represented as nothing less than an inhuman monster, a tiger constantly athirst for human blood.[23] Again, in 1799 there appeared *Les Chemises rouges,*[24] an account by A.J.T. Bonnemain of the trial and execution of those "pères de familles" who were guillotined as parricides for their alleged responsibility for the "assassination." This is a more serious recapitulation of the trial from the statements presented to the Revolutionary Tribunal, but the author's opinion is sufficiently apparent in his subtitle: *Mémoire pour servir à l'histoire du règne des anarchistes.* In the late 1790s, the foundations of the history of the Revolution were indeed being established by the writers of the right, and Bourdon was becoming indelibly marked down as a minor but malevolent villain.

Whatever influence that picture had at the time, the lives of Léonard and his brother certainly diverged sharply when 1801 began. Abandoning retirement toward the end of 1800, de Vatry re-entered the service of the Ministry of Marine as its senior administrative officer at the naval base of Lorient. Transferred from there to Le Havre, he was again dismissed by Bonaparte for predicting the failure of the expedition to Saint-Domingue (Haiti) in 1802. Then, in September 1802, he left the ministry to begin a long and honourable career in civil administration,[25] becoming (to follow him no further) prefect of Vaucluse in September 1802 and of the Maine-et-Loire from July 1805 to 1809. By contrast, the course of Léonard Bourdon's life from the coup d'état in 1799 until 1807, the date accepted as that of his death, as yet remains so obscure that certainties about it must still be combined with speculation.

One remarkable, though easily neglected, fact is that Bourdon was not one of those unfortunate men who were wrongly accused of responsibility for the attempted assassination of Bonaparte on December 24, 1800. On that occasion, an "infernal machine" (a large barrel of gunpowder) exploded on a narrow street only a few seconds after the First Consul had passed by.[26] Because at least four people were killed outright and a great many more severely injured, opinion was outraged, and Bonaparte, in a calculated frenzy, took advantage of this opportunity to insist on the deportation of 130 Jacobins, men supposedly irreconcilable revolutionaries. Although it was soon known with certainty that a group of extreme royalists had really planned and effected the explosion, the Jacobins were despatched to the Seychelles Islands "for," as Bonaparte put it, "the massacres of September, for 31 May, for Prairial, for the conspiracy of Babeuf, for all that they have done and all they might still do."[27]

There are several possible reasons why Bourdon was not included in this list of those "who have covered themselves with crime for the past ten years."[28] Possibly his name, like that of Choudieu, with whom he had been imprisoned at Ham, was one of those that the Minister of Police, Fouché, later claimed to have struck from the list.[29] Here, however, a simpler explanation seems more probable. Despite the obloquy heaped on Bourdon by reactionaries and royalists, and granted that the list compiled by the police consisted principally of men once activists in the sections, his record does not suggest that he had ever been a conspirator or even a potentially dangerous political figure.

A further possibility, not incompatible with the last, is that Bourdon was not in Paris on December 24, 1800, the date of the explosion. As in 1797, being again without employment, he might simply have been "in the country." Here Kuscinski is more positive in asserting that Bourdon had in fact been appointed a member of the administrative council of the military hospital in Toulon "un an après le coup d'État du 18 brumaire" and more explicitly in "November 1800."[30] There is, however, a difficulty about this, for Kuscinski refers only to "documents officiels," which he does not identify, and other evidence is in another respect in conflict with his statement. Whereas the *Almanach national* for the Year IX (September 1800 to September 1801) has no reference to Bourdon, that for the Year X (September 1801 to September 1802) names him explicitly as a member of the board of Directors of the military hospital at Marseille.[31] Because the entries in the annual *Almanach* presumably relate to positions held at some time before its actual publication, they tend to confirm Kuscinski's chronology and to suggest that Bourdon was given official employment (again well away from Paris) either at the close of 1800 or early in 1801. It is more difficult, however, to reconcile the supposed appointment to Toulon in 1800 with the recorded tenure of office at Marseille in 1801.

This is not to say that Bourdon was never in Toulon. On the contrary, there is both public and private proof of his presence there at a later date than that given by Kuscinski. In the first place, the *Almanach national* for the Year XI (September 1802 to September 1803) repeats the entry for 1801 that shows him at Marseille, with an additional detail identifying him as the civil administrator attached to the military board of Directors of the hospital. Thereafter, however, the entries in the *Almanach impérial* for the Years XII (1803-1804), XIII (1804-1805), and—by the abandonment of the revolutionary calendar—1806, place him at Toulon, again as the civil administrator on the board of the military hospital there. Moreover, in a letter written to "Son Excellence" the Minister of the Interior on September 27, 1804 (Vendémiaire 5, Year XIII), Bourdon explained that his period of leave in Paris was about to expire and that he would soon have to return "à mon hôpital de Toulon."[32] Although that may be thought conclusive, one other relevant item is of some supplementary interest: on December 20, 1804 (Frimaire 29, Year XIII), the police bulletin included a report from the Department of the Var that mentions Bourdon.[33] Apparently the *curé* of Solliès-Pont (near Toulon) had informed the authorities that "anarchistes" were meeting by night in his parish and attempting to subvert the troops billeted there—and "Le conventionnel Léonard Bourdon s'y est rendu." That allegation, incidentally, was soon noted as being unfounded, and the prefect of the Var obviously recognized it and others like it as the handiwork of a local crank.

That Bourdon remained at Toulon for at least three to four years (i.e., from 1803 to 1806 or 1807) is not, of course, proof that he was well settled there. Rather, such evidence as there is suggests that he tried his best to obtain a more important post closer to the centre of government. His letter of September 27, 1804, to the Minister of the Interior[34] implies that he had spent, and indeed extended, a long period of leave ("un séjour de huit mois fort inutile") in search of employment, and in itself it is a request that a new position be created for him. Noting that the Emperor had established inspectors-general for secondary schools, Bourdon suggested that the various schools of Arts et Métiers would benefit by a similar arrangement. Explaining that he had already discussed this proposal with several high officials, who had been in sympathy with it, he asked that the proposal be put before the Emperor, for he was sure that educational work was the best service that he could render to his country.

In substance, the response of the minister was that, although the suggested appointment might indeed be a useful innovation, neither finances nor circumstances made it feasible, and he added that he himself had no authority to present the proposal. Yet even such courteous finality did not deter Bourdon from trying again. In a further letter to the minister two days later,[35] he assumed that the reply meant that his application had been premature and therefore might be favourably considered when the organization of schools had progressed further. What is more, he pointed out that the minister was authorized to appoint commissioners and that the impending organization of a technical school at Trèves, of which he said he had been told by Regnault de Saint-Jean d'Angely, a member of the Council of State, was far too important a project to be left to the mercy of subordinate officials of the local administration. However, despite his persistence, Bourdon was still in 1804 as unsuccessful as ever in his efforts to obtain the sort of work that he believed he could do well.

This failure indicates the crucial problem raised by Kuscinski's positive statement that on March 12, 1807, Bourdon became a principal director of military hospitals and in that capacity followed the Grand Army into Prussia, to die at Breslau on May 29, 1807.[36] The difficulty here is that there are two very different pictures. On the one hand, we have Bourdon, a man of the Revolution who had long been unsuccessful in all his enterprises, and one who for some years past had apparently been safely relegated to a minor administrative post in a distant port; on the other hand, we have the same man suddenly appointed to a senior administrative position, which presumably entailed heavy responsibilities. Although the validity of Kuscinski's assertion may not be dependent on an explanation of this sudden transition from obscurity to prominence, the problem that it poses is worth considering.

Unfortunately there is little help from the *Almanach impérial*. As previously noted, the volume for 1806 shows Bourdon as the civil administrator on the board concerned with the military hospital at Toulon. That for 1807, however, notes that the board itself had been suppressed by virtue of the administrative orders of December 11, 1803, and July 10, 1806, which in effect replaced the local direction of all military hospitals by a central body acting through six inspectors-general. What is more, one of those named, P.F. Percy (later Baron Percy, 1754-1825), is identified in his own *Journal*[37] as being both the chief surgeon to the Grand Army from 1804 until the time of the Peninsula War and the director of its hospitals during the campaigns that led to the battles of Jena (October 14, 1806) and Eylau

(February 8, 1807). It is therefore likely that Bourdon was free for other work early in 1807, when the board at Toulon had ceased to exist, and it is possible, if less likely, that he took over Percy's responsibilities for the Grand Army's hospitals after the slaughter at Eylau. That Bourdon's name does not occur in the *Almanachs* for 1807 and 1808 might then be explained by accepting Kuscinski's dating of his death a few weeks after his appointment in 1807.

This tentative venture into medical military history (an area of specialization that apparently presents particular difficulty when the inquiry concerns a civilian)[38] thus establishes Bourdon's availability for promotion and the possibility that a vacancy was open. It does not, however, contribute directly to an explanation of his selection for higher office. Consciously or otherwise, Kuscinski suggests that this was the outcome of a direct approach by Bourdon himself. Immediately before stating that Bourdon was attached to the Grand Army, Kuscinski says that this fiery revolutionary ("ce fougueux révolutionnaire") wrote to the "vice-connétable de l'Empire" requesting the favour of an interview with the Emperor so that he could renew "le serment de fidélité à sa personne sacrée."[39] The implication, that a renegade revolutionary eventually won high office by sycophantic subservience to imperial authority, nevertheless remains open to question. Strongly in sympathy with the Montagnards, Kuscinski no doubt deplored the adoption of all formality in address, but at the time conformity with custom probably meant no more to Bourdon than it did to others or indeed than it had meant for many in the last years of the monarchy. More serious problems lie in other features of Kuscinski's entry: the date given, Germinal 5, Year XII (March 26, 1804) must be an error in transcription or printing, for the empire was not established until May 18, 1804; the office of vice-constable was apparently of later date again; and the reference given, "Collection Noel Charavay," is not one sufficiently specific for easy verification.[40] Thus, even if the authenticity of the document is accepted, all that can be learned from it is that at some time between May 1804 and March 1807 Bourdon made yet another attempt to bring himself to the notice of people who might help him to leave Toulon for a better position elsewhere.

From this fragmentary evidence, two presumptions may be advanced. One is that Bourdon did eventually succeed in attracting the attention of the Emperor. That is not unlikely, for Napoleon is well known for his almost incredible familiarity with the details of day-to-day administration. Moreover, at least in the earlier part of his period of power, he was avowedly concerned to appoint able and loyal men regardless of their political past.[41] It is also of interest that in December 1806, after the subjugation of Prussia and the occupation of Poland, he spoke furiously in Warsaw about the inadequacy and inefficiency of the army's medical administration—and typically concluded, "N'importe, il faut marcher."[42]

Implicit in this initial presumption is its successor, the supposition that, despite his efforts to leave Toulon, Bourdon had shown real ability during the years of his employment there. This ability, unfortunately, must be surmised, for the only available evidence that can here be cited to support it is a brief and caustic comment in Armand Le Corbeiller's *Le Léopard de la Révolution*. That author, whose work has been decried elsewhere in these pages, mentions (without any reference) that while Bourdon was in Toulon as a petty official he occupied himself with devising " 'lits mechaniques' et d'appareils spéciaux pour les malades."[43] Beyond that, all that can be said is that, whatever be thought of his views and judgment, Bourdon had shown himself throughout the Revolution to be intelligent, able, industrious, and energetic, and such a man might well have merited promotion after three or more years in minor office.

Although none of these considerations is conclusive, they generally suggest that the situation was not incompatible with Kuscinski's identification of the conclusion of Bourdon's career "d'après des documents officiels." Yet even this only epitomizes the problem of interpretation that is characteristic of his whole life, for it is still surprising that a man so often denigrated and so frequently frustrated should so suddenly have won a measure of recognition. It is consequently the more tragic that his hard-won success in securing an appointment offering the opportunity of rewarding work should have been followed almost immediately by his death far from France.

Of the manner of that death, nothing can be said. The assumption by some recent writers that Bourdon died "sur le champ d'honneur" can, however, be dismissed as superfluous. His life is sufficiently enigmatic without such further embroidery.

15

Conclusions

$\mathcal{H}$istory has not been kind to Léonard Bourdon. As has been indicated in these pages—and may easily be confirmed—references to him in standard works on the Revolution, and even in many more specialized monographs, are rare. Furthermore, with a few exceptions, notably the work of Auguste Kuscinski, entries about Bourdon in biographical dictionaries are repetitive and misleading. True, some serious studies of institutions, particularly the Commune of Paris of 1789 and the Convention's Committee of Public Instruction, are informative, and literature about education in this period usually includes some consideration of his school and his views about education. Almost by definition, however, such pedagogical literature is deficient in the political perspective imperative to a just appreciation of the man and his times.

Unhappily, too, scholarly biographical writing about individuals has for some time been out of fashion, and, because Bourdon was never a man of the first importance, he has suffered much by neglect. Consequently the picture of him most likely to be encountered is that of a particularly unpleasant Terrorist, "The Leopard of the Revolution." For that picture, chance is largely responsible, for Bourdon has indeed been the victim of his own survival of the Revolution. Politically active from 1789 until 1795, to say nothing of his later appearances, he incurred in succession the hostility of all those, whether Feuillants, Girondins, or Thermidorians, who condemned and opposed the course of the Revolution. Among these groups, two were particularly antagonistic to him: the notables of Orléans avowedly pursued him relentlessly because they held him responsible for all the ills that had afflicted their city in the years from 1792 to 1795; and after Thermidor the turncoat terrorists in the Convention were almost of necessity eager to discredit him as one of the few men who had rejected Robespierre but still had the courage to identify themselves with the Montagnards, the Jacobins, and the people. For both of these groups, indeed, his greatest offence was probably that of stimulating and sustaining the political and social aspirations of those whom many of the well-to-do, whether old or new, local or national, regarded as the dregs of the nation. Developed by journalists in the aftermath of 1795, and subsequently accepted by conservative and popular writers, it is this political denigration of Bourdon that has endured.

Whatever be thought of him, his life certainly merits more attention than this. Biographical writing, however, is a perilous exercise. If a person's life is to be comprehensible, something has always to be said about the changing circumstances in which it was lived, but that imperative, here the juxtaposition of Léonard Bourdon and the tremendous events of the Revolution, almost inevitably leads to magnification of the importance of the individual. Serious biography similarly demands an attempt to sympathize with the subject, but that sympathy can easily minimize a person's weaknesses and failures. In both respects, it is particularly difficult to strike a true balance in writing about Bourdon: although the records relate almost entirely to his life as a public figure, he was neither an insignificant nor an outstanding man. Indeed, because even his participation in the Revolution was intermittent, an account of it has often to be pieced together from reports about isolated and diverse episodes.

It is nonetheless worth noticing that in his day Léonard Bourdon was regarded as one who could speak with authority about the economy and about education. That is not to say that he was, or claimed to be, an original thinker. In the one case, his recipe for the redemption of the economy of France was derived directly from his father, Bourdon des Planches, and much of its attraction for him and his contemporaries sprang from the fact that des Planches had developed his ideas, and suffered somewhat for them, in the supposedly evil days of the old order. Similarly Léonard Bourdon's conception of education may be seen as his own adaptation of aspects of great eighteenth-century debate about the nature, improvement, and possible perfectibility of human beings. In this regard, however, abstract theory was of little interest to Bourdon: his strength lay in his ability to speak positively and persuasively of his experience, of his ideals, and of the importance of the practical experiment that he had initiated.

Although both the economic policy and the educational experiment were to some extent modified to meet the changing demands of their time, and although both at one point (in August 1793) seemed to be attaining full realization, both—like many other proposals—were eventually rejected and relegated to oblivion. For those failures, Bourdon must be held at least partially responsible. Certainly he failed to recognize that circumstances made his projects impractical: the costs would have been prohibitive, and prevailing opinion was as opposed to any enduring limitation of economic freedom as it was to any fundamental replacement of "instruction" by "education." Of the latter, it is sufficient here to say that Bourdon's school, la Société des Jeunes Français, like his collection and publication of the *Actions héroïques et civiques des républicains français*, flourished only during the exceptional conditions that existed during the short-lived Montagnard republic; nor could all Bourdon's efforts ever again arouse sufficient support for some second foundation. However, if such failures were implicit in the situation of France during the Revolution, then his tenacity in advocating enlightened conceptions of economic and educational reform throughout the period merits recognition and commendation. Essentially he strove in both areas to effect some reconciliation of the best interests of the individual with those of the community at large, and in this endeavour he was indeed a man representative of the Revolution.

That is also true in other respects. At the beginning of this book, it was tentatively suggested that his career might be of interest if it showed Bourdon to be one who linked the revolutionary bourgeoisie to the poor in Paris and thereby contributed to a process by which the middle class helped to bring popular democracy to birth in France. Although that proposition is far too extensive to be substantiated or refuted by any single example, some aspects of his life certainly support it. In the first place, Bourdon may fairly be regarded as a representative of the professional administrative class that existed in France before the Revolution and became predominant as it proceeded. That— unlike his brother, Bourdon de Vatry—he did not subsequently emerge as an established notable in the early nineteenth century may be thought simply a consequence of his sudden death in 1807; despite his chequered career, he was at that time well on his way to attaining respectable status. Moreover, in the last years of the old monarchy, both he and his father, educated professional men of some substance, had been convinced that changes that would make France a freer, a more prosperous, and a happier country were urgently needed, and each had zealously advocated a measure of reform that each believed would be universally beneficial. That Léonard continued in and out of season to recommend both his father's economic plan and his own educational proposals is perhaps less important than the fact that

throughout the Revolution he consistently sought to sustain and propagate his vision of the Republic as the embodiment of Liberty, Equality,
and Brotherhood.

In more material terms, too, Bourdon often concerned himself with
the general welfare of the poor, and he frequently strove to help those
afflicted by misfortune. In the first elections in 1789, he and his father
were probably unusual in their reluctance to isolate themselves from
the working people of their districts, and both men were soon involved
in the perpetual problem of replenishing the amount of grain and flour
available in Paris. Active in the countryside as an agent charged with
expediting supplies to the capital in 1789, as he was again in late 1795,
Bourdon was also soon brought into close association with the Parisian
poor as one of those responsible for identifying and securing pensions
for the men and women who had contributed and suffered most during
the attack on the Bastille. Moreover, for a few months in 1792, he was
the spokesman and champion of the *sans-culottes* of the densely populated and notoriously turbulent Section des Gravilliers in central Paris.
Thus far, at least, the suggestion that some men of a middle class were
directly involved in promoting the economic and political progress of
the poor is amply confirmed by the record of Bourdon's activities.

On the other hand, from the final months of 1792 onward, his relationship with the *sans-culottes* of Gravilliers became less intimate,
partly because, while Bourdon became a deputy, a Montagnard, and to
some extent a man of government, the section continued to develop as
an apparently independent force. Moreover, although he continued to
live and work in Gravilliers, and always had some supporters there, his
local influence was usurped by that of Jacques Roux, a man still more
personally concerned with the day-to-day economic needs of the
people in the streets and much more prone to preach and practise
direct and violent action. It is partly for this reason that Bourdon
ought to be seen primarily as a Jacobin: like Robespierre, he was ultimately more inclined to champion the underdog than to countenance
any intrusion of direct popular democracy into the management of
national affairs by patriots of proven political purity.

That is not to say that Bourdon ever turned his back on the *sans-
culottes*. Apparently he sometimes affected the manner and appearance
of one of them, and after 1792 he was occasionally associated with
popular protest, as he was most notably during the *journée* of
September 5, 1793. Moreover, and this is greatly to his credit, he was
one of the small minority of Montagnard deputies who resisted the
Thermidorian reaction in 1794 and 1795. If in this resistance he was

not as prominent as others, he was certainly consistent in supporting the cause of the people, and had he not been imprisoned as a supposedly popular leader he would surely have been one of those martyrs of Prairial whose deaths symbolized the repression of social and political democracy. In short, although he was one of those professional men who helped to bring popular democracy to birth in France, he was *not* one of those of the same class who so soon succeeded in stifling it.

If in this sustained sympathy for the poor Bourdon appears as a true revolutionary, then that should not suggest that he was either a conspiratorial figure or a man dominated by any rigid ideology. Rather, he was more typical of his time in that, having a fundamental faith in the sovereignty of the people, he encountered and responded to a succession of situations—which were sometimes abundant in promise but which were more frequently frustrating and on occasion highly dangerous. Seen in this light, the second suggestion tentatively advanced at the beginning of this book, the hypothesis that Bourdon was a man of deeply divided personality, can confidently be dismissed. That possibility arose from the contrast between his reputation as a remarkably humane educationalist and his alleged behaviour as a particularly brutal terrorist; however, that distinction has proved both artificial and superficial. For Bourdon, education and political progress were entwined ways toward a new era of human freedom and happiness. Because he soon realized that education could not prosper amid poverty and instability, nor a real republic endure amid ignorance and self-interest, he strove always to advance the same cause by following whichever road seemed most appropriate to the exigencies of an inconstant situation. True, Bourdon seldom had much freedom of choice, for during the desperate emergencies of the Year II the necessity of defending the Revolution was paramount. It is nonetheless remarkable that in August 1793, when the enactment of national residential education was practically within his grasp, he rejected it because the proposal was not founded on freedom. Moreover, he continued to fight for his own more liberal conception of education long after that goal had become unobtainable.

Nor is it legitimate to suppose that Bourdon was a singularly savage terrorist. Once mythology is cleared away, the principal charges made against him appear ill-founded. From one of these charges, his supposed brutality in Hamburg in 1798, he can be completely exonerated. Another, his alleged responsibility for the massacre of prisoners at Versailles in 1792, is reducible to the fact that he had previously condoned the abduction of those prisoners from Orléans—which is not to say that he or anyone else could have prevented it or knew what would eventually happen to the victims. Similarly his participation in the process that led to the execution of nine notable men of Orléans in 1793 does not amount to criminal conduct. His attitude toward the establishment there was defiant and may be thought provocative; his dramatization of the attack on him certainly helped to make that episode a symbolic issue at a time of intense political conflict; but his silence during the trial and in the Convention is a sufficient indication that he could not then have influenced the course of events either for good or for ill. In short, in both of these affairs at Orléans, Bourdon was a man fortuitously involved in circumstances of which the outcome was calamitous to others.

Nevertheless, he was undoubtedly a terrorist in the original sense of that word. From 1792, if not 1791, onward, Bourdon believed that exceptionally strong government was necessary for the security of France and the salvation of the Revolution, and he was correspondingly convinced that ruthless repression of the avowed enemies of the nascent new order was imperative. Of this conviction, his implacable hostility to the king is perhaps the best, as well as the most unpalatable, example—though his later support for the inauguration of the Terror and the creation of the revolutionary army of Paris is also notable. Furthermore, he continued until late in 1794 to believe that some modified form of Revolutionary Government and Revolutionary Justice was still a political necessity, and in sustaining that belief he was then unusual, though not alone.

Yet Bourdon's commitment to terror was neither exceptional nor incomprehensible. As a Jacobin, a Montagnard, and a regicide, he was only one of many such men who governed France during the most critical years of the Revolution, and in essentials his attitude was that of all but the most unscrupulously self-interested among them. These men had long believed, as had Bourdon, that immeasurable benefits for all could easily be won by the abolition of antiquated restrictions and the promotion of a few simple but fundamental reforms. Because that faith was ultimately concerned with the moral progress of humans, it inevitably had as its corollary the conviction that opposition was something essentially selfish and immoral. Moreover, this dogmatism was reinforced by the inheritance from the old monarchy of the concept of absolutism: after 1789, the sovereignty of the nation became for the revolutionaries the ultimate measure of moral as well as of political right. Thus, from that time onward, the French became a deeply divided people, the "patriots" being in a very real way at war with their enemies, "the *aristos*," whose presumed perfidy was epitomized for Bourdon and for many others by what they saw as the king's unforgivable betrayal of the new nation in 1791. Tragically, too, from 1792 to 1794, to go no further, France encountered a succession of major emergencies in a war in which it seemed to stand alone against the world. In such a situation, emotion outweighs all reason, so that the distinction between *them* and *us* becomes complete and irredeemable. When mere apathy was regarded as criminal, it is small wonder that Bourdon could turn his back on those whom he believed to be morally convicted enemies of the people.

Bourdon thus became a terrorist because he was both a patriot and an idealist. Although his idealism is more explicit in his educational writings than in any abstract political theorizing, it is evident in his conception of the Revolution as a new religion; here again the terrorist attitude is apparent in his enthusiastic adoption of dechristianization. Indeed, it is in his constant contempt for organized Christianity, and in his readiness to destroy its external signs and symbols, that he appears most obviously as an extremist. Even so, Bourdon was more concerned to proselytize than to persecute. As he showed when he was *en mission* in 1793, he believed that priests who favoured counterrevolution should be regarded as enemies of the people, whereas those who were well disposed should be tolerated until they realized that the Revolution really encompassed the true core of every creed.

As that relatively moderate attitude indicates, Bourdon in fact did more to advocate repression than to practise it. Despite Robespierre's suspicions, he ought not to be called a Hébertist, for he was always independent, and even in the crucial fall and winter of 1793-94 he sought to strengthen government, not to advance anarchical democracy. Rather, the records show that on several occasions he urged potentially violent crowds to respect their magistrates and the law. Certainly his activity *en mission* pales into insignificance in comparison with the ruthless repression enforced by men such as Joseph LeBon and Carrier, to name no others; nor are the dubious tales of his robbery of the prisoners at Orléans at all comparable to the certainty that deputies such as Barras and Fréron acquired enormous wealth by exploiting their powers as commissioners of the Convention. Although Bourdon was never in the position to use or abuse unlimited power, his conduct in the Côte d'Or and the Jura in 1793 was remarkably moderate. Endlessly energetic in striving to stimulate patriotic and revolutionary ardour, he was then indirectly responsible for many temporary arrests, and he expedited the trial of one lad already imprisoned on a capital charge, but the outcome of his visit suggests that his limited and short-lived severity sufficed only to arouse resentment. Nor should his ultimate repudiation of the Robespierrist terror in 1794 be ascribed simply to his natural interest in self-preservation, for by mid-1794 the emergency government that he had helped to establish—and that he continued to think necessary—had all too obviously become a self-perpetuating menace to the freedom of everyone, including its own Jacobin and Montagnard supporters.

There is thus a considerable difference between historical reality and the common representation of Léonard Bourdon as a cruel and treacherous terrorist. For this notoriety, he was indeed partly responsible, for he often deliberately sought to attract attention. A man strongly inclined to dramatize his own position, he was ever ready to promote popular ardour for the Revolution through patriotic festivities, and he was constantly—if sometimes deplorably—anxious to ensure that his school and his pupils were visibly in the forefront of events. On the other hand, he was vulnerable to denigration because he was an individualist who was never closely associated with any prominent political faction. Moreover, after Thermidor, when he would not protect himself by abandoning his beliefs, he remained obviously a Jacobin; yet, as Fréron realized, he was, as a schoolmaster, a man who could easily be ridiculed and abused as a revolutionary scoundrel who had finally been reduced to terrorizing his own pupils.

If, however, mythology of this sort is set aside, Bourdon emerges as a much more credible human being. The real Bourdon clearly had his faults, but even they are more interesting than those usually ascribed to him. Although he was probably unprepossessing in appearance, careless of his dress, fond of his wine and of rough rather than refined company, it was not he but Bourdon of the Oise who was a habitual drunkard. Rather, his devotion to the Jacobins suggests that despite his independence he was a man of gregarious disposition. Perhaps on that account, he was sometimes inconsistent: inclined at first to say what a particular audience hoped to hear, he had at times to modify his initial extravagances either in subsequent speeches or in private. That weakness, like his excessive but unselfish ambitions for the future of his school, and perhaps even like his attraction to children, suggests that his outlook was essentially optimistic and even simplistic. Certainly his idealism had as its counterpart some limitation of his interests and of his appreciation of practical realities. Evident in his protracted pursuit of economic and educational proposals that became ever more impractical, that deficiency is also apparent in various serious errors of judgment. In particular, Bourdon misjudged the situation in the Jura in 1793, and in 1794 he was wrong in supposing—as he apparently did—that changes in the personnel of the Committees of Public Safety and General Security would suffice to end the more tyrannical aspects of Revolutionary Government.

On the other hand, such evidence as there is suggests that Bourdon was well liked by his pupils. Certainly he was a man of liberal mind who was sincere in his determination to promote social and political progress by making education more enjoyable and more pertinent to daily life, and in that endeavour he was indeed astonishingly persistent. Sympathetic to the poor in general, he often succeeded in securing material aid for people in particularly dire need. As an independently minded Montagnard, he took little part in the daily debates of the Convention, but he was always assiduous in attending and working for those committees that concerned him, and he was from time to time remarkably energetic and effective as an agent of government in the field. On occasion, too, Bourdon was a bold and resolute participant in actions that had a considerable effect on the development of the Revolution, the most notable being the seizure of power by the Commune of the Insurrection on August 10, 1792, and the arrest of Robespierre in July 1794. As the conjunction of those two occasions suggests, Bourdon was at once a staunch supporter of repressive emergency government and a man personally much more moderate than his words and his reputation imply. Above all, despite every adversity, he remained true to his belief in the importance and eventual triumph of Liberty and Equality.

In sum, in his weaknesses and in his strengths, as in his attitudes and associations, Léonard Bourdon may fairly be regarded as a man typical of his time and representative of the Jacobin Revolution that his career illustrates so well. Although there were greater and more admirable revolutionaries, there were many others who were far worse than Bourdon. Yet his story is essentially a tragic one: from 1789 until his death in 1807, his life was constantly blighted by circumstances far beyond his control, so that his transitory triumphs repeatedly ended in frustration. Because there is no figure commemorative of him, even on the site of "his" Priory of Saint-Martin-des-Champs, now the Conservatoire National des Arts et Métiers, his only legacy remains his vision of a society that was unobtainable in his own day. In that, too, his career epitomizes many of the aspirations of the French Revolution itself.

Appendices

Appendix 1. The Conflict in the Jura

*A*fter returning to Paris in May 1793, Léonard Bourdon ceased to be directly involved in events in the Jura. The course of events there nevertheless seems to be sufficiently instructive to be noticed here, particularly because the Department of the Jura is still commonly but misleadingly described as an important centre of "federalist" disruption. On May 24, the authorities in Lons-le-Saunier, apparently with massive public support, tried to prevent or anticipate a purge of the Convention by announcing their readiness to send *suppléant* deputies and an armed force to Bourges, and they refused to recognize the authority of the National Convention after it had been purged on June 2. As is indicated in part in chapter 6 above, all that came of either attempt to rally national opinion was the despatch of delegations to adjacent departments, at best unwilling to support positive action. The Jura nevertheless remained defiant, and the possibility that this attitude might lead to some extreme conservative reaction in the department itself became clear on June 25, when guardsmen in Lons-le-Saunier forcibly closed the Popular Society there.

Nonetheless, the Jura accepted the new Montagnard Constitution by an overwhelming majority in the plebiscite held on July 14, and the department, far from encouraging the revolt in Lyon, urged that city to accept it also. Warning the Lyonnais of the danger of civil war, the delegates from Lons-le-Saunier advocated conciliation, so that the Jura was seen in Lyon and Marseille as betraying the cause of the republic.

Moreover, the "revolt" of the Jura, which amounted to a prolonged refusal to underwrite the Montagnards' seizure of power, soon became no more than a local defensive reaction to a supposed threat of invasion by forces obedient to Bassal and Garnier, the commissioners sent to the area by the Convention in mid-June. As their correspondence with Paris shows, these commissioners were bedevilled by contradictory instructions from Paris: told at first to act firmly, they were next required by the (Dantonist) Committee of Public Safety to negotiate; they were then reprimanded by the (Robespierrist) Committee for countenancing a rebellion that they should have suppressed by force. One result of this inconsistency was that exchanges with the department had to be broken off just when agreement was imminent. Furthermore, the recurrent threats alarmed the population, men stood to arms, and one man was killed and two others wounded when a small detachment of cavalrymen from Lons-le-Saunier encountered a few "*sans-culottes de l'armée dolois*" at an inn. That episode, which ended "the war against the Dolois," so compromised the department that the principal administrators fled across the frontier and the remainder capitulated to the commissioners and to the Convention on August 9.

For these and further particulars, see at the appropriate dates the various authorities and records cited in chapter 6 above, particularly H. Libois, *Délibérations de la Société Populaire de Lons-le-Saunier*, 195-96 and Appendices 46-47, pp. 392-405; D. Monnier, *Annuaire du Jura: 1856*, 53-57; and, for Bassal's letter of July 31, Aulard, *Actes*, V, 435-38. For the plebiscite, principally of interest for the conditions that the primary assemblies attached to their acceptances, AN, B. 11.14 (Isère et Jura). For the delegation to Lyon, the development of which may be followed in the series AN, AD, L 55* in each of the departments involved, notably the Doubs and the Ain, initial reference may be made to C. Riffaterre, *Le mouvement antijacobin et antiparisien à Lyon* (2 vols.; Lyons et Paris, 1912), vol. 2, pp. 353-56.

Appendix 2. The Conclusion of Bourdon's Speech on the Lepeletier Plan for Education, July 30, 1793

Qu'on accorde la priorité à ce plan; qu'on adopte même avec des modifications, *même en n'obligeant qui que ce soit à y déposer ses enfants*;[1] hâte d'en organiser l'exécution, et bientôt les avantages qui doivent en résulter seront sentis par la majorité des citoyens, qui s'empressera d'en faire jouir ses enfants. Dès lors les enfants du pauvre trouveront une nourriture saine et abondante...; dès lors les grandes routes ne seront plus couvertes de malheureux enfants qui sollicitent les secours des voyageurs et s'habituent de bonne heure au vagabondage et à la mendacité.

Les matières premières seront manufacturées partout sur le sol qui les voit naître, et nous créerons le peuple le plus industrieux qui ait encore existé.

Dès lors les enfants infortunés ... vont jouir des droits que tous les citoyns ont à une éducation égale. ... Ils recevront l'éducation des hommes libres.

La génération naissante se dégagera sur le champ de la superstition, des préjugés et des vices de la génération présente.

L'homme de génie, né dans l'obscurité, sera débarrassé, dès son aurore, de la multitude d'obstacles et d'entraves qui s'opposaient à son développement. ...

---

* Italics added. Text extracted, with some abbreviations, from J. Guillaume, *Procès-verbaux du Comité d'instruction publique de la Convention Nationale*, vol. 2, p. 184. See also note 25 to chapter 8 above.

Dès lors le choix du peuple pour les fonctions publiques ne sera plus resserré dans la limite étroite de quelques familles à qui leur äisance donnait le privilège de procurer à ses enfants une éducation qui les mettait exclusivement en état de les remplir: le peuple aura toute la latitude possible dans ses choix: il puisera dans la grande famille, dans la famille des vingt-quatre millions d'individus.

Législateurs, vous avez créé une constitution qui va consoler la terre des malheures dans lesquels le despotisme l'avait plongée, achevez votre ouvrage. Il faut maintenant créer une génération d'hommes dignes de jouir de vos bienfaits; oser l'entreprendre, et le succès couronnera infailliblement vos travaux, et le succès surpassera vos espérances. Jetez les yeux dans l'avenir: voyez ce peuple immense de sages, de héros, de vrais républicains couvrir notre immense territoire, porter dans tous les arts utiles l'industrie que vos lois les auront mis à même développer, passer de la charrue ou des ateliers dans les fonctions civiles et militaires, et retourner, après avoir honorablement remplis celles-ci, à la charrue et dans leurs ateliers. Voyez l'univers entier müri de plusiers siècles à la liberté, par le spectacle du bonheur dont jouira le peuple français.

C'est vous, législateurs, qui aurez préparé ces hautes destinées, en décrétant et organisant l'éducation commune.

Je désire que l'on ouvre la discussion sur le plan de Michel Lepeletier. . . .

Appendix 3. Notes écrites de la main de Robespierre sur différens députés à la Convention

Tous les chefs de la coalition sont des scélérats déjà notés par des traits d'immoralité et d'incivisme.

(nos. 1-4) . . .

(5) *Léonard Bourdon*. Intrigant méprisé de tous les temps, l'un des principaux complices d'*Hébert*, ami inséparable de *Cloots*; il était initié dans la conjuration tramée chez *Gobel*. Il avait composé une pièce contre-révolutionnaire, dans le sens *hébertiste*, qui devait être jouée à l'opéra, et que le comité de salut public arrêta. Rien n'égale la bassesse des intrigues qu'il met en oeuvre pour grossir le nombre de ses pensionnaires et ensuite pour s'emparer de l'éducation des élèves de la patrie, institutions qu'il dénature et qu'il déshonore. Il était aux Jacobins l'un des orateurs les plus intarissables pour propager la doctrine d'*Hébert*. *À la Convention il fut un des premiers qui introduisirent l'usage de l'avilir par des formes indécentes, comme d'y parler le chapeau sur la tête et d'y siéger avec un costume ridicule.* Il vint un jour, avec *Cloots*, solliciter la liberté des banquiers hollandais *Vandenyver*. Je les ai vus et entendus, tous deux, plusieurs fois, et *Bourdon* a eu le courage de me le nier impunément aux Jacobins.

(E.B. Courtois, Papiers inédits trouvés chez Robespierre [3 vols.;
Paris, 1828], vol. 2, pp. 16-17 [italics in original])

Appendix 4. Bourdon's Financial Claims Following the Closure of la Société des Jeunes Français, 1795-99
(see also addendum to notes to chapter 10)

A. *General Problems*

Assessment of the validity of his claims, and of the fairness of the Directory's treatment of Bourdon, is complicated by two factors.

(1) The Depreciation of the Currency: Bourdon's initial claims were in part calculated in *assignats*, the normal, and indeed compulsory, medium of exchange in 1795. In March 1796, when the *assignat* had depreciated to 1/4 of 1 percent of its nominal value, the Directory attempted to replace it with a new note based in part on the ecclesiastical lands confiscated in Belgium. This, the *mandat territorial*, was overissued as well as overvalued as equivalent to thirty assignats, and for these and other reasons it, too, depreciated rapidly, so that by the end of April 1796 it had lost 90 percent of its face value. In effect, the *mandat* then gradually died a natural death: in July, its use ceased to be compulsory; and, in February 1797, when France returned to metal coinage, it was abolished, thereafter remaining acceptable only at the "fixed rate" of 1 percent of its face value for the payment of tax arrears or for conversion into *bons* for the purchase of nationalized property.

(2) Approximation: Perhaps in the nature of the case, Bourdon's estimates of the amounts due were often indeterminate—being dependent, for example, on knowledge of the number of his pupils at different dates as well as of their ages (over or under twelve) and their status (private or subsidized, *jeunes français* or *orphelins de la patrie*). Bourdon ascribed this imprecision to the loss of his records, either when his papers were confiscated by the Committee of General Security or when his school was transferred to Liancourt. This feature is most obviously apparent in the second part of the first major assessment of his claim as shown below (for reimbursement).

B. *The Assessment of Germinal, Year IV (March 1796)*

On this occasion, the ministry first standardized Bourdon's claims in terms of the *valeur fixe* for the *assignat*, thus obtaining overall totals of 157,846 francs for various indemnities arising from the closure of his school and 10,000 francs to reimburse Bourdon for outstanding expenses allegedly incurred before its closure. Although this distinction is unrealistic, five items called *indemnities* in an initial statement by Bourdon were assessed as follows:

(1) A *claim for 26,000 francs* to supplement the amount initially granted as a subsidy for each pupil, as approved to counter depreciation of the currency. *Reduced* (as applicable only to the *orphelins de la patrie* and modified to accord with the dates of depreciation) to 11,375 *assignats* or 5,687.5 francs *valeur fixe* (hereafter VF).

(2) *A similar claim for 94.425 francs* for rising daily expenses. *Reduced* (to allow for payments previously (?) made during Bourdon's imprisonment) to 40,424, i.e., 18,191.28 VF.

(3) *A claim for 6,000 francs* for dilapidation of furnishings and property between Bourdon's arrest in Germinal and the closure of the school in Messidor III. *Disallowed* (as unproven and adequately covered by points 1 and 2 above).

(4) *A claim for 20,000 francs* for personal sacrifices and the loss of "the fruits of labour." *Disallowed* (see General Arguments below).

(5) *A claim for 39,053 francs,* or 15,000 VF, for expenses incurred for Bourdon's first school, la Société Royale d'Émulation, in 1788-89. Accepted as an obligation inherited from the monarchy and tacitly approved by the National Assembly in 1791, but *Reduced* (on the assumption that items purchased were available for la Société des Jeunes Français) to 9,000 VF.

Total recommended payment as indemnities: 32,878.78 francs, VF.

The same assessment further included seven items derived from a second statement by Bourdon. Regarded as claims for *reimbursement,* they were not related to specific sums. The ministry apparently assumed that a possible maximum of 20,000 francs could initially be considered as a claim for 10,000. These items may be briefly identified as follows.

- *Two claims for the clothing* of pupils removed to Liancourt. Although the number and value of these garments were held unproven, some liability was accepted. Recommended payment: 549 francs, VF.

- *One claim for bed linen and metal mugs,* also said to be taken to Liancourt. Value regarded as overestimated. Suggested payment: 63 francs, VF.

- *Two claims for approved printing* (of the report of the Commission of Arts and of issues of the *Heroic Actions*). Dismissed as previously separated, submitted, and paid (no dates shown).

- *One claim for a subsidy for one pupil* from September 1792 onward, the boy apparently being on Bourdon's roll but not on that of the government. Seen as insufficiently proven. Suggested payment: 862.85 francs, VF.

- *One claim for late-entry pupils* as replacements of the original intake. Seen as exaggerated in number and vague as to dates but accepted in principle. Proposed payment: 1,312.5 francs, VF.

Total proposed payment as reimbursement: 2,787.35 francs.
With *total proposed as indemnities* (as above): 32,878.78.
This gives a *combined total* of 35,666.13 francs.
(*As compared with Bourdon's claims* for 157,846 and c. 10,000, i.e., 167,846.)

Nonetheless, this report was concluded by the draft of the decree to be submitted to the Directory for the approval of payment to Bourdon of 40,000 francs for full reimbursement and full indemnity—"on ne croit pas pouvoir le traiter plus favorablement."

General Considerations

(1) The Official Argument

Enclosures apart, this report of Germinal, Year IV, fills twenty closely written foolscap pages, and much of it is concerned more with the validity of Bourdon's claims than with the specific amounts in question. As even this summary shows, the assessor obviously thought Bourdon's claims imprecise and exaggerated as far as values, periods of time, and numbers of pupils were concerned. It may, however, be more significant that he noted of several claims that Bourdon could not hold the government responsible for expenses that he had incurred "at his own risk." Essentially the official view was that Bourdon's school had always been supported provisionally as an experiment, and the failure of that experiment, manifest in the reports drawn up in Germinal and Prairial of Year III, meant that Bourdon had not fulfilled the conditions on which financial support had been granted. Thus, although some concessions might be made in view of the exceptional circumstances prevailing in 1795, the government was absolved from all liabilities save those for payments evidently in arrears.

(2) Bourdon's Argument

This appears in part in the course of this report, but it is also asserted in his own writings, of which his *Observations relatives à l'indemnité* is notable. Bourdon maintained that the report made by the Commission of Arts in June 1794—dismissed in the 1796 report as "un roman"—showed that the school was then flourishing and successful and that, despite the extreme difficulties of the time, even the inspection made on April 3, 1795, proved that the rooms were still in good order and that the pupils were generally healthy and decently clad. The deterioration in their condition apparent on June 18, 1795, when the transference of the school to Liancourt eventually took place, was in his view due to neglect of the school by the government in his absence. At that time, Bourdon said, he had even had to send money from prison to help his wife to buy food for the pupils.

Similarly he deplored the fact that no proper inventory of the furnishing and equipment of the buildings in his part of the Priory was made on April 3, 1795, and that even the inventory made on June 15-16 simply listed the property of the republic, taking little or no account of what was his. Because the dilapidation or disappearance of the contents of what was practically an open building had continued unchecked until his return to Paris in November, by that date almost everything he had was lost. Although he admitted that the confiscation of his papers made it impossible to provide positive proof of all these losses, he certainly wrote about them in high indignation. The school, Bourdon wrote, was "ma chose, dont j'étais fondateur et propriétaire." Adding that he had personally paid all the instructors, he emphasized that a principal basis of his demand for indemnification was that he had never thought any sacrifice too great to ensure that his pupils, "mes enfans adoptifs," did not suffer through the fatal depreciation of paper money. In short, Bourdon asserted that the collapse of his school was due not to any personal failure but to the hostility of his political enemies and that the consequent loss of his pupils, his property, and his prospects entitled him to compensation well beyond the simple payment of overdue accounts.

C. The Assessment Reports of 1797 and 1798

As Bourdon soon discovered, the draft of an order for payment was by no means the same thing as actual payment. His protests about his treatment and the delay of payment consequently kept the matter open, and it was the subject of two further ministerial reports. Because they covered the same ground as before, only their main features need be given here.

The Report of Thermidor, Year V (August 1797)

By this time, as G. Vautier (apparently the only historian who has touched on this tangle) has it (*Annales rév.* [1912]: 342-43), all were wearied by Bourdon's demands. The second report, which Vautier strangely calls the only available document, then reassessed the proposed settlement at 25,000 francs, *valeur metallique*, this with the note that "all things considered" Bourdon could have no further grounds for complaint. Once again, however, the order for payment remained undated, a sufficient indication that the Directory did not authorize it. Indeed, it seems that the Directors called for a full reconsideration of the claim, which was eventually effected in July 1798.

The Report of Messidor, Year VI (July 1798)

The general effect of this lengthier review was to reduce the amount allowable still further. Now the amount originally approved for the expense involved in the attempt to establish la Société d'Émulation was disallowed: "We owe him nothing for speculations which he himself admits were ill-judged." Moreover, although something was now agreed on for the dilapidation of his property while Bourdon was in prison, his call for compensation for the loss of the school itself was again dismissed as relating to an unsuccessful experiment. It was noted that "he took a chance," and the losses that he claimed were said to be sufficiently covered by the advance payment made to him for the last quarter-year of his operations. By such eliminations and reductions, the total due to Bourdon was recalculated as no more than 4,236 francs.

D. The Appeal to the Legislative Body, 1798-99

Bourdon's hopes of obtaining payment quickly were soon frustrated. In a polite letter dated October 11, 1798 (Vendémiaire 20, Year VII), the ministry informed Bourdon that, because it was not authorized to make a payment for the amount in question, application would have to be made to the Legislative Body for a special decree. Persistent as ever, Bourdon made that application, received by the Council of Five Hundred on November 8 (Brumaire 18, Year VII) and at once referred to the appropriate special commission.

Further correspondence then ensued, for on December 30, 1798 (Nivôse 10), the minister told the commissioners that the principal documents, the three earlier assessments, could not leave his office, and Bourdon himself submitted at least two letters for their consideration. As might be expected, these letters were in part a recapitulation of his case and of the way in which he had been treated, the most recent assessment here being referred to as a "revolting injustice." Of greater interest are two of his assertions: that he had been "deprived of the means of existence" for four years, and that the past three years he had been in possession of property that he had purchased from the nationalized lands, apparently in anticipation of the payment of the settlement proposed in 1796. On this last account, Bourdon particularly requested that he should be afforded the amount recommended by the ministry in 1796 with appropriate allowance for conversion of the currency, and he asked that his payment be made in *bons*, not in coinage—presumably so that he could more easily complete his purchase.

Of the conclusion of this vexatious affair, all that can be said here is that on April 13, 1799 (Germinal 24, Year VII), the Council of Five Hundred heard the report of the special commission, which formally endorsed the recommendation of the Minister of the Interior: because "Il a fait toutes les avances nécessaires à l'entretien et à l'instruction de ces élèves si intéressants" (i.e., the *orphelins de la patrie*), "la justice veut donc qu'il soit remboursé des pertes qu'il a faites" when he was forced to abandon his enterprise "par suite des evénémens révolutionnaires." The council then ordered the printing of this report . . . and adjourned.

Comment

If Bourdon ever received anything at all, it was presumably only a minimal amount: although the official attitude varied between occasional generosity and more constant parsimony, it is probable that the latter ultimately prevailed. A more striking aspect of the assessments is the variation between the reports about which parts of Bourdon's claims were or were not admissible, for that inconsistency suggests that, exaggeration and curtailment apart, there was at least some legitimate basis for most of them. Yet, as the repudiation of two-thirds of the national debt on September 30, 1797, shows, the perpetual penury of the state weighed heavily against even the most legitimate of financial grievances.

A second consideration is that Bourdon should certainly not be identified with those men who amassed great fortunes by exploiting the financial situation of the period. Whatever its legitimacy, his claim was for a comparatively small amount, and his persistence in presenting it suggests that he was in financial difficulties. Nor should his purchase, in anticipation of payment, of some small landed property be regarded as discreditable: naturally enough, when the *mandat* collapsed in 1796, "the public literally rushed on purchasable plots in order to take full advantage of this unbelievable godsend" (F. Atalion, *L'économie de la Révolution Française*, p. 229).

Sources

AN, AF III, 107. This carton contains a considerable body of correspondence, memoranda, and reports regarding Bourdon's financial claims. Particular reference may be made to nos. 235, 234, and 233 for the reports of Germinal, Year IV; Thermidor, Year V; and Messidor, Year VI; and to no. 225, the *Observations relatives à l'indemnité du citoyen Bourdon*. For the appeal to the legislative body, see also nos. 230, 229, and 228 and the *Journal des débats: conseil des cinq-cents*, 354 (no. 342, Germinal 24, Year VII).

Chronology

This list is intended to enable the reader to relate Bourdon's career to some of the main events of the period. Asterisks mark his life, and those events which concerned him most closely.

1. Before the Revolution

1754	*November 6: Léonard Bourdon born at Alençon
1758	Voltaire's *Candide*
1762	Rousseau's *Contrat social* and *Émile*
1764	Dissolution of the Society of Jesuits in France
1765	*Bourdon *père* becomes a *premier commis*
1767	*Léonard becomes "de la Crosnière"
1771-72	*Bourdon *père* loses office
1774	Accession of Louis XVI; Turgot as controller-general favours freer trade
1775	The "Flour War"
1776	*Bourdon *père* in the Bastille (September 2-19)
1776-77	Fall of Turgot; Necker in charge of finance
1778-83	France joins America in the War of Independence
1779	*Léonard an *avocat aux conseils du roi*
	*Léonard advises the St. Maur Congrégation
1782	French naval defeat at The Saintes
1783	Treaty of Versailles; Calonne becomes controller-general
1785	*Léonard resigns office of *avocat*
	*Bourdon *père*: *Projet nouveau*
1786	Commercial treaty with Britain
1788	Extensive provincial riots (e.g., Rennes, Grenoble)
August	Convocation of the Estates-General for May 1789
September 25	By legal decision, the three estates must meet separately
October 25	*Royal Council approves Bourdon's "Société d'Émulation"
December	*The *Plan* for "national" education is published
27	Royal Council doubles the size of the Third Estate

2. The "Liberal" Revolution, 1789-92

1789

February	Sieyès's *Qu'est-ce que le Tiers État?*
March	*Both Bourdons print addresses to the estates
April	*Both are elected to the Electoral Assembly of Paris
May 5	The Estates-General opens at Versailles: deadlock ensues
June 17	**The Third Estate assumes the title the National Assembly**
14	*PARISIAN RISING: THE FALL OF THE BASTILLE
16-17	Louis XVI visits Paris, accepting the Revolution
20	The Tennis Court Oath
July	The "great fear" in rural France
August 4	THE ABOLITION OF FEUDAL RIGHTS AND PRIVILEGES
10-13	*Bourdon, of the Commune of Paris, is sent to Provins He also becomes a commissioner for the identification of the victors and victims of July 14
26	THE DECLARATION OF RIGHTS
September	Constitutional conflicts and severe shortages of food *Bourdon active in the Commune's Subsistence Committee
October 5-6	THE OCTOBER DAYS
29	Decree distinguishing "active" from "passive" citizens
November 2	Nationalization of the property of the church in France
December 12	First issue of *assignats*
14-22	Reorganization of local government

1790

January	*Bourdon begins ongoing claims on government for expenses
February 8	First recorded constitution of the Jacobin Club
April 6	*The *Plan* and the *Mémoire* presented to the Commune and (May 31) to the National Assembly
17	*Assignats* become legal tender
May 21	Paris is reorganized into forty-eight sections
June 19	*Report of the Commune's "Bastille Committee"
July 12	The Civil Constitution of the Clergy
14	The first Festival of Federation
August 16	Decree reorganizing the judiciary
November 27	Decree compelling priests to take the clerical oath
December	*Bourdon listed as a member of the Jacobin Club

1791

February-March	*The Jacobin Club promotes Bourdon's proposed school
April 13	The Papacy condemns the Civil Constitution
June 20	THE FLIGHT TO VARENNES

July 16	Decree provides for reinstatement of the king on the completion of the Constitution
17	THE MASSACRE ON THE CHAMP DE MARS
July-August	*Bourdon active in reorganizing the Jacobin Club
August 27	The Pilnitz Declaration: Austria and Prussia threaten war
September 3	The National Assembly adopts the Constitution of 1791
10	Talleyrand's report on education
14	The king accepts the Constitution
30	Dissolution of the National Assembly
October 1	**Meeting of the Legislative Assembly**
7	*Renewed Jacobin support for Bourdon's proposed school
20	Brissot demands military action to disperse *émigrés*
November 9	Decree against the *émigrés* (royal veto, November 12)
29	Decree against nonjuring priests (vetoed December 19)
December 16	Brissot threatens a new insurrection
30	Robespierre (in Jacobins) opposes the demand for war
1792	
March	Formation of the "Patriot" (Brissotin) Ministry
April 20	Declaration of war on Austria
May 29	*Ministry of War subsidizes Les Jeunes Français
June 13	Dismissal of the "Patriot" ministers
20	Crowds invade the Tuileries Palace
29	LaFayette's vain attempt to close the Jacobin Club
July 8	*As president of Gravilliers, Bourdon presents an address against counterrevolution to the Legislative Assembly
July 22	Proclamation of *La patrie en danger*
28	The Brunswick Manifesto reaches Paris

3. The "Popular" Revolution, 1792-94

1792	
August	The sections of Paris admit passive citizens, and many demand the deposition of the king
9	The Legislative Assembly shelves debate on republican petitions
10-11	THE REVOLUTION OF AUGUST 10: the king is suspended, and the election of a national convention is ordered; power is divided between the Legislative Assembly and the new *Commune, of which Bourdon is at times president
17	Creation of the tribunal of August 17
19	Defection of LaFayette; Prussian army invades France
23	*Danton, the Minister of Justice, sends Bourdon to Orléans
September 2	Fall of Verdun to the Prussians
	THE SEPTEMBER MASSACRES begin in Paris

4-9	*Bourdon fails to prevent the abduction of prisoners at Orléans, who are massacred at Versailles (September 9)
9	*Bourdon becomes a *procureur* of the Commune
	*He is also chosen at Orléans as a deputy for the Loiret
20	Battle of Valmy: retreat of Prussian army
21	**Opening of the National Convention**
	Royalty is abolished
24	Conflicts begin about the power of Paris
October 10	Brissot is expelled from the Jacobin Club
13	*Bourdon joins the Committee on Public Instruction
November 5	Robespierre defends Paris and its Montagnard deputies
6	Battle of Jemappes: French conquest of Belgium
19	France offers aid to all peoples seeking liberty
December	Conflict continues concerning the trial of the king
3-13	*Bourdon speaks about his published *Opinions* on the trial
15	Decree on the treatment of occupied territories

1793

January 14-17	The Convention votes to decide the king's fate
	*Bourdon votes for immediate execution
21	THE EXECUTION OF LOUIS XVI
31	The annexation of Belgium
February 1	Declaration of war on Britain and Holland
24	Decree orders conscription of 300,000 men
March 1	War is declared on Spain
	Revolt begins in Belgium
10	Creation of the Revolutionary Tribunal
14	*Bourdon becomes a commissioner of the Convention to the Côte-d'Or and the Jura
16	The revolt of the Vendée begins
	*Bourdon is "assassinated" at Orléans
18	Battle of Neerwinden: Dumouriez falls back to France
April 5	Defection of Dumouriez
6	Creation of the Committee of Public Safety (CPS)
15	The sections demand a purge of the Convention
May 4	The first *maximum* (for price control)
10	*Bourdon again in Paris
30	Conservative Rising at Lyon
31	Insurrection in Paris
June 2	THE REVOLUTION OF JUNE 2: the Convention is purged by the Montagnards and the sections of Paris; the "federalist" wave of protests and revolt ensues
7	Lyon in open revolt
24	The Constitution of 1793 adopted by the Convention
25	*Jacques Roux assails the economic timidity of the Montagnards, and Bourdon repudiates him

June 28-July 12	*Trial by the Revolutionary Tribunal of the alleged assassins of Bourdon at Orléans
July 10	Fall of the frontier fortress of Condé, the first of many such reverses
	*Bourdon joins the Committee of Six on education
13	*The execution of the "assassins" of Bourdon
	Charlotte Corday murders Marat
18	Toulon in open revolt
27	Robespierre enters the Committee of Public Safety
30	*Bourdon's major address on residential education
August 1	*Bourdon presents the report of the Committee of Six on education
6	*Bourdon presents report on granaries
9	*Granaries plan adopted in an ineffective form
10	Festival of Unity exalts the Constitution of 1793
13	*An amended educational plan is decreed
23	General mobilization (*levée en masse*) decreed
27	Surrender of Toulon to the British
September 4-18	*Bourdon is president of the Jacobins
5	HÉBERTIST RISING IN PARIS: rule by the Terror is agreed in principle, as is a Parisian Revolutionary army; Billaud-Varenne and Collot d'Herbois join the CPS
17	The law of suspects is decreed
18	*Temporary triumph of Jacques Roux in Gravilliers
19	*Bourdon urges the recording of republican heroism
22	**Day 1, Year II**
29	The general *maximum* on prices and wages
October 5	Adoption of the Revolutionary Calendar
9	Recapture of Lyon by the Convention's forces
10	Decree sanctions Revolutionary Government until the restoration of peace
c. 12	Fabre d'Eglantine denounces the "foreign plot"
16	The execution of Queen Marie Antoinette
19	*Repeal of the August decree on residential schools
31	The execution of Brissot and the "Brissotins"
November 6	*Bourdon attacks counterrevolutionary priests
7	Abdication of Gobel, constitutional bishop of Paris
10	The Festival of Reason in Notre Dame
11	Robespierre denounces atheism as "aristocratic"
12	*The Gravilliers's demonstration against religion
23	Closure by the Commune of all churches in Paris
December 4	The law of Revolutionary Government
	The massacre of rebels begins in Lyon
7	*Bourdon charged with editing the *Recueil des actions héroïques*

5 and 15	Desmoulins's *Vieux cordelier* challenges both Hébertist extremism and official terrorism
19	Toulon falls to the Convention's army
	Law providing for universal primary education
22	*The CPS bans Bourdon's play *Le tombeau*
23	Decisive defeat of the Vendéans at Savenay
25	Robespierre's speech defining Revolutionary Government
30	The Festival of Victory

1794

January 2	*The Convention approves the first number of the *Recueil des actions héroïques*
28	*Bourdon is rebuked by Robespierre in the Jacobins
February 5	Robespierre's speech defining political morality
14	The execution of the Hébertists
March 16	*Robespierre doubts Bourdon's orthodoxy
April 5	The execution of the Dantonists
May 12	*Bourdon replaced as editor of the *Recueil des actions héroïques*
June 8	The Festival of the Supreme Being
c. 15	*Inspectors report on Bourdon's school positive
26	Battle of Fleurus: French reconquest of Belgium
July 27	(THERMIDOR 9) PROSCRIPTION OF THE ROBESPIERRISTS *Bourdon arrests Robespierre*
28	The execution of Robespierre and his associates

4. The Repression

July 30-31	Reorganization of the CPS
August 5	*Bourdon attempts to purify the Jacobin Club
September 1	Billaud, Collot, and Barère leave the CPS
15-21	*Bourdon promotes the *panthéonization* of Marat
22	**Year III begins**
October 4	*Bourdon is not re-elected to the Comité d'Instruction
13	The tribunal condemns the terrorists of Nantes
14	*Fréron's first attack on Bourdon in *L'Orateur*
28	*Bourdon's last notable speech in the Convention (an appeal for a law to curb calumny)
November 3	*Bourdon is shouted down in the Convention
9-11	*The Jeunesse d'Orée assail the Jacobin Club
11	THE CLOSURE OF THE JACOBIN CLUB
23	*Bourdon votes for the trial of Carrier
December 8	Recall of those who protested after June 2, 1793
20	Abolition of the *maximum*

1795

January 20	The French occupy Amsterdam

February 17	Treaty of La Jaunaye with the Vendéans
21	Restoration of limited religious toleration
26	Marat's body is removed from the Panthéon
March 2	Indictment of Billaud, Collot, and Barère
7	*Legendre insults Bourdon in the Convention
8	Recall of the surviving Brissotins ("Girondins")
15-24	*Bourdon again attacked in *L'Orateur*
April 1	THE PARISIAN RISING OF GERMINAL 12
	Decree deporting Billaud, Collot, and Barère
	*Bourdon is arrested and imprisoned at Ham
2	*Creuzet given charge of the Jeunes Français
5	Peace of Basle with Prussia
mid-April	Famine conditions and repression in Paris
	The White Terror in the Rhône Valley
20	*Hostile report on the state of the Jeunes Français
May 16	Peace of The Hague with Holland
20-21	THE PARISIAN RISING OF PRAIRIAL 1-2; drastic repression of "terrorists"
25	*Denunciation of Bourdon by the sections of Dijon
31	Abolition of the Revolutionary Tribunal
June 8	Death of the Dauphin, "Louis XVII"
18	*Final closure of the Jeunes Français
27	Royalist landing at Quiberon (crushed July 21)
July 22	Peace treaty with Spain
September 23	**Year IV begins**
	The Constitution of Year III is proclaimed
October 5	VENDÉMIAIRE: "ROYALIST" REVOLT IN PARIS; General Bonaparte's "Whiff of Grapeshot"
25	Stringent law against the relatives of *émigrés*
	Daunou's education law (including the higher levels)
26	Dissolution of the Convention
	*Bourdon, freed by amnesty, ineligible for re-election

5. Republican Instability, 1795-99

October 26-31	**Formation of the Councils (the Elders and the Five Hundred) and the Directory**
November	The Directors tolerate the democrats
	*Bourdon becomes a subsistence agent for Paris
16	Opening of the Panthéon Club
1796	
January	*Ministerial rejection of Bourdon's economic plan
February 19	Abolition of the *assignat*
	The Directors become less tolerant
27	Closure of the Panthéon Club (by Bonaparte)

March 30	Babeuf forms the Committee of the Equals
April 11-14	Opening of Bonaparte's Italian campaign
	*Bourdon's first claim for compensation
May 10	The arrest of Babeuf
12	*Bourdon loses office by new law on residence in Paris
July-September	*Bourdon in Brussels (? as electoral agent)
September 22	**Year V begins**
November 24	*The exclusion of all amnestied deputies from office again leaves Bourdon unemployed

1797

February 2	Bonaparte enters Mantua
March	Elections return "royalists" to the Councils
April 18	Bonaparte's preliminary peace with Austria
June-July	The Councils relax antiroyalist laws
	The Directors again seek democratic support
July-August	*Bourdon's second appeal for compensation
September 4	THE COUP D'ÉTAT OF FRUCTIDOR
	"Royalists" purged from the Directory and Councils
22	**Year VI begins**
October	*Bourdon's *Pétition* on education to the Five Hundred
	Campo-Formio: peace is made with Austria
November	Negotiations on Germany begin at Rastadt
	*Sotin, the Minister of Police, sends Bourdon to Hamburg

1798

	The Directors again restrict the democrats
February 15	Dismissal of Sotin
March	Creation of the Swiss (Helvetic) Republic
April 24	*Bourdon is recalled from Hamburg
	Elections, Year VI: large democratic gains
May	THE COUP D'ÉTAT OF FLORÉAL: elections annulled
	Bonaparte's Egyptian expedition
July	*Third report on Bourdon's claims
30	*Bourdon again proposes a new school
31	Battle of the Nile: French fleet destroyed
August 28	*Bourdon's grain project goes to a commission
September 22	**Year VII begins**

1799

March	War renewed: the second coalition against France
	*Bourdon's *La voeu de la nature*
April	Elections, Year VII: renewed democratic gains
	The Directors in difficulties
June 18	THE COUP OF PRAIRIAL: the Directory is composed anew
July-August	Emergency measures as invasions threaten
	Bonaparte abandons his army in Egypt

September 23	**Year VIII begins**
27	Masséna defeats the Russians at Zurich
October 16	Bonaparte reaches Paris
18	British evacuation of Holland
November 9-10	BONAPARTE'S COUP D'ÉTAT OF BRUMAIRE

6. The Consulate and the Empire

| December 25 | **The Constitution of Year VIII: Bonaparte is First Consul** |

1800

February	The prefectoral system is established
June 14	Marengo: Bonaparte defeats the Austrians
September 23	**Year IX begins**
November	*Bourdon is appointed to the military hospital service at Marseilles (and at Toulon, 1803-1807)
December 3	Hohenlinden: Moreau defeats the Austrians
24	"The Crime of 3 Nivôse"—a royalist attempt to assassinate Bonaparte fails

1801

January 5	Proscription of democrats as "assassins"
February 9	Peace treaty of Lunéville with Austria
July 16	The Concordat of 1801 with the Papacy

1802-1807: Some Salient Features

Because Bourdon remained remote from the main course of affairs until 1807, they are summarized below.

In 1802, the Treaty of Amiens with Britain seemed to inaugurate a general peace, and Bonaparte was able to promulgate the Concordat with the Papacy and to establish himself as consul for life (August 4, 1802). Despite the renewal of the war (the third coalition) in 1803, he then became Emperor (May 18, 1804). Until late in 1805, British supremacy at sea (consolidated at Trafalgar, October 21, 1805) thwarted the projected invasion of Britain. Abandoning that plan, Napoleon then inflicted devastating defeats on the Austrians (Austerlitz, December 2, 1805) and the Prussians (Jena, October 14, 1806) before coming to grips with the Russians at the bloody but inconclusive battle of Eylau (February 7-9, 1807). If Bourdon indeed became director of military hospitals (March 12, 1807), he may have been concerned with the aftermath of these conflicts before his death at Breslau on May 19, 1807.

Notes

Preface

1 See Raymonde Monnier, *L'Espace public démocratique: essai sur l'opinion à Paris de la Révolution au Directoire* (Paris, 1994), 147-54.

Chapter 1

1 C. Chaix d'Est-Ange, *Dictionnaire des familles françaises*, vol. 3 (Paris, 1906/1983). See also note 14 below.

2 Archives Nationales (hereafter AN), *Papiers privés*, 137AP, 21-30: *Inventaire des archives du Maréchal Ney et de sa famille conservés aux Archives Nationales* (S. de Saint-Exupéry et C. de Tourtier, Paris, 1962), 190.

3 M. Prevost et Roman d'Amat, *Dictionnaire de biographie française* (Paris, 1933/1954). C. Pancera, "Léonard Bourdon (1754-1807), Editor of the 'Collection of Heroic and Civic Actions of French Republicans,'" *History of European Ideas*, 14, no. 1 (1992), states that Bourdon was born of "a family of noble origins" (14), but I see no basis for this assumption.

4 A. Kuscinski, *Dictionnaire des conventionnels* (Paris, 1916).

5 S. Lacroix, *Actes de la Commune de Paris pendant la Révolution*, première série, 7 vols. (Paris, 1894-98), hereafter cited as *Actes*; J. Guillaume, *Procès-verbaux du Comité d'Instruction Publique de l'Assemblée Législative* (Paris, 1889)—hereafter cited as *P-V du Comité, LA*, and J. Guillaume, *Procès-verbaux du Comité d'Instruction Publique de la Convention*—hereafter cited as *P-V du Comité, Convention*, 6 vols. (Paris, 1891-1907).

6 Armand Le Corbeiller, *Le Léopard de la Révolution: l'affaire d'Orléans, 1793* (Paris, 1938).

7 *Biographie moderne ou galerie historique* (Paris, 1815); A.V. Arnault, *Biographie nouvelle des contemporains* (Paris, 1821); A. Rabbe, *Biographie universelle* (Paris, 1834).

8 A. Kuscinski, "Le Conventionnel Léonard Bourdon," *La Révolution Française*, 16 (January-June 1889): 133-34. The original entry is recorded in the Archives Departmentales de l'Orne, 3E2-001/28: Alençon, *paroisse* Notre-Dame. Some later works of reference, such as E. Boursin, *Dictionnaire de la Révolution Française* (Paris, 1893), reiterate the date 1758.

9 M. Marion, *Dictionnaire des institutions de la France aux XVIIe et XVIIIe siècles* (Paris, 1968). An indication of des Planches's increasing prosperity at the time of Léonard's birth is his acquisition in 1754 of a share in Languedoc (AN, *Minutier central des notaires*, étude XCII, liasse 589).

10 The *Almanach Royal*, an official annual publication, often necessarily shows situations that existed in the previous year. The age of Bourdon *père* is here determined retrospectively: he was sixty-six in April 1790, when his pension was confirmed by the National Assembly. See *Archives Parlementaires de 1787 à 1860* (hereafter cited as AP), première série (1787 à 1799), ed. M.J. Madival and M.E. Laurent, 2nd ed., 94 vols. (Paris, 1879-1913), 13:560.

11 M.-A. Bourdon, *À Dumaine* (Paris, 1794), British Library (hereafter cited as BL), 982.12, particularly 10.

347

12 E.g., Dr. J. Robinet, *Dictionnaire historique et biographique* (Paris, 1899).

13 Marc-Antoine asserted that he had publicly quarrelled with Thomas in the section on this occasion and that he had not seen him since then. He also denied all intimacy with another relative, a Bourdon des Planches who was apparently also named as a guard for the king by the Department of the Orne; this may perhaps be Léonard's godfather, Joseph (M.-A. Bourdon, *À Dumaine*, 10 and note).

14 G. Lefebvre, *Études Orléanaises, 1789-An IV*, 2 vols. (Paris, 1962-63), I:108, the comment being that of the *abbé* Pataud. Charles Bourdon de Saunai is perhaps the Constantin Charles de Saussay mentioned by d'Est-Ange as the fourth son of des Planches.

15 For Bourdon's denial of residence in Orléans, see Léonard Bourdon, *À ses concitoyens* (Paris, An III/1795), 3, Bibliothèque nationale (hereafter cited as BN), Lb[41] 1393. G. Walter is strangely wrong in stating (in the notes to his edition, *Histoire de la Révolution*, by J. Michelet (Paris, 1952), that Léonard's name does not appear in the official list of *avocats aux conseils* in the *Almanach*; it appears annually from 1780 to 1786, the office being held from 1779 to 1785.

16 Le Corbeiller, *Le Léopard de la Révolution*, 152, note (from information supplied to that author by a resident of the Vendée).

17 Bourdon de Vatry, Minister of Marine in 1799-1800 and in 1814, was also a notable prefect during the Napoleonic period. See M. Michaud, *Biographie universelle, ancienne et moderne*, 45 vols. (Paris, 1835), supplement to ed. of 1812, and AN, F[1b] 156/39, *Les préfets du 11 ventôse au septembre 1870: Répertoire nominatif*.

18 Marion, *Dictionnaire des institutions de la France*; R. Mousnier, *Les institutions de la France sous la monarchie absolue*, translated by A. Goldhammer, vol. 2 (Paris, 1980 ed.; Chicago, 1984), 166-67, 176-79; J.F. Bosher, "The Premiers Commis des Finances in the Reign of Louis XVI," *French Historical Studies*, 3 (1964): 475-94. Illuminating consideration of the composition and character of the *bureaux* of royal government appears in H.T. Parker, *An Administrative Bureau during the Old Regime: The Bureau of Commerce and Its Relations to French Industry from May 1781 to November 1783* (London and Toronto, 1993), particularly 14-16.

19 Kuscinski, *Dictionnaire des conventionnels*.

20 André-François Langlois (1717-81). His office of *intendant des finances* was suppressed by edict in January 1771 (M. Antoine, *Le gouvernement et l'administration sous Louis XV: dictionnaire biographique* [Paris, 1978], 145).

21 *Comité des Pensions: État des pensions . . . 1780-90*, AN, D X 1, *liasse* 8 (Calonne), and *État nominatif des pensions sur le trésor royal, 1789*, 1:414. I am indebted to Professor J.F. Bosher for guidance in locating these sources.

22 L.-J. Bourdon des Planches, *Projet pour la réunion des postes aux chevaux aux messageries* (s.l.n.d., c. 1765), BN, Lf[92] 19.

23 Charpentier and P.L. Manuel, *La Bastille dévoilée*, 4 vols. (Paris, 1789), 4:115-18.

24 G. Rudé, *The Crowd in the French Revolution* (Oxford, 1959), 24; however, cf. A. Cobban, *A History of Modern France*, vol. 1: *1715-1799* (Harmondsworth, 1961), 102.

25 L.-J. Bourdon des Planches, *Lettre à l'auteur des "Observations sur le commerce des grains"* (Amsterdam, 1775), BL, F 257.1.

26 Bibliothèque de l'arsenal, MS 12478: *Écrou de la Bastille*, 188, and, for his release, 189; F. Funck-Bretano, *Histoire général de Paris, 1659-1789* (Paris, 1903), 400, no. 5054 (*Lettres de cachet de Paris, liste des prisonniers de la Bastille*).

27 Terray was indeed still living in the vicinity of Paris, apparently being deeply involved in speculations in the grain trade, but he is more likely to have welcomed than to have opposed criticisms of Turgot's policy.

28 J. Balteau, *Dictionnaire de biographie française* (Paris, 1936).

29 Charpentier and Manuel, *La Bastille dévoilée*, 118.

30 Contemporary interest in the arrest of des Planches is apparent in the entries by L.P. Bachaumont in his *Mémoires secrètes*, 31 vols. (London, 1866), 9:234, for September 8, 14, and 26, 1776, where he commends des Planches's refusal to identify his printer, notes that des Planches was not strictly confined (being visited by his wife), and implies that the whole affair was mismanaged by the authorities.

31 F. Braesch, *La Commune du dix août* (Paris, 1911), 19.

32 The contrary argument is apparent in L.-J. Bourdon des Planches's *Adresse à la Convention Nationale sur la subsistence et sur les impositions* (Paris, 1793), BL, FR 261.17 and BN, Lb⁴¹ 1612: "Even my zeal displeased, and my initiative was followed by the suppression of the post with which I had been provided.... [M]y status was lost." This could indicate that des Planches had been transferred to another office when Langlois's bureau was eliminated in 1771, and in AN, D X 2, he is referred to once as *premier commis* of Trudaine, whose post as an intendant of finance was abolished in 1777. Des Planches was still claiming compensation in 1793 for losses suffered from the publication of his pamphlet on the posting services (F. Gerbaux et Ch. Schmidt, *Procès-verbaux des Comités d'Agriculture et de Commerce de la Constituente, de la Législative, et de la Convention*, 4 vols. [Paris, 1906-10], 4:76, for May 4, 1793).

33 See note 15 above. Robinet, *Dictionnaire historique et biographique*, says that Bourdon was an *avocat en parlement*, but he gives no source.

34 Léonard Bourdon, *Compte que les RP visiteurs et les six députés de la province de Normandie rendent au chapitre-général . . . consultation déliberé à Paris, le 29 avril 1781*, BN, Ld¹⁶ 354.

35 Controversy about the order nevertheless continued at a higher level, attacks on it in the Parlement de Paris in 1783-84 apparently being really directed against the authority of the church and the king. See H. Monin, *L'État de Paris en 1789* (Paris, 1899), 131.

36 AN, BB³ 78, dossier A.-J.-D. Bourdon. Also G. Vauthier, "Léonard Bourdon et la Société des Jeunes Français," *Annales Révolutionnaires*, 5 (1912): 331, note 2.

37 Léonard Bourdon, *Plan d'un établissement d'éducation nationale* (Orléans, 1788), BN, Rz 1767. I think it unlikely that this work was written, as Pancera asserts (note 3 above), as an assignment for the congregation; cf. Vauthier, "Léonard Bourdon et la Société des Jeunes Français," 332. For the expansion of royal military schools before the Revolution, see R.R. Palmer, *The Improvement of Humanity: Education and the French Revolution* (Princeton, NJ, 1985), 65-66, and R. Chartier, D. Julia, and M.M. Compère, *L'éducation en France du XVIᵉ au XVIIIᵉ siècle* (Paris, 1976), 217-22.

38 L.-J. Bourdon des Planches, *Projet nouveau sur la manière de faire utilement en France le commerce des grains* (Brussels, 1785), BL, FR 257.2 and BN, R 2295; and, with a prospectus, *Le monopole altéré*, BN, R 29759; L.-J. Bourdon des Planches, *Code fraternel* (s.l.n.d., 1787), BL, F 474; L.-J. Bourdon des Planches, *Bases pour taxer le pain* (s.l.n.d., 1788), BL, R 440; L.-J. Bourdon des Planches, *Au roi: lettre presentée à sa majesté le 9 déc. 1788* (London and Paris, 1789), BN, Lb³⁰ 11757.

39 Bachaumont, *Mémoires secrètes*, vol. 31, mars 6, 1786. The recommendation of the *Mercure* was reprinted in the reissue of Bourdon des Planches and Léonard Bourdon's *Projet nouveau* entitled *Aux États Generaux: subsistence et impôt* (s.l.n.d., 1788-89), BL, FR 257.21, and BN, Rp. 3808. Léonard Bourdon also published his address *Aux États Generaux: idées sur l'éducation nationale*, BL, FR 257.2, and BN, R 1452.

40 Bourdon, *Plan d'un établissement d'éducation nationale* (note 37 above). Education in general is further considered in chapter 3.

41 Agnès Thibal, "La Société des Jeunes Français de Léonard Bourdon: une expérience pédagogique sous la Révolution" (hereafter cited as Thibal, "La Société"), 2 vols., dissertation maîtrise d'histoire, Université Paris-I, 1986. Thibal, whose thesis is primarily concerned with Bourdon's school as it eventually became established in 1792, has been most generous in placing her work at my disposal. As will appear in later chapters, I have used it extensively as an indispensable work of reference.

42 At the time about which I am writing, "émulation," rivalry between students to achieve results was commonly extolled as a progressive method of instruction, often being pressed to excessive lengths. Although Bourdon's plans included the award of marks both of distinction and punishment by the pupils' general assembly, it seems certain that Bourdon thought of emulation principally in terms of participation in the life of the community.

43 E.g., F. Stuebig, "Erziehung und Gleichheit: Die Konzepte der 'Éducation Commune' in der Französischen Revolution," in *EGS Texte* (Ravensburg, 1974).

44 Léonard Bourdon, Sur l'éducation nationale: extrait d'un travail dont l'Assemblée Nationale a chargé son Comité de Constitution de faire lui le rapport (Paris, s.d.), BN, Rp. 10608. See also A. Tuetey, Répertoire général des sources manuscrits de l'histoire de Paris pendant la Révolution Française (hereafter cited as Répertoire), 11 vols. (Paris, 1890-1914), 3:582.

45 The order-in-council is appended to the Plan, the original being AN, F 17.1309, f.1 (letters patent and extract from the registers of the Royal Council of State, October 5, 1788, also given in full in Thibal, "La Société," appendix 3).

46 See chapter 2 below.

47 Siegfried Bernfeld, "Léonard Bourdons System der Anstalsdisziplin" 1788-1795," Zeitschrift fur Kinderchung, 36 (Berlin, 1930): 153-69.

48 Le Corbeiller, Le Léopard de la Révolution, 1.

49 Léonard Bourdon, Lettre au président de l'Assemblé Nationale, 1ᵉʳ novembre 1791, AN, F 17.1309, f.1 (cited in Thibal, "La Société," 41).

Chapter 2

1 Thibal, "La Société," 12, citing Archives de la Bibliothèque historique de la ville de Paris (hereafter cited as BHVP), MS 815.

2 Léonard Bourdon, Aux États-Généraux, BN, R 1452. See also Pancera, "Léonard Bourdon ... Editor" (chapter 1 above, note 3), 15.

3 At this time, many people assumed that one main feature of the reorganization of France would be the revival or establishment of provincial assemblies, which would be composed in the same way as the National Assembly. In fact, the elimination of all such bodies was one of the first steps taken toward the concentration of authority in the National Assembly, and it was one that alienated much moderate sympathy.

4 Bourdon apparently assumed that reconstituted provincial assemblies would be charged with the supervision of what would now be called public secondary education, principally provided in 1789 in the collèges of the various teaching congregations. The military schools, established in various parts of France by Louis XIV and Louis XV, were for those of noble birth, with some financial assistance for the sons of officers. They gave more attention to mathematics and military exercises; however, as Bourdon well knew, their operation was also entrusted to religious congregations such as that of Saint-Maur.

5 Léonard Bourdon with L.J. Bourdon des Planches, Aux États-Généraux: subsistence et impôt (Paris, 1788-89), BL, FR 257.21, and BN, Rp. 3808. Properly there were two separate addresses: (1) Subsistence and (2) Impôt.

6 The offer of free places is included in Bourdon's 1788 Plan d'un établissement d'éducation nationale. For the question of the real existence of Bourdon's school in 1789, see chapter 3 below.

7 J.S. Bailly and H. Duveyrier, eds., Procès-verbaux des séances et délibérations de l'Assemblée Générale des électeurs de Paris (hereafter cited as P-V des électeurs), 3 vols. (Paris, 1790), 3:373-75. See also P. Robiquet, Le Personnel municipal de Paris pendant la Révolution, vol. 1: Période constitutionelle (Paris, 1890), 68.

8 For the two decrees, Ch. L. Chassin, Les élections et les cahiers de Paris en 1789, 4 vols. (Paris, 1888-89), 1:333, 399; for consideration of the social composition of the electorate, R.B. Rose, The Making of the Sans-Culottes (Manchester, 1983), 32-33.

9 Chassin, Les élections et les cahiers de Paris en 1789, 2:319.

10 Ibid., 340; Rose, The Making of the Sans-Culottes, 25.

11 Chassin, Les élections et les cahiers de Paris en 1789, 2:317, 477.

12 Ibid., 325-30.

13 Ibid., 327-28.

14 Michael P. Fitzsimmons, The Parisian Order of Barristers and the French Revolution (Cambridge, MA, and London, 1987), 34-38.

15 The phrase, taken from a hostile journal, Montjoie's Ami du Roi, is cited, among others, by Henry E. Bourne, "Improvising a Government in Paris in July 1789," American Historical Review, 10 (1905): 280-308, particularly 285.

16 Chassin, *Les élections et les cahiers de Paris en 1789*, 2:477.

17 Bailly and Duveyrier, eds., *P-V des électeurs*, 1:v-x.

18 Ibid., 373-75; Robiquet, *Le Personnel municipal de Paris pendant la Révolution*, 146, 207; and Lacroix, *Actes*, 1:2-4, 11.

19 Bailly and Duveyrier, eds., *P-V des électeurs*, 1:89, and 2:68; Tuetey, *Répertoire*, 1:636.

20 Bailly and Duveyrier, eds., *P-V des électeurs*, 1:31-35; Chassin, *Les élections et les cahiers de Paris en 1789*, 3:156-57.

21 Léonard Bourdon, *Developpement de la motion faite dans l'Assemblée des Tiers-État de la ville de Paris le jeudi 7 mai* (s.l.n.d., Paris, 1789), BN, Lb[39] 1698.

22 Declaration on the National Assembly, June 17, 1789 (J.H. Stewart, *A Documentary Survey of the French Revolution* [New York, 1951], 87).

23 See note 18 above.

24 Gary Kates, *The Cercle Social, the Girondins, and the French Revolution* (Princeton, NJ, 1985), 34-44.

25 Robiquet, *Le Personnel municipal de Paris pendant la Révolution*, 151.

26 Lacroix, *Actes*, 1:315, 512, 516, 520.

27 Ibid., 91-92 and note. On August 4, too, Necker wrote reproachfully to the municipal officers of Provins, mistakenly dating his letter June 4 (Archives municipales de Provins, *Registre de correspondance*). Robiquet, *Le Personnel municipal de Paris pendant la Révolution*, 146, wrongly has the commissioners and the force going to Vernon; there were somewhat similar troubles there in both July and October 1789, but I have not found any reference to Bourdon on these occasions. See Kates, *The Cercle Social, the Girondins, and the French Revolution*, 30, and, for October, P.J.B. Buchez and P.L. Roux, *Histoire parlementaire de la Révolution Française*, 40 vols. (Paris, 1834), 3:239, and Tuetey, *Répertoire*, 1:357-59, nos. 3212-34.

28 Felix Bourquelot, *Histoire de Provins*, 2 vols. (Paris and Provins, 1839-40), 1:319-21. This author is well regarded, but I was unable to find documentary evidence for parts of his account. The municipal archives of Provins are at present being reclassified. See Anne Marzin, "Révolution de 1789 et manuscrits à la Bibliothèque municipale de Provins," *Provins et sa région*, no. 143, *Bulletin de la Société historique et archéologique de Provins* (1989). Also note 47 below.

29 Ibid.

30 Lacroix, *Actes*, 1:124, 240-43.

31 Ibid. Another account of this affair, anonymous and too approximate to be reliable, appears in *Expédition de Provins et aventure d'un gentilhomme enfermé dans une cave* (Paris, 1789), BL, F 424(3).

32 Bourquelot, *Histoire de Provins*, 1:321; *Le Courrier de Versailles à Paris*, 29, August 5, 1789, reports the arrival of a considerable quantity of grain from Provins on the previous day; Archives municipale de Provins, *Registre du comité municipal de Provins* in the municipal archives has details on August 16, 21, and 24 of the despatch of grain and its escort.

33 Archives municipale de Provins, *Registre du comité municipal*, August 8, 1789.

34 Mayor Bailly, who tells us that he and Lafayette arranged the military expedition to Provins, makes no mention of Bourdon or the other commissioners beyond remarking that he was sure of the wisdom of one of them, M. de la Chesnie (i.e., Chesnaye). His account of the times, however, is far from disinterested (J.S. Bailly, *Mémoires*, ed. St. A. Berville and J.F. Barriére, 3 vols. [Paris, 1821-22], 2:207-209).

35 Lacroix, *Actes*, 1:313.

36 Ibid., 1:455, 511; 2:122.

37 Ibid., 1:455, 478, 512.

38 Ibid., 208-209; Léonard Bourdon, *À Marat* (Paris, 1793 for 1792), BN, Lb[41] 2304. Cf. note 49 below.

39 Lacroix, *Actes*, 1:228-29.

40 E.g., the signature to Léonard Bourdon, *Société des Jeunes français: base d'une école centrale d'expérience* (Paris, 1791), BL, 936 f. 12(17).

41 E.g., "il assista à la prise de la Bastille" (J. Durieux, *Les Vainqueurs de la Bastille* [Paris, 1911], 31).

42 J. Flammermont, Introduction to "La journée de 14 juillet 1789," in L.-G. Pitra, *Électeur: fragment des mémoires inédites*, ed. J. Flammermont (Paris, 1892), cxciv-ccxiii; Bailly and Duveyrier, eds., *P-V des électeurs*, vol. 1, for the session July 12-14.

43 Although *Le Moniteur* for July 17-20 (*Le Moniteur: réimpression de l'ancien Moniteur* [hereafter cited as *Le Moniteur*], 32 vols. [1847-79]: 1(20), 169-72) gives a Bourdon as one of the electors' delegates sent on July 12 to try to calm the people, and gives what may be a first-hand account of events on July 14 by various electors (including a Bourdon), this could be one of three of that name. Beyond that, the evidence is negative; thus, J. Godechot, *The Taking of the Bastille*, translated by J. Stewart (London, 1970), the standard modern work, has no reference to any Bourdon.

44 Bailly and Duveyrier, eds., *P-V des électeurs*, 1:117-18. The French Guards, long garrisoned in Paris, had contributed considerably to the success of the popular revolution in July 1789.

45 Lacroix, *Actes*, 1:159, 167; 3:205.

46 Ibid., 1:228-29; 4:216, note 5 for February 26, 1790.

47 Durieux, *Les Vainqueurs de la Bastille*, 4-5; see also J. Dusaulx, *Mémoires sur le 14 juillet*, ed. St. A. Berville and J.F. Barrière (Paris, 1821), 446-47. The Conquerors of the Bastille must be distinguished from the Volunteers of the Bastille, a self-constituted unit of the citizens' militia that was eventually incorporated into the National Guard; moreover, although that unit apparently did some foraging for Paris, its name seems to have been usurped by other bands. It is perhaps one of the latter that is referred to as the "Conquerors" in the local account of events in Provins in August 1789. See Robiquet, *Le Personnel municipal de Paris pendant la Révolution*, 348.

48 Note 47 above; Lacroix, *Actes*, 6:240; AP, 16:371. See also chapter 3 below.

49 Bourdon, À Marat, BN, Lb⁴¹ 2304. Extracts from this letter, which should be dated to September 1792, when Bourdon was concerned to justify his record at a crucial electoral period, may be seen in F.-A. Aulard, *La grande encyclopédie* (Paris, 1886), 742 (entry for Bourdon).

50 See previous note.

51 Le Corbeiller, *Le Léopard de la Révolution*, 2.

52 Lacroix, *Actes*, 2:122; AP, 9:239.

53 Lacroix, *Actes*, 2:150-51.

54 L. Gottschalk and M. Maddox, *Lafayette in the French Revolution: Through the October Days* (Chicago, 1969), 333-42.

55 Lacroix, *Actes*, 2:185.

56 Ibid., 16; for the ruling, 47.

57 Ibid., 510.

58 Ibid., 3:346.

59 For this and the following paragraphs, see *Le Moniteur*, 1(77), 314, for October 23, 1789, and G. Lenotre (i.e., L.L.T. Gosselin), "Le centenaire du Mont Jura," in *Paris révolutionnaire: vieilles maisons, vieux papiers*, 6ᵉ série (Paris, 1930), 3-24.

60 D. Monnier, "Annales semi-contemporains." In *Annuaire du Département du Jura pour l'année 1850* (Lons-le-Saunier, 1849ff.), 329.

61 Lacroix, *Actes*, 2:219, 317; Robiquet, *Le Personnel municipal de Paris pendant la Révolution*, 254-55.

62 Tuetey, *Répertoire*, 2:582.

63 L.-J. Bourdon des Planches, *Association patriotique: projet de décret . . . sur les grains et les finances* (s.l.n.d., 1789), BN, Sp. 1648.

64 Gerbaux and Schmidt, *Procès-verbaux des comités d'Agriculture et de Commerce de la Constituente*, particularly 1:70.

65 Lacroix, *Actes*, 1:1517, 583.

66 Gerbaux and Schmidt, *Procès-verbaux des comités d'Agriculture et de Commerce de la Constituente*, 1:114. On February 24, 1790, when the commissioners appointed by the Subsistence Committee of the Commune eventually reported on Bourdon senior's proposals, the Commune noted that there was "nothing to discuss" (Lacroix, *Actes*, 4:197).

Chapter 3

1 Le Corbeiller, *Le Léopard de la Révolution*, 2.

2 A. Soboul, ed., *Dictionnaire historique de la Révolution Française* (Paris, 1989).

3 See above, chapter 1, note 7.

4 Lacroix, *Actes*, 4:151-52, and note; *Procès-verbaux de l'assemblée des Vainqueurs de la Bastille*, AN, C 35.298. Dusaulx, *Mémoires sur le 14 juillet*, 447, tells us that much arduous work was done by a preparatory committee, but Bourdon was not a member (Lacroix, *Actes*, 6:238).

5 *AP*, 16:371; Lacroix, *Actes*, 6:240-41 (where various and varied lists are identified); and Durieux, *Les Vainqueurs de la Bastille*, 5. For consideration of the social composition of the attackers on July 14, see Godechot, *The Taking of the Bastille*, 221-25; Rudé, *The Crowd in the French Revolution*, 57.

6 Durieux, *Les Vainqueurs de la Bastille*, 6-7, giving a letter written to Marat and published on July 2, 1790.

7 *Procès-verbal de ce qui est passé dans l'assemblée des Vainqueurs de la Bastille tenue avant-hier aux quinze-vingts* (Paris, 1790), BN, Lb³⁹ 9010; see also Lacroix, *Actes*, 6:234 (where the resolution is given at its presentation to the Commune later the same night), 248-53.

8 The fate of these men of 1789 may be indicated as illustrative of the times. Jean-Sylvain Bailly (1736-93), philanthropic astronomer, first president of the National Assembly, and first mayor of Paris, was ignominiously guillotined on the Champ de Mars, being held responsible for the massacre there on July 14, 1791. Claude Fauchet (1744-93), a priest active in the attack on the Bastille, was a notable social democrat in 1790-91; having become the bishop of Calvados and a deputy of that *département*, he was guillotined with Brissot and the Girondins. Jean Dusaulx (1728-99), once a soldier and long a scholar, was exempted from proscription with the Brissotins by Marat, who dismissed him as a harmless dotard; merely imprisoned during the Terror, he lived to become the librarian of the Arsenal. *Stanislaus Maillard* (1763-94), traditionally a particularly sinister street activist in successive *journées*—including the September Massacres—acquired still more notoriety as the head of a political security squad during the Terror. He died of consumption after being twice imprisoned on charges of corruption and brutality.

9 Durieux, *Les Vainqueurs de la Bastille*, 6.

10 Robiquet, *Le Personnel municipal de Paris pendant la Révolution*, 552-53.

11 The substance of this *affiche* is not known. See M. Tourneux, *Bibliographie de l'histoire de Paris pendant la Révolution Française*, 5 vols. (Paris, 1890-1913), 4:no. 26244, and Lacroix, *Actes*, 6:239, 304-305, 309-10.

12 E. Charavay, *L'Assemblée Électorale de Paris*, 3 vols. (Paris, 1890-1905), 1:43.

13 *AP*, 13:560.

14 L.-J. Bourdon des Planches, *Dangers du serment fédératif relativement aux subsistances et moyen d'y parer* (Paris, 1790), BN, Lb³⁹ 3731; L.-J. Bourdon des Planches, *Réclamation d'un citoyen électeur de 1789 et de 1790 pour une organisation dans le commerce des grains* (Paris, s.d.), BN, Rp. 8551 (also in the Maclure Collection); L.-J. Bourdon des Planches, *L'anti-economiste, ou moyens de rédimer les personnes et les biens du joug des impositions* (Paris, 1791), BN, Lb³⁹ 9708. The latter was accompanied by an open letter, dated September 3, 1791, to the Electoral Assembly of Paris (Tuetey, *Répertoire*, 1:3354).

15 Tuetey, *Répertoire*, 2:3497, citing AN, Y 11286, which was not available when the research for this book was being undertaken.

16 AN, *Minutier central des notaires*, étude XVII (*liasse* 1062, 28 décembre 1790), and IX (*liasse* 827, 29 décembre 1790). My synopsis indicates only what seems to be the essential feature of complex transactions. Richard C. Cobb ("La mission de Siblot au Havre-Marat," *Annales de Normandie* [1953], 177-78) notes the effect of the emigration on those working in porcelain.

17 See, e.g., the foreword (*avis*) to Léonard Bourdon's *Mémoire* (for which see note 25 below) and his *Sur l'éducation nationale* (identified above, chapter 1, note 44); also Vauthier, "Léonard Bourdon et la Société des Jeunes Français," 332.

18 Ibid., 333. The author habitually cites but does not identify documentary sources. Cf. Thibal, "La Société," 42, 49.

19 E.g., Bourdon, *Société des Jeunes français: base d'un école centrale d'expérience*, BL, 936 f. 12(17). See also note 20 below.

20 Both the conditional nature of the Order in Council and Bourdon's reaction to the hesitancy of the ministers to implement it are considered by Thibal, "La Société," 35-40, the order being given in full in her appendix 3. Pancera, "Léonard Bourdon . . . Editor," 14, has "due to the resignation of the Minister of War shortly before signing," but de Puységur held office from August 1788 to July 11, 1789.

21 Bourdon, *Plan d'un établissement d'éducation nationale*: "Je ne me suis pas dissumulé que l'établissement que j'annonce nécessitera des dépenses . . . au dessus des facultés de beaucoup de citoyens."

22 Evidence of the existence of la Société Royale d'Émulation in 1789-90 is slight. The correspondence of the royal household contains two letters of September 1789 in which references to the school seem to me to suggest that its formation was still projected (AN, O^1 500.467 and 484). Bourdon's brochure *Sur l'éducation nationale* (chapter 1, note 44 above), probably published during the second half of 1790, includes a note (5) asserting that Louis XVI and his brother, the Count of Provence, had each undertaken to subsidize one pupil; and, on July 1 and September 13, 1790, the Commune's records mention a proposal (not emanating from Bourdon) to merge the *société* and the Lycée de Paris, a suggestion that Lacroix believed was abandoned because the *société* was "more in need of help than able to give it" (Lacroix, *Actes*, 6:338, 340, 346-47). More positive proof that the *société* was abandoned lies in an official reference to it as having been "rétablie" as la Société des Jeunes Français (*Rapport présenté au Directoire Exécutif par le ministre de l'intérieur, le . . . germinal An IV*, AN, AF^{111} 107, 485:25), which is cited in a convincing consideration of the question by Thibal, "La Société," 33-43. See also notes 50-51 below and the concluding pages of this chapter.

23 Lacroix, *Actes*, 4:612. The original being lost, Lacroix cites Bourdon's reproduction of it in the records of the Jacobins (F.-A. Aulard, *La Société des Jacobins: recueil de documents* [hereafter cited as Aulard, *Jacobins*], 6 vols. [Paris, 1889-97], 3:174-75).

24 Apparently unpublished. Lacroix, *Actes*, 4:612, gives this title to Bourdon's presentation to the Commune on April 6, 1790, whereas Thibal, "La Société," 15, has it as that to the National Assembly on May 31. Probably it is simply a general description briefly recorded in the records of the assembly (AP, 16:22).

25 The full title of the *Mémoire*, the publication of which was noted in *Le Moniteur* (8:504) a year later (May 27, 1791), is *Mémoire sur l'instruction et sur l'éducation nationale, avec un projet de décret et de règlement constitutionnel pour les jeunes gens réunis dans les écoles publiques, suivi d'un essai sur la manière de concilier la surveillance nationale avec les droits d'un père sur ses enfants dans l'éducation des héritiers présomptifs de la couronne* (An II/1790-91), BN, R 22944.

26 Bourdon, *Sur l'éducation nationale.*

27 For this and for much of the following paragraphs, reference is made to two general works: H.C. Barnard, *Education and the French Revolution* (Cambridge, 1969), and the more detailed study of Palmer, *The Improvement of Humanity.*

28 Palmer establishes the theme of his study by two initial quotations from Helvétius's treatise *On Man* (1763): "L'education peut tout," and "any important reform in the moral part of education presupposes one in the form of government and of the laws" (Palmer, *The Improvement of Humanity*, 3). In and after 1789, the revolutionaries similarly assumed fundamental political change to be inseparable from corresponding changes in the purpose and character of education.

29 Lacroix, *Actes*, 4:613, note 1. Similarly Bourdon's *Mémoire* is included by Palmer, *The Improvement of Humanity*, 89-94, as the last of sixteen works collectively surveyed as representative of "the ideas of less famous persons" at this time.

30 Material for this and the following paragraphs has been derived as convenient from Léonard Bourdon's *Mémoire*; the *Projet de décret sur l'éducation nationale* (1793), BN, Le^{38} 373, that accompanied it; and *Sur l'éducation nationale*, an extract from it. (See notes 17 and chapter 1, note 44 above.) Pancera, "Léonard Bourdon . . . Editor," 16-19, surveys this material usefully from a revised edition that he ascribes to late August 1791.

31 I here concur with the assessment of Thibal, "La Société," 46.
32 Bourdon, *Sur l'éducation nationale*, 9, note.
33 Bourdon, *Mémoire*, 1-2.
34 Bourdon, *Sur l'éducation nationale*, 15.
35 Ibid. (*avertissement*).
36 Bourdon, *Mémoire*, 7.
37 Ibid., 37-38.
38 AP, 16:22.
39 Lacroix, *Actes*, 4:613, note 2.
40 Thibal, "La Société," 48, where the letter is reproduced from AN, F^{17} 1310.7.
41 Thibal, "La Société," 15; Lacroix, *Actes*, 4:615, note 2.
42 Thibal, "La Société," 15, has "in August and September (1790) he worked as a Commissioner of the National Assembly in evaluating *biens nationaux*" (at this time, properties confiscated from the regular clergy). Her source, AN, Q^2 120, indeed contains a dossier (no. 5) relating to the evaluation of the Priory of Saint-Martin-des-Champs, in which Léonard Bourdon later established his school, and successive pages are signed by a Bourdon in a hand like Léonard's. Nevertheless, in September 1795, the Convention's Committee of Public Instruction authorized the payment of 25,000 francs to "Bourdon et L. Français, entrepreneurs des bâtiments," for work done "dans les dépôts" (Guillaume, *P-V du Comité, Convention*, 6:index).
43 Tourneux, *Bibliographie de l'histoire de Paris pendant la Révolution Française*, 2:no. 7631. Marc-Antoine is also recorded in 1789 as advocating the conversion of Saint-Lazare into a parish with a hospital and a college (ibid., 3:no. 16653) and presenting the Commune with a report from his district on the courageous conduct of a captain in the National Guard in defending a baker (Lacroix, *Actes*, 1:612).
44 Lacroix, *Actes*, 4:210; 5:541; 6:225, 315, 395; 7:191. See also, e.g., AN, S 4.639: *procès* of the senior Bourdon's visit to the Augustines, June 7, 1791.
45 AP, 43:268; Gerbaux and Schmidt, *Procès-verbaux des comités d'Agriculture et de Commerce de la Constituente*, 1:317; Bourdon des Planches, *Dangers du serment fédératif relativement aux subsistences et moyen d'y parer*. In May 1790, both Bourdons, father and son, jointly sought permission to address the National Assembly about the economy, approval of their application being granted but not, apparently, implemented (AP, 43:265).
46 Robiquet, *Le Personnel municipal de Paris pendant la Révolution*, 308, 334.
47 See Rose, *The Making of the Sans-Culottes*, 86.
48 Members of the new "definitive" Commune are listed by Robiquet, *Le Personnel municipal de Paris pendant la Révolution*, 363. Bourdon des Planches soon after became an elector for Saint-Laurent in the Electoral Assembly of Paris (Charavay, *L'Assemblée Électorale de Paris*, 1:43).
49 See previous note. Unlike his father, Léonard Bourdon took the oath required of members of the old Commune denying that any financial advantages had come to them from their offices. Des Planches's failure to do so is not significant because the oath was optional for those who were also members of the *Conseil d'Administration* (Lacroix, *Actes*, 7:331, 338, 344).
50 For the accusation, see chapter 4 below. Léonard Bourdon's address at the end of 1790 appears in the membership list of the Jacobins (see next note) as "rue neuve Sainte-Avoye"—which I have taken to be an extension of the rue Sainte-Avoye, the name then given to what is now the part of the rue du Temple that lies between Blancs Manteaux and Michel le Comte (A. Franklin, *Les anciens plans de Paris*, 2 vols. [Paris, 1820], 2:52, 135 [including part of the plan of Deharme, 1763]).
51 Aulard, *Jacobins*, 1:xxxix. I have used the name Jacobins freely in this chapter for references to the Society of the Friends of the Constitution *séante aux Jacobins* in Paris, partly for convenience and partly to avoid confusion with the Société Royale d'Émulation.
52 Michael L. Kennedy, *The Jacobin Clubs in the French Revolution*, vol. 1: *The Early Years* (Princeton, 1982), 17.
53 Aulard, *Jacobins*, 2:88.
54 Ibid., 2:167-72; Lacroix, *Actes*, 4:614-15; Tourneux, *Bibliographie de l'histoire de Paris pendant la Révolution Française*, 3:no. 17178. Alexandre de Beauharnais (1760-94) was the father of

Eugène and Hortense de Beauharnais, later respectively viceroy of Italy and queen of Holland. He was executed during the Terror, ostensibly for inactivity in defending Mayence.

55 Cited by Thibal, "La Société," 50, from Rabaut Saint-Étienne, *Mémoire sur un objet préable à l'éducation nationale renvoyé au Comité des Rapports*, AN, F^{17} 1310.9. Rabaut Saint-Étienne (1743-93), a Protestant pastor, was involved in the fall of the Girondins as a member of the Commission of Twelve; outlawed as a fugitive, he was condemned and executed on identification.

56 Lacroix, *Actes*, 4:616; Thibal, "La Société," 51.

57 Ibid., 16, 51, citing AN, F^{17} 1310.9.

58 Léonard Bourdon, *Idées sur l'éducation d'un prince royal* (Paris, s.d.), BN, Lb^{39} 5167.

59 Aulard, *Jacobins*, 3:276.

60 Ibid., 2:585.

61 Ibid., 2:568; also 569, 572, and 3:87.

62 Aulard, in *La grande encyclopédie*.

63 Ibid. Bourdon claimed that he was one of forty-three Jacobins who did not desert the Club at this time: "le 17, je restais avec quarante-deux Jacobins à attendre à notre poste les menaces qui nous étaient faites." Although the course of events leading to the schism in the Club is adequately established in general histories of the Revolution, details of the part played by particular individuals in and after July 17 are elusive. The significance of Robespierre's role is still perhaps best shown in J.M. Thompson's classic biography (*Robespierre*, 2 vols. [London, 1935]), but it now seems likely that the influence of Jérôme Pétion (1756-94), who became mayor of Paris and died by his own hand as a fugitive "Girondin," was also considerable.

64 Aulard, *Jacobins*, 3:55.

65 Ibid., 3:24.

66 Ibid., 3:48, 96, 102, 116.

67 It is probably significant that at this time, before any serious breach had occurred between Robespierre and Brissot, Bourdon's name frequently occurs in the records of the Jacobins in association with men—particularly, perhaps, Collot d'Herbois—who would eventually emerge as prominent Montagnards.

68 The dating of this division is controversial. Historians generally have accepted the view that it began late in 1791, when opinions differed sharply about the expediency of open war with Austria, and thereafter grew steadily deeper. Of late, however, some writers have argued that that break was temporary and that the real breach occurred in mid-1792. See my own work, *The Girondins* (London, 1961), and Kates, *The Cercle Social, the Girondins, and the French Revolution*. For the equally vexed question of the political composition of the legislature, see also C.J. Mitchell, *The French Legislative Assembly of 1791* (Leiden, 1988).

69 Palmer, *The Improvement of Humanity*, 94-99.

70 In Bourdon's prospectus, *Société des Jeunes Français: base d'une école centrale d'expérience* (circulated by the Jacobin correspondence committee on October 7, 1791). Aulard, *Jacobins*, 3:174, note (by Bourdon), and 178.

71 Palmer, *The Improvement of Humanity*, 95.

72 Bourdon, *Mémoire*, 129-30. In his *Révolutions de France et de Brabant* (no. 93, 1-21), Camille Desmoulins asserted that Talleyrand had based a substantial part of his report on the "ingenious and profound" work of Bourdon; and, in the *Patriote français* (September 11, 1791), Brissot also said that Talleyrand in many respects "a suivi le plan tracé par M. Bourdon la Cronier [*sic*]," which was described in the preceding number as "un bel ensemble." In his reference to these entries, Palmer speaks of Brissot and Desmoulins as the friends of Bourdon, but I know of no association beyond their broad political alignment at this time. (Incidentally Desmoulins rebuked Brissot for his reservations in welcoming Talleyrand's concern for the education of girls, a part of the report that Desmoulins praised highly.)

73 Note 14 above.

74 Aulard, *Jacobins*, 3:168.

75 Ibid., 3:172 for the letter, and 173-79 for the prospectus, which is the *Société des Jeunes Français: base d'une école centrale d'expérience* in note 70 above.

76 Aulard, *Jacobins*, 3:253, December 16, 1791. Bourdon later claimed that he held this important post "pendant près de neuf mois," thus participating in the diffusion of the Jacobins' spirit throughout France (Aulard, *La grande encyclopédie*). The context suggests that this claim, of which I have not found any positive confirmation, relates principally to 1791. Bourdon signed the correspondence committe's circular of January 17, 1792, as president, but his name does not appear on that of February 15 (Aulard, *Jacobins*, 3:331, 381).

77 Ibid., 3:178. See also 267 (November 29) and M. Bouloiseau, G. Lefebvre, and A. Soboul, eds., *Oeuvres de Maximilien Robespierre*, tomes 6-10, *Discours* (Paris, 1950-67), 8:26.

78 Tuetey, *Répertoire*, 6:1632; Lacroix, *Actes*, 5:617; and Guillaume, *P-V du Comité, LA,* 10 and note 5.

79 AP, 30:50.

80 Guillaume, *P-V du Comité, LA,* 29, 35; Lacroix, *Actes*, 4:617; Tuetey, *Répertoire*, 6:1638.

81 Lacroix, *Actes*, 6:668. The list of members willing to participate in the instruction of children was again before the club on November 29 (Aulard, *Jacobins*, 3:267).

82 Lacroix, *Actes*, 4:617; Aulard, *Jacobins*, 3:275-77.

83 Thibal, "La Société," 17, citing AN, F^{17} 1309.1. Cf., e.g., Vauthier, "Léonard Bourdon et la Société des Jeunes Français," 333-34.

84 Guillaume, *P-V du Comité, LA,* 55.

85 For Condorcet's report, see Barnard, *Education and the French Revolution*, 81-95, and Palmer, *The Improvement of Humanity*, 124-29.

86 AP, 35:392.

87 Ibid., 43:265 (May 12, 1792).

88 Aulard, *Jacobins*, 3:290, 311, 386-87, 411, 418, 423, 494 (the new gun), 606.

89 Thibal, "La Société," 18 and appendix 2 (the minister's letter, from AN, AF III 107.485, folio 239). Even if costs had increased, the grant seems to have been generous, for before the Revolution the allowance per head to pupils in military schools was 700 livres (Palmer, *The Improvement of Humanity*, 66).

90 This is not in my view incompatible with recognition of antipathy between the supporters of Brissot and those of Robespierre. I would suggest both that personal alignments were still in a transitional stage and that the two groups tended to unite when counterrevolution seemed to be increasingly dangerous.

91 *Société des Jeunes Français: École républicaine établie au mois de mai 1792, au ci-devant Prieuré Saint-Martin-des-Champs par Léonard Bourdon* (a prospectus), AN, AD XVIII, 295.36; also BL, R 366.5.

92 Thibal, "La Société," 54, note 1: letter of June 1, AD (Archives Départementales) Seine, 3AZ. 148.1. Bourdon's wife, later referred to simply as "la femme Bourdon," almost certainly acted, as was not unusual, as the matron of the school. There was also a daughter, Rosalie-Michelle-Thérèse (see next note), and probably a young son, later to appear at intervals.

93 Tuetey, *Répertoire*, 5:2750, 2756 (deposition made by Léonard and his daughter Rosalie).

94 Aulard, *Jacobins*, 3:659-60.

95 Guillaume, *P-V du Comité, LA,* 369. In deciding that the Société des Jeunes Français was finally established in May-June 1792 (and thus presuming that at least some pupils were attending before the normal *rentrée* in October), I have rejected two indications of a possible earlier date. (1) In 1795, Bourdon's wife, pleading for reimbursements after the closure of the school, stated that Bourdon rented the buildings of the Priory in January 1792 and that in the course of 1792 the government sent fifty pupils to the school that he established there. Although this general statement is not incompatible with May-June as an effective date, the decisive factor is that the first lease of the Priory bears the date of April 1792 (Thibal, "La Société," 54 and note 2, citing AN, F^{17} 1144.2, and AD (Seine) DQ^z 522.396. (2) Lacroix, *Actes* 6:668-71, gives extracts from a self-justification published by Rotondo, a disreputable teacher of Italian who was arrested on July 17, 1791, and imprisoned in the Abbaye as an agitator suspected of firing a pistol at Lafayette on the Champ-de-Mars. Released on July 28, he was eventually acquitted on January 19, 1791. Curiously his ranting account of events on July 17 (Tourneux, *Bibliographie de l'histoire de Paris pendant la Révolution Française*,

4:no. 25152), which Lacroix considers to have been written while he was in prison, and published in September 1791, is signed "Rotondo, professeur au ci-devant preuré de Saint-Martin-des-Champs." Because this seems wholly incompatible with all other relevant chronology, it is possible that the document was written at a later period, for Rotondo was subsequently arrested several times before he was deported in 1798. It is also possible that his claim to have been chosen "de préférence sur plusieurs concurrents" as a teacher of English, Italian, and Latin at the Société des Jeunes Français is purely fictitious. See also G. Lenôtre (L.L.T. Gosselin), "Rotondi-Rotondo, profeseur de langues," in *Paris révolutionnaire: vieilles maisons, vieux papiers*, 2ᵉ série (Paris, 1903), 135-57.

96 See note 6, chapter 5, below.

Chapter 4

1 See notes 50 and 51 to chapter 3 above.

2 Bourdon, À Marat, BN, Lb⁴¹ 2304. The context, considered below, shows that the dating should be September 1792.

3 For this and the following paragraphs, see R. Gotlib, "Bourdon, L.J.-J. Léonard," in A. Soboul, ed., *Dictionnaire historique de la Révolution Française* (Paris, 1939); A. Groppi, "Sur la structure socio-professionnelle de la Section des Gravilliers," *AHRF*, 232 (1978): 246-76; M. Reinhard, *Nouvelle histoire de Paris: la Révolution, 1789-1799* (Paris, 1931); A. Soboul and R. Monnier, *Répertoire du personnel sectionnaire Parisien en l'An II* (Paris, 1985), 311; and Rudé, *The Crowd in the French Revolution*, particularly for the introduction and appendix 3.

4 G. Lefebvre, *La Révolution Française* (Paris, 1963), 252-53; Rudé, *The Crowd in the French Revolution*, 94, 103.

5 R.B. Rose, *The Enragés: Socialists of the French Revolution?* (Sydney, 1968), 36-39, 153.

6 I. Bourdin, *Les sociétés populaires à Paris pendant la Révolution* (Paris, 1937), 74-76; Aulard, *Jacobins*, 3:510.

7 Aulard, *Jacobins*, 4:66-67; Braesch, *La Commune du dix août, 1792* (Paris, 1911), 83, note.

8 AP, 46:251; Aulard, *Jacobins*, 4:83; see also Tuetey, *Répertoire*, 4:1179, 1413; Braesch, *La Commune du dix août*, 89; and, for the dismissal of the Directory, M. Mortimer-Ternaux, *Histoire de la Terreur*, 6 vols. (Paris, 1861-67), 2:74. On July 11, the section also participated in a joint address to the Legislative Assembly in Pétion's support (*Procès-verbaux de l'Assemblée Législative*, July 1792, 125).

9 Mortimer-Ternaux, *Histoire de la Terreur*, 2:52.

10 Ibid., 54.

11 Aulard, *Jacobins*, 4:84.

12 Ibid., 108; cf. Bouloiseau, Lefebvre, and Soboul, eds., *Oeuvres de Maximilien Robespierre*, 8:401.

13 Tuetey, *Répertoire*, 4:1372, 1373.

14 Rose, *The Making of the Sans-Culottes*, 153.

15 Ibid., 158, 160; Braesch, *La Commune du dix août*, 168.

16 Tuetey, *Répertoire*, 4:11979 (signed by Bourdon as the president of the permanent general assembly).

17 AP, 47:472. I omit in the text a reference to a further address from Gravilliers, again signed by Bourdon, marking the repudiation of distinctive insignia by the grenadiers of the section (Tuetey, *Répertoire*, 4:2025).

18 *Le Moniteur*, 13:706. See also below.

19 M. Tourneux, *Procès-verbaux de la Commune de Paris, 1792-1793* (Paris, 1894), 169 and note, 170.

20 I.e., J.-B. Louvet de Couvrai (1760-97), F.-X. Lanthenas (1754-99), and J.-H. Bancal des Issarts (1750-1826). All three men have been called Girondins, but Louvet's adherence to that group seems to date from this time, and Lanthenas later distanced himself from it. Bancal was an Austrian prisoner at the time of the Girondins' proscription.

21 The proceedings of the Quinze-Vingts Section may be followed in Buchez and Roux, *Histoire parlementaire de la Révolution Française*, 16:403-408. I have used the extract in P. Dawson, *The French Revolution* (Englewood Cliffs, NJ, 1967), 96-99.

22 E.g., A. Mathiez, *Le dix août* (Paris, 1934), 88, indicates that a similar proposal had been made in Mauconseil some days earlier.

23 It is sometimes asserted that Bourdon gave the signal for this murder, but I have not found any evidence to substantiate this allegation, which indeed seems difficult to reconcile with the known facts.

24 Braesch, *La Commune du dix août*, 272.

25 Ibid., 245-64, for the identification of those known to have been present between August 9 and 17, 1792. Braesch's consideration of the social composition of the General Council at this time follows (265-72). Bourdon de Vatry, "31 ans, employé dans l'administration de la Marine," was a delegate for the Section de Bondy and is recorded as presiding on September 2 (Tourneux, *Procès-verbaux de la Commune de Paris*, 77).

26 Tourneux, *Bibliographie de l'histoire de Paris pendant la Révolution Française*, 2:no. 6137. It is possible that Bourdon may have played some part in the arrangement by which Pétion was "protected" by being kept under guard: see M.C.M. Simpson, ed., *Reminiscences of a Regicide: Sergent Marceau* (London, 1889), 201.

27 AP, 47:641-42.

28 Tuetey, *Répertoire*, 5:18.

29 Tourneux, *Bibliographie de l'histoire de Paris pendant la Révolution Française*, 1:no. 3445.

30 Buchez and Roux, *Histoire parlementaire de la Révolution Française*, 17:91.

31 *Journal de Paris*, no. 225, August 12, 1792.

32 AD, Côte-d'Or: the letter, for which I have no more precise reference, concerns a Deslambinez, imprisoned in La Force. Dated August 17, 1792, at Paris, it is signed by L.-J. Bourdon and endorsed by Léonard Bourdon.

33 Tuetey, *Répertoire*, 5:2419 and 7:901, 914.

34 Braesch, *La Commune du dix août*, 479, 761; Mortimer-Ternaux, *Histoire de la Terreur*, 3:148. On August 25, Bourdon also presented a petition from the Commune to the Legislative Assembly calling for documents for the jury of the Tribunal of August 17 about the events of August 10 (AP, 48:697).

35 *Le Moniteur*, 13:675; E. Seligman, *La justice en France pendant la Révolution Française*, 2 vols. (Paris, 1913), 2:221; P. Caron, *La première Terreur: les missions du conseil exécutif provisoire et de la Commune de Paris*, 2 vols. (Paris, 1950-53), 1:9-10 and note 5, in which the author corrects Braesch's assumption that Bourdon was sent by the Commune.

36 E.g., Buchez and Roux, *Histoire parlementaire de la Révolution Française*, 16:29 and 131 for July 19 and 20. See also Lefebvre, *Études Orléanaises*, 2:60-61. Inevitably there are variations between sources about the exact number of prisoners. A careful scholar, Paul Huot ("Les prisonniers d'Orléans," *Revue d'Alsace* [1868], 97-114 et seq.) lists fifty-two names (100-103). I have followed G. de Cassagnac, *Histoire des Girondins et les Massacres de Septembre*, 2 vols. (Paris, 1860), 2:479-81, where the receipts of twenty-five men from the Minimes prison by Bécart and twenty-eight more from that of Saint-Charles by Fournier are reproduced.

37 Mortimer-Ternaux, *Histoire de la Terreur*, 3:362.

38 Ibid., 362-64. Lefebvre, *Études Orléanaises*, 2:61, suggests that the initiative probably came from the sections at Orléans.

39 Perroud, C., ed., *Mémoires de Madame Roland*, 2 vols. (Paris, 1905), 2:46.

40 AN, BB³ 19.5: P-V de MM. les commissaires, September 10, 1792; F.-A. Aulard, ed., *Mémoires secrètes de Fournier l'Américain* (Paris, 1890), chap. 18. Aulard concluded that these memoirs were probably written initially in Year II and printed in Year VIII. For the destruction of many of the relevant records after the Revolution and in 1940, see Lefebvre's foreword to his *Études Orléanaises*, vol. 1.

41 Aulard, ed., *Mémoires secrètes de Fournier l'Américain*, 85-87.

42 Buchez and Roux, *Histoire parlementaire de la Révolution Française*, 18:229; allegations about Bourdon's intimacy with the men of the force, which amount to a charge of subversion, are to the best of my knowledge Thermidorian: e.g., AN, F¹ᶜ III, Loiret 5: *Compte-rendu au Directoire du District d'Orléans* (Thermidor, An III).

43 BL, Tab. 443 a 3(7): *Procès-verbal du Conseil-Général de la Commune d'Orléans* (Orléans, 1792).

44 For Delessart, see (the sympathetic) F. Masson, *Le Département des Affaires Étrangères pendant la Révolution, 1787-1804* (Paris, 1877), 229-35.

45 E.g., the ill-named work of L.M. Prudhomme, *Histoire générale et impartiale des erreurs, fautes, et crimes commis pendant la Révolution Française*, 5 vols. (Paris, 1797), 4:170-84.

46 AN, F⁷ 6504, *Dossier de Fournier l'Américain*, 95, 96.

47 AN, F¹ᶜ III, Loiret 5: *Compte-rendu au Directoire du District d'Orléans*.

48 Aulard, ed., *Mémoires secrètes de Fournier l'Américain*, 88; Mortimer-Ternaux, *Histoire de la Terreur*, 3:367.

49 D. Lottin, *Recherches historique sur la Ville d'Orléans*, 2 vols. (Orléans, 1838), 1:346-51; Seligman, *La justice en France pendant la Révolution Française*, 2:267; and Bourdon's letters to the Jacobins in Paris (*Journal des débats des amis de la Constitution*, no. 99, September 3) and to Fournier, August 28, AN, F⁷ 6504, *Dossier de Fournier l'Américain*, 99.

50 Lefebvre, *Études Orléanaises*, 1:avant-propos.

51 Lottin, *Recherches historique sur la Ville d'Orléans*, 1:355-59, 389.

52 Mortimer-Ternaux, *Histoire de la Terreur*, 3:368-69, and the depositions (taken in Year III) given in his appendices.

53 P-V de MM. les commissaires.

54 Ibid., where Bourdon refers to one Cross of Saint-Louis on Fournier's horse. See also Mortimer-Ternaux, *Histoire de la Terreur*, 3:607, and F.T. Janillon, *Versailles et Quiberon* (Paris, 1916), 17.

55 AN, F⁷ 6504, *Dossier de Fournier l'Américain*, 100, 102. For the vexed question of Fournier's accounts, AN, C 170, 419, 209, and, *inter alia*, Aulard's introduction to the *Mémoires secrètes de Fournier l'Américain*.

56 AN, BB³ 19, 5, 31, and 32; Lottin, *Recherches historique sur la Ville d'Orléans*, 1:356; Mortimer-Ternaux, *Histoire de la Terreur*, 3:374 and note.

57 AN, C 170.420, *Registre des grands procurateurs*, P-V Garran-Coulon; Lottin, *Recherches historique sur la Ville d'Orléans*, 1:360-68.

58 The record of events in the *Registre des délibérations* of the Commune of Versailles (AD, Seine-et-Oise, Versailles, D1, 238-43) is cited extensively in Buchez and Roux, *Histoire parlementaire de la Révolution Française*, 18:326-48. Evidence given during the trials held in 1795 is in Seligman, *La justice, en France pendant la Révolution Française*, 2:Annexe XIV. I have found the most useful overall account to be that of Paul Huot, "Les prisonniers d'Orléans," 97-114 et seq. See also Tuetey, *Répertoire*, 5:chap. 1.

59 P. Caron, *Les Massacres de Septembre* (Paris, 1935), 382-84.

60 Roland to Fournier, September 7, 1792: AN, C 170.149; Aulard, *Mémoires secrètes de Fournier l'Américain*, 93, note 3.

61 AN, BB³ 19.d.5, deposition of Nicolas Rivière. It does not directly implicate Bourdon, one of those who signed it as a witness of its reception.

62 AN, C 170.420, P-V Garran-Coulon.

63 Ibid. See also P-V de MM. les commissaires and Lottin, *Recherches historique sur la Ville d'Orléans*, 1:368, note. Reference should also be made at this point to the heroic conduct of the mayor of Versailles, Hyacinthe Richaud: for this conduct, see the *Délibérations* of the Commune (note 58 above); G. Moussoir, *Le conventionnel Hyacinthe Richaud* (Paris, 1897), 141-56; and the account of an eyewitness, P-F. Tissot, *Histoire complète de la Révolution Française*, 6 vols. (Paris, 1836-39), 3:269-70.

64 Bourdon to the Jacobins of Paris, August 28: *Journal des débats des amis de la Constitution*, no. 99, September 3; and to Fournier, August 28, 1792: AN, F⁷ 6504, *Dossier de Fournier l'Américain*. Bourdon's attitude is that the prisoners' trials are to be expedited and that the law will soon be taking its course.

65 "Public opinion is ill informed and at least moderate in attitude": letter to the Jacobins as cited in previous note. For the summary of the situation of Orléans that follows, see Lefebvre, *Études Orléanaises*, 1:94-135, 212-51.

66 In his letter to the Jacobins on August 28, Bourdon promised that Orléans would be left "bien patriotisé."

67 Deposition of Rosalie Edouard: Mortimer-Ternaux, *Histoire de la Terreur*, 3:607.

68 Lottin, *Recherches historique sur la Ville d'Orléans*, 1:359, where "a witness" is cited as saying that Dubail said "Léonard Bourdon is a fanatic [*enragé*], his bloodthirsty views are revolting to me."

69 *Rapport de Léonard Bourdon et Prosper Dubail* (Paris, 1792), BL, F 56.11. This is the printed version of the *P-V de MM. les commissaires*, and it has an additional passage in which Bourdon notes his other activities in Orléans. See also Lefebvre, *Études Orléanaises*, 2:61.

70 Ibid., 2:82 et seq.

71 Tourneux, *Procès-verbaux de la Commune de Paris*, 105; Braesch, *La Commune du dix août*, 302; and Tuetey, *Répertoire*, 5:1084.

72 AP, 49:566-71.

73 The manuscript and the printed versions are identified in notes 40 and 69 above.

74 AN, AA 49.1404.12: Bourdon, letter to the president of the Electoral Assembly of Paris, September 18, 1792.

75 J.B. Louvet de Couvray, *La Sentinelle*, no. 52, August 21, 1792, and Kates, *The Cercle Social, the Girondins, and the French Revolution*, 238.

76 Bourdon, *À Marat*, BN, Lb^{41} 2304.

77 BN, Lb^{40} 1154 g*: *Arrêté du 23 août 1792 (Assemblée Electorale, Paris) relatif à l'inculpation faite à M. Léonard Bourdon.*

78 Charavay, *L'Assemblée Electorale de Paris*, 3:45.

79 Ibid., 128-29.

80 Ibid., 139 and note 3, 144, the accusation being given in full.

81 Ibid., 144 and note 1, 145, the justification also being given in full. On September 15, the delegates of the section reiterated this to the Legislative Assembly, which ruled the matter to be the concern of the electors (AP, 49:677-78).

82 J. Charavay, E. Charavay, and N. Charavay, Catalogue of Autographs: *Bourdon, Léonard du Loiret* (l.a.s., October 5, 1790), BL, SC 672.17246.

83 Charavay, *L'Assemblée Electorale de Paris*, 3:135 and note, giving the proceedings of the society verbatim.

84 "The electoral body decided that contrary to custom the replacements of Condorcet and Brissot would not be taken from among the alternates but would be named by a special vote" (J. Guiffrey, *Les conventionnels* [Paris, 1889], 31, note). Kuscinski, *Dictionnaire des conventionnels*, says that Bourdon owed his election to the influence of the deputy Lombard-Lachaux, then the mayor of Orléans.

85 Charavay, *L'Assemblée Electorale de Paris*, 3:609. A similar note of recognition of the commissioners' services in maintaining peace by persuasion is apparent in other communications from Orléans, e.g., *Journal des débats*, no. 100, and AN, C 165.393.68.

86 Charavay, *L'Assemblée Electorale de Paris*, 3:145. Kuscinski, *Dictionnaire des conventionnels* (for both F.-L. and L.-J.J.L. Bourdon), says that the dispute was acrimonious, it being Léonard who was really chosen by the Oise, but I have not seen any primary evidence of this conflict.

Chapter 5

1 E.g., A.C. Thibaudeau, *Mémoires sur la Convention et le Directoire*, 2 vols. (Paris, 1824), 1:11.

2 AP, 42:81-84.

3 Ibid., 95:166; *Le Moniteur*, 14:13, 62, 69, 72; Léonard Bourdon, *Projet de règlement pour la Convention Nationale, présenté au nom des commissaires* (Paris, 1792), BL, R 96.1.

4 Guillaume, *P-V du Comité, Convention*, 1:introduction; also AP, 42:480.

5 See Léonard Bourdon's *Plan d'un établissement d'éducation nationale* of 1788.

6 I take the figure six for July 1792 from L. Hennet, *Les compagnies de cadets-gentilhommes et les écoles militaires* (Paris, 1889), 159. Thibal, "La Société," 245 (citing AN, AF 111, f. 221, L. Bourdon, *La Société . . . établie en mai 1792*), has "théoriquement au minimum cinquante élèves" in July-August 1792.

7 Guillaume, *P-V du Comité, Convention*, 1:371 (appendix C), gives the extract from *Le Moniteur* of February 24, 1793—curiously the day on which the demonstration was scheduled to

begin at 9 a.m. The announcement, evidently written by Bourdon, has "La Société des Jeunes Français établie au mois août dernier. . . ."

8 Guillaume, *P-V du Comité, Convention*, 1:368 and note 3.

9 Le Corbeiller, *Le Léopard de la Révolution*, 89 (referring to about May 1793).

10 Thibal, "La Société," 55-60.

11 Guillaume, *P-V du Comité, Convention*, 1:245, 319, 335, 356, 374. We will return to one of these matters, that of the Irish college in Paris. Another concerned the long campaign of Dusaulx (for whom see note 8 to chapter 3 above) to restrict all forms of gambling.

12 *Le Moniteur*, 14:778-802, and, for a general summary of both proposals, Barnard, *Education and the French Revolution*, 103-108. Gilbert Romme (1750-95) of the Puy-de-Dôme, a staunch republican and Montagnard, was one of those who committed suicide after being sentenced to death in Prairial, Year III.

13 For Condorcet's report, see Barnard, *Education and the French Revolution*, 81-95, and Palmer, *The Improvement of Humanity*, 124-29.

14 *Le Moniteur*, 14:802-804. For Rabaut, see also chapter 3 and its note 55 above.

15 *Le Moniteur*, 14:783-84.

16 *AP*, 42:190 (Savoy); 43:53, 117 (Belgium), 208 (translation).

17 Ibid., 42:460 (Dillon); Aulard, *Jacobins*, 4:402 (Dumouriez), 515 (Kellermann).

18 *AP*, 42:408 (prisoners); 45:22 (clothing).

19 Ibid., 43:116.

20 Ibid., 42:290.

21 Aulard, *Jacobins*, 4:393.

22 Ibid., 404, 406, 409.

23 Ibid., 585-86. (The occasion involved personalities and political associations, not general issues: see L. Jaume, *Le discours Jacobin et la démocratie* [Paris, 1989], 208.)

24 Aulard, *Jacobins*, 4:328.

25 Ibid., 352 (identification of "Bourdon" questionable).

26 Ibid., 475.

27 Marat was not properly a member of the Commune of August 10, but he was afforded a complimentary seat in it.

28 *AP*, 42:438.

29 *Le Moniteur*, 14:94; *Procès-verbaux de la Convention*, 72 vols. (Paris, 1792-95), 1:125.

30 *AP*, 42:182, 31.

31 Braesch, *La Commune du dix août*, 616.

32 Cited, e.g., in A. Mathiez, *La vie chère et le mouvement social sous la Terreur* (Paris, 1927), 103.

33 Braesch, *La Commune du dix août*, 853, 857.

34 Gerbaux and Schmidt, *Procés-verbaux des comités d'Agriculture et de Commerce de la Constituente*, 3:18, 23.

35 Aulard, *Jacobins*, 4:512.

36 E.g., A. Soboul, *Le procès de Louis XVI*, Collection Archives (Paris, 1966); A. Patrick, *The Men of the First French Republic* (Baltimore, 1972); D.P. Jordan, *The King's Trial* (Berkeley, CA, 1979).

37 E.g., *Petite biographie conventionelle* (Paris, 1815); Michaud, *Biographie universelle, ancienne et moderne*.

38 Aulard, *Jacobins*, 4:689.

39 *Le Moniteur*, 14:14.

40 *AP*, 42:122, 147.

41 *Le Moniteur*, 14:754.

42 *AP*, 42:525.

43 Ibid., 43:282.

44 Léonard Bourdon, *Opinion sur le jugement de Louis Capet, dit Louis XVI* (Paris, 1792), *AP*, 44:121; BN, Le[37] 2.G.105.

45 Fitzsimmons, *The Parisian Order of Barristers and the French Revolution*, and Michael P. Fitzsimmons, *The Remaking of France* (Cambridge, 1994), to both of which I owe much.

46 Aulard, *Jacobins*, 4:549.
47 *AP*, 45:38-39.
48 Léonard Bourdon, *Réponse à Charles Villette* (Paris, 1792), BN, Lb[40] 732; Tourneux, *Bibliographie de l'histoire de Paris pendant la Révolution Française*, 2:no. 9348.
49 Michaud, *Biographie universelle, ancienne et moderne*, 303, note 2.
50 *AP*, 55:429.
51 Léonard Bourdon, *Seconde opinion sur le jugement de Louis Capet* (Paris 1792), BN, Le[37] 2.g.199; *AP*, 58:40-43.
52 Aulard, *Jacobins*, 4:621.
53 Recollections of the Earl of Lauderdale, in B. Greatheed, *An Englishman in Paris, 1803*, edited by J.P.T. Bury and J.C. Barry (London, 1953), 39.
54 Aulard, *Jacobins*, 4:625.
55 Ibid., 629. On the same evening, Bourdon consigned journalists who attacked Robespierre to a "death" of ignominious oblivion (628).
56 Ibid., 627-28.
57 Kates, *The Cercle Social, the Girondins, and the French Revolution*, 258, citing the *Bulletin des amis de la verité* of January 2, 1793.
58 Aulard, *Jacobins*, 4:670.
59 Here and in following paragraphs, I have taken the totals of voting in the Convention from Patrick, *The Men of the First French Republic*, chap. 4, and the voting by the deputations of Paris and the Loiret from the same volume, appendix 3. The votes cast by Bourdon, correctly included by Patrick, are given with his remarks in the *Procès-verbaux de la Convention*, vol. 5, as follows: **Guilt?** (215); **Appeal to Primary Assemblies?** (235); **Sentence?** (265); and **Stay of execution?** (307). All also appear in the *Le Moniteur*, vol. 15, and in *AP*, vol. 57.
60 Kuscinski, *Dictionnaire des conventionelles*, entry for Pierre Lombard-Lachaux. See also, under Sieyès, Kuscinski's attribution of the vote "La mort sans phrases" to Dyzèz (Landes), because those words have been wrongly supposed to have been used by Bourdon (as well as by Sieyès).
61 Aulard, *Jacobins*, 4:689. For the bureau, see Kates, *The Cercle Social, the Girondins, and the French Revolution*, chaps. 7 to 10, particularly 135-36.

Chapter 6

1 The Convention authorized the issue of *assignats* amounting to 400 million livres in October 1792, 800 millions in February 1793, and 1,200 millions in May 1793. Valued at 70 livres in December 1792, the 100 livres *assignat* stood at about 50 livres in May, 36 in June, 25 in July, and 22 in August 1793 (F. Aftalion, *L'économie de la Révolution Française* [Paris, 1987], 169, 178; J.M. Thompson, *The French Revolution* [Oxford, 1959], 336; and, for prices, Rudé, *The Crowd in the French Revolution*, 118, 125).
2 I use the term "local authorities" as a familiar one. Properly all local councils and their executive directories were administrative bodies without independent authority, although they were always tempted, and sometimes compelled, to assume it.
3 Most of the guardsmen were gradually redirected to the armies, but the proposal to form a permanent guard drawn from the departments was a, if not the, distinguishing feature of "Girondin" policy. For the tone of the protests, see, e.g., *Le Moniteur*, October 20, 1792.
4 The character and importance of the *enragés* have occasioned much debate. The best brief survey is Rose, *The Enragés: Socialists of the French Revolution?*, particularly chap. 3.
5 Aulard, *Jacobins*, 5:10, 13, 27, 31, 32, 63.
6 *Le Moniteur*, 15:621.
7 A. Fribourg, ed., *Discours de Danton* (Paris, 1910), 291.
8 *AP*, 60:3.
9 Ibid., 16, 25.
10 W. Doyle, *The Oxford History of the French Revolution* (Oxford, 1989), 203.
11 This view is, e.g., that of A. Mathiez, *La Révolution Française* (Paris, 1922), 370. Patrick (*The Men of the First French Republic*) is more reserved, although her classifications lend it support (24, 111, 129).

12 Doyle, *The Oxford History of the French Revolution*, 224; also, e.g., J. Gallacher, "Recruitment in the District of Poitiers," *French Historical Studies*, 3 (1963): 246-67.

13 F.-A. Aulard, *Recueil des actes du Comité de Salut Publique* (hereafter cited as Aulard, *Actes*), 28 vols. (Paris, 1889ff.), 2:302-303.

14 R. Schnerb, "Les administrateurs de la Côte-d'Or et le salut de la république en 1793," *AHRF*, 36 (1964): 22-37.

15 J. Brelot, "L'insurrection fédéraliste dans le Jura en 1793," *Bulletin de la Fédération des Sociétés Savantes Franche Comtois*, 2 (1955): 73-102; from A. Sommier, *Histoire de la Révolution dans le Jura* (Paris, 1846).

16 Patrick, *The Men of the First French Republic*, 320, 336. For C.-A. Prieur-Duvernois, usually Prieur of the Côte-d'Or, see R.R. Palmer, *Twelve Who Ruled* (Princeton, NJ, 1941); for both him and Guyton-Morveau, see Kuscinski, *Dictionnaire des conventionnels*.

17 Kuscinski, *Dictionnaire des conventionnels*; P. Libois, *Les représentants du peuple Prost et Lejeune dans le Jura en l'An II* (Lons-le-Saunier, 1936), 15-16 and passim, for the period after September 1793.

18 For the "assassination" of Bourdon at Orléans, see chapter 7 below.

19 See chapter 7.

20 *Dénunciation faite par les six sections de la Commune de Dijon . . . des crimes commis par Léonard Bourdon et Pioche-Fer Bernard des Saintes* (Dijon, An III), BL, F 846.11; also Archives Départementales de la Côte-d'Or (AD, Côte-d'Or), L 364. For Bernard, see Kuscinski, *Dictionnaire*, and R. Schnerb, "La première mission en Côte-d'Or du conventionnel Bernard de Saintes," *Annales de Bourgoyne*, 5 (1933): 45-61.

21 Unless otherwise stated, the source of reference for the proceedings of the department in the following paragraphs is F. Claudron, *Inventaire sommaire des archives départementales: Côte-d'Or, période révolutionnaire, série L* (Dijon, 1913), L 43: *Registre des délibérations du Directoire* (hereafter cited as *Directoire*), 420 et seq. for dates cited in the text.

22 L.B. Baudot, *Mouvements révolutionnaires à Dijon*, MS 1660.203, Bibliothèque municipale de Dijon. L. Huguenay, *Les clubs dijonnais sous la Révolution* (rpt. Geneva, 1978), 158-59, is not informative about Bourdon's visit.

23 AD, Côte-d'Or, L 1268, for the proclamation, and L 376 for the instruction.

24 Baudot, *Mouvements révolutionnaires à Dijon*, 203, 206.

25 AD, Côte-d'Or, L 941.

26 *Directoire*, March 30, 1793.

27 Baudot, *Mouvements révolutionnaires à Dijon*, 203.

28 N. Bazin, "Les suspects dans le District de Dijon," résumé du mémoire, *Annales de Bourgoyne*, 41 (1963), 63-75. The figure 224 excludes eighteen there classified as outsiders or not determined.

29 Jean Richard, "La levée de 300,000 hommes et les troubles de mars 1793 en Bourgoyne," *Annales de Bourgoyne*, 33 (1961): 213-51.

30 The legality of the charge has been disputed (to Bourdon's discredit) because Fondard was arrested before the Law of March 19 made his offence as one in noble service a capital crime. The extract from the judgment in Richard ("La levée de 300,000 hommes et les troubles de mars 1793 en Bourgoyne," 235) nevertheless suggests that he was liable for execution under an earlier law (October 6, 1791) for causing discord likely to lead to civil war. See also AD, Côte-d'Or, L 2: 10.44, the note of the execution, in Baudot, *Mouvements révolutionnaires à Dijon*, 206, and note 31 below.

31 These stereotyped phrases occur in brief references to Bourdon's visit in, e.g., A.C. Sabatie, *Les tribunaux révolutionnaires en Provence* (Paris, 1914), 388, and L. Passy, *Frochet, préfet de la Seine* (Evreux and Paris, 1867), 174. By way of variety, Bazin, "Les suspects dans le District de Dijon," 66, has "Bourdon . . . envoie à l'échafaud. . . ."

32 Bazin, "Les suspects dans le District de Dijon," 67; H. Wallon, *Les représentants du peuple en mission et la justice dans les départements en l'An II*, 5 vols. (Paris, 1889), 3:315-16, notes 1 and 2.

33 It is nonetheless likely that the department's definition of "suspects" on May 2 was made in anticipation of the commissioners' imminent return. Cf. *Directoire*, for April 7, 10, and 24, and L 26 for May 2.

34 Baudot, *Mouvements révolutionnaires à Dijon*, 206, 207.

35 Théodore Vernier (1731-1818), deputy to the National Assembly and to the Convention, in both of which he was respected for his age and specialization in financial problems. In 1793, he lost credit as an *appellant* and an opponent of Paris. Arrested as one of those who signed the protest of seventy-three against the arrest of the Girondins, he took refuge in the Jura and Switzerland. Subsequently a member of the Council of the Elders, of the Napoleonic Senate, and a peer of France under the Restoration.

36 The terms "district" and "department" are often also used to refer to the areas in question. They should therefore be read in their context, for it is wrong to suppose that local administrative policy was generally accepted by all those living in the relevant area.

37 In this chapter, the terms "district" and "department" usually refer to the administrative bodies, as distinct from the geographical areas and populations concerned.

38 E. Puffeney, *Histoire de Dole* (Besançon, 1882), 294 onward for the period, is predictable. Brelot, "L'insurrection fédéraliste dans le Jura en 1793," has an informative synopsis of the initial general situation.

39 For the order to Dumas, H. Libois, *Délibérations de la Société Populaire de Lons-le-Saunier du 5 novembre 1791 au 25 juin 1793* (Lons-le-Saunier, 1897), 316. Hereafter pages 1-205 of this work will be cited as *Proceedings*, but pages 206-485, which include forty-eight documentary appendices, will be cited as *Libois*, with the page.

40 Not, apparently, known to *Libois*, 317. An extract is quoted in Monnier, "Annales semi-contemporains," 344. Internal evidence indicates that this chronological account of the period was compiled by one who had youthful recollections of it.

41 *Libois*, 316-17, and, e.g., AN, AF II 112, 840.6.

42 AN, D III, 119.9 for the meetings, and AF II 112, 840.8 for the order.

43 *Libois*, 346: AN, D III (May 24, 1793).

44 For "authorities," see note 2 above. The expression "hierarchy of authority," which occurs in this chapter as it was used by the department, reflects the belief that the municipalities and districts were subordinate to the department. True of the districts, that is much more doubtful for the municipalities, the distinction being one of function rather than rank. Nevertheless, even functions often overlapped in practice, and disputes about jurisdiction were implicit.

45 L. Hennet, *L'état militaire de France pour l'année 1793* (Paris, 1903), 328.

46 AN, AF II, 247.2107.53: this return of recruitment for the Jura, April 14, 1793, shows that 920 of the quota of 1,760 men had already left. The discrepancy was explained in part by the delay in reports from Dole and Arbois.

47 *AP*, 61.373; *Libois*, 344, note. The Jura's request that the expense of the new defence force be met by the nation was evaded.

48 *Libois*, 307-15.

49 E.g., the address to the Convention of January 17, 1793: "Save the republic, or else the departments . . . will unite to do so" (ibid., 360-61).

50 See note 94 below.

51 AD, Jura, L 1087 (Registre du Conseil), April 3; *Proceedings*, 149-50, and *Libois*, 315-16; Monnier, "Annales semi-contemporains," 343.

52 *Proceedings*, 158-59; Monnier, "Annales semi-contemporains," 353-54.

53 *Proceedings*, 153; Monnier, "Annales semi-contemporains," 348.

54 *Proceedings*, 152, 154-55; Monnier, "Annales semi-contemporains," 347-48, 350-51.

55 *Libois*, 318.

56 AD, Jura, L 1087 (Registre du Conseil), April 8, 1793.

57 *Libois*, 345.

58 Monnier, "Annales semi-contemporains," 348-49; five of the six returns are AN, AF II, 247.2017.48-56, that of arms and munitions being removed.

59 AD, Jura, L 1087 (Registre du conseil), April 13 and 14.

60 *Proceedings*, 156.

61 Ibid., 164; Monnier, "Annales semi-contemporains," 355.

62 Monnier, "Annales semi-contemporains," particularly in *Annuaires du Département du Jura, pour l'année 1851*, 47-49, citing a *mémoire* written in exile; also *1848*, 140-41; *1849*, 270; *1852*, 95; M. Perrin, "Notes sur Pierre-Gabriel Ebrard," in *Travaux de la Société d'Émulation du Jura, 1848-50* (Lons-le-Saunier, 1851), 10-30; and Brelot, "L'insurrection fédéraliste dans le Jura en 1793," 77.

63 *Libois*, 344.

64 Ibid., 318.

65 Ibid., 331-33. In this connection, Mathiez, *La vie chère*, 166, notes that the Department of Doubs later protested strongly because Bourdon and Prost had ordered shipments on the Saône of grain for Besançon to be unloaded.

66 Monnier, "Annales semi-contemporains," 372.

67 AD, Jura, L 1087 (Registre du conseil), April 4, 1793.

68 AN, AF II 112.9; *Libois*, 319-22.

69 AN, AF II 182.7; AD, Côte-d'Or, L 376 and 1268.

70 Monnier, "Annales semi-contemporains," 358.

71 AN, AF II 247.66; Aulard, *Actes*, 3:341; and F.-A. Aulard, *Supplément* to *Recueil des actes du Comité de Salut Publique*, vol. 1 (Paris, 1966), 136.

72 *Proceedings*, 160, 164; Monnier, "Annales semi-contemporains," 358.

73 AN, AF II 182.28; Aulard, *Actes*, 3:417; *Libois*, 322.

74 *Proceedings*, 164.

75 Monnier, "Annales semi-contemporains," 358.

76 AN, D III, 119: Dole, 1.

77 The proposal was that the Jura should exchange the District of Dole for that of Louhans (Saône-et-Loire). It seems to have pleased the Commune of Lons but not Dole itself—possibly because Besançon would be no better than Lons (Monnier, "Annales semi-contemporains," 296).

78 AN, AF II 112.13; Aulard, *Actes*, 3:591.

79 AD, Côte-d'Or, L 26: *Directoire*, folio 87.

80 Aulard, *Actes*, 4:51-52; *Libois*, 323.

81 AN, AF II 247.2107.47; Aulard, *Actes*, 3:295.

82 I.e., the decree by which the *assignat* alone became legal tender (letter AN, AF II 247.66) and the Convention's recommendation of the "Hérault Order" by which local bodies could in effect conscript a select political militia by imposing forced loans on other individuals; however, the latter reached Bourdon so late that he could not have done much about it (despite its "good effect": letter AN, AF II 182.27). He also established at least one new Jacobin Society (Salins: Aulard, *Jacobins*, 5:184) and probably stimulated the formation of sectional revolutionary committees in Dijon (AD, Côte-d'Or, L 376; Baudot, *Mouvements révolutionnaires à Dijon*, 213).

83 AN, AF II 182.28; Aulard, *Actes*, 3:418.

84 Aulard, *Supplément*, 1:126, 136.

85 Aulard, *Actes*, 3:341.

86 Aulard, *Jacobins*, 5:184.

87 J. Jullien, *Rapport . . . sur les administrations rebelles*, October 15, 1793 (Paris, 1793), 142. Cf. *Lettre écrit de Lons-le-Saunier le 29 juin 1793 par un habitant du Jura*, BL, F 240.42.

88 Mortimer-Ternaux, *Histoire de la Terreur*, 2:447, note 5.

89 E. Dubois, *Histoire de la Révolution dans l'Ain*, 3 vols. (Bourg, 1933); Wallon, *Les représentants du peuple*, 3:232-35.

90 *Proceedings*, 162, 168; Monnier, "Annales semi-contemporains," 360.

91 *Proceedings*, 168-69; *Libois*, 333-35; Monnier, "Annales semi-contemporains," 362; AN, DC III, 120. (Anxiety about the formation of the new cavalry force in Lons was eventually to prove well founded, for on June 25 men of that force closed the club down, apparently on their own initiative (*Libois*, 391-405]).

92 AN, DC III, 119: Dole (date of exemption given as May 6); *Libois*, 348-49.

93 *Libois*, 342-43.

94 Ibid., 343-48.
95 AN, DC III, 119, for Dole, and *Proceedings*, 180-86, for Lons. Cf. the *adresse* of the Commune of Lons, BL, F 987.9, and that of its district, AN, DXL 21.40.6.
96 *Proceedings*, 368; *Libois*, 335-40; Monnier, "Annales semi-contemporains," 362; C.E. (Charmouton), *Histoire de la persécution révolutionnaire dans le Département du Jura, 1789-1800* (Lons-le-Saunier, 1893), 42 (citing Charles Nodier); E.B. Courtois, *Rapport fait au nom des commissaires chargés de l'examen des papiers trouvés chez Robespierre et ses complices* (Paris, An III), 139. G. Lenôtre (*The Tribunal of the Terror*, translated by F. Lees [London, 1909], 91-93) records a note by Réné Dumas to the public prosecutor, Fouquier-Tinville, telling him to file a letter from his brother, then in exile, pending the latter's arrest and trial.
97 *Proceedings*, 165-66, 187; Monnier, "Annales semi-contemporains," 359; Aulard, *Jacobins*, 5:202.
98 E.g., AN, F1, Jura I, but correspondence on this matter is extensive (*Libois*, 351-59, and P. Caron, *La première Terreur: les missions du conseil exécutif provisoire et de la Commune de Paris*, 1:50-53).
99 *Libois*, 360-61; Aulard, *Actes*, 1:38.
100 H. Morse Stephens, *Orators of the French Revolution*, 2 vols. (Oxford, 1892), 1:451-52.
101 Dubois, *Histoire de la Révolution dans l'Ain*, 3:203-205; H. Wallon, *La Révolution du 31 mai et le fédéralisme en 1793*, 2 vols. (Paris, 1886), 2:360, 515 (for Saône-et-Loire); M. Pigallet, *Inventaire sommaire des AD: Département du Doubs, L 55*, Délibérations du conseil* (Besançon, 1921), May 26, 1793; J. Giradot, *Le Département de la Haute-Saône pendant la Révolution*, vol. 2 (Vesoul, 1973), 221-23; and AD, Côte-d'Or, *Directoire*, May 26, 1793.
102 The Côte-d'Or is also noted for its recognition on June 17 of the purged Convention "telle qu'elle est" (*Directoire*, June 17, 1793).
103 *Libois*, 345.
104 I refer to the well-known assertion: "Il faut très impérieusement fait vivre le pauvre si vous voulez qu'il vous aide à achever la Révolution." See John Hardman, *French Revolution Documents*, vol. 2: *1792-95* (Oxford, 1973), 89.

Chapter 7

1 This aspect of the matter has long been emphasized by historians of the "classic" school. It is, however, so controversial that it must be treated with reserve and as one of several relevant factors.
2 See, e.g., the appeal of Robespierre's brother Augustin in the Jacobins on April 5, 1793 (Aulard, *Jacobins*, 5:125).
3 By this time, the expression "in insurrection" had acquired particular meaning: it being believed that in an emergency all authority reverted to the sovereign people from whom it emanated, it was possible for the Commune to assert that the shortage of food constituted an emergency and that appropriate measures could legitimately be taken regardless of existing legislation. Although defiance of government was implicit, neither massive popular action nor physical violence was necessarily involved.
4 Because in the nature of the case nothing was recorded, the existence of an agreement is necessarily speculative. It is however, presumed by Mathiez, *La vie chère*, 177, 180. Cf. N. Hampson, *A Social History of the French Revolution* (London, 1963), 176.
5 AP, 63:340 (April 25, 1793).
6 Curiously Lefebvre (*Études Orléanaises*, 2:102, note) attributed this proposal to Léonard Bourdon, whom he thought was influenced while in Orléans by the advanced radical Taboureau.
7 Gerbaux and Schmidt, *Procès-verbaux des comités d'Agriculture et de Commerce de la Constituente*, 3:126; see also 122, note. Apparently the elder Bourdon also approached the committee at this time for indemnification for his proposal regarding the posting service (ibid., 4:76, and chapter 1 above).
8 Ibid., 3:122, and Mathiez, *La vie chère*, 182, 184. The former page includes a note indicating that early in March the Section des Gravilliers discussed a plan for national granaries "which was probably drawn up or inspired by Léonard Bourdon." That is not unlikely, nor is it incom-

patible with my attribution to Bourdon *père* of the project given to the Committee of Agriculture, for both men promoted the same plan as occasion arose.

9 This again is controversial, for historians of the left long saw price control and the Montagnard Constitution as evidence that the Montagnards visualized and strove to attain a form of socialism. That view has been eroded both by a more cynical interpretation, in which these measures are seen as an amalgam of expediency and propaganda, and by increased appreciation of the extent to which initiative came "from below." Nevertheless, neither the idealism of the time nor the sincerity of some men should be discounted.

10 See the authoritative study by J. Balossier, *La commission extraordinaire des douze (18 mai-31 mai 1793)* (Paris, 1986).

11 Aulard, *Jacobins*, 5:201.

12 Ibid., 5:212 (no details being given).

13 AP, 65:38. (I here ignore episodes concerning the affair at Orléans, considered in the second part of this chapter, and an incidental comment in praise of a general who modestly declined military command [ibid., 608]). M. Slavin (*The Making of an Insurrection* [Cambridge, MA, 1986], 22) has "a sharp confrontation" between Léonard Bourdon and Lanjuinais on May 30, but I think it more probable that François Bourdon of the Oise was in question; cf. Balossier, *La commission extraordinaire des douze*, 76.

14 AP, 65:535. The voting is usually given as 279 in favour of re-establishment and 238 against it. Analysis by Patrick (*The Men of the First French Republic*, 117) substitutes 267 for and 228 against.

15 Bouloiseau, Lefebvre, and Soboul, eds., *Oeuvres de Maximilien Robespierre*, 9:537-38. Cf. a varied report of the same speech (ibid., 538-39).

16 *Bergoeing à ses commettans* (Caen, 1793), BN, Lb[41] 715.6.

17 Cf. Slavin, *The Making of an Insurrection*, 146: "there seems little doubt that they [i.e., Chabot and Léonard Bourdon] were trying to abort the insurrection." If this means that they were trying to stop or thwart the rising, I think it unlikely. The evidence itself is suspect as being a police report of allegations made by two speakers at the Cordeliers on March 12, 1794, ten months after the supposed episode; moreover, although Hébert confirmed the visit itself, he pertinently added that some people "voulait faire le procès aux patriotes qui avaient alors sauvé la République" (C.A. Dauban, *Paris en 1794 et en 1795: histoire de la rue, du club, et de la famine* [(Paris, 1868]). On the other hand, it is likely that Bourdon and Chabot were, as Montagnards, concerned to limit the insurrection, and it is possible that they were seeking to ensure that it was not controlled by the *enragé* Varlet and the small Central Revolutionary Committee—which had previously been challenged by Jacques Roux's friends in the Section des Gravilliers (Mathiez, *La vie chère*, 176). It may be relevant that on January 29, 1794, Chabot had informed the Committee of General Security that when he visited the Central Revolutionary Committee he was told in Léonard Bourdon's presence by Hébert and Chaumette that neither wanted that insurrection (that sort of insurrection?) and that they would have done things better at the Commune (Tuetey, *Répertoire général*, 11:664).

18 On May 31, the revolutionary committee of the Section des Gravilliers supplied six muskets with bayonets in response to Bourdon's request, possibly to strengthen the guard on his schoolgrounds (Slavin, *The Making of an Insurrection*, 139).

19 Reinhard, *Nouvelle histoire de Paris: la Révolution*, 282; Slavin, *The Making of an Insurrection*, 28, 36, 39; Balossier, *La commission extraordinaire de douze*, 66, 70.

20 Mathiez, *La vie chère*, 176. For Truchon, see Soboul and Monnier, *Répertoire du personnel sectionnaire Parisien en l'An II*, 319, and Braesch, *La Commune du dix août*, 147, 263, 273, and as indexed.

21 H. Calvet, "Remarques sur la participation des sections au mouvement du 31 mai-2 juin 1793," *AHRF*, 5 (1928): 366-69. Calvet estimates that the contingent from Gravilliers was exceeded only by those from Montreuil (2,946) and Quinze-Vingts (2,039).

22 AP, 65:657.

23 For the haphazard process by which these deputies were named for arrest, see my *The Girondins*, 40, 56. It is appropriate to say here that, although polarization among the deputies

evidently increased as a new rising became imminent in April and May 1793, I see no reason to alter the general contention of *The Girondins*, that "the party" was in reality a small group of individuals able to win majority support on some matters.

24 Léonard Bourdon, *À ses commettans* (Paris, 1793), BL, F 1026.3. This letter of eight pages is not included in A. Martin and G. Walter, *Catalogue de l'histoire de la Révolution Française*, 6 vols. (Paris, 1936-55).

25 The most notable protests were those written on June 6 and 19, together known as the Protest of the Seventy-Five, but similar views were expressed by many other deputies, and all have been regarded as proof of previous party membership. For criticism, see Sydenham, *The Girondins*, 44-49.

26 H. Calvet, *Un instrument de la Terreur à Paris: le Comité de Salut Public ou de surveillance du Département de Paris* (Paris, 1941), 44.

27 *AP*, 67:680-81. Remarkably Bourdon does not seem to have spoken at the Jacobins during this June. For three references to his minor activities as a deputy, see *Le Moniteur*, 16:593, 641, and the *Procès-verbaux de la Convention*, 13:246.

28 The quotations are taken from Palmer, *Twelve Who Ruled*, 34-35. For the translated text of the Declaration of Rights and the Constitution, see Stewart, *A Documentary Survey of the French Revolution*, 455-58, 458-68.

29 For this address (J. Roux, *Adresse à la Convention Nationale* [Paris, 1793], not in Martin and Walter, *Catalogue de l'histoire de la Révolution Française*) and its sequel, the best source is W. Markov, ed., *Jacques Roux: Scripta et Acta* (Berlin, 1969), 480-81 et seq. A translation of the record in *Le Moniteur* (16:747-48) is in P.H. Beik, *The French Revolution* (New York, 1970), 261-62. See also *AP*, 67:459; Mathiez, *La vie chère*, 215, 223, 232, 241; and Rose, *The Enragés: Socialists of the French Revolution?*, 44-46.

30 Note 29 above, particularly Markov, ed., *Jacques Roux: Scripta et Acta*, 492, 520.

31 A. Soboul, *Les sans-culottes parisiens en l'An II* (Paris, 1962), 64.

32 I here refer particularly to Le Corbeiller, *Le Léopard de la Révolution*. As the title shows, this book is a detailed account of Bourdon's "assassination," and I have on occasion drawn upon it in this chapter. It is, however, a work to be used with caution, for the writer is violently hostile to Bourdon and indiscriminate in his assertions. The value of the details that he gives is, moreover, offset by the complete absence of references.

33 See below, chapter 12 onward.

34 Lefebvre, *Études Orléanaises*, 2:62 onward, particularly 96-99.

35 Ibid., *avant-propos*.

36 Lottin, *Recherches historique sur la Ville d'Orléans*, 2:26-28: *Adresse des citoyens composent la garde nationale d'Orléans à la Convention Nationale, 18 mars 1793*. Apparently most of the 579 men supposed to have signed this address later denied all knowledge of it (ibid., 28 note, and *AP*, 62:255).

37 Léonard Bourdon, *Exposé des faits relatifs à l'assassinat commis à Orléans le 16 mars 1793, et réponse au rapport du Comité de Législation* (Paris, 1793), BN, Le[38] 259.3.

38 It soon became common for deputies on mission to go outside their allotted areas in response to immediate emergencies.

39 In mid-May, the existence in Orléans of a "comité vendéen" was exposed. Its members were alleged to be sending funds and military information to the rebels in the Vendée (Lottin, *Recherches historique sur la Ville d'Orléans*, 2:104).

40 Bourdon, *Exposé des faits relatifs à l'assassinat commis à Orléans*, 2-3.

41 For this and the two following paragraphs, see Lefebvre, *Études Orléanaises*, 2:81 onward, and Debal, *Histoire d'Orléans et de son terroir*, vol. 2: J. Vassort et C. Poitou (Roanne, 1982), 153-55.

42 Lefebvre, *Études Orléanaises*, 2:87. From 1792 onward, the right of sectional assemblies to meet continuously "in emergency" was crucial to popular power.

43 Ibid., 97. By the Law of February 24, 1793, local administrations were required to begin conscription if at the end of three days the required quota had not been met by voluntary enlistments.

44 Ibid., 80.

45 Ibid., 88, and *AP*, 68:684, for the description given by Fouquier-Tinville at the Revolutionary Tribunal: "des commis des marchands, clercs de procureurs, domestiques et gens attachés aux négotiants et autres citoyens faibles."

46 Bibliothèque municipale d'Orléans, MS 565.85: *L'abbé Pataud, Notes relatives à l'histoire d'Orléans*, including the *Déclaration du président du Département du Loiret sur les événements du 16 mars 1793* (given below as Benoist, *Déclaration*).

47 Bourdon, *Exposé des faits relatifs à l'assassinat commis à Orléans*, 3. "Feuillantisme," a term of political abuse, refers to constitutional monarchists.

48 Lottin, *Recherches historique sur la Ville d'Orléans*, 2:26. The *Adresse* of the guardsmen suggests that Bourdon's "dangereuse et bruyantes diatribes" at the Popular Society on March 15 and 16 preceded an attempt to storm the town hall on March 16. Le Corbeiller (*Le Léopard de la Révolution*, 22-23) cites inflammatory passages to the same effect from the speech on Saturday, March 16, but whatever source was used must be one of hearsay, for all the records of the society were destroyed in 1795 by order of the district "to avoid perpetuating hatreds" (Lefebvre, *Études Orléanaises*, 1:*avant-propos*).

49 Benoist, *Déclaration*. Le Corbeiller (*Le Léopard de la Révolution*, 16) identifies the boy as "le jeune Raimond, gamin de quatorze ans," the brother of a widow of Orléans who had become one of Bourdon's pupils in September 1792. Other instances of the presence of a child in Bourdon's entourage occur, and hostile authors hint at perversity. Kindness, and Bourdon's constant determination to advertise his school, should also be considered.

50 *AP*, 60:357: Bourdon, *Déclaration faite aux autorités constituées d'Orléans le 17 mars 1793*. The warning was given by Vigoureux.

51 Benoist, *Déclaration*. Lottin, *Recherches historique sur la Ville d'Orléans*, 2:9, identifies the two offenders as Olivier de la Roussellière and Robert Tassin Duchêne. Both men eluded pursuit, probably with the aid of relatives at the town hall. For the letters of Saint-André and Lacoste to the municipality and to the Convention on this matter, see Aulard, *Actes*, 2:497.

52 Lottin, *Recherches historique sur la Ville d'Orléans*, 2:27: *Adresse des citoyens*.

53 Bourdon, *Exposé des faits relatifs à l'assassinat commis à Orléans*, 8, note, and supporting letter dated Vendémiaire 26, Year III, by Bernard de Saintes and Guimberteau appended to Bourdon, *À ses concitoyens*.

54 Benoist, *Déclaration*.

55 Lottin, *Recherches historique sur la Ville d'Orléans*, 2:14 note, lists twenty names from the deposition of Johanet, one of those subsequently tried by the Revolutionary Tribunal. The actual composition of the party is yet uncertain, for one of those named, President Benoist, emphasized in his *Déclaration* that he withdrew when the dinner ended. The names of Nicole and Besserve occur among those noted as extreme democrats by Lefebvre, *Études Orléanaises*, 2:59.

56 Bourdon, *Exposé des faits relatifs à l'assassinat commis à Orléans*, 5,

57 Benoist, *Déclaration*.

58 Bourdon, *Exposé des faits relatifs à l'assassinat commis à Orléans*, 5. In his *Déclaration faite aux autorités constituées d'Orléans le 17 mars 1793*, Bourdon has "many citizens in uniform with red facings" (*AP*, 60:356).

59 Bernard and Guimberteau in the letter attached to Bourdon, *À ses concitoyens* (1795), BN Lb41 1393.

60 Cf. note 17 above.

61 For this and the following paragraphs, see Bourdon's *Déclaration faite aux autorités constituées d'Orléans le 17 mars 1793*, which is substantially the same (Bourdon, *Exposé des faits relatifs à l'assassinat commis à Orléans*, 7-10).

62 Note 19 above. The word *mensongère* is written into the title by Lottin (*Recherches historique sur la Ville d'Orléans*, 2:13) and those who have copied him. Le Corbeiller (*Le Léopard de la Révolution*, 27 and 69) suggests that the guardsmen were simply seeking to take Bourdon before the municipal officials in the town hall.

63 *AP*, 60:474: *Lettre du maire: Extrait des registres du conseil-général de la commune d'Orléans, le 16 mars 1793*. See also the municipality's *Observations de la Municipalité d'Orléans* on Bourdon's *Déclaration faite aux autorités constituées d'Orléans le 17 mars 1793*.

64 Letter appended to Bourdon, À ses concitoyens.

65 Extrait des registres: AP, 60:475.

66 Letter of March 17, 1793, Procès-verbaux de la Convention, March 18, 34; Le Moniteur, 15:732.

67 Letter of March 19, AP, 60:472.

68 March 17, 1793, AP, 60:474, and Extrait des registres, ibid., 476.

69 Bourdon, Exposé des faits relatifs à l'assassinat commis à Orléans, 10-13.

70 Aulard, Actes, 2:448. The activity at this time of Collot d'Herbois—who was perhaps less prominent in Orléans than his colleague Laplanche—is reviewed in P.L. Mansfield's doctoral thesis "The Missions of Collot d'Herbois: A Study in His Political Career" (Macquarie University, NSW, 1985), 118-25.

71 Note 15 above. The passage is quoted, inter alia, by Lottin, Recherches historique sur la Ville d'Orléans, 2:19, note.

72 Bourdon's critics have not failed to exploit this alleged theft (Lottin, Recherches historique sur la Ville d'Orléans, 2:33; Le Corbeiller, Le Léopard de la Révolution, 50). The statement of expenses made by Bourdon and Prost for their mission to Côte-d'Or and the Jura, published in 1795, nevertheless has a footnote stating (1) that the carriage officially supplied to them in Paris was left with the postmaster at Dijon and returned by him; (2) that the carriage supplied to Bourdon by the authorities in Orléans (and presumably used by both men from Dijon onward) was returned to the postmaster in Paris; and (3) that the latter's receipts for both vehicles were held. Incidentally the statement also shows the return of a balance of 2,231 livres of the 9,000 given to them for their mission (Léonard Bourdin, Convention Nationale, compte de l'emploi des sommes reçues par Léonard Bourdon et Prost . . . mars 14 à mai 24, 1793 [Paris, Pluviôse, An III], Maclure Collection, no. 1157).

73 Le Moniteur, 15:732, 759.

74 Ibid., 739-41. The Committee of General Defence was the forerunner of the Committee of Public Safety.

75 Ibid., 732. This page also has Bourdon's first letter from Orléans (of March 17) without its final sentence, which notes that the authorities in Orléans "font les recherches les plus actives" (Procès-verbaux de la Convention, March 18, 1793, 35).

76 E.g., Tallien et Goupilleau, from Blois, March 17 (Aulard, Actes, 2:381); Jeanbon and Lacoste (ibid., 497-99); for the use of the term rixe, to which Prieur drew attention in the Convention, see Le Moniteur, 15:732, and the Justification of the mayor and the municipal officers.

77 Procès-verbaux de la Convention, March 18, 1793, 54-57; Le Moniteur, 15:736.

78 Lottin, Recherches historique sur la Ville d'Orléans, 2:33 onward, including a list of those under arrest on May 21, 1793 (105). For the measures taken by the Convention's commissioners, AP, 61:511-13, 613-14, and 62:154-55.

79 Lefebvre, Études Orléanaises, 2:98-99; Debal, Histoire d'Orléans, 156.

80 Le Publiciste, nos. 147 and 148 of March 19 and 20, 1793 (Marat: Collection complète du journal [Tokyo, 1967]); J.M. Girey (for J.-P. Brissot), Le Patriote français, nos. 1314, 1323, 1371, and 1380 for March 19 and 28, and May 16 and 25, 1793.

81 AP, 60:599-600, 602, and 63:383. See also Buchez et Roux, Histoire parlementaire de la Révolution Française, 25:179, for Tallien's attitude on March 24.

82 Le Moniteur, 16:474 (sic), and Petition à la Convention par les citoyennes d'Orléans (Paris, 1793), BL, FR 5722. The four new commissioners were Lesage, Mariette, Duval, and Beauprey. According to Mortimer-Ternaux (Histoire de la Terreur, 6:479), Lesage reported that trouble arose on March 16 because Bourdon had insulted and tried to shoot a sentinel.

83 Le Moniteur, 16:424.

84 Ibid., 427-28. According to Louvet, the women had first approached those in authority at a civic banquet at Orléans, where they were forced to join in the dancing before being pelted with dishes and driven out with blows.

85 Rapport de J.-B. Noel, sur l'affaire Léonard Bourdon, in Étienne Noel, Jean Baptiste Noel, conventionnel (Cosne-sur-Loire, 1966), 120-23.

86 AP, 65:604.

87 Bourdon, Exposé des faits relatifs à l'assassinat commis à Orléans, 1.

88 Ibid., 14-23.

89 Le Corbeiller, *Le Léopard de la Révolution*, 97-99.

90 For brief accounts, see E. Campardon, *Le Tribunal Révolutionnaire de Paris*, 2 vols. (Paris, 1886), 1:52-56; H. Wallon, *Histoire du Tribunal Revolutionnaire de Paris*, 2 vols. (Paris, 1900), 1:64-67; Lenôtre, *The Tribunal of the Terror*, 69-70. The only previous collective trial was that of twenty-seven men and women supposedly implicated in the "Breton Conspiracy," of whom twelve were condemned to death.

91 Le Corbeiller, *Le Léopard de la Révolution*, 105-106. The story that Tassin de Montcourt was accused because he was mistaken for his brother seems to be untrue: the charges against him were that he, being in the town hall, withdrew when Bourdon was assaulted and that he had valid blank passports in his possession—which might explain the disappearance of those who insulted Jeanbon Saint-André.

92 *AP*, 68:684-93.

93 Cf. Le Corbeiller, *Le Léopard de la Révolution*, 108-10.

94 *AP*, 18:693. According to Montane, the president of the Tribunal, the verdict was carried by one vote amid general lamentations. Although that is not improbable, his evidence is somewhat suspect, being given at the trial in 1795 of the public prosecutor, Fouquier-Tinville; moreover, Montane himself was dismissed from the presidency in July 1793 for failing to sequester the property of those condemned on July 13 (Wallon, *Histoire du Tribunal Révolutionnaire de Paris*, 1:66; Campardon, *Tribunal Révolutionnaire de Paris*, 1:54).

Remarkably the list of the names of the condemned men given by Wallon and Campardon coincides with that of A.J.T. Bonnemain, *Les chemises rouges* (Paris, An VII/1799), but not with the formal judgment given in the *AP*, 18:691 (where two of those elsewhere shown as acquitted are among the condemned and vice versa). Of those listed in the *AP*, none was a youth; six were apparently men of some rank and substance; and, although only three were said to have laid hands on Bourdon, all were alleged to have been in his vicinity when the attack occurred.

95 I refer particularly to the description given by Harmand de la Meuse, *Anecdotes relatives à . . . la Révolution*, which is cited, *inter alia*, by C.A. Dauban, *La démagogie à Paris* (Paris, 1868), 269-70, as being based on personal recollection. Kuscinski, *Dictionnaire des conventionnels*, however, dismisses the anecdotes as "inept inventions." Le Corbeiller's story (*Le Léopard de la Révolution*, 137) that Pauline, the ten-year-old daughter of the widowed Gellet-Duvivier, one of those condemned, vainly threw herself at Bourdon's feet, clasping Bourdon about the knees as he left the chamber, comes from the journalist L.M. Prudhomme, *Histoire générale et impartiale des erreurs, fautes, et crimes commis pendant la Révolution Française*, 5:201. I have not yet found the source of Le Corbeiller's assertion (*Le Léopard de la Révolution*, 109, 134) that the relatives of the condemned also approached "la citoyenne Vicaire," whom he assumed to be Bourdon's mistress, and that she herself pleaded in vain with Bourdon.

96 *AP*, 68:647.

97 This episode, which is not well documented, is not mentioned by either of the principal authorities (Campardon and Wallon on the Tribunal) or by Le Corbeiller. It is, however, referred to briefly by Kuscinski, *Dictionnaire des conventionnels* (entry for Bourdon), and by Dauban, *La démagogie à Paris*, 269, who remarks that the Convention then returned to its agenda "une seconde fois." It is included in Bouloiseau, Lefebvre, and Soboul, eds., *Oeuvres de Maximilien Robespierre*, 9:620-21. I take the exclamation of Gaston from the *Journal de Perlet*, no. 296 (347), and from the *AP*, 68:657 (which does not refer to Robespierre).

98 *Léonard Bourdon, représentant du peuple, à ses concitoyens* (Paris, An III), BL, F22*:23, a response to the attacks made by Fréron in *L'Orateur du peuple*.

99 *Le Moniteur*, 15:732. See also, e.g., the use of the same expression on April 11 by Julien of Toulouse and his colleagues (*AP*, 61:613).

Chapter 8

1 Above, chapter 5.

2 *Procès-verbaux de la Convention*, 8:203, and *Adresse de la Société des Jeunes Français, 24 mars 1793* (Paris, 1793), BL, RF 57.15.

3 A. Tuetey, *L'assistance publique à Paris pendant la Révolution*, 4 vols. (Paris, 1897-1917), 3:567.

4 It is commonly said that two-thirds of the departments revolted against the Montagnard Convention after the Revolution of May 31, 1793. The truth is far more complex, for praises, protests, and retractions long flowed into Paris from innumerable local administrative and political groups, and even in September no one really knew which areas were loyal and which were not. See M.J. Sydenham, "The Republican Revolt of 1793: A Plea for Less Localised Local Studies," *French Historical Studies*, 12 (1981): 120-38, particularly 134, note 45.

5 Six of the original Committee of Nine, including Danton, were not re-elected on July 10, 1793. Membership was then Barère; Lindet; Hérault de Séchelles; Couthon; Saint-Just; Jeanbon Saint-André; Prieur de la Marne; Thuriot; and Gasparin, who was replaced by Robespierre on July 27.

6 *AP*, 69:193.

7 "Bulletin du Département du Jura, 3 août 1793," in G. Guigue, *Procès-verbaux de la Commission Populaire de Rhône-et-Loire* (Trevaux, 1899), Annexe XLVIII:501.

8 *Mémoire* of Ebrard, cited by D. Monnier, in *Annuaires du Département du Jura, pour l'année 1851*, 133.

9 *AP*, 69:591; *Le Moniteur*, 17:258-59.

10 Ibid., 17:259.

11 See appendices.

12 Guillaume, *P-V du Comité, Convention*, 2:introduction, iii.

13 Ibid., 2:2; *AP*, 68:422.

14 Guillaume, *P-V du Comité, Convention*, 2:v, ix, 30. After initial changes, the six were Grégoire; Lakanal; Ruell; Couppé; Bourdon; and Robespierre, who was later replaced by Pons.

15 Clause 22 of the Declaration of Rights of 1793 (Thompson, *French Revolution Documents*, 241); see also Bouloiseau, Lefebvre, and Soboul, eds., *Oeuvres de Maximilien Robespierre*, 9:581, and Palmer, *The Improvement of Humanity*, 137.

16 Guillaume, *P-V du Comité, Convention*, 2:34-61.

17 Ibid., 31. Apparently Robespierre borrowed the plan from Michel Lepeletier's younger brother, Felix, who, not being a deputy, was seeking permission to unveil it himself in the Convention. The editors of the *Oeuvres de Maximilien Robespierre* (9:621, note) suggest that Robespierre had Felix's consent. Palmer (*The Improvement of Humanity*, 138) has "Robespierre, by a strategem, obtained. . . ."

18 Guillaume, *P-V du Comité, Convention*, 2:34-61, and below, note 19. Various aspects of the Lepeletier Plan are considered by Barnard, *Education and the French Revolution*, 119-23; A. Léon, *La Révolution Française et l'éducation technique* (Paris, 1968), 140-44; R.J. Vignery, *The French Revolution and the Schools: The Educational Policies of the Mountain, 1792-94* (Madison, WI, 1965), 84-88; and, for perhaps the best-balanced assessment, albeit one that hardly does justice to Bourdon, Palmer, *The Improvement of Humanity*, 119-23.

19 Bouloiseau, Lefebvre, and Soboul, eds., *Oeuvres de Maximilen Robespierre*, 10:10-42.

20 Léon, *La Révolution Française et l'éducation technique*, 142-43; Barnard, *Education and the French Revolution*, 122.

21 Bourdon, *Projet de décret sur l'éducation nationale*, BN, Le[38] 373, and Maclure Collection 1042.17.

22 Palmer, *The Improvement of Humanity*, 135-37; Barnard, *Education and the French Revolution*, 111-18.

23 "Examination" here relates primarily, if not entirely, to questioning to ascertain whether counterrevolutionary attitudes were being inculcated.

24 Thibal, "La Société," 4, 178, and, for emphasis on Bourdon's concern for apprenticeship, 202-207. Pancera, "Léonard Bourdon . . . Editor," 21, emphasizes Bourdon's interest at this

time in national primary education. He also stresses Bourdon's ardent desire that the schools foster the formation of character and civic morality, an aspect of Bourdon's *Reports* that has been more fully considered in earlier chapters of the present text.

25 An extract is given here in the appendix (Léonard Bourdon, *Discours sur l'instruction commune prononcé dans la séance du 3 juillet 1793* [Paris, s.d./1793], BN, Le[38] 322; Guillaume, *P-V du Comité, Convention*, 2:178-85). Poorly printed, the original title page should read 30 juillet, which of course conforms to the historical context.

26 Léonard Bourdon, *Rapport de Léonard Bourdon prononcé le 1 août 1793* (Paris, 1793), BN, Le[38] 372; Guillaume, *P-V du Comité, Convention*, 2:206-13.

27 Bouloiseau, Lefebvre, and Soboul, eds., *Oeuvres de Maximilien Robespierre*, 10:69-70.

28 AP, 80:125; *Le Moniteur*, 17:392. I say "apparently" because the phraseology here is somewhat ambiguous, and Bourdon's insistence on instruction seems to be inconsistent with his usual stress on the importance of education. Presumably even some instruction seemed to be preferable to none at all.

29 Fribourg, ed., *Discours de Danton*, 532-36. For the expression "Bourdon-Danton compromise," see Vignery, *The French Revolution and the Schools*, 87.

30 AP, 67:26.

31 Guillaume, *P-V du Comité, Convention*, 2:676, note.

32 Palmer, *The Improvement of Humanity*, 137, 146.

33 Fribourg, ed., *Discours de Danton*, 533.

34 *Supra*, particularly chapters 1, 2, 5, and 7.

35 Aftalion, *L'economie de la Révolution Française*, 185.

36 Ibid., 183-85.

37 *Infra*, note 39.

38 Bouloiseau, Lefebvre, and Soboul, eds., *Oeuvres de Maximilien Robespierre*, 10:45.

39 Léonard Bourdon, *Organisation des greniers nationaux: Rapport fait au nom des Comités d'Agriculture et de Salut Publique* (Paris, s.d./1793), BN, Le[38] 423. Also, AP, 70:347, and Mathiez, *La vie chère*, 291-95. The following paragraphs also derive from the *Rapport*.

40 Aulard, *Jacobins*, 5:331-32. Discussion of the plan was deferred.

41 Cf. chapter 1 above.

42 Notably the notorious law of July 26, 1793, moved by Billaud-Varenne, by which hoarding was made a capital crime (Stewart, *A Documentary Survey of the French Revolution*, 469).

43 The most obvious criticism of these proposals is that they did not deal directly with the principal evil of the time, inflation caused by the massive printing of paper money to finance the war.

44 Aftalion, *L'economie de la Révolution Française*, 191.

45 Mathiez, *La vie chère*, 295-96.

46 Ibid., 295-97.

47 Ibid., 297-98.

48 AP, 72:548. For preliminary announcements of this, see ibid., 328, and *Le Moniteur*, 17:442. Also *La vie chère*, 306-309.

49 *La vie chère*, 378, note.

50 Ibid., 378-79.

51 Soboul, *Les sans-culottes parisiens en l'An II*, 158.

52 *Procès-verbaux de la Convention*, 18:218; *Le Moniteur*, 17:366, 468; Aulard, *Jacobins*, 5:389-406.

53 AP, 70:130; *Le Moniteur*, 17:307.

54 *Le Moniteur*, 17:422.

55 Ibid., 432; AP, 72:378.

56 AP, 72:623.

57 Including ibid., 46, 247, and *Le Moniteur*, 17:317.

58 AP, 72:251. See also *Le Moniteur*, 17:599-600, for September 9, 1793.

59 AP, 72:338.

60 Ibid., 70:282.

61 Ibid., 73:104; *Le Moniteur*, 17:508.
62 Aulard, *Jacobins*, 5:329.
63 For this and the following paragraph, see Soboul, *Les sans-culottes parisiens en l'An II*, 91-150.
64 Ibid., 145 and note, 212, and Markov, ed., *Jacques Roux: Scripta et Acta* (no. 78), 543-44; also 554 for Truchon's part in the arrest of Roux.
65 Aulard, *Jacobins*, 5:330 (August 5).
66 For the situation in the Jacobins, June-September, see Craig W. Dotson, "The Paris Jacobin Club in the French Revolution" (unpublished doctoral dissertation, Queen's University, Kingston, ON, 1974), 427-55.
67 In its context, the comment probably refers particularly to Vincent and the placing of men of the Cordelier Club in the Ministry of War (Aulard, *Jacobins*, 5:329).
68 Ibid., 338.
69 See James A. Leith, *Media and Revolution* (Toronto, 1968), 67.
70 Soboul, *Les sans-culottes parisiens en l'An II*, 109-16, particularly 114.
71 Aulard, *Jacobins*, 5:383 (August 30).
72 AP, 70:346.
73 Aulard, *Jacobins*, 5:351.
74 Ibid.
75 Dotson, "The Paris Jacobin Club in the French Revolution," 448-51.
76 Aulard, *Jacobins*, 5:383 (August 30); Bouloiseau, Lefebvre, and Soboul, eds., *Oeuvres de Maximilien Robespierre*, 10:86-87.
77 Rose, *The Enragés: Socialists of the French Revolution?*, 46-47, and note 81 below.
78 Soboul, *Les sans-culottes parisiens en l'An II*, 165-66.
79 Ibid., 168, 170. Aulard (*Jacobins*, 5:389) nevertheless has "Desfieux rend compte de la mission dont il avait été chargé au commencement de la séance, en compagnie de Léonard Bourdon."
80 Soboul, *Les sans-culottes parisiens en l'An II*, 170.
81 Ibid., 172.
82 AP, 73:392.
83 Hardman, *French Revolution Documents*, 355-57.
84 AP, 73:414, 417-18.
85 Accounts of the day may be found in Soboul, *Les sans-culottes parisiens en l'An II*, 170-73; Doyle, *The Oxford History of the French Revolution*, 251; and, in more detail, Palmer, *Twelve Who Ruled*, 45-54.
86 AP, 73:418. On this occasion, the unidentified Jacobin delegates presumably did not include Bourdon.

Chapter 9

1 Aulard, *Jacobins*, 5:426.
2 Bouloiseau, Lefebvre, and Soboul, eds., *Oeuvres de Maximilien Robespierre*, 10:122. The translation is that of Palmer, *Twelve Who Ruled*, 71.
3 Stewart, *A Documentary Survey of the French Revolution*, 479-81.
4 Aulard, *Jacobins*, 5:passim, for the period in question, and Dotson, "The Paris Jacobin Club in the French Revolution," 440-58.
5 Aulard, *Jacobins*, 5:390.
6 Ibid., 533 et seq.
7 AP, 73:492-93. No particular committee was specified, but that of General Security, regarded as lax, was renewed on the same day, September 9.
8 Aulard, *Jacobins*, 5:395-96.
9 Ibid., 396.
10 Palmer, *Twelve Who Ruled*, 59.
11 Aulard, *Jacobins*, 5:503, for November 9.
12 AP, 68:497, 498. See also Aulard, *Actes*, 6:328.
13 *Le Moniteur*, 17:625, for September 9.

14 Ibid., 533 (*sic* for 593), for September 6. See also 651 for September 13 and the proposal of the arrest of all those of the first levy of conscripts who had not departed.

15 Aulard, *Jacobins*, 5:426.

16 Ibid.

17 The link with Léonard Bourdon is problematic: writing in support of a Captain Constant, who was not appointed, de Vatry noted that Constant had not time to see Léonard (Richard C. Cobb, *Les armées révolutionnaires* [Paris, 1961], 115-16, and Cobb, "La mission de Siblot au Havre-Marat," 177-78).

18 *Le Moniteur*, 17:342, and Aulard, *Jacobins*, 5:494. Bourdon was probably generalizing the application of several specific decrees.

19 Aulard, *Jacobins*, 5:446.

20 *Le Moniteur*, 18:98.

21 Ibid., 343.

22 Ibid., 342, 495.

23 Ibid., 209. Miscellaneous minor matters in which Bourdon took some interest in these weeks may be found in AP, 74:113, 664; *Le Moniteur*, 17:711-12; and Aulard, *Jacobins*, 5:393, 411, 427, 493.

24 Ibid., 5:473.

25 *Le Moniteur*, 17:651, and 18:98.

26 Aulard, *Jacobins*, 5:440.

27 Ibid., 404.

28 See, initially, Kuscinski, *Dictionnaire des conventionnels*, for F.-L. Bourdon, and R.R. Monnier, "Rossignol," in A. Soboul, ed., *Dictionnaire historique de la Révolution Française* (Paris, 1989).

29 Aulard, *Jacobins*, 5:399-400.

30 See the chapters on Pauline Léon and Claire Lacombe in Rose, *The Enragés: Socialists of the French Revolution?*, 56-64, 65-72.

31 Aulard, *Jacobins*, 5:404, for September 13.

32 Ibid., 406-407, for September 16.

33 *Le Moniteur*, 18:285.

34 Rose, *The Enragés: Socialists of the French Revolution?*, 63.

35 On October 3, 1793, forty-five people were indicted as participants in the so-called Brissotin conspiracy. Robespierre resisted calls for the addition of the "Seventy-Three" (actually seventy-five) others who had signed the protests of June 6 and 19 against the arrests effected on June 2 (*Le Moniteur*, 18: 32, 37, 38).

36 Ibid., 200-206, 212-13, 220-22.

37 Ibid., 224, and Sydenham, *The Girondins*, 216.

38 The figure twenty-one suggests an attempt to meet the Parisian demand in the spring of 1793 for the punishment of twenty-two "unfaithful deputies." The deficiency should have been filled by "Égalité," the Duke of Orléans, but he, having been imprisoned in Marseille, was brought to Paris too late for the collective trial. He was executed on November 6.

39 *Le Moniteur*, 18:224-68, for the report of the trial.

40 Ibid., 259-60, for the evidence given by Bourdon.

41 Bourdon's statement referred to Brissot and L. Vigée (Viger), who were in court, and to F. Buzot, B. Lidon, J. Pétion, J.B. Noel, and J. Rabaut Saint-Étienne, who were not. Of the latter, all save Noel were among those expelled from the Convention on June 2. Noel and Rabaut were eventually guillotined, and the other three absentees killed themselves.

42 The word *apparently* is used here because this part of the evidence is given briefly in reported speech.

43 For the steps by which pressure was brought to bear for an end to the trial, see Aulard, *Jacobins*, 5:484; *Le Moniteur*, 18:265 and note, 290-91.

44 *Le Moniteur*, 18:261.

45 AN, W 295.246.15, a document not easily legible.

46 See chapter 6 above.

47 Aulard, *Jacobins*, 4:460, and Kuscinski, *Dictionnaire des conventionnels*.

48 *Le Moniteur*, 18:427.
49 Lefebvre, *Études Orléanaises*, 2:66-67.
50 Guillaume, *P-V du Comité, Convention*, 2:310, 333, 343, and (later) 398.
51 Ibid., 310, 356; AP, 73:342.
52 Guillaume, *P-V du Comité, Convention*, 2:355-56, 360, and, for March 1793, 1:374, 398; *Le Moniteur*, 17:593.
53 R. Hayes, *Ireland and Irishmen in the French Revolution* (Dublin, 1932), 49-62.
54 W. Benjamin Kennedy, "Duckett, Wm., 1768-1841," in J.O. Baylen and N.J. Gussman, eds., *Biographical Dictionary of Modern British Radicals, 1770-1830* (Sussex, 1978). I am indebted to Dr. Kennedy for drawing my attention to this entry.
55 AP, 74:238; *Le Moniteur*, 17:680.
56 Barnard, *Education and the French Revolution*, 126.
57 Guillaume, *P-V du Comité, Convention*, 2:xxvi.
58 Palmer, *The Improvement of Humanity*, 163-68. This survey of the origins of the Paris Plan should be compared with earlier works by other authors, which suggest that it actually emanated from some members of the committee.
59 Ibid., 161; Barnard, *Education and the French Revolution*, 124-25.
60 As note 55 above.
61 Vignery, *The French Revolution and the Schools*, 96-100.
62 Bourdon, *Projet de décret sur l'éducation nationale*, Articles XXXI onward, particularly XLIV and XLV.
63 *Le Moniteur*, 18:373.
64 Léon, *La Révolution Française et l'éducation technique*, 181; Tourneux, *Bibliographie de l'histoire de Paris pendant la Révolution Française*, 2:no. 6432. The nomenclature is confusing, and the difficulty is probably increased by loose contemporary reference. Properly the school usually called that of Liancourt (from its foundation by the Duke of Rochefoucauld Liancourt) was the École des Enfants de l'Armée; that of the Chevalier Pawlet was initially the École des Orphelins Militaires and later the École des Orphelins de la Patrie (or the École/Institut de Popincourt); Bourdon's *jeunes français* may appear as *les enfants*—or even *les orphelins*—*de la patrie*; and those entrusted to him on November 8 were *les orphelins des défenseurs de la patrie*.
65 *Le Moniteur*, 18:380.
66 Thibal, "La Société," 246.
67 AP, 74:239. On September 15, the Department of Paris drew the deputies' attention to the plight of two young blacks, Avril and Oger Azéma, who had reached France after escaping death by violence in Saint-Domingue. At Bourdon's instigation, the assembly ordered that they be enrolled as *orphelins de la patrie*. Cf. note 64 above.
68 Thibal, "La Société," 204-205.
69 *Le Moniteur*, 17:700. Also AP, 74:402, and Guillaume, *P-V du Comité, Convention*, 2:454-55.
70 Ibid., 2:592, 594 note, 606.
71 D. Julia, *Les Trois couleurs de tableau noir: la Révolution* (Paris, 1981), 208.
72 *Le Moniteur*, 18:434; Aulard, *Jacobins*, 5:509, is briefer.
73 E.g., N. Ravitch, "Liberalism, Catholicism, and the Abbé Grégoire," *Church History*, 36 (1967): 422.
74 Guillaume, *P-V du Comité, Convention*, 3:159 note, 255 note. The rejected text was probably prepared initially by Thomas Rousseau, a songwriter (Julia, *Les Trois couleurs de tableau noir*, 209).
75 J. McManners, *The French Revolution and the Church* (London, 1969), 87. The author does not include Bourdon among those whom he describes to illustrate this view.
76 M. Vovelle, "Dechristianisation," in Samuel F. Scott and Barry Rothaus, vol. 1 of *Historical Dictionary of the French Revolution*, 2 vols. (Westport, CT, 1985). Various perspectives of this extensive topic appear in a special number of the *Annales Historiques de la Révolution Française* (50, no. 233 [July-September, 1978]: 1950.
77 M. Vovelle, "Déchristianisation," in A. Soboul, ed., *Dictionnaire historique de la Révolution Française* (Paris, 1989).

78 F.A. Aulard, cited by Soboul, *Les sans-culottes parisiens en l'An II*, 286.

79 *Le Moniteur*, 18:50.

80 Ibid., 122, 137; S. Bianchi, "Chaumette," in A. Soboul, ed., *Dictionnaire historique de la Révolution Française* (Paris, 1989), 213-14.

81 *Le Moniteur*, 18:122.

82 Ibid., 366; Aulard, *Jacobins*, 5:497.

83 *Le Moniteur*, 18:362.

84 Bourdon to the Commune of Paris, August 29, 1792, *Le Courrier français*, July-August, 1792, BN, Lc² 158, no. 244.

85 Chapter 6 above.

86 see chapter 1 above for Léonard Bourdon's *Plan d'un établissement d'éducation nationale* of 1788; Thibal, "La Société," 145-48.

87 AN, AF II, 182, 6, printed in *Libois*, 333-35. For my ascription of this to Bourdon, rather than to C. Prost, see chapter 6 above.

88 These popular societies or clubs should be distinguished from the popular societies in the provincial towns that were affiliated with the Jacobins; see Soboul, *Les sans-culottes parisiens en l'An II*, 274 et seq. The Central Committee is obscure and controversial: Mathiez (*La Révolution Française*, 465), sees it as a powerful body; Soboul (*Les sans-culottes parisiens en l'An II*, 291) is briefly hostile. Cf. S. Bianchi, "La déchristianisation en l'An II," *AHRF*, 50 (1978): 368, who speaks more sympathetically of a popular movement.

89 See note 82 above.

90 Markov, ed., *Jacques Roux: Scripta et Acta*, 543-52, 598; Rose, *The Enragés: Socialists of the French Revolution?*, 47 and note.

91 Soboul, *Les sans-culottes parisiens en l'An II*, 294. It seems to me that Soboul experienced some difficulty in reconciling his general thesis, that of the crucial importance throughout Year II of the *sans-culottes* as the initiating force in the Revolution, with his conclusion that they were not foremost in advocating dechristianization, and that he consequently tends to cast others for that role.

92 A. Mathiez, *La Révolution et l'église* (Paris, 1910), 80. The accusation is also accepted, at least by implication, by the editors, Bouloiseau, Lefebvre, and Soboul, of the *Oeuvres de Maximilien Robespierre*, 10:193. Lefebvre, *La Révolution Française*, 377, cautiously says "certains extrémistes."

93 L'abbé Grégoire, *Mémoires*, vol. 2 (Paris, 1857), 31-32. For the threat to Grégoire himself, see Lord Ashbourne, *Grégoire and the French Revolution* (London, 1932), 64.

94 Soboul, *Les sans-culottes parisiens en l'An II*, 291. The same author's more general study, *La première république* (Paris, 1968), 85-86, nevertheless speaks of the men of the Central Committee accompanied by Cloots and Léonard Bourdon. Cf. note 91 above. For Gobel ("Cloots and Pereyra came to find me at eleven o'clock, when I was in bed and already asleep"), see the *Bulletin du Tribunal Révolutionnaire*, part 4, no. 35 (Paris, 1794).

95 L'Abbé Lambert, "Relation," *L'Ami de la religion, Journal ecclesiastique, politique, et litteraire*, 136 (1848): 239-40.

96 G. Duval, *Souvenirs de la Terreur de 1788 à 1793*, 4 vols. (Paris, 1841-42), 4: 116-17. Although this account has been challenged by various scholars (e.g., H. Baulig, "Anacharsis Cloots, conventionnel," *La Révolution Française*, 61 [1901]: 116), its essentials seem to be more acceptable than some lurid details. Because Léonard Bourdon is not named as present at the alleged conference, its accuracy is not here crucial, but I cite it as illustrative of the participation of the Dantonist group, which was emphasized by Mathiez, *La Révolution et l'église*, particularly 66-77.

97 *Le Moniteur*, 18:371.

98 Ibid., 368.

99 Grégoire, *Mémoires*, 32 et seq.

100 P. Pisani, *L'église de Paris et la Révolution*, vol. 2 (Paris, 1909), 77. *Le Moniteur*, 18:372, includes the episode of the flag but not the request for a procession.

101 *Le Moniteur*, 18:401.

102 Ibid., 420.
103 W. Markov and A. Soboul, *Die Sansculloten von Paris* (Berlin, 1957), 206-208.
104 McManners, *The French Revolution and the Church*, 88.
105 AP, 79:336. The Convention did not approve this proposal.
106 Bouloiseau, Lefebvre, and Soboul, eds., *Oeuvres de Maximilien Robespierre*, 10:194-201; see also Aulard, *Jacobins*, 5:527.
107 A notable example is Robespierre's letter (for the Committee of Public Security) of October 27, 1793, to André Dumont (G. Michon, *Correspondance de Maximilien et Augustin Robespierre* [Paris, 1926], 203).
108 Bouloiseau, Lefebvre, and Soboul, eds., *Oeuvres de Maximilien Robespierre*, 10:197.
109 This statement is not derived only from Robespierre's speech on November 21, 1793, but generally from the views that Robespierre expressed on both earlier and later occasions. See, particularly, the speech on March 26, 1792 (ibid., 8:234), to which he referred on November 21, 1793.
110 For an indication of the complexity of the "foreign plot," see N. Hampson, "François Chabot and His Plot," *Royal Historical Society Transactions*, 5th series, 26 (1976): 1-14.
111 From about this point the word "Club" seems more appropriate to contemporary usage than is the term "Society." It also limits confusion with other societies, e.g., the Jeunes François.
112 Reinhard, *Nouvelle histoire de Paris: la Révolution*, 304.
113 Aulard, *Jacobins*, 5:554.
114 *Le Moniteur*, 18:666.
115 *Le tombeau des imposteurs et l'inauguration du Temple de la Verité: sans-culottide dramatique en trois actes mêlée de musique par les citoyens Léonard Bourdon, Moline, et Valcour* (Paris, An II), BL, 11738 k 2 (4).
116 Aulard, *Actes*, 9:582, for the imposition of the ban on December 22, 1793. See also 16:87 for the repeal of this measure on August 14, 1794.

Chapter 10

1 C. Sellier and P. Dorbec, *Guide explicatif du Musée Carnavalet* (Paris, 1903), no. 399 on p. 152. A reproduction may be seen in P. Sagnac, *La Révolution de 1789*, 2 vols. (Paris, 1934), 2:279. Bourdon also appears in the engraving by J.-J.-F. Tassart of the picture *La nuit du 9 au 10 Thermidor* by F.-J. Harriet (obit 1805), which is of the period but in which youthful features seem to be simply stylized.
2 J.M.B. Renouvier, *Histoire de l'art pendant la Révolution*, 2 vols. (Paris, 1863), 2:371-72.
3 E.g., the frontispiece in Le Corbeiller, *Le Léopard de la Révolution*.
4 E.B. Courtois, *Papiers inédits trouvés chez Robespierre*, 3 vols. (Paris, 1828), 2:20-21, which is given as appendix 3 of the appendices below. The preceding notes about Bourdon de l'Oise were obviously written later than June 8, 1794, the day of the Festival of the Supreme Being.
5 M.-A. Bourdon, *À Dumaine (10 pluviôse II)*, 6.
6 Aulard, *Jacobins*, 5:523-24; *Le Moniteur*, 18:484, for November 19; AP, 80:26-27, 43; *Le Moniteur*, 18:613, for December 6. See also chapter 9, note 18, above.
7 Tuetey, *L'assistance publique à Paris pendant la Révolution*, 4:395.
8 AP, 82:73-74, 401-402. The wounded soldier was presented by the *orphelins de la patrie*, which may refer to the pupils of Pawlet.
9 See the masterly survey by Palmer, *Twelve Who Ruled*.
10 See A. Goodwin, "The Underworld of the French Revolutionary Terror," in *Memoirs and Proceedings of the Manchester Literary and Philosophical Society, 1954-55* (Manchester, 1954-55), 38-56, particularly 47-49.
11 AP, 82:74; Aulard, *Jacobins*, 5:569.
12 Cobb, *Les armées révolutionnaires*, 784.
13 AP, 82:206, 236. Minor matters raised by Bourdon in December-January appear in ibid., 81:248 and 83:310-11.
14 Aulard, *Jacobins*, 5:629-30; *Le Moniteur*, 19:348.
15 Aulard, *Jacobins*, 5:663, 665.

16 Ibid., 674. The reality of these abuses is confirmed by Paganel, who visited the Invalides for the Convention's Comité de Secours; see P. Paganel, *Essai historique et critique sur la Révolution Française*, vol. 2 (Paris, 1815), 49. For minor interventions by Bourdon in February and March 1794, see Aulard, *Jacobins*, 5:642, and *AP*, 86:498.

17 P. Caron, *Paris pendant le Terreur* (Paris, 1943), 199.

18 Aulard, *Jacobins*, 5:617; *AP*, 83:559; sanctioned by the Committee of Public Instruction (Guillaume, *P-V du Comité, Convention*, 3: 335-36).

19 Soboul, *Les sans-culottes parisiens en l'An II*, 757.

20 Aulard, *Jacobins*, 5:684.

21 Ibid., 693.

22 Ibid, 693-95.

23 Soboul, *Les sans-culottes parisiens en l'An II*, 881, suggests that Robespierre's annoyance arose because Couthon's proposal was an initial step toward control of the Commune by the Revolutionary Government. The arrest of Chaumette on March 18 may support that suggestion, but I see no reason to suppose that on March 16 Bourdon was concerned to protect the Commune.

24 In taking this to be the end of the episode, I follow Bouloiseau, Lefebvre, and Soboul, eds., *Oeuvres de Maximilien Robespierre*, 10:395, and Aulard, whose editorial note (*Jacobins*, 5:692) identifies his source as the *Journal de la Montagne*. The report of the police agent Dugas (P. Caron, *Paris pendant la Terreur*, 342-43) adds that Bourdon tried to defend himself but was shouted down "when he had the effrontery to deny before three thousand people that he had said what he had."

25 There is an undercurrent of allegation implying that Bourdon was associated with Chabot, who was arrested on November 27, 1793, and executed with the Dantonists on April 5, 1794. Although one of Chabot's letters from prison mentions Bourdon's advocacy of toleration for Jews (*AP*, 86:466), the allegation does not seem significant.

26 Quoted from Palmer, *Twelve Who Ruled*, 291.

27 Bouloiseau, Lefebvre, and Soboul, eds., *Oeuvres de Maximilien Robespierre*, 10:445.

28 Stewart, *A Documentary Survey of the French Revolution*, 515-19, gives the text of the law. For commentaries on it, see Barnard, *Education and the French Revolution*, 128-32, and Palmer, *The Improvement of Humanity*, 179-83.

29 This was in part because many deputies were determined to prevent the emergence of professional teachers as a new corporate body, but Bouquier himself spoke on December 11 of clubs, festivals, and so on as "inexhaustible sources of instruction," as an "organisation— simple and sublime, as the people have created it" (Barnard, *Education and the French Revolution*, 131).

30 *AP*, 85:320, 356; Guillaume, *P-V du Comité, Convention*, 3:335-42.

31 Palmer, *The Improvement of Humanity*, 182.

32 Clauses 1 and 2 of Section 3; see Stewart, *A Documentary Survey of the French Revolution*, 517.

33 See chapter 9 above.

34 *AP*, 82:586.

35 Guillaume, *P-V du Comité, Convention*, 3:258.

36 Ibid., 3:292; Julia, *Les Trois couleurs du tableau noir*, 210.

37 Guillaume, *P-V du Comité, Convention*, 3:332; Aulard, *Actes*, 11:177, where the figure given is 50,000, probably by a printing error. Cf. the foreword to no. 5 of the *Recueil des actions héroïques et civiques des républicains français* (Paris, An II/1793), BN, Lc² 39.

38 Barnard, *Education and the French Revolution*, 129; E. Kennedy, *A Cultural History of the French Revolution* (New Haven, CT, 1989), 356-57.

39 Julia, *Les Trois couleurs de tableau noir*, 208.

40 Quoted here from the foreword to the first number of the *Recueil des actions héroïques et civiques*, as above.

41 R.T. Lindet, usually "Thomas Lindet," the constitutional bishop of Evreux, was the brother of J.-B.-Robert Lindet of the Committee of Public Safety. E.-J.-M. Aoust, once the Marquis

d'Aoust, is sometimes called Daoust; see Kuscinski, *Dictionnaire des conventionnels*; Guillaume, *P-V du Comité, Convention*, 4:introduction.

42 *Recueil des actions héroïques et civiques*, 1:foreword, Bourdon's speech to the Convention of December 16, 1793.

43 Ibid., 7-8.

44 Ibid., 13.

45 Ibid., 20.

46 Ibid., 22.

47 See Guillaume, *P-V du Comité, Convention*, vol. 4, for these two months (indexed in vol. 6, particularly 211).

48 Ibid., 4:398, 421; Thibaudeau, *Mémoires sur la Convention et le Directoire*, 1:79. Thibaudeau, more active in the Convention after Thermidor than before, is notable for his work with Bonaparte on the Council of State during the Consulate.

49 Pancera, "Léonard Bourdon . . . Editor," 13.

50 *Recueil des actions héroïques et civiques*, 1:14, 17, 20, 22.

51 Julia, *Les Trois couleurs de tableau noir*, 212.

52 Pancera, "Léonard Bourdon . . . Editor," 24.

53 It may be significant that on June 12, 1794, an official circular, of which 10,000 copies were printed, appealed for accounts of striking deeds and prescribed a format for the recital of details (Julia, *Les Trois couleurs de tableau noir*, 210).

54 Thibaudeau, *Mémoires sur la Convention et le Directoire*, 1:80.

55 Julia, *Les Trois couleurs de tableau noir*, 213.

56 Guillaume, *P-V du Comité, Convention*, 4:462.

57 Ibid., note, in which Guillaume suggests that Bourdon remained suspect to many after Robespierre's attack on him in March.

58 Ibid., 3:336.

59 Thibaudeau, *Mémoires sur la Convention et le Directoire*, 1:76.

60 Thibal, "La Société," 245-46.

61 AN, F 17.1012 (dossier 6). See also note 64 below.

62 Tuetey, *L'assistance publique publique à Paris pendant la Révolution*, 3:568.

63 AN, AF II. 67 (dossier 491), f. 2; Hennet, *Les compagnies des cadets gentilhommes et les écoles militaires*, 159-60.

64 AN, F 17.1012 (dossier 6). It contains returns and reports on the number of pupils in Bourdon's school, from which the sums to which Bourdon was entitled for different three-month periods were calculated. Several of these reports emphasized the fact that administrative changes had led to the growth of arrears and that payment in full had become imperative.

65 For much of this part of this chapter, I am indebted to the meticulous research of Thibal, "La Société." For this paragraph, 244-49 relate to the number of pupils; 251-54 to their age range; 183-85 and 271-76 to their instructors; and 201-36 to the curriculum.

66 Ibid., 179-82. Apart from the prospectus that accompanied the original *Plan* in 1788, the two most commonly encountered are Léonard Bourdon, *Société des Jeunes Français: École républicain établi au mois de mai 1792*, and *Société des Jeunes Français: base d'une école centrale d'expérience* (Paris, 1791), BL, Fortescue Collection, R 366.5 and 936.f12 (17) respectively.

67 Aulard, *Actes*, 10:331.

68 Thibal, "La Société," 207.

69 Aulard, *Actes*, 11:222. Both this order and that of January 20 are cited verbatim by Léon, *La Révolution Française et l'éducation technique*, 133-34.

70 Guillaume, *P-V du Comité, Convention*, 3:332, 333; see also Thibal, "La Société," 205, including note 8, and 206. Pancera, "Léonard Bourdon . . . Editor," 24, has only 1,200 copies, probably by an error in printing.

71 Dauban, *Paris en 1794 et en 1795*, 64.

72 F. Fortunet, "Enfant trouvé," in Soboul, *Dictionnaire historique de la Révolution Française*, is in my view conclusive. A further reason for regarding Dauban's identification as mistaken is the entry in P. Caron, *Paris pendant la Terreur*, 417, where another police agent describes a

march of "les élèves de la Patrie, ci-devant les enfants de la Pitié," during which the children, evidently young, are permitted a period of play in a park. Caron, a scholarly editor, simply suggests that they may have been either "enfants de la République" or Bourdon's pupils. Moreover, these children wore uniforms of blue and white, whereas occasional references to the jeunes français ("the couriers of Léonard Bourdon") specify the Parisian colours of red and blue.

73 AP, 90:482-83. See also Addendum, following note 114 below.

74 Ibid., 87:592.

75 L. Tuetey, Procès-verbaux de la Commission des Arts, 2 vols. (Paris, 1912-18), 1:224; Guillaume, P-V du Comité, Convention, 4:700 (a request on June 27, 1794, for regular inspections).

76 Le Moniteur, 20:731-32.

77 Rapport des députés nommés par la Commission des Arts, AN, AF[111] 107.485, f.12. Given in full by Thibal, "La Société," annexe I. This was received by the commission "with satisfaction" (Tuetey, Procès-verbaux de la Commission des Arts, 1:247) and is noted in brief in Guillaume, P-V du Comité, Convention, 4:704.

78 Ibid.

79 AN, F[17] 1012.6 (dossier 16). Léon, La Révolution Française et l'éducation technique, 181. The decision was not in fact effected.

80 This is implicit in the statement made by Bourdon's wife, "la citoyenne Bourdon," in April 1795 (Léon, La Révolution Française et l'éducation technique, 133).

81 AN, AF[17] 1012.5.

82 Given in Thibal, "La Société," 2:223, from AD, Seine, *3AZ 148. Léon, (La Révolution Française et l'éducation technique, 133) notes that Bourdon then also requested a garden and a gymnasium.

83 Thibal, "La Société," 2:225, from AN, F[17] 1331b 9. Bourdon's first request to the Committee of Public Instruction was on December 17, 1793 (Guillaume, P-V du Comité, Convention, 2:168).

84 This decree, if such it was, is elusive. Thibal ("La Société," 282) has "according to the Organisation de la Société des Jeunes Français," one of several papers appended to the Rapport des députés nommés par la Commission des Arts, (note 77 above).

85 Tuetey, Procès-verbaux de la Commission des Arts, 1:58-59, 113.

86 Ibid., 184.

87 Ibid., 138, 163, 172, 183-84, 303; Guillaume, P-V du Comité, Convention, 3:373. Thibal ("La Société," 285-89) has a detailed survey of what is known of these acquisitions.

88 Ibid., 183; Guillaume, P-V du Comité, Convention, 4:429.

89 Thibal, "La Société," 284-85, 289.

90 Ibid., 292-93.

91 Many deputies are said to have moved continually in order to avoid any obvious association with others (R. Hesdin, The Journal of a Spy in Paris [London, 1895], 195). Apart from the occasions on which Bourdon read the Recueil des actions héroïques et civiques to the Convention, his only interventions between mid-March and Thermidor were on March 31, May 13, and June 1, and they were on minor matters.

92 Bouloiseau, Lefebvre, and Soboul, eds., Oeuvres de Maximilien Robespierre, 10:542-86.

93 According to the report of the Swiss journalist Cassat on August 16, 1794 (G. Walter, La conjuration du neuf thermidor [Paris, 1974], 431).

94 Aulard, Jacobins, 6:241-42.

95 See appendix 3.

96 I here follow the editors of Oeuvres de Maximilien Robespierre, 10:606 (save in the spelling of Féraud, as in Kuscinski's Dictionnaire des conventionnels), who give six names and note the addition of Bourdon de l'Oise; they add that one paper reported the nomination of twelve (see AP, 93:564, and Pièce C, which suggests—from the request of Barras, as reported by Perlet—that those chosen may have been supposed to know the geography of Paris). Some sources give the name Ferrand in place of Féraud, but that seems improbable.

97 This conclusion is derived from comparison of the biographies given in Kuscinski, *Dictionnaire des conventionnels*, but cf. note 96 above.

98 Féraud and Fréron gave the Convention brief reports of their activities, as did Legendre, who effected the closure of the (Robespierrist) Jacobin Society (R.T. Bienvenu, *The Ninth of Thermidor* [Oxford, 1968], 215, 217-20).

99 Ibid., 222-28, from P.-F.-J.-N. Barras, *Memoirs of Barras*, edited by G. Duruy, vol. 1 (London, 1895), 236-48.

100 *AP*, 93:594; Bouloiseau, Lefebvre, and Soboul, eds., *Oeuvres de Maximilien Robespierre*, 10:610, note 1.

101 Soboul, *Les sans-culottes parisiens en l'An II*, 996-1021.

102 Walter, *La conjuration du neuf thermidor*, 376.

103 Ibid., 173-74.

104 AN, F^7 4432 (dossier 6); see also Soboul, *Les sans-culottes parisiens en l'An II*, 1008.

105 AN, F^7 4432 (dossier 6); Soboul, *Les sans-culottes parisiens en l'An II*, 1006.

106 The records of the Section des Arcis do not seem to refer to Bourdon. Those of the Section de Marat (once Théâtre Français) note a visit by Léonard Bourdon, who gave "an energetic address" urging the people not to visit the Convention until it was less busy but to report the names of unworthy officials and of patriots who had been wrongly imprisoned. He is also reported as promising that the remains of Marat would be interred in the Panthéon, from which he said they had been excluded by the jealousy of Robespierre. These details match Léonard's position before and after Thermidor, but his visit—if, indeed, he is rightly named—does not conform to what is known of his movements *before* his report to the Convention (AN, F^7 4432.9, and Walter, *La conjuration du neuf thermidor*, 243).

107 Soboul, *Les sans-culottes parisiens en l'An II*, 1003, 1005.

108 Ibid., 1024.

109 C.-A. Méda, *Précis historique des événements qui se sont passés dans le soirée du neuf thermidor* (Paris, 1802); also Walter, *La conjuration du neuf thermidor*, 372-78.

110 Walter, *La conjuration du neuf thermidor*, 379-84.

111 P. Sainte-Claire Deville, *La Commune de l'An II* (Paris, 1946), 294-99.

112 Historians generally agree that Robespierre attempted suicide. An interesting speculation is that his brother Augustin shot him with the pistol already used by Lebas and then hurled himself from the balcony.

113 Soboul, *Les sans-culottes parisiens en l'An II*, 994-95, 997; Rudé, *The Crowd in the French Revolution*, 136-41.

114 Soboul (*Les sans-culottes parisiens en l'An II*, 903 and note 79) notes an address to the Convention from the Section Fontaine-de-Grenelle on Floréal 18 (May 7, 1794) recording the suspension of activity by la Société des Amis-des-Lois-Révolutionnaires. Printed, it was apparently signed "Léonard Bourdon, ex-président," and Soboul refers to Bourdon as the "ancien président de la société." He then explains the suspension as the result of pressure from the Jacobin Society (of which Léonard Bourdon had been a president) against a potential rival and adds: "on sait l'animosité du premier [i.e., Léonard Bourdon] surtout pour le mouvement populaire." Given in isolation, this strange statement suggests either an aberration or another instance of mistaken identity at some level. I know of no other connection of Léonard with that part of Paris.

Addendum: The Cost of the School (see also appendix 4)

(1) The total sum demanded by Bourdon for clothing the *orphelins des défenseurs de la patrie* at this time is indeterminate, because neither the number nor the ages of these boys is known. (2) The general charge that the Société des Jeunes Français was unduly costly seems to be somewhat severe. Granted that 300,000 livres was allotted to the three "national" schools, Bourdon's share should have been about 100,000 for the year or 25,000 for each quarter. More specifically, Bourdon could claim the sum originally approved, that of 1,000 per pupil per year, or 250 per quarter, so that a claim for 95 pupils for the three months ending in June would amount to 23,750. He appears, in fact, to have claimed 26,618 for that

period, a difference of some 3,000, apparently for clothing new pupils; a similar sum of 3,000 above the basic claim for 69 pupils was made for the first quarter of the year, this sum apparently for the upkeep of the building. These figures suggest that Bourdon's demands were high but not inordinately so; that they were increasing with the growth of his school; and that over a full year Bourdon would ask for rather more than one-third of the total approved for the three schools. The evidence, which I take from AN, F^{17} 1012.5 and 6, is not easily interpreted.

Chapter 11

1 For this and the two following paragraphs, see Doyle, *The Oxford History of the French Revolution*, 281; D. Woronoff, *The Thermidorean Regime and the Directory, 1794-1799*, translated by J. Jackson (Cambridge, 1984); G. Lefebvre, *The Thermidorians*, translated by R. Baldick (London, 1965); and, in more detail, A. Mathiez, *After Robespierre: The Thermidorian Reaction*, translated by C.A. Phillips (New York, 1965).

2 Re-election was to be by one-quarter of each committee every month. Political conflict soon focused on the fate of the remaining members of the great Committee of Public Safety, i.e., Billaud-Varenne, Collot d'Herbois, and Barère, who retired from office on September 1, and Carnot, Lindet, and Prieur of the Côte-d'Or, who retired on October 6. (Two of the original twelve, Jeanbon Saint-André and Prieur of the Marne, were deprived of their places in Thermidor because they were then away from Paris on missions, and four—Robespierre, Saint-Just, and Couthon—had then died, as had Hérault, who had been executed with the Dantonists in April.)

3 *Le Moniteur*, 21:395.

4 Aulard, *Actes*, 16:87.

5 H. Gough, *The Newspaper Press in the French Revolution* (Chicago, 1988), 118-21; F. Gendron, *La Jeunesse Dorée* (Québec, 1987), 34-39.

6 Mathiez, *After Robespierre: The Thermidorian Reaction*, 37-40. According to Kuscinski, *Dictionnaire des conventionnels*, Lecointre's whole career began and ended in denunciations: "Ce fut chez lui une monomanie, une habitude exempte de tout discernement."

7 *Le Moniteur*, 21:577; Aulard, *Jacobins*, 6:364.

8 Ibid., 6:302; see also 307-11, 334, 353.

9 Ibid., 289-93.

10 Ibid., 319; *Le Moniteur*, 21:439.

11 Dotson, "The Paris Jacobin Club in the French Revolution," 603-604.

12 Lefebvre, *The Thermidorians*, 21-22.

13 *Le Moniteur*, 21:691; Aulard, *Jacobins*, 6:417 (September 5, 1794).

14 It is usual (e.g., Gendron, *La Jeunesse Dorée*, 90) to ascribe the initiative simply to the Jacobin Society. The difficulty is that its record indicates only that "un membre," supported by many others, promoted the plan (Aulard, *Jacobins*, 6:423, for September 7, 1794). Ian Germani (*Jean-Paul Marat, Hero and Anti-Hero of the French Revolution* [Lewiston, NY, and Queenston, ON, 1992], 192) refers to Bourdon as "the festival's creator."

15 Brumaire 24, An II; Guillaume, *P-V du Comité, Convention*, 5:17. See also below, note 21.

16 Ibid.

17 Ibid., 14-15.

18 Being a member of the committee without a specific function in August, Bourdon retained his position at its partial renewal by lot on August 26 and was attached to the Public Morale Section on September 7 (Guillaume, *P-V du Comité, Convention*, 4:introduction, 990, and 5:13).

19 AN, F^7 4432, 9.

20 Guillaume, *P-V du Comité, Convention*, 5: 16-17, for the initial outline of the proposal, and 59-61 for its development. The latter was published in Léonard Bourdon, *Rapport fait au nom du Comité d'Instruction Publique sur la fête du cinquième sans-culottide* (BN, Le^{38} 940, Paris, s.d./1794).

21 Ibid., 38-39.

22 Ibid., 17-19.

23 Germani (*Jean-Paul Marat, Hero and Anti-Hero*, 188-90) has a lively account of the events of the day.

24 F.-A. Aulard, *Paris pendant la réaction thermidorienne et sous le Directoire*, 2 vols. (Paris, 1898), 1:123.

25 Ibid., 120.

26 Aulard, *Jacobins*, 6:502, and Germani (*Jean-Paul Marat, Hero and Anti-Hero*, 192), who cites the *Journal de la Montagne* for Vendémiaire 3, Year III.

27 See the authorities cited in note 1 above, particularly Mathiez, *After Robespierre: The Thermidorian Reaction*, 58-67. Ironically the worst terrorists at Nantes were known as the Compagnie Marat.

28 *Procès-verbaux de la Convention*, 50:74.

29 Mathiez, *After Robespierre: The Thermidorian Reaction*, 61; Lefebvre, *The Thermidorians*, 26-27.

30 Guillaume, *P-V du Comité, Convention*, 4:990 (August 27, 1794).

31 Aulard, *Jacobins*, 6:441 (September 10, 1794).

32 Ibid., 6:501-503; *Le Moniteur*, 22:44.

33 Lefebvre, *The Thermidorians*, 35-36; Gough, *The Newspaper Press in the French Revolution*, 120.

34 Edited and probably written mainly by Dussault, it was a new series reviving that of the same title in 1790.

35 Guillaume, *P-V du Comité, Convention*, 5:118 (Vendémiaire 14/October 5, 1794).

36 BN, Lc² 392, *L'Orateur du peuple*, issue of Vendémiaire 23, Year III.

37 *Le Moniteur*, 22:252.

38 Aulard, *Paris pendant la réaction thermidorienne*, 1:196.

39 Mathiez, *After Robespierre: The Thermidorian Reaction*, 70-78; Lefebvre, *The Thermidorians*, 29-30. See also R.B. Rose, *Gracchus Babeuf: The First Revolutionary Communist* (Stanford, CA, 1978), 162-65.

40 The episode provides a neat example of the selective nature of Jacobin democracy. Thus, on August 26, Dufournay and Réal told the Jacobin Society that the proposal of the Society of the Évêché for the election of revolutionary committees by the people was dangerous, and Maure said explicitly that it would tend "à jeter une grande défaveur sur les patriotes" (Aulard, *Jacobins*, 6:385-86).

41 Mathiez, *After Robespierre: The Thermidorian Reaction*, 56-57.

42 *Le Moniteur*, 22:314; Aulard, *Jacobins*, 6:599-600.

43 *Le Moniteur*, 22:378; Aulard, *Jacobins*, 6:613-15 (October 28, 1794).

44 Ibid., 6:613-15.

45 Bourdon, *À ses concitoyens*, BL, F22*:23. See also above, chapter 7.

46 Bourdon, *À ses concitoyens*, BL, F22*:23, and above, chapter 7.

47 Ibid.

48 *L'Orateur du peuple*, Brumaire 19, Ventôse 25, Germinal 4, An III.

49 *Le Moniteur*, 22:378; Aulard, *Jacobins*, 6:613-15.

50 Ibid., 6:621.

51 Ibid., 627; *Le Moniteur*, 22:416.

52 Aulard, *Jacobins*, 6:627. When one of the dismissed women appealed to the club later in the day, Bourdon praised her and her companions for their care of the sick but advised them against further inquiry.

53 Ibid., 635.

54 The authoritative work is that of Gendron, *La Jeunesse Dorée*.

55 *La Jeunesse Dorée*, e.g., 34, 43.

56 Aulard, *Jacobins*, 6:633.

57 *Le Moniteur*, 20:442.

58 Ibid., 439, and Aulard, *Jacobins*, 6:638.

59 *Le Moniteur*, 22:442.

60 November 11, 1794; see note 66 below.

61 Aulard, *Jacobins*, 6:640.

62 Ibid., 643.

63 Gendron, *La Jeunesse Dorée*, 46-47.

64 Aulard, *Jacobins*, 6:646-47.
65 Ibid., 647-48.
66 Ibid., 669. The relevant proceedings of the Convention appear in Aulard, *Jacobins*, 6:649-77, being taken from *Le Moniteur*, 22:473 onward.
67 Aulard, *Jacobins*, 6:651-54.
68 Ibid., 655.
69 Lefebvre, *The Thermidorians*, 44-45; Gendron, *La Jeunesse Dorée*, 48-50.
70 Aulard, *Jacobins*, 6:677.
71 Ibid., 675.

Chapter 12

1 Guillaume, *P-V du Comité, Convention*, 5:461. The exception to the general statement is Bourdon's vote for the indictment of Carrier, noted here in chapter 11.
2 Debal, *Histoire d'Orléans*, 160.
3 BL, R 578.11 (Vendémiaire 16, Year III).
4 D. Tonnesson, *La défaite des sans-culottes* (Oslo and Paris, 1959), 149.
5 Ibid., 58, 94-95, for the Electoral Club.
6 Ibid., 149 and note 39, for Vertbois. Cf. Mathiez, *After Robespierre: The Thermidorian Reaction*, 170.
7 Ibid., 97; Gendron, *La Jeunesse Dorée*, 52.
8 The reader should appreciate that the interpretation here is my own. The more general view is that the centre was soon indistinguishable from the right. Although in this chapter I have drawn much from the meticulous research of Gendron, I have not accepted his view (89, 131, and passim) that the Convention, even including the Thermidorians, soon became dominated by the Jeunesse Dorée.
9 Gendron, *La Jeunesse Dorée*, 83-84. For the background, se_ G. Lefebvre, *The Thermidorians*, 53 et seq.
10 Gendron, *La Jeunesse Dorée*, 90, 93-105; Tonnesson, *La défaite des sans-culottes*, 117-18; Germani, *Jean-Paul Marat, Hero and Anti-Hero*, 197-204.
11 Gendron, *La Jeunesse Dorée*, 106.
12 For what follows, see ibid., 114-20, and corresponding police reports in Aulard, *Paris pendant la réaction thermidorienne*, 1:466, and A. Schmidt, *Tableau de la Révolution Française*, 2 vols. (Leipzig, 1867-70), 1:237, 243-45; 2:283.
13 AN, F^{17} 4612 (dossier Bourdon); Gendron, *La Jeunesse Dorée*, 116 and note 386.
14 Aulard, *Paris pendant la réaction thermidorienne*, 1:513; Gendron, *La Jeunesse Dorée*, 125. *Le Messager du Soir*, which printed the report, was a right-wing paper edited by I. Langlois, a recognized leader of the Jeunesse Dorée (J.D. Popkin, *The Right-Wing Press in France, 1792-1800* [Chapel Hill, NC, 1980], 44-45).
15 For this affair, Gendron, *La Jeunesse Dorée*, 121-23; Aulard, *Paris pendant la réaction thermidorienne*, 1:534-39, 545. For Armonville, who apparently accepted police advice and ceased wearing his red cap in public, see Kuscinski, *Dictionnaire des conventionnels*.
16 *Le Moniteur*, 23:629.
17 Ibid., 24:19. See also Soboul, *Dictionnaire historique de la Révolution Française*, 280. Four days later (March 23/Germinal 3), Bourdon complained to the Committee of Public Safety about different charges made in a pamphlet entitled *Grande arrestation de Léonard Bourdon, qui s'est assassiné lui-même*. His letter, of course futile, is of interest because he said that he could give a day-to-day account of his conduct since 1789 and that "le genre d'occupations auquel je me suis consacré avec quelque succès n'est pas la carrière d'un ambitieux et d'un intrigant" (Thibal, "La Société," 28, citing BHVP, MS 815, fol. 65).
18 *L'Orateur du peuple*, BN, L^2 392c, no. XCI for Ventôse 25 (March 15), and XCV for Germinal 4 (March 24).
19 I have not thought it desirable to trouble the reader with frequent references to the many publications of Bourdon des Planches, which are often either undated or arbitrarily assigned to a year, usually 1793. In general, too, these writings reiterate in one form or another Bour-

don *père*'s constant plea for internal free trade tempered by the control of distribution by a government agency with a monopoly of external purchasing. Those most obviously pertinent to early 1795 are *Adresse à la Convention Nationale sur la subsistence et sur les impositions* and *Du pain, du pain, et moyen d'en avoir: lettre sur la subsistence et sur les impositions et finances à Cambon* (Paris, 1795), these being respectively BN, Lb⁴¹ 1612 and 1613.

20 Soboul, *La première république*, 166, notes that there were 8,000 million *assignats* in circulation in December 1794 and 11,000 million in May 1795. For a strong statement of the view that this, not the abolition of price controls, was the principal cause of other evils, see Aftalion, *L'économie de la Révolution Française*, 221-24. Depreciation appears in the fall in value of a 100-livre *assignat* from 24 livres in November 1794 to 14 in February 1795 and 8 by March 20 (Mathiez, *After Robespierre: The Thermidorian Reaction*, 166); or, with the effects of scarcity, in the actual cost of bread, which rose from 25 sous for the loaf in March to 6 livres by mid-April and 16 livres by mid-May (Rudé, *The Crowd in the French Revolution*, 144).

21 Mathiez, *After Robespierre: The Thermidorian Reaction*, 160; Rudé, *The Crowd in the French Revolution*, 149.

22 Gendron, *La Jeunesse Dorée*, 140, 149-51, 166-75.

23 Tonnesson, *La défaite des sans-culottes*, 160-61. The trial was entwined with the constitutional question because adoption of the Constitution of 1793 would mean the closure of the Convention and the transference of the trial to a new national assembly, as Merlin de Thionville proposed on March 28 (Lefebvre, *The Thermidorians*, 102).

24 Ibid.

25 Mathiez, *After Robespierre: The Thermidorian Reaction*, 172.

26 E.g., Woronoff, *The Thermidorean Regime and the Directory*, 15.

27 The main points are made briefly by Lefebvre, *The Thermidorians*, 103-104, where the final scene is dismissed as a "pitiful scuffle." For a fuller account of the day, see Gendron, *La Jeunesse Dorée*, 178-84.

28 R. Levasseur, *Mémoires de René Levasseur (de la Sarthe), ex-Conventionnel*, 4 vols. (Paris, 1829), 4:205, 208-209; P.-R. Choudieu, *Mémoires et notes de Choudieu*, edited by V. Barrucand (Paris, 1897), 301-302.

29 Tonnesson, *La défaite des sans-culottes*, 172-76.

30 Ibid., 353-54, where Tonnesson notes a report written on Germinal 25 (April 14) by the Director of a jury investigating the troubles in Gravilliers at the end of March. It stated that fifty-three witnesses had so far been heard but that their evidence "n'offre des faits très précis que contre le représentant Léonard Bourdon" and six other citizens. Because these facts remain unknown, Tonnesson concludes that they might have shown either that Bourdon was associated with the principal agitators beforehand or that he only became involved once the disturbances had begun. Although not insignificant, this material has seemed to me too indefinite to be included in my text. C. Dupuy, *Les électeurs parisiens de 1792 dans la Section des Gravilliers* (Maîtrise, Paris–I, 1988) (seen in abstract form only), has Bourdon as one of the two most active of fifteen electors of Gravilliers who were proscribed after Germinal and Prairial, but she gives no details of his activity.

31 Levasseur, *Mémoires*, 4:217.

32 Tonnesson, *La défaite des sans-culottes*, 213 and note 63, which gives the names of the signatories of the demand. Two of the "great criminals," Collot d'Herbois and Billaud-Varenne, were deported to Guiana, where they died in 1796 and 1819 respectively. Similarly sentenced, Barère contrived to remain concealed in France, as had Vadier.

33 Levasseur, *Mémoires*, 4:218. Gendron (*La Jeunesse Dorée*, 184) suggests that the six were those who had been particularly abusive of the Jeunesse Dorée during the afternoon.

34 *Le Moniteur*, 24:120.

35 "Battelier à Albert, 21 Germinal," *La Révolution Française*, 75 (1922): 60-63; Tonnesson, *La défaite des sans-culottes*, 212.

36 AN, F⁷ 4672 (dossier Bourdon), which includes the relevant orders of Germinal 12 and 13 as well as material relating to the sealing of Bourdon's papers in Prairial and Messidor. See also Tonnesson, *La défaite des sans-culottes*, 213, and Gendron, *La Jeunesse Dorée*, 187.

37 Bourdon de Vatry was absent from the Section de la République, "having gone to join those who wanted to save his brother" (Tonnesson, *La défaite des sans-culottes*, 213, note 92, citing Biblio. Victor Cousin, ms. 118, fol. 70).

38 Kuscinski, *Dictionnaire des conventionnels*.

39 Tonnesson, *La défaite des sans-culottes*, 214-16, which may be compared with Gendron, *La Jeunesse Dorée*, 186-89, or with the account in the right-wing *Courrier Républicain* given in Aulard, *Paris pendant la réaction thermidorienne*, 1:634.

40 Choudieu, *Mémoires*, 310, has "un peu de désordre et du tapage."

41 Tonnesson, *La défaite des sans-culottes*, 218-20.

42 Kuscinski, *Dictionnaire des conventionnels*, includes Amar, but AN, BB³ 29 (dossier Choudieu), no. 5, concerns the carriage used for the removal of the other three. They were forgotten when the general amnesty was announced in late October and were not freed until eight days later.

43 Aulard, *Actes*, 24:295. In June 1793, Blaux was one of those who signed the Protest of the Seventy-Five against the proscriptions of June 2, a convenient but, as I have argued elsewhere, misleading classification of party membership (Sydenham, *The Girondins*, 43-45, 219).

44 *Le Moniteur*, 24:239, for Germinal 28 (April 17).

45 Ibid., 522.

46 *Procès-verbaux de la Convention*, 63:198; Aulard, *Actes*, 24:204. See also chapter 6, note 19, above.

47 Lesage was one of the twenty-nine deputies placed under guard on June 2, 1793 (Sydenham, *The Girondins*, 216). For the quotation, see Kuscinski, *Dictionnaire des conventionnels*.

48 *Le Moniteur*, 24:130; Guillaume, *P-V du Comité, Convention*, 6:31-32.

49 *Le Moniteur*, 26:132.

50 Léon, *La Révolution Française et l'éducation technique*, 182. Palmer (*The Improvement of Humanity*, 164 note) mentions his participation in the Parisian plan for education in the summer of 1793.

51 Guillaume, *P-V du Comité, Convention*, 5:61; Barnard, *Education and the French Revolution*, 158. Instruction was of course secondary to conservation. For the allocation of the Priory to the Conservatoire, see AN, AD VIII, 29.

52 AN, F 171012, 9 and 6; also Thibal, "La Société," 246.

53 Tuetey, *L'assistance publique à Paris pendant la Révolution*, 3:568, 570-72.

54 Léon, *La Révolution Française et l'éducation technique*, 182, note 88.

55 Guillaume, *P-V du Comité, Convention*, 4:873 and 909, note 2, for August 20, 1794, and 5:564 for March 4, 1795.

56 As in notes 48-49 above.

57 AN, AF III, 107.27, and see below.

58 AN, AD VIII, 29. The report was in part incorporated in that presented to the Convention of May 19 (Floréal 30), for which see AF III, 107.25, and Guillaume, *P-V du Comité, Convention*, 6:217-21. It is also cited in part by Vauthier, "Léonard Bourdon et la Société des Jeunes Français," 331-43, 340-42.

59 Ibid.

60 Plaichard told the Convention that mothers bearing babies still at the breast appealed daily to the committee and that some of those at Bourdon's school were less than three years old (Guillaume, *P-V du Comité, Convention*, 6:217). Thibal ("La Société," 251-54) has an analysis of the age range of the pupils, but unfortunately it could not be related to a specific period.

61 Léon, *La Révolution Française et l'éducation technique*, 249. Pancera ("Léonard Bourdon . . . Editor," 13-33) suggests that "during the prairial insurrection in Paris 'his' students protested against the Convention," citing AN, F¹⁷ 1010 (dossier 6). This does not seem likely to me, but I have not seen the dossier.

62 Note 58 above.

63 AN, AD VIII, 29; Guillaume, *P-V du Comité, Convention*, 6:217.

64 Note 75 below.

65 Mathiez, *After Robespierre: The Thermidorian Reaction*, 44, and the works cited in note 20 above.

66 Madame Bourdon was initially repulsed by the Committee of Instruction, being told to approach that of Finance. See Guillaume, *P-V du Comité, Convention*, 6:119-20, and, for her letter, 122.

67 Ibid., 127, 129, 149, and, for further references, the Index under Institut des Jeunes Français (80); also, Tuetey, *L'assistance publique à Paris pendant la Révolution*, 3:573. Thibal ("La Société," 305) calculates that at intervals Creuzot received 70,000 livres for the school (including pens, ink, and paper) before its closure in mid-June.

68 Léon, *La Révolution Française et l'éducation technique*, 77, 177-79.

69 Ibid., 177.

70 Guillaume, *P-V du Comité, Convention*, 6:221.

71 Ibid., 233, 256.

72 Ibid., 268-71; Vauthier, "Léonard Bourdon et la Société des Jeunes Français," 338.

73 Léon, *La Révolution Française et l'éducation technique*, 78, 179-82.

74 Guillaume, *P-V du Comité, Convention*, 6: 293, 295-96.

75 AN, AF III, 107:27 and 28, given in part by Vauthier, "Léonard Bourdon et la Société des Jeunes Français," 338-40.

76 Like Crouzet, Mahérault had been a professor at the Collège du Panthéon, and the two had collaborated in promoting educational reform in 1793 (Palmer, *The Improvement of Humanity*, 164 note and 210).

77 Including Paulet, who might be the Paulin to whom Bourdon gave prominence in the demonstration against Christianity in 1793; see chapter 9 above.

78 These figures for the condition of clothing have, for simplicity, here been obtained by amalgamating various minor classifications.

79 In the original, reference is made to *la Galle*, *l'acreté dans le sang*, and *la Gourme*, which I have not attempted to translate. I take them to be the effects of malnutrition, probably related to scurvy.

80 Written in as from Versailles but actually from Saint-Sulpice (see Tuetey, *Procès-verbaux de la Commission des Arts*, 2:340).

81 As was recognized in the inventory. It seems that these papers were initially sealed and stored in Gravilliers but that the seals were officially lifted twice. By an order dated Prairial 21 (June 9, 1795), they were searched (with what success?) for correspondence that might "reasonably establish" evidence of Bourdon's links with the agitators of the section, evidence that was to be sent to the Military Commission. Then, on Messidor 22 (July 10), all (else?) was to be sent to the Committee of General Security (AN, F[7] 4612:37).

82 Thibal, "La Société," 301. Pages 272-315 contain a searching scrutiny of many aspects of conditions in the school.

83 Ibid., 283-85.

84 Guillaume, *P-V du Comité, Convention*, 6:289, has his officious offer on June 14 to investigate Bourdon's administration of the school. For the report that he wrote on Messidor 3, see AN, F[7] 4612:37. See also note 81 above.

85 Julia, *Les Trois couleurs du tableau noir*, 289; Léon (*La Révolution Française et l'éducation technique*) concludes that the character of the first school of Arts et Métiers owed less to Liancourt than to the schools of Pawlet and Bourdon. I am also indebted to C.R. Day ("The Making of Mechanical Engineers in France: The Écoles d'Arts et Métiers, 1803-1914," *French Historical Studies*, 10 [1978]: 439-60) for personal guidance about the background to this period.

Chapter 13

1 *Le Moniteur*, 26:346. A few of those concerned in the rising of Vendémiaire were excluded from the amnesty, which may have applied to as many as 30,000 "terrorists."

2 A. Mathiez, *Le Directoire* (Paris, 1924), 25; G. Lefebvre, *The Directory*, translated by R. Baldick (Paris, 1937; London, 1964), 3.

3 Paragraph derived from Kuscinski, *Dictionnaire des conventionnels*, for those named.

4 Thibal, "La Société," 29, 279-80, citing AD, Seine, DQ[10] 522.396 (Direction des Domaines, dossier Léonard Bourdon).

5 See Doyle, *The Oxford History of the French Revolution*, 319, for Boissy d'Anglas's statement for the constitutional committee on June 23, 1795. For the Constitution, see Stewart, *A Documentary Survey of the French Revolution*, 572-612, and G. Lefebvre, *La France sous le Directoire, 1795-1799* (Paris, 1977/1984), 45-73.

6 Stewart, *A Documentary Survey of the French Revolution*, 613-14.

7 Lefebvre, *The Thermidorians*, 203-204, and Lefebvre, *La France sous le Directoire*, chap. 1, particularly 14.

8 Mathiez, *Le Directoire*, 76, 140.

9 A. Schmidt, *Paris pendant la Révolution d'après les rapports de la police secrète, 1789-1800*, 2 vols. (Paris, 1880), 2:483-84.

10 Bibliothèque municipale de Provins, *Léonard Bourdon, commissaire du gouvernement pour l'execution de la loi du 22 Brumaire: Melun, 30 Brumaire An 4* (MS 181?).

11 Kuscinski, *Dictionnaire des conventionnels*.

12 I. Woloch, *Jacobin Legacy: The Democratic Movement under the Directory* (Princeton, NJ, 1970), passim.

13 Although the term "Jacobin" (sometimes written as "jacobin" or more recently as "Neo-Jacobin") is usual, I have deliberately chosen to avoid it in this later period because it was frequently used as a term of abuse more or less synonymous with "terrorist." Moreover, the distinction between the Jacobins of 1793-94 and those of 1795 onward is open to interpretation. My use of the less evocative term "democrat" is not intended to imply that those so named necessarily favoured either universal suffrage or any limitation of sovereign authority. The word *moderate* is inevitably relative.

14 Mathiez, *Le Directoire*, 140-41; Lefebvre, *La France sous le Directoire*, 98-99.

15 C. Proquenard, "La Société du Panthéon," *La Révolution Française*, 33 (1897): 318-48; Mathiez, *Le Directoire*, 141-59.

16 Proquenard, "La Société du Panthéon," 329; Mathiez, *Le Directoire*, 147. The one exception was J.-B. Drouet, who as postmaster of Sainte-Ménehould had thwarted the flight of the royal family in 1791.

17 Aulard, *Paris pendant la réaction thermidorienne*, 2:374.

18 Ibid., 386; Schmidt, *Paris pendant la Révolution*, 2:444. For a general summary, see also his 1:124-37.

19 Ibid., 2:483.

20 Ibid., 484, 486; Aulard, *Paris pendant la réaction thermidorienne*, 2:33, 438. There is some ambiguity here between the agents' observations and their synopses of press reports, the particular reference being apparently to an independent republican paper, *L'Ami des Lois*.

21 Schmidt, *Paris pendant la Révolution*, 1:127, 2:453; Aulard, *Paris pendant la réaction thermidorienne*, 2:400. Vadier, one of the four "great criminals" indicted for their part in the Terror, had escaped deportation by concealing himself until he was saved by the amnesty.

22 Aulard, *Paris pendant la réaction thermidorienne*, 2:405.

23 Schmidt, *Paris pendant la Révolution*, 2:530.

24 The literature is extensive. I have relied principally on Rose, *Gracchus Babeuf: The First Revolutionary Communist*.

25 J.B. Robert Lindet (1746-1825), the driving force behind the economic policy of the Committee of Public Safety in 1793-94, was embittered by the Thermidorian Reaction. Mathiez (*Le Directoire*, 150) holds him particularly responsible for the failure of the Directors' policies at the end of 1795.

26 This issue included the notorious Manifesto of the Plebeians. See Rose, *Gracchus Babeuf: The First Revolutionary Communist*, 211-14, for an analytical summary; for the original, see, e.g., J. Godechot, *La pensée révolutionnaire en France et en Europe, 1780-99* (Paris, 1964), 255-71.

27 The trial of sixty-five alleged conspirators, of whom forty-seven were present, opened on February 20 and concluded on May 24, 1797. Babeuf and one other, A.-A. Darthé, were condemned and executed, and seven others, notably F. Buonarroti, were sentenced to deportation. The remainder—mostly *sans-culottes*, but including some more notable figures (among whom were three of those Montagnards proscribed with Bourdon in Germinal, Year III: Amar, Chasles, and Choudieu)—were acquitted.

28 A. Debidour, *Recueil des actes du Directoire Exécutif*, vol. 1 (Paris, 1890), 494 and note.

29 AN, AF III, 341, no. 49 for Nivôse 26, Year IV, and no. 50 for Nivôse 29.

30 Ibid., as endorsement of the letter of Nivôse 26. See also Debidour, *Recueil des actes du Directoire Exécutif*, 452-53.

31 Ibid., as cited by Bourdon in the letter of Nivôse 29.

32 *Biographical Anecdotes of the Founders of the French Republic*, 2 vols. (London, 1797-98), 2:304-306 (BL, 613d. 32).

33 Mathiez, *Le Directoire*, 218; AN, AF III, 107.225.15, Léonard Bourdon, *Observations relatives à l'indemnité du citoyen Bourdon* (Paris, n.d./1798-99).

34 Extract from the *Nouvelles Politiques*, no. 350 of Fructidor 16, Year IV, included in the *Mémoire* cited in note 38 below.

35 Léonard Bourdon, *Discours prononcé le 9 Thermidor An IV* (Brussels, 1796), microfilm, University of British Columbia Library, Vancouver.

36 As I understand the matter, the title, in use between 1791 and c. 1804, originally reflected the revolutionaries' belief that in their new world the law would be so simplified that almost anyone could defend himself or another. Subsequently, as the legal profession was gradually reinstated, it became broadly equivalent to recognition as one qualified to practise law. See Fitzsimmons, *The Parisian Order of Barristers and the French Revolution*, passim.

37 Bourdon, *Discours prononcé le 9 Thermidor An IV*.

38 For this and the following paragraphs (unless otherwise stated), my source is the *Mémoire du citoyen Antoine Joseph Braeckenier, rédacteur de l'impartial Bruxellois, défendeur, contre Léonard Bourdon, actuellement en cette ville, demandeur* (Brussels, 1796), BL, F 969.16. It gives the author's account of the case and an assortment of material compiled by him from the French press.

39 Lefebvre, *La France sous le Directoire*, 264.

40 Ibid.

41 Thibaudeau, *Mémoires sur la Convention et le Directoire*, 2:152-53.

42 Kuscinski, *Dictionnaire des conventionnels*, entry for Mallarmé, F.-R.-A., 1755-1831.

43 Mathiez, *Le Directoire*, 237.

44 See chapter 15 below.

45 BN, Charavay Collection of Autographs, XXXVIII, carton 290, no. 42826, letter dated Nivôse 6, Year V (de Vatry deplores the divisions in France, congratulates himself on the confidence the Minister [of Marine] has in him, and hopes that measures he has in mind will benefit the colonies).

46 Woloch, *Jacobin Legacy*, 170.

47 Appendix 4.

48 Bourdon, *Observations relatives à l'indemnité*. For *bons*, see Aftalion, *L'economie de la Révolution Française*, 231.

49 *Le Moniteur*, 27:748.

50 F. Barthélemy (1747-1830), a diplomat of royalist sympathies, replaced Letourneur as a Director in May 1797. Exiled to Guiana, he escaped and eventually became eminent in the service of Napoleon and Louis XVIII.

51 See, e.g., my *The First French Republic, 1792-1804* (London, 1974), 147-48.

52 AN, F⁷ 6151: *Police Générale: Affaires politiques, plaque 8: Léonard Bourdon à Hambourg*, no. 503: Bourdon to Merlin de Douai, Germinal 25, Year VI. Further references to Bourdon's reports to Merlin are given only by number (e.g., F⁷ 6151, no. 503).

53 P.A. Merlin (1754-1838), "de Douai," an exceptionally able jurist, became known as "Merlin-Suspect" for his part in drafting the Law of Suspects in September 1793. Having been Minister of Police and Minister of Justice before Fructidor, he then replaced Barthélemy as a Director. A dominant figure until June 1799, he later held high office during the Consulate and the Empire.

54 AN, F⁷ 6151, no. 434, Bourdon's account endorsed as correct by Sotin. See also nos. 395-96, report from the *bureau particulière* to the Minister of Police, Frimaire, Year VII.

55 The one report appears in *Le Moniteur*, 29:151, and the other is in the original edition (Paris, 1798), no. 144 (579). Both entries relate to Pluviôse 24, Year VI (February 12, 1798), but neither volume includes both statements.

56 W. Markov ("Babeuf, le babeuvisme et les intellectuels allemands 1796-97," in *Colloqué international de Stockolm, 21 aôut 1960: Babeuf et les problèmes du babeuvisme* [Paris, 1963], 196, note 76) points out that the records of the period in Hamburg were mostly destroyed in the great fire of 1842. Markov adds that an abridgement by an unknown archivist (c. 1846) states that Bourdon's visit prompted the Senate to pay its debts to France to be rid of "cet émissaire inquiétant."

57 A. Sorel (*L'Europe et la Révolution Française*, 8 vols. [Paris, 1885-1904], 5:298) notes that on February 23, 1798, Bonaparte urged the Directors to abandon the projected invasion of England and to secure Hanover and Hamburg. S.S. Biro (*The German Policy of Revolutionary France*, 2 vols. [Cambridge, MA, 1957], 2:817-25 and 962-63) argues convincingly that French resentment of Hamburg's wealth and independence was outweighed by appreciation of its value as a neutral centre.

58 Comte de Neuilly, *Souvenirs et correspondance* (Paris, 1865), 160 and, for the quotations that follow, 160-61.

59 Ibid.

60 For this paragraph, AN, as above, F⁷ 6151, nos. 399, 408, 412, 430, 484, 493, and Archives des Affaires Étrangères, *Correspondance diplomatique de Hambourg*, Supplément, 266, 268.

61 Neuilly, *Souvenirs et correspondance*, 161.

62 AN, F⁷ 6151, nos. 422 and 430-33.

63 Ibid., nos. 430, 497. Cf. L. Sciout, *Le Directoire*, 4 vols. (Paris, 1895-97), 3:668-79.

64 AN, F⁷ 6151, no. 434. Cf. no. 486 and *Correspondance diplomatique de Hambourg*, 113:470.

65 AN, F⁷ 6151, nos. 399, 430, 491, 492. See also Kennedy, "Duckett, William (1768-1841)."

66 Roberjot to Talleyrand, Germinal 13, Year VI; *Correspondance diplomatique de Hambourg*, 113:no. 8.

67 *Correspondance diplomatique de Hambourg*, 112:363ff. for the *procès-verbal* of the meeting and Bourdon's address.

68 Ibid., 461, 462.

69 For this sequence, ibid., 112:no. 6; 113:nos. 8, 22, 39; and AN, F⁷ 6151, no. 415.

70 Instructions to Roberjot, Pluviôse 26, Year VI (February 14, 1798), *Correspondance diplomatique de Hambourg*, Supplément, 260-62.

71 Ibid., 112:23.

72 AN, F⁷ 6151, nos. 434 and 503, for Bourdon's increasing concern about his lack of money.

73 Ibid., nos. 399, 420, 443, 492; *Correspondance diplomatique de Hambourg*, 112:34; 113:15, 17.

74 AN, F⁷ 6151, no. 490.

75 Ibid., nos. 394, 484.

76 Ibid., nos. 460 and, for the elusive papers, 419, 500-502, 504-14.

77 *Correspondance diplomatique de Hambourg*, Supplément, 292.

Chapter 14

1 Kuscinski, "Le Conventionnel Léonard Bourdon," 133-34.

2 Kuscinski, *Dictionnaire des conventionnels*, 82.

3 Patrick, *The Men of the First French Republic*, 9.

4 "Avertissement," in Kuscinski, *Dictionnaire des conventionnels*, i and iv.

5 AN, F¹⁷ 6745.18.

6 The junction of the rue de Bourgoyne and the rue (Saint-) Dominique lies behind the Palais Bourbon, once la Maison de la Révolution and now the National Assembly. Bourdon gives the number 1514, but the duration of his stay is unknown.

7 *Le Moniteur*, 29:360.

8 Bibliothèque historique de la ville de Paris: H. 89, *Table de P-V du Conseil des Anciens et du Conseil des Cinq-Cents*, vol. 1: A-L (Paris, 1808), 98.

9 The Constitution of Year III: Title II: no. 16 (Stewart, *A Documentary Survey of the French Revolution*, 577).

10 *Table de P-V du Conseil des Anciens et du Conseil des Cinq-Cents*, 1:115.

11 Léonard Bourdon, *Pétition au Conseil des Cinq-Cents sur l'Education Commune* (Paris, s.d./1797), BN, Rp. 7818. A brief notice of this appears in the *Journal des hommes libres*, no. 161, Brumaire 6, Year VI, BN, Lc² 734-35.

12 Léonard Bourdon, *Le voeu de la nature et de la Constitution de l'An III sur l'éducation générale . . .* (Paris, s.d./1799), BN, Rp. 13880.

13 Léon (*La Révolution Française et l'éducation technique*, 182, note 87) refers to an initial letter to the administration of the Seine on Ventôse 29, Year VII (March 19, 1799); Vauthier ("Léonard Bourdon et la Société des Jeunes Français," 343) has the presentation date as March 29.

14 Bourdon, *Le voeu de la nature*, 13. This passage, in its immediate context, is rightly cited by Pancera as the conclusion of his article "Léonard Bourdon . . . Editor," 29.

15 Kuscinski, *Dictionnaire des conventionnels*.

16 Stewart, *A Documentary Survey of the French Revolution*, no. 126, 616-19: decree relating to primary schools, November 17, 1794; Barnard, *Education and the French Revolution*, 174-77.

17 Ibid., 181-82; Palmer, *The Improvement of Humanity*, 236-41.

18 Vauthier, "Léonard Bourdon et la Société des Jeunes Français," 313, citing Michaud, *Biographie universelle, ancienne et moderne*, 305, note 1. The adverse letter from the administrators of the Seine to the Commission of the Council of Five Hundred, AN, Af. III, 107.223, is cited by Thibal, "La Société."

19 *Journal des débats, Conseil des Cinq-Cents*, Germinal 24, Year VII (April 13, 1799). See appendix 4.

20 Napoleon's letter of September 19, 1797, to Talleyrand (J.M. Thompson, *Napoleon's Letters* [London, 1964], 65).

21 See the standard biographies, notably Arnault, *Biographie nouvelle des contemporains*; Michaud, *Biographie universelle, ancienne et moderne*); and Hoeffer, *Nouvelle biographie générale* (1853).

22 Prudhomme, *Histoire générale et impartiale des erreurs, fautes, et crimes commis pendant la Révolution Française*, 4:170-84 and 5:191-203.

23 For these two occasions, see chapters 4 and 7 above.

24 Bonnemain, *Les chemises rouges*.

25 See note 21 above; J. Savant, *Les préfets de Napoléon* (Paris, 1958), 12, 252, 316; and J. Savant, *Les ministres de Napoléon* (Paris, 1959), 16.

26 M.J. Sydenham, "Le crime de 3 Nivôse (24 December 1800)," in J.F. Bosher, ed., *French Government and Society, 1500-1800: Essays in Memory of Alfred Cobban* (London, 1973), 295-320.

27 Ibid., 309, from A.C. Thibaudeau, *Bonaparte and the Consulate*, edited by G.K. Fortescue (London, 1908), 66.

28 Ibid.

29 Ibid., 310. Both Choudieu and Lecointre were in some danger, but both were able to live in retirement, the one in Holland and the other in the Seine-et-Marne.

30 Kuscinski, "Le Conventionnel Léonard Bourdon," 134.

31 Most, though not all, of the relevant volumes of the *Almanach* are available in the *Maclure Collection of Revolutionary Materials*, edited by J.D. Hardy, Jr., et al. (Philadelphia, 1966).

32 AN, F¹² 1084 (dossier Compiégne).

33 E. d'Hauterive, *La police secrète du première empire*, 2 vols. (Paris, 1908), 1:215. A reference in vol. 2 to the accidental death of "la femme Bourdon" is unfortunately not specific enough for firm identification.

34 As note 32 above.

35 Ibid., the second letter being attached to the first.

36 Here and below, the entries in Kuscinski, *Dictionnaire des conventionnels*, and in Kuscinski, "Le Conventionnel Léonard Bourdon," should be consulted jointly.

37 Baron P.F. Percy, *Journal des campaigns*, edited by E. Longin (Paris, 1904). See also J. Rieax and J. Hassenforder, *Histoire de service de santé et du Val-de-Grace* (Paris, 1951). Both volumes give useful background without referring to Bourdon.

38 My own initial visits to Toulon, to Val-de-Grace (where the archivists were most helpful), and to Vincennes were made in vain. Possibly further research would be more profitable, but the

fact that Bourdon was neither a doctor nor a soldier, but a civilian administrator, is a difficulty.

39 Kuscinski, *Dictionnaire des conventionnels.*

40 My perusal of the collection of the catalogues of autographs offered for sale over many years by E. Charavay and Company produced various interesting items but not that which Kuscinski mentions. The company does not keep old records of items purchased.

41 For these points, initial reference may be made to Sydenham, *The First French Republic*, 230, 240.

42 Percy, *Journal des campaigns*, 124-26.

43 Le Corbeiller, *Le Léopard de la Révolution*, 152.

Bibliography

Save for isolated exceptions, the sources and books listed here appear in the notes given to the text. They indicate both the vast amount of material that exists for the period of the French Revolution and the quality of the work done by others, particularly historians who have collected, classified, and published so much invaluable documentary evidence. Because my subject has involved the pursuit of much that proved peripheral to it, my debt to many previous scholars is considerable.

Although necessarily limited by time and circumstance, the research for this book has been complete in the sense that it became subject to the law of diminishing returns. Further avenues for exploration certainly exist, the principal possibilities being the *Minutier Central* and AD Seine (for further details of Bourdon's family and property); the records of the Committee of General Security and, at Vincennes, of the Commission for the Movement of the Armies (for more about the operation of la Société des Jeunes Français); and the Institut d'Histoire de la Révolution Française (for the sources used by A. Kuscinski). However desirable, such further inquiry is, in my view, unlikely to alter the substance of the present text to any significant extent.

Manuscript Sources

Archives Nationales

Minutier central des notaires, étude XCII, *liasse* 589: Bourdon des Planches, purchase of property in Languedoc, 1754. Études XI, *liasse* 827, 28 décembre 1790, and XVII, *liasse* 1062, 29 décembre 1790: Bourdon des Planches, payment of debt with reservation of property right.

Papiers privés: 137AP, 21-30: *Inventaire des archives du Maréchal Ney et de sa famille conservés aux Archives Nationales* (S. de Saint-Exupéry et C. de Tourtier, Paris, 1962), 190.

Series C: *Assemblées Nationales*

C 35.298: *Procès-verbaux de l'assemblée des Vainqueurs de la Bastille.*

C 165. *Pièces diverses:* 393.68: *Assemblée Electorale, Orléans.*

C 170. *Papiers de la haute cour d'Orléans,* inc. 419 (*Roland à Fournier,* September 7, 1792), and 420 (*Registre des grands procurateurs,* P-V Garran-Coulon).

Series D: *Comités des Assemblées*

D III. *Comité de Législation:* 119: *Jura:* 9 (Dole); 182, 28 (Dole, I).

D X 1: *Comité des Pensions: État des pensions . . . 1780-90, liasse* 8 (Calonne); see also D X 2 and the *État nominatif des pensions sur le trésor royal, 1789* (1:414).

D XLI: *Correspondance:* 21.40.6: *Adresse, District de Lons-le-Saunier.*

Series F: *Versements des Ministères*

F1: 1: *Ministère de l'Intérieur: Correspondance: Jura* I.

F[1b] 156/39: *Intérieur: Administration Générale, fonctionnaires préfectorale, An VIII—1880. Répertoire nominatif.*

F[1c] III, *Loiret* 5: *Compte-rendu au Directoire du District d'Orléans,* Thermidor, An III.

F[7]: *Police Générale:* 4612 (dossier Bourdon); 4432: *Troubles, conspirations;* 6151: *Affaires politiques: Bureau particulier: Léonard Bourdon à Hambourg;* 6504, including *Dossier de Fournier l'Américain.*

F[12]: *Commerce et Industrie:* 1084; *Écoles d'Arts et Métiers, dossier Compiégne.*

F[17]: *Mélanges:* 1012: *Déspenses, Instruction publique;* 1309: *Comité d'Instructon Publique de la législative: enquête . . . de 1790-91:* fol. 1: *Léonard Bourdon, lettre au président de l'Assemblée Nationale,* to which is appended the *Royal Order in Council of 5 October 1788, et al.;* 6745: *Instruction publique, enseignement secondaire.*

Series O[1]: *Maison du roi sous l'ancien régime*

500: 467 and 484: *Correspondance* September 1789.

Series Q[2]: *Domaines*

Biens nationaux: 120.5: *Saint-Martin-des-Champs.*

Series S: *Biens des établissements réligieux supprimés*

S4: 639: *Augustines, r. neuve St.-Étienne du Mont.*

Series W: *Juridictions*

Tribunal révolutionnaire: Affaires jugées: 295.246.15. *Manuel,* P.L.

Series AA: *Lettres diverses*

AA 49: 1404.12: Bourdon, letter to the president of the Electoral Assembly of Paris, September 18, 1792.

Series AF II: *Comité de Salut Public*

AF II: 17.1012: *Instruction publique;* AF II 67: *Instruction publique;* AF II 112: *Missions: Jura:* 840.6 and 8; 182: *Bureau du Midi,* 27 and 28; 247: *Guerre: Armée du Rhin:* including 48-56 (returns of recruitment, etc., from the Jura, 1793).

Series AF III: *Directoire exécutif*

AF III. 107: *Instruction publique* (financial reports 233-35, and 225. 15: *Observations relatives à l'indemnité du citoyen Bourdon*); 341. 49-50: letter/reply, Bourdon to Directors, Nivôse 30, Year IV, 485. *Société des Jeunes Français, rapport présenté par le ministre de l'intérieur, le . . . germinal An IV.*

Series BB: *Ministère de la Justice*

BB³ *Affaires criminelles*: 19.5. *Haute cour nationale*, inc. *P-V de MM. les commissaires*, September 10, 1792; and 29: *Membres de la Convention*, dossier Choudieu; 78: *Justice Révolutionnaire*: dossier A.-J.-D. Bourdon.

Series AD: *Textes imprimées*

Administratives: VIII: *Instruction publique*, 29 (Prieuré Saint-Martin).

AD Côte-d'Or

L 26: *Directoire*, fol. 87.
L 364: *Dénunciation faite par les six sections de Dijon.*
L 376: *Arrété* issued by Bourdon and Prost, April 2, 1793.
L 1268: *Proclamation*. . . . See also L 26: 941, and L 2: 10.44.

AD Jura

L 1087: *Registre du conseil.*

Archives des Affaires Étrangères

Correspondance diplomatique de Hambourg, vols. 112, 113, and Supplément.

Bibliothèque de l'arsenal

MS 12478: *Écrou de la Bastille.*

Bibliothèque historique de la ville de Paris

Imprimé: H. 89, *Table de P-V du Conseil des Anciens et du Conseil des Cinq-Cents*, vol. 1: A-L (1808).

Bibliothèque municipale de Dijon

MS 1660.203: L. Baudot: *Mouvements revolutionnaires à Dijon.*

Bibliothèque municipale d'Orléans

MS 565.85: *L'abbé* Pataud, *Notes relatives à l'histoire d'Orléans.*

Bibliothèque municipale de Provins

Registre du comité municipal de Provins (for August 1789); *Registre de correspondance* (for the same, and for *Léonard Bourdon, commissaire du gouvernement pour l'execution de la loi du 22 Brumaire: Melun, 30 Brumaire An 4* (MS 181?). (See Anne Marzin, "Révolution de 1789 et manuscrits à la Bibliothèque municipale de Provins," *Provins et sa région*, no. 143, *Bulletin de la Société historique et archéologique de Provins* [1989].)

Bibliothèque nationale
The Charavay Collection of Autographs, XXXVIII, carton 290, no. 42826.

Primary Sources, Printed
(Unless otherwise stated, all references are to publication in Paris.)

Pamphlets
Unless otherwise stated, references are to the Bibliothèque nationale (BN) and to the Croker and Fortesque Collections in the British Library (BL). Occasional reference is also made to the microfilm Maclure Collection of revolutionary materials (University of Pennsylania).

Publications of the Bourdon Family (given, as far as possible, in their chronological order of publication)

Bourdon, Léonard

Compte que les RP visiteurs et les six députés de la province de Normandie rendent au chapitre général . . . consultation déliberé à Paris, le 29 avril 1781, BN, Ld^{16} 354.

Plan d'un établissement d'éducation nationale (Orléans, 1788), BN, Rz 1767.

Aux États-Généraux: subsistence et impôt (with L.-J. Bourdon des Planches, s.l.n.d., 1788-89), BL, FR 257.21, and BN, Rp. 3808, and BL, FR 257.21.

Aux États-Généraux: idées sur l'éducation nationale (s.l.n.d., 1788-89), BL, FR 257.2, and BN, R 1452.

Developpement de la motion faite dans l'Assemblée des Tiers-État de ville de Paris le jeudi 7 mai (s.l.n.d., 1789), BN, Lb^{39} 1698.

Mémoire sur l'instruction et sur l'education nationale, avec un project de décret et de règlement constitutionnel pour les jeunes gens . . . suivis d'un essai sur la manière de concilier la surveillance nationale avec les droits d'un père sur ses enfants dans l'éducation des héritiers présomptifs de la couronne (An II/1790-91), BN, R 22944.

Société des Jeunes français: base d'une école centrale d'expérience (1791), BL, 936, f. 12(17).

Sur l'éducation nationale: extrait d'un travail dont l'Assemblée Nationale a chargé son Comité de Constitution de faire lui le rapport (Paris, s.d.), BN, Rp. 10608.

Idées sur l'éducation d'un prince royal (s.d./1791), BN, Lb^{39} 5167.

Société des Jeunes Français: École républicaine établie au mois de mai 1792 au ci-devant Prieuré Saint-Martin-des-Champs par Léonard Bourdon (1792), BL, R 366.5 (see also AN, AD XVIII, 295.36).

Adresse de la Section des Gravilliers à l'Assemblée Nationale, présentée le 8 juillet 1792 (signed Léonard Bourdon, président; BN, Le^{33} 3 X 62).

Rapport des commissaires envoyés auprès de la haute cour nationale à Orléans (with Prosper Dubail: September 1792), BN, Lb^{39} 10909. See also AN, BB^3 19.15.

À Marat (1793 for 1792), BN, Lb^{41} 2304.

Projet de réglement pour la Convention, présenté au nom des commissaires (1792), BL, R 96.1.

Opinion sur le jugement de Louis Capet, dit Louis XVI (1792), BN, Le^{37} 2.G.105.

Réponse à Charles Villette (1792), BN, Lb^{40} 732.

Seconde opinion sur le jugement de Louis Capet (1792), BN, Le^{37} 2.g.199.

Copie de la Déclaration faite aux autorités constituées d'Orléans le 17 mars 1793 (1793), BN, Lb^{41} 587.

À ses commettans (1793), BL, F 1026.3.

Exposé des faits relatifs à l'assassinat commis à Orléans le 16 mars 1793, et réponse au rapport au Comité de Législation (1793), BN, Le^{38} 259.

Projet de décret sur l'éducation nationale (1793), BN, Le^{38} 373.

Discours sur l'instruction commune prononcé dans le séance du 3 juillet 1793 (s.d./1793; read: 30 juillet), BN, Le^{38} 322.

Rapport de Léonard Bourdon prononcé le 1 août 1793 (1793), BN, Le^{38} 372.

Organisation des greniers nationaux: rapport fait au nom des Comités d'Agriculture et de Salut Publique (s.d./1793), BN, Le^{38} 423.

Le tombeau des imposteurs et l'inauguration du Temple de la Vérité: sans-culottide dramatique en trois actes mêlée de musique par les citoyens Léonard Bourdon, Moline, et Valcour (Paris, An II/1793), BL, 11738 k 2 (4).

Recueil des actions héroïques et civiques des républicains français (An II/1793), BN, Lc^2 39.

Rapport fait au nom du Comité d'Instruction Publique sur le fête du cinquième sans-culottide (s.d./1794), BN, Le^{38} 940.

À ses concitoyens (An III/1795), BN, Lb^{41} 1393; also BL, F22*:23, another copy.

Convention Nationale, compte de l'emploi des sommes reçues par Léonard Bourdon et Prost . . . mars 14 à mai 24, 1793 (Paris, Pluviôse, An III), Maclure Collection, no. 1157.

Discours prononcé le 9 Thermidor An IV (Brussels, 1796), microfilm, University of British Columbia Library, Vancouver.

Petition au Conseil des Cinq-Cents sur l'Éducation Commune (s.d./1797), BN, Rp. 7818.

Le voeu de la nature et de la Constitution de l'An III sur l'éducation générale . . . (s.d./1799), BN, Rp. 13880.

Bourdon des Planches, L.-J. (Selected)

Projet pour la réunion des postes aux chevaux aux messageries (s.l.n.d., c. 1765), BN, Lf^{92} 19.

Lettre à l'auteur des "Observations sur le commerce des grains" (Amsterdam, 1775), BL, F 257.1.

Projet nouveau sur la manière de faire utilement en France le commerce des grains (Brussels, 1785), BL, FR 257.2 and BN, R 2295, and, associated with this, a prospectus Le monopole altéré (BN, R 29759).

Code fraternal (s.l.n.d., 1787), BL, F 474.

Bases pour taxer le pain (s.l.n.d., 1788), BL, R 440.

Au roi: lettre presentée à sa majesté, le 9 déc. 1788 (London and Paris, 1789), BN, Lb^{30} 11757.

Aux États-Généraux: subsistence et impôt (with Léonard Bourdon, as above).

Association patriotique: projet de décret . . . sur les grains et les finances (s.l.n.d., 1789), BN, Sp. 1648.

Dangers du serment fédératif relativement aux subsistences et moyen d'y parer (1790), BN, Lb^{39} 3731.

Réclamation d'un citoyen électeur de 1789 et de 1790 pour une organisation dans le commerce des grains (s.d./1791), BN, Rp. 8551.

L'anti-economiste, ou moyens de rédimer les personnes et les biens du joug des impositions (1791), BL, FR 261.17 and BN, Lb^{39} 9708.

Adresse à la Convention Nationale sur la subsistence et sur les impositions (1794-95), BN, Lb^{41} 1612.

Du pain, du pain, et moyen d'en avoir: lettre sur la subsistence et sur les impositions et finances à Cambon (An III), BN, Lb^{41} 1613.

Bourdon de Vatry, M.-A.

M.-A. Bourdon, *À Dumaine* (Paris, 1794), BL, 982.12.

Other Pamphlets

Adresse de la Commune de Dole, BL, F 987.99.

Adresse de la Société des Jeunes Français, 24 mars 1793 (Paris, 1793), BL, RF 57.15.

Arrêté du 23 août 1792 (Assemblée Electorale, Paris) relatif à l'inculpation faite à M. Léonard Bourdon, BN, Lb⁴⁰ 1154 g*.

Bergoeing à ses commettans (Caen, 1793), BN, Lb⁴¹ 715.

Braeckenier, Antoine Joseph. *Mémoire du citoyen Antoine Joseph Braeckenier, rédacteur de l'impartial Bruxellois, défendeur, contre Léonard Bourdon, actuellement en cette ville, demandeur* (Brussels, 1796), BL, F 969.16.

Dénunciation faite par les six sections de la Commune de Dijon . . . des crimes commis par Léonard Bourdon et Pioche-Fer Bernard de Saintes (Dijon, An III), BL, F 846.11.

Expédition de Provins et aventure d'un gentilhomme enfermé dans une cave (Paris, 1789), BL, F 424.

Lettre écrit de Lons-le-Saunier le 29 juin 1793 par un habitant du Jura (Lons-le-Saunier, 1793), BL, F 240.42.

Observations de la Municipalité d'Orléans (Orléans, 1793), BN, Lb⁴¹ 587.

Pétition à la Convention par les citoyennes d'Orléans (1793), BL, FR 5722.

Procès-verbal de ce qui est passé dans l'assemblée des Vainqueurs de la Bastille tenue avant-hier aux quinze-vingts (1790), BN, Lb³⁹ 9010.

Procès-verbal du Conseil-Général de la Commune d'Orléans (Orléans, 1792), BL, Tab. 443 a 3(7).

Journals

Bulletin du Tribunal Révolutionnaire, part 4, no. 35 (Paris, 1794).

Journal de Paris, no. 225, August 12, 1792.

Journal de Perlet, no. 296.

Journal des débats des amis de la Constitution, no. 99, September 3, 1792.

Journal des hommes libres, no. 161, Brumaire 6, An VI/October 26, 1797.

La Sentinelle, no. 52, August 21, 1792.

Le Courrier français, no. 244, July-August 1792.

Le Courrier de Versailles à Paris, no. 29, August 5, 1789.

Le Moniteur: réimpression de l'ancien Moniteur (32 vols., 1847-79) and, where shown, *Gazette national ou moniteur universel* (9 vols., 1789-1810).

L'Orateur du peuple, Vendémiaire 23, Brumaire 19, Ventôse 25, Germinal 4, An III.

Le Patriote français, journal libre (1789-93).

Le Publiciste, nos. 147, 148 (Marat: *Collection complète du journal* [Tokyo, 1967]).

Révolutions de France et de Brabant (1789-92).

Published Collections of Documents

Aulard, F.-A. *La Société des Jacobins: recueil de documents*. 6 vols. Paris, 1889-97.

_____. *Recueil des actes du Comité de Salut Publique*. 28 vols. Paris, 1889ff. vol. 1, Paris, 1966.

_____. *Supplément* to *Recueil des actes du Comité de Salut Publique*. Vol. 1. Paris, 1966.

_____. *Paris pendant la réaction thermidorienne et sous le Directoire*. 2 vols. Paris, 1898.

Bailly, J.S., and H. Duveyrier, eds. *Procès-verbaux des séances et délibérations de l'Assemblée Générale de électeurs de Paris*. 3 vols. Paris, 1790.

Beik, P.H. *The French Revolution*. New York, 1970.

Bouloiseau, M., G. Lefebvre, and A. Soboul, eds. *Oeuvres de Maximilien Robespierre*. Tomes 6-10: *Discours*. Paris, 1950-67.

Buchez, P.J.B., and P.L. Roux. *Histoire parlementaire de la Révolution Française*. 40 vols. Paris, 1834.

Dawson, P. *The French Revolution*. Englewood Cliffs, NJ, 1967.

Debidour, A. *Recueil des actes du Directoire exécutif*. Vol. 1. Paris, 1890.

Fribourg, A., ed. *Discours de Danton*. Paris, 1910.

Funck-Bretano, F. *Histoire générale de Paris, 1659-1789*. Paris, 1903.

Gerbaux, F., and Ch. Schmidt. *Procès-verbaux des Comités d'Agriculture et de Commerce de la Constituente, de la Législative, et de la Convention*. 4 vols., Paris, 1906-10.

Godechot, J. *La pensée révolutionnaire en France et en Europe, 1780-99*. Paris, 1964.

Guigue, G. *Procès-verbaux de la Commission Populaire du Rhône-et-Loire*. Trevaux, 1899.

Guillaume, J. *Procès-verbaux du Comité d'Instruction Publique de l'Assemblée Législative*. Paris, 1889.

_____. *Procès-verbaux du Comité d'Instruction Publique de la Convention*. 6 vols. Paris, 1891-1907.

Hardman, J. *French Revolution Documents*. Vol. 2: *1792-95*. Oxford, 1973.

Lacroix, S. *Actes de la Commune de Paris pendant la Révolution*. Première série. 7 vols. Paris, 1894-98).

Libois, H. *Délibérations de la Société Populaire de Lons-le-Saunier du 5 novembre 1791 au 25 juin 1793*. Lons-le-Saunier, 1897.

Markov, W., ed. *Jacques Roux: Scripta et Acta*. Berlin, 1969.

Markov, W., and A. Soboul. *Die Sansculloten von Paris*. Berlin, 1957.

Maclure Collection of Revolutionary Materials. Catalogue. Edited by J.D. Hardy, Jr., et al. Philadelphia, 1966.

Michon, G. *Correspondance de Maximilien et Augustin Robespierre*. Paris, 1926.

Roberts, J.M. *French Revolution Documents*. Vol. 1: *1787-92*. Paris, 1966.

Schmidt, A. *Paris pendant la Révolution d'après les rapports de la police secrète, 1789-1800*. 2 vols. Paris, 1880.

_____. *Tableau de la Révolution Française*. 2 vols., Leipzig, 1867-70.

Soboul, A. *Le procès de Louis XVI*. Collection Archives. Paris, 1966.

Stewart, J.H. *A Documentary Survey of the French Revolution*. New York, 1951.

Thompson, J.M. *French Revolution Documents, 1789-1794*. Paris, 1948.

_____. *Napoleon's Letters*. London, 1964.

Tourneux, M. *Procès-verbaux de la Commune de Paris, 1792-1793*. Paris, 1894.

Tuetey, A. *L'assistance publique à Paris pendant la Révolution*. 4 vols. Paris, 1897-1917.

Tuetey, L. *Procès-verbaux de la Commission des Arts*. 2 vols. Paris, 1912-28.

Memoirs

Bachaumont, L.P. *Mémoires secrètes*. 31 vols. London, 1866.

Bailly, J.S. *Mémoires*. Edited by St. A. Berville and J.F. Barrière. 3 vols. Paris, 1821-22.

Barras, P.-F.-J.-N. *Memoirs of Barras*. Edited by G. Duruy. London, 1895.

C.-A., Méda. *Précis historique des événements qui se sont passés dans le soirée du neuf thermidor*. Paris, 1802.

Choudieu, P.-R. *Mémoires et notes de Choudieu*. Edited by V. Barrucand. Paris, 1897.

Dusaulx, J. *Mémoires sur le 14 juillet*. Edited by Berville and Barrière. Paris, 1821.

Duval, G. *Souvenirs de la Terreur de 1788 à 1793.* 4 vols. Paris, 1841-42.

Fournier, C. [Claude]. *Mémoires secrètes de Fournier l'Américain.* Edited by F.-A. Aulard. Paris, 1890.

Greatheed, B. *An Englishman in Paris, 1803.* Edited by J.P.T. Bury and J.C. Barry. London, 1953.

Grégoire, *l'abbé. Mémoires.* Vol. 2. Paris, 1857.

Levasseur, R. *Mémoires de Réné Levasseur (de la Sarthe), ex-conventionnel.* 4 vols. Paris, 1829.

Méda: *see* C.-A., *supra.*

Neuilly, Comte de. *Souvenirs et correspondance.* Paris, 1865.

Paganel, P. *Essai historique et critique sur la Révolution Française.* Vol. 2. Paris, 1815.

Percy, Baron P.F. *Journal des campaigns.* Edited by E. Longin. Paris, 1904.

Perroud, C., ed. *Mémoires de Madame Roland.* 2 vols. Paris, 1905.

Pitra, L.-G. *Électeur: fragment des mémoires inédites.* Edited by J. Flammermont. Paris, 1892.

Simpson, M.C.M., ed. *Reminiscences of a Regicide: Sergent Marceau.* London, 1889.

Thibaudeau, A.C. *Mémoires sur la Convention et le Directoire.* 2 vols. Paris, 1824.

_____. *Bonaparte and the Consulate.* Edited by G.K. Fortescue. London, 1908.

Other Contemporary Sources

Almanach Royal (1774-91); *National* (1792-1802); *Impérial* (1805-13).

Archives Parlementaires de 1787 à 1860, première série, 1787 à 1799. Edited by M.J. Madival and M.E. Laurent. 2nd ed. 94 vols. Paris, 1879-1913.

Charpentier and Manuel, P.L. *La Bastille dévoilée.* 4 vols. Paris, 1789.

Charavay, J., E. Charavay, and N. Charavay. Catalogue of Autographs: *Bourdon, Léonard du Loiret* (l.a.s., October 5, 1790), BL, SC 672.17246.

Courtois, E.B. *Rapport fait au nom des commissaires chargés de l'examen des papiers trouvés chez Robespierre et ses complices.* Paris, An III. Also published in *Papiers inédits trouvés chez Robespierre.* 3 vols. Paris, 1828.

Journal des débats, Conseil des Cinq-Cents. Particularly no. 342, Germinal 24, An VIII/April 13, 1799.

Jullien, J. *Rapport . . . sur les administrations rebelles.* Paris, 1793.

Procès-verbaux de l'Assemblée Législative. 1791-92.

Procès-verbaux de la Convention. 72 vols. 1792-95.

Secondary Sources
Dictionaries and Works of Reference

Antoine, M. *Le gouvernement et l'administration sous Louis XV: dictionnaire biographique.* Paris, 1978.

Arnault, A.V. *Biographie nouvelle des contemporains.* Paris, 1821.

Aulard, F.-A. *La grande encyclopédie.* Paris, 1886.

Balteau, J. *Dictionnaire de biographie française.* Paris, 1936.

Biographical Anecdotes of the Founders of the French Republic. 2 vols., London, 1797-98, BL, 613d 32.

Biographie moderne ou galerie historique. Paris, 1815.

Boursin, E. *Dictionnaire de la Révolution Française.* Paris, 1893.

Claudron, F. *Inventaire sommaire des archives départementales: Côte-d'Or, periode révolutionnaire, série L.* Dijon, 1913.

Chaix d'Est-Ange, C. *Dictionnaire des familles françaises.* Vol. 3. Paris, 1906/1983.

Guiffrey, J. *Les conventionnels*. Paris, 1889.

Hoeffer, Dr. *Nouvelle biographie générale*. Paris, 1853.

Kuscinski, A. "Le Conventionnel Léonard Bourdon." *La Révolution Française*, 16 (January-June 1889): 133-34.

_____. *Dictionnnaire des conventionnels*. Paris, 1916.

Marion, M., *Dictionnaire des institutions de la France aux XVIIe et XVIIIe siècles*. Paris, 1968.

Martin, A., and G. Walter, *Catalogue de l'histoire de la Révolution Française*. 6 vols. Paris, 1936-55.

Michaud, M. *Biographie universelle, ancienne et moderne*. 45 vols. Paris, 1835. Supplement to ed. of 1812.

Mousnier, R. *Les institutions de la France sous la monarchie absolue*. Translated by A. Goldhammer (Paris, 1980 ed.). Vol. 2. Chicago, 1984.

Petite biographie conventionelle. Paris, 1815.

Pigallet, M. *Inventaire sommaire des AD: Département du Doubs, L 55*, Délibérations du conseil*. Besançon, 1921.

Prevost, M., and Roman d'Amat. *Dictionnaire de biographie française*. Paris, 1933/1954.

Rabbe, A. *Biographie universelle*. Paris, 1834.

Robinet, Dr. J. *Dictionnaire historique et biographique*. Paris, 1899.

Scott, Samuel F., and Barry Rothaus. *Historical Dictionary of the French Revolution*. 2 vols. Westport, CT, 1985.

Sellier, C., and P. Dorbec. *Guide explicatif du Musée Carnavalet*. Paris, 1903.

Soboul, A. *Dictionnaire historique de la Révolution Française*. Paris, 1989.

_____, and R. Monnier. *Répertoire du personnel sectionnaire Parisien en l'An II*. Paris, 1985.

Tourneux, M. *Bibliographie de l'histoire de Paris pendant la Révolution Française*. 5 vols. Paris, 1890-1913.

Tuetey, A. *Répertoire général des sources manuscrits de l'histoire de Paris pendant la Révolution Française*. 11 vols. Paris, 1890-1914.

Works Concerning Education

Barnard, H.C. *Education and the French Revolution*. Cambridge, 1969.

Bernfeld, Siegfried. "Léonard Bourdons System der Anstaldisziplin, 1788-1795." *Zeitschrift fur Kinderchung*, 36 (Berlin 1930): 153-69.

Chartier, R., D. Julia, and M. Compère. *L'éducation en France du XVIe au XVIIIe siècle*. Paris, 1976.

Hennet, L. *Les compagnies de cadets-gentilhommes et les écoles militaires*. Paris, 1889.

Julia, D. *Les Trois couleurs de tableau noir: la Révolution*. Paris, 1981.

Kennedy, E. *A Cultural History of the French Revolution*. New Haven, CT, 1989.

Léon, A. *La Révolution Française et l'éducation technique*. Paris, 1968.

Monnier, Raymonde. *L'Espace publique démocratique: essai sur l'opinion à Paris de la Révolution au Directoire*, particularly 147-52. Paris, 1994.

Palmer, R.R. *The Improvement of Humanity: Education and the French Revolution*. Princeton, NJ, 1985.

Pancera, C. "Léonard Bourdon (1754-1807), Editor of the 'Collection of Heroic and Civic Actions of French Republicans.'" *History of European Ideas*, 14, no. 1 (1922): 13-33.

Stuebig, F. "Erziehung und Gleichheit: Die Konzepte der 'Éducation Commune' in der Franzosischen Revolution." In *EGS Texte*. Ravensburg, 1974.

Thibal, Agnès. "La Société des Jeunes Français de Léonard Bourdon: une expérience pédagogique sous la Révolution." 2 vols. Dissertation (maîtise d'histoire), Université Paris–I, 1986.

Vauthier, G. "Léonard Bourdon et la Société des Jeunes Français." *Annales Révolutionnaires*, 5 (1912): 331-43.

Vignery, R.J. *The French Revolution and the Schools: The Educational Policies of the Mountain, 1792-94*. Madison, WI, 1965.

Other Secondary Sources

Aftalion, F. *L'economie de la Révolution Française*. Paris, 1987.

Ashbourne, Lord. *Grégoire and the French Revolution*. London, 1932.

Balossier, J. *La commission extraordinaire des douze (18 mai-31 mai 1793)*. Paris, 1986.

Baulig, H. "Anacharsis Cloots, conventionnel." *La Révolution Française*, 61 (1901): 116.

Bazin, N. "Les suspects dans le District de Dijon." Résumé du mémoire. *Annales de Bourgoyne*, 41 (1963): 63-75.

Bianchi, S. "La déchristianisation en l'An II." *AHRF*, 50 (1978): 341-71.

Bienvenu, R.T. *The Ninth of Thermidor*. Oxford, 1968.

Biro, S.S. *The German Policy of Revolutionary France*. 2 vols. Cambridge, MA, 1957.

Bonnemain, A.J.T. *Les chemises rouges*. Paris, An VII/1799.

Bosher, J.F. "The Premiers Commis des Finances in the Reign of Louis XVI." *French Historical Studies*, 3 (1964): 475-94.

Bourdin, I. *Les sociétés populaires à Paris pendant la Révolution*. Paris, 1937.

Bourne, Henry E. "Improvising a Government in Paris in July 1789." *American Historical Review*, 10 (1905): 280-308.

Bourquelot, Felix. *Histoire de Provins*. 2 vols. Paris and Provins, 1839-40.

Braesch, F. *La Commune du dix août, 1792*. Paris, 1911.

Brelot, J. "L'insurrection fédéraliste dans le Jura en 1793." *Bulletin de la Fédération des Sociétés Savantes Franche Comtois*, 2 (1955): 73-102.

Calvet, H. *Un instrument de la Terreur à Paris: le Comité de Salut Public ou de surveillance du Département de Paris*. Paris, 1941.

————. "Remarques sur la participation des sections au mouvement du 31 mai-2 juin 1793." *AHRF*, 5 (1928): 366-69.

Campardon, E. *Le Tribunal Révolutionnaire de Paris*. 2 vols. Paris, 1886.

Caron, P. *Les Massacres de Septembre*. Paris, 1935.

————. *La première Terreur: les missions du conseil exécutif provisoire et de la Commune de Paris*. 2 vols. Paris, 1950-53.

———— *Paris pendant la Terreur*. Paris, 1943.

Cassagnac, G. de. *Histoire des Girondins et les Massacres de Septembre*. 2 vols. Paris, 1860.

C.E. (Charmouton), *Histoire de la persécution révolutionnaire dans le Département du Jura, 1789-1800*. Lons-le-Saunier, 1893.

Charavay, E. *L'Assemblée Électorale de Paris*. 3 vols. Paris, 1890-1905.

Chassin, Ch. L. *Les élections et les cahiers de Paris en 1789*. 4 vols. Paris, 1888-89.

Cobb, Richard C. *Les armées révolutionnaires*. Paris, 1961.

————. "La mission de Siblot au Havre-Marat." *Annales de Normandie* (1953): 177-78.

Cobban, A. *A History of Modern France*. Vol. 1, *1715-1799*. Harmondsworth, 1961.

Le Corbeiller, Armand. *Le Léopard de la Révolution: l'affaire d'Orléans, 1793*. Paris, 1938.

Dauban, C.A. *La démagogie à Paris*. Paris, 1868.

————. *Paris en 1794 et en 1795: histoire de la rue, du club, et de la famine*. Paris, 1868.

Day, C.R. "The Making of Mechanical Engineers in France: The Écoles d'Arts et Métiers, 1803-1914." *French Historical Studies*, 10 (1978): 439-60.

Debal, J. *Histoire d'Orléans et de son terroir*. Vol. 2: J. *Vassort et C. Poitou*. Roanne, 1982.

Deville, P. Sainte-Claire, *La Commune de l'An II*. Paris, 1946.

Dotson, Craig W. "The Paris Jacobin Club in the French Revolution." Unpublished doctoral dissertation, Queen's University, Kingston, ON, 1974.

Doyle, W. *The Oxford History of the French Revolution*. Oxford, 1989.

Dubois, E. *Histoire de la Révolution dans l'Ain*. 3 vols. Bourg, 1933.

Dupuy, C. *Les électeurs parisiens de 1792 dans la Section des Gravilliers*. Mâitrise, Paris–I, 1988.

Durieux, J. *Les Vainqueurs de la Bastille*. Paris, 1911.

Fitzsimmons, Michael P. *The Parisian Order of Barristers and the French Revolution*. Cambridge, MA, and London, 1987.

————. *The Remaking of France*. Cambridge, 1994.

Franklin, A. *Les anciens plans de Paris*. 2 vols. Paris, 1820.

Gallacher, J. "Recruitment in the District of Poitiers." *French Historical Studies*, 3 (1963): 246-67.

Gendron, F. *La Jeunesse Dorée*. Québec, 1987.

Germani, I. *Jean-Paul Marat, Hero and Anti-Hero of the French Revolution*. Lewiston, NY, and Queenston, ON, 1992.

Giradot, J. *Le Département de la Haute-Saône pendant le Révolution*. Vol. 2. Vesoul, 1973.

Godechot, J. *The Taking of the Bastille*. Translated by J. Stewart. London, 1970.

Goodwin, A. "The Underworld of the French Revolutionary Terror." In *Memoirs and Proceedings of the Manchester Literary and Philosophical Society*, 38-56. Manchester, 1954-55.

Gotlib, R. "Bourdon, L.J.-J. Léonard." In A. Soboul, *Dictionnaire historique de la Révolution Française*. Paris, 1939.

Gottschalk, L., and M. Maddox. *Lafayette in the French Revolution: Through the October Days*. Chicago, 1969.

Gough, H. *The Newspaper Press in the French Revolution*. Chicago, 1988.

Groppi, A. "Sur la structure socio-professionelle de la Section des Gravilliers." *AHRF*, 232 (1978): 246-76.

Hampson, N. "François Chabot and His Plot." *Royal Historical Society Transactions*, 5th series, 26 (1976): 1-14.

————. *A Social History of the French Revolution*. London, 1963.

Hauterive, E. d'. *La police secrète du première empire*. 2 vols. Paris, 1908.

Hayes, R. *Ireland and Irishmen in the French Revolution*. Dublin, 1932.

Hennet, L. *L'état militaire de France pour l'année 1793*. Paris, 1903.

Hesdin, R. *The Journal of a Spy in Paris*. London, 1895.

Huguenay, L. *Les clubs dijonnais sous la Révolution*. Rpt. Geneva, 1978.

Huot, P. "Les prisonniers d'Orléans." *Revue d'Alsace* (1868): 97-114.

Janillon, F.T. *Versailles et Quiberon*. Paris, 1916.

Jaume, L. *Le discours jacobin et la démocratie*. Paris, 1989.

Jordan, D.P. *The King's Trial*. Berkeley, CA, 1979.

Kates, Gary. *The Cercle Social, the Girondins, and the French Revolution*. Princeton, NJ, 1985.

Kennedy, Michael L. *The Jacobin Clubs in the French Revolution*. 3 vols. Princeton, NJ, 1982-84.

Kennedy, W. Benjamin. "Duckett, Wm., 1768-1841." In J.O. Baylen and N.J. Gossman, eds., *Biographical Dictionary of Modern British Radicals, 1770-1830*. Sussex, 1978.

Lambert, *l'abbé*. "Relation." *L'Ami de la religion, Journal ecclesiastique, politique, et litteraire*, 136 (1848): 239-40.

Lefebvre, G. *The Directory*. Translated by R. Baldick. Paris, 1937; London, 1964.

_____. *Études Orléanaises, 1789-An IV*. 2 vols. Paris, 1962-63.

_____. *La France sous le Directoire, 1795-1799*. Paris, 1977/1984.

_____. *La Révolution Française*. Paris, 1963. Translated as *The French Revolution*. 2 vols. London and New York, 1962, 1964.

_____. *The Thermidorians*. Translated by R. Baldick. London, 1965.

Leith, James A. *Media and Revolution*. Toronto, 1968.

Lenôtre, G. (i.e., Gosselin, L.L.T.). *Paris révolutionnaire: vieilles maisons, vieux papiers*. 2ᵉ série, Paris, 1903; 6ᵉ série, Paris, 1930.

_____. *The Tribunal of the Terror*. Translated by F. Lees. London, 1909.

Libois, P. *Les représentants du peuple Prost et Lejeune dans le Jura en l'An II*. Lons-le-Saunier, 1936.

Lottin, D. *Recherches historique sur la Ville d'Orléans*. 2 vols. Orléans, 1838.

Mansfield, P.L. "The Missions of Collot d'Herbois: A Study in His Political Career." Unpublished doctoral dissertation, Macquarie University, NSW, 1985.

Markov, W. "Babeuf, le babeuvisme et les intellectuels allemands, 1796-97." In *Colloqué international de Stockholm, 21 août 1960: Babeuf et les problèmes du babeuvisme*. Paris, 1963.

Masson, F. *Le Département des Affaires Étrangères pendant la Révolution, 1787-1804*. Paris, 1877.

Mathiez, A. *After Robespierre: The Thermidorian Reaction*. Translated by C.A. Phillips. New York, 1965.

_____. *Le Directoire*. Paris, 1924.

_____. *Le dix août*. Paris, 1934.

_____. *La Révolution et l'église*. Paris, 1910.

_____. *La Révolution Française*. Paris, 1922.

_____. *La vie chère et le mouvement social sous la Terreur*. Paris, 1927.

McManners, J. *The French Revolution and the Church*. London, 1969.

Mitchell, C.J. *The French Legislative Assembly of 1791*. Leiden, 1988.

Monin, H. *L'État de Paris en 1789*. Paris, 1899.

Monnier, D. "Annales semi-contemporains." In *Annuaires du Département du Jura*. Lons-le-Saunier, 1849ff.

Mortimer-Ternaux, M. *Histoire de la Terreur*. 6 vols. Paris, 1861-67.

Moussoir, G. *Le conventionnel Hyacinthe Richaud*. Paris, 1897.

Noel, Étienne. *Jean-Baptiste Noel, conventionnel*. Cosne-sur Loire, 1966.

Parker, H.T. *An Administrative Bureau during the Old Regime: The Bureau of Commerce and Its Relations to French Industry from May 1781 to November 1783*. London and Toronto, 1993.

Palmer, R.R. *Twelve Who Ruled*. Princeton, NJ, 1941.

Passy, L. *Frochet, préfect de la Seine*. Evreux and Paris, 1867.

Patrick, A. *The Men of the First French Republic*. Baltimore, 1972.

Perrin, M. "Notes sur Pierre-Gabriel Ebrard." In *Travaux de la Société d'Émulation du Jura, 1848-50*, 10-30. Lons-le-Saunier, 1851.

Pisani, P. *L'église de Paris et la Révolution*. Vol. 2. Paris, 1909.

Popkin, J.D. *The Right-Wing Press in France, 1792-1800*. Chapel Hill, NC, 1980.

Proquenard, C. "La Société du Panthéon." *La Révolution Française*, 33 (1897): 318-48.

Prudhomme, L.M. *Histoire générale et impartiale des erreurs, fautes, et crimes commis pendant la Révolution Française*. 5 vols. 1797.

Puffeney, E. *Histoire de Dole*. Besançon, 1882.

Ravitch, N. "Liberalism, Catholicism, and the Abbé Grégoire." *Church History*, 36 (1967): 419-39.

Reinhard, M. *Nouvelle histoire de Paris: la Révolution, 1789-1799*. Paris, 1931.

Renouvier, J.M.B. *Histoire de l'art pendant la Révolution*. 2 vols. Paris, 1863.

Richard, Jean. "La levée de 300,000 hommes et les troubles de mars 1793 en Bourgoyne." *Annales de Bourgoyne*, 33 (1961): 213-51.

Rieax, J.J., and J. Hassenforder, *Histoire de service de santé et du Val-de-Grace*. Paris, 1951.

Robiquet, P. *Le personnel municipal de Paris pendant la Révolution*. Vol. 1: *Période constitutionelle*. Paris, 1890.

Rose, R.B. *The Enragés: Socialists of the French Revolution?* Sydney, 1968.

————. *Gracchus Babeuf: The First Revolutionary Communist*. Stanford, CA, 1978.

————. *The Making of the Sans-Culottes*. Manchester, 1983.

Rudé, G. *The Crowd in the French Revolution*. Oxford, 1959.

Sabatie, A.C. *Les tribunaux révolutionnaires en Provence*. Paris, 1914.

Sagnac, P. *La Révolution de 1789*. 2 vols. Paris, 1934.

Savant, J. *Les ministres de Napoléon*. Paris, 1959.

————. *Les préfets de Napoléon*. Paris, 1958.

Schnerb, R. "Les administrateurs de la Côte-d'Or et le salut de la république en 1793." *AHRF*, 36 (1964): 22-37.

————. "La première mission en Côte-d'Or du conventionnel Bernard de Saintes." *Annales de Bourgoyne*, 5 (1933): 45-61.

Sciout, L. *Le Directoire*. 4 vols. Paris, 1895-97.

Seligman, E. *La justice en France pendant la Révolution Française*. 2 vols. Paris, 1913.

Slavin, M. *The Making of an Insurrection*. Cambridge, MA, 1986.

Soboul, A. *La première république*. Paris, 1968.

————. *Les sans-culottes parisiens en l'An II*. Paris, 1962.

Sommier, A. *Histoire de la Révolution dans le Jura*. Paris, 1846.

Sorel, A. *L'Europe et la Révolution Française*. 8 vols. Paris, 1885-1904.

Stephens, H.M. *Orators of the French Revolution*. 2 vols. Oxford, 1892.

Sydenham, M.J. "Le crime de 3 Nivôse (24 December 1800)." In J.F. Bosher, ed., *French Government and Society, 1500-1800: Essays in Memory of Alfred Cobban*, 295-320. London, 1973.

————. *The Girondins*. London, 1961.

————. *The First French Republic, 1792-1804*. London, 1974.

————. "The Republican Revolt of 1793: A Plea for Less Localised Local Studies." *French Historical Studies*, 12 (1981): 120-38.

Thompson, J.M. *The French Revolution*. Oxford, 1959.

————. *Robespierre*. 2 vols. London, 1935.

Tissot, P.-F. *Histoire complète de la Révolution Française*. 6 vols. Paris, 1836-39.

Tonnesson, D. *La défaite des sans-culottes*. Oslo and Paris, 1959.

Vovelle, M. "Déchristianisation." In A. Soboul, ed., *Dictionnaire historique de la Révolution Française* (Paris, 1989), and in Samuel F. Scott and Barry Rothaus, vol. 1 of *Historical Dictionary of the French Revolution*, 2 vols. (Westport, CT, 1985).

Wallon, H. *Histoire du Tribunal Révolutionnaire de Paris.* 2 vols. Paris, 1900.

_____. *Les représentants du peuple en mission et la justice dans les départements en l'An II.* 5 vols. Paris, 1889.

_____. *La Révolution du 31 mai et le fédéralisme en 1793.* 2 vols. Paris, 1886.

Walter, G. *La conjuration du neuf thermidor.* Paris, 1974.

_____, ed. *Histoire de la Révolution,* by J. Michelet. Paris, 1952.

Woloch, I. *Jacobin Legacy: The Democratic Movement under the Directory.* Princeton, NJ, 1970.

Woronoff, D. *The Thermidorian Regime and the Directory, 1794-1799.* Translated by J. Jackson. Cambridge, 1984.

Index

Deputies to the National Convention are identified by (C).

"Abolition of Feudalism," 27, 30
Abrancourt, d', Minister of War, 81
Alençon, 3
Almanach Royal, 4-6, 9; *National* 315-16; *Impérial*, 316-18
Altona, 300, 305
Amar, Jean-Pierre-André (C), 135, 272-73, 286, 292
Amelot de Chaillou, J.-A., Secretary of State, 8
Annales heroïques: see *Recueil des Actions*
Amnesty of 1795, 263, 276, 285
Antwerp, 313
Aoust, Eustache-J.-M., *marquis d'* (C), 225
appel nominal, 111, 144
appel au peuple, 108-11; *appelants*, the, 111, 120, 141, 193
Arena, Barthélémy, deputy 1791-92, 258
armies: of the Alps, 313; of the Centre, 69; of the Interior, 292; of the Moselle, 229; of the Rhine, 180
Armonville, Jean-Baptiste (C), 267-68
Artois, C.-A., *comte de* (later Charles X), 9, 265
Arts et Métiers (Conservatoire), 277, 328
Arts et Métiers (École), 284; others, 316
Assemblies, National:
 The Estates General, 12, 16, 18-21, 25, 37

The National (Constituent) Assembly (1789-91), 23, 25, 32, 34, 37-38, 95; Committees: Agriculture and Commerce, 37, 51; Constitution, 50, 54-55; Instruction, 58; Pensions, 41, 43, 51
The National Legislative Assembly (1791-92), 41-42, 44, 47, 50-51, 54, 56-59, 70-72, 74, 76-77, 81, 87, 92, 95, 97-99; Commission of Twenty-one, 72, 198; Committees: of Legislation, 255; Public Instruction, 59, 60, 68
The National Convention (1792-95): elections to, 87-90; powers, 91; initial situation, 93, 96-99; trial of Louis XVI, 102-12; and follow on: 116, 118-19, 133, 137, 140-49, 157, 159-63, 165-70, 172-76, 178, 180-89, 193-96, 198, 200-205, 208-209, 211, 214, 217-18, 220-24, 230, 232, 236-38 (Thermidor), 241, 243, 245-47, 249-50, 253-54, 258, 260, 262, 263-65, 267, 270-73, 277, 280, 285 (closure), 287, 299, 309, 312, 325, 328; Commissions: Constitutional, 264; of Six, 169-73, 201, 203; of Twelve 143-44, 198; Committees, "governing"; of General Security, 168, 180, 195, 211-12, 218, 236-38, 245-46, 254, 260-61, 266-68, 273, 282, 286; of